Civilization in the West

CRANE

brinton

Civilization in the West

Part 1   From the Old Stone Age to the Age of Louis XIV

Third Edition

Prentice-Hall, Inc.,   Englewood Cliffs, New Jersey

JOHN B.

christopher

University of Rochester

ROBERT LEE

wolff

*Archibald Cary Coolidge
Professor of History,
Harvard University*

8 95

Civilization in the West
THIRD EDITION
Part 1: From the Old Stone Age
to the Age of Louis XIV
Brinton, Christopher, and Wolff

Design by Walter Behnke

Maps by J & R Services

Library of Congress Cataloging in Publication Data

Brinton, Clarence Crane, 1898–1968.
  Civilization in the West.

  Includes bibliographical references.
  1. Civilization—History. I. Christopher,
John B., joint author. II. Wolff, Robert Lee,
joint author. III. Title.
CB59.B7 1973   901.9   72-10621
ISBN 0-13-134981-3 (v. 1)

10 9 8 7 6 5 4 3 2 1

PRENTICE-HALL INTERNATIONAL, INC., London
PRENTICE-HALL OF AUSTRALIA, PTY. LTD., Sydney
PRENTICE-HALL OF CANADA, LTD., Toronto
PRENTICE-HALL OF INDIA PRIVATE LTD., New Delhi
PRENTICE-HALL OF JAPAN, INC., Tokyo

Preface

This third edition of *Civilization in the West* may serve as the sole reading for a single quarter or semester survey course. For a more leisurely survey, extending over two or more quarters or semesters, we think it offers an account brief enough to permit students wide supplementary reading. For the first time the book is available both in a single casebound edition and as two paperbacks, the break coming between Chapter 9, "The Arts and Sciences in the Classical and Baroque Age," and Chapter 10, "The Eighteenth-Century Economy and the Enlightenment."

While basing this revision on our more detailed *A History of Civilization,* fourth edition (Prentice-Hall, 1971), we have reworked and rearranged the material from the parent volumes, and we have also made additions to bring the book abreast of events and of scholarship. Those familiar with the previous edition will find changes throughout the new volume, especially at the beginning and at the end.

The introduction, "What Good Is History?," is new. The first chapter takes into account the startling new discoveries and interpretations of the Old Stone Age published during the last year, which are likely to revolutionize our attitudes toward prehistoric man. The materials on Rome in Chapter 2 have been considerably revised and expanded. In Chapters 3 and 4 wholly new sections have been provided on literature and the arts, considering the latest discoveries of archaeology and theories of art historians and historians of literature. Throughout the book a vigorous effort has been made to give appropriate new emphasis to social, as well as political and intellectual, history.

Chapters 9 and 10 represent a complete reworking of a single chapter in the earlier edition. Chapter 9 emphasizes the *theme* of the Great Century, and limits itself to culture and science, singling out the major innovations and giving new treatment not only to literature, art, and music, but also to religion, and reevaluating some of the most important individuals of the period. Chapter 10, focusing first on the economy, enables the reader to approach the intellectual phenomenon of the Enlightenment only after he is already aware of the major changes in trade, agriculture, and industry. In subsequent chapters full account has been taken of new scholarship on the French Revolution and on the nineteenth century; the sequence of major topics has been altered to gain greater clarity; the traditional emphasis on the Revolutions of 1848 has been challenged and new propositions have been argued. In Chapter 14, new interpretations of the industrial revolution, of Darwinism, and of literary realism and naturalism have been incorporated.

We have given a much fuller treatment to the world since 1945, three chapters (17, 18, and 19) replacing a single chapter in the earlier edition. The first two now deal with the quarter-century between 1945 and 1970, discussing not only international relations but the domestic history of the major powers and of the emerging third world. The third—Chapter 19—tentatively propounds the thesis that in 1970 the "postwar" period can be said to have ended, and that events of the past two years will in the future be considered as the beginning of a major series of changes: a real thaw in a pattern of international relations that had seemed eternally frozen. This chapter discusses those aspects of human affairs that have changed, and notes the many others that have not. In the wholly new final chapter (20) we concentrate on the revolutionary developments in the cultural and intellectual history of the twentieth century, giving particular emphasis to psychology and to experimentation in the arts. It may be worth emphasizing that these last two chapters (19 and 20) do not appear in the parent volume in any form, but were written especially for this book.

Throughout the book the sections on art history have been more fully illustrated, and many more works have been keyed directly to the text. The maps have been thoroughly revised, with what we hope will be found pleasing as well as useful results. In fact, we trust that the reader will find the physical aspect of this new edition particularly satisfying.

We should like here to express our gratitude to the members of the Project Planning Department at Prentice-Hall who have applied their skills and energies most generously and effectively: Walter Behnke, who designed the book; Helen Maertens, who handled its production; and Rita M. Ginsburg and Winifred M. Schneider, who laid out the pages. Once again it has been a delight to have the privilege of working with Cecil Yarbrough, Project Planning editor, who has given us not only technical assistance but many valuable substantive suggestions as well.

Contents

Maps

Illustrations

What Good Is History?

A little less than two centuries ago, just about the time of the American Revolution, a learned Englishman, Edward Gibbon, had completed a new volume of his famous work, *The Decline and Fall of the Roman Empire,* and called upon a royal duke, a brother of King George III, to give him a copy. The duke accepted the present with the remark "Another damned thick book. Always scribble, scribble, scribble. Eh, Mr. Gibbon?"

If you stop to think about it, there was really very little that Gibbon could say in reply. He might have pointed out that the earlier volume had been a bestseller, and was on the dressing tables of most of the fashionable ladies of the duke's acquaintance. But that would probably not have changed the duke's opinion very much. The duke was bored by history, and that was that. There have always been people like the duke and there always will be. Nor have they always been merely stupid, as one must admit that the duke was. The first Henry Ford, inventive genius whose cheap cars changed the whole way of life of twentieth-century America, once remarked feelingly "History is bunk," and there is no reason to think that he did not mean it or that he ever changed his views. And Henry Ford in his own way was brilliant. An even more brilliant man, a deeply original thinker in the field of psychology, an active scholar and colleague of one of the authors of this history book you are reading, once said with deep feeling "I hate history." It is true that he said it at a cocktail party, but he surely meant it. Once his listener had overcome the shock of hearing so extravagant a statement from such a source, the remark became even understandable.

Like the duke and Henry Ford, the psychologist was made uncomfortable by history. How many complications we could avoid if we did not know anything about the past: what our forefathers in America and our ancestors in other countries and men and women in civilizations other than our own had done in their lives. If we could ignore everything that had happened yesterday or the day before or last year or ten or a hundred or a thousand years ago, we could face our own problems cleanly, without trying to hark back and solve them by remembering and acting upon some precedent. Or could we? We could avoid the clutter of past thinkers' unreliable, fumbling, inappropriate efforts to work things out, and so avoid a war, clean up a mess, end injustice (if any) by the sheer fresh, simple use of our own brilliant intuition. Or could we? If indeed we could, why should we bother about the past? Yet if it were merely boring (as the duke said) or bunk (as Henry Ford said) we really could ignore it, and it would not only not be necessary to study it, or a good idea to reflect upon it: it would be forgotten and better forgotten. Yet it is not forgotten, it is remembered; it somehow will not go away, and people do keep on trying to guide themselves by its lessons.

By introducing a necessary complication into human calculations, the past, or our memory of it, prevents the solution of human problems by simple, straightforward, direct means: it gets in the way of neatness, and somehow fogs things up, irritating our friend the psychologist. Remembrance of the past, of what happened to us the last time we crossed the street against the traffic light, of what happened to our father in the Korean War, or what happened to *his* father in the stock market crash of 1929 cannot help affect us every day, as we go for a walk, think about Vietnam, or contemplate investing in a speculative stock. Whether we get useful or nonuseful signals from our memories of the past, good or bad advice, is another question. One traffic crossing is not the same as another; two wars are not the same; maybe the fact that grandpa was burned by speculating in 1929 should not stop us from trying the same kind of thing today, because times have changed, haven't they? Or haven't they? That is the thing that continues to puzzle us. And if times have changed, how ought the change to affect our decisions?

When one begins to contemplate this as a problem, one can sympathize with the psychologist, if not share his views. We simply cannot escape the past, at least in the sense of our own immediate memories and the memories of those whom we have known. But of course this is a long way from the study of the past. If we cannot prevent ourselves from acting at least partly in accordance with our knowledge of past experience—our own and that of others—we can at least not bother to find out about more remote things, things that happened in more distant times and places to people we never heard of. We do not *need* to study history. And many today echo in their own way the voices of the duke, of Henry Ford, and of the psychologist. Usually they say that history is not "relevant." Are they right? Is it "relevant?" What good is it?

A team of doctors in the Panama Canal Zone at the beginning of the present century found ways to defeat the deadly disease of yellow fever. Of course they had studied biology, chemistry, and medicine. History would hardly have helped them much, except possibly in giving them knowledge of the failures of previous scientists or of the dreadful toll past yellow fever epidemics had taken. Other scourges like polio have more recently yielded to similar researches. Who can question the "relevance" of studies that lead to results like these? We would cheerfully agree that history is simply not "relevant" in the same way. No matter how hard we study the past history of racial discrimination, for instance, and no matter how much we know about the evils it has wrought, our knowledge will not lead directly to its elimination from the hearts of other men, although indeed such knowledge may help us conquer it in ourselves. So even here, "relevance" by no means disappears.

It is often said, of course—so often that practically everybody who reads this will expect us to be saying it at just this moment—that we can solve the problems of the present—or even the future—by using the lessons of the past. True, a person who has recovered from being run over after crossing the street against a red light will quite probably wait for the light the next time. This past experience has solved a present problem. But as soon as the problem becomes more than an individual one, involving, say, national policy, the statement about the lessons of the past needs to be modified at once. The United States fought in World War I in 1917 and 1918. Should we therefore have been able to avoid fighting in World War II, which in fact we found ourselves doing between 1941 and 1945? The answer can only be that the lessons of history are never so clear. Everything changes, so that the range of problems the second time is very different from the range of problems the first time. It is not like a single person facing the same red light twice. The intersection has changed, the lights are different colors, and the rules are not the same. In 1941 we faced the Japanese as enemies; they had been on our side in World War I. In 1941 we faced a Germany under Hitler quite different from the Germany of the Kaiser of World War I. Our mere act of participation in the First World War could not teach us how to avoid the Second.

On a more complex level, of course, perhaps we could have learned some lessons that we did not learn. Instead of participating in international organizations to keep the peace after World War I—the League of Nations—the United States stayed out of the League, which never managed to become an effective agency against war. People often say that had the United States joined the League, it would have been able to prevent World War II. But this is far from clear. After World War II, we did join the United Nations, successor to the League. But the United Nations has not proved any more effective with us than the League proved without us: wars continue to be fought, and the United States itself has been involved in two major ones, in Korea and in Vietnam, since World War II ended. While it is true that World War III has so far indeed been avoided, that is probably more due to the general belief that the existence of nuclear weapons means that mankind might well be exterminated in such a war than to any other factor. And that belief is hardly a lesson from history.

If complex problems never present themselves twice in the same or even in recognizably similar form, if—to borrow a frequent image from the military world—our generals always prepare for the last war instead of the next war, then does the study of history in fact offer mankind any help in solving its problems? The answer is, surely, yes: but only in a very limited way. It does offer a rich collection of clinical reports on human behavior in various situations—individual and collective, political, economic, military, social, cultural—that informs us in detail how the human race has at times conducted its own affairs, and that surely suggests ways of handling even distantly similar problems in the present. President Truman's secretary of state, the former chief of staff General George Marshall, once remarked that nobody could "think with full wisdom and deep conviction" about the problems of the 1950's who had not reflected upon the fall of Athens in the fifth century B.C. He was thinking of the extraordinary history of the Peloponnesian War between Athens and Sparta written just after the war was over by Thucydides the Athenian, a participant in the struggle. There were no nuclear weapons, no telecommunications, not even any guns and gunpowder, in the fifth century B.C.; the logistics of the war were altogether primitive, yet one of the most distinguished leaders of American military and political affairs twenty-three hundred years later found Thucydides indispensable to his thinking about the problems of the United States.

History, then, can, though only roughly, only approximately, show the range—or the spectrum—of human behavior, with some indication of its extremes and averages. It can, though again by no means perfectly, show how and within what limits human behavior changes. This last is especially important for the social scientist, for the economist, the sociologist, the applied anthropologist. For if these experts studied only the people and institutions existing today, they would have but imperfect notions of the real capacities of human beings. They would be like biologists with no knowledge of the contributions of historical geology and paleontology to their understanding of organic evolution. History, then, provides materials that even the aspiring leader of men into new ways and new worlds—the prophet, the reformer, or the columnist—will do well to master before he tries to lead us into those new ways.

For it can tell us something about what human material can stand and what it cannot stand, just as the many contributory sciences and technologies involved can tell the engineer what stresses his metals can stand. The historian, incidentally, knows that human beings can stand a lot—much more than any metal. History can give an awareness of the depth of time and space that should check the optimism and the overconfidence of the reformer. Millions of man-hours, for example, are wasted in the process of teaching children to read English, with its absurd spelling and its over-refined punctuation. Yet the slightest background of history will show that human societies usually resist changes like the reform of spelling, or accept them only in times of revolution, as when the metric system was introduced during the French Revolution; or under dictatorship, as when the Turkish alphabet was changed from Arabic to Roman by the twentieth-century dictator Atatürk.

You may still wish to reform our spelling, even though you know these historic difficulties; but if you have learned from history, you will never look at the problem of getting English-speaking peoples to change their spelling as if it were a problem like that of designing a superhighway. You will, or should, however, learn through the study of history something about the differences between *designing* such a highway, an engineer's job, and getting the highway built, a much more complicated job for government experts, economists, businessmen, contractors, workers of many kinds of training, politicians local, state, and national, conservationists and other pressure groups, and ultimately a problem for us as taxpayers and voters.

So, if you are willing to accept a "relevance" more difficult to see at first than the immediate applicability of science, and more remote than direct action, you will have to admit that history is "relevant." It may not actually build the highway or clear the slum, but it can give enormous help to those who wish to do so. And failure to take it into account may bring about failure in the sphere of action. We are not, you notice, making grandiose claims for history. Nor do we think we can convince those among you who already hate it, like the professor of psychology, although maybe we have a chance with those of you who so far agree only with Henry Ford or with Gibbon's duke. There is, however, one undeniable fact that will help us, and that we hope will help you: many people actively *enjoy* history.

Whether it is historical gossip they prefer (how many lovers did Catherine the Great of Russia actually take during a given year and how much political influence did their activity in the imperial bedroom in fact give them?), or the details of historical investigation (how does it happen that the actual treasures found in a buried Viking ship correspond to those described in an Anglo-Saxon poetic account of a ship burial?), or more complex questions of cause and effect (how influential have the writings of revolutionary intellectuals been upon the course of actual revolutions?), or the relationships between politics and economics (how far does the rise and decline of Spanish power in modern times depend upon the supply of gold from the New World colonies?), or cultural problems (why was it classical Greek and Roman art and literature that men revived in the earliest period of modern times, instead of turning to some other culture or to some altogether new experiment?), those who enjoy history will read almost greedily to discover what they want to know. And having discovered it, they may want to know how we know what they have learned, and turn to far more detailed and scholarly accounts than we have been able to provide here, or even to those sources closest in time to the persons and questions concerned, and presumably the best informed. So we know in advance that some of you already like history, for whatever reason, and we know too that others of you will soon be hooked. Unashamedly we admit it: the study of history can be enormous fun. Otherwise why should we have scribbled away and produced another damned thick book?

The historical record is most imperfect, and even the labors of generations of scholars have not filled it out. Notably, historians until quite recently have usually been more interested in the pomp and drama of the lives of the great than in the conditions of life for the masses. Battles and treaties have studded their pages. They have studied with care political and religious behavior, it is true, and within the last few generations they have studied economic behavior. Until recently they have paid less attention to social behavior and to folkways. Since the historians of one generation make the historical record that is handed down to later historians, our record is very faulty and cannot always be improved. No one can ever conduct a sort of retrospective Gallup Poll, for instance, to find out just what millions of fifteenth-century Frenchmen thought about Joan of Arc. Yet our ignorance must not be exaggerated either. As you can learn from any manual of historiography—that is, the history of the writing of history—historians have in the last few hundred years built up a technique and a body of verifiable facts that have made history, not an exact science, but a useful body of knowledge.

History is no longer merely past politics—and past wars; it is "past everything." Geographically, it is no longer just the history of Europe and North America; it is the history of the whole world.

No sensible person will deny that these newer interpretations have greatly enriched and deepened the study of history. On the other hand, this new history is much more complex, difficult, and unwieldy than was the old. When you add China, India, the Aztecs, and a lot more in space, and add the centuries back to ancestral subhumans in time, and add all the innumerable activities of all men to the dramatic activities of a few in politics and war, you create an unmanageable mass of detail, and the result is sometimes a longer and more arid catalog of details than the lists of kings, queens, presidents, consuls, generals, popes, and cardinals that used to fill the older histories. After all, a list of poets, or even of inventors, is not in itself very illuminating; and even a hasty epithet or two—"ethereal" Shelley, "sweet-voiced" Keats, "ingenious and laborious" Edison—adds very little.

The present book is in part—though only in part—a reaction against the attempt to cover all the past everywhere on earth. We hope to retain the best of the old and add the best of the new. As for space, we shall concentrate on the history of one part of the world, the Europe sometimes scornfully called "a small peninsula of Asia." We shall trace the expansion of that Europe as Europeans explored, settled, colonized, and traded in all parts of the globe. But we shall be concerned with non-European peoples only as they and their histories impinged on the development of European cultures. We are not motivated by any self-worship, certainly not by any contempt for Asians or Africans, but rather by a desire to get our own record straight. We are not against the study of "world history," but we do hold that it is unwise to begin with world history; we think it wiser to know one's own civilization well before one tries to understand all others. As for time, after a very brief look at the ages-long prehistoric past of Western man and the beginnings of his history in the Near East, we shall be mostly concerned with the last two thousand years or so.

Obviously, this is not all a good American citizen of the second half of the twentieth century needs to know about the past of *Homo sapiens.* But it is an essential part of what he needs to know, probably the part he *most* needs to know if he is to face the problems of human relations on this planet.

In discussing the past of our own civilization, we shall try manfully to see our forebears in their religious and cultural lives, and engaging in all their manifold social and economic activities. But "what really happened" still primarily means to us, as we think it must to all who are writing an introductory work, politics: politics in the sense of past government, past domestic policy, past foreign policy, and therefore—as always—past wars and past peace. So it will be around the political lives, political expediencies, political inventions, and political behavior of men from the first civilizations to the present that we hope to organize this work.

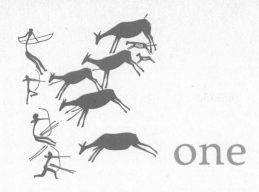

one

Man's First Civilizations

I
Before Writing

History and Prehistory

Within the lifetime of men now in their forties and fifties, archaeology, with the new tools supplied by other sciences, has revolutionized what human beings know about the remoter past of our earth and the people who live on it. Discoveries continue at a rapid pace. In the 1930's, '40's, and '50's, no writer could have put on paper many of the major statements in this chapter. In the 1980's and '90's, perhaps even sooner, our successors will know enough to dispute or modify or at least greatly add to what we here set forth.

It may at first seem strange that our concepts of the distant past are changing much faster than our concepts of the periods much closer to us in time and much better known. But when we consider the ways in which we know about the past we can quickly see that—far from strange—this is entirely natural. If we want to know about something—almost anything—that happened, let us say, during the American Revolution, we have the letters of George Washington and his contemporaries, the written records of the British government that tried to suppress the American colonists' rebellion, the proceedings of the Continental Congress, the Declaration of Independence, and literally thousands of other *written sources*—diaries, memoirs, documents, newspapers, propaganda leaflets—that take us instantly into the minds of the men of that time and enable us to work out for ourselves what probably happened. And if we cannot go directly to these written sources for history, we have hundreds of books written since the events of the Revolution by the historians who have been interested in it and who have set down their view of what happened, for us to accept or challenge, but at least to consider. New sources may be discovered and fresh light thrown on some event we thought we understood: we may find out that Paul Revere's teacher at school had been reading radical pamphlets (something that previous students had not known) and that this helped prepare Paul as a youth for his famous ride. But the new sources probably would not force us to reject or even to reconsider everything we had learned before they were discovered.

Most of the sources we would read about the American Revolution would be written in English. But if we wanted to find out about the part played by Lafayette and Rochambeau we would soon find ourselves compelled to read documents in French; if we asked ourselves why a Pole, Tadeusz Kościuszko, joined the American side, we might have to learn Polish—and Russian and German—in order to find out. If we were interested in the ideas of Thomas Jefferson, we would have to study several of his favorite classical authors—who wrote in Greek or Latin—and, though we would find translations available, we might feel it important to read them as Jefferson did, in the original. But whatever the problems of learning languages, or of trying to decide which of two contradictory accounts of the same event to follow, or of interpreting what we might find (this is what George III *said;* but what did he *really* think?), we would always be dealing with abundant written sources in languages that modern men know how to read.

For events two thousand years or more before the American Revolution, or less well known, or taking place in Europe or Asia, we would still usually have written sources, in Persian or Sanskrit, Greek or Latin or Chinese, sometimes fragmentary instead of full, sometimes so biased as to be unreliable, but written. Where possible we would supplement these with all kinds of other evidence: the coins that rulers struck with pictures or inscriptions on them that might tell us things we could not find out any other way; the statues or paintings or poems or songs of the age that might reflect the attitudes of the artists and their society more surely than a document; indeed, anything that we could find from the period and the place to supplement our written sources.

But suppose our written sources were written in a language we could not read? Or suppose we had no written sources at all? As we move backward in time through human history these problems confront us more and more urgently. The discovery of texts written in both a known and a previously unknown language has over the last couple of centuries enabled scholars to read the language of the Egyptians, and those of the peoples of the ancient Mesopotamian river valleys in the Near East, although uncertainties often remain. Brilliant use of the techniques of cryptography in the 1950's cracked one of the two scripts commonly used in ancient Crete and on the Greek mainland. But the earlier Cretan script remains to be deciphered. Nobody has yet cracked Etruscan, the language—written in Greek letters—of the people that ruled in Italy before the Romans.

And of course there were long, long, *long* centuries and millennia before man had learned to write at all. Only his bones and the bones of his animals and some of the things he made remain to tell us about him: they are our only sources. The recent development of the carbon-14 technique, whereby radioactive carbon is used to enable us to date ancient objects within a couple of centuries, has proved to be a great help in straightening out chronology. Nothing seems surer, however, than that scholars will find many more new objects and new ways of dating them and so will enable our successors to write with more certainty than we about our earliest ancestors.

In the seventeenth century, an Anglican archbishop named Ussher carefully worked out from data given in the Bible the date of the creation of the world by God. It proved to be precisely 4004 B.C.; so if you added the sixteen hundred or so years since the birth of Christ, you came up with a figure of under six thousand years for the age of our earth. We smile now at the generations that accepted Ussher's views—though everybody did so until the nineteenth century—because all of *us* know that the earth is billions of years old and that organic life may go back several billion years. Beginning in 1959, a series of digs in equatorial east central Africa in and around Olduvai Gorge turned up fragments of a small creature that lived between nineteen and fourteen million years ago, christened *Kenyapithecus* ("Kenya ape"), who seems to have made crude tools. He may not be a direct ancestor of man, but like man may have branched off from a primate ten million years older still, and still more primitive. By about two million years ago a creature more like true man had made his appearance, *Homo habilis,* "the skillful man." A mere quarter of a million years later came *Zinjanthropos,* who was perhaps related to a manlike animal about the size of a chimpanzee, but with a larger brain, called *Australopithecus* ("southern ape"). *Australopithecus* was a vegetarian (to judge by his teeth), and seems to have ceased evolving and come to a dead end, while *Homo habilis,* who ate meat, continued to evolve in the direction of true man, *Homo sapiens,* "the man who knows." All these manlike animals had larger skulls, with more brains, than apes. In another three-quarters of a million years (we are now down to a moment in time about a million years ago or a little less) the later remains of *Homo habilis* begin to look like those of a being long known as Java man, who lived about 700,000 B.C. First found in Java in the late 1880's and christened *Pithecanthropus erectus* ("ape-man that stands erect"), he is now recognized as a true man, far from an ape, and renamed *Homo erectus.* A somewhat later stage is represented by Peking man of about 500,000 B.C., who has advanced well beyond *Homo habilis.*

Much more is being learned and will continue to be learned, as the origins of manlike beings and of true men continue to be studied. Especially we should like to know about the stages by which *Homo erectus* evolved into *Homo sapiens,* who appeared in Europe first only about thirty-seven thousand years ago. When he arrived there in a fashion still unknown, he entered into a land of forests and plains that had already been occupied for perhaps a hundred thousand years by Neanderthal man, named for the Rhineland valley where his remains were first discovered but spread far more widely, leaving remains, for example, also in the mountains of what is today eastern Iraq. Probably far less apelike than the traditional reconstructions of his skull have shown him to be, Neanderthal man was not yet *Homo sapiens.* We cannot yet locate him accurately on a hypothetical family tree, but he probably represents another offshoot from the main trunk. A recent excavation of a Neanderthal burial has shown that the corpse was placed on a heaping bouquet of flowers, an attention more delicate than one would have expected.

Even though we can identify our remote ancestors so many hundreds of thousands of years before Ussher thought the world was made, we know so little about what was happening during all those hundreds of millennia before Ussher's creation date of 4004 B.C. that for the historian—as distinguished from the anthropologist—almost all of that time belongs to "prehistory." We can be certain that during those long, long centuries the advance of the human animal was enormously slow. The first real tools were stones that he used to chip other stones into useful instruments. And it was by stone weapons and tools that early man lived for hundreds of thousands of years: lived in a stone

Stag hunt: cave painting from Cueva de los Caballos, Spain.

age as the terms that scholars use to describe his life make abundantly clear.
Down to roughly 8000 B.C.—varying by a few thousand years or so according to the region one is describing—man lived in the Old Stone Age—Paleolithic. By about 8000 B.C. in some places—much later in others—he passed into a New Stone Age, Neolithic, marked by certain great changes that we shall consider in a moment. By about 3000 B.C. we are at the beginning of the Bronze Age, and of even greater transitions to new forms of human life and society. And still later came the Iron Age. Wrong though Archbishop Ussher is about the age of the earth, he is nonetheless ironically almost right about what a historian can say about the period before 4004 B.C.

Paleolithic man left remains scattered widely in Europe and Asia, and took refuge in Africa from the glaciers that periodically moved south over the northern continents and made life impossible there. Wherever he went, he hunted to eat, and fought and killed his enemies. He learned how to cook his food, how to take shelter from the cold in caves, and eventually how to specialize his tools: he made bone needles with which to sew animal hides into clothes with animal sinews; he made hatchets, spears, arrowheads, awls.

One day in 1940, when two boys in southwest France went hunting rabbits, their pet dog suddenly disappeared down a hole and did not come back. Following the dog, they literally fell into an underground grotto, hidden for thousands of years. The light of their torches revealed an extraordinary series of paintings on its limestone walls and roofs, of animals portrayed in brilliant colors with astonishing realism and artistry: deer, bison, horses, and others. These were the achievement toward the end of the Paleolithic period of Cro-Magnon man, true *Homo sapiens,* often standing as tall as six feet four inches and with a large brain. Lascaux, where the paintings were found, became one of the great tourist centers of Europe. By 1960, despite all the precautions of the authorities, the breath of so many thousands of visitors gazing in awe and wonder began to damage the pictures, which had been sealed away from moisture for so many millennia; so the cave has had to be closed to the public. At Altamira, in northern Spain, similar contemporary cave pictures, not quite so splendid, had long been known, but had suffered somewhat from early souvenir hunters. Long exposed to air and changing temperatures, they are happily immune to moisture, and now remain the most easily visible monument of the great skills of Paleolithic man. There are many other caves with late Paleolithic paintings, but perhaps none so spectacular as Lascaux and Altamira.

We can only guess but not know for certain why the Paleolithic artist painted the pictures. Did he think that by putting animals on his walls he could improve his chances in the hunting field? Would their pictures give him power over them, and so ensure his supply of food? Were the different animals also totems of different families or clans? Sometimes on the walls of the caves we find paintings of human hands, often with a finger or fingers missing. Were these hands simple testimony of appreciation for one of man's most extraordinary physical gifts: the hand with its apposable thumb (not found in apes), which alone made tool-making possible? Or were they efforts to ward off evil spirits by upholding the palm or making a ritual gesture? Or were they prayers by hunters and warriors that they should not suffer mutilation of their fingers or that they might retain their strength despite some mutilation they had already suffered? Paleolithic man occasionally produced small female statuettes, sometimes overemphasizing the breasts, buttocks, and sexual organs (and sardonically called Venuses by modern archaeologists). Were these fertility symbols? or love charms?

Painting of a bull from the cave at Lascaux, ca. 12,000 B.C.

Until the late 1960's, such questions were the only ones that scholars had asked about the achievements of Paleolithic man, and hypothetical answers the only possible ones. But in addition to the cave paintings, and the Venuses, and the tools—known in such variety and with such increasing skill of manufacture from about 35,000 B.C. to about 8000 B.C.—archaeology had yielded up a rich variety of other finds. Prompted by some regular scratched markings on a bone from equatorial Africa carbon-dated at 8500 B.C., an inquiring scholar named Alexander Marshack has since 1965 reexamined the vast amount of material in European collections, and has made some amazing discoveries which he has judiciously explained by reaching hypotheses about Old Stone Age man that are absolutely new.

Marshack found numerous objects—a mammoth tusk, bones of various animals, a pebble, several short staffs of ivory, a pair of eagle bones—dating from perhaps 32,000 B.C. to 12,000 B.C. on which markings appeared in sequences like those on his initial bone tool from Africa, markings whose sequence and intervals he could interpret as notations recording lunar periods. Sometimes only one or two lunar months had been observed, sometimes six, sometimes an entire year. With the passing of the millennia, the Paleolithic craftsman learned to make the notations more complex, sometimes engraving them in a cross-hatched pattern that looks like mere decoration until one learns to read it, sometimes adding extra angled marks at important dates.

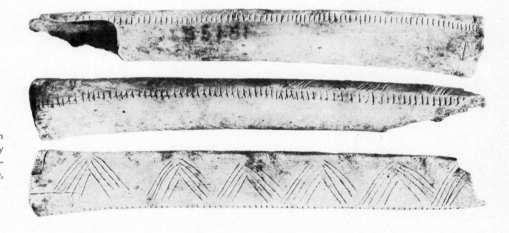

Three faces of an eagle bone with the markings interpreted by Alexander Marshack as lunar notation: from southwest France, ca. 13,000 B.C.

Once one realizes that late Old Stone Age man may well have been keeping a kind of calendar to enable him to predict the regular seasonal changes from year to year, and that therefore he was presumably regulating his hunting life and his other activities, such as the preparation of skins for clothing, one gets such a vivid new perspective on the quality of his mind and his perception of the importance of time in his life that the "mystery" of his extraordinary skills becomes far less mysterious. In the later Paleolithic art objects, the marks that Marshack has interpreted as time notations sometimes *accompany* artistic representations of animals. Where we find on the same piece of ivory from southwest France a budding flower, sprouting plants, grass snakes, a salmon, and a seal—which appeared in spring in the local rivers—Marshack proposes that we regard the object as a kind of symbolic representation of the earth's reawakening after winter; and when such symbols of springtime appear with

Naked woman holding a bison horn, with its crescent shape, and thirteen marks corresponding to the lunar months of the year: from southwest France, ca. 22,000 B.C.

the lunar calendric notation, we are looking at something very like an illustrated calendar. Other spring events celebrated in the art include the rutting of stags and bison.

In the same way, perhaps the "goddess" images should not be dismissed as "sexual" in any simple sense. In a hunting culture, a female image, with its suggestion of the female processes, serves to recapitulate the procession of the seasons. Certain animals—reindeer, bison, horses—appear on the artifacts associated with females; others—bears and lions—with males. Some representations can be interpreted as sacrifices. The men of the late Old Stone Age apparently had a mythology that involved tales of the hunt, successful and unsuccessful, a ritual that involved killing and sacrifice, and a deep awareness and knowledge of the passing of time in the world around them and in the bodies of animals and of mankind. A nude figure of a woman holding a bison horn that looks exactly like a crescent moon and is marked with thirteen lines, the number of lunar months in a year, we may now perhaps salute as mankind's first recognizable true goddess, the forerunner of the bare-breasted Neolithic lunar goddess we have long known as the Mistress of the Animals, who appears with crescent, fish, flower, plant, bird, tree, and snake, and with a consort who plays sun to her moon and hunts the animals of nature and of myth. Though Old Stone Age man remains a dim and remote figure to us, Marshack's researches for the first time make him recognizable as fully man.

The New Stone Age

The advance from the Old Stone Age (Paleolithic) to the New (Neolithic) was marked by certain major changes in man's way of life, all first found in the Near East. One of these was the domestication of animals for food. Man had tamed dogs and used them in the hunt long before; but when he kept goats, pigs, sheep, and the ancestors of our cows in pens, he could eat them when their meat was young and tender without having to hunt them down when they were hardest to overtake. Parallel with this went the first domestication of plants for food—a kind of wheat and barley. Finally—and this always seems to have been the last step—man turned his shelter into a house, and settled down to live in it. Once he had done all these things, he had made the transition to the New Stone Age. And accompanying these fundamental steps went the practice of a new art, the baking of clay vessels—pots and bowls and storage jars—much easier to make, of course, than stone ones. It is chiefly by studying the surviving varieties of such clay vessels and their fragments, and the types of glazes and decoration the potters used, that modern scholars have been able to learn how to date the sites where men lived in the times before writing, and often even later. Recent excavations in the Near East have pushed back our previous earliest Neolithic dates; and with the boundaries between periods thus in flux and the terms intended only to be useful and not to confuse, it is probably better here not to try to fix any firm boundaries between late Paleolithic and early Neolithic.

At Jericho in Palestine during the 1950's, archaeologists excavated a town radiocarbon-dated at about 7800 B.C. that extended over about eight acres and included perhaps three thousand inhabitants. These people lived in round houses with conical roofs—the oldest permanent houses known—and they had a large, columned building in which were found many mud-modeled figurines of animals and modeled statues of a man, woman, and male child; it was almost surely a temple of some kind. All this dates from a time when people did not yet know how to make pots, which appear only at a later stage. In Çatalhüyük in southern Turkey, discovered only in 1961 and dating to 6500 B.C., the people had a wide variety of pottery, grew their own grain, kept sheep,

Neolithic figurine shaped like a phallus but carved as a female figure: from Tepe Yahya, Iran.

and wove their wool into textiles. A female sculptured in relief in the posture of giving birth to a child, a bull's head, boars' heads with women's breasts running in rows along the lower jaws, and many small statuettes were all found together in what we can be sure was their shrine. The bull and a double ax painted on a wall seem to look forward to main features of the better-known religion of ancient Crete, as we shall see.

Far to the east, in modern Iraq (ancient Mesopotamia, "between the rivers" Tigris and Euphrates) lay Jarmo, to be dated about 4500 B.C., a third Neolithic settlement. A thousand years later than Jarmo, about 3550 B.C., and far to the south, at Uruk on the banks of the Euphrates River, men were using the plow to scratch the soil before sowing their seeds, and were already keeping the accounts of their temple in simple picture-writing. This was the great leap forward that took man out of prehistory and into history. Similar advances are found in Egypt too, at roughly the same time. But archaeology seems to show that Mesopotamia took the lead, and indeed that it was from Mesopotamia that major cultural contributions—especially the all-important art of writing—penetrated into Egypt and gave the Egyptians a great push into history.

Still further to the east, in various parts of modern Iran, archaeologists during the 1960's have found several of these early Neolithic sites, some of which seem to go back in time as far as Jericho or even before—although no city so large or complex or advanced has been found from the eighth millennium B.C. The sites are scattered, and many of them are located in the highlands, indicating that the Neolithic revolution was not necessarily confined, as had usually been thought, to river valleys. Many of these Iranian discoveries are still unpublished, and much work remains to be done. But from 6000 B.C. there are several sites in northwest Iran rather like Jarmo, giving plenty of evidence of domesticated animals and grains. And even earlier, probably, perhaps around 7000, in the region of southwest Iran very near the Mesopotamian eastern border there are mud-brick houses and the same clear evidence of goat- and sheep- and cereal-raising. In a totally different region, in south central Iran, a brand-new site was discovered in the summer of 1967 at Tepe Yahya, where the earliest settlement in a large mound proved to be a Neolithic village of about 4500 B.C. Here along with the animal bones and cereal remains archaeologists found in a mud-brick storage area not only pottery and small sharpened flints set in a bone handle to make a sickle but an extraordinary sculptured figurine of dark green stone, which is simultaneously a female figure and a phallus.

The Neolithic people of the Near East were not necessarily any more intelligent than those elsewhere. Indeed, Neolithic remains have been found also in many places in the Mediterranean region, and even far to the north. But in those places climate was far less favorable, and even when Neolithic man managed to triumph over his environment—as in the lake settlements of Switzerland, where he built frame houses on piles over the water—the triumph came later (in this case about 2500 B.C.). In Australia and New Guinea and in South America there are people today who still live in the Neolithic Age. It was the inhabitants of the more favored regions who got to the great discoveries first. It was they who learned copper-smelting and the other arts of metallurgy, and who thus led the human race altogether out of the Stone Age—and into the Bronze Age. And it was they who first lived in cities. Writing, metallurgy, and urban life: these are the marks of civilization. Soon after these phenomena appeared in the Tigris–Euphrates valleys, along the Nile, and in Iran they appeared also in the valley of the Indus, and along certain Chinese rivers. But since it is not to India or China but to Mesopotamia and Egypt that we can trace our own civilization, it is to these that we must now turn, with some words on Iran as well.

II

The Valley Peoples and Iran

Mesopotamia and Elam

SUMERIANS   The most recent discoveries have led some scholars to believe that the first Mesopotamian inventors of writing may have been a people whom the later Babylonians called Subarians. Traditionally they came from the north. In any case, by about 3100 B.C. they seem to have been overpowered, and were certainly superseded in southern Mesopotamia by the Sumerians, whose name became synonymous for the region immediately north of the Persian Gulf, in the fertile lower valleys of the Tigris and Euphrates and in the land between them. Here the Sumerians were already well established by the year 3000. They had invented bronze, an alloy of copper and tin that could be cast in molds, and they now made tools and weapons of it. Thus they had moved mankind into the Bronze Age, a momentous development. They lived in cities; they had begun to accumulate and use capital; and they wrote. We have known about the Sumerians for only a hundred years. Archaeologists working at Nineveh in northern Mesopotamia in 1869 found many Babylonian inscribed clay tablets, which they could read because the inscriptions were written in a known Semitic language (Akkadian). But some of the tablets also had writing in another language that was not Semitic, and was previously unknown. Some of these inscriptions made reference to the king of Sumer and Akkad, and so a scholar suggested that the new language be called Sumerian. But it was not until the 1890's that archaeologists digging far to the south of Nineveh found many thousands of tablets inscribed in Sumerian only. Since then, excavations have multiplied; the material has poured in; by working from known Akkadian to previously unknown Sumerian, scholars have pretty well learned how to read the Sumerian language.

If the Sumerians did not invent writing on clay, at least they perfected it, using at first a kind of picture-writing, and over the thousand years between 3000 and 2000 B.C. developing a phonetic alphabet. With a reed pen they impressed into the wet clay tablet little wedge-shaped marks, producing a script that we call cuneiform from the Latin *cuneus,* meaning a wedge. The first thousand years of Sumerian history we know from tens of thousands of these tablets that are mostly economic or administrative in content. It is not until the second thousand years (after 2000 B.C.) that we get purely literary materials, but five thousand tablets from that period do provide us with them, some short, some very long, some of them not yet transcribed or translated.

In the earliest days, the Sumerians governed themselves through a council of elders, who derived their authority in turn from a general assembly of all the adult free men. This assembly, which decided on such questions as making war and peace, sometimes would grant supreme authority to an individual leader for a limited time. This arrangement—which seems astonishingly "modern" and "democratic" to us—apparently did not last long, and was replaced by one-man rule in each city. But the human ruler acted only as the representative on earth of the god of the city. In this capacity the ruler built temples to the god to keep him appeased, and especially to obtain his divine protection against the floods that often swept torrentially down the river valleys in the springtime with disastrous results for the people in their way.

The lives and religion and literature of the peoples of Mesopotamia were pervaded by terror of floods: it is virtually certain that the story of the flood in Genesis echoes the ancient tradition of the Sumerians that told of a single disastrous flood from which only a remnant of the people was saved, and from which (about 2900 B.C.) everything later was dated. The Sumerians devised an elaborate system of canals not only for irrigation but to control the force of the floods, and each city required the blessing of its god on its labors. Toward the south, near the Persian Gulf, the problem became one of drainage, to halt the flow of salt water that would have ruined the fields.

Indeed, it took the toil of many centuries for the Sumerians to transform the bleak marshes of the river valleys into fertile and productive farmland, dotted with prosperous cities, each with its own political bureaucracy and its religious institutions; and, as with all human societies, each passing through occasional oppressions, upheavals, and political overturns many of which are recorded by surviving inscriptions. Cities warred with one another, and about 2350 B.C. we find the first inscription recording the ambition of one city ruler to rule the entire region, to be the first universal monarch in history. Moreover, the Sumerians had to fight against infiltrating Semites from the Arabian deserts to the west and the hills to the north. And they campaigned eastward too, against "Elam," the peoples living in what today is western Iran. About 2300 Sargon, king of Akkad, a Semite from the north, conquered the Sumerian ruler of Uruk, and he and his successors called themselves kings of Sumer and Akkad, perhaps indicating that a fusion of the non-Semitic Sumerians and the Semitic Akkadians may have already begun. By about 2100, when scholars date the end of the Early Bronze Age, Sargon's descendants had lost their power, and for a time there was no force to unify the petty states.

In taking the lead against invaders, Gudea, ruler of the city of Lagash, united the Sumerians about 2050 B.C. Soon after he died, Ur replaced Lagash as the capital city, and for a century its rulers played the role of universal monarch. They again called themselves kings of Sumer and Akkad. Much of what we know about the Sumerians comes from the recent systematic excavation of Ur. Very recently a portion of a series of statutes promulgated by the ruler Ur-Nammu (about 2000 B.C.) has been discovered, providing fixed punishment for certain crimes, such as a fine of five shekels of silver for the rape of a virgin slave girl without her owner's consent. Ur-Nammu is thus the first known true lawgiver for an entire people. And Ur enjoyed a brief period of great prosperity based on a farflung trade, a systematic tax system carefully recorded, and a revival of learning. But a decline set in, and Ur's subject cities fell away; invading Elamites from the east destroyed it, but an Amorite general profited by Ur's destruction and the end of Sumerian power, as we shall see. The center of political might shifted to the north.

In addition to their city gods, the Sumerians worshiped a god of the heavens, a god of the region between heaven and earth (the air, hence storms and winds), and a god of earth. Another trinity included gods of the sun and moon, and a goddess of the morning star, who was also associated with fertility. With this female deity was associated a young male god who died and was reborn as a symbol of the seasons.

Here, in the first religion recorded in sources that we can read and therefore interpret surely, we find elements common to all subsequent efforts of men to deal with the supernatural. It was Enki, god of earth and of wisdom, for instance, who poured the water into the two great fertilizing rivers, Tigris and Euphrates, and stocked them with fish; who created grain, filled the land with cattle, built houses and canals, and set subgods over each enterprise.

The Sumerian gods were portrayed in human form, and lived recognizably human lives, with rivalries among themselves. Sumerians also believed in a multitude of demons, mostly bad. From the very earliest days in Mesopotamia, various arts were apparently employed in an effort to foretell the future. The entrails of slaughtered sheep or goats were carefully observed, and texts survive that list the meaning of the various configurations these might assume. Interpreting dreams was also an important method, and the stars were observed, ever more scientifically but always with the purpose of obtaining omens. Because the temples of the city god and other gods actually owned most of the land, most of the population worked as serfs of the temple. But the produce of the land was distributed as pay to them.

Life was highly diversified: blacksmiths, carpenters, and merchants now appear alongside the hunters, farmers, and shepherds of the older days. Fathers exercised many rights over their children. The society was monogamous, and women held a high position. Punishments seem mild relative to those later found in the Babylonian society that grew out of the Sumerian; in Sumer, they consisted mostly of fines.

In many epic poems, the Sumerians celebrated the brave exploits of Gilgamesh, a mighty hero. He undertook perilous journeys, fought and overcame dreadful monsters, and performed great feats of strength. But even Gilgamesh, strong though he was, had to die; and a mournful tone, which scholars recognize as typical of the society, pervades Sumerian literature: hymns, lamentations, prayers, fables, and even schoolboy compositions.

Yet a Sumerian proverb sagely says,

Praise a young man, and he will do whatever you want;
Throw a crust to a dog, and he will wag his tail before you.

Obviously these were people who observed each other keenly; they are very recognizably of the same human breed as ourselves. In their literature they often dealt with the seeming injustice of this life, where even righteous men who lead good lives must suffer. We can recognize the type of the future Old Testament Job, and the moral is the same: glorify god, await the end of life, which will set you free from earthly suffering.

Sumerian art was entirely religious, official in intent and impersonal in style. It changed very little for a millennium and more. The Sumerians built their temples of baked brick. In the shrine was an altar against a wall; other rooms and an outer courtyard were later added. The most striking feature of the temple was that the whole structure was set upon a terrace, the first stage toward a multiplication of terraces, each above and smaller than the last, with the sanctuary at the top, reached by stairs from terrace to terrace. This was the ziggurat, the typical Mesopotamian temple, whose construction itself suggests the rigidly hierarchical Sumerian social order. It was a great ziggurat that suggested the tower of Babel to the author of Genesis. Sumerian tombs were simple chambers, but were often filled with objects intended for use in the afterlife, which Sumerians envisioned as mournful and dreary. Their statuary consisted of clothed human figures, solemn and stiff, with large, staring eyes: gods were shown as larger than kings, and ordinary human beings as smaller. On monumental slabs (steles), on plaques, and especially on seals the Sumerians showed themselves skillful at carving in relief.

Figure of a Sumerian dignitary.

NEW DISCOVERIES IN IRAN   Since 1967, the mound at Tepe Yahya in south central Iran, which contained the Neolithic city we have already mentioned, has also yielded startling finds from a later period. Here, five hundred miles east of the Mesopotamian region traditionally accepted as the birthplace of writing, archaeologists have turned up clay tablets dating to about the year 3500 B.C.— at least as early as, and perhaps even slightly earlier than, the early Sumerian writings. And at Tepe Yahya, the language of the tablets is what scholars call proto-Elamite, not Sumerian or Semitic but the earliest form of the language spoken in Elam, later Iran. In 1972 the tablets had not yet been read, but they are probably commercial records, since they were found in what appeared to be a storehouse, along with pottery storage jars. They were surely written where they were found, since similar tablets still blank were found with them.

Tepe Yahya, its discoverers believe, was a center of the soapstone manufacturing industry, and served as a midpoint between the civilizations growing up in Mesopotamia and that much further to the east in the valley of the Indus. Another such midpoint appears to have been the island of Bahrein in the Persian Gulf. It will undoubtedly be many years before the details of such ancient trade and other relationships have been thoroughly investigated, and all conclusions are for the moment still tentative. But it is at least likely that the men of the Tigris and Euphrates valleys had such hitherto undemonstrable relationships with the men of the Indus valley, and that various centers in Iran were the midpoints. And at any rate the discovery of the proto-Elamite writings of so early a date, and of the soapstone industry of Tepe Yahya, are in themselves sensational brand-new developments in the exploration of the ancient Near East.

AKKADIANS: BABYLONIANS AND ASSYRIANS   Now that scholars have learned so much about the Sumerians, they have realized the enormous debt to Sumer owed by the people who succeeded them as rulers of Mesopotamia: the Semitic Akkadian-speakers, to whom belonged first the Babylonians and then their successors, the Assyrians, both originally descended from the nomads of the Arabian desert. Power first passed to the Semites as we saw with Sargon the Great (2300 B.C.), and returned to them after an interlude, about 2000 B.C., with the invasions of the Amorites from the west.

Since 1935 excavations at Mari in the middle Euphrates valley have turned up a palace with more than 260 rooms containing many thousands of tablets throwing much new light on the Amorite kingdom. Mari was one of its main centers, and the documents we have, mostly from the period between 1750 and 1700 B.C., consist of the royal archives, and include the official letters to the king from his own local officials scattered through his territories and from other rulers of local city-states and principalities many of which were previously unknown to scholars. Among the correspondents was an Amorite prince named Hammurabi, who just before 1700 B.C. made his own Babylonian kingdom supreme in Mesopotamia. His descendants were able to maintain their power in Babylon and the regions surrounding it down to about 1530, but had to give up Hammurabi's great conquests.

Hammurabi's famous code of law, engraved on an eight-foot pillar, though in part modeled on its Sumerian predecessors, exhibits a much harsher spirit in its punishments. Yet, as its author, the king boasted not of his warlike deeds but of the peace and prosperity he had brought. The code reveals a strongly stratified society: a patrician who put out the eye of a patrician would have his own eye put out; but a patrician who put out the eye of a plebeian only had to pay a fine. Yet perhaps it is most important to note that even the plebeian had rights that, to a degree at least, protected him against violence from his betters. Polygamy and divorce have now made their appearance. The code, in fact, is just about what we would expect: it shows a harmonious grafting of Semitic practice and needs in a changing society upon the original qualities of Sumerian inspiration and orderliness.

New nomads, this time from the east (Iran), the Kassites, shattered Babylonian power about 1530; and, after four centuries of relatively peaceful Kassite rule, supremacy in Mesopotamia gradually passed to the far more warlike Semitic Assyrians, whose power had been rising, with occasional setbacks, for several centuries in their great northern city of Assur. About 1100 their ruler Tiglath-pileser reached both the Black Sea and the Mediterranean on a conquering expedition north and west, after which he boasted that he had become "lord of the world." Assyrian militarism was harsh, and the conquerors regularly transported into captivity entire populations of defeated cities. By the eighth century the Assyrian state was a kind of dual monarchy: Tiglath-pileser III (744–727), their ruler, also took the title of ruler of Babylonia, thus consciously accepting the Babylonian tradition. He added enormous territory to the Assyrian dominions. During the 670's B.C. the Assyrian king Esarhaddon invaded and conquered Egypt. Then in turn the mighty Assyrian Empire fell to a new power, the Medes (Iranians related to the Persians), who took Nineveh (612 B.C.) with Babylonian and Palestinian help.

For less than a century thereafter (612–538) Babylonia experienced a rapid, brilliant revival, during which King Nebuchadnezzar built temples and palaces, made Babylon a wonder of the world, with its famous hanging gardens, and overthrew Jerusalem and took the Hebrews into captivity. But in 539, the Hebrew prophet Daniel showed King Belshazzar the moving finger on the wall of the banquet chamber that told him his kingdom was to be given to the Medes and the Persians. Daniel was right, of course, and Cyrus the Great of Persia took Babylon, ending the history of the Mesopotamian empires after two and a half millennia at least.

In addition to their cuneiform writing, the Babylonians and Assyrians took much of their religion from the Sumerians. The cosmic gods remained the same, but the local gods of course were different, and under Hammurabi one of them, Marduk, was exalted over all other gods and kept that supremacy thereafter. The religious texts left behind outnumber those of the Sumerians and give us a more detailed picture of Babylonian–Assyrian belief: demons became more numerous and more powerful, and a special class of priests was needed to fight them. Magic practices multiplied; soothsayers consulted the livers of animals in order to predict the future. All external happenings—an encounter with an animal, a sprained wrist, the position and color of the stars at a vital moment—had implications for one's own future that needed to be discovered. Starting with observation of the stars for such magical purposes, the Babylonians developed substantial knowledge of their movements, and the mathematics to go with it. They even managed to predict eclipses. They could add, subtract, multiply, divide, and extract roots. They could solve equations, and measure both plane areas and solid volumes. But their astronomy and their mathematics remained in the service of astrology and divination.

Like the Sumerians, the Babylonians were a worried and a gloomy people, who feared death and regarded the afterlife as grim and dusty, in the bowels of the earth. Even this depressing fate could be attained only if the living took care to bury the dead and to hold them in memory. Otherwise one had only restlessness and perhaps a career as a demon to look forward to. In Babylonian literature we find Marduk the center of an epic of the creation; we encounter Gilgamesh again, in a more coherent epic than that of the Sumerians, in which he declines a goddess's offer to make him a god because he knows he is sure to die.

Similarly in art the inspiration remains unchanging, but some variations appear: unlike the Sumerians, the Babylonians in some regions had access to stone, and so now incorporated columns in their buildings; and especially the Assyrians showed greater interest, as one would expect, in scenes of combat. In Assyria too one finds the orthostat, a statue inserted into a wall, and so appearing in high relief; typical Assyrian versions appear as bulls, lions, and fantastic winged beasts. Jewels, gold, and ivory-carving now reached new and extraordinarily beautiful heights, as shown especially in the finds at Nimrud.

Egypt

CHARACTER OF THE SOCIETY   What the Tigris and the Euphrates rivers did for the land between them—Mesopotamia—the Nile River, rising in the hills of Ethiopia and flowing a thousand miles north through Egypt into the Mediterranean, did for the strip of land along its banks on both sides, beyond which, east and west, stretched the dry and inhospitable sands of desert. Nobody can be certain how many millennia had passed in which the people along the Nile had slowly learned to take advantage of the annual summer flood by tilling their fields to receive the silt-laden river waters, and by regulating its flow, but about 3000 B.C., at approximately the time when the Sumerian civilization emerged in Mesopotamia, the Egyptians had reached a comparable stage of development. Much better known to us than Mesopotamia—most of us even as small children already knew about the pyramids, the sphinx, and King Tut's tomb—Egypt was the other ancient valley civilization that made major contributions to our own.

No sweeping generalizations about peoples and societies are ever wholly acceptable; yet, speaking roughly, scholars who have studied the sources for both Egypt and Mesopotamia and who have compared the two often note that the Egyptians were generally more cheerful and confident than the gloomy and apprehensive Sumerians, Babylonians, and Assyrians; more tolerant and urbane and less harsh and obdurate; more speculative and imaginative and less practical and literal-minded; and—despite the long centuries of apparent sameness—more dynamic and less static in their attitudes and achievements. Life after death the Egyptians regarded as a happy continuation of life on earth with all its fleshly pleasures, not as a dismal eternal sojourn in the dust. When we think of Mesopotamian art we think of temples made of brick and of public monuments; when we think of Egyptian art we think of tombs made of stone and of private monuments. The Mesopotamians have left few statues, the Egyptians many. The Mesopotamian rulers—both the early city lords and the later kings who aspired to universal monarchy—were agents of the gods on earth; the Egyptian rulers from the beginning were themselves regarded as gods. The Mesopotamians were historically minded, the Egyptians not. So, despite the many similarities between the two societies, and the mutual influences we know to have passed from one to the other—though chiefly in the direction of Egypt from Mesopotamia—each had its own distinct characteristics.

Because Egyptian territory consisted of the long strip along the banks of the Nile, it always was hard to unify. At the very beginning—3000 B.C.—we can distinguish two rival kingdoms—Lower Egypt: the Nile Delta (so called because it is shaped like the Greek letter of that name), the triangle of land nearest the Mediterranean where the river splits into several streams and flows into the sea; and Upper Egypt: the land along the course of the river for eight hundred miles between the Delta and the First Cataract. Periodically the two regions were unified in one kingdom, but the ruler, who called himself king of Upper and Lower Egypt, by his very title recognized that his realms consisted of two somewhat disparate entities, one looking toward the Mediterranean and outward to the other civilizations growing up around its edges, and the other more isolated by its deserts and more self-regarding. The first unifier, perhaps mythical, was a certain Menes, whose reign (about 2850 B.C.) scholars take as the start of the first standard division of Egyptian history, the Old Kingdom (2850–2200).

OLD, MIDDLE, AND NEW KINGDOMS   When the king is god, his subjects need only listen to his commands to feel sure they are doing the divine will. As each Egyptian king died, his great sepulchral monument in the form of a pyramid told his subjects that he had gone to join his predecessors in the community of gods. The largest of the pyramids took several generations to build, and involved the continual labor of thousands of men, a token that the society accepted and took pride in the divinity of its rulers. A highly centralized bureaucracy carried out the commands of the king. A stratified society worked for him. His forces advanced at times westward into the Libyan desert, and at other times—drawn by the pull that we find exerted on every ruler of Egypt from Menes to President Sadat—east and north into Palestine. The Old Kingdom was first disturbed and eventually shattered by a growing tendency among district governors to pass their offices on to their sons, who in turn tended to strike out on their own or at least to regard their territories as hereditary fiefs and thus to weaken the central authority. At the same time we know the priests of the Sun had also made good their claims to special privileges that helped diminish royal power. After an interim period of disorder lasting perhaps two centuries (2200–2000), a new dynasty (eleventh of the thirty in Egyptian history) restored unity in what is known as the Middle Kingdom (2100–1800), distinguished for its rulers' land-reclamation policies and its victories abroad.

To the south, the hostile Nubians were defeated and their movements controlled by the building of frontier fortresses. Palestine and Syria came under Egyptian influence. The bureaucracy flourished. Thebes ceased to be the capital, as a new city was founded south of Memphis, from which government could be exercised more effectively; the provincial governorship became hereditary, but had to be confirmed by the king; and the king's son at the age of twenty-one became co-ruler with his father. The king himself was less remote and more eager to be regarded as the shepherd of his people.

But secessionist movements took control of Egypt and the growing internal weakness combined with a foreign invasion and conquest put an end to the Middle Kingdom about 1800 B.C. The conquerors were called Hyksos, Asian nomads of uncertain origin who imported the war chariot and perhaps the bow. The Egyptians hated their rule, which lasted something over a century, and eventually rallied behind a new dynasty (the seventeenth) to drive out the invaders. By about 1550 and the eighteenth dynasty the task was accomplished and the New Kingdom (1550–1085) well launched. The five centuries of the New Kingdom saw extraordinary advances: in foreign affairs, the Egyptians engaged in a struggle for Syria and Palestine not only with the great powers of Mesopotamia but with the mountain and desert peoples who lived between the two great valley civilizations. The Egyptian ruler (now called pharaoh) Thutmose I reached the Euphrates on the east, and marched far south into Nubia (what we today call the Sudan). Thutmose III (1469–1436) fought seventeen campaigns in the East, and even crossed the Euphrates and

Pillars of the temple at Karnak.

The pharaoh Akhenaten and his wife Nefertiti offer gifts to the sun god Aten.

beat his Mesopotamian enemies on their own soil. The walls of the great temple of Karnak preserve his own carved account of his military achievements and the enormous tribute paid him by his conquered enemies. It is his obelisk, popularly known as Cleopatra's Needle, that stands in Central Park in New York. The Egyptians established their own network of local governors throughout the conquered territories, but ruled mildly, and did not, as the Assyrians were soon to do, deport whole masses of the population into captivity. The building program of the eighteenth dynasty was a vast one.

It was the pharaoh Amenhotep IV (1379–1362) who caused a major internal upheaval in the successful New Kingdom by challenging the priests of the sun god Amen, who had become a powerful privileged class. Amenhotep urged the substitution for Amen of the sun disk, Aten, and, even more dramatic, commanded that Aten alone be worshiped and that all the multitude of other gods, whom we shall shortly discuss, be abandoned. Amenhotep changed his name to Akhenaten, "Pleasing to Aten," in honor of his only god. Some have seen in this famous episode a real effort to impose monotheism on Egypt; others doubt this. To mark the new policy, Akhenaten and his beautiful wife Nefertiti, whose statue is widely reproduced, ruled from a new capital in Amarna. Amarna gives its name to the "Amarna age" (ca. 1417–ca. 1358). Nearby, beginning in the 1880's A.D., were found the famous Tell-el-Amarna letters, a collection of about four hundred tablets including the diplomatic correspondence of Akhenaten and his father with the rulers of western Asia, in many languages, an invaluable source for scholars.

Akhenaten's effort to overthrow the entrenched priesthood led to internal dissension and the loss of external strength. His son-in-law, Tutankhamen (1361–1351), was eventually sent to rule in Thebes, city of the priests of Amen, with whom he compromised: this was "King Tut," the discovery of whose tomb with all its magnificent contents was the sensation of the 1920's. With Akhenaten's death, the new religious experiment collapsed, and the pharaohs

21

strove to make up for the interval of weakness by restoring their foreign conquests.

About 1300 B.C. we find Ramses II (nineteenth dynasty) reaching a treaty with a people from Asia Minor, the Hittites. This treaty, of which we have texts both in Egyptian and Hittite, called for a truce in the struggle for Syria and provided for a dynastic marriage between the pharaoh and a Hittite princess. The interlude was short, however, and soon after 1200 B.C. the New Kingdom in its turn suffered severely as the result of an invasion of the eastern Mediterranean shores by mixed bands of Sea Peoples, probably including ancestors of the later Greeks and Sicilians, and others.

Now Egypt entered into a period of decline, marked by renewed internal struggles for power between the secular authorities and the priests, and among local and central rulers. Then came the Assyrian conquest of the seventh century, the Persian conquest of 525 B.C., and the conquest by Alexander the Great of Macedonia in 331 B.C.

RELIGION   Religion was the most powerful force animating Egyptian society, and it was so complicated a religion that modern authorities are hard put to describe it. One of the greatest writes that if one asked an ancient Egyptian "whether the sky was supported by posts or held up by a god, the Egyptian would answer: 'Yes, it is supported by posts or held up by a god—or it rests on walls, or it is a cow, or it is a goddess whose arms and feet touch the earth.'" * So the Egyptian was ready to accept overlapping divinities, and to add new ones whenever it seemed appropriate: if a new area was incorporated into the Egyptian state, its gods would be added to those already worshiped.

From the beginning, Egyptian cults included animals, totems perhaps: sheep, bulls, gazelles, and cats, still to be found carefully buried in their own cemeteries. As time passed, the figures of Egyptian gods became human, but often retained an animal's head, sometimes an animal's body. Osiris, the Egyptian god best known to most of us, began as a local Nile Delta deity. He taught mankind agriculture; Isis was his wife, and animal-headed Set his brother and rival. Set killed Osiris; Isis persuaded the gods to bring him back to life, but thereafter he ruled below (obviously a parallel to the fertility and vegetation-cycle beliefs we have already encountered in Mesopotamia and will encounter in Greece). Naturally enough, Osiris was identified with the life-giving, fertilizing Nile, and Isis with the receptive earth of Egypt.

Horus the sun defeated the evil Set after a long struggle. But Horus was only one kind of sun god: there was also Re, later joined with Amen, and still later Aten, as we saw. The moon god was the ibis-headed Thoth. In the great temple cities like Heliopolis, priests worked out and wrote down hierarchies of divinities. Out in the villages all the forces of nature were deified and worshiped: one local god was part crocodile, part hippopotamus, and part lion, a touching and economical revelation of what simple farmers along the river-banks had to worry about. However numerous the deities, Egyptian religion itself was unified; unlike a Sumerian temple, however, which was the political center of its city, and for which the population toiled, the Egyptian temple had a limited religious function.

The Egyptians were preoccupied with life after death. They believed that after death each human being would appear before Osiris and recount all the bad things he had *not* done on earth: "I have not done evil to men. I have not ill-treated animals. I have not blasphemed the gods," and so on, a negative

* J. A. Wilson, in *The Intellectual Adventure of Ancient Man* (Chicago, 1943), p. 44.

confession, to justify his admission into the kingdom of the blessed. Osiris would then have the man's heart weighed, to test the truth of his self-defense; and he would be admitted or else delivered over to judges for punishment.

Egyptians believed not only in body and soul, but in *ka,* the indestructible vital principle of each human being, which left the body at death but could and did return at times. That is why the Egyptians preserved the body in their elaborate art of mummification: so that the ka on its return would find it not decomposed; and that is why they filled the tombs of the dead with all the objects that the ka might need or find delightful on its return to the body. Otherwise it might come back and haunt the living.

CIVILIZATION   We know Egyptian civilization so intimately because of the great number of inscriptions, which give us the historical materials, and of papyri (fragments of the ancient material the Egyptians wrote on, made of the pith of a water plant), which give us the literary materials. Yet what we have represents a smaller percentage of what once existed and of what may yet be found than does our collection of Mesopotamian literature on its carefully copied myriad clay tablets. The Egyptian language first yielded its secrets only in the 1820's, when the French scholar Champollion first saw on a late obelisk that several Greek personal names were repeated in the Egyptian hieroglyphics (literally, "sacred writing"). With these as a start, Champollion turned to a famous trilingual inscription, the Rosetta Stone, found in the Nile Delta in 1799, which bears the same text in Greek, in hieroglyphics, and in another script used in Egypt after hieroglyphics had gone out of fashion. The Rosetta Stone was soon deciphered, and the lessons learned have been applied to all the texts discovered before and since. Visitors to the British Museum can still see the extraordinary slab that made it possible for men of the nineteenth and twentieth centuries A.D. to understand ancient Egypt.

The famous Egyptian *Book of the Dead* brings together stories of the gods and hymns and prayers, and teaches us much of what we know of Egyptian religion. The Egyptian literature we have includes no epic story of a hero comparable to Gilgamesh, a mortal who cannot quite attain immortality, no doubt because the Egyptians confidently did expect to attain it, whether heroic or not. But it does include love songs, banquet songs, and what we would call fiction, both historical and fantastic. "If I kiss her," says an Egyptian lover, "and her lips are open, I am happy even without beer," * a sentiment that seems irreproachably up to date even at the distance of three millennia. "Enjoy thyself as much as thou canst," says a banquet song, "for a man cannot take his property with him,"† though actually nobody ever tried harder than the Egyptians to do so. The historical romance of Sinuhe tells the story of an Egyptian noble who was forced by intrigue into exile in Asia (early Middle Kingdom, ca. 1980 B.C.), was elected chief of a tribe there, won a magnificent single combat against a local champion, and, at the end, full of longing for Egypt, was happily recalled by the pharaoh and richly dressed, honored, and given a pyramid of his own for his future sepulcher. In another story we hear of the young man who resisted a lady's advances only to find that she was accusing him of having made advances to her: a predicament similar to that of Joseph in Egypt itself as reported by the Old Testament, and to many similar tales in the folklore of other peoples.

* A. Erman, *Literature of the Ancient Egyptians,* trans. A. M. Blackman (London: Dutton, 1927), p. 244.

† J. H. Breasted, *The Dawn of Conscience* (New York, 1933), pp. 163–164.

Egyptian Art

We have all seen pictures
of Egyptian pyramids and temples,
gigantic sculptured pharaohs
and divinities, and the
rich and ostentatious gold
and jewels of a splendid
sepulcher like King Tut's. The
use of stone in building,
the skillful use of great spaces,
the skillful portraiture
of individuals rather than types,
the obelisks and sphinxes, the
absence of perspective: these are
familiar characteristics
of Egyptian art.

Relief of cattle fording a stream: from the tomb of Ti, an official of the Fifth Dynasty, ca. 2350 B.C.

The pyramids of Gizeh.

Above left: Painted-limestone head of Nefertiti, wife of Akhenaten. Above right: Akhenaten himself.

Right: The brother and sister-in-law of Ramose, a high official in the service of the pharaoh Amenophis III, portrayed at a banquet. From the walls of the tomb of Ramose in Thebes: ca. 1375 B.C.

Below: Limestone sculpture of a scribe with his roll of papyrus: ca. 2400 B.C.

The temple of Idfu, third century B.C., best preserved of the Egyptian temples.

But less well known are the many scenes of ordinary country or family life that characterize Egyptian painting and that show a characteristic enjoyment and even a sense of humor distinctly not found in Mesopotamia. On the wall of an Egyptian tomb a young man and his wife sit happily playing checkers or listening to music or watching the dancing girls. A thief steals a cow while the herdsman's eyes are elsewhere; a crocodile waits for a baby hippopotamus to be born so that at last he may have his lunch. The people who lived along the Nile all those millennia ago speak to us clearly, and we listen with fascination and recognition.

Old Kingdom relief of a crocodile hungrily awaiting the birth of a hippopotamus: from Saqqara.

III
Peoples Outside the Valleys

For well over a thousand years after their first flourishing the peoples of the valley civilizations had held the stage virtually alone. But the Hyksos invasion of Egypt (ca. 1800), the Kassite invasion of Mesopotamia, and the Hittite attacks on both have already warned us that the men of the mountains and deserts outside the valleys had begun to compete fiercely with the more settled valley societies. The outsiders too had centuries of history behind them, still not well known to scholars, but by 1500 B.C. the Kassites in southern Mesopotamia, the Hurrians with their state of Mitanni in northern Mesopotamia and smaller states in southeastern Anatolia (modern Turkey), and the Hittites in the remainder of Anatolia had all emerged as rivals both to Babylon and to Egypt.

All of them had strong Indo-European ethnic elements: that is, elements of a strain that will become predominant in Iran, and later in the Mediterranean and the West. All of them were ruled by kings, but their kings were neither the Mesopotamian agents of god on earth nor the Egyptian deified monarchs: rather they ruled as the most powerful among a noble class that controlled the instruments of conquest—horses and chariots—and shared the fruits of conquest, dividing new land among themselves. We begin now to find records, not only of war between these newly emerging peoples and the settled valley societies, but also of their diplomatic exchanges and their peace settlements.

For communication everybody used Akkadian, a Semitic tongue often foreign to both parties in a negotiation. The Egyptians, for example, corresponded in it with the peoples who ruled Syria, who did not speak it either. As with the language and the cuneiform letters in which it was written, so with the culture generally: the outside peoples were deeply influenced by Mesopotamian religion and literature and art. Though the outsiders dealt severe blows to the valley societies and sometimes seemed temporarily to have overthrown them, the valley societies—Mesopotamia and Egypt—did not in fact succumb during the centuries from 1500 to 1200 B.C., when the threat was greatest.

The Hittites

Until the twentieth century A.D., we knew the Hittites only from a few mentions in other sources—Uriah, whom King David so reprehensibly arranged to have killed in battle in order to keep his wife Bathsheba, was a Hittite, for instance. But the discovery of the Hittite capital, Hattusas, now called Boğazköy, in the high plateau of Anatolia revealed several thousand tablets, largely cuneiform in script and written not only in the Indo-European Hittite language but in many others as well. These finds enable us to date at about 1700 B.C. the emergence of a strong Hittite kingdom, with its Indo-European ruler and aristocracy in control over the native Anatolian population; to note its great conquests between 1700 and ca. 1590, its resumption of successful expansion toward Babylon about 1530, its internal crises and recovery about 1500 with the first of the hereditary monarchs, and its height under Suppiluliumas (1380–1346), contemporary of Akhenaten, who took advantage of Egyptian weakness to assert his own strength.

Surely it was no coincidence that Suppiluliumas began after his intimate contact with the Egypt of Akhenaten to insist that he be addressed as "my Sun" and to use the solar disk as a symbol. Henceforth Hittite sovereigns were deified, but only after death: it is from about this time that the written sources

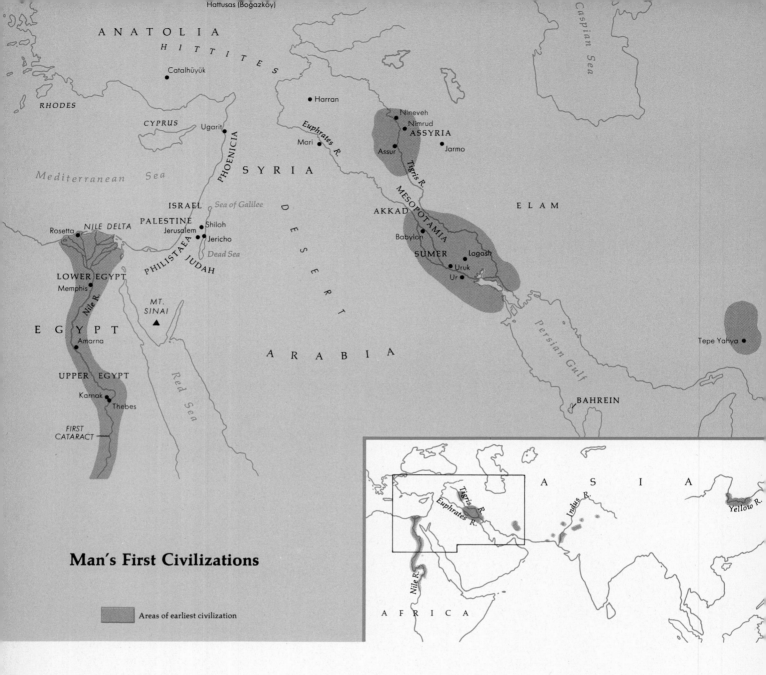

Hattusas (Boğazköy)

Man's First Civilizations

Areas of earliest civilization

we have begin to speak of a king as "becoming a god" at death. The onslaught of the Sea Peoples that damaged the Egyptian New Kingdom about 1200 also put an end to the centralized Hittite state, although various smaller "neo-Hittite" petty principalities continued to exist in Asia Minor in the face of Assyrian expansion down to the late eighth century B.C.

To Hittite religion the native Anatolians, the Indo-European Hittite upper crust, the Mesopotamians, and the Egyptians all made contributions: foreign gods were made welcome and domesticated. Once part of Hittite religion, no matter where they had originally come from, they received homage in forms derived from Mesopotamia. But there were differences here too: women played a more prominent role in Hittite religion and society than they did either in Mesopotamia or in Egypt. And alone among the peoples of the ancient Near East, the Hittites cremated their kings.

This has reminded scholars that in Homer's *Iliad* the Trojans cremated their dead prince Hector and that Troy itself stood on the edge of Anatolia and so would have been close to areas of predominant Hittite influence. When to this is added the fact that Hittite sources apparently refer to the Achaeans (the name that Homer gives his Greeks) and to Troy, many have been tempted to see a close historical connection between the Hittites and the tale told by Homer.

That portion of Hittite literature which is preserved is full of Mesopotamian echoes, but it is distinguished by its sober official histories, which—alone up to that time among the literary works of the ancient Near East—sought to determine and record the motives of the rulers for their actions. The treaty, too, as a special literary and diplomatic instrument, was apparently a Hittite invention. Hittite architecture expressed itself in fortresses on peaks, which became the nuclei of cities. Otherwise, the buildings show Mesopotamian influence, as does the sculpture; but the Hittites produced no monumental human statues.

Hurrians, Canaanites, Philistines, Phoenicians

Far less well known than the Hittites and still posing many unsolved problems are the Hurrians, whose state, called Mitanni, was established about 1500 B.C. in northern Mesopotamia and lasted only about a century and a third. No local archaeological finds comparable to Boğazköy for the Hittites have yet turned up; and what we know about the Hurrians comes from Egyptian, Hittite, Amorite, and western Palestinian documents. Like the Hittites, the Hurrians had an Indo-European ruling class, and worshiped some Indo-European deities. Their great importance was to act as intermediaries between the great civilization of Mesopotamia and the less advanced peoples to the north and west, especially the Hittites.

Besides the mountains of Anatolia and northern Mesopotamia, the deserts of Syria (the Old Testament land of Canaan) gave rise to a number of Semitic peoples who from time to time invaded the valley societies. Indeed, the Akkadians themselves, both Babylonians and Assyrians, and the Amorites as well had first emerged into history along this path. But there remained behind, of course, other Semitic peoples who never penetrated into the valleys, and who created societies of their own along the Syrian coast of the Mediterranean and in its hinterland.

At Ugarit on the coast—in the northern portion called Phoenicia—archaeologists in 1929 found the royal palace of a Canaanite state that flourished between 1400 and 1200 B.C., complete with tablets in a northwest Semitic tongue—Ugaritic—containing several poems highly important for our knowledge of the religion and culture of the people, and also the archives of official correspondence, including a treaty with the Hittites written in Akkadian and showing that the Canaanites were under Hittite domination. Though extremely important because of its farflung relationships with contemporary states and as a forerunner of the Phoenicians, Ugarit was only one of many Canaanite city-states, and it went down in the general chaos of 1200 B.C. caused by the Sea Peoples' invasion. Among these invading Sea Peoples, we know, were the Indo-European Philistines, who settled to the south of the Canaanites and gave their name to Palestine.

The Canaanites apparently matched their extreme political localism with extreme religious localism, and they seem often not to have taken much trouble to sort out their gods: several gods presided over any given department of life, and gods were sometimes masculine and sometimes feminine, as if nobody was quite sure or cared very much. If this seems primitive, the impression is reinforced by the Canaanite practices of human sacrifice and religious prostitution. The supreme Canaanite god was El, whose name simply means "god" and who is little known. Baal, on the other hand, whose name means "lord," was a storm god—like the Sumerian god of the air, the region between heaven and earth. Baal and his wife Astarte, like Osiris and Isis in Egypt and parallel figures in Mesopotamia, symbolized the seasons and cyclical fertility.

In the period after 1300 the Phoenicians, still another Semitic people, flourished along the coast south of Ugarit, and carried on a brisk trade with the western Mediterranean, founding Carthage as a colony about 800 B.C. The Phoenicians (whose very name comes from the word for the Tyrian purple dye made from shellfish found along the coast of their capital, Tyre) thus brought their Semitic tongue (Punic) more than halfway to the Straits of Gilbraltar, through which in fact their ships had often sailed. Many Phoenician names, as we shall see, appear among the names the Greeks gave to their gods; and the Phoenician alphabet, a real advanced alphabet, not, like cuneiform, a collection of signs that stood for whole syllables, and perhaps inspired by Ugaritic, became the immediate ancestor of the Greek alphabet.

Land of Canaan, Baal, Philistines: these names have been familiar to us all since childhood. For we have now come into the place and time of the Old Testament, and are prepared to understand some of the regional and cultural background of the Hebrews, who in turn were to pass on so much to the peoples of Europe and America.

The Hebrews

HISTORY AND THE OLD TESTAMENT   With the Hebrews we have reached our first people whose history is recorded in a series of books providing a consecutive story over many centuries. This is of course the Old Testament, which includes much besides the historical accounts in Genesis, Exodus, Joshua, Judges, Samuel, and Kings: genealogy and ritual law (Numbers, Leviticus, and Deuteronomy), tales (Ruth and Job), proverbs (Proverbs, Ecclesiastes), prophetic utterances (Isaiah, Jeremiah, and the rest), and lyric poems (The Psalms, The Song of Songs). Because for many centuries these books were held by Jew and Christian alike to express the literal and sacred truth, it was not until relatively recently that scholars began to apply to them the same test of authenticity that they apply to ordinary works of history. Nineteenth-century scholars found much material in the Old Testament that they took to be legendary and mythical, and they often questioned its historical accuracy. But most such doubts have tended to be dispelled in our own time, as hard archaeological evidence has piled up in support of the general narrative that the Old Testament gives us. It is true that the Old Testament was not written down as the events happened, that many of its earliest portions were compiled long after the event, that the writings were not arranged in their present form until the second century B.C., and that many folklore elements can be easily identified. But the weight of the evidence tends to confirm the biblical story.

Even the biblical account of the mist-shrouded beginnings of the Hebrews now seems authentic: they may well have migrated from Ur "of the Chaldees" sometime after 1950 B.C., when that Sumerian center in southern Mesopotamia was destroyed, northwest to the prosperous center of Harran. Abraham then may well have migrated westward into "Canaan," as Genesis says. The accounts in Genesis of the origins of the universe and the racial origins of the Hebrews, and the stories of Eden, the Flood, and the Tower of Babel all fit into the supposition of a northern Mesopotamian—and no other—place of residence for the Hebrews before about 1500 B.C., when the westward migration took place. Probably a racial mixture including some non-Semitic elements

Jehu, king of Israel, paying homage to King Shalmaneser III of Assyria: a panel from Nimrud, 841 B.C.

(Hurrian?) from the beginning, the Hebrews may well be the same as a people called Khapiru who appear beginning about 1900 B.C. in the cuneiform tablets and in both Hittite and Egyptian sources as raiders, wanderers, and captives. Historians also are convinced that some of the Hebrews at least did live for several centuries in the Nile Delta during the Hyksos period, before Moses (whose name is Egyptian) became their leader and led them about 1300 B.C. to within sight of the Promised Land. Even the miraculous crossing of the Red Sea in Exodus is not incompatible with the shallow waters, the reedy growth, and the winds of the region.

Outsiders battering their way back into Canaan against the entrenched resistance of those who already lived there, the Hebrew confederation of tribes was held together by the new religion that Moses gave them—the Ten Commandments, the ark of the covenant, the many observances that God prescribed. Gradually by ruthless conquest they added to their holdings (Joshua took Jericho about 1230 B.C.), and after the period of the Judges—when many minor leaders directed Hebrew affairs and battles were fought against Canaanites and Philistines—the loose confederation became a monarchy in about 1020 B.C., when the prophet Samuel chose Saul to be the first king. Saul's son-in-law, rival, and successor, David, so well known to us by the virtually contemporary account (1000–960 B.C.) in the Book of Samuel, united the kingdom and strengthened it. His luxury-loving son Solomon brought the Palestinian kingdom of the Jews to new heights of prosperity, but even then it was small in size and resources compared to Sumer, Babylon, Assyria, or Egypt.

But Solomon (960–922 B.C.) lacked the character of David, and in 933 B.C. the kingdom split in two: the northern kingdom of Israel (933–722 B.C.), stronger but lacking the great center of Jerusalem, and the southern kingdom of Judah (933–585 B.C.), which held Jerusalem but had little real strength. The Assyrians destroyed Israel in 722 B.C., and the Babylonians—then, as we have seen, experiencing a brief revival—destroyed Judah in 586 and took the Jews into captivity. When the Persians under Cyrus the Great in turn conquered Babylonia and freed the Jews to return to Palestine after 538, the Jews no longer had a state, but a religious community only. From then on they were held together by religion alone, and depended politically on one empire or another: in succession, the Persian, the Macedonian, the Roman.

RELIGION   Indeed, had it not been for their extraordinary religion, the Hebrews would seem to us just another people of the ancient Near East, less numerous than most, less talented artistically than any. But of course we would probably not know much about them had it not been for their religion, which gave them and us the books of the Old Testament and an enduring tradition. Many of the most fundamental ideas of Hebrew religion go back to the days when the Hebrews were still nomads, before they had adopted a settled life. Thus God's commandments to Moses on Mount Sinai that "Thou shalt have no other gods before me," "Thou shalt not make unto thee any graven image," and "Thou shalt not take the name of the Lord thy God in vain"—which long preceded the settlement in Palestine—determined three fundamental and permanent aspect of Judaism that were new among Near Eastern religions.

The religion of the Hebrews was monotheistic, recognizing only a single god. Despite the experiment of Akhenaten in Egypt and a few Babylonian texts that try to associate all divine power with the chief god, Marduk, alone, the Jews were the first to insist that their god was the only god, and a universal god. Second, the Jews were forbidden to represent him in sculpture or painting—which was an enormous contrast with all other religions of the ancient world. More than that: they were forbidden to make *any* images of living beings, flesh, fish, or fowl, no doubt because their leaders feared that if they did make such images, they would end by worshiping them; and so from these earliest days their art was confined to nonrepresentational subjects. When they deviated from this law, as they sometimes did, it was usually because of the influence upon them of neighbors whose traditions did not forbid animal or human representations in art. Third, the religion of the Hebrews from the beginning would regard the *name* of God—Yahweh or Jehovah, meaning "he causes to be," or "the creator"—as literally not to be spoken, a reverence quite different from any we have found in other ancient Near Eastern religions. From the nomadic period of Hebrew life also come the feast of the Passover, with its offering of a spring lamb and of unleavened bread, celebrating the escape from Egypt; the keeping of the sabbath on the seventh day; the annual day of expiation (Yom Kippur); and other holy days still honored by the Jews in our own times.

The Old Testament swarms with episodes in which the Hebrews proved unable to keep the first commandment, broke away from the worship of the single God, tried to propitiate other gods, and were punished. Yet however often they disobeyed, the first commandment remained the central feature of their religion. With monotheism from the first went morality, as shown in the remaining commandments forbidding murder, adultery, stealing, false witness, and covetousness of one's neighbor's property. Jehovah himself, both merciful and righteous, creator of all things, was human in form, but was not visible to the human eye. Unlike the gods of all the other peoples, he did not lead a human life; he had no family; he dwelt, not in a palace like a human palace only more splendid, but in heaven. When he wished to speak to the leader of his people, he descended onto a mountaintop (Mount Sinai) or into a burning bush or into the space left for him by his own direction between the wings of the cherubim to be set atop the sacred box in which the Ten Commandments on their two tablets of stone were to be kept.

This was the ark of the covenant, built by artisans to the special orders of God as relayed by Moses. The covenant was the special pact between God himself and his chosen people, all the tribes of the Hebrews, in tribal confederation, held together by their regard for this most sacred of objects. Kept at first in a very special tent, a portable tabernacle, the ark moved with the

Hebrews, first to Shiloh, where the Philistines captured it about 1050 B.C., and then into the temple built for it by Solomon in Jerusalem, a royal chapel, whose decorations included many that violated the commandment about graven images. Solomon's temple was built by a Canaanite architect using Phoenician models, showing the increasing influence of non-Israelite peoples on the cult.

There were prophets (men called by God) among the Jews from the beginning; but they naturally multiplied during the division of the people into the two kingdoms of Israel and Judah. They summoned the people to return to the original purity of the faith and to avoid the paganism that seemed to be threatening if Canaanite influences continued. In ecstasy perhaps brought on by dances, they solemnly warned of fearful punishment to come if the people did not heed them. After the punishment, however, the prophets (notably Isaiah) promised that Israel would rise again, and that a descendant of David would appear as the Messiah to usher in a new golden age. The disaster came, of course, with the Babylonian captivity; and now that the prophecies of evil had been fulfilled, the prophet Ezekiel had a vision of new life being breathed into the dead bones of Israel, and urged the preparation for its restoration. (It was in exile, in the sixth century B.C., that the sacred writings were selected and arranged in a form not unlike the Old Testament we know.) The captivity once over, the priests became the dominant figures in the restored community, with its rebuilt temple but without a state of its own. They strove deliberately to return to what they believed to be the practices of their remote ancestors.

As one would expect, there was much about Hebrew society that recalls what we have already observed about the remaining peoples of the ancient Near East. The father exercised supreme authority within the family; polygamy and divorce were permitted; and, as among the Hittites, a widow married her dead husband's brother. The Hebrews had slaves, but a Hebrew slave could be made to serve no more than six years. A man who had injured his slave was required to set him free. Otherwise the law of an eye for an eye, a tooth for a tooth, held sway. Yet the general prescriptions, such as the Commandments, and even some of the specific regulations—not to wrong strangers, not to exact usurious interest for a loan, to help one's enemies as well as one's friends—strike an ethical note deeper than any found in the earlier Mesopotamian Near East, and presage the Christian principles that would—within another half-millennium—emerge from this Hebrew society.

IV
Crete and Mycenae

Minoans before Mycenae

Among the notable finds in Ugarit was an ivory relief of a bare-breasted goddess, holding wheat ears in each hand and seated between two goats standing on their hind legs. She is like nothing from Mesopotamia or Egypt, but she greatly resembles the goddesses frequently found on the large Mediterranean island of Crete, on the westernmost fringe of the Near East, where there developed beginning about 2600 B.C. the last of the Bronze Age civilizations we shall consider, preceded, like the others, by untold numbers of centuries of gradual Stone Age advance. Cretan civilization is often called Minoan, after Minos, the legendary founder of the local dynasty, whose monarchs were all called Minos after him.

Sir Arthur Evans, the British archaeologist whose brilliant work in Crete in the first half of our own century enabled modern scholars to appreciate

Minoan society at its true worth, divided the culture into three main periods, Early Minoan (ca. 2600–ca. 2000), Middle Minoan (ca. 2000–1600), and Late Minoan (ca. 1600–1100); and each of these three is regularly further subdivided three times to enable easy discussion of the objects found. For all such dating pottery is the key. Different styles found at different levels permit scholars to work out a chronological framework. In Crete such dating is of surpassing importance, partly because we have not yet learned how to read the earliest writing, some of it in hieroglyphics and some of it in a script known as Linear A. The number of Linear A tablets is relatively small compared with the tens of thousands of Mesopotamian writings at our disposal; and no inscription has yet been found written in both Linear A and a known language: Crete has no Rosetta Stone. Since they cannot read the writing, scholars who try to reconstruct Cretan society in its early phases have nothing to go on except the objects uncovered by the archaeologist. Of these the greatest are the palace of Minos at Knossos (Heraklion), found and partly reconstructed by Evans, and other palaces and tombs in other parts of the island.

The Cretans were—we think—not Indo-Europeans but descendants of Anatolian immigrants to the island. Pottery and seals found on Crete show that the Cretans were in touch with both Egypt and Mesopotamia. In fact, this was a busy maritime people, whose ships not only plied the Mediterranean but presumably managed to defend the island against invaders, since none of the palaces was fortified. Expanding at the expense of other islanders, the Cretans had garrisons and even colonies abroad, a Bronze Age overseas empire on a small scale exacting tribute from other powers.

The Palace of Minos is a Middle Minoan triumph, resting on earlier foundations, characterized by many rooms, a great staircase, strikingly beautiful wall frescoes (recovered from the ruins in fragments), massive columns, many six-foot-tall stone storage jars for olive oil or wine, and an elaborate plumbing system with pipes, running water, and ventilation. So complex was the palace that Evans himself believed—probably rightly—that he had discovered that building that had inspired the ancient Greek legend of the Labyrinth, the palace on Crete with a system of rooms and corridors so mazelike that nobody could find his way without a guide or a thread to drop behind him so that he might later retrace his steps.

Minoan craftsmen produced delicate pottery hardly thicker than an eggshell, decorated with birds, flowers, and marine animals; ivory or pottery statuettes of the bare-breasted goddess, who sometimes holds a snake in each hand; and many paintings of bulls, some showing young athletes—girls and boys—leaping over a bull's back, in what was clearly something like a ritual game. Athenian legend (no doubt a memory of tribute of grain once sent to Crete) said that their ancestors had been forced to send each year young men and maidens to be sacrificed by the Cretans to their half-man, half-bull monster called the Minotaur (a Minos-bull, supposedly the fruit of a union between the Cretan queen Pasiphaë and a bull). This reminiscence too, and the fact that many pairs of bull horns have been found in Knossos and elsewhere, illustrate the importance of the animal in the Cretan religion, in which a double ax, found in many sizes, from full-sized models in bronze to tiny miniatures in gold, also played a role. The word *labyrinth* itself means "place of the double ax" (*labrys*).

Society at Knossos, at least from the Middle Minoan period on, was elegant. Sophisticated court ladies wearing embroidered dresses and gold or silver necklaces enjoyed dances or strolled about viewing the fountains, the carefully laid-out flower beds, and the rock gardens. But Crete had its troubles too,

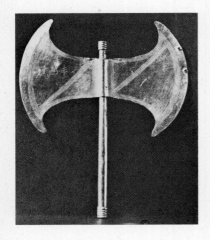

Gold votive ax found in a cave near Knossos.

Ruins of the Palace of Minos at Knossos.

though conjecture must help us in any effort to say just what they were. Was it natural catastrophes (earthquakes, tidal waves, and fires) that destroyed the palace of Minos a little after 1600 B.C., and again about 1500, and a third time about 1400? Or did invading Hyksos, on their way out of Egypt after their occupation, do the damage of 1600? Did mainland Greeks, crossing from the north, cause the destruction of 1500? Nobody can be quite sure about the earlier destructions, which were repaired; but the last disaster may well be attributable to actions of mainland Greeks.

Mycenaeans and Minoans

In Greece too, Bronze Age civilization had taken root. Greece was a largely barren land, mountainous, and divided into small valleys and plains, separated from each other but none of them far from the sea. From the earliest times the inhabitants took advantage of the rugged coasts and islands, with their many shelters and good harbors, to sail from place to place, seldom if ever losing sight of land, profiting by the exchange of olive oil and wine for grain and metal and slaves. About 2000 B.C. the village Bronze Age culture of the inhabitants—who were not Indo-Europeans but, like the Cretans, presumably a mixture of Stone Age indigenous peoples and Anatolians who had invaded about 3000 B.C.—was interrupted by the invasion from the north of the first true Greeks: Indo-Europeans, who first destroyed and then settled, no doubt intermarrying with the previous inhabitants. This society had one of its chief centers at Mycenae in the Peloponnesus, suitably situated to control land trade and not far from the sea.

The Mycenaeans were led by warrior chieftains, but they also engaged in commerce with Crete. Minoan objects have been found in the famous royal tombs at Mycenae that perhaps span the century from 1600 to 1500 B.C. In fact, so profound was the Minoan influence at work upon the arts of the mainland that scholars speak now of the Minoanization of mainland Greece. The most celebrated objects are the great gold masks of the warrior princes buried in the tombs and the daggers inlaid with various metals that show hunting scenes of astonishing realism and beauty. When the great German archaeologist Heinrich Schliemann found these in the 1870's he was looking for the tomb of the Homeric hero Agamemnon, and thought that he had found it. But, as we shall see, Agamemnon actually lived about three hundred years later. Egypt and Anatolia too shared in the Mycenaean trade, but the chief influences in mainland Greece were Minoan.

Interchange, we now believe, went both ways. Mycenaean Greeks visited Crete as traders or even as tourists; perhaps they observed the absence of physical fortifications that left Knossos vulnerable. Then (it is conjectured) they moved in and seized power, perhaps about 1480, presumably having first built their own fleet. No longer did they need to send to Knossos whatever tribute is remembered in the Minotaur legend. Indeed, they now controlled the very center of the civilization that had already taught them so much. Certain military innovations now took place in Crete: chariots were introduced and arrows stored for large bodies of troops, but the invaders built no fortifications, presumably because they expected no new invasion. In the palace of Minos the Greeks installed a throne room of the type they were accustomed to build in their own mainland palaces. But, most important, the Minoans showed them how useful it was to keep records; and since Linear A, devised for a non-Indo-European language from Anatolia, would not do, the scribes presumably invented a new script—Linear B—in which to write the language of the conquerors: Greek. On the other hand, Linear B may have been developed gradually out of Linear A.

It is the very existence of this new script, and the conclusive proof worked out only in 1952 by Michael Ventris that in fact it *is* early Greek, that has made possible the foregoing tentative reconstruction of events that are still somewhat uncertain. Of course Evans had found the Linear B tablets in great numbers in his Cretan excavations; but no such tablets were known *from mainland Greece* until 1939, when an American scholar, Carl Blegen, discovered the first of what proved to be a large collection of them in Pylos, where he was excavating a Mycenaean palace, and since then many more have turned up elsewhere in Greece, including some in Mycenae itself. Acting on the assumption that it was probably Greek (since he now knew that Greeks were keeping records in it on the mainland), Ventris used the techniques of cryptography to demonstrate that the signs in the language each represented a syllable (not a single letter), and then cracked the code. The thousands of Linear B tablets have by no means all been read even now, and by no means all readings are certain; but Greek it is. It is too bad in some ways that the tablets are mostly prosaic inventory lists of materials stored in the palaces or of persons in the royal services.

But the disappearance in Crete of Linear A, and the substitution for it about 1460 B.C. of the new Linear B (Greek), points clearly to a Mycenaean occupation of the island that preceded the last great violent destruction of about 1400 and lasted almost a century. We cannot be sure to what degree the new Greek rulers of Knossos were independent of direct authority from the mainland: they may have been subordinate Mycenaean princes. The great palace of Knossos and a number of other major Cretan centers were burned down about 1400, apparently after looting. We do not know who did it. Perhaps the Cretans rose against their Greek masters and burned down their own cities; though it has been plausibly suggested that such an act would have invited fierce reprisals and continued occupation after reconstruction. There was no reconstruction. Instead there was permanent disruption. So perhaps it was the Mycenaeans themselves who—in revenge against Cretan rebelliousness which may have made the island ungovernable—decided to cut their losses and destroy the Cretan centers and sail away. Or perhaps it was a volcanic upheaval of the seabed. The recent rediscovery (1967) and present active excavation of a Minoan city on the volcanic island of Santorin (Thera) to the north of Crete may furnish us with new evidence and enable us to decide the question one way or another. We do know that after the disaster of 1400 B.C. Crete remained rich and populous but lost its Mediterranean importance, which passed definitely to the aggressive mainland peoples.

Mycenae, 1400–1100 B.C.

We still know relatively little about Mycenaean politics and society. We can tell from excavated gold treasures that Mycenae itself was wealthy, which is not surprising considering that it had conquered Crete. But the Mycenaeans seem not to have been overseas empire builders even in the sense that the Cretans had been; their occupation of Crete may well have been undertaken by an invading captain who retained power for himself in Crete, however much of its revenue he sent back home. The Achaeans (Greeks) of whom the Hittite sources speak may well not have been the Greeks of Mycenae at all but Greeks of Rhodes, another island principality. And there were other settlements in the Peloponnesus itself—Pylos, Tiryns (the latter very close to Mycenae)—which seem to have been extensive too, and perhaps under local rulers equally powerful but bound in alliance to the Mycenaeans: a kind of loose confederacy among equals seems to fit best with the evidence. Each of the cities was walled. The walls of Mycenae survive, with their famous Lion Gate showing the two great sculptured beasts who lean forward to face each other, separated by a slender column, over the huge lintel above the gateway.

Tombs from the period before 1400 B.C. are of two sharply distinct types: those carefully built to take the bodies of kings and important noblemen, and simple burial places for the rest of the population. Tombs from the period between 1400 and 1200 show a rise in the general wealth: more chamber tombs with more gifts to the dead found in them. Similarly at Mycenae itself, Tiryns, Pylos, Athens, and Thebes there arose now great palaces as community centers, with workshops, storage areas, guardrooms, and lesser dwelling houses attached. Others certainly existed, and more will be found. Good roads with bridges and culverts connected the main towns, and good water-supply systems characterized them. Artisans attached to the palace built and repaired chariots, made jars to hold the wine and oil, tanned leather, wrought bronze in the forge, made bricks, and sewed garments; workmen stored goods for preservation and for sale and exchange. A Mycenaean palace was a business-like (and noisy) place. The Linear B tablets preserve records of special royal furniture most elaborately inlaid in ivory, glass, and gold: like the Egyptian pharaohs, the Mycenaean rulers obviously valued things most when they took a lot of time and effort to make. Smaller than the great palaces on Crete, those of the Mycenaeans on the mainland nonetheless testify to the vibrant life of an advanced society. One of the richest hoards, containing treasures in gold

The Lion Gate of Mycenae.

and jewels and bronze made over a period of five centuries, was found in a private house in Tiryns: it was obviously the stolen booty of a Mycenaean grave robber with a fine taste in antiques, who like all men before and since could not take his possessions with him.

Mycenaean religion remains a puzzle. Unlike Crete, where shrines and evidence of worship are everywhere, the Greek mainland furnishes no separate shrines at all, although there are some fragments of an altar in the great room or the courtyard of the palaces, and some portable altars have been found. The reason is that the Greeks, unlike the Cretans, made burnt and blood offerings to their gods. Gems found in the Mycenaean royal tombs clearly show Cretan deities and religious scenes; so the Cretan goddess was also revered on the mainland. The Linear B tablets from Pylos kept records of offerings made to certain gods—Poseidon, the god of the sea, Ares, the god of war, Artemis, the moon goddess, and even Zeus and Hera, to later Greeks the ruler of the gods and his consort. But there are other gods who did not survive the Dark Age to come and so do not appear in classical Greece.

The most famous Mycenaean exploit of the three centuries 1400–1100 was of course the Trojan War, now dated either about 1250 or about 1200 B.C., known to every Greek of the classical period from the poems of Homer written down four to five centuries after the event, and known in some measure to all civilized westerners ever since. This was a great expedition led by the king of Mycenae, Agamemnon, in command of a fleet and an army contributed by the other towns and islands of Mycenaean Greece, against Troy, a rich city on the northwest coast of Asia Minor (Anatolia) not far from the mouth of the Dardanelles, the straits that lead from the Aegean into the Sea of Marmora. The Trojans were Indo-Europeans like the Greeks but not so advanced: they did not write or paint their own pottery; they seem to have had few contacts with their neighbors in the Aegean, the Cretans, or their neighbors in Anatolia, the Hittites. They had a powerfully fortified city, and they traded with mainland Greece (many Mycenaean objects have been found in the ruins of Troy), though what they gave in exchange is not certain: perhaps horses, grain, purple dye, silver, and textiles.

Scholars now dismiss as romance the famous tale of the rape by the Trojan prince Paris of Helen, wife of Menelaus, Mycenaean prince of Sparta, and the war of revenge that followed; and we must believe instead that the Mycenaean expedition was undertaken for plunder of the Trojan citadel. Romantic too— or at least unproven—are the traditions that the siege lasted ten years and that great numbers of ships and men were involved. Agamemnon's force won, and burned Troy. Excavation carried on first by Schliemann and later by other scholars shows that the Troy destroyed by Agamemnon's famous expedition was probably a patched-up reconstruction of a richer Troy that may well have suffered destruction in an earlier Greek attack about 1300.

The gold Mycenaean death mask known as the Mask of Agememnon.

Soon after the siege of Troy there began the upheaval in the Mediterranean world to which we have already several times referred, the great raiding expeditions of the Sea Peoples that eventually—among other things—shattered the Egyptian New Kingdom and the Hittite state and left the Philistines washed up on the shores of Palestine. Egyptian and Hittite sources show that there were perhaps Greeks among the Sea Peoples, but we cannot tell where these "Achaeans" (or "Argives") and "Danaans" came from. In this period of raiding and migration the general violence did not spare Mycenaean Greece, which began about 1200 to suffer a great wave of destruction.

The great palaces were burned, some perhaps by fellow Mycenaean Greeks, others perhaps by fragments of other Sea People little better than pirates who landed and conducted hit-and-run raids, and still others perhaps by a new wave of Greek invaders from the north, adding to the general confusion now by entering the Mycenaean society as conquerors. These last were the Dorians, whom scholars can later identify by their special dialect of Greek in inscriptions but who at the beginning were illiterate. It took them a century to obtain mastery in Greece. To them scholars used to attribute most of the destruction that ushered in the Dark Age that began about 1100, but probably much of the destruction preceded their invasion and made it easier.

The Dark Age; Homer

With the destruction of the Mycenaean cities there set in at least three centuries that are called the Dark Age: dark in that we have little conclusive evidence from them to give us a picture of the life, and dark also in that the interlude surely marked a great series of steps backward in Greek civilization. Literacy vanished, for example. It is sometimes argued that Linear B was too clumsy a script ever to have been useful for anything much beyond keeping business records and that in any case only a very small proportion of Mycenaean Greeks (perhaps five percent) could ever have been able to read and write in it; so that its disappearance now was a positive benefit, for when literacy returned it would be in the new Greek alphabet taken from the Phoenicians. Even this argument would, however, concede the end of progress and the reversion to more primitive conditions characteristic of the Dorian domination. The political units of the Mycenaean world, already small, gave way to still smaller communities.

There were, we know, migrations of Greeks from Greece itself to the Aegean coasts of Asia Minor: to the central region (later called Ionia) that emerges into daylight again about 800 B.C.; and other Greeks, speaking other dialects, into the regions to the north (Aeolic) and south (Doric) of Ionia. In the hinterland behind these regions lived the Anatolian peoples in their own kingdoms: Lydia, Caria, Phrygia. Other Greeks on the mainland were lucky enough to miss the full impact of the Dorian invasion, notably the Athenians, whose later leadership of Greece, once the Dark Age cleared, may perhaps be attributable to a head start gained in this way.

The end of the Dark Age is closely tied in with the writing down of the Homeric poems, the *Iliad* and the *Odyssey*. Did the same person commit both to writing? Was it Homer? Did the *Iliad* precede the *Odyssey?* No certain answer can be given to these questions, but it seems highly likely that at some time between 850 and 750 B.C. (some say even later) both were recorded permanently, and we may as well call the man who did it Homer. Together the two great epics represent only a fraction of the epic material that existed in the Dark Age; there were many other tales of the great deeds of heroes. Minstrels who accompanied themselves on stringed instruments sang the separate songs to audiences around the banquet tables in a princely palace, or to a gathering of villagers in a public square, or to soldiers around a campfire. The songs that together make up the much longer epics that have come down to us were no doubt among the most popular, and the minstrel who put them down was selecting from his repertory the stories that had best stood the test of performance.

The *Iliad* tells the story of a single incident that took place during the siege of Troy: the wrath of the Greek hero Achilles, who stopped fighting and sulked in his tent because the commander Agamemnon had taken from him a Trojan girl captive. Agamemnon had allowed himself to be persuaded to restore to her family his own captive girl, and so made up for his loss by taking Achilles' prize away. While Achilles refused to fight, the great combat continued, and eventually, when Hector the Trojan prince had killed Achilles' best friend and comrade-in-arms, Patroclus, Achilles returned to the battle and in turn slew Hector, whose body at the very end he returned to Hector's sorrowing father, old King Priam. The *Odyssey* tells of the ten-year wanderings of another Greek hero, Odysseus, after the siege of Troy was over; of the extraordinary places and peoples he visited on his way back to his home on the island of Ithaca, where his faithful wife Penelope awaited him despite the attention of many suitors, and whence their son Telemachus had set out in order to find his father.

Put in this summary form, the two stories perhaps seem blunt and commonplace. But a deep humanity pervades both. Despite the continual bloody fighting in the *Iliad,* the modern reader—like all before him—is moved by the terror of Hector's baby son, Astyanax, when he sees his father with his fierce plumed war helmet on, until Hector takes it off and shows the child who it really is; feels the truth of the passage when the old men of Troy admit that Helen—beautiful as a goddess—was well worth all the fuss; shares the grief and dignity of Priam as he begs Achilles to return Hector's body for decent burial; and appreciates Achilles' courteous generosity to an enemy when he reluctantly agrees. The romantic *Odyssey,* with its lotus eaters, sirens, men turned to swine by enchantment, and fierce one-eyed giant, provides similar moments of high human drama in the actual homecoming of Odysseus in disguise, and the responses of his favorite dog and his old nurse, or in the sorrow of the beautiful island princess Nausicaa, first seen playing ball on the beach with her maidens, when she finds that Odysseus will not stay and be her lover.

In both poems, the gods—now the standard collection of Greek divinities: Zeus, Hera, Apollo (the sun), Artemis (the moon), Ares (war), Poseidon (the sea), Aphrodite (love), Athena (wisdom), and the rest—play an intimate part in the affairs of the mortals, intervening in the fighting to give victory to their favorites, supplying Achilles with an extraordinary shield on which are displayed many scenes in cunning metalwork, saving Odysseus from the perils of his voyage. The gods and goddesses on Olympus are only a little more outsize than the heroes; they live thoroughly human lives, quarreling over the affairs of the mortals and giving way to fits of bad temper. The epics take the reader into the world of a heroic age, like the later and lesser epics that reflected other heroic ages: such as *Beowulf* or *The Song of Roland* (see Chapter 4).

We hear at every turn and in great detail about the armor, ships, houses, domestic arrangements, and social behavior of the personages. It has always been a great temptation for scholars to reconstruct Mycenaean society from Homer. But Homer was writing five hundred years after the Trojan War. How far back did even a powerful oral tradition reach? In describing Odysseus' bed was he describing a real Bronze Age Mycenaean bed or the kind of bed that a prince would have slept in in his own day or a little before? Sometimes archaeology helps us here; more often it either does not help or adds to the confusion, as when the word that Homer uses for Nestor's drinking cup (*depas*) is found scratched on a Mycenaean storage jar far too big for anyone to drink from. Was Homer sometimes consciously trying to show his readers a world five hundred years earlier than theirs, and if so to what extent and in what passages? How safe are we in using him as a historical source?

To these largely unanswerable questions scholars give varying answers; but most in recent years have preferred to use Homer sparingly if at all. Yet there is the long interpolated Catalog of the Ships in the *Iliad* that lists the contingents supplied to the Greek armies by the various Greek settlements and names their commanders. Many authorities think it is a genuine Bronze Age document that provides hard, usable evidence with regard to the diverse political organization of Mycenaean society: partly by city, partly by the captain the people follow, partly by tribe. So too the description of Odysseus' household as including more than fifty slaves is taken as an indication of the prevalence of slavery in Mycenaean times, and conclusions are reached from episodes in Homer with regard to the inheritance of royal power and the existence of assemblies of elders. Other scholars would reject such conclusions as dangerous. But whether we use Homer as history or not, the Greeks themselves from his time on certainly did so, and formed their own conception of their ancestral past from the *Iliad* and the *Odyssey*. Together with the Old Testament, some of which was being committed to writing at about the same time, these two poems form the greatest literary and cultural and spiritual legacy of ancient man.

Indeed, certain modern scholars would maintain that both Homeric and Hebrew civilization grew directly from a common eastern Mediterranean background, and they point to many parallels in action and attitude. In many respects archaeological evidence serves to suggest that this viewpoint probably deserves a wider acceptance than it has yet won.

Reading Suggestions on Man's First Civilizations

PREHISTORY

J. Pfeiffer, *From Galaxies to Man: A Story of the Beginnings of Things* (Macmillan, 1959). A good popular account of recent evolutionary concepts.

A. L. Kroeber, *Anthropology*, 2 vols. (*Harcourt). A masterly review; the first volume deals with biology and race, and the second with culture patterns and processes.

J. Hawkes, *Prehistory* (*Mentor). A recent and highly respected survey.

L. S. Leakey, *Adam's Ancestors: The Evolution of Man and His Culture* (*Torchbooks). By the expert who discovered remains of man's remote ancestors in Africa.

Alexander Marshack, *The Roots of Civilization* (McGraw-Hill, 1972). Recent, magnificently illustrated (and controversial) account of brand-new research into the artifacts and mental processes of Paleolithic (Old Stone Age) man.

R. Coulbourn, *The Origins of Civilized Societies* (Princeton, 1959). A scholarly, readable, and stimulating study.

W. F. Albright, *From the Stone Age to Christianity* (*Anchor). Superb survey of a field that has been much altered by modern scholarship.

THE NEAR EAST

William W. Hallo and William Kelly Simpson, *The Ancient Near East: A His-*tory (*Harcourt). Up-to-date survey, not always easy to read.

H. Frankfort, *The Birth of Civilization in the Near East* (*Anchor). A brief and stimulating essay by an expert in the area.

S. Moscati, *The Face of the Ancient Orient: A Panorama of Near Eastern Civilization in Pre-Classical Times* (*Anchor). Good introductory survey.

L. Woolley, *Beginnings of Civilization* (*Mentor). Sequel to the survey by Miss Hawkes, above.

C. C. Lamberg-Karlovsky, *Excavations at Tepe Yahya, Iran 1967–1969* (Peabody Museum, Harvard University, 1970). The first progress report on very important new discoveries.

G. Bibby, *Four Thousand Years Ago* (Knopf, 1962). A most readable account of the crucial millennium from 2000 to 1000 B.C.

H. Frankfort et al., *Before Philosophy* (*Penguin). Admirable essays in the intellectual history of the ancient Near East.

H. B. Parkes, *Gods and Men: The Origins of Western Culture* (*Vintage). Perceptive survey of early religions.

M. E. L. Mallowan, *Early Mesopotamia and Iran* (*McGraw-Hill). By the archaeologist husband of Agatha Christie.

S. N. Kramer, *History Begins at Sumer* (*Anchor). Introduction by an expert.

J. Lassoe, *People of Ancient Assyria* (Barnes & Noble, 1963). An attempt to show the Assyrians as more than mere militarists.

O. R. Gurney, *The Hittites,* 2nd ed. (*Penguin). Survey of a people rescued from almost total oblivion by archaeology.

J. A. Wilson, *The Culture of Ancient Egypt* (*Phoenix). The best single-volume study of the subject.

J. H. Breasted, *History of Egypt* (*Bantam). By a celebrated Egyptologist of another generation, and still worth reading.

C. Desroches-Noblecourt, *Egyptian Wall Paintings from Tombs and Temples* (*Mentor). An informative sampler.

H. M. Orlinsky, *The Ancient Jews,* 2nd ed. (*Cornell University). A good introductory manual.

L. Finkelstein, ed., *The Jews: Their History, Culture, and Religion,* 3rd ed., 2 vols. (Harper, 1960). Comprehensive; popular in the best sense.

Cyrus H. Gordon, *Introduction to Old Testament Times* (Ventnor, 1953) See note on Gordon's writing under next heading.

CRETE AND EARLY GREECE

L. R. Palmer, *Mycenaeans and Minoans* (Knopf, 1962). Controversial reassessment in the light of the Linear B tablets. J. Chadwick, *The Decipherment of Linear B* (*Vintage). By Ventris' collaborator.

C. W. Blegen, *Troy and the Trojans* (Praeger, 1963), and Lord William Taylour, *Mycenaeans* (Praeger, 1964). Clear scholarly introductions.

Emily Vermeule, *Greece in the Bronze Age* (University of Chicago, 1964).

Cyrus H. Gordon, *Before the Bible* (Collins, 1962) and *Ugarit and Minoan Crete* (Norton, 1966). Drawing highly daring parallels between ancient Near Eastern and Homeric civilization.

two

The Classical World

I

The Greeks before the Persian Wars

In the first chapter, seeking to chronicle and understand man's experience from his beginnings down to about 850 B.C.—or in some instances a few centuries later—we have concentrated primarily on the ancient Near East, and we have examined as well the Minoan-Mycenaean civilization that grew up on Crete and on the mainland of Greece, peripheral to the Near East but closely connected with it. Sometime about 850, the focus for chroniclers and interpreters like us shifts away from the Near East to a people that has hitherto been peripheral: the Greeks. Of course, the Near East after 850 continues to engage our attention: indeed, we have already noted the military adventures of the Assyrians in the eighth and seventh centuries and the Babylonian captivity of the Hebrews and their release from it by the Persians in the sixth. The Persians we shall soon encounter again. But for fresh ideas, for new contributions to our own heritage, for new attitudes toward the outside world and toward man himself it is the Greeks who move to the center of the stage between the ninth and the third centuries B.C.

What the Greeks Were Like The Greeks were different from the other peoples we have come to know. For one thing, they were more curious: it is still proverbial that a Greek always wants to know some new thing, and that he will ask questions tirelessly of anybody who knows something he does not yet know himself. Where does the stranger come from? how big is his family? how much money does he have? what does it cost to live in his country? The questions may range from such relatively superficial personal matters—the answers to which will only temporarily satisfy the questioner's thirst for all knowledge—to the most fundamental problems abstract or practical: how do we really know what we *think* we know? what is the universe made of? what causes men to suffer fevers? what are the various possible ways for men to live together and govern themselves? and the myriad other questions to which there may be no real answers but only a multitude of approximations, any one of which will please some Greeks and none of which will please them all; so the argument can continue and the fun rage unchecked.

Then too, the Greeks were less otherworldly than the other peoples. The Mesopotamians and Egyptians—though with differing attitudes—both concentrated their attention upon the life to come; the Greeks were far more interested in life on earth. They did not deny that death was inevitable, and they suffered the fears and anxieties common to the human lot; but they had no feeling of hopelessness with regard to earthly life, and found it delightful to engage in tackling its manifold problems. The Hebrews submitted to the will of an all-powerful single god, who directed not only the footsteps of the entire people but the lives of each of its individual members; the Greeks had no such divinity and no such law, and so man himself, human reason, and human answers to human problems took a central place in their hearts and minds. Gods of course they had, and proper service to the gods they felt it seemly to render; indeed they would often, even usually, attribute human action to the influence of a god; but one gets the feeling that for them this was often only a manner of speaking. They say "Ares [the god of war] strengthened the hero's arm for the deadly spearthrust" when they seem to mean little more than "the hero summoned up all the strength of his muscular right arm, and let the enemy have it with a spear."

We often hear that the Greeks invented democracy: literally, government by the people. Indeed they did, but they also invented oligarchy: government by the few; and aristocracy: the rule of the best, or noblest or richest; and they also produced many refinements on rule by one man, which they called a tyranny even when it was mild and just and popular. Moreover, although they invented democracy, they had terrible difficulties in making it work. Fierce political infighting between rival groups and rival politicians characterized their political life at intervals almost from the beginning. Rather than absorb a political loss at home, a Greek politician would often intrigue with a foreign enemy.

Modern students have often taken their picture of Greek politics in general from the superb speech that Pericles, the most celebrated of the leaders of Athens, made in 430 B.C. over the Athenian soldiers killed in the first year of a great war against Sparta (see p. 57), as reported in the history of the war by the historian Thucydides. Praising Athenian democracy, Pericles said that at Athens the law guaranteed equal justice to all, that talent and not wealth was the Athenian qualification for public service, that Athenians expected of everybody a lively interest and participation in public affairs. In fact, his picture corresponded more to an ideal world than to the real Athenian world, where the courts were often markedly prejudiced, where wealth remained an important qualification for office, and where individual political ambition burned as hotly and was often pursued as ruthlessly and unscrupulously as anywhere on earth. In the tough world of Athenian politics one can without much effort see strong parallels to human behavior in other, more modern democracies. The Greeks invented democracy but seldom practiced it; when they did, it usually fell far short of their own ideals as expressed by Pericles. We know their politics in great detail—more fully than those of any people we have yet considered.

Then too, the Greeks had far more humor than any of the other peoples, who, as we have seen—except for an occasional bit of playfulness the Egyptians reveal in their art—were by and large a solemn lot. The Greeks enjoyed laughter, whether playful and gentle or raucous and cruel. The American musical comedy *Of Thee I Sing,* which in the 1930's satirized our powerless vice-presidency and our tendency to be sentimental over politics, or Gilbert and Sullivan operettas that poked fun at the civilian head of Queen Victoria's Nay-vee or lampooned the aesthetic movement of which Oscar Wilde was the symbol, echo themes in the Greek comedies of Aristophanes. But Aristophanes is also capable of the violence and vulgarity and indecency typical of much recent American political satire, as, for example, Philip Roth's book on President Nixon, *Our Gang.* Touches of Charlie Chaplin and of the Marx Brothers make Aristophanes instantly understandable and delightful. Brilliant, funny, energetic, inventive, opinionated, arrogant, and immensely quarrelsome, the Greeks are the first people of the ancient world whom we can feel we actually know.

Revival after the Dark Age

For the Greeks the Dark Age began to dissipate about 850 B.C., with the renewal of contact between the mainland and the Near East: Phoenicia, whose trade continued brisk, lay close to the Greek island of Cyprus, where Mycenaean culture had continued after the Dorians had ruined it on the mainland. Objects from Phoenicia now appear in mainland Greece; and the earliest traces of the Phoenician alphabet as adapted to the writing of Greek are now dated about 825 B.C. New letters were added for peculiarly Greek sounds. The general disorders of the Dark Age were coming to an end, and orderly life began to resume. New styles of pottery also testify to the renewal of communications. Greece proper now received the Homeric poems, first written down in the Ionian Greek settlements of Asia Minor, and bringing back to the mainland the sense of its glorious and heroic past.

In Greece itself, the poet Hesiod, writing in the language of Homer and in the same meter, in his *Works and Days* (ca. 800 B.C.) set down the proper rules of life for the small farmer, and scolded his own brother, who had tried to grab more than his fair share of the family estate. Hesiod also wrote a genealogy of the gods *(Theogony),* giving the traditional view of the way the universe had come into being: the gods were the children of earth and heaven, and had themselves created mankind. Preaching justice, human and divine, Hesiod's verse reflected the religious ideas of the Greeks in an early phase, perhaps partly under the influence of the oracle at Delphi, a mountain shrine of the sun god Apollo in central Greece where a divinely inspired prophetess gave advice to all comers. The invading Dorians had become particular sponsors of the shrine at Delphi. To this earliest period of the revival also belongs the foundation of a famous Greek institution, the Olympic games, held every four years beginning with 776 B.C. at Olympia, shrine of Zeus in the western Peloponnesus.

The Polis: Sparta

The chief social and political form to emerge in reviving Greece was the *polis* or city-state (pl., *poleis*), which had begun in the Greek settlements of Asia Minor, and consisted of the municipality itself and the territory surrounding it: small in size and in population, often centering on a fortress built on a hill— the high city or Acropolis. It was in the Dorian centers—first Crete, and then especially Sparta on the mainland—that such city-states first emerged. The

Vase in the geometric style of the eighth century B.C., after the close of the Dark Age. It shows a prothesis, or lying-in-state of the dead.

one at Sparta is of course responsible for the overtones that the word *Spartan* still has in our ordinary language today.

Here, in what the philosopher Aristotle later called "an association of several villages which achieves almost complete self-sufficiency," only the upper five to ten percent of the population were citizens. Descendants of the Dorian conquerors, they were the rulers, hereditary landowners, and soldiers. The overwhelming majority of the people belonged to the *helot* class, farm laborers bound to the soil, servants of the ruling group. In between was a free class called *perioikoi* ("dwellers around"), descendants of the pre-Dorian residents of neighboring areas, who lived in the villages under Spartan control and had personal freedom but no right to participate in politics or to intermarry with the Spartans. The ruling Spartans lived in constant fear of revolution; they kept their secret agents planted among the helots to report subversive talk, and indeed barely managed to put down a helot uprising in the late seventh century.

The constitution, which the Spartans attributed to a divinely inspired lawgiver, Lycurgus, dating perhaps from about 825 B.C., provided that there should be two kings, descendants of two rival Dorian families. Real political power came to reside in five *ephors* (overseers) elected annually by an assembly of all Spartan citizens over thirty, excluding, of course, all women, helots, and perioikoi. In addition, there was a kind of council of thirty elders representing the more powerful families.

War dominated Spartan thinking. The males lived under military discipline from the age of seven, when a boy was taken from his parents and taught reading and music and running and fighting. Weak-looking babies were abandoned to die. So that there might be healthy children, girls too were given strenuous training. Adult males lived in the barracks until they were thirty, though they might marry at twenty, but they dined in the mess hall until they were sixty. It was a harsh, bleak life, "Spartan" in its merits and in its defects.

The army was excellent and the citizens were patriotic and able to bear misfortune. The need to keep hostile neighbors under control led the Spartans also to introduce clumsy iron bars as money in order to make ordinary commercial pursuits as unattractive and difficult as possible.

Their earliest poets wrote fine, sensitive lyrics, but soon this art vanished, and war songs first, and then no poetry at all, replaced it. The Spartans were not artists, but fighters. A barracks state, Sparta reminds twentieth-century students of the fascist states of the 1920's and 1930's.

Colonization

Together with the establishment of city-states there took place a large-scale movement of Greek colonial expansion. The city-states of Asia Minor and of Greece proper sent out naval expeditions of their citizens to plant new settlements in non-Greek areas where there was no power strong enough to prevent it: around the edge of the Black Sea, along the African shore of the Mediterranean in what we now call Libya, in Sicily and along the Italian coasts (which the Romans later called *Magna Graecia*, "Great Greece"), and as far west as the coasts of France and Spain. Each new colony became a new city-state, independent of its mother city but bound to it by sentimental and economic ties and by similar political and religious practices. It was no doubt overpopulation and internal strife in the settled cities together with the wish for trade and adventure that advanced the colonizing movement. Trebizond in Asia Minor, Panticapaeum in the Crimea, Byzantium (later to be Constantinople and still later Istanbul) at the Black Sea Straits, Syracuse in Sicily, Naples in southern Italy, Marseilles in southern France, and Cadiz beyond the Straits of

Gibraltar on the Atlantic southern coast of Spain are among the famous cities that started their lives as Greek colonies (see map, p. 53).

Such foundations, and many others, combined with the decline of Egypt and the Assyrian conquests in western Asia, set off a whole new period of Mediterranean trade focusing on Greece. First one of the Greek cities and then another would assume prominence in the busy traffic: the Dorian-founded settlements on Crete, Rhodes, Corinth (with its strategic position at the isthmus that attaches the Peloponnesus to northern Greece), Megara: all became powerful and prosperous, as to a lesser extent did many other cities. By the mid-seventh century, coins, invented in the Anatolian kingdom of Lydia, had begun to be struck on the island of Aegina in Greece, where silver was the only precious metal available, and soon this convenient system spread westward. The coins of Aegina had turtles on them, those of Corinth foals, those of Athens from the sixth century onward the owl of Athena, goddess of the city.

Athens

The owl, sacred to Athena, appeared on Athenian coins from the sixth century. This silver coin is from the fifth century.

DRACO AND SOLON   Athens—which had never undergone a Dorian occupation—did not become a polis as soon as Sparta and Corinth, but lingered as an old-fashioned aristocratic tribal state, dominating the large surrounding hinterland of Attica. It was divided territorially into plains, hills, and coastal land, and politically into four tribes, each of which had three brotherhoods *(phratries)* or territorial subdivisions *(trittyes)*. Within each phratry a further distinction was drawn between those who owned and worked their farms (the *clans*)—which were the earliest category—and the *guildsmen,* later in origin, who belonged to an association of artisans or merchants. The clans included numerous related families or households of varying degrees of nobility. Land descended in the clan and might not be alienated. With it went a deep attachment to the local religious shrines, whose priests were clansmen. The guildsmen were citizens but not aristocrats, and presumably could sell or transfer their property. Each mature male was admitted into a phratry either as a clansman or as a guildsman.

Three *archons* (leaders or principal persons)—one of whom managed religious affairs, one military affairs (the polemarch), and one civil affairs—were joined in the seventh century by a board of six recording archons, making nine in all. Each was elected for a year, at the end of which all nine automatically became members of the Council of the Areopagus (the hill of Ares, god of war, in Athens), the chief judicial and policy-making body. Although a general assembly of all the people directly elected the archons and so the future members of the Areopagus Council, only clansmen—people of birth and wealth—not guildsmen, could be elected.

Already ancient in the seventh century B.C., these political arrangements were challenged in 632 by a young noble's plot to seize power, which led to a scandal when his followers were massacred though they had taken sanctuary at the altar of Athena. The noble family held responsible for the sacrilege was banished, and in 621 a specially appointed official, Draco, published the first Athenian law code, famous for its severe penalties: hence our term a "Draconian" measure. Harshest of all were the laws on debt: a bankrupt clansman could never sell off or mortgage his land, but was compelled to mortgage the produce of it to the debtor. Thus he would oblige himself and his heirs to work it indefinitely for somebody else, and in effect would lose his own freedom. Bankrupt guildsmen actually became the property of their creditors, as slaves. The growing inequity of this system led to civil strife.

In the 590's the reformer Solon freed both the clansmen and guildsmen

Head of the bronze statue of a charioteer from the sanctuary of Apollo at Delphi, ca. 470 B.C.

then suffering these penalties for debt, canceled current debts, and abolished the harsh system. He repealed almost all Draco's laws, and published a new code. He tried to improve the general prosperity by emphasizing the need to abandon complete economic dependence on agriculture and to foster a lively new commerce. He even offered citizenship to citizens of other poleis who would come to work in Athens. He opened the most important offices of state to rich guildsmen as well as rich clansmen: money, not birth, now counted chiefly.

He is also said to have founded a new body, the Council of Four Hundred, consisting of one hundred members from each of the four tribes, all named by Solon himself, to act as an inner circle of the general assembly of the people, preparing the materials for discussion and making recommendations for action: the general assembly now could not act without such a recommendation; but it could vote against it, and it still elected the archons. And Solon also made it a kind of court, by selecting a panel of assembly members by lot to review the work of the magistrates.

Introducing these democratic innovations but keeping both the older aristocratic election only of the rich to magistracies and the oligarchic power of the few in the Council of the Areopagus, Solon's reforms were really a radical set of compromises. In one of his own poems he says of his actions: "I stood holding my stout shield over both parties [the poor and the rich]; I did not allow either party to prevail unjustly." By justice Solon meant more than legal justice; he meant what we would call social justice. Though some of his fellow Athenians jeered at him for not taking advantage of his extraordinary powers to line his own pockets, he answered (again in a poem) that "money flits from man to man, but honor abides forever." Urging the Athenians to abide by his laws for a hundred years, he withdrew from the scene for a decade.

PEISISTRATUS AND CLEISTHENES   Civil strife at once began again. Athenians seem to have lined up in accordance with both region and class: the plains people being mostly aristocrats who felt Solon had gone too far, the hill people mostly poor farmers who felt he had not gone far enough, and the coast people mostly artisans who thought he was about right. In 561 B.C. their quarrels gave Athens into the hands of a "tyrant," as the Greeks called a dictator, however benevolent: Peisistratus, a noble, who had made himself leader of the hill people. In and out of office for some years, Peisistratus owed his final return in 546 to vast sums of money that he had made from the silver mines on his estates in the north, and to mercenary troops from Argos whom he hired with his wealth. Peisistratus and his sons dominated Athens until 510 B.C.

Though Solon's constitutional measures had not prevailed, his economic policy made Athens rich, as Athenian pottery became the best and most sought-after in Greece. Peisistratus—who collected ten percent of all revenues for his personal fortune—pushed commercial success still further, partly by shrewd alliances with other poleis. At home, his was the only party. He exiled those aristocrats who refused to support him; he would often keep the son of a noble family as a hostage to ensure the family's loyalty. Having come to power as leader of the poor, he made them loans, embarked on a lavish program of public works to be sure there were jobs for all, subsidized the arts, and increased the magnificence of state religious celebrations. His sons, who succeeded him on his death in 527 B.C., followed his policies; but of course the noble families whom their father had displaced continued opposition, often from exile. When Hipparchus, one of the sons, was assassinated for personal reasons in 514 B.C., executions multiplied, government grew more tyrannical, and the exiled nobles came back in 510 B.C. By 508 Cleisthenes, one of the exiles, who appealed for the support of the guildsmen—already so much favored by Peisistratus—succeeded in his turn in coming to power by promises of constitutional reform.

These he fulfilled by striking at the political influence of the clans in elections, and giving the guildsmen equal weight. Using as the basic new political unit an old territorial division called a *deme,* a small area something like a ward in a modern city, Cleisthenes ordered all citizens registered as voters within their demes, irrespective of their origins, thus giving the guildsmen equal franchise with the clansmen. Whoever was a member of a given deme in the year 508–507 B.C. remained so permanently, and so did his descendants even if they moved away.

Cleisthenes also rezoned Attica into three new regions that did not coincide with the former coast, hill, and plain. He regrouped the demes into trittyes that, unlike the twelve older trittyes, were in general not compact and adjacent, but chosen from all three territorial subgroupings. Finally, by drawing lots he put every three trittyes together into a political "tribe." Instead of the four old racial (or genuinely tribal) tribes, there were ten of these new political tribes whose membership cut across the old family and regional and class lines. Each of these new, nontribal, artificial tribes had members from each of the three new territorial divisions, and the former influence of the noble families had been effectively cut down. Cleisthenes had invented a fundamental tool of democracy: the gerrymander.

Each deme annually elected a number of its members (proportionate to its population) as its representatives, and from them the new ten tribes selected by lot fifty each to be members of the new Council of Five Hundred, replacing Solon's Council of Four Hundred. Solon had given Athenians equality before the law; Cleisthenes gave them equality at the ballot box. The four old racial or tribal tribes, the old brotherhoods, the clans, continued to play a major part in religious and social life, but their political role was over.

Of course, the system was clumsy. The archons continued to administer, except that now (501) the whole Assembly of the People elected ten generals a year to serve as operational commanders under the polemarch. The Council of the Areopagus (ex-archons) retained its powers and its aristocratic complexion. Archons and generals continued to be aristocrats, and though they were often able, experienced, and patriotic, they struggled with each other for power and prestige, and tended to become the chiefs of rival factions. These rivalries would lead individuals to take different positions at different times in their careers. Cleisthenes himself had fluctuated between supporting and opposing the family of Peisistratus, had worked with and against both Spartans and Persians, and had at one time appealed to the nobles, at another to the people. These switches in loyalty were normal in Athenian politics but naturally increased its instability.

The ten groups of fifty tribal members of which the Council of Five Hundred was made up each governed in continual session for a tenth of the year (roughly thirty-six days), and the chairman of the committee of fifty that was sitting at any given time was selected afresh by lot every day. During each continual thirty-six-day session the committee members *(prytaneis)* lived in a special state building and were fed at public expense. They could summon the remaining councilors to a full session whenever they wished. No citizen between the ages of thirty and sixty could be a member of the council more than twice or chairman of a day's session more than once. Thus, with swiftly changing large groups of citizens receiving responsibilities for short times, almost any citizen could hope to enjoy the experience at some time during his life. Fortified by their new constitution giving all citizens a stake in the community the Athenians were prepared for their famous historic confrontation with the Persian Empire.

II

Persia and the Greeks, to 478 B.C.

The Persian Empire

We have already encountered the Medes, an Indo-European people of the Near East, who in 612 B.C. cooperated with the briefly recovering Babylonians to destroy Nineveh and bring down the hated empire of the brutal Assyrians. We have also seen the Medes' southern relatives, the Persians, destroy Babylon (538) and allow the captive Hebrews to return to Jerusalem. It was Cyrus, the Persian ruler (550–529 B.C.) of the southern province, the captor of Babylon and liberator of the Jews, who attacked his northern kinsmen the Medes and took their capital (Ecbatana, south of the Caspian Sea), and so began a meteoric rise toward universal empire, the last and greatest to come out of the ancient Near East.

Uniting his territory with that of the Medes and bypassing Babylon, Cyrus moved westward into Anatolia, absorbed the Lydian kingdom of the rich king Croesus, and then attacked and conquered the Greek cities of Ionia along the Aegean coast. Next he moved east all the way to the borders of India, conquering and annexing as he went, but imposing no such tyranny as the Assyrian. Instead of deporting whole populations, Cyrus allowed them to worship as they pleased, and to keep on governing themselves in their own way under his representatives. The fall of Babylon led to the Persian conquest of Syria. Cyrus' son Cambyses (529–522 B.C.) invaded and conquered Egypt, and died on his way home to put down a revolution, which his brother-in-law and successor Darius (521–486 B.C.) succeeded in quelling.

It was Darius who subdivided the empire into twenty provinces *(satrapies),* each with its political governor, its military governor, and its tax collector, but each allowed to maintain its religion and local customs. Royal agents crossed and crisscrossed the vast area from the Aegean to the Indus, collecting intelligence for the king. Darius took from the Lydians the practice of coining money and introduced it into all his dominions. The highway system was a marvel, a great network whose largest thread was the royal road that ran more than sixteen hundred miles from Susa, Darius' capital, to Sardis, the chief city of Lydia. It is likely that Darius himself introduced Zoroastrianism, the religion of Zarathustra, who had died only a generation earlier. In any case, Darius himself accepted the religion, and paid honors to its great god Ahuramazda without repudiating other gods.

Zoroastrianism began as a monotheistic faith, proclaiming the one god Ahuramazda, whose chief quality was his wisdom. He is the only intellectual deity we have so far encountered, and the other divinities around him were not gods and goddesses but abstract qualities such as Justice and Integrity, which he had created. It was the existence of evil in the universe that led Zarathustra to imagine that life was a constant struggle between a good spirit and an evil spirit, *both* subordinate to Ahuramazda. A wise man will ponder and then choose the good way; a foolish man will choose the evil way; and the supreme spirit will reward the wise and punish the foolish.

Intellectual and abstract, lacking ritual and priesthood, early Zoroastrianism was perhaps too impersonal and rarefied for a popular faith, and was modified after its founder's death. By identifying Ahuramazda with the good spirit, the next generations in effect demoted the supreme god, who was now no longer the ruler over the evil spirit (Ahriman) but only a contender with him. From a monotheism the religion became dualistic (giving comparable power to good and evil) and also revived elements of earlier polytheism, as old deities and ceremonies reappeared and a powerful priesthood asserted itself. At the moment of Darius' reign, however, the religion was still in its earliest phase.

The Ionian Cities;
The Threat to Greece;
Marathon

The one thing that the new Persian rulers would not allow their subjects was political freedom, which was precisely what the now captive Ionian Greek cities most valued. Their prosperity also declined, as the Persians drew toward Asia the wealth of the trade routes that had formerly enriched the Aegean towns. By 513, the Persians had crossed the Bosporus on a pontoon bridge, sailed up the Danube, and moved north across modern Romania into the Ukraine in a campaign against the nomadic people called Scythians. Though indecisive, the new advance into Europe alarmed the Greeks, who were now receiving overtures for an alliance from the Scythians: it looked as if Darius would move south against European Greece from his new base in the northern Balkans.

Some of the Greek poleis—Sparta and her allies—were hostile to the Persians; but there were others that had pro-Persian rulers. One of Peisistratus' sons, Hippias, had taken refuge with the Persians, who were backing his return to Athens, but about 505 B.C. the Athenians refused to accept him, and soon afterwards decided to give help to the captive Ionian cities in their resistance to Persian rule. The Ionians then rebelled; with Athenian help they burned down Sardis, the former Lydian capital and now headquarters for the Persians in Asia Minor (499 B.C.). Encouraged, many other Greek cities joined the rebellion.

But the Persians struck back, and by 495 B.C. had defeated the ships of the Greek cities in the Aegean; they burned the most important Ionian city— Miletus—massacred many of its men, and deported its women and children. By 493 B.C. the Ionian revolt was over, and in the next two years the Persians extended their authority along the northern coasts of Greece proper, directly threatening Athens. It was probably Hippias who advised the Persian commanders whom he was accompanying to land at Marathon, in a region once loyal to his father Peisistratus, only about twenty-five miles north of Athens. There a far smaller Athenian force decisively led by Miltiades defeated the Persians and put an end for ten years to the Persian threat to Greece. Because the Spartans had been celebrating a religious festival during which military operations were taboo, they had been unable to participate in the fighting; only the much smaller polis of Plataea had sent a thousand troops to join the ten thousand Athenians. The credit for driving off the Persians therefore went primarily to Athens. Darius now planned a much greater invasion, but first an Egyptian uprising and then his death (486) delayed it. His successor Xerxes (486–465), having subdued the Egyptians in 485, resumed the elaborate preparations.

The 480's

By the time Xerxes was ready to try again, the Athenians had removed their hero Miltiades from an active role in their affairs. Like other Athenian leaders he had had the usual varied career: at one time pro-Peisistratus, at another anti-, at one time pro-Persian, at another the hero of Marathon. A leader of the nobles, he was eventually brought down by a rival faction.

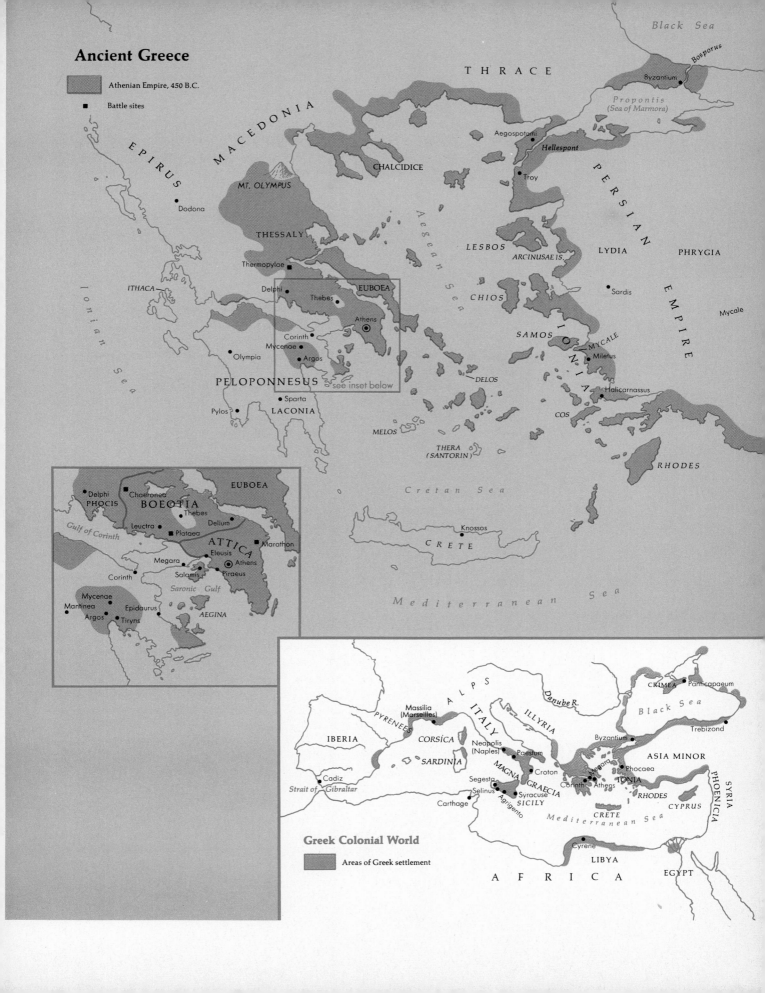

Ancient Greece

Athenian Empire, 450 B.C.

■ Battle sites

Black Sea

T H R A C E

Byzantium

Bosporus

Propontis (Sea of Marmora)

Aegospotami

Hellespont

M A C E D O N I A

CHALCIDICE

Troy

E P I R U S

MT. OLYMPUS

Aegean Sea

LESBOS

ARGINUSAE IS.

LYDIA

PHRYGIA

Dodona

THESSALY

CHIOS

Sardis

Mycale

Thermopylae

Delphi

Thebes

EUBOEA

Athens

SAMOS

MYCALE

Miletus

Ionian Sea

ITHACA

Corinth

Mycenae

Olympia

Argos

DELOS

Halicarnassus

PELOPONNESUS

see inset below

COS

Sparta

Pylos

LACONIA

MELOS

THERA (SANTORIN)

RHODES

Cretan Sea

Knossos

C R E T E

Mediterranean Sea

Inset (upper)

Delphi

PHOCIS

Chaeronea

BOEOTIA

EUBOEA

Gulf of Corinth

Thebes

Leuctra

Delium

Plataea

ATTICA

Marathon

Megara

Eleusis

Corinth

Salamis

Athens

Piraeus

Saronic Gulf

Mycenae

Epidaurus

AEGINA

Mantinea

Argos

Tiryns

Greek Colonial World

Areas of Greek settlement

Black Sea

CRIMEA

Panticapaeum

ALPS

Danube R.

Massilia (Marseilles)

PYRENEES

ITALY

ILLYRIA

Trebizond

IBERIA

CORSICA

Byzantium

ASIA MINOR

SARDINIA

Neapolis (Naples)

Paestum

MAGNA

Croton

Megara

Phocaea

IONIA

Segesta

GRAECIA

Corinth

Athens

Cadiz

Selinus

Syracuse

SICILY

RHODES

CYPRUS

Strait of Gibraltar

Agrigento

SYRIA

Carthage

Mediterranean Sea

CRETE

PHOENICIA

Cyrene

LIBYA

EGYPT

A F R I C A

It was probably now (488 B.C.) that some leader first invented the famous practice known as ostracism. The word comes from *ostrakon,* a fragment of a clay pot on which the individual citizens scribbled the name of any politician they wished to exile from the city for a period of ten years. Apparently a majority of a meeting of 6,000 citizens (i.e., 3,001 votes) was needed to ostracize. The 480's—the decade of preparation for Xerxes' expected attacks—was the decade of ostracism par excellence: many hundreds of the original clay potsherds still exist with the names of prominent politicians written on them, a sort of negative ballot. The citizens ostracized the leaders of the Peisistratid party and many other politicians. By 480 a leader named Themistocles had emerged as the popular choice to lead the resistance to the new Persian invasion.

After 487 the nine archons were no longer elected by the people but selected by lot from a preliminary list, drawn up by the demes, of five hundred candidates, who still had to be among the richer citizens. This reform further reduced the influence of the aristocratic clans. Moreover, it gradually reduced the influence of the Council of the Areopagus, since more and more its members became men chosen in the new way. Because the generals were still elected, the old political rivalry for the archonship now shifted to the office of general, and factional struggle continued.

New supplies of silver were discovered in the nick of time, and Themistocles persuaded the Athenians to use the money to build a new fleet instead of passing it out among the citizens, a decision that probably determined the outcome of the Persians' new effort, and that incidentally suited the poor, who built the ships and rowed them and whose fortunes were associated with the navy. As the leading military power of Greece, Sparta took over the leadership of the anti-Persian Greek poleis, which together formed an anti-Persian League with a congress of delegates from the individual cities and a unified command. Knowing that its forces would be greatly outnumbered (perhaps 110,000 against 500,000 Persians), the League did not try to defend the northern cities, where the Persian cavalry could operate freely, but instead abandoned them.

Xerxes Invades

In 480 B.C., Xerxes' huge army, its supply lines greatly overextended and its speed slowed down by its very numbers, crossed into Europe and swung south into Greece, while a fleet, possibly of three thousand ships of various sizes, sailed along the coast. At the pass of Thermopylae in central Greece a Greek traitor showed the Persians how to outflank the defenders, but a small army of Spartans—only three hundred strong—defended the pass to the last man, taking a terrible toll of the Persian infantry. A storm, a battle, and a second storm cut the Persian fleet in half. The Delphic oracle had mysteriously prophesied that Athens would be destroyed but had advised the Athenians to put their trust in their "wooden walls." Themistocles succeeded in persuading the Athenians that the message meant they should abandon the city and rely upon their fleet—their wooden ships—for their defense.

Athens was accordingly evacuated, except for the defenders of the Acropolis, whom Xerxes' men killed as they plundered the city. But the fleet in the narrow waters of the harbor of Salamis off Athens awaited the Persian attack, despite fierce debate and disagreement among the Greeks. Themistocles eventually sent a misleading message to the Persians pretending that he would betray the Greeks, and so persuaded them that it was safe to attack. The Greek fleet—helped by deserters from the Persians who revealed Xerxes' battle plans—won a smashing victory, which Xerxes himself watched from a great throne set up on shore. Xerxes had to withdraw from Greece, for autumn was setting in. In the next year (479) at Plataea the united Greek forces numbering more than a hundred thousand men defeated the Persian troops once again.

The maintenance of Greek unity was most impressive: in spite of the thousands of personal and municipal rivalries among the Greeks, all members of the League had kept the oath "I shall fight to the death, I shall put freedom before life, I shall not desert colonel or captain alive or dead, I shall carry out the generals' commands, and I shall bury my comrades-in-arms where they fall and leave none unburied." A wildly individualistic people had shown that they could put the general interest ahead of all else. Soon afterwards at Mycale (478 B.C.) the Greeks scored another victory on land and sea. The Persians, as it turned out, had been stopped forever, although peace was not formally made until 448, and at many times during those three decades the threat of renewed invasion hung over the heads of the Greeks.

III

The Athenian Empire, 478–404 B.C.

Postwar Reorganization

When the Athenians began to rebuild and refortify Athens, the Spartans asked them to stop, arguing that the new walls might be useful to the Persians if they ever again invaded Greece; but Themistocles, as ambassador to Sparta, trickily played for time until the walls had already been built. The episode serves as a symbol of Athens' unwillingness to let Sparta, as the strongest military power, take the lead in planning for the future defense against Persia. It was indeed Athens, after 478 the strongest naval power, that organized the new Greek alliance, designed to liberate the Ionian cities still subject to Persia and to maintain the defenses. Athens contributed most of the ships, but the other cities were assessed contributions in both ships and money. The treasury of the alliance was on the island of Delos; so the alliance is called the Delian League. It scored a major victory over the Persians in Asia Minor about 467 B.C.

About 472 Themistocles was ostracized. While in exile, he was charged with corruption; he fled to the Persians, was given rich revenues, and died in the service of Xerxes' son and successor. Immensely able, Themistocles somehow seemed not quite trustworthy. He accurately foresaw the great danger that lay ahead for Athens: the long-range threat from Sparta. Like Miltiades, he lost the confidence of the Athenians after he had done them invaluable service.

In 462 a new reform further democratized Athenian government: the Areopagus Council was shorn of its powers, while the Council of Five Hundred and the Assembly were the beneficiaries. Though put through largely by Ephialtes, the reform was partly inspired by a brilliant young aristocratic politician named Pericles (a grandson of Cleisthenes). By about 457 the patriotic and incorruptible Pericles had become the leading Athenian politician, responsible for the many military and naval operations conducted simultaneously against the Persians (chiefly in Egypt: an expensive failure), against the Spartans, and against certain members of the Athenian alliance itself who resented the dictatorial ways of Athens.

At home Pericles pushed democracy, inaugurating a system of state pay, first for the jurymen (drawn from a panel six thousand strong, six hundred from each tribe) and later for those rendering other services to the state. State service was thus transformed from an acitivity that the poor could not afford to one that they welcomed. In order to limit the number of those eligible for such payment, Pericles also now limited Athenian citizenship to those both of whose parents were Athenian. The money to pay all these people could come only from the allies.

From Alliance to Empire

In fact, Pericles was gradually turning the Athenian alliance into an empire, with the subject members providing the money for Athens, which in turn would defend them all, and would be able to challenge Sparta. In 454 the treasury of the alliance was moved from Delos to Athens, and became in effect a major Athenian resource. Since 470, no ally had been allowed to secede. During a truce with the Spartans (451–446 B.C.), the Athenians, operating in the Aegean, increased the number of their allies (about 170 cities at the peak), and in 448 made a peace with Persia that liberated the Ionian cities and bound the Persians not to come within three days' journey of the coast.

Athenian settlements were founded on the territories of some allied states, and Athenian coinage was standard. Resentment against Athens was naturally widespread among the allies. But in 446–445 a new thirty years' treaty with Sparta provided that neither side would commit aggression against the other. Both had lost the good will of the other Greek poleis: Athens was now ruling an empire by force and its services against the Persians seemed less magnanimous; Sparta had suffered defeats and its reputation was dimmed.

The thirty years' truce, as it turned out, lasted only for fifteen (446–431). It was a prosperous period, during which Pericles continued to dominate the affairs of state, but he was elected general democratically every year. He had at his disposal the large surpluses in the imperial treasury, which mounted in these years of peace, and which with Athens' other revenues were much more than enough to pay the 10,000 rowers of the warships, the 700 officials, the 500 councilors, the 6,000 jurors, and many others. Pericles embarked upon a great program of public works, of which the two most famous buildings were the celebrated Parthenon (the temple of Athena Parthenos, the virgin) and the Propylaea (monumental gateway), both on the Acropolis. After one had mounted the steps that led up to the Propylaea, and passed through it, one saw at the top of the hill the giant bronze statue of Athena sculptured by Phidias, a personal friend of Pericles, and behind it and to the right rose the entrance portico of the magnificent new temple. Inside was another statue of Athena, this one in gold and ivory, also by Phidias.

There were plenty of jobs available in the building program, and slaves as well as freemen participated and were well paid. There was money and opportunity for everybody: for the 30,000 resident aliens *(metics),* who had to pay a special tax, and were not allowed to own land or participate in politics, but engaged in commerce and contributed to the city's and their own good fortune; for the 200,000 slaves, whose lot was easier than it was elsewhere, and who were often set free; and most of all for the 168,000 Athenian citizens (4,000 upper class, 100,000 middle class, and 64,000 lower class).*

The Peloponnesian War

THE FIRST FIFTEEN YEARS, 431–416 B.C.   The splendid civilization of Athens in the fifth century depended upon the continued exercise of complete control over the subject poleis in the empire. A growing number of incidents in which the Athenians ruthlessly asserted their power alarmed the Spartans: if they did not fight soon, they feared, they might not be able to win. They tried to force the Athenians to make concessions, but Pericles, with the support of the Assembly, said only that Athens would consent to have all disputed questions arbitrated.

* All such statistics are mere approximations. No exact figures can be given.

In 431 began the ruinous Peloponnesian War (431–404 B.C.). The Spartans invaded Attica in order to force a military decision. Pericles countered by withdrawing the entire population within the city walls, which had been extended to include the suburbs and to give access to the sea. He intended to avoid pitched battles with the superior Spartan troops on land, and to match his defensive policy on land by an offensive policy at sea, launching seaborne raids against enemy territory and inviting naval battles.

These tactics worked well in the first year of the war; but in 430 a terrible plague broke out in Athens, where the whole population of Attica was cooped up with no sanitation. In 429 Pericles himself died of it, leaving Athens without the trusted leader who could make even unpopular policies acceptable. The plague raged until the end of 426, and cost Athens about a third of its population, including its best troops. It did not deter the Athenians from continuing the war, however, with general though costly success at sea and even, contrary to Pericles' policies, on land.

By 424, Athens could probably have ended the war on favorable terms, and the upper and the middle classes that had suffered most from it were eager to do so: it was their lands in Attica that the Spartans ravaged, and their members who made up most of the land forces that did the heavy fighting. But the lower classes, identified with the fleet, which was still in fine condition, hoped for even greater gains, and wanted to continue the war, and since they now dominated the city's politics, the war continued.

Not until 421 could the peace party conclude the Peace of Nicias (so called after its leader), which provided that each side restore captured places and prisoners, and remain at peace with the other for fifty years. This was soon supplemented by an actual Spartan–Athenian alliance, also concluded for fifty years but intended chiefly to give each power a chance to put its own alliance in order while secure from an attack by the other. The war had been marked by numerous acts of brutality on both sides: prisoners were slaughtered and enslaved, and agreements broken in a way that contemporaries felt to be blameworthy.

ALCIBIADES AND FAILURE   The peace lasted only five years, 421–416 B.C., which saw the gradual rise to eminence in Athenian politics of Pericles' nephew, Alcibiades, a brilliant, ambitious, dissolute, and unstable youth, who succeeded the demagogic Cleon as leader of the lower-class war party against the restrained and unglamorous Nicias. Athenian efforts to support Argos against Sparta only ended in the defeat of Argos and Athens and the strengthening of Spartan prestige. By killing all the adult males of the island of Melos and enslaving the women and children as a punishment for Melos' insistence on staying neutral in the war (415), Athens underlined its own ruthlessness. By deciding, against Nicias' prudent counsel, to send off a large naval expedition to Sicily to attack the great Greek city of Syracuse (which had opposed Athens in the past, and was the ally of Selinus, a town engaged in a war with Segesta, an ally of Athens), the Athenian assembly once again followed Alcibiades' lead—he said there would be great glory in it, and that all Sicily and then Greece would become subject to Athens.

Yet the project bore no real relationship to the politics of mainland Greece, and the Athenians had little sound military intelligence about Sicily. Just before the expedition sailed, a scandal broke out in Athens: the statues of Hermes that stood before the doors of temples and houses were mutilated in the night (the sexual organ was broken off), and Alcibiades—who was known to have committed similar sacrilege before when in a wild and dissipated

Charioteer: silver coin from Syracuse, fifth century B.C.

mood—was suspected. But he went off to Sicily, as co-commander with his opponent, the unwilling Nicias, of the greatest naval expedition ever sent out by a Greek polis. Before the fleet reached Syracuse, Alcibiades was recalled to stand trial for the mutilation of the Hermae; but he escaped to Sparta.

The siege of Syracuse was long drawn out (414–413), enormously expensive, and a total failure: Nicias and other leaders were captured and killed. While it was going on, Sparta, now advised by Alcibiades (who also seduced the wife of the Spartan king), renewed the war at home and sent troops to help the Syracusans. The Spartans also stirred up the Ionian cities to revolt against Athens. The Persian satraps in Asia Minor, hoping to regain sea-coast towns lost so long before, joined with the Spartans. Alcibiades, who had worn out his welcome in Sparta, now joined the Persians.

Ironically enough the balance of power between the two great Greek poleis that in 490 and 480–479 had so gloriously expelled the Persians from Greece was now, in 412, held by the very same Persians. Alcibiades tried to blackmail the Athenians by telling them that if they would install an oligarchic government he would return and exercise his influence with the Persians on their behalf; while the Spartans promised the Persians that, in exchange for paying for their fleet, they would permit the cities of Ionia to fall into Persian hands once more.

Civil strife accompanied by assassinations of those who opposed a change in the constitution created a turbulent atmosphere in Athens. A group of conspirators first prevailed on the Assembly to appoint a team to draft a new oligarchic constitution, and then persuaded a rump session to accept the recommendation that the existing officials be dismissed. A group consisting of five presidents appointed a hundred associates, who in turn co-opted three hundred more, and this now became the new Council of State, which ousted the former Council of Five Hundred by an armed but bloodless coup d'état. The new Four Hundred could summon at will a new Five Thousand, ostensibly to replace the traditional assembly of all the citizens. The democratic forces still controlled the fleet.

The leading oligarchs would now have liked to proceed at once to peace with Sparta, and probably intended that the Five Thousand should never be summoned. From exile, Alcibiades, however, indicated his preference for their summoning. After a naval defeat, the citizens actually deposed the oligarchic Four Hundred and elected the Five Thousand—all upper class—which governed the city from 411 to 410 B.C., when, after some Athenian successes at sea, democracy was restored.

Alcibiades continued to command Athenian naval forces at sea without returning home until 407, when he came to Athens and was absolved for the mutilation of the Hermae; but the Spartan fleet defeated him in 406, and he went into retirement on his estates along the Hellespont (the modern Dardanelles), where he was murdered three years later by Spartan and Persian agents. His career vividly illustrates the vulnerability of the Athenian democracy to a plausible, charming, talented scoundrel. Another weakness—the temptation to yield to impulse—was displayed soon afterwards, when the Athenians had defeated the Spartan fleet (at Arginusae) but had suffered heavy casualties, and the Council was intimidated by the mourning families of the drowned soldiers into ordering the collective executions of six generals on the charge of not rescuing the troops in the water. The Council paid no attention to the fact that one of the generals had himself been swimming for safety at the time. The people later regretted their act, but the generals were dead.

In the final naval action of the war, the Spartans captured most of the Athenian fleet empty on a beach in the Hellespont while the sailors were hunting food on shore (Aegospotami, 405), and the Spartan infantry rounded up thousands of Athenian prisoners, of whom three thousand were executed as direct reprisal for recent Athenian atrocities. Starving, blockaded by land and sea, its alliance in ruins as the allies had defected or joined the Spartans, Athens had to surrender. Some of the Spartan allies wanted to punish the Athenians as the Athenians had punished the Melians, but the Spartans refused. The Athenians had to demolish their long walls, abandon their empire, surrender their fleet, and undertake to follow the Spartan lead in foreign policy. But they were not massacred.

IV

The Fourth Century B.C. and the Hellenistic Age

Spartan Domination

As the victors, the Spartans found themselves dominant in a Greece where polis hated polis and, within each polis, faction hated faction. From Ionia, which the Spartans had sold back to Persia as the price of victory, the Persians loomed once more as a threat to the whole Greek world. By midcentury the new state of Macedonia in the north menaced the Greeks. Perhaps wiser or more vigorous leaders would have been able to create some sort of federation among the individual poleis that could have withstood the Persians and the Macedonians, and, still later, the Romans. But since this did not happen, it seems more likely that the polis as an institution was no longer the appropriate way for the Greek world to be organized. Perhaps it was too small, too provincial, too old-fashioned to keep the peace and give men room for economic advancement and intellectual growth.

Sparta proved as unable as Athens to manage Greece. The Spartan government, suitable for a state that had no job but war, was largely in the hands of the elders, too conservative to meet new challenges. Gold and silver had found their way into the simple agricultural economy whose founders had preferred to use bars of iron as exchange. Many Spartans for the first time found themselves disfranchised for debt, and so relegated to the status of "inferiors." They joined the helots and perioikoi as part of a discontented majority at precisely the moment when Sparta needed more "equals"—full, enfranchised, fighting citizens. Away from home the Spartans could neither free the cities of the former Athenian Empire in which they had installed governments of their own oligarchic type, nor occupy them satisfactorily.

At Athens, for example, an oligarchy of thirty (the Thirty Tyrants) at the instigation of the extremist Critias instituted a reign of terror not only against democrats associated with past regimes but also against moderate oligarchs. In 403 an invading force of exiled democrats killed Critias and touched off a brief civil war. At Athens they restored democracy, but the Thirty Tyrants and their sympathizers were set up as a Spartan puppet state nearby at Eleusis. Nobody was allowed to move between the two separate Athenian states. In 401 the Athenians treacherously killed the generals of the Eleusis armies, and the two states were reunited. It was the government of this insecurely reestablished Athens that tried and condemned the philosopher Socrates in 399 B.C. (see p. 76).

The Spartans could not pose as the leaders of Greece and simultaneously keep their bargain with the Persians to sell Ionia back to them; yet if they went back on this bargain, the Persians would start a new war. So in 401 B.C., when the younger brother of Artaxerxes II, king of Persia—Cyrus the Younger, governor of Asia Minor—rebelled against Artaxerxes and asked for Spartan aid, Sparta gave it to him. Cyrus was soon killed in a battle deep in Mesopotamia, and his Greek troops were left high and dry in the heart of Persia. Their disciplined march north to the shores of the Black Sea and the Greek city of Trebizond on its shore forms the substance of a book called the *Anabasis* ("The March Back") by the Athenian Xenophon, one of their officers. The episode left the Spartans at war with Persia.

The Spartans did not unite their land and sea commands, but gave the Persians time to build a fleet, which they put under an Athenian admiral, Conon. The Persians also bribed Thebes, Corinth, Argos, and Athens to stir up so much trouble against Sparta that Spartan troops had to be recalled from Persia to fight a new war in Greece proper. It lasted eight years (to 386); saw the self-assertion of Thebes; seemed to produce the threat of a renewed Athenian Empire; and ended in stalemate, as the Persians and Spartans finally got together and imposed a peace ("The King's Peace," 386 B.C.) by which the Persians resumed control of all Greek states in Asia, and the rest were autonomous.

Thebes Rises to Leadership

Raising money from their allies and hiring mercenaries to intimidate all resistance, the Spartans systematically disciplined and punished the cities that dared resist, installing an oligarchy at Thebes (382) and in lesser places, breaking their promise to respect the autonomy of all Greek cities. A group of Theban democratic exiles conspired to overthrow the pro-Spartan regime there (379 B.C.), and when the Spartans tried to punish them, a new war broke out, in which Athens participated after 377 as the leading power in a new anti-Spartan League of many Greek cities.

By 371, the Spartans were ready for peace, a guarantee of independence to all Greek states, and disarmament. But the wording of the treaty gave Persia and Athens the leading roles as guarantors, and deliberately limited the Thebans to signing for Thebes only, not for their own league of allies (the Boeotian League). So Epaminondas, the chief Theban delegate, refused to sign, and soon afterward roundly defeated the Spartans at the battle of Leuctra. Cities subject to Sparta began to oust their oligarchic governments and install democracies. Epaminondas followed up his successes by two invasions of the Peloponnesus (369, 368), which destroyed Spartan power in its own homeland. Ugly and tyrannical, Spartan power vanished from Greece unmourned. It was no credit to Athens that in the final stages she helped Sparta out of fear of Thebes.

As head of the Boeotian League, Thebes under Epaminondas not only had a democratic government of its own, but treated its allies rather as equals than as subjects, and so commanded a true federation rather than an empire like the first Athenian alliance or the Spartan alliance. Other local leagues of cities followed the Boeotian example and were affiliated with Thebes. Warfare continued despite the effort of the Persians to dictate a general peace (367), as the Athenians reverted to their former imperialist practices and installed colonies of Athenian settlers on the soil of conquered cities. The Thebans fought in the Peloponnesus, in the north, against Athens at sea, and finally in the Peloponnesus again, where an alliance of Sparta and Athens and several other poleis met them in battle at Mantinea (362).

Epaminondas was killed at a moment when his forces were winning, but they stopped fighting when they heard of his death, and their enemies got away. All hope that Thebes could put an end to the interminable fighting among Greeks died with Epaminondas, a leader of extraordinary military talent and political generosity, who preferred leadership to domination but whose own people, the Boeotians, largely deserved their reputation elsewhere in Greece as country bumpkins, uncultivated and crude, with a strong streak of ruthlessness which even Epaminondas could not always control.

Though a new league of city-states was now formed (362) to end war and to enable the Greeks as a whole to determine their foreign policy, Athens continued to act as the rival of Thebes and to play the traditional political game of alliance-building within the League. Though ineffective, the League was an important effort to create something like a United States of Greece. Without its restraints, Thebes found itself broken in war against the city of Phocis, whose general had seized the shrine of Delphi and used the accumulated funds there to create a large army of mercenaries (354). For its part Athens strove to reconstruct its old Aegean empire, but in 357 many of its most important outposts rebelled, and Athens was forced to grant them freedom in 355. Athens was exhausted and broke and weak.

Ironically enough, the inability of the Greek cities to give up fighting was almost surely due in part to general prosperity. Whereas during the fifth century only Athens and Sparta had been able to afford large armies and navies, during the fourth many other cities grew rich enough to support such forces. Brisk Mediterranean commerce brought wealth to the distant Greek settlements from the Crimea to Spain; it was not only goods that flowed but also slaves and mercenary troops: it is estimated that shortly after midcentury the Persians alone had fifty thousand Greek troops fighting in their armies.

Many of the devices of modern capitalism to make international trade easier now first made their appearance: banking and credit, insurance, trade treaties, and special privileges. Private wealth grew rapidly, and was widely distributed. Slaves increased in number; we know of several people who owned more than a thousand of them; by 338 b.c. there may have been as many as 150,000 in Attica, working in the mines and at other occupations. All this prosperity meant that states quickly recovered from defeats in war and could quickly afford to try again. Patriotism became more and more a matter of cutting up the melon of profits. At the same time, the poor grew poorer; unwilling to declass themselves by engaging in the manual labor that was now the work of slaves, they became vagrants or mercenary soldiers.

Macedon

North of Thessaly, and extending inland into areas that are today part of Yugoslavia and Albania, lay the kingdom of Macedon, with a considerable coastline along the Aegean. The Macedonians were a mixture of peoples including some of Greek origin; they were organized into tribes, worshiped some of the Greek gods, and spoke a native language that the Greeks could not understand although it included many words of Greek origin. Their hereditary kings—who were also elected by the people—claimed Greek descent; indeed they believed they were descendants of the hero Herakles, son of Zeus himself.

The king spoke Greek as well as the native language, had title to all land, and ruled absolutely so long as he was not charged with treason (when the people might depose him). He was advised by councilors who were selected from among the nobles of each tribe and felt themselves to be his social equals. Although the Greeks had planted some poleis along the Macedonian shore, and although Greek cultural influence and Greek trade had penetrated deeply into Macedon by the fourth century, Macedon did not copy Greek political institutions but kept its own, much more nearly like those of Mycenaean Greece in the days of Agamemnon. Traditionally the Macedonians relied on cavalry in war, but in the fourth century they added foot soldiers in order to fight their neighbors from the west and north, the Illyrians (probable ancestors of the Albanians of today). Both Athens and Sparta interfered and intrigued in internal Macedonian affairs.

THE ACHIEVEMENT OF PHILIP   In 359, a prince of the ruling house, Philip, became regent for his infant nephew, the king. Having lived for three years as a hostage in Thebes, where he knew Epaminondas, Philip knew all about Greek affairs. He applied Theban military principles to his army (emphasizing infantry tactics), led it in person, defeated the Illyrians and various rivals for power within Macedon, was elected king in his own right, and broke the power of Athens in the territory neighboring his own to the east (359–354 B.C.). He exploited the rich gold and silver mines in his kingdom, and struck his own coinage. He scored successes in Thessaly and in Thrace, where he threatened Athenian possessions along the shore of the Hellespont (354–351).

Athenian politicians viewed Philip's advance with mixed feelings. Some favored him, others opposed. It was not until he had won still more territory and begun to use a fleet successfully that the famous Athenian orator Demosthenes began to warn against the threat from Macedon. But Philip had annexed the peninsula of Chalcidice and detached the big island of Euboea, close to Attica itself, from its Athenian loyalties.

At that point he suggested peace and an alliance with Athens, which was reached with the approval even of Demosthenes (346), though Philip meanwhile had secured control over the Delphic oracle. He was moving south and consolidating his power as he came. By 342, the Athenians had acquired new allies in the Peloponnesus. In retaliation Philip moved into Thrace (modern Bulgaria) to cut off the Athenian grain supplies coming from the Black Sea and to avert a new Persian–Athenian alliance. Once again Demosthenes pressed for war, and Athens took military action in Euboea (341, 340). By late 339 Philip was deep in Greece once again, only two days distant from Attica. Demosthenes now arranged an eleventh-hour alliance with Thebes. Protesting at intervals his wishes for peace, Philip totally defeated the Athenian-Theban alliance at Chaeronea in Boeotia (338 B.C.). He occupied Thebes, which had surrendered, but spared Athens a military occupation on condition that the Athenian alliance be dissolved and an alliance with Macedon adopted. He showed leniency, and proved that in fact he had never intended to destroy Athens, as Demosthenes had maintained.

Philip's victories aroused in many the hope of a unified Greece. At Corinth in 337 B.C., all the poleis except Sparta met and organized a league that called itself "The Greeks," all members of which bound themselves to stop fighting and intervening in each other's affairs. This was a far more closely knit body than the abortive league of 362 (see p. 61). It immediately allied itself with Macedon, and then joined with Philip in a declaration of war on Persia to revenge the sacrilege of Xerxes' invasion of 143 years earlier. Philip was to command the expedition. By 336 B.C. the advance forces of the army were already liberating the Ionian cities from Persia. But Philip, aged only forty-six, was now mysteriously assassinated.

Philip's accomplishments greatly impressed his contemporaries, who realized that no such powerful consolidated state as his Macedon had ever existed west of Asia. Instead of allowing the resources of Macedon to be dissipated in flashy conquests, he organized the people he conquered, both in the Balkan area from the Adriatic to the Black Sea and in Greece. He kept

Alexander the Great depicted on a four-drachma silver coin of about 300 B.C. with the horns of Amen.

morale high in the army, and had the various contingents from the various regions competing to see who would do the best job. He differentiated his troops into more specialized units for diverse tasks in war, and he personally commanded whichever unit had the roughest assignment. He could appreciate the strengths of his Greek opponents, and when he had defeated them he utilized their skills and made sure of their loyalty by decent treatment. By his final effort to unify them against their traditional Persian enemy, he associated himself with the ancient patriotic cause that so many of them had so often betrayed but that obviously still had great appeal for them. Though he felt himself to be part of Greek civilization, he reminds many students of the Greece of an earlier age than his own, a kind of Homeric hero in the flesh almost a thousand years after the siege of Troy.

THE ACHIEVEMENT OF ALEXANDER   Philip's son Alexander the Great belongs to legend as much as to history. Alexander loved war, politics, athletics, alcohol, poetry, medicine, and science. He was only twenty when he came to the throne. Within a dozen years he led his armies on a series of triumphal marches that won for Macedon the largest empire yet created in the ancient world. He began by crushing a Greek revolt led by Thebes (335 B.C.), whose entire population he sold into slavery (he did not massacre the males, as the

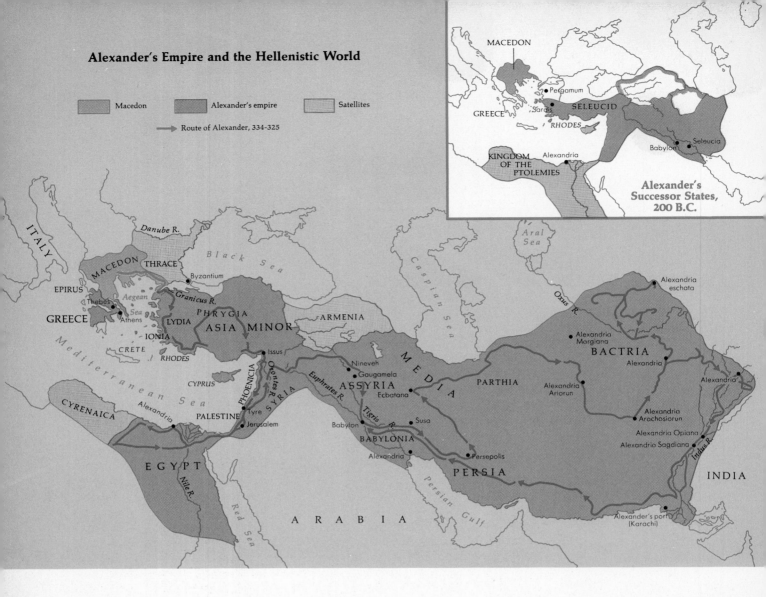

Alexander's Empire and the Hellenistic World

Macedon   Alexander's empire   Satellites

→ Route of Alexander, 334-325

Alexander's Successor States, 200 B.C.

MACEDON

GREECE   Pergamum   SELEUCID

Sardis

RHODES

KINGDOM OF THE PTOLEMIES   Alexandria

Babylon   Seleucia

ITALY

Danube R.

MACEDON   THRACE

Black Sea

Byzantium

EPIRUS

Thebes   Granicus R.

GREECE   Aegean Sea   Athens   PHRYGIA

LYDIA   ASIA MINOR   ARMENIA

IONIA

CRETE   RHODES

Issus

Aral Sea

Caspian Sea

Oxus R.

Alexandria eschata

CYPRUS

Mediterranean Sea

Orontes R.   SYRIA

Euphrates R.   Nineveh   Gaugamela   ASSYRIA

MEDIA   PARTHIA

Alexandria Margiana

BACTRIA

Alexandria

Alexandria

CYRENAICA

Alexandria

PHOENICIA   Tyre   PALESTINE

Jerusalem

Babylon

Tigris R.   Ecbatana

Susa

BABYLONIA

Alexandria

Alexandria Ariorun

Alexandria Arachosiorun

Alexandria Opiana

Alexandria Sagdiana   Indus R.

EGYPT

Nile R.

Red Sea

ARABIA

Persian Gulf

Persepolis

PERSIA

INDIA

Alexander's port (Karachi)

Spartans and Athenians often did). Next he crossed the Aegean into Asia Minor to continue the war of the Greek League against Persia, and recapture the Ionian cities. He defeated the Persians at the river Granicus (334 B.C.), and took over Ionia, where he established democracies in the poleis. In territories belonging to the Persians he took title to all land, thus replacing the Persian king, whom he defeated again at Issus (333 B.C.), and so opened up Syria. He reduced Tyre by siege, and refused King Darius' offer of a Persian princess and all territory west of the Euphrates.

Egypt was next, and it fell easily. Here he founded the great port of Alexandria in the Nile Delta (332), a Greek city from the beginning. But he paid his respects to the Egyptian divinities, and allowed himself to be treated as a god, according to the Egyptian way. Then he marched east and defeated the Persians again in Mesopotamia (Gaugamela, near Nineveh, 331 B.C.). The Persian Empire was smashed. Alexander sacrificed to Marduk in Babylon, and ordered his temple restored; the Persians had destroyed it. Vast mopping-up operations continued in Persia proper (330-327), as Alexander's armies seized the chief cities and all the Persian royal treasure—perhaps half a billion dollars in cash. But he treated the Persian royal family with great courtesy, and acted toward his new subjects just as a king of Persia would have done. The Persian nobles came to acknowledge him as king by the grace of Ahuramazda. In fact, Alexander *was* king of Persia, just as he was pharaoh of Egypt, king of Babylon, king of Macedon, and commander *(hegemon)* of the Greek League.

Far out in Central Asia, Alexander fell in love with and married the daughter of a local chieftain, who joined forces with the conqueror (327 B.C.). This marriage enhanced the new loyalty of the Persians to him, but it helped to strain the loyalty of his own Macedonian noble companions, who also disliked Alexander's own occasional adoption of Persian dress and Persian custom to please his new subjects. Though enjoying his role as "Great King," Alexander, who had paid his respects to the shade of his ancestor Achilles at Troy before he began his Eastern campaigns, and whose favorite reading was the *Iliad,* thought of himself as Greek. But the issue was involved in an alleged plot against Alexander, for which Philotas, the son of the most powerful single Macedonian noble, Parmenio, was executed, and soon afterward Alexander had Parmenio himself killed. And later, Alexander in a drunken fury killed another of his own Macedonian generals for having taunted him with his Persian ways. There was much truth in the charge, and Alexander continued to purge Macedonians who resisted his orientalization.

The tensions of the conquest did not diminish its efficiency: new levies of troops came out from Europe and were raised in Asia; new roads were built, and new towns sprang up, each named after Alexander. Believing that India was the last region in Asia, that it was small, and that after India one would come upon Ocean, via which one could perhaps return to Europe by sea, Alexander next set out to conquer India (327 B.C.) from a base in what is now Afghanistan. He soon found himself doing battle with the hill tribes and with princes of Kashmir and Punjab (now Pakistan). At first the Indian war elephants terrified Alexander's cavalry and his men, but soon the Macedonians learned how to defeat them, and won many victories. Alexander moved on east; but India was not small, as he had thought, and his troops eventually mutinied. Alexander had to give in, and call off any further advance (326 B.C.). He led his troops on riverboats down the Indus southward toward the Indian Ocean, fighting all the way, and sacrificing a gold cup to Poseidon when he reached the ocean shore. Several new Alexandrias were founded, including the town that is now Karachi (Pakistan), before Alexander led his forces westward again across the southern Persian deserts back to Susa (324).

Here he conducted a purge of those he suspected of treason, and dramatically pursued his plan to combine the best features of the Macedonian and the Persian nobilities by staging a mass marriage between eighty Macedonian officers and eighty Persian noblewomen. He himself took a new Persian wife, and blessed the unions of ten thousand Macedonian troops with Persian women. Those who wished to return home were sent off well rewarded; but Alexander kept their wives in Persia and planned to use their children as the nucleus of a future army of mixed blood that would owe everything to him. A great double naval expedition from the mouths of the Tigris–Euphrates eastward along the shore of the Persian Gulf to India, and westward around Arabia (never yet circumnavigated) to Egypt, was in preparation at Babylon, where Alexander had great dockyards built. From the Greeks, who had enjoyed a longer period of internal peace than any for over a century, Alexander asked for divine honors: apparently he wanted to become a god. In 323 B.C., at Babylon, he caught a fever and died, aged thirty-three.

Imagination can hardly conceive of what Alexander might have accomplished had he lived: he might well have made Greece the center of his empire, and would surely have been able to conquer the two states in the western Mediterranean already looming on the horizon as powers there: Carthage and Rome. He respected all races and religions, and believed in decent politics and a booming economy. Each of the Alexandrias he settled with Greeks and planned as a center for the diffusion of Greek culture. A superb general, a clever governor of subject peoples, a pious believer in the Greek gods, a passionate man with a strong streak of megalomania, Alexander astonished his contemporaries, and it is little wonder that he became to later generations the hero of a great cycle of romances that circulated in every country, in every language, and among every people, down virtually into our own day.

Heirs of Alexander

As soon as the news of Alexander's death was known, his faithful generals began a fierce scramble for portions of his empire. They combined against each other in various shifting alliances, and arranged many intermarriages and murders, in a period of kaleidoscopic political and military change. By about 300 B.C. three dynasties had emerged as supreme, each in a different portion of the empire: the Ptolemies in Egypt, the Seleucids in Asia, and the Antigonids in Macedon and Greece. In addition, there were various lesser kingdoms, chiefly in Asia Minor. Fighting continued almost without interruption until the rising power of Rome began to challenge them and to destroy and then absorb them one by one.

In Egypt the Ptolemies followed the ancient pattern of government, turning themselves into successors of the pharaohs. They became gods, they sometimes married their sisters, they exploited the agricultural wealth of the country to the limit. They claimed title to all land, some of which was farmed by peasants directly for their benefit and some let out to temples or to military settlers or officials. The Ptolemies' own land gave them all its produce except what was needed to feed the farm workers. Land let to others paid the Ptolemies a percentage of the wheat. Oil, flax, and papyrus were royal monopolies. No tree in Egypt could be cut down without royal permission. The Ptolemies governed largely through their Greek officials, who poured into Egypt for several generations after Alexander's death. Even the armies of the first three Ptolemies were made up wholly of Greeks. It was not until 217 B.C. that Egyptian troops participated in the wars of the dynasty, which were directed chiefly against the Seleucids of Asia for the possession of Syria, and against the Antigonids for islands of the Aegean and the Anatolian coasts.

Alexandria, the capital, was built between the Mediterranean and a great lake connected by canals with the Mediterranean and the Nile, and the Nile in turn with the Red Sea. The city had harbors on both the Mediterranean and the lake, with port and dock facilities; it had broad streets, luxurious palaces, a famous library with approximately a million volumes—its catalog alone filled 120 volumes. In the "museum," scholars, freed from all duties by state subsidies, conducted their researches ("fat fowls in a coop," a skeptical poet called them). The towering white stone lighthouse four hundred feet high was regarded as one of the wonders of the world, and had a broad ramp to the first platform so wide that two horsemen could pass. This was the biggest city of the ancient world until Rome eventually outstripped it; there were perhaps a million inhabitants of Alexandria in the first century B.C., some of them living in multistoried apartment houses. Alexandria was far too big to be a polis; but its Greek population had its own political organization, as did the Jews and the Egyptians. At Alexandria stood also the Ptolemies' big barn, where all the royal grain was stored after it had come down the Nile.

The Egyptian population lived under its own law, and was judged in its own courts. Those who were discontent with the system that exploited them so thoroughly—and there were many—had no escape except to take sanctuary in a temple; and the government always tried to reduce the number of temples that had the right to provide sanctuary. For a long time the Greek population, with its own language, law courts, culture, and ways of life, did not mingle with the Egyptians, but remained a large collection of foreigners who were getting rich as fast as they could. By the early second century Greek immigration had tapered off, Greek–Egyptian intermarriages had begun, and the army was more Egyptian and less effective. Rome began to intervene; disorganization set in; and by 118 B.C. Ptolemy VII had to issue a series of decrees calling for reform that show how far the system had begun to disintegrate.

Seleucus I was also one of Alexander's generals, who began as governor of Babylon and eventually won control over all of Alexander's Asian lands except northern and western Asia Minor and the Indian regions in the east, which had to be given up by 303 B.C. Seleucid territorial holdings fluctuated a good deal, however. We know much more about the Ptolemaic kingdom than about the Seleucid because many papyri have survived in the dry climate of Egypt that preserve details of economic and social life; no such source exists for Asia. The Seleucids' Ionian territories centered on the former Lydian capital of Sardis, their Syrian territories on the new city of Antioch-on-Orontes in northern Syria, and their Mesopotamian territories on the new city of Seleucia not far from Babylon. As the heirs of the ancient Near Eastern empires, the Seleucids used the former Assyrian and Persian administrative forms, revived Babylonian religion and Babylonian literature, still written in cuneiform. Some scholars believe that by deliberately sponsoring a Babylonian religious revival the Seleucids were seeking a counterweight to Zoroastrianism, the Persian faith. It does appear that the Seleucids failed to achieve what Alexander had so well begun: the securing of Persian cooperation in managing the huge Asian territories.

The Seleucids could not count on deification, like the Ptolemies, nor could they create in Asia anything like the extremely centralized Ptolemaic system of exploitation. In Asia, unlike Egypt, there was too vast an area to be governed, there were too many varied traditions of authority, too many local governors to be considered. The Seleucids instead did something the Ptolemies did not do: they founded Greek cities, and sponsored their development. To do this they gave up large areas that were their own royal land, and they also transferred the land of powerful individual landowners to the cities. In such cases the lot of the peasant improved, as he ceased to be private property and gained his freedom. The Greek cities were military colonies, with money and land given by the king, and settlement, housing, financial, and other questions delegated to a military governor. The settlers received land, and were required to serve in the army in exchange.

Like Alexander the Seleucid rulers named the cities for themselves; there were many Antiochs named for the Antiochus who had been Seleucus I's father and whose name continued to be given to many of the monarchs of the dynasty; there were also Seleucias, Laodiceas named after Seleucus' mother, and Apameas named after his wife. Some of the earlier Alexandrias now had their names changed to Antioch. The multiple founding of Greek cities all over Asia was a bold attempt to solve the problem of military security, and it failed partly because there were not enough Greeks available to populate the cities and man the armies, partly because the Seleucids did not command the loyalty of the Persian population.

As for Macedon and Greece, the family that won there were the Antigonids, descendants of Alexander's governor of the western Anatolian province of Phrygia. It was not until 276 B.C., almost half a century after Alexander's death, that the son of the first Antigonus, known as Antigonus Gonatas, was accepted as king of Macedon. Antigonus Gonatas had defeated the marauding Gauls, Celts (Indo-Europeans) from distant western Europe who were now migrating eastward along the Danube and bursting southward from the wilder and unsettled portion of the Continent on raids into Italy, Greece, and eventually Asia Minor, where they were given a kingdom of their own called Galatia. Having protected Greece from the Gauls (277 B.C.), Antigonus proved a successful ruler in Macedon.

Though the Greek cities were now grouped together into two leagues, the Aetolian and the Achaean, larger in membership and more representative in their joint rule than the Athenian and Spartan alliances of earlier times, they fought against each other and against the Antigonid kings of Macedon with the usual Greek vigor; so that by the 220's the Greeks were largely independent of Macedon. Athens had become famous largely as a university town, and usually stayed out of the perpetual brawls of the other cities. But Sparta, true to its traditions, tried to take over the Achaean League, and would have succeeded had not the Macedonians been brought back into Greece in 222, to defeat the Spartans finally. By the 220's, however, Rome had begun the interventions in the Greek world which were quickly to lead to conquest.

Buildings in the caravan city of Petra, in present-day Jordan, were carved directly into the red rock hills.

V
The Civilization of Greece

The Gods

The Olympian gods are already old acquaintances, whom we first learned to know in Homer. The citizens of a polis naturally had special devotion for the divinity who had founded it: Athens for Athena, Sparta for Zeus, but they worshiped the other gods as well. Everybody worshiped the goddess of the hearth, Hestia, the protectress of each individual person's own home and fireside. Births and deaths in a family, solemn political actions in the state, were accompanied by religious rites. Poleis in large numbers grouped together in special devotion to regional shrines: the temple of Apollo at Delphi and of Zeus at Olympia we know; Zeus had another shrine at Dodona. The Olympic games were followed by others held in honor of Apollo at Delphi, of Poseidon the sea god on the Isthmus of Corinth. At the games religious solemnities

Bronze statue of Zeus or Poseidon, fifth century B.C.

accompanied the sports: racing, jumping, throwing the discus, wrestling. The winners were crowned with laurel, as were those who won drinking contests or beauty contests or contests for the best poem or musical composition, including hymns to the god, which retold the myths that surrounded his birth and life, almost as if he were a human hero.

Two Greek cults of particular importance began outside the ordinary worship of the Olympian gods: that of Demeter at Eleusis near Athens, and that of Dionysus. Demeter (the name means literally "earth-mother") was the goddess of fertility and of the harvests: her daughter (by Zeus), Persephone, was snatched away by the god of the underworld, and had to spend a third of the year with him: the months of barrenness, late autumn and winter. Every spring she returned, and the fields became fertile again. Like the Mesopotamians from Sumer on and like the Egyptians, and perhaps even like late Old Stone Age man, the Greeks too invented a story to account for the miracle of rebirth every spring. At Eleusis Demeter was worshiped in ceremonies that all initiates swore to keep secret. We know few of the details, but certainly there was a kind of ritual drama in which the initiates acted out the sorrow of the goddess searching for her lost daughter; there was a ritual meal, with communion in bread and water; and there was a sacred purifying bath in the salt waters of the nearby sea. Probably the participants expected that they would enjoy some sort of afterlife.

Dionysus, the god of wine, was not Greek in origin, but a northern foreigner, who also stood for fertility in its more openly sexual aspects: his celebrants originally carried phalluses in his procession, and were themselves often dressed as goats. In its original form the cult inspired its followers with wild frenzy in which they tore up and ate the flesh of living animals, and so acted out the devouring of the god himself. The cult was tamer in Greece, where songs were early written for the god.

Tragedy

From these songs there developed at Athens the art of tragedy: the word means "goat song" and shows the close connection with the god Dionysus. At first largely sung by a chorus and formally religious in tone, the tragedies later began to deal with more personal human problems, and individual actors' roles became more and more important. The first competition to choose the best tragedy was sponsored by Peisistratus in 534 B.C., and annual contests were held thereafter. Many hundreds of tragedies were written; comparatively few have survived in full—probably the best—and we have fragments of others. The later Greek philosopher Aristotle believed that it was the purpose of tragedy to arouse pity and terror in the spectators; to purge or purify them by causing them to reflect on the fearful punishments that highly placed men and women brought upon themselves by their own sins, the worst of which was hubris, arrogance.

The first, and some would still say the greatest, of the three chief tragedians whose works survive was Aeschylus (ca. 525–456), of whose seventy-odd tragedies we have seven. The earliest in time was *The Persians* (472 B.C.), in which Aeschylus explained the defeat of the Persians as the result of Xerxes' efforts to upset the international order established by the gods, and of the arrogance by which he offended Zeus. The audience could ponder recent history (it was only seven years since the Persians had been defeated) and consider the moral reasons for their own victories: such a play would tend to sober up any fire-eater who thought one Greek could lick ten Persians.

In *Prometheus Bound,* Aeschylus dealt with the punishment inflicted by Zeus upon Prometheus the Titan, who had stolen fire as a gift to mankind and

The theater at Epidaurus, built around 330 B.C.

who now lay chained to a rock while a vulture pecked at his liver. Zeus behaved tyrannically—he was new to the job of being king of the gods when Prometheus committed his offense—and only gradually learned to temper his wrath with mercy. Just as Xerxes had offended against the proper order of things by trying to impose Persian rule on Greece, so Prometheus had, even out of good will, offended by trying to get mankind the great gift of fire too soon. In the trilogy *The Oresteia,* all three plays of which survive, Aeschylus dealt with the ghastly tragedies in the family of Agamemnon, who sacrificed his daughter Iphigenia to get a favorable wind to go to Troy, was murdered by his unfaithful wife Clytemnestra on his return, and was avenged by his son Orestes, who killed his mother on the order of Apollo. Orestes suffered torments by the Furies, and was acquitted by a court presided over by Athena; but only Zeus succeeded in transforming the Furies into more kindly creatures. Crime and punishment, remorse and release, a benevolent god over all: these Aeschylus portrayed in lofty, moving verse.

Sophocles, the second of the three greatest tragedians (496–406), wrote many tragedies, of which only ten survive. He believed deeply in Athenian institutions and in the religion of his fellow Greeks, and took an active part in the public life of Periclean Athens. In his *Antigone,* the niece of Creon, tyrant of Thebes, defied her uncle's harsh decision that the body of her brother, killed while leading a rebellion, must be exposed to be devoured by beasts of prey. Proclaiming that divine law required decent burial, she disobeyed Creon, and caused the proper ceremonial earth to be sprinkled on the body. She knew she would die for her defiance, but she acted in obedience to her conscience and resisted the dictator. The *Antigone* has carried its message of the sanctity of the individual conscience down the centuries, proclaiming the superiority of what is eternally right and decent to any mere dictator's brutal whim.

Living to be ninety, Sophocles saw the ruin brought by the Peloponnesian War, and his last tragedy, *Oedipus at Colonus,* produced after his death, dealt with the old age of the famous Theban king who in ignorance had killed his father and married his mother, and had torn out his own eyes in horror when he discovered what he had done. A blind beggar, outcast, Oedipus now knew that he could not have avoided the pollution of his unwitting crimes, and that his self-mutilation too was justified. Tempered by years of suffering, he sought sanctuary to die, and received it from Theseus, king of Athens: Oedipus' tomb would forever protect the Athenians against Thebes. Reflecting upon the terrible story of Oedipus and on the trials of all human life, Sophocles' chorus sang that for mankind the best thing is never to be born, and the next best to die as soon as possible after birth: the passions of youth, the blows dealt one in middle life, and the anguish of old age are not worth it.

Nineteen plays remain of the many written by the third and last of the great Attic tragedians, Euripides (ca. 480–406), who focused more upon human psychology, with far less emphasis on divine majesty. More realistic in their introduction of children, slaves, and other characters upon the scene, his plays were also more romantic in their exploration of the far reaches of the human mind. The *Hippolytus* showed the uncontrollable sexual passion of a decent woman—Phaedra—for her ascetic stepson Hippolytus, who rejected it as he would all passion. She was ashamed of her lust but, as in the case of Potiphar's wife and Joseph, accused Hippolytus of having attacked her; he was executed, she committed suicide. The *Medea* showed a woman so far gone in agony brought about by rejection of her love that she killed her children in a fit of madness. The *Alcestis* showed a husband so selfish that he gladly accepted the offer of his devoted wife to die for him so that she might prolong his life; and then suffered agonies of remorse at his folly, when he had lost her.

The *Trojan Women* presented the sufferings of the women of Troy at the hands of the Greeks. It was staged in the same year as the Athenian atrocity at Melos, and must have caused the audience many uncomfortable moments of self-questioning. The *Bacchae* explored the excesses of religious ecstasy: in a frenzy a queen tore her own son to bits, thinking he was a lion. Was Euripides saying that men under the impulse of strong emotion were beasts, or that the old religion had too much that was savage in it, or only that the young king had defied the god and his hubris had brought him a fate that he well deserved?

Comedy

Comedy, like tragedy, also began at the festivals of Dionysus. Aristophanes (ca. 450–ca. 385) has left eleven complete plays and parts of a twelfth. Besides making his audience laugh, he hoped to teach them a lesson through laughter. A thoroughgoing conservative, Aristophanes was suspicious of all innovation. In *The Frogs,* for instance, he brought onto the stage actors playing the parts of the two tragedians Aeschylus (then dead) and Euripides (still alive). The god Dionysus himself solemnly weighed verses from their plays on a giant pair of scales. Every time, the solemn, didactic, and old-fashioned Aeschylus outweighed the innovating, skeptical, febrile, modern Euripides: a tragedian's duty, Aristophanes thought, was to teach.

In *The Clouds* Aristophanes ridiculed the philosopher Socrates, whom he showed in his "think shop" dangling from the ceiling in a basket so that he could voyage in air and contemplate the sun. Aristophanes meant to call attention to the dangers offered to Athenian youth by the Sophists (see p. 75). His identification of Socrates with them was somewhat unfair; but, like the others, Socrates taught young men to question the existing order, and he was therefore fair game.

Aristophanes opposed the Peloponnesian War not because he was a pacifist but because he thought it unnecessary. In *Lysistrata* the women denied themselves to their husbands until the men made peace, and in other plays Aristophanes denounced the Athenian politicians, including Pericles himself, for going to war. In *The Birds* the leading characters set off to found a Birdville (Cloud-cuckoo-land) to get away from war. In one of his later plays, of which we have only two, the women took over the state and proposed to share all the men among them, putting prostitutes out of business; in the other, Poverty and Wealth appeared in person and argued their cases.

These later plays provided a transition to the New Comedy of the fourth century, gentler and more domestic. We have several New Comedies by Menander, including one published for the first time only in the late 1950's. The drama was of course only one form that Greek poetic genius took. From the earliest days, the Greeks were the masters of lyric poetry as well (we have quoted one or two of Solon's own poems above, p. 49): among the most celebrated are poems of love by the poetess Sappho, of war by Spartan poets in the very early days, and of triumph in the games by Pindar.

History

A large proportion of what we know about the Greeks before and during the Persian Wars we owe to the industry and intelligence of Herodotus (ca. 484–420), who began to write his history as an account of the origins and course of the struggle between Greeks and Persians, and expanded it into an inquiry into the peoples of the whole world known to the Greeks. Born in Halicarnassus on the Ionian coast of Asia Minor, Herodotus was a great traveler, who visited Egypt, Italy, Mesopotamia, and the lands around the Black Sea, collecting information and listening to whatever stories people would tell him about their own past and about their present customs. He recorded what he learned, much of it of course tinged with myth, and he loved a good story; but he was both experienced and sensible, and he often put his reader on his guard against a story that he himself did not believe but set down in order to fill out the record.

Some have tended to scoff a little, especially at Herodotus' tales of a past that was remote even when he was doing his research; but these doubters have often been silenced by recent archaeological finds. Herodotus, for instance, said that the founder of Thebes, the semimythical Cadmus, was a Phoenician who had brought Phoenician letters with him from Phoenicia to Greece, where he founded Thebes about 1350 B.C., or about 900 years before Herodotus' own day. Herodotus added that Cadmus' dynasty was ousted about 1200 B.C. This was often disbelieved. But in A.D. 1964 archaeologists at Thebes found in the palace of Cadmus a large collection of fine cuneiform seals, one of which was datable to 1367–1346 B.C. These instantly demonstrated the high probability of Herodotus' account of Cadmus' origin, date of arrival, and bringing of letters. Even the date of the ouster was verified, since the seals were in a layer of material that had been burned about 1200 B.C. and had survived because they were already baked clay. Herodotus wrote so well and so beguilingly that we would read him with delight even if he were not so reliable. Nor was he a mere collector and organizer of material. Though he wandered far, he never lost sight of his main theme: the conflict between east and west, which he interpreted as a conflict between despotism and freedom.

Always coupled with Herodotus we find the equally intelligent but very different historian Thucydides (ca. 471–ca. 400), who wrote the account of the origins and course of the Peloponnesian War. The difference between the two arose partly from their subject matter: Herodotus was dealing largely with events that had happened before his own time, and he had to accept traditions and often hearsay accounts. Thucydides was dealing largely with events in which he himself had been a participant: he was an unsuccessful general on the Athenian side in the war, and had been punished for his defeat; but he remained impersonal, scientific, and serious, collecting and weighing his information with the greatest care. Though he followed Herodotus' custom of putting into the mouths of his leading characters words—sometimes long speeches—that represented what they might have said rather than what they actually said, he notified his readers that they must realize what he was doing: the actual words were not available, but the arguments on both sides of any issue could be revived and written up in the form of speeches. Pericles' funeral oration of 430 B.C. with its praise of Athenian democracy is perhaps the most famous; but Thucydides also wrote for the Melians, about to suffer terrible slaughter and enslavement at Athenian hands, all the moving arguments appropriate to those who were about to be massacred.

As deep a student of human psychology as any of the tragedians, Thucydides found in men and nations the cause of war; he knew as much about war and human behavior as anybody since has been able to learn. He wrote as a loser, but not as a mere loser in a sporting event, where time, and perhaps a return match, will assuage the hurt: Thucydides had seen his own Athens, so admirable in its best qualities, brought down by the Spartan militarists. He hoped that human intelligence would in the future realize how risky war was and what damage it did to the highest human values, but he knew that human nature would always respond to certain challenges by force, and that the lessons of the past were hard to learn. He wrote in pain and in iron detachment. His narrative of the great military events, such as the siege of Syracuse, Alcibiades' ill-conceived project, moves with great speed and well-concealed artistry. The much less talented and more pedestrian Xenophon, author of the *Anabasis* (see p. 60), wrote—in the *Hellenica*—a continuation of Thucydides' work down to the year 362 B.C. And the still less talented Arrian, writing very late but basing his work largely on the now lost account by Ptolemy I himself, has left us an account of Alexander's campaigns.

But for the century or so that followed the death of Alexander we have no historical work comparable with the histories of Herodotus, Thucydides, Xenophon, or Arrian. Therefore, we know the period less intimately than any since the Dark Age. It is only with the decade of the 220's that we once again encounter a narrative history, and then its author and his purpose themselves symbolize the change that has taken place. He was Polybius, a Greek who wrote in Greek but who had spent much time in Rome, where he had become an admirer and agent of the Romans, and the subject of his book was the rise to power of Rome. That he began his account with the year 221 B.C. clearly suggests that by that date the focus of world affairs had begun the shift from Greece to Rome.

Science and Philosophy

Possessed of inquiring, speculative minds, the Greeks showed a deep interest in science. Stimulated by their acquaintance with Egyptian science, the Ionians and later the European Greeks, though they lacked instruments to check and refine their results, correctly attributed to natural rather than supernatural causes a good many phenomena. They knew that the Nile flooded because annual spring freshets took place at its source in Ethiopia. They decided that the straits between Sicily and Italy and Africa and Spain had been caused by earthquakes. They understood what caused eclipses, and knew that the moon shone by light reflected from the sun. Hippocrates of Cos (ca. 460–377) founded a school of medicine, from which there survive the Hippocratic oath, with its high concept of medical ethics, and detailed clinical accounts of the symptoms and progress of diseases so accurate that modern doctors have been able to identify cases of diphtheria, epilepsy, and typhoid fever.

The mathematician Pythagoras (ca. 580–500) seems to have begun as a musician interested in the mathematical differences among lyre strings needed to produce various notes. The theorem that in a right-angled triangle the square of the hypotenuse is equal to the sum of the squares of the other two sides we owe to the followers of Pythagoras. They made the concept of numbers into a guide to the problems of life, elevating mathematics almost to a religious cult, perhaps the earliest effort to explain the universe in abstract mathematical language. Pythagoras is said to have been the first to use the word *cosmos*—harmonious and beautiful order—for the universe. Earlier Greeks had found the key to the universe in some single primal substance: water, fire, or air; and Democritus (460–370) decided that all matter consisted of minute, invisible atoms.

When Alexandria became the center of scientific research, the astronomer Aristarchus, in the mid-third century, concluded that the earth revolves around the sun, a concept not generally accepted till almost two thousand years later, while his younger contemporary, Eratosthenes, believed that the earth was round, and estimated its circumference quite accurately. Euclid, the great geometrical systematizer, had his own school at Alexandria in the third century B.C., and his pupil Archimedes won a lasting reputation in both theoretical and applied physics, devising machines for removing water from mines and irrigation ditches ("Archimedes' screw," a hand-cranked device, is still in use in Egypt), and demonstrating the power of pulleys and levers by single-handedly drawing ashore a heavily laden ship. Hence his celebrated boast: "Give me a lever long enough and a place to stand on, and I will move the world." In the second century, Hipparchus calculated the length of the solar year to within a few minutes.

Greek scholars were usually not specialists like those in a modern university. The same man would study and write books on physics, mathematics, astronomy, music, logic, and rhetoric. Rhetoric became an increasingly important subject, as the Greeks reflected on their own language and developed high standards of self-expression and style. The subject really began with political oratory, as politicians wished to make more and more effective speeches—particularly essential in wartime, when the population was excited anyhow, and each leader strove to be more eloquent than the last. These multipurpose scholars who in the fifth and fourth centuries B.C. taught people how to talk and write and think on all subjects were called Sophists: wisdom-men. Sophists generally tended to be highly skeptical of accepted standards of behavior and morality, questioning the traditional ways of doing things.

How could anybody really be sure of anything?, they would ask, and some would answer that we cannot know anything we cannot experience through one or more of our five senses. How could you be sure that the gods existed if you could not see, hear, smell, taste, or touch them? Perhaps you could not know, perhaps they did not exist after all. If there were no gods and therefore no divine laws, how should we behave? Should we trust laws made by other men like us? And what sort of men were making laws and in whose interest?

Maybe all existing laws were simply a trick invented by powerful people—members of the establishment—to protect their position. Maybe the general belief in the gods was simply a "put-on," invented by clever people to whose interest it was to have the general public docile. Not all Sophists went this far, but in Athens during the Peloponnesian War many young people, already troubled by the war or by the sufferings of the plague, were ready to listen to suggestions that the state should not make such severe demands upon them. Such young people would have burned their draft cards if they had had any, and their troubled parents, god-fearing and law-abiding, greatly feared the Sophists as the corrupters of the youth.

It is only against this background that we can understand the career and the eventual fate of Socrates (469–399 B.C.), whose method was that of the Sophists—to question everything, all the current assumptions about religion, politics, and behavior—but who retained unwavering to the end his own deep inner loyalties to Athens and to God. Socrates wrote no books, and held no professorial chair; but we know him well from contemporary reports, chiefly those of his pupil Plato. Socrates was a stonemason who spent his life talking and arguing in the Assembly, in public places, and in the homes of his friends in Athens. He thought of himself as a "gadfly," challenging everything anybody said to him and urging people not to take their preconceptions and prejudices as truths. Only a never-ending debate, a process of question and answer—the celebrated "Socratic method"—could lead human beings to truth. Reasoning led Socrates to conclude that man was more than an animal, that he had a mind, and, above all, that he had a true self, a kind of soul or spirit. Man's proper business on earth was to fulfill this true soul and cultivate the virtues that were proper to it—temperance, justice, courage, nobility, truth. Socrates himself listened to the voice of God that spoke within him.

We have already seen Socrates in his basket in midair in Aristophanes' *Clouds.* Of course he irritated and alarmed those who were worried about the youth of the day, and who thought of him as just another Sophist and one of the most vocal and dangerous. So when he was about seventy years old he was brought to trial on charges of disrespect to the gods and corrupting the youth of Athens. He argued that he had followed the prescribed religious observances and that he wanted only to make men better citizens; and he defended his gadfly tactics as necessary to stir a sluggish state into life. But a court of 501 jurors voted the death penalty by a narrow margin. Socrates could have gotten off by suggesting that he be punished in some other way. Instead he ironically asked for a tiny fine, and forced the court to choose between that and death. It condemned him again. Socrates drank the poison cup of hemlock, and waited for death serenely optimistic: he was "of good cheer about his soul." Many contemporaries and most men since have recognized that he was the victim of hysteria following a dreadful war.

Thereafter, it was Plato (ca. 427–347) who carried on his work. Plato founded a school in Athens, the Academy, and wrote a large number of celebrated dialogues: earnest intellectual conversations, in which Socrates and others discuss problems of man and the human spirit. Much influenced by the Pythagoreans, Plato retained a deep reverence for mathematics, but he found cosmic reality in Ideas rather than in numbers. As man has a "true self" (soul) within and superior to his body, so the world we experience with our bodily senses has within and superior to itself a "true world," an invisible universe or cosmos. In the celebrated dialogue *The Republic,* Plato has Socrates compare the relationship between the world of the senses and the world of Ideas with that between the shadows of persons and objects as they would be cast by firelight on the wall of a cave, and the same real persons and objects as they would appear when seen in the direct light of day. So man sees the objects—chairs, tables, trees—of the world as real, whereas they are only reflections of the true realities—the universals—the Idea of the perfect chair, table, or tree. So man's virtues are reflections of ideal virtues, of which the highest is the Idea of the Good. Man can and should strive to know the ultimate Ideas, especially the Idea of the Good.

This theory of Ideas has proved to be one of the great wellsprings of Western thought and has formed the starting point for much later philosophical discussion. Moreover, in teaching that the Idea of the Good was the supreme excellence and the final goal of life, Plato was advancing a kind of monotheism and laying a foundation on which pagan and Christian theologians both would build.

Politically, Athenian democracy did much to disillusion Plato: he had seen its courts condemn his master Socrates. On his travels he had formed a high opinion of the tyrants ruling the cities of Magna Graecia. So when Plato came to sketch the ideal state in *The Republic,* his system resembled that of the Spartans. He recommended that power be entrusted to the Guardians, a small intellectual elite, specially bred and trained to understand Ideas, governing under the wisest man of all, the Philosopher-King. The masses would simply do their jobs as workers or soldiers, and obey their superiors.

Plato's most celebrated pupil was Aristotle (ca. 384–322), called the "master of those who know." Son of a physician at the court of Philip of Macedon, and tutor to Alexander the Great, Aristotle was interested in everything. He wrote on biology, logic, literary criticism, political theory, ethics. His work survives largely in the form of notes on his lectures taken by his students; despite their lack of polish, these writings have had a prodigious later influence. He wrote 158 studies of the constitutions of Greek cities. Only the study of Athens survives.

Aristotle concerned himself chiefly with things as they are. The first to use scientific methods, he classified living things into groups much as modern biologists do, and extended the system to other fields—government, for example. He maintained that governments were of three forms: by one man, by a few men, or by many men; and that there were good and bad types of each, respectively monarchy and tyranny, aristocracy and oligarchy, polity and democracy (mob rule). Everywhere—in his *Logic, Poetics, Politics*—he laid the foundation for later inquiry. Though he believed that men should strive and aspire, he did not push them on to Socrates' goal of self-knowledge or to Plato's lofty ascent to the Idea of the Good. He urged instead the cultivation of the golden mean, the avoidance of excess on either side: courage, not foolhardiness or cowardice; temperance, not overindulgence or abstinence; liberality in giving, not prodigality or meanness.

Later, in the period after Alexander, two new schools of philosophy developed, the Epicurean and the Stoic. Epicurus (341–270) counseled temperance and common sense, carrying further the principle of the golden mean. Though he defined pleasure as the key to happiness, he ranked spiritual joys above those of the body, which he recommended should be satisfied in moderation. The Stoics, founded by Zeno, got their name from the columned porch *(Stoa)* in Athens where he first taught. They preferred to repress the physical desires altogether. Since only the inward man counted, the Stoics preached total disregard for social, physical, or economic differences among men. They became the champions of slaves and other social outcasts, anticipating to some degree one of the moral teachings of Christianity.

The Arts

The incalculably rich legacy left by the Greeks in literature was well matched by their achievements in the plastic arts. In architecture, their characteristic public building was rectangular, with roof supported by fluted columns. Over the centuries, the Greeks developed three principal types or orders of columns, still used today in "classical" buildings: the Doric column, terminating in a simple, unadorned square flat capital; the Ionic, slenderer and with simple curlicues (volutes) at the four corners of the capital; and the Corinthian, where acanthus leaves rise at the base of the volutes. Fluting gives an impression of greater height than the simple cylindrical Egyptian columns.

No matter what the order of the columns, a Greek temple strikes the beholder as dignified and simple. On the Acropolis of Athens, the Parthenon, greatest of all Doric temples, rose between 447 and 432 B.C. as the crowning achievement of Pericles' rebuilding program. By means of subtle

Far left: Archaic Greek sculpture: sixth-century Kore (statue of a girl) from Chios, with the posture and serene smile typical of the period.

Left: Roman marble copy of Polyclitus' statue of a spearbearer (The Doryphorus). The original was sculpted ca. 450–440 B.C., at about the time that Phidias was at work on the Acropolis.

The Parthenon.

devices—slightly inclining the columns inward so that they look more stable, giving each column a slight bulge in the center of the shaft so that it does not look concave—the building gives the illusion of perfection. In the triangular gable ends that crowned its front and back colonnades (the pediments) and on the marble slabs between the beam ends above the columns (the metopes) stood a splendid series of sculptured battle scenes, whose remains are now in the British Museum (the Elgin Marbles). Originally, the Parthenon and its statues were brightly painted. The building survived almost undamaged until 1687, when a Venetian shell exploded a Turkish powder magazine inside.

The achievement of Phidias and the other sculptors of the Periclean Age (see p. 56) had gradually developed from the "archaic" statues created a century or more earlier, usually of young men rather rigidly posed, with their arms hanging at their sides and a curiously uniform serene smile on their lips. Probably influenced by Egyptian models, these statues have great charm for moderns, who sometimes find the realism of the finished classical work rather tiresome. Phidias' great gold and ivory statues of Athena and the Olympian Zeus long ago fell to looters. So did most of the Greeks' sculpture in bronze; but every so often a great bronze statue is fished out of the sea or (as happened in 1959) is found under the pavement of a street being excavated for a sewer.

Three goddesses from the east pediment of the Parthenon (ca. 437-431 B.C.), part of the Elgin Marbles in the British Museum.

Though Greek painting as such has almost disappeared, we know from written texts that public buildings were adorned with paintings of Greek victories and portraits of political and military leaders. Moreover, the thousands of pottery vases, plates, cups, and bowls that have been discovered preserve on their surfaces—in black on red or in red on black—paintings of extraordinary beauty and of great variety. They show mythological scenes, illustrations to the *Iliad* and *Odyssey,* and the daily round of human activity: an athlete, a fisherman, a shoemaker, a miner, even a drunk vomiting while a sympathetic girl holds his head.

In the Hellenistic age sculpture became more emotional and theatrical: compare the Laocoön group, with its writhing serpents crushing their victims, to Polyclitus' statue of a spearbearer. The Venus de Milo and the Winged Victory of Samothrace are two of the most successful Hellenistic works of art; but there are a good many imitative and exaggerated efforts that are regarded as comparative failures. In literature, too, beginning with Menander's New Comedy, vigor and originality ebbed, while sophistication and a certain self-consciousness took over.

The painted inside of a drinking cup (kylix) of the sixth century, showing Dionysus in a boat.

Hellenistic sculpture: The Laocoön Group. First-century B.C. marble, eight feet tall.

Such a summary account of the splendors of Greek civilization runs the risk of creating the impression that the Greeks were supermen living in a paradise of physical and cultural triumphs. In fact, of course, few Greeks could understand or follow the ideas of a Plato or an Aristotle, or could afford to spend a great deal of time at the games, at the theater, or arguing with Socrates. Most Greeks worked hard, and their standard of living would seem extremely low today. In all of Athens at its height we know of only one establishment that employed over a hundred workmen. Even wealthy Athenians resided in small, plain houses of stucco or sun-dried brick: nobody until the Hellenistic period lived pretentiously. Athens was a huddle of mean little streets; there was little or no drainage; lighting was by inadequate, ill-smelling oil lamps. Inside a smithy or a pottery, it was so hot that the smith or potter often worked naked, as we know from vase paintings. But relaxation was at hand: a musician might play in the smithy; and the climate made outdoor living agreeable much of the year.

On the one hand, the Greeks discovered or invented democracy, drama, philosophy. But on the other, they clung to their old-fashioned religious rituals and could not make themselves give up civil war between their city-states. The freedom-loving Athenians executed Socrates. Though they formulated the wisdom of "Know Thyself" and the golden mean, created a beautifully balanced and proportioned architecture, and organized an education that trained the whole man, intellectual and physical, they too often exhibited hubris, the unbridled arrogance that they felt to be the most dangerous of mortal vices. And, as it did in the tragedies of the stage, so in their own lives, their hubris brought nemesis upon them. Their achievements, however, have lived after them, inspiring most of the values that Western man holds dearest.

VI

The Romans

The Early Republic

The Romans cherished the legend that after the fall of Troy, Aeneas, a Trojan prince, half divine, led his fugitive followers to Italy and founded Rome on the banks of the Tiber. The poet Vergil (70–19 B.C.) immortalized the story in his *Aeneid,* written as Roman imperial glory approached its zenith. And as Vergil borrowed from Homer, so Rome borrowed extensively from the older Greek and Near Eastern civilizations. The tale of the mythical Aeneas symbolizes the flow into Italy of Greeks and Near Easterners as well as Rome's debt to the Greco-Oriental world. Yet Rome did not achieve greatness on borrowed capital alone. The practical Romans were builders, generals, administrators, law-givers.

Compared geographically with Greece, Italy enjoys certain natural advantages: the plains are larger and more fertile, the mountains less of a barrier to communications. The plain of Latium, south of the site of Rome, could be farmed intensively after drainage and irrigation ditches had been dug; the nearby hills provided timber and good pasturage. The city of Rome lay only fifteen miles from the sea and could share in the trade of the Mediterranean; its seven hills overlooking the Tiber could be easily fortified and defended.

To the south, as we know, by the year 600 B.C. Greek colonies dotted the shores of Italy and Sicily: this was Magna Graecia. To the north, the dominant power was held by the Etruscans, a mysterious people, surely foreigners in Italy, perhaps from Asia Minor (and so the source of the Aeneas legend) who had invaded the peninsula and conquered the region north of Latium by 700

Part of an Etruscan wall painting from the Tomb of the Bulls, Cormeto, Italy.

B.C. They extended their power southward, surrounding Rome, and then seized it soon after 600. Although we have rich Etruscan remains—pottery, weapons, sculpture, painting, mostly found in tombs—nobody has yet altogether deciphered the language: the Etruscans wrote in Greek letters, but it is not Indo-European. No key like the Rosetta Stone has turned up, and so far no expert like Ventris has turned up either. But most of the ten thousand existing inscriptions are very short: even if one could read them, one might not learn very much. The Etruscans were expert farmers and miners, they built huge stone walls around their settlements, and they practiced divination, foretelling the future from observing flocks of birds in flight or from examining the entrails of an animal slain as a sacrifice. Their tomb decoration seems to show that, like the Egyptians, they believed in an afterlife similar to this one, and that they accorded their women a more nearly equal status with men than was usual in ancient society. They also enjoyed gladitorial combat as a spectacle, a taste that the Romans borrowed from them.

When the Etruscans moved into Latium and took over Rome, the people they conquered were apparently Latin tribesmen, descendants of the prehistoric inhabitants of the peninsula. Under its Etruscan kings, Rome prospered during the sixth century. The Etruscans built new stone structures and drained and paved what became the Forum. But the native population resented foreign rule, and joined with other Latin tribes in a large-scale rebellion. The traditional date for the expulsion from Rome of the last Etruscan king, Tarquin the Proud, is 509 B.C. What he left behind was an independent Latin city-state, still including some Etruscan notables, much smaller than Athens or Sparta, sharing Latium with other city-states. Yet in less than 250 years Rome would dominate the entire Italian peninsula.

We can understand this success only if we examine Roman institutions. Once they had ousted Tarquin, the dominant aristocratic forces at Rome set up a republic. Only the well-established land-owning families, the *patricians* (Latin *pater*, "father")—perhaps not more than ten percent of the population—held full citizenship. The remaining ninety percent were *plebeians* (Latin *plebs*, "the multitude"), who included those engaged in trade or labor, the smallest farmers, and all those who were debtors as the result of the economic upheaval after the expulsion of the Etruscans. The plebeians had no right to hold office; they could amass as much money as they pleased, however, and wealthy plebeians would eventually lead the campaign to gain political emancipation for their class. Fifth-century Rome, then, was not unlike sixth-century Athens before the reforms of Cleisthenes.

The patrician class supplied the two consuls, the executive chiefs of state who governed jointly for a term of a year, enjoying full *imperium,* supreme political power. Each had the right of veto over the other; so that both had to support a measure before it could be put through. Ordinarily they were commanders of the army, but in wartime this power was often wielded, for a period not longer than six months, by an elected *dictator.* (Despite the modern meaning of the term, in the Roman republic it meant a commander who had obtained his authority constitutionally and had to give it up when his term was over.) The consuls usually followed the policies decided on by the Senate, a body consisting of about three hundred members, mostly patricians and all ex-officials like the members of the Athenian Council of the Areopagus, and wielding such prestige that it comes first in the famous Roman political device: S.P.Q.R.—*Senatus Populusque Romanus* (The Senate and the People of Rome). The reigning consuls were themselves senators, and appointed new senators. The Romans had another deliberative body, the Centuriate Assembly, based on the century, the smallest unit (a hundred men) of the army. Although some plebeians were surely present, the patricians dominated the deliberations of this body also. It enjoyed a higher legal prerogative but less actual power than the Senate, although it elected the consuls and other officials, and approved or rejected laws submitted to it by both the consuls and the Senate.

Before a man could be chosen consul, he had to pass through an apprenticeship in other posts. The job that led directly to the consulate was that of praetor (*prae-itor,* the one who goes in front). Elected by the Centuriate Assembly for a term of a year, the praetor served as a judge; he often had an army command, and later a provincial governorship. At first there was only one praetor; but the number later rose to eight. Men seeking election as praetor or consul wore a special robe whitened with chalk, the *toga candida,* whence our word "candidate." From among the ex-consuls, the Assembly elected two censors, for an eighteen-month term, who took a census to determine which of the population was qualified for army service. They also secured the right to pass on the moral qualifications of men nominated for the Senate, barring those they thought corrupt or too luxury-loving, whence the connotation of our words "censor" and "censorship."

This regime was well designed to carry on the chief business of the Roman state: war. The Roman army at first had as its basic unit the phalanx, about 8,000 foot soldiers, armed with helmet and shield, lance and sword. But experience led to the substitution of the far more maneuverable legion, consisting of 3,600 men, composed of 60- or 120-man bodies called maniples or handfuls, armed with the additional weapon of the iron-tipped javelin, which was hurled at the enemy from a distance. Almost all citizens of Rome had to serve. Iron discipline prevailed; punishment for offenses was summary and brutal, but the officers also understood the importance of generous recognition and reward of bravery as an incentive.

The plebeians naturally resented their exclusion from political authority. As early as the 490's, they threatened to withdraw from Rome and to found nearby a new city-state of their own, and when this tactic won them a concession, they continued to use it with great effect on and off during the next two hundred years. First (494) they got the right to have officials of their own, the tribunes of the people, to protect them from unduly harsh application of the laws. By 457 there were ten of these. The plebeians also (471) gained their own assembly, the Tribal Assembly (so named because of the subdivision of the plebeian population into tribes), which chose the tribunes and had the right, like the Centuriate Assembly, to pass on new laws. Next they complained that the patrician judges could manipulate the law for their own purposes because it had never been written down. So in 451 the consuls ordered the (extremely severe) laws engraved on wooden tablets—the Twelve Tables, beginning the epochal history of Roman law.

In the early days of the Republic, debt meant that a plebeian farmer would lose his farm and be forced into slavery. Property therefore accumulated in the hands of the patrician landowners. The plebeians obtained legislation limiting the size of an estate that any one man might accumulate, abolishing the penalty of slavery for debt, and opening newly acquired lands to settlement by landless farmers. The farmer-debtor problem, though eased, remained to plague the Romans to the end. During the fifth and fourth centuries, the plebeians won the right to hold all the offices of the state, even that of consul (366 B.C.). They also forced the abrogation of the laws that forbade their intermarriage with patricians. The fusion of wealthy plebeians and patricians formed a new class, the *nobiles,* who were to dominate the later republic as the patricians had the earlier.

Roman Expansion

In a long series of wars the Romans made good their supremacy over the other Latin towns, the Etruscan cities, and the half-civilized tribes of the central Apennines (the mountain backbone of the peninsula). Early in the third century B.C. they conquered the Greek cities of southern Italy. Meanwhile, in the north, a Celtic people, the Gauls (see p. 68), had crossed the Alps and settled in the Lombard plain; their expansion was halted at the little river Rubicon, which formed the northern frontier of Roman dominion. In conquered areas the Romans sometimes planted a colony of their own land-hungry plebeians. Usually they did not try to force the resident population into absolute subjection, but accepted them as allies and respected their institutions. The cities of Magna Graecia continued to enjoy home rule. Some of the nearest neighbors of Rome became full citizens of the republic, but more often they enjoyed the protection of Roman law as part citizens who could not participate in the Roman Assemblies. So the expansion of Rome in Italy demonstrated imaginative statesmanship as well as military superiority.

The conquest of Magna Graecia made Rome a near neighbor of the Carthaginian state. Carthage—modern Tunis—was originally a Phoenician colony, but had long since liberated itself from its motherland and expanded along the African and Spanish shores of the Mediterranean and into the western parts of Sicily. Ruled by a commercial oligarchy, Carthage held a virtual monopoly of western Mediterranean trade. When the Carthaginians began to seize the Greek cities in eastern Sicily also, the Sicilian Greeks appealed to Rome. So the Romans launched the First Punic (from the Latin word for Phoenician) War, 264–241.

The Romans won by building their first major fleet and defeating the Carthaginians at sea. They forced Carthage to give up all claim to eastern Sicily and to cede western Sicily as well, thus obtaining their first province outside the Italian mainland. Seeking revenge, the Carthaginians used Spain as the base for an overland invasion of Italy in the Second Punic War (218–201). Their commander Hannibal led his forces across southern Gaul and then over the Alps into Italy, losing in the snow many of the elephants he used as pack animals. In northern Italy he recruited many Gauls, and won a string of victories as he marched southward, notably at Cannae (216 B.C.). But gradually the Roman general Fabius Cunctator ("the delayer") exhausted the Carthaginians. His "Fabian" strategy was to refrain from an all-out battle while eating away at the Carthaginians by attacking their supplies and patrols.

In 202 B.C., Hannibal was summoned back to defend Carthage itself against a Roman invading force under Scipio. Scipio won the battle and the title "Africanus" as a reward. The Romans forced the Carthaginians to surrender Spain (where the native population resisted for another two centuries), pay a large sum of money, and promise to follow Rome's lead in foreign policy. Hannibal fled to the court of the Seleucid king Antiochus III. Although Carthaginian power had been broken, the speedy recovery of the city's prosperity alarmed a war party at Rome, which agitated for its complete destruction. Cato the censor and senator would end each of his speeches with the words "Delenda est Carthago" ("Carthage must be destroyed"). In the Third Punic War (149–146) the Romans leveled the city, sprinkled salt on the earth, and took over all its remaining territory.

While the Punic Wars were still going on, Rome had as early as 230 B.C. become embroiled in the Balkans and in Greece, sending ships and troops at

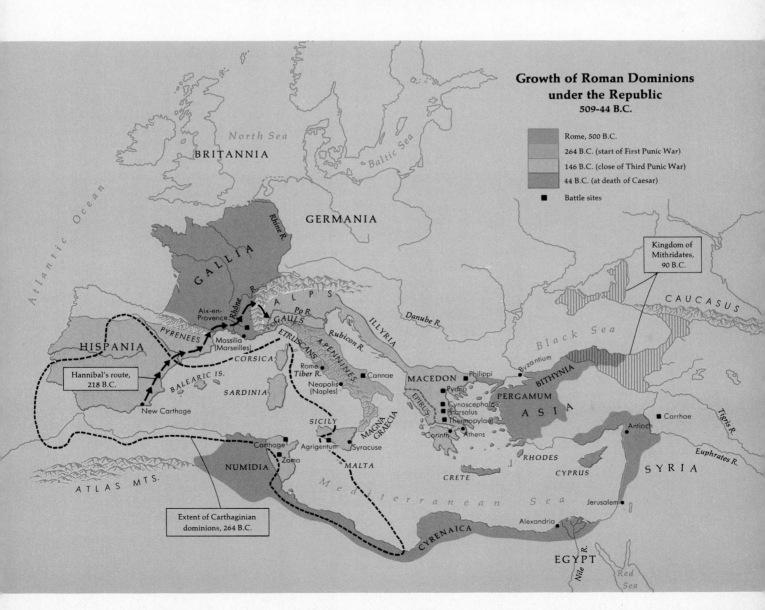

Growth of Roman Dominions under the Republic
509–44 B.C.

Rome, 500 B.C.
264 B.C. (start of First Punic War)
146 B.C. (close of Third Punic War)
44 B.C. (at death of Caesar)
■ Battle sites

first to put down the Illyrian pirates who were operating in the Adriatic from bases in what is now Albania, and then intervening again in 219 to punish an unruly local ally. The Greeks were grateful to Rome, and admitted Romans to the Eleusinian mysteries and the Isthmian Games (see pp. 70, 69). But Philip V (221–178), Antigonid king of Macedon, viewed with great suspicion Roman operations on his side of the Adriatic. He tried to help Hannibal during the Second Punic War, but a Roman fleet prevented him from crossing to Italy, and many of the Greek cities, opponents of Philip but not yet of Rome, came to Rome's aid in the fighting that ensued, helping to defeat him in the First Macedonian War (215–205).

Not anxious as yet to expand on the eastern shores of the Adriatic, Rome contented itself with establishing a series of Illyrian buffer states. But Philip kept intervening in these, and the Romans feared for their loyalty. And in 202, several powers—Athens, Ptolemy V of Egypt, his ally Attalus, king of the powerful independent kingdom of Pergamum in Asia Minor, and Rhodes, head of a new naval league—appealed to Rome to intervene again against Philip V. In the Second Macedonian War (200–197) Rome defeated Philip's armies on their own soil (Cynoscephalae, 197) and forced him to withdraw from Greece altogether and become an ally of Rome. At the Isthmian Games of 196, a solemn Roman proclamation declared that the Greeks were free. Two years later, after more fighting (chiefly against Sparta), the Roman armies left Greece and a largely disillusioned population. Antiochus III (223–187), Seleucid king in Asia, profited by the defeat of Macedon to take over the Greek cities on the Aegean coast of Asia Minor and to cross into Europe and campaign there. Hoping to keep Greece as a buffer against him, and worried at his advance, the Romans, who had their hands full with wars in Spain, kept on negotiating with him. But Antiochus, who had with him the refugee Hannibal, challenged the Romans in Greece, hoping but failing to win wide native support. At Thermopylae in 191 B.C. the Romans defeated Antiochus, and then invaded Asia, forcing Antiochus in 188 to surrender all the Seleucid holdings in Asia Minor. Hannibal escaped, but poisoned himself in 183 as he was about to be surrendered to Rome. Rome had become the predominant power in the Greek world.

For the next forty years, the Romans found themselves obliged to arbitrate the constantly recurring quarrels among the Greek states. Rebellions forced repeated armed intervention. Philip V's son and successor, Perseus (179–168), seemed to threaten to unite Greece against the Romans, and in the Third Macedonian War (171–168) he was eventually captured and his forces were routed at the decisive battle of Pydna (168). Rome imposed a ruthless settlement, breaking Macedon up into four republics and exiling from Greece many who had sympathized with Perseus. Twenty years later, after intervening against a leader called Andriscus who pretended he was a son of Perseus, the Romans annexed Macedon (148 B.C.), their first province east of the Adriatic; and two years after that they defeated a desperate uprising of the Achaean League, and marked their victory by a particularly brutal sack of Corinth: all the men were killed, the women and children were sold as slaves, and the city was leveled. It was the same year as the total destruction of Carthage. The Romans henceforth governed Greece from Macedon, but did not yet annex it as a province. Internal fighting in Greece came to an end; there was a religious and economic revival. Rome's prestige was now so great that in 133 the king of Pergamum, whose family had been helpful allies of the Romans—and much hated elsewhere for that reason—left his flourishing Asia Minor state to Rome in his will.

As Roman territory increased, signs of trouble multiplied. The republic allowed a few overseas cities to retain some self-government, but usually organized its new territories as provinces under governors appointed by the Senate. Some of the governors proved oppressive and lined their own pockets, but as long as they raised recruits for the army and collected taxes, they had a free hand. In Italy, pressure mounted from Rome's allies, who demanded full citizenship and a share in the new wealth flowing into the capital. With the gradual exhaustion of Italian soil, grain had to be imported from Africa; former Italian grainfields were transformed into mixed farms or large cattle ranches run by slaves, whom only big landowners could afford. While veterans of overseas fighting and retired governors accumulated money and slaves as the spoils of conquest, more and more small farmers lost their land and became penniless and resentful refugees in the city of Rome.

The proprietors of *latifundia* (big estates), the successful generals and governors, and certain merchants and contractors who had built roads for the state or furnished supplies to the army combined to form a new class of very rich men, called *equites* (knights) because they could afford to equip themselves for service in the cavalry, the most expensive branch of the army. Yet the *nobiles* dominated the Senate, increasingly influential because it had managed the Punic Wars successfully. Among the senators themselves, those who were content with things as they were called themselves *optimates,* while those who found themselves unable to get things done their way sometimes tried to get support from the people at large in the Tribal Assembly, and so got from their opponents the name *populares.* Social tensions became acute: an old fashioned conservative nobilis like Cato, for instance, hated the rich men's taste for the luxurious new ways of life imported from Greece and the East. The political machinery of a small city-state could not cope with the problems of empire, of social tension, and of economic distress.

Two noble brothers named Gracchus, grandsons of Scipio, hero of the First Punic War, emerged during the late 130's and the 120's as the champions of the dispossessed. Tiberius Gracchus, who served as tribune of the people in 133 B.C., and Gaius, who held the post from 123 to 121, sought to increase the role of the tribunes and the Tribal Assembly at the expense of the Senate. The wild beasts, said Tiberius, have their dens, but the Roman soldiers have not a clod of earth to call their own. The brothers wanted to limit the size of estates that could be owned by one family, to resettle landless farmers either abroad or on state-owned lands in Italy that had been leased to capitalist farmers, and to give the city poor of Rome relief by allowing them to buy grain from the state at cost. Politically, they wanted to give certain judicial posts to the equites, to extend Roman citizenship to all Latins, and to raise other Italians to Latin status.

The efforts of the Gracchi failed. Of their economic program only the proposal to sell the Roman people cheap grain was adopted. In the succeeding centuries the state had to lower the price until the poor were getting their bread free. This in itself reveals the failure of the resettlement program: had the dispossessed farmers actually received new allotments, the number in the city needing cheap bread would have fallen off sharply. The agrarian capitalists, after being forced by the Gracchi to give up some of the land they rented from the state, were soon expanding their holdings once more. The latifundia had to come to stay. Moreover, on the political side, the Senate resented the extension of rights to the equites, and balked at granting citizenship to other Italian cities (eventually, after an uprising in 91–88, this had to be done).

Meantime, politics turned unconstitutional and violent. Tiberius Gracchus ousted a tribune of the people who was blocking his program; both brothers defied precedent and ran for reelection as tribunes. The senators themselves resorted to murder to stop the Gracchi and assassinated Tiberius in 133; in 121 Gaius killed himself to avoid a similar fate. Were the Gracchi high-minded "New Dealers" blocked by the vested interests of the senators, or unstable radicals whose high-handed methods only added to the discord? Probably both; at any rate the deadlock between Gracchan reformism and senatorial conservatism moved Rome toward autocracy.

After the Gracchan interlude, political leadership passed to generals who cared less for principle than for power. In the provinces the misrule of the governors provoked uprisings. Along the frontiers, at the end of the second century B.C., Germanic tribes were threatening. In 88 B.C. in Asia Minor, Mithridates, the king of Pontus, seized the Roman province of Asia, and provoked the massacre of eighty thousand Romans.

A general victorious in the chronic provincial warfare would celebrate in Rome with a great "triumph," a parade of his successful troops and of their prisoners and booty that would dazzle the public. And the troops, properly rewarded by their commanders, became loyal to them rather than to the state. The prescription for political success at Rome was to make a record as a successful general.

Political Generals: Marius, Sulla, Pompey, Caesar

The first of the generals to reach power was Marius, leader of the populares, who had won victories against the Numidians in North Africa—in what is now eastern Algeria (111–105)—and against a group of Celtic and Germanic peoples called the Cimbri and Teutones, who had caused a great deal of trouble before he beat them at what is now Aix-en-Provence in southern France (102). Violating the custom that a consul had to wait ten years before serving a second term, Marius had himself elected five times between 108 and 103 B.C. He began a major reorganization of the army by abolishing the old requirement that a Roman citizen must pay for his own equipment, a rule that had automatically excluded the poor. Now that the state furnished the equipment, professional soldiers gradually replaced the former citizen soldiers, who in the past had gone back to their normal peacetime occupations once the fighting was over. When the Senate nullified a law extending Roman citizenship to citizens of all other Italian cities, the cities rose in a rebellion that threatened Rome with the loss of her Italian power. After this savage war for independence (called the Social War from *socius,* "ally"), the secessionists were mostly pacified by the year 89, but only by the gradual extension of Roman citizenship to all of Italy.

When Rome went to war against Mithridates in 88 B.C., Marius emerged from retirement and demanded the command. But the Senate chose Sulla, a younger general who was an optimate, and a bloody civil war broke out between the supporters of the two. Marius died in 86, and Sulla defeated Mithridates in 84, and then returned to assume the office of dictator. On the way to and from the east, his forces plundered Zeus's treasury at Olympia and Apollo's at Delphi, and sacked Athens for having sympathized with Mithridates. The Romans brought back Greek sculpture, painting, books, and other loot.

It took Sulla two years of bloody fighting to establish himself in power, and he took fierce reprisals against his opponents. He tried to move the Senate back into its ancient position as the chief force in political life. He put through laws designed to curb the rise of new younger politicians. He curtailed the powers of the tribunes and the Tribal Assembly. He broke all precedent by prolonging his tenure as dictator beyond the prescribed six months. He did retire in 80 B.C., but the Senate proved unable to govern.

Within ten years, Pompey, a ruthless and arrogant young veteran of Sulla's campaigns who had won victories first in Spain and then at home against a slave rebellion led by Spartacus (73–71), rose to power, becoming consul in 70 B.C. before he had reached the minimum legal age. With his colleague Crassus, a millionaire, Pompey forced the Senate to restore the tribunes and the Tribal Assembly to their old power. He became grand admiral of Roman naval forces against the troublesome pirates of the Mediterranean. After defeating them (67 B.C.), he took command of a new war against Mithridates, who had attacked Rome again in order to prevent the Romans from picking up a neighboring kingdom (Bithynia) in Asia Minor that had been left them in the will of the king. By 65 B.C. Pompey had driven Mithridates into exile at the court of his son-in-law, Tigranes, king of Armenia, who had also begun to acquire portions of Asia Minor. Mithridates committed suicide in 63 B.C., and Pompey reorganized Asia Minor into Roman provinces and subject kingdoms. Syria too, where the last effective Seleucid had died in 129 B.C., had largely fallen to Tigranes by 83, and Pompey now made it a Roman province (64 B.C.). He even took Jerusalem in that year. The western fringe of Asia was now virtually Roman, and much new revenue soon flowed to Rome.

On his campaigns Pompey enjoyed unprecedented special powers, forced through against much senatorial opposition, and huge resources in men and money. Foreseeing a showdown on his return, Crassus tried to build up his own power by vainly calling for the annexation of Egypt. And in 63 there took place a celebrated conspiracy at Rome, led by Catiline, leader of a group of discontented and dispossessed nobles who had been the victims of Sulla's purges and who now planned a revolution and a comeback. The consul and famous lawyer Cicero discovered the plot and arrested the plotters, some of whom he illegally had executed. His speeches in the Senate against the ringleader, Catiline, have given much instruction and some pain to generations of schoolboys. Cicero hoped to cooperate with Pompey in governing Rome and ending Roman domestic quarrels, but he lacked the family background and personal following necessary to get to the very top in Rome, and Pompey was not responsive.

Having returned to Rome as a private citizen (62 B.C.), Pompey returned to politics because the Senate would not ratify his Eastern settlement or give the usual land grants for his veteran troops. He joined in a triumvirate, or team of three men, with Crassus and Gaius Julius Caesar, a man of enormous energy and talent, and impeccable ancestry. Caesar became consul in 59 B.C. Pompey married Caesar's daughter; Pompey's soldiers received large land grants to the south, near Naples, and the eastern Mediterranean settlement was confirmed. Caesar became governor of the southern strip of Gaul (modern France), which Rome had annexed some sixty years earlier, and other lands rich in revenue. In Gaul, between 58 and 50 B.C. he conquered the area corresponding to most of modern France and Belgium, then inhabited by farming and cattle-raising tribes, and even crossed the English Channel to punish the Celtic Britons for helping their fellow Celts in Gaul, though he did not try to conquer Britain permanently. Caesar's successes meant that, like Italy and Spain, the future France would have a civilization firmly based on Rome and a language based on Latin. In order to give his achievements maximum publicity in Rome, he now wrote his *Commentaries on the Gallic Wars* (a lot easier reading than Cicero).

While Caesar was busy in Gaul, Crassus became governor of Syria, where he became involved in war against the Parthians, a dynasty that had risen in Persia to replace the Seleucids. At Carrhae in Mesopotamia in 53 B.C. the Parthians defeated and killed Crassus. The triumvirate had begun to fall apart even before that, as Pompey's wife, Caesar's daughter Julia, died in 54 B.C. Pompey, who had been commander in Spain, stayed in Rome as the most powerful politician there, and became sole consul in 52 B.C. The former chief of Pompey's private gang now murdered the chief of Caesar's faction in Rome. This was Clodius, who had been acting to protect Caesar's interests in his absence, and had once succeeded in getting Cicero exiled for a period. A revolution in Gaul kept Caesar busy in 52 and 51 B.C.; when it was over, Caesar faced Pompey for supremacy.

In 49 B.C. Caesar defied an order from the Senate to stay in Gaul, and led his loyal troops south across the Rubicon river boundary. Within a few weeks, he was master of Italy. He then won another war in Spain, and in 48 B.C. defeated Pompey's troops at Pharsalus in Greece, to which most of the Senate had fled with Pompey. Pompey was later murdered in Egypt by troops of Ptolemy XII. Caesar now traveled to the East and to his famous love affair with Ptolemy's sister, Cleopatra. After new victories over former troops of Pompey's in Asia Minor, North Africa, and Spain, he returned to Rome in triumph in 45 B.C. Less than a year later, on the Ides of March, 44 B.C., he lay stabbed to death on the floor of the Senate at the foot of Pompey's statue. His assassins included patriots troubled at his assumption of supreme power and his destruction of the Roman constitution, and others who were merely disloyal or jealous.

But during his brief period of dominance Caesar had carried further the subversion of the institutions of the republic that Marius and Sulla and Pompey had begun. Unlike Sulla, he was always merciful to conquered enemies. But as dictator he arrogated to himself many of the powers that usually belonged to the consuls, the tribunes, and the high priest. He had packed the Senate with his own supporters. He showed a deep interest in the social and economic problems of Rome: he gave his veterans grants of land in outlying provinces; he tried to check the importation of slaves into Rome because they took work from free men; he made gifts to the citizens from his own private fortune, and then sharply curtailed the dole of grain that the Gracchi had instituted, forcing the creation of new jobs. He issued the first gold coins and reformed the calendar to bring it into line with the solar year. At the moment of his death he was projecting a great public works program: Tiber valley flood control, a trans-Apennine highway, and a canal through the Isthmus of Corinth in Greece. The rank and file of the Romans seem to have regarded him as a benefactor, the restorer of order and prosperity. His opponents said he was planning to be crowned as king and they may have been right. They also accused him of wishing to be worshiped as a god, and here—so far as Rome was concerned—they were probably wrong. But he was personally autocratic and had ridden roughshod over the Roman constitution.

After Caesar's death, the conspirators found the public hostile to them, and were forced first to accept a compromise with his supporters and then to flee the hostile mob, goaded to fury by the fiery funeral oration given Caesar by his aide the unscrupulous consul Mark Antony, who had got hold of Caesar's private papers, including his will, by which he left a legacy to every individual Roman citizen. But to Antony's distress three-quarters of Caesar's huge fortune went to Octavian, his shrewd and able grandnephew, still only nineteen years old. After some civil strife between their forces, Octavian and Antony, with a third former aide of Caesar, Lepidus, formed the "second triumvirate," this time formal and official, and divided territory and power between themselves. They raised money by executions and confiscations, and defeated the forces of Caesar's murderers (Philippi, 42 B.C.) led by Brutus and Cassius, who both committed suicide. But rivalry between Octavian and Mark Antony continued, interrupted for a time when Antony married Octavian's sister. By 36 B.C. Lepidus had been dropped; Octavian controlled the entire West, and Antony, in the East, had begun *his* famous affair with Cleopatra. Claiming that Caesar's young son by Cleopatra was the legitimate heir to Rome, and assigning provinces to Cleopatra herself and to his own children by her, Antony clearly posed a threat to Octavian, and in 33 B.C. the triumvirate was not renewed. Military action soon followed, and at Actium, off the western coast of northern Greece (31 B.C.), Octavian's ships won a critical naval battle. Antony and Cleopatra committed suicide. Rome thus acquired Egypt, the last of the great Hellenistic states to disappear. Egypt would not become a Roman province, but the personal property of Octavian and his successors, the Roman emperors, administered for them by their agents. And Octavian had become master of the entire Roman heritage. The republic had come to an end.

VII
The Roman Empire

*Augustus and His
Immediate Successors*

Octavian was too shrewd, too conscious that he was heir to a long tradition, to startle and alienate the people of Rome by formally breaking with the past and proclaiming an empire. He sought to preserve republican forms, but at the same time to remake the government along the lines suggested by Caesar, so that Rome would have the machinery to manage the huge territories it had acquired. After sixty years of internal strife, the population welcomed a ruler who could guarantee order. Moving gradually, and freely using his own huge personal fortune, now augmented by the enormous revenues of Egypt, Octavian paid for the pensions of his own troops, and settled them on their own lands in Italy and abroad. He was consul every year; imperator; governor in his own right of Spain, Gaul and Syria; and princeps, first, among the senators. In 27 B.C. the Senate bestowed upon him the new title of Augustus ("revered one") by which he was thereafter known to history, although he always said his favorite title was the traditional one of princeps.

Of course he had far more power than anybody else, but since he called himself the restorer of the republic, Romans could feel that they were again living under republican rule. In 23 B.C. the Senate gave him tribunician power, "larger" powers than those held by any other provincial governor, and the right to introduce the first measure at any meeting of the Senate. It was he who summoned the Senate, to which he gave a small inner steering committee, on which he sat. To the Senate he appointed men he thought able, regardless of their birth. He created a civil service where careers were open to talent. Having endowed a veterans' pension department out of his own pocket, he created two new taxes—a sales tax of one-hundredth and an estate tax of one-twentieth—to support it. His social laws made adultery a crime, and encouraged large families. He paid for the construction of splendid new buildings, boasting justly that he had found Rome a city of brick and had left it a city of marble. He also gave it its first police and fire departments, and improved the roads throughout Italy. The army, now numbering about 300,000 men, was stationed in permanent garrison camps on the frontiers, where the troops in peacetime worked on public projects such as aqueducts or canals.

Augustus reached a settlement with the Parthians in the East, and thus probably averted an expensive and perhaps a dangerous war. In 4 B.C., Herod, a client king of Jewish faith who governed Judea, died, and the Romans took over Judea and ruled through a Roman procurator, who remained outside Jerusalem as a concession to the Jews. They retained their freedom of worship, did not have to serve in the Roman armies, and were allowed not to use coins bearing "graven images," the portrait of Augustus. Under Augustus, most of Spain and Portugal were permanently pacified, and the Romans successfully administered Gaul. In what is now Switzerland and Austria and eastward along the Danube Augustus campaigned, extending Roman power into present-day Hungary, Yugoslavia, and Bulgaria, all the way to the Black Sea.

But in the year A.D. 9 the Roman armies suffered a disaster in Germany, when the German tribesmen under Arminius (or Hermann) wiped out three legions (perhaps sixteen or seventeen thousand men). Now an old man, Augustus made no effort to avenge the defeat, and so the Rhine frontier proved to be the final limit of Roman penetration into north-central Europe. Thus the Germans never did become Romanized, a fact that had fateful consequences for all the subsequent history of Europe.

The Roman provinces were now probably better governed than under the republic. Regular census-taking permitted a fair assessment of taxes. In Gaul the tribes served as the underlying basis for government; in the urbanized East, the local cities performed that function. Except for occasional episodes, Augustus had done his work so well that the celebrated *Pax Romana*—the Roman Peace—lasted from his assumption of the title "Augustus" in 27 B.C. until A.D. 180, more than two hundred years. It was an enormous boon. Whatever may have been Augustus' faults of character, one must cheerfully admit that he should be remembered as he wished to be remembered: he had maintained the Roman state firmly and had laid long-lasting constitutional foundations for its future.

When he died in A.D. 14, the only possible surviving heir was his stepson, Tiberius, son of his wife Livia by her first husband. Gloomy and bitter, Tiberius reigned until A.D. 37, emulating Augustus so far as possible during the first nine years but thereafter becoming involved in the efforts of a certain Sejanus (commander of the Praetorian Guard, a specially privileged body of troops founded by Augustus, and now stationed in Rome itself) to secure the succession to the throne. Absent from Rome for long periods, Tiberius became deeply unpopular, despite the fact that he reduced taxes and took steps to make interest-free loans available to debtors. His grand-nephew and successor Caligula (37–41), however, was perhaps insane and certainly brutish. The number of executions mounted, and the emperor enriched himself with the property of his victims. He made elaborate preparations for the invasions of Germany and of England, but in fact did nothing in Europe, while he convulsed Judea by insisting that his own statue be set up in the rebuilt temple. Caligula was assassinated A.D. 41.

His uncle Claudius (41–54), youngest of Tiberius' nephews and the best of the first four emperors to succeed Augustus despite physical weakness and a miserable early life, was a learned student of history and languages—he even knew Etruscan—and strove to imitate Augustus by restoring cooperation with the Senate. He added to the number and importance of the bureaucracy by dividing his own personal staff of bureaucrats—mostly freedmen by origin—into regular departments or bureaus not unlike those in modern governments. So the private imperial civil service made strides in his reign. Claudius was generous in granting Roman citizenship to provincials. Abroad, he departed

Marble head of Augustus as a youth.

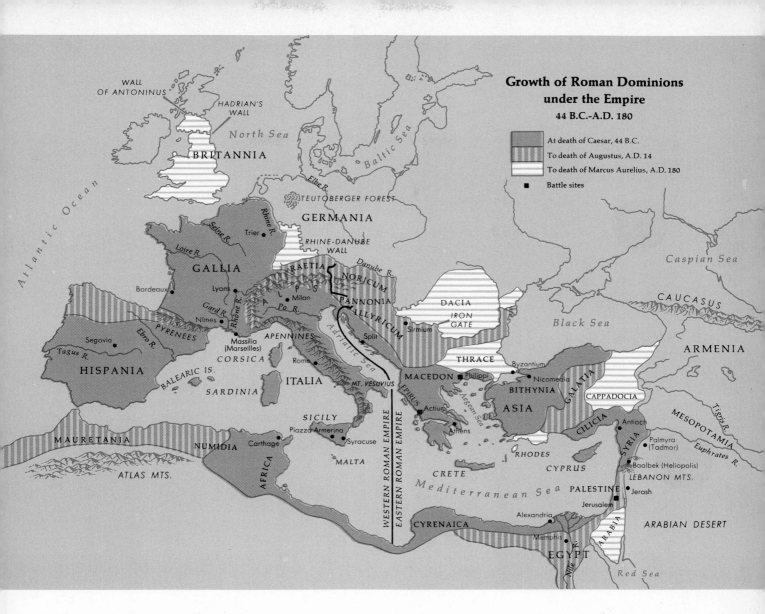

Growth of Roman Dominions under the Empire

44 B.C.-A.D. 180

- At death of Caesar, 44 B.C.
- To death of Augustus, A.D. 14
- To death of Marcus Aurelius, A.D. 180
- ■ Battle sites

from Augustus' principles, and added to Roman territory the region that is now Morocco, and certain smaller areas (Thrace and Lycia) in the Balkans and in Asia Minor. And A.D. 43 he invaded Britain, ninety-eight years after Julius Caesar's first invasion. Southeast England became the province of Britain, whose frontiers were pushed outward toward Wales. The conspiracies of Claudius' fourth wife, Agrippina, to obtain the succession for her son by an earlier marriage, Nero, culminated in her poisoning Claudius himself in 54. Nero (54–68) recompensed her by having her murdered in 59.

Dissolute and insanely proud of his own artistic talents, Nero sang, played the harp, acted, and drove a chariot at Roman public spectacles, which he wanted to transform into something like the Greek Olympic games. He had his mother put to death, murdered his wife, and married his mistress, whom he later kicked to death in a fit of temper. He did not start the great fire that burned down much of Rome in 64, nor did he fiddle while Rome burned; indeed he personally took part in the efforts to put the fire out, and did what he could for those who had been left homeless. But the dispossessed did blame him, and to find a scapegoat he accused the new sect of the Christians, now for the first time attracting attention at Rome. Their secret meetings had led to charges of immorality against them, and Nero persecuted them to take attention away from himself.

There were serious revolts in Britain in 61, but the chief threat in the provinces arose in Judea, where Roman rule had alternated between extremes of tolerance (Augustus) and intolerance (Caligula). There were rival sects among the Jews, who detested each other and the Christians. Nobody except the small upper class supported Roman rule, and the Romans had too few troops to keep order. In 66, after the Jewish high priest refused to sacrifice to Jehovah for the special benefit of Nero, and a group of Jewish zealots massacred a Roman garrison, there was open warfare. The Roman general Vespasian had made much progress in the reconquest of Palestine when Nero found himself faced with a rising in Gaul and Spain of troops loyal to the governor, Galba. When the Senate proclaimed Galba emperor, Nero committed suicide (68).

From Nero to Marcus Aurelius (68–180)

Augustus' first four successors are called the Julio-Claudian emperors. Each had been a member, though sometimes a distant one—of the family of Julius Caesar and Augustus. But now the line had run out wretchedly in Nero, and the Senate and people of Rome learned that emperors could be found in other families and chosen in other ways. In 68–69 alone, four emperors, each a general supported by his own troops, ruled in rapid succession. The first three all died by violence, and the fourth was Vespasian, who had left his son Titus in command of the campaign in Palestine, where in 70 the Roman troops would sack Jerusalem and destroy the rebuilt temple. Vespasian (69–79) founded the second Roman imperial dynasty, the Flavian, the throne passing successively to his two sons, Titus (79–81) and Domitian (81–96). Competent in every way, Vespasian added new blood to the Senate by appointing numerous non-Romans, especially Spaniards. He put through financial reforms, subdued a rebellion in Gaul, made gains in Britain, and managed to stave off the potential uprisings of other generals' troops against him by using some soldiers to build public works, stationing others in dangerous areas of the frontier, and keeping the numbers concentrated in any one place too few to encourage an ambitious commander to rebel. It was in the brief reign of Titus that Vesuvius, the great volcano overlooking the Bay of Naples, erupted, and wiped out the population of the provincial town of Pompeii, leaving behind all the famous remains that testify so eloquently about daily life there. Domitian was a suspicious tyrant, seeing conspirators against him everywhere, and forcing the Senate to approve his own execution of suspects. In 96 a palace conspiracy brought him down.

When an emperor died, the Senate—so subservient during his lifetime—had the power of appointing his successor. In 96 they chose a mild sixty-five-year-old official named Nerva (96–98), who had no children and therefore could not found a dynasty. He promptly ended Domitian's persecutions of Jews and Christians, founded a new charity that gave loans to farmers in Italy to provide food for orphans, and most particularly discovered a method of providing for the succession: he adopted as his son, and so nominated as his successor, the great general Trajan (98–117), who succeeded him peacefully when he died. This was the first of a series of four successive fortunate adoptions that gave the empire its most prosperous and peaceful years at home, 98–177. Abroad, in a series of successful but expensive campaigns, Trajan moved north of the Danube into Dacia—part of the Romania of to-

Ruins of Hadrian's Wall in Northumberland.

day—which in 106 became a Roman province; but to the east, his campaigns across the Euphrates against the Parthians ended in failure in 115. A massive revolt of the Jews confronted Trajan's successor, his nephew Hadrian, when he succeeded his adoptive father in 117.

Hadrian (117–138), widely experienced as a soldier and administrator and a highly cultivated man, put down the Jewish uprising. He realized that Roman communication lines would always become too extended by efforts to cross the Syrian desert against the Parthians; so he wisely abandoned Trajan's war against them, and eventually made peace with them. He made himself generally popular by canceling all private debts to the government, furthering charities, and putting on great spectacles in the circus. Among his advisers were some able lawyers who helped him adjust taxes and control prices in bad years, and improve the legal position of slaves and soldiers. They codified all past decisions of the praetors, for the first time enabling a citizen to know when he ought to sue somebody, and assuring him of uniform procedures.

Hadrian believed that all the provinces should be equal under Roman imperial benevolence, with himself as the "father of the fatherland" *(pater patriae).* So he caused each of the armies for provincial defense to be recruited within the province itself. And he himself lived much away from Rome: in Britain (where he built across the island the famous defensive system of walls and ditches still called Hadrian's Wall, to contain invasions from the Scots and Picts to the north), in southern France, in Spain, in Morocco, in Asia Minor, in Greece, in Tunisia and Libya, in Greece again, in Syria and Palestine (where he replanned Jerusalem and changed its name, forbade circumcision, and had to put down another Jewish uprising), and in Egypt. Everywhere he inspected the troops and defenses, built buildings, and made himself known to the population, and everywhere except Palestine he was admired. After a decade abroad, he returned to Rome, where he began to build "Hadrian's Villa" at nearby Tivoli, something like a World's Fair exposition ground with whole areas built in his favorite Greek and Egyptian styles.

His successor, Antoninus (138–161), called Pius because he was so loyal an adoptive son to Hadrian, himself immediately adopted as his future successor his own nephew Marcus Aurelius (161–180). It is with these two "Antonine" emperors that many articulate contemporary Romans believed that they had reached the peak of good government and agreeable living, and boasted that from Rome a feeling of security emanated throughout the world, preserved because of the eternal vigilance of Roman troops along the distant river frontiers, the Rhine, the Danube, and the Euphrates. Civil strife was surely absent, great public buildings continued to rise, and those who were comfortable had never been more comfortable. In Rome and, more widely, in Italy, the Antonine monarchy showed great concern for the less privileged, and softened the worst pains of poverty. Egypt, as always, continued to be ruthlessly exploited. Unlike Hadrian, Antoninus Pius never left Italy, and the boasted watch of the troops along the frontiers grew slacker after Hadrian's death. Marcus Aurelius therefore found himself forced to campaign in Dacia and against the Parthians. Though victorious, he permitted some barbarians to settle inside the Roman frontiers and to be enrolled in the Roman armies, thus undermining the traditional defensive system.

A Century of Decline (180–284) and the New Empire (284–337)

Commodus (180–192), the genuine son of Marcus Aurelius, ended the line of fortunate adoptions, and proved to be a throwback to Caligula, Nero, or Domitian, a tyrant without talent. In the end, his closest advisers murdered him, and after two other emperors had been installed and murdered by the Praetorian Guard within a year, Septimius Severus (193–211), a native North African, commander of the Roman troops in what is now Hungary, marched his army into Rome and disbanded the guard, replacing it by a new elite body chosen from his own officers. He emerged successfully from the first civil strife Rome had known in more than a century, and rewarded his armies for their loyalty in a campaign against the Parthians (Mesopotamia was added as a province) by rewarding them with better food, better pay, and better conditions: his legionaries might marry native women and married legionaries might live off the base. Killed campaigning in Britain, Septimius Severus was succeeded by his two sons, one of whom (Caracalla, 211–217) killed the other, and embarked on a series of other atrocious crimes until he was assassinated. He is also remembered for an edict of 212, which extended citizenship to all freeborn inhabitants of the empire, a natural climax to the earlier acts gradually expanding the circle of Roman citizens, but also a money-raising device, since all new citizens would be liable to inheritance taxes from which noncitizens were exempt.

Caracalla's sixteen immediate successors were all assassinated in their turn, forming an unedifying parade of almost uniformly incompetent rulers. Between 235 and 284 twenty-five of the twenty-six Roman emperors died by violence. Most of them were chosen by their troops, held power briefly, and were in turn supplanted in the same way. Attracted by Roman weakness, and pushed from behind by other people on the move, the barbarians crossed the Roman frontiers at many points. The emperor Decius was killed in battle by them (252). The emperor Valerian was captured (260) by the Persians (the Sassanian dynasty had succeeded Parthian rule there), and died or was killed in captivity. Plagues raged, whole provinces temporarily escaped from the central authority, population fell off, public order virtually vanished. The tide began to turn with the reign of Aurelian (270–275), the "restorer of the world," and definitively with the accession of Diocletian (284–305). But to turn the tide demanded a thoroughgoing series of reforms, internal as well as external. Diocletian and his successors, especially Constantine, did put through such reforms, although we do not know exactly when some of the new measures

Fourth-century Sassanian cameo showing the defeat and capture of Valerian by the king of Persia in 260.

were adopted. The result is usually called the new empire, but what looks new about it often proves to have been instead a return to earlier practice. It was the combination of all the experiments that was certainly new.

Under Diocletian there evolved gradually—each step resulting from local emergencies in one part or another of the empire—a system that when complete was called the tetrarchy, or rule by four men. Diocletian as Augustus first appointed a talented officer as Caesar, an action often taken previously, and then was forced by circumstances to promote him to Augustus, or co-emperor, though it was understood that Diocletian was the senior Augustus. Soon each Augustus had in turn appointed a Caesar of his own, whom he also adopted as his son. Such adoption too, we know, was an old practice. It was understood that the two emperors would eventually abdicate, each to be succeeded by his own Caesar, who upon becoming Augustus would appoint a new Caesar as his son and eventual successor. The scheme was obviously designed to assure a peaceful succession and to end the curse of military seizures of the throne. The empire, though in practice ruled by four men—a tetrarchy—still in theory remained a single unit.

This was particularly important, because accompanying the gradual establishment of the tetrarchy there was a territorial shift in administration, as each of the four new rulers took primary responsibility for his own large area. Diocletian made his headquarters at Nicomedia, on the eastern shore of the Sea of Marmara, in western Asia Minor, and from there governed Asia Minor, Syria, and Egypt, plus Thrace in Europe, the whole becoming the prefecture of the East. His Caesar had his headquarters at Sirmium in what is now Yugoslavia, and governed from there the Balkans including Greece, which became the prefecture of Illyricum. Diocletian's co-Augustus, the junior emperor Maximian, had his headquarters at Milan, and from there governed Italy and North Africa, together with parts of what is now Austria, which became the prefecture of Italy. And *his* Caesar had his headquarters at Trier (Treves) on the Moselle River, and governed Gaul, Spain, and Britain, which became the prefecture of Gaul. Diocletian remained supreme over the others.

The tetrarchy of Diocletian, co-rulers of the Roman Empire: sculpture in St. Mark's, Venice.

What is of course most obviously striking is that not even the prefecture of Italy was governed from the imperial capital of Rome. The new imperial territorial reorganization exposed as a hollow sham the ancient pretense that the emperor shared power with the Senate. Diocletian simply walked out on Rome, leaving the citizens with their free bread and circuses. It is of great importance too that he chose the East as the site of his own headquarters. Diocletian indeed now adopted the full trappings of oriental monarchy: he wore silk robes of blue and gold to symbolize the sky and the sun; he sprinkled his hair with gold dust to create the nimbus when the light shown down upon him. His clothes glittered with jewels; he wore ruby and emerald bracelets, necklaces, and rings; his fingernails were gilded; and his boots—which were to become *the* new symbol of imperial power—were of purple leather. He entered his throne room carrying a golden scepter topped with a golden ball—the earth—on which was seated a Roman gold eagle with a sapphire in its beak—the heavens. Servants followed sprinkling the air with perfume, and fan bearers spread the scent abroad. Every person in the room sank to the floor until Diocletian was seated on his throne, after which the privileged might kiss the hem of his garment.

The first Augustus would have been revolted. Occasionally Rome had seen similar displays, notably under the perverted Elagabalus, himself the priest of a Syrian sun god, but even in its degenerate days Rome always hated such display, and Elagabalus was murdered. Diocletian's pomp had nothing to do with effeminacy or perverted tastes: he was a rough Balkan soldier. Rather he was making a deliberate attempt to elevate the prestige of the emperor—the divine and deified emperor—so high that his divinity would not be shaken by the ambitions of his rivals. It was no accident that Diocletian chose the additional surname Jovius, thus associating himself with Jupiter (Jove), the ruler of the gods.

No mere mechanical reorganization and geographical regrouping of forces could have prevented the recurrence of military uprisings. Diocletian now firmly separated the military from the civil power, so that the generals and colonels in command of local garrisons throughout the empire had no local political authority. The new civil officials whom he appointed had no military authority. Moreover, Diocletian subdivided the old provinces, so that the number of provinces rose to over one hundred, each of course vastly smaller than a province had formerly been; and these in turn were regrouped into twelve so-called dioceses, which made up the four great prefectures. The bureaucracy grew enormously: the various financial departments, the secret service, the post, and foreign relations each had its own structure, and the top officials became a kind of advisory body, almost a Cabinet. While an individual Roman senator might find a place in such a system, it was independent of the Senate as such, and as a body the Senate continued only as a group of privileged magnates. Diocletian also adapted military tactics to a new age, introducing heavy-armed cavalry for the first time, and inventing a flexible system of frontier defenses that made it possible for troops to move rapidly to a point where danger threatened.

Diocletian and Constantine also took steps to deal with the economic misery and social unrest that had accompanied the political and military disorders of the later third century. By using as a unit of land measurement for tax purposes the amount of land that could be cultivated by a single farm laborer, and by trying to force the farm laborer to stay put, work his land, and pay his taxes, the new empire greatly stimulated the growth of the class of rural resident called the colonus, who was attached to the soil. He was not a slave, and could not be sold apart from the land he cultivated, but when it was sold he went with it. Other men in other walks of life also were bound to their various jobs, and sons to their fathers' jobs after them. Sons of bakers had to become bakers, sons of goldsmiths goldsmiths. In his efforts to stabilize the economic situation, Diocletian also tried to fix prices, but was thwarted by black-marketing and riots.

At the lowest territorial administrative level, the civitas (each city and portions of the surrounding countryside), the city senators (curiales) had to make up out of their own pockets any difference between the tax payments assessed for the civitas and the amount actually collected. From being an honor, the position of curialis became a burden, and curiales too had to be compelled to stay in their posts, to do their duty, and to pass their jobs on to their eldest sons. Society in the new empire became more rigidly stratified than ever before in Roman history. The combination of this increased social stratification with oriental despotism, a huge bureaucracy, and a continuing dependence on the military made ordinary life extremely bleak: corruption, violence, inequity, individual despair were frequent. The Roman Empire survived in both East and West (though the days of the Western empire proved numbered), but its citizens were probably unhappier than ever before.

Diocletian retired in 305 and left his half of the empire to his Caesar; and he forced his fellow Augustus, Maximian, to do the same. Each of the new Augusti in turn named a Caesar; but the system now broke down, as the four top officials began to struggle against each other for supreme power. By 324, Constantine, who had begun as the son of the Western Caesar, boss of Gaul, emerged as sole Augustus, and the empire was reunited. Though the tetrarchy did not survive, the other reforms of Diocletian and his immediate successors certainly helped to stave off collapse. But, of course, they did not prevent it.

Few subjects have been more debated than the reasons for the decline of the Roman Empire. The celebrated eighteenth-century historian Edward Gibbon blamed Christianity, charging that it destroyed the civic spirit of the Roman by turning his attention to the afterlife and away from his duties to the state. Michael Rostovtzeff, a learned Russian scholar writing in the 1920's and 1930's, attributed the decline in part to the constant pressure of the underprivileged masses to share in the wealth of their rulers, of which there was not enough to go around anyhow. Gibbon and Rostovtzeff each reflected his own time and experience, Gibbon the anticlerical rationalism of the eighteenth century, Rostovtzeff the bitter lesson of the Bolshevik Revolution in his native Russia. Others have emphasized the influx of Greeks and Orientals into Roman society, and intimated that the original "pure" Roman racial virtues were thus diluted, a view shared by few reliable historians. Still others have talked of climatic change, but with little evidence.

Economically, losses in population caused by plagues and civil war crippled agriculture, already hampered by backward methods. The growing concentration of land in large estates and the absorption of free farmers into the status of coloni diluted Roman prosperity, already suffering from feeble purchasing power and inflation. Psychologically, the masses became alienated from their rulers: the substitution of the mercenary for the old citizen-soldier testified to the decline of the old Roman patriotism. Yet even with all these factors, it would be hard to imagine Roman decline without the terrific pressure of outside forces: the third and fourth centuries were the time when the barbarian world began to move, and it was the barbarian threat that eventually brought about the collapse of the Roman structure in the West while permitting its survival in the East in a modified form.

Colossal head of the emperor Constantine.

VIII
The Civilization of Rome

In the years following the end of World War II, when American military power emerged as the decisive force in European affairs, many Europeans unkindly compared the Americans to the Romans and themselves to the Greeks. The Americans, they felt, were uncultivated boors without much of a civilization of their own, but with a great deal of impressive military hardware, trying to tell newly weakened peoples with old and proud military and political traditions how to run their affairs, and at the same time goggling admiringly at the surviving monuments of European culture.

It is of course true that American civilization is newer, and that if Americans wish to see ancient temples, medieval castles, and cathedrals, they must go to Europe to do so. But the parallel breaks down in many places. America did not attack and conquer Europe or attempt to govern it. Rome did these things to Greece. America was founded by Europeans, and inherited its civilization from them; so that Homer, Dante, and Shakespeare are as much a part of our tradition as of theirs. Rome was not founded by Greeks. And if many Americans regarded Europe as a museum for their entertainment and instruction, was it not because they recognized themselves as part of the same tradition rather than because they had found something new and different?

However faulty the modern part of the parallel may be, one ancient generalization still holds true: Greece, though conquered, took her conqueror captive. Indeed, Greek influence from Magna Graecia affected the Romans long before they conquered Greece itself. In the arts, the Romans found virtually their entire inspiration in Greek models. In literature the Greeks supplied the forms, and often much of the spirit, but the best Roman literary achievements could not be mistaken for Greek works: they have a Roman spirit and quality. In science and engineering the Romans had greater natural talent than the Greeks, as they did in law and the arts of government.

The Greece the Romans gradually conquered was not the Greece of Homer or Pericles; so that the Romans, for example, did not imitate the Greek tragedians of the fifth century B.C.: there was no Roman Aeschylus, Sophocles, or Euripides. This was the Greece of the decades after the death of Alexander, of the New Comedy of Menander, not the Old Comedy of Aristophanes, when literature—much of it produced in Alexandria—was more artificial, more purely charming and graceful, often trivial, less grand, less concerned with the central themes of human existence. The surviving Alexandrian epic, Apollonius Rhodius' *Argonautica,* which tells of the adventures of the mythical hero Jason on his way to find the golden fleece, was a scholar's careful (and not very successful) effort to be Homeric long after the heroic age was over. When the Romans first began to imitate the Greeks, the greatest Greek works, though deeply respected, were no longer being written: it was a lesser age.

Before the first contacts with the Greeks, of course, the Romans, in their central Italian provincial agricultural city-state, had already evolved their own religion, the worship of the household spirits, the lares and penates, that governed their everyday affairs, along with those spiritual beings that inhabited the local woods and springs and fields. Like the Greek Hestia, the Roman Vesta presided over the individual hearth, and had in her service the specially trained Vestal Virgins. From the Etruscans the Romans took the belief, which they never abandoned, in divination: they too foretold the future through observing the flight of birds (the auspices) and examining the entrails of animals (the auguries). From Greece there came the entire Olympic collection of gods and goddesses, some of them merging their identities in existing divinities, and most of them changing their names. Zeus became Jupiter, Hera Juno, Poseidon Neptune, and so on, though Apollo remained Apollo. But the Romans had nothing like the Greek Olympic games or the festivals of Dionysus that had led to the writing of Athenian tragedy and comedy.

Julius Caesar, as we know—and after him most of the emperors beginning with Augustus—was deified after death, and Augustus consented to be worshiped jointly with Rome at the great altar in Gaul. But in the imperial cult as in other religious observances, except for certain notable festivals each year, the individual Roman took little part. The official priests performed most rites, headed by their chief priest, the pontifex maximus, a title and role taken over by the emperors themselves. The state religion early lost its appeal for the Romans, and, since there was no reason why they could not worship as many other gods as they chose in addition, after rendering due veneration to the ordinary deities, including the emperor, Rome early imported cults from other places, chiefly the East, which competed for popularity. Since Christianity eventually joined and won the competition, we postpone discussion of its competitors until the next chapter, where we can more easily examine the reason for its victory.

Literature

Quintus Ennius (239–169 B.C.), who was born and brought up in Magna Graecia, naturally turned to Homer for inspiration when he put into epic form his patriotic account (the *Annales*) of Roman successes down to his own time. Although only fragments (in all between six and seven hundred lines) are preserved, we have enough to appreciate Ennius' thoroughly Roman admiration for the military virtues, and to understand his lasting influence on later Roman writers. Just as Ennius used Homeric verse to celebrate Roman toughness and resilience, Plautus (254–184 B.C.) and Terence (190–159 B.C.) found their inspiration in the Greek New Comedy of Menander. Plautus was the more raucous and knockabout: it was he who wrote the play about the two sets of twins, masters and servants who are always being taken for each other, that Shakespeare eventually imitated in *A Comedy of Errors.* And other characters from Plautus—the rich but stupid young gentleman with an immensely clever and resourceful valet, the money-grubbing miser—recur throughout the course of western European—and Russian— literary history. Gentler and milder in every sense, Terence stuck closer to the Greek originals, but was not a success in his own day. After Plautus and Terence, various Roman authors tried to write comedies with a native Italian inspiration, but none of their work survives. In addition to these sophisticated works, the Romans enjoyed crude farces of the kind that had always been staged in the villages.

During the late republic appeared two of Rome's greatest poets, Lucretius (96–55 B.C.) and Catullus (84–54 B.C.), alike only in their mastery of their chosen verse forms and the genuineness of their emotions. Lucretius—a serious disciple of the Greek philosopher Epicurus—wrote a long poem, *On the Nature of Things (De Rerum Natura),* putting into moving poetry his master's beliefs that there is no human survival after death, and that the gods—far from governing the affairs of men—do not intervene at all. The universe is made of atoms, whose motions and behavior are governed by fixed laws, right out to the edges, the "flaming walls of the universe," except that men control their own actions. Catullus, looking to certain Alexandrian poets of the emotions, wrote passionate love lyrics recording his feelings for his mistress Clodia (sister of the tribune Clodius), to whom he gives the name of Lesbia. Sometimes playful and charming, as in the poems addressed to Lesbia's pet sparrow or celebrating the first days of returning spring, sometimes bitter and obscene (Lesbia was unfaithful and made Catullus miserable), these brief poems, in a meter new to Rome, seem to some readers the highest achievement of Roman literature. Catullus also wrote a long, sustained, and extraordinarily gripping poem about the exaltation and self-mutilation of the devotees of Cybele, the great mother goddess of Asia Minor, and her consort Attis, whose cult was becoming popular at Rome.

In Cicero (106–43 B.C.), whom we have already so often encountered in his role as a lawyer and politician, the late republic produced its greatest writer of prose. His oratorical skill of course furthered his career as a successful lawyer and politician; his speeches in the courtroom or in the Senate were carefully prepared and effective pleas. He deliberately won his listeners with an occasional quick injection of a witty or ironical phrase into an otherwise somber and stately passage. He carefully studied not only what he wanted to say but how he could choose the most effective—sometimes the most unexpected— words in which to say it, and how he could combine them into a rhythmical and pleasing pattern, so that the sound and the sense would combine to make his point irresistibly. As the recognized supreme master of the art, he also wrote treatises on oratory. We also have almost a thousand letters that Cicero wrote to his friends and acquaintances, and some of their answers to him. The correspondence includes not only exchanges of letters with the most important Roman public figures of the period but also many intimate letters to Cicero's best friend, Atticus, that reveal his personal joys and sorrows.

Philosophically, Cicero in large measure agreed with the views of the Stoics as modified by Greek teachers who had adapted the originally abstract and remote concepts of Stoicism to Roman taste by allowing for the exercise in ordinary life of the Stoic virtues and admitting that one can have some virtues without possession of all knowledge. Cicero, himself not an original thinker, deliberately helped popularize these ideas in his philosophic essays—on Old Age, on Friendship, on the Nature of the Gods, and on other political and social subjects. Into the Latin language he introduced for the first time terms capable of conveying the meaning of the Greek concepts he was discussing. His fellow Romans first learned from him about the concept of a "natural law," for example, that existed independent of all human legislative actions, or a "law of nations" that should regulate the relationships of different peoples toward each other. The influence of these Ciceronian works radiated far into future human history: the early Christian church fathers went to school to Cicero, as did the humanists of the Italian Renaissance, and the men who made the eighteenth-century revolutions in America and in France and who wrote the Declaration of Independence and the Constitution of the United States.

It was the writers of the Age of Augustus who gave Rome its literary Golden Age. And, as in the other enterprises of his era, Augustus himself took an active part in recruiting and subsidizing talent, even genius, to proclaim the glories of the new era, his new era. Vergil (70–19 B.C.) in his *Georgics* and *Eclogues* followed the models of Greek pastoral poetry, and praised the pleasures and satisfactions of rural life. Written before Augustus reached political supremacy, these poems helped Augustus advance his later program of propaganda to get men back to the farm. He persuaded Vergil to write the *Aeneid,* the great epic of Rome's beginnings, in which the poet could "predict" the future glories that Augustus' rule would bring. Though designed in part to please Augustus, these passages nontheless reveal Vergil's own sincere and intense patriotism. Vergil often reflects upon the sacrifices that necessarily accompany a rise to greatness, on sorrow, and on death.

His fellow poet Horace (65-8 B.C.) had more humor, and expressed a greater variety of feelings in a greater number of meters. In short poems on more limited subjects he too praised the joys of rural life and the virtues of moderation, but also in more solemn terms celebrated the Roman qualities of quiet toughness, the simple life, the traditional religious attitudes. Ovid (43 B.C.-A.D. 17) gave worldly advice—often cynical—on the art of love; and elsewhere told the stories of the mythical transformations reported in Greek myths, as various divinities became birds or animals or plants. Ovid died in exile because of his involvement in a scandal affecting the granddaughter of Augustus.

To match in prose Vergil's epic of Rome's early days and to stress again the virtues that had made Rome great, the historian Livy (59 B.C.-A.D. 17) set out to write a prose history of the city from the moment of its founding. Only 35 of the 142 books into which he divided his work have come down to us complete, but we have summaries of the missing portions—most of the second and all of the first century B.C. Livy could use as his sources the compilations of many Roman writers now lost; but for the earliest periods he had to fall back on legend. He knew the difference between reliable and unreliable accounts, but often had only the latter available, and so used them. Vividly written, his work was indeed very long, and soon was put into *Reader's Digest* form for the unambitious. The future emperor Claudius had Livy as his tutor, and it would probably be safe to attribute Claudius' own success as emperor to the training he received from the historian.

The insistence on the great Roman virtues reflected an uneasy sense of their decline. In the period after Augustus, as the government became more arbitrary and autocratic, and writers began to fear the consequences of expressing themselves too freely, disillusionment set in. Moreover, the general admiration for the achievements of the Augustan writers, especially Vergil, became so intense that poets were often content to try to imitate the authors of the Golden Age, and to suppress their own originality. The greatest of all the Roman historians, Tacitus (ca. 55-117 A.D.), himself a master of prose style, was convinced that Romans had degenerated. In his *Germania* he wrote an essay ostensibly in praise of the rugged and still primitive way of life of the German barbarians, but in fact an acid commentary on the qualities the Romans had once had and had now lost. Similar disillusionment pervades his works of history, originally covering the period from Tiberius to Domitian, but not entirely preserved. Brilliant and prejudiced, allowing his personal opinions to color his accounts (sometimes in ways we cannot surely check), he was the greatest of the writers of the period between Tiberius and Hadrian, known as the Silver Age.

Silver Age poets included notably Seneca, Nero's tutor, by birth a Spaniard, a Stoic philosopher, and author of nine tragedies imitating Greek originals but far more bombastic and sensational. Seneca perhaps also wrote an extant satire on Claudius—a man easy to poke fun at, especially after he was dead, but morally worth several Senecas and any number of Neros. Seneca's nephew, Lucan, wrote an epic poem *(The Pharsalia)* about the struggle between Caesar and Pompey. In successive generations, Persius (34-62 A.D.) and Juvenal (50-130) satirized contemporary society, and, as satirists often do, overstated the case: Juvenal enjoyed painting the vulgarities and wretchedness, the cruelties and greed of Rome in the harshest colors. His crass characters the Romans would have met frequently not only on the streets but in the pages of a famous obscene novel, the *Satyricon,* attributed to one of Nero's court officials, Petronius, which has an unforgettable episode of a wild banquet given by a newly rich ex-slave.

Law

The legal code published on the Twelve Tables in the fifth century B.C. reflected the needs of a small city-state, not those of a huge empire. As Rome became a world capital, thousands of foreigners flocked to live there to pursue their businesses, and of course they often got into disagreements with each other or with a Roman. But Roman law developed the flexibility to adjust to changing conditions: the enactments of the Senate and Assemblies, the decrees of each new emperor, and the decisions of the judges who were often called in as advisers—all of these contributed to a great body of legal materials.

It was the praetors, the chief legal officers, who heard both sides in every case, and determined the facts before turning over the matter to the judex, a referee, for decision. The judices had to develop a body of rules for deciding cases that were not covered by existing law. As they dealt with many different breeds of foreigners, they worked out a body of legal custom common to all of them, the law of the peoples *(jus gentium),* that would be acceptable to all comers. As each new praetor took office for a year, he would announce the laws by which he intended to be bound, usually following his predecessors, and adding to the body of law as necessary. Romans too gradually acquired the benefits of the law of the peoples.

The expert advisers (jurisconsults) to both praetor and judex felt an almost religious concern for equity: it was the spirit rather than the letter of the law that counted. This humane view found support in the philosophical writings of the Stoics, who believed as we saw that above all manmade law stood a higher "natural" law, divinely inspired, and applying to all men everywhere. In practice, of course, judges were often ill trained, the emperors brutal or arbitrary; Roman law could be used to exalt the authority of the state over the individual. Yet the law recognized the rights of the citizen, afforded legal redress even to slaves, and gave wide scope to local legal practices. Its superiority made it victor over other legal systems; the law of much of western Europe today goes back to its provisions.

Engineering and Medicine

The Romans devised a formula for making concrete from sand, lime, silica, stone, and water. They combined this concrete with large stones in building roads and bridges so well designed and so long-lasting that even today a few are still in use. The network of roads spread throughout the empire, making travel overland swift and easy. The Romans went to great trouble and expense to provide their cities with pure and abundant water. A dozen aqueducts served Rome itself, and from Constantinople to Segovia aqueducts form the most spectacular Roman ruins. The concern for water reflected a real interest in bathing and in hygiene: the Romans had the highest sanitary standards known in Europe until the nineteenth century.

Roman surgeons made a variety of ingenious instruments for special operations, including the Caesarean operation—supposed (probably wrongly) to have been first performed at the birth of Julius Caesar—to deliver babies unable to be born normally. The Romans invented the first hospitals, military and civilian. Much superstition survived in Roman medicine, and it was the Greeks, notably Galen (A.D. 131–201), who continued to make the chief theoretical contributions, compiling medical encyclopedias and diffusing learning.

What Galen did for medicine, his contemporary Ptolemy of Alexandria did for ancient geography; both remained the chief authorities on their subjects down to the sixteenth century. Some learned Romans followed the Alexandrian Eratosthenes in believing that the earth was round. Pliny the Elder in the first century A.D. made observations of ships approaching the shore to support this hypothesis: it was the tip of the mast that appeared first to an observer on shore and the hull last, a proof, Pliny felt, that the surface of the earth was curved.

Architecture, Sculpture, and Painting

Roman architecture borrowed the Greek column, usually Corinthian, but made wide use also of the round arch, originated by the Etruscans, and from this developed the barrel vault, a continuous series of arches like the roof of a tunnel which could be used to roof over large areas. The Romans introduced the dome, and a splendid one surmounts the Pantheon at Rome, built to honor the divine ancestors of Augustus. Roman structures emphasized bigness: the Colosseum seated 45,000 spectators; the Baths of the emperor Caracalla accommodated thousands of bathers at a time (its ruins are still used for grand opera); Diocletian's palace at Split in modern Yugoslavia contains most of the modern city inside its walls. All over the Middle East and North Africa, as well as western Europe, one finds amphitheaters, temples, villas, and other monumental remains of the Roman domination.

Relief of a Roman battle on the Column of Trajan, Rome.

Roman statues, though derived from Greek and Hellenistic models, often had a realism all their own, as in the cases of imperial portrait busts. In a sculptured frieze running spirally up a monumental column the victories of the emperor Trajan are vividly recorded. Of Roman painting we have chiefly the pretty—sometimes obscene—wall decorations of the villas at Pompeii (the resort town near Naples that was literally buried in A.D. 79 by the sudden eruption of Vesuvius that covered it in a rain of hot ash), and the mosaic floors of public and private buildings, where a favorite subject was a hunting scene in the landscape of the Nile, with crocodiles and hippopotamuses among the papyrus plants. The recently discovered imperial villa at Piazza Armerina in Sicily has a superb series of these floors, including a scene of bathing girls in bikinis tossing a beach ball from hand to hand.

A Final Appraisal

Tacitus was certainly right in thinking that Rome had lost some of its traditional virtues with its conquest of huge territories, its accumulation of wealth, and its assumption of imperial responsibilities. Nevertheless, the first two centuries of the empire mark the most stable and prosperous era that had yet occurred in human history. No doubt, the profits of flourishing commercial life were unevenly distributed, and there were glaring contrasts between riches and poverty. But many of the harshest aspects of ancient society elsewhere were softened at Rome: slaves could obtain their freedom more easily; women had more rights and commanded more respect (we have much evidence of harmonious family life, though there were more divorces perhaps than at any time until our own day); physical comforts were abundant for those who could afford them.

In Rome itself, however, great areas were slums: six- and seven-story wooden tenements that burned down repeatedly and were rebuilt despite building codes and fire departments. Worst of all was the chronic urban unemployment: at the height of the Pax Romana, perhaps half the population of the capital was on the bread dole. The inhabitants also were given free circuses in the form of chariot races and gladiatorial combats, and the poor squandered their pennies on betting. Bloodshed exerted a morbid fascination: criminals were crucified and even burned alive on the stage as part of spectacles to entertain the populace, and in the last century of Roman life these shows had become so popular that they had superseded the circus, despite the protests of the occasional horrified citizens, pagan or Christian.

Though the structure of the Roman state would disappear in the West by the end of the fifth century A.D., Roman influence has given a permanent shape to western Europe. Italian, French, Spanish, Portuguese are all languages derived from Latin, and our own English tongue is a hybrid with almost as many Latin as Germanic words. Roman legal concepts provided the foundations of respectability for many a squalid barbarian society. Rome itself, finally, would become the capital of Christianity and its administrative organization a model for the structure of the Church.

Reading Suggestions on the Classical World

GREECE: GENERAL ACCOUNTS

M. I. Finley, *The Ancient Greeks* (*Compass). Compact and perceptive introduction to Greek life and thought.

C. E. Robinson, *Hellas: A Short History of Ancient Greece* (*Beacon). By a good scholar.

M. I. Rostovtzeff, *Greece* (*Galaxy). A famous older account, now somewhat outdated.

J. B. Bury, *A History of Greece to the Death of Alexander the Great,* 3rd ed. rev. (Macmillan, 1951). Another celebrated older account, stressing war and politics.

N. G. L. Hammond, *A History of Greece to 322 B.C.,* 2nd ed. (Oxford University, 1967). A good up-to-date survey.

R. M. Cook, *The Greeks till Alexander* (Praeger, 1962). Well-illustrated survey, stressing material accomplishments.

THE GREEK POLIS

V. Ehrenberg, *The Greek State* (*Norton). Solid scholarly introduction.

A. Andrewes, *The Greek Tyrants* (*Torchbooks). Informative comparative survey of emerging constitutions.

A. H. M. Jones, *Athenian Democracy* (Praeger, 1957). An up-to-date interpretation.

A. E. Zimmern, *The Greek Common-*

wealth (*Galaxy). A celebrated and sympathetic older account, stressing especially Athens.

H. Michell, *Sparta* (*Cambridge University). A comprehensive and sympathetic survey.

Kathleen Freeman, *Greek City-States* (*Norton). Excellent overview, focusing on states other than Athens and Sparta.

A. G. Woodhead, *The Greeks in the West* (Praeger, 1962), and J. M. Cook, *The Greeks in Ionia and the East* (Praeger, 1963). Two volumes in the series "Ancient Peoples and Places," also reminding us that the Greek world was not limited to Athens and Sparta.

GREEK CIVILIZATION

W. Jaeger, *Paideia,* 3 vols. (Oxford University, 1939–1944). An advanced study of Greek culture and ideals (*Vol. I, Galaxy).

C. M. Bowra, *The Greek Experience* (*Mentor). As seen by a literary scholar.

A. Bonnard, *Greek Civilization,* 3 vols. (Macmillan, 1957–1961). Stimulating chapters on a wide range of topics.

W. K. C. Guthrie, *The Greeks and Their Gods* (*Beacon). Detailed but engrossing study of the origins and nature of Greek religion.

F. M. Cornford, *Before and After Socrates* (*Cambridge University). A first-rate short introduction to science and philosophy in Greece.

J. B. Bury, *The Greek Historians* (*Dover). Appraisals by a celebrated English historian.

Rhys Carpenter, *The Esthetic Basis of Greek Art* (*Indiana University). Analysis by an expert.

THE HELLENISTIC WORLD

W. W. Tarn, *Alexander the Great* (*Beacon). Hero worship that protests too much.

W. W. Tarn and G. T. Griffith, *Hellenistic Civilization,* 3rd ed. (St. Martins, 1952). A comprehensive survey.

M. Rostovtzeff, *The Social and Economic History of the Hellenistic World* (Clarendon, 1941). Detailed study by a great historian.

ROME: GENERAL ACCOUNTS

M. Rostovtzeff, *Rome* (*Galaxy). Excellent scholarly survey, though a little outdated.

A. E. R. Boak, *A History of Rome to 565,* 5th ed. (Macmillan, 1965). A standard textbook.

C. E. Robinson, *Apollo History of Rome* (*Apollo). A clear introduction.

T. Mommsen, *The History of Rome* (*Philosophical Library). Detailed study by a great nineteenth-century scholar; still worth reading.

M. Grant, *The World of Rome* (World, 1960). Handsomely illustrated introduction to imperial Rome.

R. H. Barrow, *The Romans* (*Penguin). Sound popular survey.

THE ETRUSCAN BACKGROUND AND THE ROMAN REPUBLIC

O. W. von Vacano, *The Etruscans in the Ancient World* (*Indiana University). Careful study of the archaeological evidence.

R. Bloch, *The Etruscans* (Praeger, 1958). Briefer and well-illustrated volume in the series "Ancient Peoples and Places."

———, *The Origins of Rome* (Praeger, 1960). Another volume in the series, taking the story to the early fifth century B.C.

H. H. Scullard, *Roman Politics, 220–150 B.C.* (Clarendon, 1951). Detailed study of the era when Rome began to dominate the Mediterranean world.

———, *From the Gracchi to Nero* (*Barnes & Noble). Up-to-date, clear, and balanced history of the later republic and early empire.

R. E. Smith, *The Failure of the Roman Republic* (Cambridge University, 1955). A provocative essay that is critical of the Gracchi.

THE ROMAN EMPIRE

R. Syme, *The Roman Revolution* (*Galaxy). The transformation of state and society under Caesar and Augustus.

H. T. Rowell, *Rome in the Augustan Age* (Oklahoma University, 1962). Sympathetic appraisal of Augustus and his work.

T. W. Africa, *Rome of the Caesars* (*Wiley). The first two centuries of the empire interpreted through biographies of its leaders.

M. P. Charlesworth, *The Roman Empire* (*Galaxy). Informative sketch.

Stuart Perowne, *Hadrian* (Norton, 1960). Lively modern treatment.

Anthony Birley, *Marcus Aurelius* (Little, Brown, 1966). The latest monograph.

S. Dill, *Roman Society from Nero to Marcus Aurelius* (*Meridian). A classic of social history.

ROMAN CIVILIZATION AND DECLINE

M. Clarke, *The Roman Mind* (Cohen & West, 1956). Studies in the history of thought from Cicero to Marcus Aurelius.

M. Wheeler, *Roman Art and Architecture* (*Penguin). Clear and well illustrated.

H. Mattingly, *Roman Imperial Civilization* (*Anchor). Through a study of coins.

E. Gibbon, *A History of the Decline and Fall of the Roman Empire* (*many editions, usually abridged). The earliest chapters of this famous classic relate to the third and fourth centuries.

M. Rostovtzeff, *The Social and Economic History of the Roman Empire,* 2nd ed. (Clarendon, 1957). Magnificently illustrated detailed study, with speculations on the reasons for Roman decline.

R. M. Haywood, *The Myth of Rome's Fall* (*Apollo). Scholarly survey of the centuries of decline.

A SAMPLING OF SOURCES AND FICTION

W. H. Auden, ed., *The Portable Greek Reader* (*Viking).

The Iliad, trans. R. Lattimore (*Phoenix).

W. J. Oates and E. O'Neill, Jr., eds., *The Complete Greek Drama,* 2 vols. (Random House, 1938). A selection may be found in *Seven Greek Plays* (*Vintage).

The Dialogues of Plato, trans. B. Jowett (Clarendon, 1953).

The Works of Aristotle, ed. W. D. Ross (Clarendon, 1908–1931).

Thucydides, *History of the Peloponnesian War,* trans. B. Jowett (*Bantam).

Mary Renault, *The King Must Die* (*Pocket Books). A novel set in Mycenae and in Minoan Crete.

———, *The Last of the Wine* (*Pocket Books). A novel set in Athens at the time of the Peloponnesian War.

B. Davenport, ed., *The Portable Roman Reader* (*Viking).

N. Lewis and M. Reinhold, *Roman Civilization,* 2 vols. (*Torchbooks). Including both selections from the sources and enlightening comments on them.

Vergil, *The Aeneid,* trans. R. Humphries. (*Scribner's).

Marcus Aurelius, *Meditations* (*several editions).

Bryher, *The Coin of Carthage* (*Harcourt). Novel set against the Second Punic War.

———, *The Roman Wall* (*Vintage). Novel set on the Alpine frontier in the era of decline.

Bernard Shaw, *Caesar and Cleopatra* (*Penguin). Drama depicting Caesar as wise and very talkative.

Shakespeare, *Julius Caesar.*

———, *Antony and Cleopatra.* With a devastating portrait of the ambitious youth who later became Augustus.

———, *Coriolanus.* A thoroughly disenchanted view of republican Roman politicians.

three

The Making of a New World: To the Year 1000

I

The Christian Revolution in the Roman World

The Spirit of the Times

Greek scientific theory and Roman technical skills had brought the ancient world to the threshold of an industrial age. Heron of Alexandria, who we think lived at about the beginning of the Christian era, had even discovered the engineering usefulness of steam pressure in a boiler, and conceived a model of a fire engine, including the piston. It would have been only a short step to the building of steam devices. Why did more than 1700 years pass before man took that step?

One answer is that slave labor was working so well that nobody thought labor-saving devices were desirable, but this seems an unsatisfactory explanation. Another answer might be that people thought of Heron's devices only as toys because science, in Alexandria, like literature, had become a mere game played by a small circle of erudite people uninterested in practical applications of their research. The Alexandrian upper classes were grateful to the Romans for providing stability and prosperity and in no mood even to imagine an industrial revolution. And, as for the rulers of Rome, science formed no part of their education, and scattered statements show that they scorned what we would call research. The emperor Tiberius once executed a man who had invented a process for making unbreakable glass. Although the earlier advance of science in the Greek and Hellenistic world had given rise to small groups of rationalists who believed in improving their lives by using their reasoning powers, even these minorities seem virtually to have disappeared. Everywhere in Rome the student can observe mounting pessimism and a lack of faith in man's ability to work out his own future.

The old gods seemed powerless to intervene; life appeared to be a mere matter of luck. And so, beginning as early as the third century B.C. and gathering increasing momentum later on, the cult of the goddess Fortune became immensely popular in the Mediterranean world: chance governed everything; today's prosperity might vanish tomorrow; the best thing to do was to enjoy luck while it lasted. Closely related was the belief in Fate: what happened was inevitable, because it had been fated from the beginning; when you were born, the moment of your death was already fixed. Some, like Cicero, protested that men could contribute to their own fate and so take advantage of fortune; Vergil attributed both fate and fortune to the will of the divine providence; but most Romans, like Tacitus, seem to have felt helpless to change their own fates or to influence events.

ASTROLOGY   To escape this feeling, most Romans came to believe that the movements of the heavenly bodies influenced the fortunes and the fate of men and governed the decisions they made. Thus the science of astronomy became lost in the false speculation of astrology. If you could do nothing to change your destiny, you could at least try to find out what it might be by consulting an expert astrologer. He would study the seven planets (Saturn, Jupiter, Mars, the Sun, Venus, Mercury, the Moon), each of which had its own will, character, sex, plants, numbers, and animals, and each of which was lord of a sphere. Seven transparent but impenetrable concentric spheres, with Earth at the center, cut man off from heaven. Each planet had its own day: hence the seven-day week. Seven itself became a mystic number: there were seven ages of man, seven wonders of the world. Then too there were the twelve Houses of the Sun, constellations of stars through which the sun passed on his path around the earth: the signs of the Zodiac.

From the position of the heavenly bodies and the signs of the Zodiac at the moment of your conception or birth, astrologers would draw up a horoscope foretelling your fate. The Roman emperors, like most of their subjects, profoundly believed in astrology. Especially valuable for the art of prophecy were unnatural events: the appearance of a comet, the birth of a monster. Similarly, men believed in all sorts of magic, and tried by its power to force the heavenly bodies to grant their wishes.

NEW CULTS: CYBELE, ISIS, MITHRA   The state religion of the Olympian gods and of the deified emperor still commanded the loyalty of many Romans, who regarded the proper observance of its rites as the equivalent of patriotism. But the old faith no longer allayed the fears of the millions of people believing in blind fate and inevitable fortune. More and more, men sought for a religion that would hold out the hope for an afterlife better than the grim life here on earth. So, along with astrology and magic, a large number of mystery religions began to appear in Rome.

All the new faiths taught that a human being could save his soul by uniting it with the soul of a saviour, who in many cases had himself experienced death and resurrection. Union with the saviour was accomplished by a long initiation, with purifications, ritual banquets, and other ceremonies. The candidate gradually cast aside human unworthiness, the god would enter him, and so after death he would be saved. It was perfectly possible to join as many of these cults as one liked and yet continue to practice the state religion.

The Greeks had had such cults, in the rites of Demeter at Eleusis and in the mysteries of Dionysus. The rites of Dionysus, now called Bacchus, became popular at Rome, celebrating as they did the animal side of human nature and the abandonment of all restraint. On hundreds of Roman sarcophagi can be seen the Bacchic procession, celebrating the joys of drink and sex. But the cult of Bacchus was too materialistic to satisfy all Romans.

One of its major competitors was the cult of the great mother goddess Cybele, transplanted from Asia Minor. Her young husband, Attis, died and was reborn annually (like Demeter's daughter, Persephone). Attis was thus a symbol of renewed fertility. The rites of Cybele included fasting, frenzied processions, and the self-flagellation and even self-mutilation of the priests. The first temple to Cybele at Rome dated from 204 B.C., but the zenith of the cult came in the second century A.D. and later, when it spread to the West. By that time the rites included the slaughter of a bull above a pit into which the initiate had descended in order to be bathed by the blood.

Even more popular—especially among women—was the cult of the Egyptian Isis, whose consort, Osiris, also died and was reborn each year. All feminine elements, both lascivious and chaste, were concentrated in an elaborate ritual of worship for Isis, the loving mother goddess, who promised her adherents personal immortality.

Roman relief of the slaughter of a bull (taurobolium) in Mithraism.

From Persia via Asia Minor came the cult of the god Mithra, allied to the supreme powers of good and light and so connected with the Sun. The male initiates passed in succession through seven grades of initiation (corresponding to the seven planets and named after animals), qualifying for each by severe tests. Baptism and communion were also part of the ritual. Unconquered, physically tough, and self-denying, Mithra became a model for the Roman soldier, to whom he held out the hope of salvation. Mithraism had no priests and welcomed the gods of other cults; it tended to absorb the other sun-worshiping cults, including that of Apollo, into one new cult, often heartily supported by the emperor. From London to Alexandria and from the Rhine to the Euphrates, temples of Mithra, with altars and statues, have been found.

Christianity

But no single one of the mystery religions appealed to men and women of all classes at Rome. Mithraism, which perhaps had the most adherents, excluded women and lacked love and tenderness. Christianity competed with these cults in the Roman world for more than three centuries after the death of its founder, with no assurance that it would triumph. Sharing some things in common with them, it also possessed qualities they lacked.

THE HISTORICAL JESUS   Jesus was born in Palestine sometime between the years we call 8 and 4 B.C., and was crucified probably A.D. 29, or 30, or 33. There are no sources absolutely contemporary with his life, but Paul's Epistle to the Corinthians was written about A.D. 55, the Gospel according to Mark about 65, Matthew and Luke and Acts probably about 80–85, and John about 100. Late in the second or early in the third century these texts were revised in Alexandria. We have no canonical Christian text written down before this revision. Before the year A.D. 60 a collection of the sayings of Jesus himself existed, written in Aramaic, the Semitic language that he spoke; this is lost. In addition, many other texts existed that were not regarded as canonical. Among them we may note the so-called *Gospel of Thomas,* of which fragments were found in Egypt in 1945 and 1946, consisting of 114 sayings attributed to Jesus, and dating from the early second century.

Thus, because we have no precise, contemporary accounts, the exact details of the preachings of Jesus during his own lifetime cannot always be determined. But the general nature of his message is clear enough. Although he appealed to the poor, the unlearned, and the weak, he was no simple social revolutionary, no revivalist, no ascetic. He preached the enjoyment of the good things of this world, an enjoyment freed from rivalry, ostentation, and vulgarity. He was kind but stern: good intentions are not enough; "he that heareth and doeth not is like a man that without a foundation built a house upon the earth. . . ." Above all Christ preached gentleness and love: humility, honesty, toleration, charity; but he warned that "wide is the gate, and broad is the way, that leadeth to destruction." Though he preached that men should turn the other cheek, he also said that he came not to bring peace, but a sword.

CHRISTIAN IDEAS   From Jesus' preaching there emerged theological conclusions of great importance: he spoke of his Father in heaven, referred to himself as the Son of Man, and taught that God the Father had sent him to redeem mankind from sin. Those who hearkened and led decent lives on earth would gain eternal bliss in heaven; those who turned a deaf ear and continued in their evil courses would be eternally damned in hell. The Gospels add that Christ (the word means "the anointed one") had died on the cross as the supreme act of redemption, that he had risen from the dead on the third day, and that he would soon return, during the lifetime of some of his hearers, to end this world in a final Day of Judgment. So the earliest Christians expected the second coming of Christ momentarily, and thought little of their earthly lives. Soon the literal expectation of Christ was transformed into a more mystical expectation of "the Comforter."

Christ was miraculously born of a virgin mother. He was baptized in the waters of the Jordan, and his followers too were baptized by their priests. He himself had given bread and wine to his followers, and told them that it was his body and blood. The virgin mother, the purifying bath, and the mystical sacrificial meal of communion recall elements that were present in the various mystery cults, as of course does the promise of eternal life. But the Christians held in contempt the excesses of the cult of Cybele, for example, and regarded Mithraic baptism and sacred communion as fiendish parodies of their own practices. Moreover, Jesus' sacrifice of his life for mankind and the intimacy with God promised during the future eternal life gave Christianity an immediacy and an appeal that no mystery religion could duplicate. Christ's message of love—for man, woman, and child, for the weak and lowly—supplied the tenderness so lacking in the world of every day.

By the third century the ritual act of communion—the sacrament of the Eucharist or Mass—had become the central symbol of Christianity. It was the action that made the individual Christian actually partake of his God and feel the wonder of salvation, just as by his baptism he had been figuratively washed clean of the sin that has at birth stained all men since Adam chose to disobey God. Baptism made one a Christian; the Eucharist, if taken reverently, kept one a Christian, provided one's behavior was also suitable. Because Christ by his crucifixion had atoned for the sin of Adam, the individual Christian might now also be saved.

Besides baptism and the Eucharist, five other ritual acts eventually came to be regarded as sacraments. These were confirmation, by which a child was brought into the Church when he had reached the age at which he could understand Christian doctrine; penance, by which the repentant sinner was given a temporal punishment by the priest and was granted absolution (but the performance of the penance could not guarantee salvation, since it might not have satisfied God's justice); extreme unction, the last rites for the dying; matrimony; and, for the priest, ordination.

JUDEAN BACKGROUNDS Christianity was born in the Kingdom of Judea, ruled over by a Hellenized Jewish dynasty loyal to Rome. Jesus was himself a Jew, and his followers inherited with his own teaching the uncompromising monotheism of the Old Testament, the Jewish tradition of regular education of the faithful, the belief that they formed a chosen people, the acceptance of authority, and the constant indoctrination of the faithful with a code of behavior. The Gospels of Matthew and Luke in particular refer to Christ as the Teacher of Righteousness.

New light on these specifically Palestinian traditions in Christianity may be provided by the so-called Dead Sea Scrolls, which were discovered in caves in Palestine beginning in 1947. The scrolls, dating from the mid-third century B.C. into the Christian era, contain among other manuscripts fragments of the teachings of a heretical Jewish sect, the Essenes, who lived in an isolated community and shared their property; their buildings were destroyed by the Romans A.D. 68. The Dead Sea Scrolls make repeated reference to a Teacher of Righteousness, a Suffering Just One, in whom some see a forerunner of Christ. Although after the Teacher's death, probably a violent one, his followers did not claim that he had been the Messiah awaited by the Jews, there is one passage in which the Teacher spoke of himself as producing a man-child who would have all his own powers. The New Testament makes no reference at all to the Essenes, and Jesus may have had no contact with them or with their tradition, yet the scrolls reveal a reforming movement within Judaism that had much in common with later Christianity. In Christ's own time, the Pharisees, the more adventurous-minded of the two warring sects of Jews, had already developed a belief in a Messiah and in an afterlife.

PAUL AND THE APOSTLES   To the entrenched Jews of Palestine and to the occupying Roman power, Jesus seemed subversive because he did not accept the existing order of things. Amid circumstances the details of which are still debated, he met his martyrdom. After his crucifixion, the small band of his immediate followers began enthusiastically to spread the good news (Evangel) of his teachings and his future second coming. Palestine and Syria were ready to receive their message. Saul of Tarsus, a Jew converted to Christianity by a vision beheld on the road to Damascus, was renamed Paul, and took the lead in giving the new faith its first organization: the earliest Christian church.

Jesus had proclaimed that he had not come to change the Law of the Jews. Non-Jews, though attracted by the appeal of Christianity, did not wish to comply with the details of the Old Testament prescriptions: for example, they did not want to be circumcised or to abstain from pork. Paul said that Greeks and Syrians need not follow the Law in these and other prescriptions. "The letter killeth," said Paul, "but the Spirit giveth Life." It was not the letter of the Law of the Jews that would save the Christian, but the spirit of the faith in a single God as interpreted by his son. Paul was at once a mystic, who would transcend the world and the flesh, and a practical human being, who knew how to advise ordinary men and women about the problems of their daily lives. He never preached denial of this world, yet he urged that man be constantly aware of the next. He expressed this as the mystic union of Christ and the Christian, "Always bearing about in the body the dying of the Lord Jesus, that the life also of Jesus might be made manifest in our body" (II Corinthians 4:10). Not mere animals, not mere men, Christians are children of God both mortal and immortal. While on earth they must live in the constant imperfections of the flesh; after death, if they have been true Christians, they are destined to eternal bliss.

Paul, of course, was not one of the twelve apostles, the actual companions of Christ, who, according to tradition, separated after the crucifixion to preach the faith in the four quarters of the earth. Peter, it was believed, eventually went to Rome itself, and was martyred there. Since Paul too had the same fate, the Church of Rome had both Peter and Paul as its founders. By the year 100, the new faith had penetrated into many of the eastern territories of Rome and was beginning to find a niche in the West. But it was still a small, obscure, poor sect, and only a visionary could have predicted its triumphant future.

PERSECUTIONS   Why were Peter and Paul and others martyred? If Rome could tolerate such a multitude of other sects, why not the Christians? Because, alone among the many sects, they would not sacrifice before the statue of the emperor and thus fulfill their patriotic duty as Romans. The emperor was not *their* god, and they were ready to incur the punishment of death for not worshiping him. Had they consented to perform this act, which violated the consciences of no other sect, the Christians could have carried on their own ceremonies undisturbed. But they would not, and therefore they had to conduct their services in secret. The Roman authorities suspected them of great vices: incest, murder, infanticide.

So it was natural for the emperor Nero, in A.D. 64, to punish the Christians by terrible cruelties and, as Tacitus says, to seek a scapegoat for the fire. According to tradition, Peter and Paul perished at that time. After Nero,

Christian in a Roman toga: mural from a Roman catacomb.

persecutions took place only sporadically. When Pliny the Younger, a special representative of Trajan (reigned 98–117) in Asia Minor, asked what to do about Christians, Trajan replied that Pliny should make no effort to hunt them out, but that when they were denounced they should be punished unless they denied their religion and supported that denial by worshiping the gods. Christian willingness to undergo martyrdom rather than worship the gods was regarded by most pagan Romans, including the Stoic emperor Marcus Aurelius (reigned 161–180), as a kind of exhibitionism. Marcus Aurelius persecuted the Christians both in Asia Minor and in Gaul. In the third century, as the Roman world seemed to be coming apart at the seams, persecutions became more frequent and more severe; Diocletian (reigned 284–305) was especially harsh.

The Triumph of Christianity

But the church throve on repeated martyrdoms. And by 313, Licinius and Constantine, the successors of Diocletian, agreed that the Christians would be let alone. In 312 Constantine himself had a religious experience akin to Paul's on the Damascus road: just before going into battle, the emperor saw in the heavens the sign of a cross against the sun and the words "conquer in this." He put the sign on the battle standards of his army, won the battle, and attributed the victory to the god of the Christians. Though the story has often been challenged, there is little evidence for the counterargument that Constantine acted because he simply foresaw the eventual triumph of Christianity. He continued to appease the sun god as well as the god of the Christians, but he regarded himself a Christian. Soon he found that, as the first Christian emperor, he must try to settle the severe quarrels that had broken out among Christians. A little more than half a century after Constantine's death in 337, and in spite of the celebrated attempt of the pagan emperor Julian (reigned 361–363) to turn back the clock, Christianity became the sole tolerated religion in the Roman Empire.

Why did Christianity triumph? It was at the beginning a despised sect of simple enthusiasts in a rich, well-organized, sophisticated society. Yet it took over the society. In general, we may postulate the need for a religion of love in the savage world of Rome; and in particular we have noted some of the advantages that Jesus' teachings gave Christianity over the mystery cults, which often seem to have degenerated into mere mumbo-jumbo. The cult of Isis lacked a missionary priesthood, that of Mithra any priesthood at all. Isis was chiefly for women, Mithra altogether for men. The Evangel was really "good news," with its promise of personal immortality, its admonition to behave with kindness and with love to one's fellow human beings, its lofty moral code. The Church provided a consoling and beautiful and dramatic ritual, and the opportunity to become a part of the exciting, dangerous, and thoroughly masculine task of spreading the gospel. The would-be convert could find in it ideas and rites closely related to those of Egyptians, Greeks, and Jews. It was at Ephesus, site of the shrine of the peculiar virgin mother goddess known as Diana of the Ephesians, that the quarrelsome Christian theologians of the fifth century would proclaim the Virgin Mary the mother of God.

Men will continue to debate, as they do with all major turning points in history, the causes for the triumph of Christianity and will argue over whether the primary cause was its oldness, its newness, its concept of love, or its capacity for adaptation. But scholars agree that in addition to all of these, Christianity greatly benefited from the organization that the early Christians desired for their church.

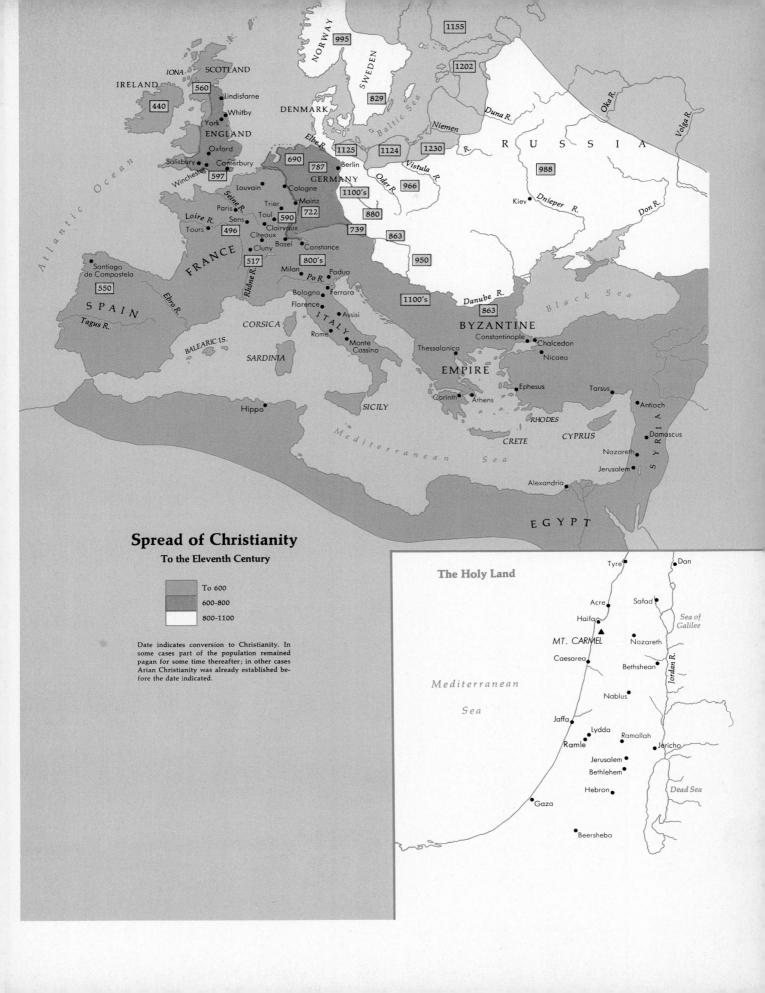

Spread of Christianity

To the Eleventh Century

	To 600
	600-800
	800-1100

Date indicates conversion to Christianity. In some cases part of the population remained pagan for some time thereafter; in other cases Arian Christianity was already established before the date indicated.

The Holy Land

ORGANIZATION OF THE CHURCH   To maintain order, the Christian community clearly needed some authority to discipline, or even oust, misbehaving individuals. It had to organize in order to survive in the midst of an empire committed in principle to its suppression. Prophets, or teachers, appeared in the very first churches, the informal groups of Christians organized by the missionaries, and soon elders, overseers and presidents followed.

More and more, the overseer (Greek *episkopos*) appeared in authority over a compact administrative area, his *see.* This was the bishop, who became the key figure in church administration. Each see claimed to have been founded by one of the original apostles; and its bishop thus held office through apostolic succession. Since it had been Christ himself who had chosen the apostles, every bishop, in effect, became a direct spiritual heir of Christ. Groups of bishoprics or episcopal sees often were gathered together into larger units, owing obedience to an archbishop, a head overseer *(archiepiskopos).* Just as the bishop often had his headquarters in a Roman *civitas,* or city-state unit, and exercised authority over the churches in the countryside roundabout, so the archbishop governed the *civitates* from a mother city, a *metropolis,* usually the capital of a Roman province, and his "see" was called a province.

At the top of the hierarchy stood the bishop of the imperial capital, Rome itself, the father of them all, *papa* or pope, who claimed supreme authority. The prestige of Rome contributed powerfully to his claim. So did the association of Peter and Paul with Rome. Christ had said to Peter, "Thou art Peter and upon this rock I will build my church," a celebrated Greek pun, since the word for Peter is *Petros* and that for rock *petra.* Because Peter had been martyred in Rome, the bishops of that city could claim that Christ himself had picked Rome as the rock upon which to build: a claim that was embodied in their "Petrine theory." The bishops of the great cities of the eastern Mediterranean, Alexandria and Antioch, however, claimed to exercise a paternal rule equal in authority to that of the pope. They called themselves patriarch (fatherly governor). Still later, after Constantinople had been made the imperial capital (A.D. 330), its bishop, also a patriarch, would oppose papal claims to supremacy.

With the departure of imperial government from Rome, the popes gradually made themselves more and more responsible for the government of the great city. And as the barbarians began to pour in and Rome itself came under attack, the pope became the symbol of the old Roman regularities and certainties, a rock indeed. A succession of outstanding men became bishop of Rome, notably Leo the Great (reigned 440–461), a theologian, a splendid administrator, and a brave man, who saved the city from the Hun, Attila. By the time of the break-up of the Roman Empire, in the fifth century, nobody in the West would have disputed the claim of papal supremacy; the papacy had emerged as the firmest institution in a new and terrible world.

The government of the Church thus exhibited important characteristics. First, it had arisen gradually, in response to need. Second, the Church strengthened its organization by utilizing the existing political machinery of the Roman Empire, placing its major officials in centers that were already administrative capitals. Third, the bishops and archbishops, meeting in councils, determined which religious ideas or practices would be accepted and which rejected, which writings were truly Christian and which false. In this way the Church selected from other writings the twenty-seven canonical books of the New Testament, written in Greek, and the Old Testament writings as preserved in a Greek translation from the Hebrew. In the Greek church today, these versions are still in use; in the Roman church, the Latin version called the Vulgate, made by Saint Jerome in the fourth century, is used. Many of the writings that the Church rejected have survived. Though not canonical, they have much interest for the modern historian and theologian.

Each individual bishop presided over several churches. Each church was under the care of a priest (Greek *presbyteros,* elder), who had been qualified by special training and by the ceremony of ordination. The area served by each church and its priest came to be known as the parish. In the early church the office of deacon, often held by a man who had other occupations besides the service of the church, had much importance. In some of the early churches, the congregation itself elected its officers, and the church was governed by boards of elders (presbyteries); but the system of appointment from above prevailed over that of election, although the congregation was often consulted. Before long, then, the distinction between those who were merely faithful worshipers (the laity) and those who conducted the worship and administered the affairs of the church (the clergy) became well defined. Despite frequent rumbles of protest during the two thousand years of Christianity, and despite differences of degree in the Christian churches, the distinction between laity and clergy is maintained in almost all.

From the time of the conversion of Constantine, the election of bishops became a matter of particular concern to the state. In order to retain the initiative, the officials of the church worked to put the election of each new bishop into the hands of the clergy of the cathedral (episcopal church) of his see. Practice remained uneven, however. Sometimes the citizens simply gave assent to an accomplished fact by approving elections; and at other times they had real power, as when Roman mobs under the sway of rival political leaders controlled the choices to the papal throne. Since bishops often exercised actual governing power and had their own law courts, lay rulers often insisted on approving or even selecting them. The problem of the degree to which laymen could participate in the choice of the bishops remained acute down into the eleventh century, as the popes strove to have the ultimate say.

This struggle, as we shall see, raged only in western Europe. In the East, for more than a thousand years, the successor of the Roman emperors at Constantinople actually wielded supreme authority over both church and state, and had the final say in the appointment of bishops.

MONASTICISM   Deacons, priests, bishops, archbishops, all serve the laity of this world, and are called *secular* clergy (Latin *saeculum,* "world"). Early in the history of the Church, however, another kind of devotee to Christianity appeared in Syria and Egypt—the monk, a man who felt that he must deny the urges of his own flesh and become an ascetic. Monks would leave civilization behind and go into the desert to live in solitude, meditation, and prayer, subsisting on the minimum of food and drink. By the third century, there were a good many of these hermits, who enjoyed reputations for extreme holiness and often competed with each other in torturing themselves or in self-denial; some lived in trees or in holes in the ground, others on the tops of columns.

To keep the extremists from using the cloak of holiness to cover un-Christian self-assertion, certain leaders, such as Saint Anthony, early collected groups of monks around themselves and formed communities, living by a rule. The Greek saint Basil (329–379) wrote the most famous of these rules, which became standard in the Greek church and still regulates Greek monasticism today. Basil prescribed celibacy and poverty but combatted the dangers of extreme asceticism by requiring that the monks work in the fields or

From a Coptic monastery in Egypt: the Virgin and saints.

elsewhere to make their communities as self-supporting as possible. Because, after Basil, monks lived by a rule, they are known as the *regular* clergy (Latin *regula,* "rule"), as contrasted with the secular clergy.

Similarly, in the West the problem was met by the rule of Saint Benedict, who founded the great abbey at Monte Cassino in southern Italy about 529. His Latin rule, like Basil's Greek rule, prescribed hard work for all and urged the monks to try to be tolerant of each other's interests and infirmities. In the West particularly, the monks broke new ground around their monasteries, acted as pioneers in opening up the wilderness, performed missionary service among the still unconverted heathen tribes, and did much charitable and medical work among the poor and the sick. In both East and West scholarship early became one of the recognized occupations for monks, and the monastic scribe, who copied the works of the ancients and built up the library of his foundation, helped preserve the literature of the past.

Tensions often arose between secular and regular clergy, each feeling that its own work was more valuable to Christianity as a whole. Constant care and strict government were needed to maintain the high ideals of the monasteries and of the convents for women that soon appeared. This continuing need prompted the successive monastic reform movements that played a major role in Christian history. The abbots of the greater monasteries often participated, along with the bishops, in the councils of the Church that helped form Christian doctrine and frame the rules of Church observance and discipline.

Heresy

The early centuries of Christianity saw a series of struggles to define the accepted doctrines of the religion—orthodoxy—and to protect them against the challenge of rival doctrinal ideas—heresy. The modern student must make a major effort of the imagination to understand how such seemingly trivial issues generated such heat. Men believed that their future salvation depended upon the proper definition and defense of religious belief and practice. In addition, bitter political, economic, and national issues often underlay disputes that took a theological form.

GNOSTICS AND MANICHAEANS   Men have always had difficulty in understanding and explaining how evil can exist (as it obviously does) in a physical world created by a good God. The Gnostics affirmed that only the world of the spirit is real (and good); the physical world is evil, or an evil illusion. Thus they could not accept the Old Testament, whose God created this world; they regarded him as a fiend or decided that this world had been created by Satan. Nor could they accept Jesus' human life and work in this world, an essential part of Christian belief. The sharp distinction that the Gnostics drew between the evil present world and the good world of the spirit is often called *dualist.* Clearly heretical, the Gnostics focused on Christ's miracle-working and on other sorts of magic. Among them there arose a sharp distinction between an elite, whose members led especially pure lives, and the ordinary flock, less able to bear self-denial or the mysteries of the faith, who usually worked hard to support the elite.

Closely related to Gnosticism were the ideas of Mani, a third-century Mesopotamian prophet who also echoed the dualistic views of the Persians and preached that the God of light and goodness and his emanations were in constant conflict with the god of darkness, evil, and matter and his emanations. These Manichaean views became immensely popular, especially along the North African shores of the Mediterranean during the third and fourth centuries. The Christians combatted them, and throughout the Middle Ages tended to label all doctrinal opposition with the term *Manichaean.* Yet the dualist ideas persisted, more or less underground, and cropped up every few decades for a thousand years and more.

DONATISTS AND ARIANS   Within Christianity itself heresy sometimes involved very practical problems. The emperor Constantine faced the so-called Donatist movement in North Africa. The movement arose because, during the Roman persecutions of the Christians, a number of priests had lacked the courage to court martyrdom and had instead handed over to the Roman authorities the sacred books. After the persecutions had come to an end, these "handers-over" *(traditores)* had resumed their role as priests. Donatus, bishop of Carthage, and his followers maintained that the sacraments administered by such a *traditor* were invalid. While one can understand Donatus' wish to punish weakling or collaborationist priests, one can also see that, once a believer suspected the validity of the sacraments as received from one priest, he might suspect it as received from any other. Amidst much bitterness and violence Constantine finally ruled that, once a priest had been properly ordained, the sacraments administered at his hands had validity even if the priest had himself acted badly.

Heresy also arose over essentially philosophical issues. Such was Arianism, named after Arius, a priest of Alexandria who early in the fourth century put forth the view that if God the Father had begotten God the Son (through God the Holy Ghost), then God the Son, as begotten, could not have exactly the same nature as God the Father but must be somehow inferior to, or dependent upon, or at least later in time than his begetter. It is difficult to refute this position on the basis of logical argument alone. But Arius' view threatened to belittle the divinity of Christ as God the Son and to separate Christ from the

Trinity. Arius' bitter opponent, Athanasius, bishop of Alexandria, fought him passionately, disdaining logic and emphasizing mystery. Athanasius and his followers maintained that Christians simply had to take it as a matter of faith that Father and Son are identical in nature and that the Son is equal to, independent of, and contemporaneous with the Father; even though the Father begat the Son, it is heresy to say that there was ever a time when the Son did not exist. In the Greek East especially, this abstract philosophical argument was fought out not only among churchmen and thinkers but in the barbershops and among the longshoremen. The fact that most people did not understand what they were talking about did not prevent their rioting against their opponents.

After trying hard to stay out of the quarrel and urging the bishops to stop discussing it, Constantine realized that it would have to be settled. He himself summoned in 325 the first council of the whole Church, a council called ecumenical (from the Greek *oikoumene*, "the inhabited world"), at Nicaea, across the straits from Constantinople. A large majority of the bishops decided in favor of the Athanasian view, which was then embodied in the famous Nicene Creed, issued with all the force of an imperial decree by Constantine himself. Having presided over the council, against his will he found himself assuming the role of head of the Church, giving legal sanction to a purely doctrinal decision and so playing the role both of caesar and of pope. This "caesaropapism," in fact, became the tradition of empire and Church in the East.

But the decree of Nicaea did not dispose of Arianism. Arians disobeyed; Constantine himself wavered; and his immediate successors on the imperial throne were Arians. Between 325 and 381, there were thirteen more councils that discussed the problem, deciding first one way, then another. One pagan historian sardonically commented that one could no longer travel on the roads because they were so cluttered up with throngs of bishops riding off to one council or another. Traces of Arianism remained in the empire for several centuries after Nicaea, and, because the missionary Ulfilas preached the Arian form of Christianity to the barbarian Goths beyond the frontiers of the empire, the heresy was spread among many Germanic peoples.

THE TWO NATURES OF CHRIST   Long before Arianism disappeared, a new and related controversy had shaken the Eastern portion of the empire to its foundations. Exactly what was the relationship of Christ the God and Christ the man? He was both man and God, but just exactly how was this possible? And was the Virgin Mary—a human woman—perhaps the mother only of his human aspect; or if not, how could a human being be the mother of God? The extreme positions were that of the dyophysites (two-nature-ites), who separated the human nature of Christ from the divine and so refused to regard the human virgin as the mother of God, and that of the monophysites (one-nature-ites), who argued that the human and divine natures were merged, but carried their thesis so far that they almost forgot Christ's human attributes and tended to make him a god only. Again the dispute flared up in physical violence in the East; again the decision hung in the balance; again the emperor (Marcian, reigned 450–457) called an ecumenical council, at Chalcedon, near Constantinople, in 451. Supported by the pope, the council condemned monophysitism and, like the Council of Nicaea, took a mystical rather than a rational decision: the true believer must believe in the two natures of Christ, human and divine, coexisting yet not distinct from each other; the Virgin is properly called the mother of God.

But like the decision at Nicaea, the decision at Chalcedon did not completely or definitively dispose of the opposition. Monophysites were concentrated in the provinces of Egypt and Syria and expressed the deep resentment of the ancient Mediterranean cities of Alexandria and Antioch against the new domination by the upstart Constantinople. So, partly because it was identified with what we would call nationalism, monophysitism did not die out, and the emperors strove to deal with it by one compromise or another. But, since there were no monophysites in the West, the Roman church regarded the issue as closed; every time an emperor at Constantinople tried to appease his Egyptian and Syrian monophysite subjects, he would be condemned by the pope for heresy. The problem remained unsolved.

The disaffection of the monophysite provinces of Syria and Egypt was to facilitate their conquest in the seventh century by the new religion of Islam. To this day there are still monophysite Christians in Egypt and Syria. The continuing quarrel illustrates the lasting political impact that theological disagreement sometimes provides.

Literature and Thought in the First Christian Centuries

Though a good deal of dislike and mutual misunderstanding had always characterized the attitudes of Greeks and Romans toward each other, Roman admiration for Greek literature and art had given its stamp to the works of Roman writers and artists. The triumph of Christianity tended to contribute, as we have seen, new sources of misunderstanding and tension to the relationships between Easterners and Westerners. The political division imposed by Diocletian and repeated by many of his successors expressed the undoubted geographic distinction between Eastern and Western provinces. As the barbarian inroads began increasingly to disrupt communications and threaten all the established institutions in the West, the opportunities for Westerners to know Greek and embrace the great classical tradition were fewer. In the Eastern provinces few except soldiers and professional administrators had ever spoken or read Latin, though it remained the official language of legislation at Constantinople down through the fifth century. Despite the growing division, however, the literature and art of the late Roman and early Christian world may be treated as a single whole.

In this period letters declined and almost disappeared in the pagan West. In the East a few passionate devotees of the old gods and opponents of Christianity still made their voices heard, notably the teachers of the nephew of Constantine, the young Julian, who became emperor in 361. In a brief reign of two years, Julian, embued with classical philosophy in its more mystical forms, tried to restore the old beliefs, reviving the sacrifices in the temples, forbidding Christians to teach, threatening new persecutions, even trying to construct a kind of hierarchy to give to the pagan faiths the efficiency of the Christian church. Julian himself wrote satirical and moralistic essays and orations on behalf of his program, which was doomed to failure, but which has always interested poets and novelists as well as scholars.

Christian letters began to take the center of the stage. In the East, many of the best writers devoted much energy to polemical writings on the burning doctrinal questions and disputes of the day. In both East and West the best minds among Christians faced the problem of how to treat the classical heritage. A few thinkers, mostly in the West and especially at first, advised against the reading of anything but Scripture, for fear of pagan error. They later came to acknowledge that one had to read the great pagans of the past in order to be able to refute pagan philosophical ideas. Still, there was always the danger that in the pleasure of reading a delightful classical author one might forget that the prime concern was to expose his errors and refute his arguments. The

Saint Jerome in His Study: a panel by Jacopo di Paolo da Bologna (1384–1426).

Greek Christians worried far less about this problem, and in the fourth century the three great Cappadocian fathers (so called from the province of Asia Minor where they were born)—Basil, author of the monastic rule; his brother, Gregory of Nyssa; and their friend, Gregory of Nazianzos—all had an excellent classical education and used the techniques of the pagan philosophers in discussing religious ideas.

Jerome, who studied with Gregory of Nazianzos, produced the Latin Bible, the Vulgate, as the climax of a life of devoted scholarship that had made him the master of Hebrew and Greek as well as Latin. Ambrose (ca. 340–397), a Roman civil servant who became bishop of Milan, wrote many theological works and commentaries, Christianizing much that he found in the classics, particularly in Cicero; he transformed Cicero's Stoic concept of duty to the state into a Christian concept of duty to God. Ambrose put his own preaching into practice when he publicly humiliated the emperor Theodosius I (reigned 379–395) and forced him to do penance for savagely punishing some rioters. The act symbolizes the Western Church's insistence that, in matters of morals and of faith, the Church would be supreme, an attitude that ran exactly counter to the practice already growing up in the East.

Augustine (354–430), the greatest of the Western church fathers and a native of North Africa, himself had been a Stoic, a Manichaean, and a Neoplatonist before he studied under Ambrose and was converted to Christianity. He then became bishop of the North African city of Hippo, and engaged in energetic controversy with heretics. He was the author of *Confessions,* a vivid and mystical autobiography, and of *The City of God,* which he wrote to refute the pagan argument that Christianity had led to the decline and the misfortunes of Rome. He easily showed that pagan empires innocent of Christianity had often fallen in the past, and he then moved far beyond the specific controversy to outline a complete Christian philosophy of history.

Augustine maintained that God's plan for humanity involved a continuing struggle between the community of those who will be saved, God's community or city, *civitas Dei,* and the community of those who reject God, the earthly community, *civitas terrena.* Ultimately, of course, the triumph of the city of God is assured; its members will be saved, while those of the earthly city will be damned. Since human history is all a preparation for the last judgment, the individual should turn his will toward God, and with the help of divine grace may so order his earthly life by decency, tolerance, trust, and discipline that he may deserve and receive heavenly citizenship hereafter. The help of the divine grace, Augustine taught, was necessary to fortify human wills (even those that had already chosen God) because original sin (inherited from Adam) had turned man away from God, and God's grace must help him to return. At times Augustine's argument led him to minimize the value of good works, or even of the sacraments, for the achieving of salvation: he came near to a belief in predestination: the belief that God has chosen in advance an elect company of men for salvation. The later church fathers did not follow Augustine, but insisted that both good works and grace were essential to salvation.

So to the Christian, although the heavenly city is the goal, his conduct and attitudes in the earthly city have the utmost importance. He must curb his pride and ambition, control his natural appetites, and avoid yielding too exclusively to the pull of family ties. This does not mean the annihilation of self in extreme asceticism, but rather the combination of control of self with love and kindness for others: all others, high and low. The Christian must love even the sinner, though not the sin. Nor may he, out of softness, attribute sin to environment or temporary influences; sin is *there,* and will be permanent in the earthly city. Nor may a Christian trust too fully the experiences of his senses alone, and try to explain all phenomena by reason and by naturalistic arguments. He must have faith, "the substance of things hoped for, the evidence of things unseen." He must not try to put himself in the place of God, who alone can "understand" the universe. Instead he must believe in God, for then he can feel that the universe is not the puzzling or hostile place it seems to men who do nothing but reason. Yet he must also strive to improve the world around him and the other human beings who live in it, in order to make the earthly city as nearly as possible resemble the city of God.

II
The Barbarian Onslaught

The Barbarians

Even the centuries of the Pax Romana were filled with combat against the barbarians on the far side of the Rhine–Danube line. Tacitus lectured his fellow Romans on the instructive contrast between their own soft degeneracy and what he regarded as the simple toughness and harshness of the Germans. His account of them, partisan though it may be, is the fullest report we have on their tribal life before their first major breakthrough to the Roman side of the frontier, which did not take place until the fourth century. In spite of Tacitus' fears, it was apparently not so much Roman decline that opened the way to the Germans as sheer pressure on the Germans from other tribes that drove them in panic to try to cross the Roman borders, by force if necessary.

Indo-European in language, like the Greeks, the Romans, and the Celts, the Germans seem to have dwelt originally along the shores of the Baltic, both on the Continent and in Scandinavia. Very early in ancient times they migrated southward. When the Romans first began to write about them, they were already divided into tribes, but had no overall political unity. One group of Germanic tribes, the Goths, had settled in what we now call Romania, on the north side of the Danube boundary, and in the adjacent plains of what is now southern Russia, the Ukraine. In the fourth century, conditions in central Asia about which we still know almost nothing precipitated a fierce Asian people known as the Huns into the territory of the Goths. Living on horseback for days, traveling swiftly, and reveling in cruelty, the Huns started a panic among the Goths and other tribes. The shock waves, beginning in the last half of the fourth century, continued throughout the fifth and into the sixth. They shattered the Roman structure in the West and left its fragments in barbarian hands. The Eastern territories suffered much less, and the imperial tradition continued uninterrupted in Constantinople.

In addition to barbarian military raids, penetrations, and conquests, there were slower and more peaceful infiltrations lasting over long periods. Moreover, before, during, and after the invasions, individual barbarians joined the Roman side, often rising to high positions defending the old empire against their fellow barbarians. The Romanized barbarian became as familiar a figure as the barbarized Roman.

VISIGOTHS, VANDALS, ANGLO-SAXONS   When the Hunnic push against them began, one tribe of Goths, the Visigoths, or West Goths, petitioned to be allowed to cross the Danube and settle in Roman territory, on the south bank, in what we would call Bulgaria. The Roman border guards took cruel advantage of their fear and hunger; and soon there were many desperate Goths milling

Bronze Irish crucifix, ca. 750.

around only a few miles from Constantinople. In the year 378, at Adrianople, the mounted Goths defeated the Roman legions of the Eastern emperor Valens, who was killed in battle. More and more Goths now freely entered the empire. Unable to take Constantinople or other fortified towns, they proceeded south into the Balkans, ravaged Greece, including Athens, and then marched north again around the head of the Adriatic and south into Italy. In 410, their chieftain Alaric sacked Rome itself, and died soon afterward. His successors led the Visigoths north across the Alps into Gaul, and then south again across the Pyrenees into Spain.

Here, in the westernmost reaches of the continental Roman Empire, after their long wanderings, the Visigoths founded a Spanish kingdom that would last until the Muslim invasions of the seventh century. In southern Gaul they had a large area (Aquitaine) given them by the Western Roman emperor Honorius (reigned 395–423), into whose family their king married; but this area they would lose in less than a century to a rival German tribe, the Franks. Since the Visigoths were Arians, they had some difficulty in ruling the orthodox Christians among their subjects.

Almost simultaneously with the Visigothic migration, another Germanic people, the Vandals, crossed the Rhine westward into Gaul and moved southward into southern Spain, where they settled in 411. The Roman governor of North Africa made the mistake of inviting them across the straits to help him in a struggle against his Roman masters. The Vandals came in 429, but soon seized North Africa for themselves. They moved eastward across modern Morocco and Algeria and established their capital at Carthage. Here they built a fleet and raided the shores of Sicily and Italy, finally sacking Rome (455) in a raid that has made "vandalism" synonymous to this day with the worst forms of violence. Like the Visigoths, the Vandals were Arian, and they, too, often persecuted the orthodox.

Under pressure on the Continent, the Romans early in the fifth century began to withdraw their legions from Britain. Into the gap thus made began to filter Germanic tribes from across the North Sea in what we would now call north Germany and Denmark. Angles, Saxons, and Jutes, coming from an area that had undergone little Roman influence, were still heathen. In England they established their authority over the Celtic Britons and soon founded seven Anglo-Saxon kingdoms, of which Northumbria and Mercia successively became the most important. Scotland and Wales remained Celtic, as of course did Ireland, which was in large measure converted to Christianity in the fifth century by Catholic missionaries from Gaul.

Ireland escaped the first great wave of barbarian invasions, and its Celtic church promoted learning, poetry, and the illumination of manuscripts such as the famous *Book of Kells,* one of the wonders of the era. By the end of the sixth century Catholic Christianity was moving into England from two directions at once: Celtic Ireland and Rome. The differences between the two were mostly matters of practice, such as the determination of the date of Easter, and, though hotly debated, these questions were eventually settled.

HUNS, OSTROGOTHS   Not only the Germanic peoples but the Asian Huns themselves participated in the onslaught on Roman territories. Emerging into Europe from the East early in the fifth century, the Huns soon conquered what we would call Romania, Hungary, and parts of Yugoslavia, Poland, and Czechoslovakia. Under their domination lived a large collection of German and other tribes, and the Hunnic rulers extracted tribute money from the Roman emperors at Constantinople. Under Attila, in the middle of the fifth

THE MAKING OF A NEW WORLD:
TO THE YEAR 1000

124

century, this savage horde pressed westward, crossed the Rhine, and met with defeat in Gaul in 451 at the hands of a Roman general in a battle usually called Châlons. Pope Leo the Great persuaded Attila to withdraw from Italy without attacking Rome.

Like many nomad empires, that of the Huns fell apart after the death of the conquering founder (453). A plague decimated their ranks, and many withdrew into Asia once more. But other related Asian peoples, nomads and pagans like the Huns, and Mongol in appearance, entered Europe before the age of the barbarian invasions was over: Avars in the sixth century, Bulgars in the sixth and seventh, and Magyars or Hungarians in the ninth, for example. The Magyars eventually set up a lasting state in the Danubian plain, and their Europeanized descendants still inhabit modern Hungary. As the first Asian invaders, the Huns had not only begun the movement of the Germanic tribes but had helped to smash Roman domination in central Europe.

Among the German tribes liberated by the collapse of the Hunnic Empire, the first to make a major impact were the Ostrogoths (East Goths). They moved into the general disorder left in Italy after the last of the Western emperors, Romulus Augustulus (the little Augustus), had been dethroned by his barbarian protector Odovacar in 476, the date often chosen for the end of the Roman Empire in the West. Actually, like his immediate predecessors, Romulus Augustulus had been an ineffectual tool of the nearest barbarian general who could command loyal troops. Roman imperial power, however, continued uninterruptedly in the East; in fact, the emperor Zeno in Constantinople had hired the Ostrogoths to intervene in Italy on his behalf against Odovacar.

The leader of the Ostrogoths, Theodoric, had been educated in Constantinople, and admired both Greek civilization and the Roman Empire as an

Early eighth-century relief of a German warrior.

institution. For most of his long rule in Italy (489–526) he was content to serve as nominal subordinate to Zeno and his successors in the East, as a kind of governor of Italy. He was also king of his own Gothic people, and established his capital at Ravenna. Like many other Christianized German tribes, the Ostrogoths were Arian. In the eyes of the popes and of the Italians, they were heretics as well as German foreigners. Although Theodoric hoped to impose upon his subjects the civilization of the empire, he did not have enough time to bring about any real assimilation. Moreover, toward the end of his reign, Theodoric, who had made dynastic marriages with the Vandal and other Germanic ruling houses, became suspicious of the empire and planned to go to war against Constantinople.

Many other barbarian peoples participated in the breakup of Roman territory and power in the West during the fifth and sixth centuries, but failed to found any lasting state. They remain mere tribal names: Sciri, Suevi, Alamanni—the German forests seem to have had an inexhaustible supply of them. There were two other German tribes, however, whose achievements we still remember: the Burgundians, who moved into the valleys of the Rhone and Saône rivers in modern France in the 440's and gave their name to a succession of "Burgundies," varying in territory and government, and the Franks, from whom modern France itself derives its name.

Destined to found the most lasting political entity of any of the Germanic tribes, the Franks appeared first as dwellers along the lower Rhine. They engaged in no long migrations, but simply expanded gradually from their native seacoast and river valleys until eventually they were to create an empire that would include most of western Europe except for the Iberian peninsula and the British Isles. Clovis (reigned 481–511), descendant of the house of Merwig or Merovech, called Merovingian, was the founder of Frankish power. He defeated successively a Roman army (486), the Alamanni (496), and the Visigoths of Aquitaine at the battle of Vouillé, in 507. Much of modern France and northwest Germany and the Low Countries thus became Frankish.

The most important factor in Clovis' success, aside from his skill as a general, was his conversion to Christianity, not as an Arian heretic but as an orthodox Catholic. This gave him the instant support of the clergy of Gaul, especially of the powerful bishops of Aquitaine, who welcomed the Franks as a relief from the Arian Visigoths. Probably the greatest liability of the Franks was their habit of dividing up the kingdom between the king's sons in every generation. This meant not only a constant parceling out of territory into petty kingdoms and lordships but constant secret intrigues and bloody rivalries among brothers and cousins and other relatives who strove to reunite the lands. Merovingian history forms one of the most sordid and savage chapters in the whole record of Western society.

By the end of the seventh century, the Merovingian kings themselves became so degenerate that they are known as *rois fainéants* (do-nothing kings). Real powers had been delegated to their chief officials, the "mayors of the palace," a title showing the close connection between household service of the monarch and actual government. By the eighth century one particular family had made this office hereditary from father to son—the Carolingians (from *Carolus,* Latin for Charles). One of the mayors, Charles (reigned 714–741), called Martel, "the hammer," organized the Frankish nobles into a dependable cavalry and in 732 near Tours defeated a roving band of Muslims that had been raiding northward from Spain. There was no real danger that the Muslims would absorb the Franks, yet since Tours was the farthest north

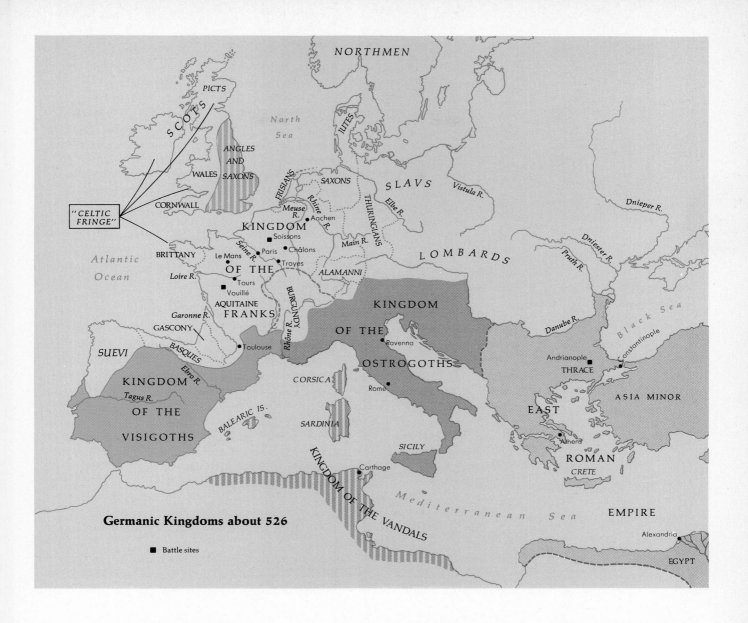

Germanic Kingdoms about 526

■ Battle sites

Map labels: NORTHMEN · PICTS · SCOTS · North Sea · JUTES · SLAVS · Vistula R. · Dnieper R. · ANGLES AND SAXONS · WALES · CORNWALL · FRISIANS · SAXONS · THURINGIANS · Elbe R. · Rhine R. · Meuse R. · Aachen · Main R. · LOMBARDS · Dniester R. · "CELTIC FRINGE" · KINGDOM OF THE · Soissons · Châlons · ALAMANNI · Pruth R. · BRITTANY · Seine R. · Paris · Troyes · Le Mans · FRANKS · Loire R. · Tours · Vouillé · BURGUNDY · KINGDOM · Danube R. · Black Sea · Constantinople · Atlantic Ocean · AQUITAINE · Rhône R. · OF THE · Ravenna · Andrianople · THRACE · Garonne R. · GASCONY · Toulouse · OSTROGOTHS · EAST · ASIA MINOR · SUEVI · BASQUES · Ebro R. · CORSICA · Rome · KINGDOM · Tagus R. · OF THE · SARDINIA · ROMAN · Athens · CRETE · VISIGOTHS · BALEARIC IS. · SICILY · KINGDOM OF THE VANDALS · Carthage · Mediterranean Sea · EMPIRE · Alexandria · EGYPT

in Europe that the Muslims ever came, the battle is a landmark in Western history. Charles Martel's son, Pepin the Short (reigned 741–768), assumed the title of "king of the Franks" and consolidated the kingdom once again. Pepin's adventurous policy with regard to Italy initiated a whole new chapter in Western history.

ITALY FROM THEODORIC TO PEPIN   Soon after the death of Theodoric, the great emperor Justinian launched from Constantinople an ambitious effort to reconquer the major areas of the West that had been lost to the barbarians. The imperial forces overthrew the Vandals first, and then, before consolidating the reconquest of North Africa, invaded Italy from Carthage, via Sicily. For almost twenty years (535–554) savage and destructive warfare ravaged the peninsula, as Justinian's troops fought the Ostrogoths. The towns and countryside of Italy were depopulated, and the survivors reduced to misery. Justinian's proclamation of an imperial restoration (554) was hollow. In the same year, imperial forces took a portion of southern Spain from the Visigoths.

THE MAKING OF A NEW WORLD:
TO THE YEAR 1000

Only three years after Justinian's death, a new Germanic tribe, the Arian Lombards, entered Italy (568) from the north. They easily conquered the north Italian plain that still bears their name (Lombardy), and established a kingdom with its capital at Pavia. Further to the south, they set up two duchies (Benevento and Spoleto). Italy lay once again in fragments. Still under imperial domination were the capital of Ravenna and territory surrounding it, the island settlement of Venice, Rome, Naples, and the toe and heel of the peninsula, as well as Sicily. The emperor at Constantinople appointed a governor called the exarch who had headquarters at Ravenna and was particularly charged with organizing the defense of Italy.

But Constantinople was far away; dangers threatened the emperors from the East, and they often could not afford to pay much attention to Italy's needs or send money and troops to help the exarchs fight the Lombards. In this situation, the Church emerged more and more as the protector of the Catholic population, the bishops often receiving privileges from the Arian Lombard conquerors that conferred upon them virtual governing rights in the towns. Among the bishops, the pope of course took the lead, and, among the popes, the most remarkable in every way was Gregory I, the Great (reigned 590–604).

Child of a rich and aristocratic Roman family, Gregory abandoned worldly things and became a monk and founder of monasteries. His administrative talents were extraordinary: he served as papal ambassador to the court at Constantinople before becoming pope, against his will, in 590. Besides his religious duties, he had to take virtually full responsibility for maintaining the fortifications of Rome, for feeding its population, for managing the great financial resources of the Church and its lands in Italy, for conducting diplomatic negotiations with exarchate and Lombards, and even for directing military operations. It was he who sent the mission to Britain (596) that began the conversion of the Anglo-Saxons. Gregory had an exalted conception of papal power, and stoutly defended its supremacy over the Church in his letters to the emperor and to the patriarch at Constantinople.

During the seventh and early eighth centuries the alienation between the empire in the East and the papacy was greatly increased by religious disagreements and a related political and economic dispute. And simultaneously, the Lombards gradually consolidated and expanded their power, taking Ravenna in 751 and putting an end to the exarchate. Menaced by the Lombards and unable to count on help from Constantinople, Pope Stephen II in 753 paid a visit to King Pepin of the Franks.

In exchange for papal approval of his title of king, Pepin attacked the Lombards and forced them to abandon Ravenna and other recent conquests. Then he gave these lands to the pope, as the celebrated "Donation of Pepin." Of course the lands did not belong to Pepin but to the emperor at Constantinople, but this did not prevent Pepin's disposing of them. Together with Rome itself and the lands immediately around it, the Donation of Pepin formed the territory over which the pope ruled as temporal sovereign down to the nineteenth century. These were the Papal States, and Vatican City is their present-day remnant. Pepin's son, Charles the Great (Charlemagne), finished off the Lombard kingdom in 774 and assumed the Iron Crown of Lombardy.

From the papal point of view, the new alliance with the Franks marked the end of dependence upon the empire and the beginning of the papacy as a temporal power. The Franks, too busy to take over these Italian lands themselves and no doubt also aware of the pious responsibilities that they had acquired when they became the protectors of the Church, did not try to dominate the popes. Soon after Pepin's donation, the clerks of the papal chancery forged "proof" that Pepin had only been confirming a gift of lands to the Church made long ago by the emperor Constantine. The forgery stated, in addition, that Constantine directly declared that the papal power, as divine, was superior to his own imperial power, which was only earthly; that the see of Peter should rule over the other sees (including Antioch, Alexandria, Constantinople); and that the pope alone should rule in questions of faith. For about seven hundred years, until the Italian Renaissance scholar Lorenzo Valla (see Chapter 6) proved it a forgery, men believed that this extraordinary document was genuine.

CHARLEMAGNE AND HIS SUCCESSORS   Pepin's son, Charlemagne (768–814)—so his contemporary biographer tells us—was a vigorous, lusty, intelligent man who loved hunting, women, and war. All his life he wore Frankish costume and thought of himself as a Frankish chieftain. Although he kept pen and ink under his pillow, he could never teach himself how to write. He spoke Latin, however, and understood some Greek. He sought to iron out the conflicts between two codes of law that governed his people but had to leave this project unfinished. A great conqueror, Charlemagne turned his armies east and crossed the Rhine. In campaigns lasting more than thirty years, he conquered the heathen Saxons living south of Denmark, and converted them at sword's point to Christianity. Monks and priests followed his armies.

Charlemagne made the first successful invasion of Germany. This spawning ground of the barbarians who had shattered Roman society in the West then began the long, slow process of assimilation to Western civilization. In addition to the lands of the Saxons, Charlemagne added to his domain the western areas of modern Czechoslovakia (Bohemia), much of Austria, and portions of Hungary and Yugoslavia; the eastern boundaries of his realm reached the Elbe River in the north, and the Danube, where it turns sharply south below Vienna. Along these wild eastern frontiers he established provinces (marks or marches). His advance into eastern Europe brought him victories also over the Asian Avars, successors to the Huns along the lower Danube. Far to the west, Charlemagne challenged Muslim power in Spain and set up a Spanish march in what is today Catalonia. A defeat of his rear guard at the pass of Roncesvalles in the Pyrenees in 778 formed the theme of the heroic epic *The Song of Roland (Chanson de Roland),* composed several centuries later.

By the end of the eighth century, Charlemagne had reunited under Frankish rule all of the Western Roman provinces except for Britain, most of Spain, south Italy, Sicily, and North Africa, and had added to his domains central and eastern European areas that the Romans had never possessed. On Christmas Day 800 the pope himself, Leo III, crowned Charlemagne emperor in Rome. So mighty was the tradition of Roman empire and so great its hold on the minds of men that, more than three centuries after the disappearance of Romulus Augustulus, last of the Western emperors, the chief bishop of the Christian church, seeking to honor and recognize his mighty Frankish patron, automatically crowned him emperor of Rome. Even before the coronation a poet in Charlemagne's own circle had hailed him as "Augustus."

It is quite possible that Charlemagne himself was surprised and not altogether pleased by the coronation; he probably relished his title, but he almost surely disliked the role played by the pope and the implication that the pope had the right to choose and crown emperors. The true successors of Augustus, the Roman emperors at Constantinople, were horrified at the insolence of the barbarian Charlemagne in assuming the sacred title.

Detail of a fourteenth-century reliquary bust of Charlemagne.

THE MAKING OF A NEW WORLD:
TO THE YEAR 1000

Within his territories Charlemagne was, by virtue of his consecration, a sacred ruler, with spiritual rights and duties as well as temporal ones. His lofty concept of his office and his personal power enabled him to govern the Church—even in matters of doctrine—more in the style of Constantine or other Eastern emperors than any other Western monarch. He himself named Louis the Pious, by then his only living son, his successor in 813; the pope had no part in the ceremonies.

Charlemagne's government was very simple: it was only the accidental deaths of his other sons that prevented a standard Frankish division of the heritage. The king's personal household staff were also the government officials: the chamberlain, the count of the stable (constable), and so on. On major decisions the emperor conferred with great nobles of state and church, but he told them what he (and they) were going to do rather than asking them for advice and permission. Since the Franks, like other Germans, believed that law *existed* and could not be made by men, even Charlemagne could not in theory legislate. But he did issue instructions to his subjects, divided into subheadings or chapters and therefore called *capitularies,* which usually dealt with special administrative problems. It was a highly personal rule.

Charlemagne's territories included about three hundred counties, each governed by a count, those in former Roman territory corresponding to the lands of a civitas. The count had to maintain order, render justice, and recruit and command soldiers. Alongside the count, the bishop of the diocese and the various local magnates might have considerable powers of their own on their own lands. Only a powerful king could keep the local authorities from arrogating too much power to themselves. Charlemagne required his counts to appoint teams of judges, called *scabini,* whose appointment he would then ratify, and who would actually take over much of the count's role in rendering justice. He also sent out from his own central administrative staff pairs of royal emissaries (the *missi dominici*), usually a layman and a cleric, to investigate local conditions and correct abuses. As representatives of the emperor, they could overrule the count.

The Carolingian Empire depended too much upon Charlemagne personally; he had assembled more territory than could be effectively governed, in view of the degeneration of administrative machinery and of communication since Roman days. Under his less talented successors, the old Frankish habit of dividing up lands and authority among the heirs to the throne reasserted itself. Quarrels over the allotment of territory raged among brothers and cousins. The title of emperor descended to a single heir in each generation, but as early as the middle of the ninth century it had become an empty honor.

One episode in the struggle among Charlemagne's grandsons deserves special notice: the Strasbourg Oaths of 842. Two of the grandsons, Charles the Bald and Louis the German, swore an alliance against their brother, the emperor Lothair. Each swore in the language of the other's troops: Louis in a Latin-like language on its way to becoming French, which scholars call Romance, and Charles in Germanic. Of course this does not mean that there was a France or a Germany in 842: only that the western and eastern Frankish lands spoke divergent tongues. But the symbolism is a striking sign of things to come in European history. Charles and Louis could hardly have chosen a more appropriate place than Strasbourg—center of Alsace, a bone of contention between modern France and Germany—to swear their bilingual oath. In the ninth century, however, there were as yet no national states in Europe. Indeed, instead of coalescing into large national units, the Frankish dominions were even then in the process of breaking up into much smaller ones. As the

SCANDINAVIA

North Sea

Baltic Sea

Oder R.

Elbe R.

**Partition of the Empire
by the Treaty of Verdun, 843**

KINGDOM
OF CHARLES
THE BALD

KINGDOM
OF LOTHAIR

KINGDOM
OF LOUIS

IRELAND

SCOTLAND

NORTHUMBRIA

Whitby

KINGDOM
OF DENMARK

ANGLO-SAXON
KINGDOMS

WALES

MERCIA

EAST
ANGLIA

CORNWALL

WESSEX

ESSEX

SUSSEX KENT

London

Canterbury

SAXONS

Cologne

Aachen

Rhine R.

Elbe R.

BOHEMIA

BRITTANY

Seine R.

Soissons

Verdun

Paris

Strasbourg

Danube R.

MORAVIA

S L A V S

Loire R.

Fontenoy

Poitiers

Besançon

BAVARIA

CARINTHIA

PANNONIAN
MARCH

A V A R S

AQUITAINE

Geneva

Lyons

MARCH
OF FRIULI

Drava R.

Rhône R.

BURGUNDY

LOMBARDY

Po R.

Venice

Pavia

Ravenna

Danube R.

BULGARS

SPANISH MARCH

Roncesvalles

Arles

Marseilles

Ebro R.

DONATION

OF

PEPIN

Rome

CROATS

Spalato

SLAVIC PEOPLES

Adriatic Sea

THRACE

Constantinople

EMIRATE
OF
CORDOVA

Barcelona

Thessalonica

CORSICA

Monte Cassino

Naples

DUCHY
OF
BENEVENTO

BALEARIC IS.

SARDINIA

B Y Z A N T I N E

E M P I R E

Carolingian Empire

Kingdom of Charlemagne, 768

Acquired by Charlemagne to 814

Areas tributary to Charlemagne's empire

Byzantine Empire

■ Battle sites

SICILY

Mediterranean Sea

CRETE

power of the central Frankish state was frittered away in family squabbles, smaller entities, duchies or counties, emerged as virtually autonomous units of government, many with names we still recognize as belonging to provinces of modern France or Germany: Champagne, Brittany, Saxony, Bavaria.

Charlemagne's conquests in Germany had for the first time brought into the area of Western civilization the breeding ground of many of the barbarians. Still outside lay Scandinavia, from whose shores there began in the ninth century a new wave of barbarian invasions that hit Britain and the western parts of the Frankish lands with savage force. The Northmen conducted their raids from small ships that could easily sail up the Thames, the Seine, or the Loire. Their appetite for booty grew with their successes, and soon they organized fleets of several hundred ships, ventured further abroad, and often wintered along a conquered coast. They ranged as far south as Spain, penetrated into the Mediterranean through the Straits of Gibraltar, and raided Italy. To the west they proceeded far beyond Ireland, and reached Iceland and Greenland. Some possibly reached as far as Canada or New England, although scholars still debate the validity of the scanty evidence we have of this.

The longing for booty may not by itself account for the Norse invasions. Polygamy was common among the upper classes of the pagan Scandinavians (the lower ones could not afford it), and it is probable that the younger sons of these Viking chiefs either had to leave home or stop living in the style to which they had grown accustomed. This possible cause for the Norse expansion is suggested by the fact that even after the Vikings had conquered their first European base of settlement, the younger sons continued to go abroad to plunder and to settle.

Their first captured base was the region along the lower Seine River, which is still called Normandy after these Northmen. In 911, the Frankish king was forced to grant the Norse leader Rolf (or Rollo) a permanent right of settlement. The Normans became an efficient and powerful ruling class—in fact, the best administrators of the new "feudal" age. From Normandy soon after the year 1000 younger sons went off to found a flourishing state in the south Italian and Sicilian territories that still belonged to the Eastern Roman Empire. From Normandy in 1066 Duke William and his followers conquered England.

Kinsmen of these Norsemen who had settled in Normandy also did great deeds. In the 860's the first wave of Viking invaders crossed the Baltic Sea to the territory that is now Russia, and penetrated deep inland to the south along the river valleys. They conquered the indigenous Slavic tribes, and, at Kiev on the middle Dnieper, consolidated the first Russian state.

While the Normans were raiding and developing Normandy, the Danes were almost paralleling their achievements in the British Isles. They seized the Irish ports and coasts; the Celtic inhabitants fought back fiercely and eventually assimilated the Danes, but the brilliance of Irish culture had suffered a fatal interruption. In England, too, the savage Danish attacks on the northern and eastern shores soon led to settlement. The chief organizer of defense against the Danes was the Anglo-Saxon kingdom of Wessex under Alfred the Great (871–899). Although Alfred finally defeated the Danes, he was not strong enough to expel them, and had to concede the whole northeast of England to them, a region thereafter called the Danelaw.

Far more advanced at this stage than the Danes, the Anglo-Saxon kingdom was governed through the royal household and clerical staff. The king's great council, the *witenagemot,* made up of important landholders, churchmen, and officials, advised him when he asked for advice, acted as a court, and elected

An early tenth-century Irish sculptured cross, "the Muire-adach Cross."

and deposed kings. The king could count on revenue from his own estates, and also from a special tax imposed for defense against the Danes, called the Danegeld. He also received two-thirds of all the fines imposed by local courts. His army was still the old Germanic host *(fyrd),* in which every landholder was obliged to serve, but he also had additional household troops. Anglo-Saxon institutions in the tenth century were not very different from those of the Franks before Charlemagne or those of any settled Germanic tribe.

Soon after the turn of the eleventh century, new waves of Danes scored important successes under the command of Canute (Knut), the king of Denmark. In 1016 Canute was chosen king of England by the Anglo-Saxon witenagemot. Able ruler of a kind of northern empire (he was also king of Norway), Canute allied himself with the Roman church, and brought Scandinavia into the Christian community. His early death (1035) without competent heirs led to the breakup of his holdings, and England reverted to a king of the house of Alfred (Edward the Confessor). The work of Canute in England, though it did not last, belongs with that of the Normans and, in Russia, of the Norsemen, as an example of the political and administrative ability so widely demonstrated by the Scandinavians once they had settled down.

Carolingian Decline

By the end of the ninth century, the power of the Carolingians in their German territories had frittered away in the face of domestic challenge by ambitious local magnates and foreign threats from Norsemen, Slavs, and the Asian Magyars, who poured into the Hungarian plain in the mid-890's. When the last nominal Carolingian ruler, Louis the Child, died in 911, the German magnates elected the duke of Franconia as King Conrad I (reigned 911–918). The most important units in Germany became the duchies—Franconia, Saxony, Swabia, and Bavaria—each under its autonomous ruler. Conrad I failed to control either the other dukes or the Magyars and finally nominated his strongest enemy, Henry, duke of Saxony, to succeed him. Henry's son, Otto I (936–973), both checked the rival dukes and, at the battle of the Lechfeld, 955, defeated the Magyars.

Master of his German territories, Otto next sought to revive the title of emperor, which had passed from one shadowy Carolingian prince to another until it lapsed in 924. Deep in decline after the reign of the great pope Nicholas I (858–867), the papacy had fallen into the hands of rival Roman noble families, corrupt, wicked, and ineffectual. Without strong central administration and under attack from Muslims and Magyars, Italy had become anarchic. Yet Rome, even at its lowest depths in the mid-tenth century, continued to act as an irresistible magnet for those seeking supreme power. Like Charlemagne almost two hundred years before him, Otto went to Italy. He had himself crowned by the degenerate and dissipated Pope John XII (962), then had John deposed for murder and installed his own candidate on the papal throne. He forced the Roman aristocracy to promise that imperial consent would hereafter be necessary to papal elections, and renewed the Donation of Pepin and the subsequent grants of the Carolingians to the papacy. Though the papacy for the next hundred years was hardly more than an instrument manipulated by Otto's German successors, Otto's action ensured the continuity of the papacy as an independent institution; it also tightly linked the political fortunes of Germany and Italy for centuries to come.

In the western Frankish lands, which we may now call France, Carolingian partitioning, strife, and feebleness led to the fragmentation of both territory and power among ambitious landowners. As early as 887 one faction of these magnates chose a non-Carolingian, Odo, count of Paris, as king, and civil war between him and the Carolingian claimant added to the chaos. For the next century the families of the two rivals alternated in power. Finally, in 987 the magnates elected as king a descendant of the early count of Paris, Hugh Capet, who founded the dynasty that would last almost to our own time. (When Louis XVI went to the guillotine in 1793, his executioners called him Citizen Capet.) In 987, however, several of the nobles who chose Hugh were actually more powerful than he.

Europe about 1000

About the year 1000, then, England was a centralized monarchy; France was nominally ruled by an elected king who was feebler than his great supporters; Germany was divided into duchies, one of which had asserted its supremacy and claimed the old imperial title; and Italy still remained anarchic, but a revived papacy had begun to emerge. Out of the debris of the Roman Empire, buffeted by two waves of barbarian invasions and held together only by their common Christian faith, these major fragments had begun to take on, even as early as this, certain features that we can still recognize today. Elsewhere, the Scandinavian kingdoms had imposed order on the turbulent peoples who had made the Viking expansion, and the little Christian kingdoms in the north of Spain were only beginning their struggle with the Muslim tide that had engulfed the peninsula.

In the East, the empire, with its direct descent from Rome and its Greco-Oriental character, still stood firm at Constantinople after many shocks. It had started its work of Christianizing those Slavic peoples nearest to it—the Bulgarians, the Russians, the Serbs. The western Slavs—Czechs, Poles, Croats, and others—and the Magyars, lying between the Germans and the influences radiating from Constantinople, had received the attention of Roman missionaries. By the year 1000 there was already visible a fateful line of demarcation between the Western Catholic world and the Eastern Orthodox world, with its different alphabet and its different outlook.

III
Feudal Europe

Historians have long referred to the centuries between the fifth and the fifteenth as the Middle Ages (or medieval)—that portion of man's history in the West that lies between ancient and modern. The half-millennium we have begun reviewing—roughly between 500 and 1000, the early Middle Ages—is often called the Dark Ages. Scholars no longer maintain, as they once did, that the period represents the debasement of high human values and thus spiritual darkness, but it is true that our sources are so scanty that we remain at least partly in the dark as to what happened and how we are to interpret it. Yet we can discern in the Dark Ages elements in human institutions surviving from Roman times, together with innovations introduced by the barbarians and changes linked with conversion to Christianity. The settled inhabitants of western Europe and the invaders underwent a long period of slow mutual adjustment, as new and old ways of regulating human affairs competed and often combined with each other.

Feudalism: The Rulers

To these widely varied social and political combinations scholars give the name *feudalism*. Feudal institutions were the arrangements—personal, territorial, and governmental—between persons that made survival possible under the conditions that obtained in western Europe during the Dark Ages. The arrangements were made between important people who were concerned with maintaining order; feudal institutions involved the governors—the upper classes, both laymen and clerics—not the masses of the population. Because central authority was no longer able to maintain itself locally, local authority had to be improvised to replace it. But because the processes and their results were anything but systematic, we do not use or recommend the outmoded term *feudal system.*

One of the most influential arrangements between persons was the war band of the early Germans, the *comitatus,* as Tacitus called it in Latin—the leader commanded the loyalty of his followers, who banded together for fighting and winning of booty. All the Germanic barbarians appear to have had this institution; the Anglo-Saxon word for its chieftain, *hlaford,* is the origin of our word *lord.* In the Roman provinces, too, local landowners had often built their own private armies, while in Rome itself the magnates had their groups of *clients,* to whom they acted as *patron* and gave legal protection. When a humble man wanted to enter the client relationship, he asked for the *patrocinium* of the great man and secured it by performing the act of *commendation,* commending or entrusting himself to the patron. He remained free, but obtained food and clothing in exchange for his services, whatever they might be. If the man was of the upper classes, he was called *fidelis.* By the Carolingian period, the term *vassus,* originally denoting a man of menial status, had come to mean a man who rendered military service to his patron, or lord. Vassalage meant no disgrace; it was the status gained by the act of commendation. So a combination of old Germanic and old Roman practices contributed to new relationships described in new terms.

With regard to land, a Roman patron sometimes had retained the title to a piece of property but granted a client the temporary use of it, together with the profits to be derived from it so long as he held it, often for life. The Romans used the term *precarium* for this kind of tenure, and the Carolingian rulers commonly adopted the old practice—sometimes using the old Roman term, sometimes the newer *beneficium,* benefice, to describe the land temporarily held by the vassal in exchange for service. By the year 1000 the act of becoming a vassal usually meant that a man got a benefice; indeed he might refuse faithful service or loyalty unless he were satisfied with the land he received. The feeble later Carolingians and their rivals outbid each other in giving benefices to their supporters in order to obtain armed support and service. This was one of the practices that depleted the royal estates.

In the later Carolingian period, the benefice came to be called *feudum,* a fief, the term that has given us the words *feudal* and *feudalism.* As it became a fief, the benefice also became hereditary: though title to it remained with the lord who granted it, the fief itself passed, on the death of a vassal, to the vassal's heir, along with the vassal's obligations to serve the lord and his heirs.

The man who received a fief often got with it certain governmental rights over the farmers who lived and worked on the lands that made it up. This practice too had its precedents: in late Roman times, the emperors often granted an *immunity* to their own estates, an understanding that the people who lived on these lands would not be visited by imperial tax collectors or other law-enforcing officials. Because the immunity exempted the inhabitants from onerous duties, it was hoped that the farmers would enjoy their privileged status and therefore stay put and supply the emperor with needed produce. The Frankish kings adopted this practice, sometimes extending it to lands of the Church and even to those of private proprietors. By the tenth century the immunity meant that the king undertook to keep his officials off the privileged lands, and that the holder of the lands would perform such governmental functions as collecting taxes, establishing police arrangements, and setting up a court, of which he might keep the profits.

From late Roman times, too, came the local offices of duke and count; originally military commanders, they took over increasing civil authority as the power of the central government relaxed. In Frankish times they might be very powerful rulers, kings in all but name. In the disorders of the Carolingian decline, these offices gradually became hereditary; at the same time, the dukes and counts became the vassals of the Carolingians. So the title and office, the duties of the vassal, and the fief (or territory of the office) all became hereditary.

VASSALS AND LORDS   Feudalism and feudal practice did not extend uniformly over all of Europe. Northern France and the Low Countires were the most thoroughly feudalized areas, Germany perhaps the least. Everywhere some pieces of land never became fiefs, but remained the fully owned private property of the owners; these were called *allods*. Feudal practices varied from place to place, and they developed and altered with the passage of time. But certain general conceptions were held pretty much everywhere.

One of the most significant was that of contract: the lord—or *suzerain,* as he was often called—owed something to the vassal just as the vassal owed something to the lord. When they entered upon their relationship the vassal rendered homage to his lord and promised him aid and counsel. That is, he would appear, fully armed, and participate as a knight in the lord's wars (subject perhaps to limits on the number of days' service owed in any one year); and would join with his fellow vassals—his "peers," or social equals— to form the lord's court that alone could pass judgment on any one of them. He might also be required at his own expense to entertain his lord for a visit of specific length, and to give him money payments on special occasions—the marriage of the lord's eldest daughter, the knighting of his eldest son, or his departure on a crusade. The vassal also swore fealty (fidelity) to his lord. And the lord was understood to owe, in his turn, protection and justice to his vassal.

If the vassal broke this contract, the lord would have to get the approval of the court made up of the vassal's peers before he could proceed to punishments such as forfeiture, depriving the vassal of his fief. If the lord broke the contract, the vassal was expected to withdraw his homage and fealty in a public act of defiance before proceeding to open rebellion. Sometimes the contract was written, sometimes it was oral. Sometimes the ceremony included a formal investiture by the lord: he would give his kneeling vassal a symbol of the fief that was being transferred to him, a twig or a bit of earth. When lord or vassal died, the contract had to be renewed with his successor. The son of a vassal, upon succeeding to his father's fief, often had to pay relief, a special, and often heavy, cash payment like a modern inheritance tax. If the vassal died without heirs, the fief would escheat, or revert to the lord, who could bestow it on another vassal or not as he saw fit. If the heir was still a minor, the lord exercised the right of wardship or guardianship until he came of age; this meant that the lord received the revenues from the fief, and if he was unscrupulous he could milk it dry.

Within a feudal kingdom, the king occupied the top position in a theoretical pyramid of society. Immediately below him would be his vassals, men who held fiefs directly from the king, called tenants-in-chief. But they in turn would be feudal lords: that is, they would have given out various parts of their own property as fiefs to their own vassals. These men, the king's vassals' vassals, would be the king's "rear vassals," and so at the next lower level of the theoretical pyramid. But they too would often have vassals, and so on, for many more levels—a process called *subinfeudation*.

Practice was more complicated still. A tenant-in-chief might hold only a very small fief from the king and not be a very important person at all, while a vassal's vassal's vassal might be rich and powerful. The dukes of Normandy, who were vassals to the king of France, were for some centuries much stronger than their overlord. An individual might receive fiefs from more than one lord, and so would be vassal to more than one lord, owing homage and fealty to both. What was he to do if one of his lords quarreled with another and went to war? To which one would he owe priority? This kind of thing happened very often: one Bavarian count had twenty different fiefs held of twenty different lords. Gradually, there arose a new concept, that of a *liege* lord, the one to whom a vassal owed service ahead of any other; but in practice the difficulties often persisted. Even though feudal law became more and more subtle and complex, this was an era when the force of arms counted for more than legality.

MANORIALISM   All the complicated arrangements we have been discussing directly involved only the governing persons who fought on horseback as mounted knights and whose fiefs consisted of landed property known as manors or estates. Even if we include their dependents, the total would hardly reach 10 percent of the population of Europe. Most of the other 90 percent of the people worked the land. In late Roman times, the large estate, owned by a magnate and worked by tenant farmers, was called a *latifundium*. The tenant farmers or *coloni* were often descendants of small landowners who had turned over their holdings to the magnate in exchange for a guarantee of protection and a percentage of the crop. While the coloni were personally free, not slaves, they could not leave the ground they cultivated, nor could their children.

If the coloni lived in groups of houses close together, the latifundium could be described as a *villa.* Though conditions varied widely, we shall not be far wrong if we think of the late Roman latifundium becoming the medieval manor, the late Roman villa becoming the medieval village, and the late Roman coloni becoming the medieval serfs. As we shall see, the early German village community also contributed to the new social structure. While the Roman landed estate had often produced its food for sale at a profit in the town and city, the long centuries of disorder beginning with the barbarian invasions led to a decline of commerce, of cities, and of agriculture for profit. The medieval manor usually produced only what was needed to feed its own population.

The oldest method of cultivation was the two-field system, alternating crops and fallow so that fertility could be recovered. Later, especially in grain-producing areas, a three-field system was devised—one field for spring planting, one for autumn planting, and the third lying fallow. Originally, oxen pulled the plow, but the invention of the horse collar (so that the horse would not strangle on the old-fashioned strap around his neck) and the use of horseshoes (which allowed the horse to plow stony soil that hurt the oxen's feet) helped make it possible to substitute horses for oxen. So did the increasing use of tandem harnessing, enabling the horses to work in single file instead of side by side. A heavy-wheeled plow made its appearance in advanced areas.

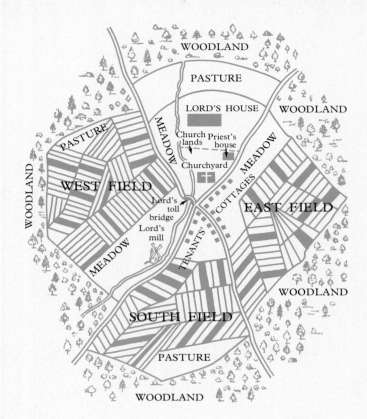

The following labels appear on the manor plan:

WOODLAND

PASTURE

LORD'S HOUSE

WOODLAND

PASTURE

Church lands — Priest's house

WOODLAND

MEADOW

Churchyard

WEST FIELD

MEADOW

COTTAGES

EAST FIELD

Lord's toll bridge

Lord's mill

TENANTS'

MEADOW

WOODLAND

SOUTH FIELD

WOODLAND

PASTURE

WOODLAND

Plan of a medieval manor; the solid strips are the lord's demesne.

The pattern of agricultural settlement varied from region to region. But so far as a typical manor existed, each of its peasant families had holdings, usually in the form of scattered long strips, in the big open fields. In theory this gave each family a bit of good arable land, a bit of the less good land, a bit of woodland, and so on. The strips might be separated from each other by narrow, unplowed *balks,* but there were no fences, walls, or hedges. The lord of the manor had his own strips, his *demesne* (perhaps a quarter to a third of the land), reserved for the production of the food that he and his household needed. The peasants had to work this land for the lord, often three days a week throughout the year, except perhaps in harvest time, when the lord could have exclusive call on their services until his crops were safely in the barns.

In exchange for permission to pasture their beasts in the lord's meadows, the peasants performed other duties. They paid to have their grain ground at the lord's mill and their bread baked in his oven. They often had to dig ditches or maintain the roads. They could not marry or allow their daughters to marry outside the manor without the lord's permission and usually the payment of a fine. They were bound to the soil, a hereditary caste of farm laborers, serfs. But they were not slaves; the lord could not sell them; they and their children descended with the land to the lord's heirs. On such a manor the peasants would live in a cluster of houses close together. A big manor might have several such villages, with perhaps isolated farmsteads in addition. On the other hand, a single village might lie partly in one manor and partly in another belonging to a different lord.

The organization of the countryside by manors was earliest developed in eastern France and in parts of Italy and Germany. Even at its height, it did not include some parts of these and other European countries. But in the large areas where manorialism did prevail, the old Roman landlord's economic power over his tenants had fused with the traditional Germanic village chief's political power, and, by the eleventh century, with the governing rights that the lord received with his fief. The deep respect for custom tended to prevent the lord's extorting from his peasants more work or more food than they traditionally owed him; but they had no rights, and nowhere to appeal in cases where the lord was oppressive. Custom prevailed in the lord's court, when he or his steward sat in judgment on the tenants, enforcing the traditional rules of the village community. Custom regulated the bargaining agreements reached among the peasants for the use in common of plows and plowteams. Custom no doubt retarded inventiveness and stifled initiative, but it was the only thing that gave a serf the sense that he was protected against exactions and cruelties.

The Civilization of the Early Middle Ages in the West

The achievements of the West in letters and the arts during the centuries of the barbarian onslaught were feeble indeed by comparison with those of Greek, Hellenistic, or Roman civilizations, or indeed with those of the contemporary eastern Mediterranean world, Christian and Muslim. This is exactly what one would expect in a new world where the masters usually did not have the taste or the judgment to patronize writers or artists, and where life was too turbulent to give men much leisure for the exercise of creativity. Communications became far more precarious than in the Greco-Roman world, as roads and the postal system deteriorated and sea transport became more uncertain. Cities—centers of culture and of the commerce that made culture possible—subsided into ruined shells of their former splendor. Technical skills were lost—the art of sculpture, for example, as the celebrated realism of the ancients gave way to something so crude in the representation of the human body that one finds it hard to believe that men deliberately carved in that style because they wanted to be symbolic. Lost too was the command over language: nobody spoke good Latin any more, and few could write it, and the slowly developing vernacular tongues—the Romance-French or the proto-German—were not yet used in a literary way.

Yet many barbarians loved and admired the Roman world that their fellow barbarians were engaged in destroying, and some made a conscious effort to keep alive the Roman literary and artistic tradition. Moreover, the invading tribesmen brought with them art forms of their own—in poetry, sculpture, and painting—that have only recently begun to win the appreciation they deserve. In the cultural realm, as in the realm of institutions, one finds an amalgam, a new combination of old elements. We shall meet no Homer, no Vergil, no Phidias in these centuries, but the writers and artists—many of them anonymous—living under different pressures and expressing themselves in different ways—deserve our study and our admiration.

WRITING IN LATIN   In Italy, where under the rule of the Ostrogothic king Theodoric the fight against the loss of the classical heritage was waged most vigorously, two distinguished intellectuals emerged as its leaders: Boethius and Cassiodorus. Boethius (ca. 480–524), unlike most of his contemporaries, knew Greek as well as Latin. He was an authority on mechanics and on music, and he held high political office. He planned a Latin translation of Plato and Aristotle, which was the first effort among Christian thinkers to use Aristotle's logical methods in dealing with Christian theology. And he wrote original works on the art of argument. These labors would serve as inspiration not to the men of his own times, most of whom had little interest or ability in philosophical discourse, but to scholars and thinkers who lived six hundred and more years after his death, when philosophical disputation on theological questions became the fashion, and, indeed, the chief sign of an intellectual revival.

Had Boethius survived to complete his work of rendering the greatest Greek philosophers into Latin, perhaps western Europe would not have been denied these materials for another half-millennium, and intellectual development in the West might have been speeded. But Theodoric imprisoned Boethius on a charge of treasonable plotting against him, and after keeping him in jail for a year executed him at the age of forty-four. While in prison, Boethius wrote *The Consolation of Philosophy,* part verse, part prose, in which philosophy herself appears to him and consoles him by reminding him how fickle fortune is, and how transitory and relatively worthless are earthly triumphs. A moving book, written in excellent Latin, it became a popular schoolbook for generations of medieval students.

Cassiodorus lived much longer (ca. 490–580), and managed to stay in Theodoric's good graces, acting as his secretary of state and collecting his official correspondence. Cassiodorus hoped to found a Christian university in Rome. Thwarted by the disorders of Justinian's reconquest of Italy, he eventually founded a monastery in southern Italy, and prescribed the study of the classics as a means to strengthen and advance Christian education. His monks copied by hand not only the Bible but the best pagan Latin authors—Cicero, Vergil, and the others—and Cassiodorus helped them by writing a book on how to spell. He followed Cicero too in writing a book on the human soul.

Far more typical of the period were the views of Pope Gregory the Great (reigned 590–604), who had no use for the classics despite his good education. Gregory's own style was crude and vigorous, and everything he wrote had its practical purpose. His commentary on the Book of Job was designed to make people behave better; his *Dialogues,* which included a life of Saint Benedict, were written to make the monastic life popular. More than a thousand letters of Gregory survive, written to correspondents all over the Christian world, and dealing with every sort of problem in the management of the Church and its relationship to secular rulers. Modern scholars turn to these documents as a wholly unparalleled source of information for the early Middle Ages.

In Gaul, a highly Romanized province, there remained well into the period of the barbarian invasions a cultivated circle of upper-class landowners and churchmen, who still wrote letters to each other in Latin, and lived an old-fashioned life on their country estates. But this Gallo-Roman culture virtually disappeared with the Frankish triumph. From the Merovingian period we have the Latin hymns of Fortunatus, and the somewhat childlike history by Gregory (538–594), bishop of Tours and chronicler of the savage crimes of the Frankish ruling house. In Spain, Isidore (ca. 570–636), archbishop of Seville, wrote a kind of encyclopedia, *The Etymologies,* which became the standard reference book for several hundred years. It reflects both Isidore's learning, which was extraordinary for his time, and his superstition and ignorance, which were more typical.

For a different spirit one must turn to Ireland and England, where the seventh century—elsewhere in Europe the low point of intellectual activity— saw a genuine revival. The monasteries provided a refuge for booklovers and a shelter for their books; and the combined influence of the Celtic and the Roman traditions brought fruitful results.

A page from Alcuin's edition of the Vulgate.

Of a large number of cultivated men, the greatest was Bede (ca. 672–735), who could read Greek, knew the works of the church fathers, and produced the remarkable *Ecclesiastical History of the English People,* covering the period 597–731; this is an invaluable source for the student, written in a Latin of astonishing vigor and purity. Churchmen from this separate cultural world of Britain made possible a revival on the Continent under Charlemagne, who supplied the necessary interest and patronage.

Alcuin of York (d. 804), who had studied under a pupil of Bede, came to the court of Charlemagne in 782 and helped transform the palace school into a serious and practical educational institution where men studied the seven liberal arts as then understood—grammar, rhetoric, and dialectic; arithmetic, geometry, astronomy, and music. Alcuin wrote much himself, and also took the lead in biblical scholarship and in improving the handwriting of the scribes in monasteries, thus ensuring a regular and increasing supply of legible books. The survival of much of Latin literature we owe directly to the efforts of Carolingian scribes. Many other poets, scholars, and historians joined Alcuin in making the palace school a center not only for learning but for agreeable and interesting conversation, in which Charlemagne enjoyed taking part. The foundations laid by these men permitted their successors in the next two generations to write personal letters, history, poetry, and even ambitious works on theological and ethical questions.

WRITING IN THE VERNACULAR: "BEOWULF"   It was in England too—where the Latin veneer was thinner than anywhere on the Continent—that the Angles, Saxons, and Jutes produced the first European literature in a vernacular language, which we call Anglo-Saxon or Old English. Sometimes they translated: Boethius' *Consolation of Philosophy* was rendered into Old English, and King Alfred the Great himself translated Bede's *Ecclesiastical History.* But by far the most remarkable Old English literary monument is *Beowulf,* a poem of about 3,200 lines, preserved in only a single manuscript in the British Museum written down about the year 1000. But *Beowulf* was originally composed much earlier, sometime between 680 and 800. Scholars argue as to the place of its composition, its authorship (one author or several?), and its author's religion (Christian or pagan?). Described as "a museum for the antiquarian, a sourcebook for the historian, a treatise for the student of Christian thought, and a gymnasium for the philologist," it is also unmistakably a magnificent poem.

It begins in Denmark, and tells of the building by King Hrothgar of his great hall, and of the savage attacks upon his men by a monster called Grendel. The hero Beowulf, a Geat from southern Sweden, comes to Denmark, and kills not only Grendel but Grendel's even more terrifying mother, who is destroyed at the bottom of the lake in which she lives. Having become king of his own people, Beowulf at the end of his long life is slain in a victorious combat with a dragon who has stolen a hoard of treasure and is ravaging the country. The poem ends with Beowulf's funeral ceremonies: his body is placed with his favorite possessions in a ship: one like it was found in 1939, treasures and all, at Sutton Hoo in eastern England. *Beowulf,* like the *Iliad* and *Odyssey,* exalts the ideal of heroic behavior. But the climax of Beowulf's heroism is death and burial. Though the poet tells us that Grendel's mother and thus Grendel also are descendants of Cain, he never mentions Christ or the Incarnation, the Crucifixion, or the Resurrection. The Christianity of the poem seems to have been superficially grafted on to a pagan stem. Although the later Old French *Song of Roland* has a somewhat similar spirit, there is no surviving vernacular poem of the same period as *Beowulf* that is truly comparable to it.

The Arts

In the arts, as in literature, the story is one of a very gradual transition away from Roman forms, thoroughly standardized and understood in all the continental provinces, and adapted to Christian needs and uses for at least two centuries before the barbarians arrived, toward newer achievements introduced as the barbarians themselves became more cultivated. The early great churches of such important imperial cities as Milan (San Lorenzo) or Trier were still the large rectangular basilicas taken over from the secular architecture of the Romans, but for certain smaller Christian structures, especially baptisteries, then built detached from the main church, innovations were tried: some were square, with corner niches and a drum (Fréjus, in southern France), others were polygonal (Albenga, in northern Italy), and rich mosaic decoration was characteristic. As soon as a barbarian tribe was firmly established in its new territory, its kings as a matter of prestige built churches, often small, it is true, but generally imitative of the Roman models. Most of these have disappeared, but we know from contemporary written accounts and from archaeological research that they often had domes, and tin or gilded bronze roof tiles that shone in the sun. In Merovingian times, marble quarries were worked, especially in southwest France, and fine stone capitals and slabs were even exported.

From the Visigothic occupation in Spain there survive several churches, such as the seventh-century San Pedro de la Nave near the Portuguese frontier, whose architecture is late Roman but whose sculpture is clearly unclassical and in a new mood: in a capital showing the sacrifice of Isaac,

Right: The sacrifice of Isaac: capital at San Pedro de la Nave. The hand of God, representing the voice of the Lord, emerges from the heavens at the critical moment to stop Abraham from killing his son.

Below: Exterior of the seventh-century Church of San Pedro de la Nave.

the hand of God emerges
from the heavens representing
the voice of the Lord
telling Abraham to hold his
upraised hand and spare his son.

For a still-existing Merovingian
building one must examine
the seventh-century Baptistery
of St. John at Poitiers,
later remodeled to some extent,
but still clearly showing
its debt to late Roman buildings,
even though the sculptural
decoration and the
ornamentation in terra-cotta
are now far cruder. At Poitiers
too is the underground
mausoleum of a seventh-century
abbot, Mellebaude, modeled on the
Gallo-Roman tomb chambers in
which such a noble as Sidonius,
for example, or indeed any
of his ancestors for centuries
before him, might have been
buried. In very good Latin

The Baptistery of St. John, Poitiers.

*Cutaway drawing of the underground mauso-
leum of Abbot Mellebaude, Poitiers.*

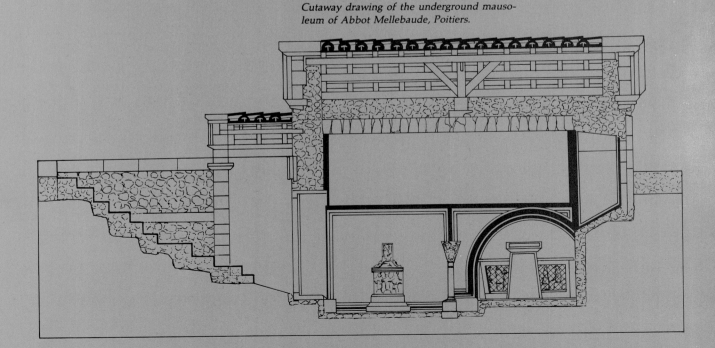

The sculptured figures in Mellebaude's tomb: the two thieves who were crucified with Christ, bound to their crosses.

on the wall are painted inscriptions,
well lettered, one of which says
"Everything goes from bad to worse,
and the end of time is near,"
a quite un-Roman sentiment that
reflects the pessimism of
men who felt the degeneration of
the times they lived in. Even
more representative of a new era
is a sculptured representation
in the tomb chamber itself:
the two thieves crucified with Christ,
each bound to a cross of his own
that no Roman sculptor could
have carved, so primitive
are the figures, so staring the eyes,
so crude the execution. Here,
as for example in certain
sculptured slabs of the same period
found in excavations at St. Denis,
just outside Paris (a most ancient and
celebrated church in which
French kings were later buried),
one sees unmistakably
the barbarian hand working in a
tradition that is all its own.

Also still almost miraculously
preserved at Poitiers by the nuns
at the Abbey of the Holy Cross
is a small carved wooden bookstand
owned by a Merovingian queen,
Radegund, at the end of the sixth
century. In the center of the carved
reading surface is a lamb,
representing Christ, and in each

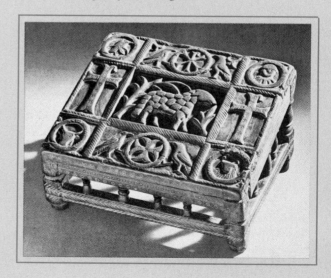

The carved wooden bookstand of the saintly Merovingian queen Radegund.

corner is the symbol of one of the four apostles, an eagle's head for John and a man's for Matthew, a bull's for Luke and a lion's for Mark. At the top, between two doves, is the Greek monogram for Christ, while at bottom, between two doves, is a cross in a circle. Along the sides two crosses in still another form balance each other. The whole is simple and harmonious, and thoroughly Mediterranean in inspiration, but in execution perhaps more primitive, showing possibly the limitations of a barbarian woodcarver, and suggesting—if one is impressionable—both the piety and the ingenuousness of a Christian barbarian queen.

Two sculptured tombs in the crypt (underground chapel) of Jouarre, east of Paris, further illustrate the complexity of the era. The tomb of Agilbert, of the late seventh century, with its extraordinarily vivid and poignant representation of men and women praying at the Last Judgment, their arms upraised, is so unlike all other sculpture of the period in its intensity that it has been conjectured that the artist was an Egyptian Christian, one of those known to have fled from the Arab Muslim conquest. By contrast, the tomb of Theodechilde, of the first half of the eighth century, with its splendid carved shells and beautifully lettered Latin inscription, is in the fullest Roman tradition. Jouarre had close connections with Britain, and its sculptures have been compared with those of the early sculptured crosses of Ireland and northern England, where it is possible also that Egyptian influences had penetrated.

Below: Detail from the tomb of Agilbert in the crypt of Jouarre: women praying at the Last Judgment.

Right: From the tomb of Theodechilde at Jouarre: detail of carved shells and Latin inscription.

Not only Egypt but the Byzantine Empire too made
its contribution to the art of the West during these centuries.
There were of course the great monuments built
in Rome and Ravenna itself by Greeks or artists trained
in the Greek school, dating back to the sixth century,
all well known. But this was imperial territory down to 751.
More striking are the frescoes in the tiny church
in a remote village in northern Italy, Castelseprio, where
the bishops of Milan had a summer residence.
Totally unknown until 1944, these were revealed
when some soldiers scraped the plaster off the wall.
Although there is still much debate among
scholars as to the date when they were painted, it
seems probable that they belong to the eighth or early ninth
century, and they reflect a classical revival that had been
taking place at Byzantium itself since the seventh century.
Compared with the figures of the tomb of Mellebaude,
these frescoes reveal an extraordinary sophistication.

*Adoration of the Magi: fresco in the
Chapel of St. Mary, Castelseprio, Italy.*

*Jeweled clasp from Spain, in the shape of
an eagle.*

To find clear-cut examples of the kind of art
the barbarians brought with them, it is easiest to turn
to the "minor arts" of goldsmithing and jewelry. As the Huns
drove before them into Europe the Germans who
had settled along the shores of the Black Sea, the Germans
brought with them objects made there by local
craftsmen working in an Iranian or other Eastern tradition,
and characterized by brilliant color and the use of gems
(often from as far away as India) or colored glass
for ornamentation. Once inside the borders of the Roman
Empire, the tribesmen, notably the Ostrogoths, naturally
retained their taste for this sort of thing, and
presumably artists they had brought with them as well
as their own craftsmen continued the tradition. Many of these
marvelous (and altogether unclassical) objects have been
found in barbarian graves in central Europe, and also
in Gaul, Spain, and Italy. An eagle-shaped clasp
from Spain is a fine example of a not uncommon
type of ornament of this school.

*One of the jeweled gold bookcovers for the Bible that Gregory
the Great gave to the Lombard queen Theodelinde.*

To understand the influences exerted by the Byzantine outpost of the exarchate at Ravenna, we
must make a point often overlooked: between 642 and 752 virtually all the popes were themselves
Greek or Syrian by origin. These Eastern popes surely sponsored further imports from the East and
fostered a continued popularity of Eastern objects. The magnificent jeweled gold bookcovers made
probably in Rome for the Bible that Pope Gregory the Great himself gave to the Lombard queen
Theodelinde provide a convincing example. Four large jewels in the corner of each cover are
actually classical portrait gems, often now taken out of some treasured collection to embellish this
sort of artwork of a quite different tradition.

The jeweled gold crown of the Visigothic king Recceswinth.

From later in the seventh century comes the jeweled gold crown of the Visigothic king Recceswinth, one of a large collection of Visigothic royal crowns, of which several can be seen in the Cluny Museum in Paris. Similar jeweled objects—a purse, a harp, and weapons—were found in the great Sutton Hoo ship burial in Essex, England, in 1939, to which we have referred in connection with *Beowulf.* To those astonished archaeologists and students of Old English poetry who first looked at the Sutton Hoo find, it must have seemed as if they were seeing illustrated in real life the lines of the poem that tell how

. . . then they laid their dear lord,
the giver of rings, deep within the ship
by the mast in majesty; many treasures
and adornments from far and wide were gathered there.
I have never heard of a ship equipped
more handsomely with weapons and war-gear,
swords and corselets; on his breast
lay countless treasures that were to travel far with him. . . .*

* Reprinted by permission of Farrar, Straus & Giroux, Inc.,
and Macmillan & Co., Ltd. from Kevin Crossley-Holland's translation of *Beowulf.*
Translation © 1968 by Kevin Crossley-Holland; introductory matter
© 1968 by Bruce Mitchell.

And the presence in the royal funeral ship at Sutton Hoo of a massive round silver plate made at Byzantium in the period 491–518, and of two silver spoons with Greek inscriptions, helped to emphasize the continuous contacts between the barbarians and the East.

It was, indeed, the influences from the East, greatly stimulated by the influx of barbarians, that led to the gradual abandonment of the realistic representation of men and beasts in art. Imported Byzantine silver, ivories, and textiles, as well as the Byzantine monuments like those of Ravenna, on Italian soil, surely helped speed the change in styles. Though the story of Eastern influences and its expression by Western artists is a complicated one, it is strikingly exemplified by an extraordinary row of six stucco statues of saints that decorates the front of a small church (Santa Maria in Valle) at Cividale in northern Italy. These saints were carved by sculptors whose skills would have permitted them to do anything they chose. The stiff ceremonial garments obviously cover genuine human bodies; and though hieratic positions are preferred for the figures, the detail is deliberately realistic. Scholars now date these remarkable statues to about the year 800 and ascribe them to Byzantine artists working in Italy.

In strong contrast is the almost abstract effect of a relief of the Adoration of the Magi on the altar of Duke Ratchis, in the same small town of Cividale, ascribed to native Lombard craftsmen and to a period a little more than half a century earlier. Here we are almost back to the primitive quality

Above left: Three of the six statues of saints at the Church of Santa Maria in Valle, Cividale.

Above right: Adoration of the Magi: relief on the altar of Duke Ratchis, Cividale.

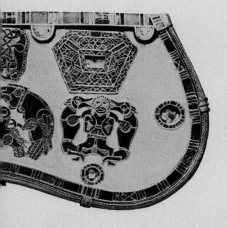

Left: Part of a seventh-century purse cover, with gold, garnets, and enamel, from the ship burial at Sutton Hoo, England.

Seventh-century German tomb slab: on one side a warrior, on the other Christ.

of the two thieves in Abbot Mellebaude's tomb at Poitiers. But we have come the full distance and more when we consider a seventh-century German tomb slab (stele) now at Bonn. On one side the warrior stands sword in hand, about to be bitten by the serpent of death; on the other, Christ stands over his tomb with a halo (but also with a spear!).

Although in a few cases, such as the paintings at Castelseprio and the stucco saints at Cividale, we have found monuments reflecting powerful classicizing influences, we must wait until the Carolingian period for a full revival. Surviving monuments in Italy gave the artists some of their inspiration, and Charlemagne's desire and ability to attract the best craftsmen from anywhere in Europe enabled them to put it into effect. Paintings and mosaics in Roman churches—Santa Maria Antiqua and Santa Maria Maggiore in particular, dating to the fifth and sixth centuries, illustrated for the men of the eighth and ninth centuries, as they do today, what could be made of Christian subjects treated in the classical style.

Wall paintings and mosaics are fixed monuments, and only a traveler can visit them if they are widely separated from each other; but books are transportable, and it was largely through book illustration—the famous illumination of manuscripts—that inspirations from one region and one school intermingled in other regions with influences from other schools. So north Italian books in which all these classical and Byzantine influences had been brought to bear traveled across the Alps, into Gaul, and into Britain with Gregory the Great's missionaries: there actually survive two illustrations from a Bible that came along on the expedition, which together with other books and objects, now lost or unidentifiable, brought the Mediterranean traditions into England, already exposed to them indirectly by the Celtic missionaries from Ireland. And in due course the same influences penetrated into Germany by the same route, where artists under the Ottonian emperors would pick them up.

Illustrative of this north Italian school of painting, so influential in transmitting its influences northward, is a drawing from a manuscript of a book of church law (early ninth century) at Vercelli. Constantine the Great is shown on his throne at the Council of Nicaea with the bishops who signed its decrees, while below the throne, books propounding the Arian heresy are being burned.

Book illustration: Constantine at Nicaea, from a canon-law book at Vercelli.

To the "Carolingian Renaissance," notably marked by manuscript illustration, the specifically barbarian contribution came not in the form of figure drawing, either of persons or of animals, but in the decorative geometric patterning that often characterized barbarian craftsmanship in the metal objects we have discussed. It appears as well in the contemporary written descriptions of other objects (Beowulf was given by a Dane a sword whose "iron blade was engraved with deadly twig-like patterning"—ll. 1458–1459—which we are specifically told was an heirloom); and it reappears in book illustration with the breathtaking patterns to be seen in the great Celtic manuscripts: the Books of Durrow, Echternach (brought from Britain to Germany), Lindisfarne, and Kells, executed in the seventh and eighth centuries. A page with interlace border from the earliest of these, the Book of Durrow, shows Saint Matthew in a cloak of complex checkerboard design; both border and cloak are of barbarian inspiration. The Celtic missionaries who went from Ireland to the Continent and founded the monastery at Bobbio in Italy took these talents with them, and there learned what the indigenous craftsmen had to teach them. By the time we reach the celebrated Book of Kells the earlier stiffness of the human figure is gone, and the geometric patterns have enriched themselves and proliferated; in some cases the birds and fish that were used by continental artists for ornamentation also appear. Coptic influences from Egypt, and even Iranian ones can also be seen in some of the manuscript illuminations produced just before the time of Charlemagne, notably at the French monastery of Corbie.

Charlemagne himself made five trips to Italy, which have been called "the stages by which Frankish culture climbed to the level of Carolingian culture," deepening and carrying further the connection begun by Pepin. Lombards from northern Italy joined the Anglo-Saxons like Alcuin at a court that had no permanent residence during the long years of continual campaigning, but that settled in 794 at Aachen, where the new royal (soon imperial) residence was built at forced-draft speed. From Rome and Ravenna there poured in exciting works of art, many of which have of course disappeared, like the equestrian statue of Theodoric, itself an imitation of that of Marcus Aurelius. We have preserved a model in bronze of a similar statue of Charlemagne himself. In the chapel at Aachen, Charlemagne's marble throne is still in place.

To Aachen came Romans, Lombards, Greeks from southern Italy and probably from Byzantium itself, Syrians, Anglo-Saxons, Irishmen, Spaniards from the Visigothic parts of Spain, Jews, Arabs, and every sort of inhabitant of Gaul and Germany. Architects and artisans—including, perhaps, some Greeks—were striving to create a kind of synthesis between the imperial palace in Constantinople and the papal residence in the Palace of St. John Lateran in Rome. Charlemagne especially enjoyed receiving foreign travelers, who came from everywhere, many of them, especially officials, bringing rich gifts—relics, books, textiles, jewels. In 796 arrived the treasure captured from the Avars, who had been pillaging for two centuries. It filled sixteen oxcarts. The most sensational present was sent in 802 by the caliph at Bagdad, Harun al Rashid: the famous white elephant, Abu'l Abbas, who became a general favorite at Aachen, and whose bones remained a wonder for many centuries after he died. Harun also sent Charlemagne a marvelous clock of gilded bronze, with twelve mounted mechanical knights who on the stroke of noon emerged from twelve little doors that shut behind them. Silken tents, perfumes, oriental robes abounded. The exotic atmosphere of the court remained a vivid memory for many centuries after the glory had departed. Charlemagne had a good many beautiful daughters, whom the gentle aging Alcuin nicknamed "the crowned doves that flit about the chambers of the palace," and against whom he warned his students.

Saint Matthew, from the Book of Durrow.

Saint John, from the Book of Kells.

In a New Testament made expressly
for Charlemagne in the early 780's and richly
illustrated, the dedication verses
read "Charles, the pious king of the Franks
with Hildegard his glorious wife
ordered me to write down this work,"
and the simple words conceal
only momentarily the appearance of a new
factor in early medieval art, the presence
and determination of a powerful
royal patron that provided a wholly
new stimulus to artists. A portrait of Christ
from this early manuscript reflects
the influence of paintings recently done
at Rome. It is only one of literally hundreds
of miniature paintings from surviving
Carolingian books, among which scholars
distinguish between those painted
at court and those produced
in provincial centers. Similarly the art
of the worker in precious metals and jewels
flourished with new vigor, and that
of the bronze-founder—having virtually
perished—was revived at Aachen, where
the still-existing grillwork around the gallery
of Charlemagne's palace-chapel illustrates
the development of a variety of styles,
and where great bronze doors,
several with ornamental lion's-head handles,
testify to classicizing influence at work.
And these and all the other
currents can be seen in ivory carvings
of the period.

With the Carolingian artistic explosion
and its continuation in modified form
by the Ottonians, after a lapse
during the decline of the early tenth century,
we have returned to monuments far better
known to students than those
of the earlier so-called "darker" ages, upon
which we have therefore concentrated
our attention, in an effort to restore
the balance in a summary account.

*Interior of the Chapel of Charlemagne at Aachen,
with grillwork in a variety of styles.*

CHRISTIANITY

F. Cumont, *The Oriental Religions in Roman Paganism* (*Dover). An introduction to the general religious climate in which Christianity took root.

A. Schweitzer, *The Quest of the Historical Jesus,* new ed. (Macmillan, 1948). Fascinating examination of the question of the historicity of Jesus by the celebrated medical missionary.

M. Burrows, *The Dead Sea Scrolls* (Viking, 1955). Of the many books on the subject perhaps the most useful.

A. D. Nock, *St. Paul* (Oxford, 1955). A classic treatment.

S. J. Case, *The Social Origins of Christianity* (University of Chicago, 1923). Relating ideas and the environment.

E. R. Goodenough, *The Church in the Roman Empire* (Holt, 1931). Brief, balanced account for the beginning student.

R. Bultmann, *Primitive Christianity in Its Contemporary Setting* (*Meridian). Good scholarly treatment.

A. H. M. Jones, *Constantine and the Conversion of Rome* (*Collier). Short and impartial account.

W. H. C. Frend, *Martyrdom and Persecution in the Early Church* (*Anchor). Scholarly and readable study.

C. N. Cochrane, *Christianity and Classical Culture* (*Galaxy). Stimulating.

K. S. Latourette, *Christianity through the Ages* (*Harper College Paperbacks). Overview by a sympathetic historian.

C. Dawson, *Religion and the Rise of Western Culture* (*Image). Excellent Catholic survey to the thirteenth century.

A. McGiffert, *A History of Christian Thought* (*Scribner's). Good account from the Protestant standpoint.

H. B. Parkes, *Gods and Men: The Origins of Western Culture* (*Vintage). Clear and sympathetic.

R. M. Pope, *The Church and Its Culture* (Bethany, 1965). A brief and sympathetic account, with a full, up-to-date bibliography.

THE BARBARIAN ONSLAUGHT

J. M. Wallace-Hadrill, *The Barbarian West: The Early Middle Ages, A.D. 400–1000* (*Torchbooks). Up-to-date.

J. B. Bury, *The Invasion of Europe by the Barbarians* (*Norton). An older and very good short account.

E. A. Thompson, *The Early Germans* (Oxford, 1965). Up-to-date survey.

F. Lot, *The End of the Ancient World and the Beginnings of the Middle Ages* (*Torchbooks). Balanced assessment by a French historian writing more than a generation ago.

C. Dawson, *The Making of Europe* (*Meridian). Scholarly review by a Catholic historian.

S. Dill, *Roman Society in the Last Century of the Empire* (Macmillan, 1898) and *Roman Society in Gaul in the Merovingian Age* (Macmillan, 1926). Still very much worth reading.

J. Boussard, *Civilization of Charlemagne* (*McGraw-Hill). Brings together materials difficult to obtain in English.

R. Winston, *Charlemagne: From the Hammer to the Cross* (*Vintage). The best biography in English.

H. Fichtenau, *The Carolingian Empire: The Age of Charlemagne* (*Torchbooks). A competent study.

H. Pirenne, *Mohammed and Charlemagne* (Norton, 1939). Defense of the highly controversial thesis that the Arab conquest of the Mediterranean harmed western Europe more than the German invasions had done.

F. M. Stenton, *Anglo-Saxon England,* 2nd ed. (Clarendon, 1950). Authoritative.

P. H. Blair, *Roman Britain and Early England, 55 B.C.–871 A.D.* (*Norton) and *Introduction to Anglo-Saxon England* (*Cambridge). More recent scholarly studies of early medieval England.

J. Bronsted, *The Vikings,* rev. ed. (*Pelican). Up-to-date assessment of the Norse invaders.

FEUDALISM

C. Stephenson, *Medieval Feudalism* (*Cornell). Simple introductory manual.

F. L. Ganshof, *Feudalism* (*Torchbooks). More advanced introduction.

M. Bloch, *Feudal Society,* 2 vols. (*Phoenix). A masterpiece.

J. Clapham and E. Power, eds., *The Cambridge Economic History,* Vol. I (Cambridge University, 1941). A scholarly study of medieval agrarian life.

A. Dopsch, *The Economic and Social Foundations of European Civilization* (Harcourt, 1937). An important work revising notions of the breakdown that occurred after the "fall" of Rome.

L. J. Daly, *Benedictine Monasticism: Its Formation and Development through the Twelfth Century* (Sheed & Ward, 1965). A valuable history.

C. Brooke, *Europe in the Central Middle Ages, 962–1154* (Holt, 1964).

LITERATURE AND THE ARTS

M. L. W. Laistner, *Thought and Letters in Western Europe, A.D. 500 to 900* (*Cornell). A good scholarly study.

Gregory of Tours, *History of the Franks,* trans. O. M. Dalton (Clarendon, 1927). Merovingian cultural decadence vividly illustrated.

Venerable Bede (Beda Venerabilis), *Ecclesiastical History of the English Nation* (Dutton, 1954). Useful translation.

R. W. Chambers, *Beowulf: An Introduction to the Study of the Poem,* suppl. C. L. Wrenn, 3rd ed. (Cambridge, 1959). A full scholarly summary.

Beowulf, trans. Kevin Crossley-Holland (Farrar, 1968). Good translation.

J. Hubert, J. Porcher, and W. F. Volbach, *Europe of the Invasions* (Braziller, 1969). Excellent pictures, good brief text.

SOURCES AND FICTION

The student may want to read portions of the New Testament, of which several translations are available.

H. S. Bettenson, *Documents of the Christian Church* (*Oxford). Admirably edited collection.

P. R. Coleman-Norton, ed. *Roman State and Christian Church* 3 vols. (S.P.C.K., 1966). Translations of the key documents down to 535.

St. Augustine, *Confessions* (Sheed & Ward, 1947) and *The City of God,* trans. G. E. McCracken, 7 vols. (Harvard, Loeb Classical Library).

Bryher, *The Roman Wall* (Pantheon, 1954). Novel of the Roman Alpine frontier under German pressure.

four

The Medieval World: Western Europe

I

The Society and Its Economy

The Turning Point
of the Eleventh Century

The eleventh century proved to be a major turning point in the social and economic life of the West, although nobody alive at the time could have been fully conscious of what was happening. As the raids of the Northmen tapered off, most of western Europe found itself secure against outside attack. By the end of the century, western Europe was able to take the offensive and invade the lands of Islam in the Crusades (see Chapter 5). During the eleventh century, the population grew rapidly. Although scholars cannot really account for this, it may have reflected the greater security of the individual and his increased expectancy of life. By modern standards, of course, human beings were still exposed to dangers from plague, famine, and violence that seem to us fantastic.

The larger population needed more food and more land. Pioneers felled trees, drained swamps, opened up new areas for farming. When forests or marsh lay within a manor, a lord would often offer special inducements to his serfs to get them to undertake the extra heavy labor of clearing and farming it. Sometimes a group of peasants would move into a new region that had lain empty before, and would clear it and farm it by introducing the usual strip system. If such uninhabited land belonged to a lord, he might invite peasants to colonize it and would offer them freedom from serfdom and the chance to pay a money rent instead of the usual services. This would bring profit to the lord and great advantages to the emancipated serf.

New technology helped to improve the farmer's life. Farmers adopted some devices that had been known earlier, such as the heavy wheeled plow and the use of horses to draw it. Windmills made their first appearance on the European landscape, especially in flat areas like the Low Countries where there was no falling water to run a watermill. Slowly the anonymous inventors of the Middle Ages perfected systems of gears that would turn the millstones faster and produce more meal in less time.

Trade and Town

During the eleventh century also, and as part of the same general development, trade began slowly to revive. Medieval farmers were helpless in the face of a bad harvest year, and plenty or scarcity varied widely from region to region. It was the natural thing to bring surpluses into areas of famine and sell them at high prices to the hungry. The first new commercial centers arose in places such as Venice and the Low Countries, where the local farms could not feed the increasing population. Even in the Dark Ages, such trade had never disappeared altogether, but now the incentives to increase its scale were pressing.

When the proprietor of a manor found that year after year he could make large sums by selling a certain crop, he began to plant more and more of that crop and to use the money gained by its sale to buy the things he was no longer raising. Once he had more money than he needed for necessities, he began to think of how to spend it on something extra, a luxury. Such a demand quickly creates its supply: what was once a luxury comes to seem a necessity. Thus, for example, the people of Flanders, living in an area that was poor for growing grain but good for raising sheep, sold their raw wool, developed a woolen-manufacturing industry, and imported the food they needed.

The recovery of commerce and the beginnings of industries stimulated the growth of towns. Old Roman towns like London and Marseilles revived. New towns grew around a castle (*bourg* in France, *burgh* in England, *burg* in Germany), especially if it was strategically located for trade as well as for defense. And so the resident *bourgeois, burgesses,* or *burghers* enter the language as castle dwellers, but soon become recognizable as residents of towns, engaged in commerce. Protected by the lord of the castle, or sometimes by the abbot of a local monastery, the townsmen built walls and pursued their trade. They would band together into guilds to protect themselves from brigands on the roads, and to bargain with the lord of the next castle, who might be showing unpleasant signs of confiscating their goods or charging indecently high tolls whenever they crossed his land. Grouped in a guild, merchants could often win concessions: if the lord they were bargaining with seemed unreasonable, they might threaten to take a route across the lands of some less rapacious lord and pay a more moderate toll.

Mutual advantage soon led proprietors, including kings as well as lesser lords, to grant privileges to the townsmen by issuing a charter. Although the contents of such documents varied, most of them guaranteed free status to the townsmen; even an escaped serf within the town would acquire freedom if he could avoid capture for a year. The charter might also grant the townsmen the right to hold a perpetual market, to transfer property within the town walls, and to have their lawsuits tried in a town court by town custom, which slowly developed into a whole new kind of law, the *law merchant.*

Industry followed commerce into the town. The merchant, with his experience of distant markets, learned how to buy raw material, to have workmen do the manufacturing wherever it was cheapest, and to sell the finished products wherever he could get the best price. The workmen also soon began to organize themselves into craft guilds, which provided medical care and

Drapers' hall, Ghent, begun in the fifteenth century.

burial for the members, and often fixed minimum wages, the standards of quality of the product, and even the prices that were to be asked.

Enterprise was neither free nor private. It was highly regulated, not only as an effort to reduce outside competition but also as a reflection of the ideas of the age. Men believed that a "just price" for a pair of shoes included the cost of the leather and the thread, the amount needed to sustain the shoemaker at his usual standard of life while he made the shoes, and a small addition to pay the seller for his time and trouble. To make money in the modern sense of charging all that the traffic would bear was in theory to cheat the customer. No doubt many medieval customers were in fact cheated in this sense, but the ethics of the time condemned the action. Finance capitalism—the use of money to make money, the investment of funds at interest—was condemned as usury.

Town and Countryside

In their turn, the towns greatly affected the overwhelming mass of the population who remained in the countryside, who now had a place to sell their surplus and so an incentive to produce it. Some peasants saved enough cash to buy their freedom; some fled to the town in the hope of acquiring freedom, or at least in the hope that their children might acquire it. The very word *cash* suggests a most important development, the flourishing of a money economy instead of the economy of barter. Barter still continued, but as the magnates came to want more and more manufactured or imported or luxury goods, they wanted cash rather than services: a serf's labors would produce more grain, but not the money to buy a piece of armor. So the lord would let the peasant pay him cash, and would forgive (commute) the serf's obligation to work on the lord's land. More demand for money led to more money in circulation, and to a slowly inflationary rise in wages and prices.

With the increase in demand for goods, large-scale fairs became a regular feature of medieval life. Some of them brought together merchants and products from a relatively narrow region, but others attracted men and goods from all over the European world. In Champagne, in northeastern France, for example, there were several great annual fairs each year. The count of Champagne collected a fee from the towns for the privilege of holding the fair as well as the revenues from a special court set up to try cases that arose during its course. As large-scale transactions became more frequent, it became less practical for merchants to carry around large amounts of cash, and during the thirteenth century merchants came to use a written promise to pay instead. Acceptance of these bills of exchange, a kind of primitive check, often made it unnecessary to transport money at all, since a Parisian creditor of a London merchant could call upon a Parisian debtor of the same merchant to pay the amount owed.

II

Monarchy in the Medieval West

With the gradual changes in the economy and the society of western Europe went changes also in its political life. As always in politics the central question is: who has the power? In France, often regarded as the most feudal area of Europe, the monarch successfully asserted his superiority over his vassals. In England, the kings, having made good their superiority, were forced by their vassals to dilute it. In Germany, the nobles in the end became little rulers, each in his miniature realm. We now turn to the histories of these peoples in the centuries between the eleventh and the fourteenth and to their different experiences, which largely determined their future political development and their national character in our own day.

France: Hugh Capet through Philip the Fair (987–1314)

THE CAPETIANS   Chosen king of France by the nobles in 987, Hugh Capet came of a family that for a century had been disputing the throne with the feeble surviving Carolingians (see Chapter 3). His own domain was the Île de France, a compact strip of land including Paris and its environs, and extending south to the Loire at Orléans. It was smaller than the domains of any of the great feudal lords, his vassals, who chose him as king: the dukes of Normandy or Burgundy or Aquitaine, the counts of Flanders, Anjou, Champagne, Brittany, or Toulouse. This may have been one of the reasons they could elect him. More powerful than he, they might defy him by withholding the military service, the feudal dues, and the counsel that they owed him.

Yet the Capetians proved to have certain advantages. Hugh's male line continued to inherit the throne for almost 350 years. At first the kings secured the election and coronation of their eldest sons during their own lifetimes, until, by the end of the twelfth century, the hereditary principle was firmly established. The king alone had no suzerain. Moreover, his office gave him a special sanctity: crowned and anointed with holy oil, he seemed to the people partly divine, "the eldest son of the Church." The Church became his partner; he defended it and it assisted him. He nominated bishops to sees near Paris, and the bishops took an oath of fealty to him. Finally, Hugh Capet's domain, though small, was compact and easily governed; he and his successors concentrated their attention on it.

While the duke of Normandy was conquering England, or relatives of the duke of Burgundy were making themselves kings of Portugal, Hugh Capet's descendants were doggedly clearing the brigands from the roads in the Île de France, forcing royal authority upon its inhabitants, and adding territory to it piecemeal. The officers of the royal household became the king's advisory and administrative staff—the *curia regis,* or king's court. By the early twelfth century, the king had prevented these important jobs from becoming hereditary in one family, and had begun to appoint men of his own choice as royal servants. Suger, abbot of St. Denis, a man of humble birth, faithfully served Louis VI (reigned 1108–1137) and Louis VII (reigned 1137–1180) for several decades. Louis VI introduced royal appointees known as *prévôts* (provosts) to administer justice and taxation in the royal lands. He granted charters to rural pioneers and to new towns, recognizing that the monarchy would gain by new settlements. In these ways the French kings began their long and important alliance with the middle class. By the time of Louis VII, the king had acquired such prestige that far-off vassals in the south of France were appealing to him to settle local disputes.

Then, in the late twelfth century, the monarchy had to face the challenge posed by its Norman vassals. Though Duke William had conquered England in 1066 and thus gained resources that made him much stronger than the king of France, he was still vassal of the Capetians for Normandy. In the early twelfth century an English queen married another great vassal of the king of France, the count of Anjou; and their son, King Henry II of England (reigned 1154–1189), ruled England, Normandy, Anjou, Maine, and Touraine, in what is sometimes called the Angevin Empire. Worse still, Henry II married Eleanor of Aquitaine, heiress to all of southwest France, whom Louis VII had divorced in 1152 because she had not borne him a son. Henry II now had more than half of France, and added Brittany and other territories. The survival of the French monarchy was in question.

The tomb figure of Eleanor of Aquitaine in the abbey church of Fontevrault, France.

PHILIP AUGUSTUS AND TERRITORIAL EXPANSION   Philip II (reigned 1180–1223), called Philip Augustus, used both cunning and force to win a major first round in the struggle. He supported Henry II's rebellious sons against him and then plotted against Henry's son, Richard the Lionhearted, when he became king of England. He also married a Danish princess in the hope of inheriting the Danish claims to the English throne and utilizing the Danish fleet. In 1200, a year after Richard's brother John became king of England, Philip used feudal law against him: John had foolishly married a girl who was engaged to somebody else; her father complained to Philip, and Philip summoned his vassal John to answer the complaint. When John failed to appear, Philip quite legally declared his fiefs forfeit, and planned to conquer them on behalf of a rival claimant, John's nephew, young Arthur of Brittany. When John murdered Arthur (1203), he lost his sympathizers on the Continent, and played into Philip's hands. In 1204 John had to surrender Normandy, Brittany, Anjou, Maine, and Touraine.

Driven out of France north of the Loire, the English retained only Aquitaine. In 1214, at the battle of Bouvines, Philip defeated an army of English and Germans, and made good his territorial gains. The lands John had lost became part of the French royal domain, and the Duchy of Normandy, in royal hands, could serve as a model of administrative efficiency for the rest of France.

The next major conquest took place in the southern territories of Languedoc and Toulouse, whose inhabitants spoke a dialect differing from northern French. Many of them were heretics. This region had become the center of the Cathari (Greek, "pure ones"), also called Albigensians after the town of Albi, one of their strongholds. Albigensian beliefs derived ultimately from those of the Manichaeans (see Chapter 3) which had spread, often secretly, from the eastern Mediterranean via the Balkans to northern Italy and southern France. Believing that all matter was created by the forces of evil, the Albigensians held that the earth itself, the body of man, wood, water—anything material— was the work of the devil. So they denied the humanity of Jesus, repudiated the adoration of the cross, and forbade infant baptism, the Mass, and other sacraments. Though strongest among the lower classes, they often had the support of individual nobles.

In 1208 the pope proclaimed a crusade against the Albigensians, and hundreds of northern French nobles rushed south to kill the heretics and steal their property. Philip Augustus himself did not intervene at first. But by the year of his death (1223), after fifteen years of bloody warfare, he saw the chance of annexation and sponsored an expedition under his son Louis VIII (reigned 1223–1226). By the 1240's the royal armies and a special church court, the Inquisition, had driven the heresy underground; in 1249, when the last count of Toulouse died, his lands went—by marriage—to the brother of the king of France.

THE DEVELOPMENT OF ROYAL GOVERNMENT As the royal lands increased, royal government grew in efficiency. Philip Augustus collected detailed information of just exactly what was owing him from the various royal fiefs. He systematically tried to reach over the heads of his own vassals and make *their* vassals dependent on him. He made his vassals promise to perform their feudal duties or else surrender themselves as prisoners. If they did not, the Church would lay an interdict on their lands, depriving the inhabitants of the sacraments and the other comforts of religion (the people feared this punishment more than any other). Philip bought as many estates as he could. He insisted on providing husbands of his own choosing for great heiresses, who in those violent days often survived several husbands and paid the king handsomely each time he married them off.

Philip Augustus supplanted the prévôts, whose lands and offices had tended to become hereditary and who were often abusing their powers. The new officials—called *baillis* (bailiffs) in the north and *sénéchaux* (seneschals) in the south—received no fiefs, and their office was not hereditary. They did not reside in their administrative areas, but traveled about enforcing the royal rights, rendering justice on the king's behalf, and collecting money owed to the king. Baillis and sénéchaux were salaried royal civil servants, removable at the king's will and dependent upon his favor. As a further check upon them, Louis IX (reigned 1226–1270) made it easy for complaints against them to be brought to his attention, and appointed still other new officials to take care of the caretakers. These were the *enquêteurs* (investigators), rather like Charlemagne's *missi dominici*, who had supervisory authority over the baillis and sénéchaux and toured the country inspecting their work. By this system of royal officials the king could interfere with almost all local and private transactions, exact his just due, and supply royal justice at a price.

New business swamped the old curia regis. For the monarchy of Louis IX and his successors to have depended on the household officers, as the immediate successors of Hugh Capet had been able to do, would have been a little like the United States government today trying to get along with no filing system except an old chest of drawers belonging to George Washington. So the old household began to differentiate itself into departments, most of which dealt with the needs of the king and his retainers, clergy, and advisers. When a major policy decision needed to be made or when a major lawsuit needed to be tried, the king could summon all his vassals (lay and clerical) for counsel. When they joined the rest of the curia regis and sat in judgment on a lawsuit, the enlarged body was called a *parlement,* a high judicial tribunal.

As law grew more complex, trained lawyers had to handle more and more of the judicial business. At first they explained the law to the vassals sitting in judgment, and then, as time passed, they formed a court and arrived at decisions themselves in the name of the king. By the fourteenth century this court was called the Parlement de Paris. When the curia regis sat in special session on a financial matter or audited the reports of royal income and expenditure, it was acting as a kind of government accounting bureau. By the fourteenth century this was called the *chambre des comptes,* the chamber of accounts. More and more it, too, needed full-time employees: clerks, auditors, and so on. Though the king got money from his lands, from customs dues and tolls, and from fees of all kinds paid by vassals for justice or for exemption from outmoded feudal services, he could not levy regular taxes on his subjects. The nobles became accustomed to the regular paying of feudal aids, but bitterly objected to anything else, such as two royal efforts (1145 and 1188) to collect special taxes as a penalty from those who stayed home from a crusade.

SAINT LOUIS   The medieval French monarchy reached its highest point with Louis IX. Generous and devout, almost monastic in his personal life, he was made a saint by the Church in 1297, less than thirty years after his death. Yet personal piety did not prevent him from defending royal prerogatives against infringements by his own bishops or by the papacy. In 1247 he would not let the pope assess the churches of France for money and men to fight papal military campaigns. Louis showed the same hardheaded spirit in his dealings with the towns, old allies of the Capetians, where the lower class of tradesmen resented the concentration of authority in the small merchant upper class. The crown intervened, not on behalf of the poor and humble, but for the purpose of ensuring the regular flow of funds to the royal coffers. In 1262 Louis required that the towns present annual accounts. The very form of the decree illustrates Louis's strong assertion of royal prerogative: it was a new kind of enactment, the *ordonnance,* a royal command issued for all of France without the previous assent of the vassals. By ordonnance the king also forbade private warfare and declared that royal money was valid everywhere in the realm.

By Louis's day Frenchmen preferred royal justice, and appeals from lower feudal courts flowed in to the parlement. The royal court alone could try cases of treason and breaking the peace. To the parlement the crown brought in townsmen, the king's *bourgeois,* and so extended royal justice to the towns. Sitting under an oak tree in the forest of Vincennes outside of Paris, Saint Louis made himself available to all his subjects and listened to all disputes. Foreigners too came to prize his justice. He settled quarrels in Flanders, Burgundy, Lorraine, and Navarre, and in 1264 was invited to judge a dispute

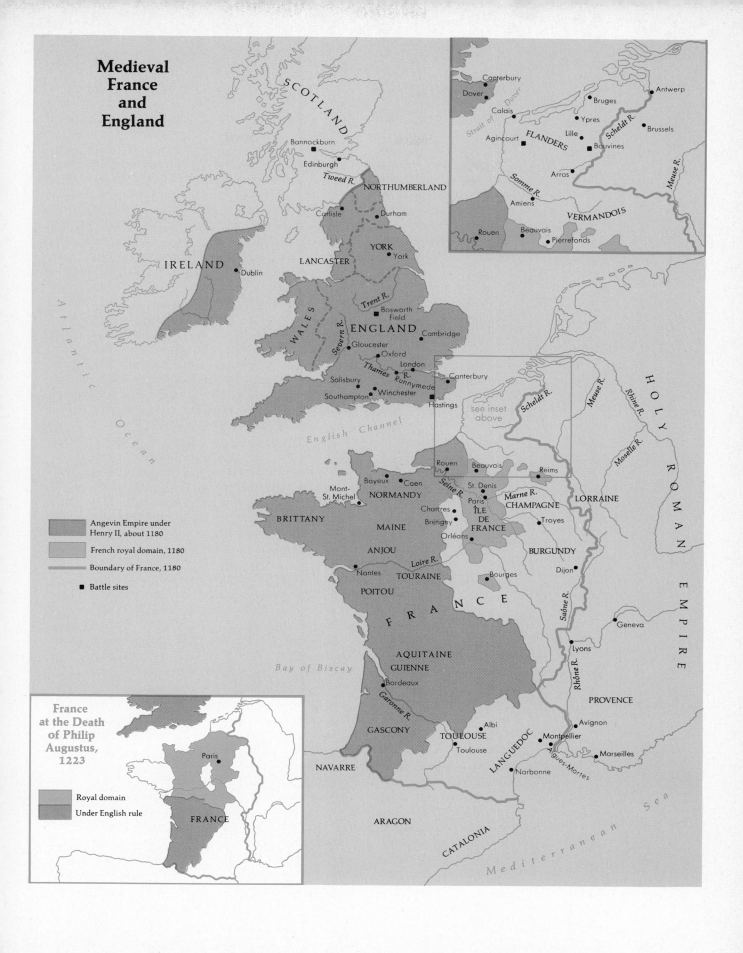

Medieval France and England

Legend

- Angevin Empire under Henry II, about 1180
- French royal domain, 1180
- Boundary of France, 1180
- ■ Battle sites

France at the Death of Philip Augustus, 1223

- Royal domain
- Under English rule

FRANCE

Main map labels

SCOTLAND

Bannockburn
Edinburgh
Tweed R.
NORTHUMBERLAND
Carlisle
Durham

IRELAND
Dublin

LANCASTER
YORK
York

Trent R.
Bosworth Field
ENGLAND
Cambridge
WALES
Severn R.
Gloucester
Oxford
London
Thames R.
Salisbury
Runnymede
Southampton
Winchester
Canterbury
Hastings
see inset above

Atlantic Ocean

English Channel

Mont-St. Michel
Bayeux
Caen
NORMANDY
Rouen
Beauvais
Reims
St. Denis
Seine R.
BRITTANY
MAINE
Chartres
Paris
Marne R.
CHAMPAGNE
LORRAINE
ÎLE DE FRANCE
Brétigny
ANJOU
Orléans
Troyes
Nantes
TOURAINE
BURGUNDY
POITOU
Bourges
Dijon

F R A N C E

Bay of Biscay

AQUITAINE
GUIENNE
Geneva
Bordeaux
Lyons
Garonne R.
Saône R.
PROVENCE
GASCONY
Albi
Avignon
Rhône R.
TOULOUSE
Montpellier
Toulouse
LANGUEDOC
Marseilles
NAVARRE
Aigues-Mortes
Narbonne

ARAGON

CATALONIA

Mediterranean Sea

HOLY ROMAN EMPIRE
Scheldt R.
Meuse R.
Rhine R.
Moselle R.

Inset (top right)

Canterbury
Dover
Calais
Strait of Dover
Bruges
Antwerp
Ypres
Lille
Scheldt R.
Brussels
Agincourt
FLANDERS
Bouvines
Arras
Somme R.
VERMANDOIS
Amiens
Rouen
Beauvais
Pierrefonds
Meuse R.

Inset (bottom left)

Paris

between King Henry III of England and the English nobles. In the conception and enactment of his special God-ordained role as king, Saint Louis reached a height attained by no other monarch.

THE SYSTEM HARDENS: PHILIP THE FAIR   After the death of Saint Louis, and especially during the reign of his grandson Philip IV (1285–1314), called "the Fair" because of his good looks, the French royal system experienced a kind of hardening—a loss of new forms of expression. This hardening is notable throughout the medieval world during the late thirteenth and early fourteenth centuries. Where Saint Louis had been firm and just, Philip the Fair was aggressive and ruthless. The towns, the nobles, the Church all suffered as he and his ubiquitous agents invaded long-standing rights.

Much of this undermining went on in a series of courtroom battles, as the king's lawyers perverted old rules in order to push royal claims to the uttermost. The royal agents asserted that if a case was begun in a royal court it had to be completed there, no matter where it legally belonged. They urged plaintiffs to claim on any and all occasions that they had been denied justice in the court of a feudal lord and so to bring their cases before the king's court. They exploited the rule that the loser of a suit could call the judge "wicked and false" and appeal to the next higher court, where the first judge would become the defendant. By using this device in the great lords' courts, the king's men could bring the great lords themselves before the king's court. The system of royal justice was swallowing up the system of feudal justice.

And, as the new cases flowed in, the parlement became ever more specialized and professionalized. The *chambre des requêtes* (chamber of petitions) handled all requests that the royal court intervene; the *chambre des enquêtes* (chamber of investigations) would establish the facts in new cases. In the *chambre des plaids* (chamber of pleas) the lawyers actually argued the cases, and judgments were handed down. Members of the parlement traveled to the remotest regions of France, bringing royal justice to the king's own domain, and more and more taking over the machinery of justice in the great feudal lordships.

At the same period, the most intimate advisers of the king in the curia regis, whom he regularly consulted, became differentiated as the narrow or secret council, while the larger groups of advisers, consisting of the remaining lords and high clerics, were called the full council. In 1302, for the first time, representatives of the towns attended a meeting of this large council. At the moment when townsmen first participated, a transition began to a new kind of assembly, later called the Estates-General. An estate is a social class; traditionally, the clergy was the first estate, the nobility the second, and the townsmen the third. When all three estates were present, an assembly became an Estates-General. Though the clerics and nobles acted as individuals, the townsmen came as chosen delegates from the corporations of their municipalities, and so acted as representatives.

THE STRUGGLE FOR MONEY   Needing money for his wars, Philip the Fair summoned the estates to obtain their approval for his preparations to raise it. He usually would not fix an amount because the contributor would have the right to bargain with him. Medieval man felt that no action was proper unless it had always been customary; so that whenever the king wanted to do something new he tried to make it seem like something old. Often a protest that a given effort to raise money constituted "an unheard-of exaction" would suffice to frustrate his efforts. One of Philip's most effective techniques was to demand military service from a man and then let him escape it by paying a specific amount assessed on his property. Philip asked regularly for sums that had in the past been demanded only occasionally. He also took forced loans, debased the coinage, and levied new customs dues and royal taxes on commercial transactions.

Need for money led to a fierce quarrel with the papacy. When Philip claimed the right to tax the clergy for defense, Pope Boniface VIII (reigned 1294–1303) forbade kings to do so without his consent (1296). Philip then forbade the export from France of all precious metals, severely threatening the financial position of the papacy. Boniface backed down in 1297, agreeing that Philip could tax the clergy in an emergency. But in 1300, when Philip's courts tried a French bishop accused of treason, the pope publicly claimed the right to intervene in the affairs of any land ruled by a wicked king; Philip in reply called the pope "your fatuousness." Boniface now proclaimed that every human creature, in order to be saved, must be subject to the pope, and threatened to excommunicate Philip, who had sent a band of thugs to kidnap Boniface. They burst into the pope's presence and so humiliated the old man, who was over eighty, that he died not long afterward from the shock. Philip then obtained the election of a French pope, who never even went to Rome. Thus began the "Babylonian Captivity" of the papacy at Avignon in southern France (1305–1377).

Money also lay at the root of Philip's famous attack on the Knights Templars, originally an order of crusading warriors, who now had a rich banking business. In order to avoid paying the Templars what he owed them, Philip accused them of vicious behavior, brought them to trial, and in 1312 succeeded in having the order abolished. He arrested the Jews of France, stripped them of their property, and expelled them; he also persecuted the agents of the Italian bankers. His agents collected and kept all the debts owing to his victims.

Just before Philip died in 1314, his encroachments led to a kind of taxpayers' strike, in which the towns joined with the local lords in protest against his having raised money for a war and then having made peace instead of fighting. Louis X (reigned 1314–1316) calmed the unrest by returning some of the money and sacrificing some of the unpopular bureaucrats. He also issued a series of charters confirming the rights of his vassals yet not putting a permanent check on the advance of royal power. Since taxation was still connected with military service, the king's unquestioned feudal right, the king could declare an emergency, summon his vassals to fight, and then allow some of them to commute the service for money. Nor did the French nobles keep a committee (as the English had done) to see to it that the king kept his promises. The French monarch of the early fourteenth century continued to enjoy a position at home more powerful and centralized than that of any other western European ruler.

England: William the Conqueror through Edward I (1066–1307)

WILLIAM THE CONQUEROR William, duke of Normandy, who crossed the Channel and defeated the Anglo-Saxons at Hastings in 1066, displayed in his new kingdom the full Norman genius for government. As victor, he could retain or modify or add to the Anglo-Saxon institutions that he found: the thirty-four counties or shires with their sheriffs, the courts of shire and hundred (a subdivision of a shire), the *witenagemot* or royal council, the Danegeld, and the *fyrd* or militia. William assumed the ownership of all the land in England. He kept about one-sixth as royal domain, gave about half as fiefs to his great Norman barons, and returned to the Church the quarter that it had held

A scene from the Bayeux Tapestry, ca. 1073–1083, depicting William's Normans defeating the Anglo-Saxons at Hastings.

before. Although many of his barons subinfeudated their lands, their vassals owed military service only to William, and swore primary allegiance to him (in the Salisbury Oath, 1086). The bishops and abbots also owed him feudal services. He permitted no castles to be built without a royal license, forbade private war, and allowed only royal coinage. He levied the Danegeld, summoned the fyrd as well as the feudal array, and kept the Anglo-Saxon system of courts. He gave the sheriffs authority at the expense of other local officials and bound them closely to the crown.

In sum, the Conqueror respected English custom and law but superimposed the Norman feudal structure; the sheriffs provided continuity between the old and the new. The Norman curia regis superseded the Anglo-Saxon witenagemot; it gave counsel, tried the cases of the great vassals, and performed duties in the shires. In 1086 William ordered a careful survey of all landed property in England. Its record, the unique Domesday Book, included for each piece of land a full statement of past and present ownership and all resources: forests, fishponds, cattle, so that the king's men might find more revenue if possible. As for the Church, William paid the accustomed dues to Rome, but refused to acquiesce when the pope asked to be recognized as feudal suzerain of England (none of the Anglo-Saxon kings had ever acknowledged papal sovereignty). William left the English monarchy in 1087 stronger than the French would be for more than two centuries.

William's immediate successors extended the system. More and more they paid their administrators fixed salaries, since payments in land (fiefs) often led the recipient to try to make his office hereditary, and since clerical administrators might feel the rival pull of papal authority. Within the curia regis, the king's immediate advisers became a "small council." The royal *chancery* or secretariat grew in size, since the king was also duke of Normandy and had much business on the Continent. As vassals were allowed to give money payments (*scutage,* "shield money") to commute their military service, and as other forms of revenue became available, the first specialized treasury department came into existence. This was the *exchequer,* so called because the long table on which the clerks rendered the semiannual audit of the royal accounts was covered with a cloth divided into checkerboard squares representing pounds, shillings, and pence. Norman administration was grasping and efficient.

Between 1135 and 1154 civil war raged between rival claimants for the throne, William's granddaughter Matilda, wife of County Geoffrey of Anjou, and her cousin Stephen. Despite the temporary anarchy, Matilda's son,

Henry II (reigned 1154–1189), found the firm foundations for powerful monarchy intact when he succeeded to the throne. He destroyed more than 1,100 unlicensed castles that had sprung up during the civil war. Once again money rolled in: from scutage plus special fees for the privilege of paying it, from fines, from aids, from payments by the towns, from a new tax paid by knights who did not want to go on a crusade.

HENRY II AND THE COMMON LAW   Despite the universal feeling that law was what had always existed and that the function of government officials was simply to discover and tell what this was, Henry II was able to make a major contribution to legal institutions by developing new combinations of old instruments. In England the baronial courts, lay and ecclesiastical, often competed for jurisdiction with the Anglo-Saxon hundred and shire courts. Henry's subjects therefore welcomed the chance to obtain uniform royal justice, administered under a law common to all England—hence the common law. Only the king could give Englishmen better ways of settling their quarrels among themselves than the old trial by ordeal or trial by battle, which relied on God's intervention to defend the innocent and punish the guilty.

How did Henry II go about this? First of all, by writs. If somebody seized a subject's property, the victim could buy quite cheaply a royal writ, an order from the king directing a royal official to listen to the plaintiff's case. Then, by juries. The official would assemble a group of twelve neighbors who knew the facts in the case; they were sworn (juré), and then they decided whether the plaintiff was the true owner of the property, thus rendering a verdict (veredictum, a thing spoken truly). This jury was different from a modern trial jury: its members were people presumed to know the facts already. Similar machinery of writ and jury enabled a man to recover an inheritance or a man falsely held as a serf to win his freedom. The writ and the jury were both old; but their use in combination, and the flexibility permitted by a variety of writs, created new procedure. A decision by a royal judge in effect became law without new legislation in the modern sense. No matter who won, the royal exchequer profited, since the loser paid it a fine.

Henry II extended the system by sending itinerant justices to the shires to try all pending cases. The sheriff brought before the justices a group of sworn men from each hundred and township to report all crimes since the last visit of the justices and to say who they thought was guilty in each case. This was the jury of presentment (since it presented the names of suspects), the ancestor of our grand jury. With all the refinements of old instruments, proof of guilt was still the ordeal by cold water: if the accused, with hands and feet tied, floated in a pool of water blessed by a priest, he was guilty; if he sank, he was innocent.

Henry II failed in his effort to extend royal justice at the expense of the Church. He appointed his friend and chancellor, Thomas à Becket, archbishop of Canterbury, but Becket at once refused to yield the Church's rights. King and archbishop quarreled over which should have the authority to deal with churchmen charged with crimes, "criminous clerks." Henry maintained that clerics should be indicted in the royal courts, and, when convicted in the bishop's court, handed back once more to the royal authorities for punishment. Becket resisted this royal encroachment, and appealed to the pope for support. The quarrel lasted six years, and the issue was compromised. But Henry, in a fit of temper, asked whether nobody would rid him of Becket, and four of the king's knights then murdered Becket in his own cathedral. Henry had to undergo a humiliating penance and concede that the Church had sole right to punish clerics: *benefit of clergy,* the principle was called. Also he had to agree that litigants in church courts could appeal directly to Rome without royal intervention or license. While this was a severe defeat, the king still would not allow the pope to tax English clerics directly. Only two years after the murder, Becket became a saint, and pilgrimages to his miraculous tomb at Canterbury became a standard part of English life.

Henry's own sons, Richard the Lionhearted (reigned 1189–1199) and John (reigned 1199–1216), made his last years miserable by their attacks on his possessions in France. Yet his work had been so well done that, although Richard spent less than six months of his ten-year reign in England, the royal bureaucracy functioned efficiently in his absence. Its main task was collecting huge sums of money to pay for Richard's crusade, his ransom from captivity, and his wars against Philip Augustus. By the time John came to the throne, Richard had squandered the royal resources and angered the barons. The greedy and tyrannical John also had to face Philip Augustus, and he engaged in a furious new quarrel with the papacy.

JOHN AND MAGNA CARTA   Innocent III, greatest of the medieval popes, intervened in a disputed election to the archbishopric of Canterbury, and when John exiled the members of the cathedral chapter and seized the property of the see, the pope put all England under an interdict (1208) and excommunicated John (1209). He threatened to depose him, planned to replace him with a Capetian, and encouraged Philip Augustus's project of invading England. Fearing that his own vassals would not stay loyal, John gave in (1213). He accepted the pope's candidate for the see of Canterbury, and agreed to restore church property and to reinstate banished priests. But he was forced to go much further than this: he recognized England and Ireland as fiefs of the papacy, and did homage to the pope for them while agreeing to pay an annual tribute to Rome. The pope had won a startling victory, and from now on supported John in his domestic quarrel with the English barons.

This quarrel became acute after the French had won the battle of Bouvines (1214). "Since I have been reconciled to God, and have submitted to the Roman church," John exclaimed at the news of Bouvines, "nothing has gone well with me." About a third of the English barons were hostile to him, not only because of his ruthless ways of raising money but because of his habit of punishing vassals without trial. After Bouvines they renounced their homage to him and drew up a list of demands, most of which they made him accept on June 15, 1215, at Runnymede. John promised to send out to all the shires of England under the royal seal a legal document in the form of a grant or conveyance, the Great Charter, Magna Carta, with sixty-three clauses listing the specific concessions that the barons had extorted from him. John agreed to reform his exactions of scutage, aids, and reliefs; he promised uniform weights and measures (especially important to townsmen), and free elections to bishoprics.

Why do English and American historians and politicians often call this medieval statement of the special interests of the feudal class the foundation stone of our present liberties? Partly because in later centuries some of its provisions received new and expanded meanings. For instance, the provision "No scutage or aid, save the customary feudal ones, shall be levied *except by the common consent of the realm*" in 1215 meant only that John would have to consult his great council (barons and bishops) before levying extraordinary feudal aids. Yet this could later be expanded into the doctrine that all taxation must be by consent, that taxation without representation was tyranny—which

A fourteenth-century manuscript illumination showing King John hunting deer.

would have astonished everybody at Runnymede. Similarly, the provision "No freeman shall be arrested or imprisoned, or dispossessed or outlawed or banished or in any way molested; nor will we set forth against him, nor send against him, unless by the lawful judgment of his peers and by the law of the land" in 1215 meant only that the barons did not want to be tried by anybody not their social equal, and that they wished to curb the aggressions of royal justice. Yet it was capable of later expansion into the doctrine of due process of law, that everybody was entitled to a trial by his peers.

John's medieval successors reissued the charter with modifications some forty times. Under the Tudor monarchy in the sixteenth century it was ignored, and Englishmen did not appeal to it until the civil war of 1642–1649 (see Chapter 8). Then, some of the enemies of Charles I could interpret it in the same inaccurate modern way that we often do. "This is that which we have fought for," said one of them; another, better informed, found in it "many marks of intolerable bondage." So Magna Carta's lasting importance lies partly in its later misinterpretation. But even when we admit this, we must also recognize that the charter rested upon two underlying general principles that justify our gratitude to its baronial sponsors: the king is subject to the law, and if necessary he can be forced to observe it.

HENRY III AND THE BARONS   John instantly tried to break the promises he had made; the pope supported him, declaring the Charter null and void; John's enemies supported Philip Augustus, and a French army landed and briefly occupied London. But John died in 1216, and the barons rallied to his nine-year-old son Henry III (reigned 1216–1272) and expelled the French from England. Henry appointed many Frenchmen to high administrative posts, and the pope appointed Italians to the highest posts in the English church. The English barons deeply resented the foreigners, and at times refused Henry money or tried to limit his powers. In the 1250's Henry undertook to conquer Sicily as a kingdom for one of his sons, and to subsidize his brother as a candidate for the Holy Roman Empire, both very expensive undertakings. Bad harvests and new papal demands for money finally precipitated a new revolt of the barons in 1258.

They came armed to the session of the great council, and a committee of twenty-four issued a document called the Provisions of Oxford, which required the king to submit all his requests to a council of fifteen barons. The committee took over the high posts in the administration and replaced the great council with a baronial body of twelve. They seemed to be founding a baronial tyranny perhaps worse than the king's own. The barons expelled the foreigners but quarreled among themselves; the pope declared the Provisions of Oxford null and void, and Henry III resumed his personal rule. But in 1263 came civil war, as Simon de Montfort took command of the baronial party, defied an arbitration by Saint Louis in favor of the king, captured Henry III himself (1264), and set up a regime of his own, based on the Provisions of Oxford. It came to an end when Henry's heir, Edward, defeated and killed Simon de Montfort in 1265 and restored the king to his throne. For the last seven years of Henry's reign (1265–1272) as well as for his own long reign (1272–1307), Edward I was the real ruler of England.

PARLIAMENT   Historians turn to these turbulent years of baronial opposition to Henry III for the earliest signs of the greatest contribution of the English Middle Ages to mankind—Parliament. The word itself is French, and means "a talking," any kind of discussion or conference. We have encountered it as applied to the French curia regis acting as a court. In England too, in the thirteenth century, the word seems to have meant a session of the king's large council acting as a court, just as the Anglo-Saxon witenagemot had sometimes acted. Feudal law imported by the Normans traditionally reinforced the king's right to get aid and counsel from his vassals. The Norman kings made attendance at the great council compulsory: it was the king's privilege, not his duty, to receive counsel, and it was the vassal's duty, not his privilege, to offer it.

Yet contrary to their own intentions, the kings gave the barons the feeling that they had the right to be consulted, as the scutage and aid provision of Magna Carta shows. Since the kings more and more consulted only the small council of intimate and permanent advisers and called the great council only occasionally, the barons on the great council felt excluded and affronted. The rebels against Henry III in 1258 demanded that the great council should meet three times a year, and they called it a parliament. When Henry III regained power, he continued to summon the great council, the parliament, as well as his small council.

As England grew more prosperous in the thirteenth century, two new classes began to appear at sessions of the great council, or parliament. These were the *knights of the shire,* members of the landed gentry, not direct vassals of the king, and *burgesses* or townsmen. When the king asked for money at the great council and his vassals assented, they would try to raise much of what they owed from *their* vassals; so the subvassals also naturally came to feel that they should assent to the levies. In the early thirteenth century, these knights of the shire had already brought information regularly to itinerant justices, and had otherwise spoken on behalf of their shires. When in 1254 the king summoned two knights from each shire to a great council, or parliament, it can hardly have been felt as a major innovation.

Similarly, burgesses had regularly presented accounts or legal documents on behalf of their towns, and in 1265, when Simon de Montfort summoned an assembly of his supporters, he included burgesses as well as knights of the shire. Scholars no longer think of "Simon de Montfort's parliament" as a representative body in any modern sense, or of Simon himself as a champion of democratic representation. But his parliament did establish precedent: the simultaneous presence of shire and town representatives made it the first true ancestor of the modern House of Commons. Not all later parliaments had shire and town representatives, and not all assemblies attended by them were parliaments. The knights and burgesses had no "right" to come to parliament; no doubt they often felt it a nuisance and an expense to come, rather than a privilege. But gradually under Edward I and his successors, it became customary for them to attend.

EDWARD I   Edward I not only accomplished the final conquest of Wales (1283), which had been begun by Henry II, but three times strove to add Scotland to the English crown, dying during his last effort against the rebellious Robert Bruce (1307). In 1314, Bruce defeated Edward's son and heir, Edward II (reigned 1307–1327), at Bannockburn, and Scotland and England remained separate monarchies until 1603, when a Scottish king (James VI) became king of England (James I) as well.

At home Edward I emerged as a great systematizing legislator, causing the laws to evolve in a way that would not have been possible for his custom-shackled predecessors. The experts in the small council now formulated a series of statutes, elaborating and expanding the machinery of government. The Second Statute of Westminster (1285) assured a great landowner that no tenant to whom he had granted an estate could dispose of it except through inheritance. This is what we would call entail. The Statute of Mortmain (French, "dead hand," 1279) prevented the transfer of land to the Church without the consent of the suzerain. Once the Church had a piece of land, it placed a "dead hand" on it and could hold onto it forever; so lay landowners were reluctant to see portions of their holdings transferred to clerics. These statutes reflect an England in which the old feudal relationship was less and less a matter of a vassal giving military aid and more and more a matter of landlord–tenant relationships. Both statutes redounded to the interests of landlords.

Edward also went a long way to assert that all rights held by others derived from the crown. By the writ *quo warranto* ("by what authority") he commanded all the barons to explain where they had got their rights to any franchise or privilege—such as a hundred court—that they might possess. Some franchises he revoked, but he was mainly concerned to show that only the king could give them or take them away. As royal justice increased its business, specialized courts made their appearance, all of them the offspring of the curia regis. The Court of Common Pleas took cases between subjects, the Court of King's Bench took crown and criminal cases, and the Court of Exchequer took disputes concerning royal finance.

Edward asserted the crown's permanent right to share in export and customs dues, a valuable source of income in this period of flourishing trade. He expelled the Jews from England in 1290; they were not allowed to return until the mid-seventeenth century. He required all freemen to equip themselves appropriately for military service; if you had a certain minimum amount of property you *had* to become a knight (distraint of knighthood), serve on horseback, and so become subject to feudal dues. Baronial opposition naturally arose again, and in 1297 Edward had to confirm Magna Carta and promise not to tax without consent.

Edward's parliament of 1295 included not only the barons, higher clergy, knights of the shire, and burgesses, but representatives of the lower clergy. It is called the Model Parliament, although the lower clergy did not always attend later parliaments. In the royal summons to its members we find a famous clause, "What touches all should be approved by all," an echo of a provision of Roman law, apparently accepting the principle that consent to taxation was necessary. In 1297 Edward declared that the "good will and assent of the archbishops, bishops, and other prelates, earls, barons, knights, burgesses, and other freemen of our realm" were *essential* to a royal levy. Often in later years this principle would be reasserted, and Parliament sometimes made a king confirm it before it would grant him funds.

In England by the early fourteenth century, the monarchs had met with a corporate baronial opposition that had forced consultation upon them, and had begun to create brand-new institutions out of old ones. The regular presence of knights and burgesses at parliaments had gradually made them more and more nearly indispensable to the king's business. The contrast with the French monarchy is a striking one.

Germany and the Empire (911–1273)

THE SAXON MONARCHY   As the Carolingian Empire gradually began to disintegrate, the local administrators of five east Frankish areas—Franconia, Saxony, Thuringia, Swabia, and Bavaria—took the title of duke (army commander) and organized their regions as military units. They chose one of their own number, Conrad, duke of Franconia, as king in 911, on the extinction of the Carolingian line. Each duke made himself a hereditary ruler, took control of the Church in his own duchy, and tried to assert his own domination over the royal administrators—the counts—still active on his lands. After a severe struggle, King Henry I (reigned 919–936) of the house of Saxony and his descendants made good the power of the monarchy, reestablished royal control over the counts, and regained the right to appoint bishops.

To govern Germany, the Saxon kings relied largely on the bishops. Churchmen were better educated than laymen, and could not pass on their offices to their sons as the counts tried to do. Even the papacy welcomed the stability of such a system, and recognized the right of the German king to appoint his own bishops. The kings gave special protection to church lands, exempting them from the authority of the counts. Within their own domains, the bishops administered justice and were in fact invested with the powers of counts. Tenants of church lands made up three-quarters of the royal army, while the Church furnished much of the royal revenue. Churchmen shared largely in the *Drang nach Osten,* the German push to the east: the defeat of the Magyars (955) and the advance into Slavic lands along and across the Elbe and Saale rivers. German bishoprics, with Magdeburg as the chief, were established in the new regions, and the Slavs there were christianized.

When King Otto I (reigned 936–973) became emperor in 962 (see Chapter 3), he created for Germany a grave new series of problems. Although the old concept of the Roman Empire as the one true secular power continued uninterruptedly at Constantinople, in the West *emperor* had come to mean a ruler who controlled two or more kingdoms but who did not necessarily claim supremacy over the whole inhabited world. For a German king to call himself emperor meant that he was asserting authority over Italy—weak and divided—and usually Burgundy as well as Germany. If Otto I had not assumed the imperial title, he faced the danger that one of the other German dukes might do so and thus nullify the royal struggle to control them all. Self-defense and consciousness of being the heir to the Carolingians probably motivated Otto I as much as the urge for conquest. In any case, the German monarchs henceforth regularly claimed the imperial title and intervened in Italy.

Otto III (reigned 983–1002), brilliant grandson of Otto I, had a Byzantine mother from whom he probably inherited some of the older conception of empire. His seal read *Renewal of the Roman Empire.* In Rome he tried to restore the Roman imperial palace, titles, and glory, in the hope of winning the support of the old aristocracy. He also installed German officials on Italian church lands, and appointed German bishops to Italian sees in an effort to create in Italy the kind of system he had at home. He did not neglect the affairs of Germany, and his German contemporaries seem to have approved of his Italian involvement. By the early eleventh century it was taken for granted that the German king had the right to be king of Italy and emperor. German intervention ended Italian anarchy and raised the level of the papacy from its tenth-century degeneration. But as the emperors sponsored reforming movements within the Church, they set in motion forces that would make the papacy a world power and bring about their own eventual ruin.

SALIAN GOVERNMENT   When the Saxon dynasty died out in 1024, the widow of the last Saxon nominated Conrad II (reigned 1024–1039), of the Salian dynasty from Franconia, as his successor. Conrad experimented with ruling through the counts and allowing their offices to become hereditary, in an effort to enlist their support against the pretensions of the great dukes. But the counts felt rather more oppressed by the centralizing tendencies of the crown than by the dukes, and the experiment was a failure. Conrad's successors did maintain

North Sea

Danzig
PRUSSIA

Lübeck
Hamburg
Bremen
Elbe R.
POMERANIA
Vistula R.
Weser R.
FRIESLAND
SAXONY
BRANDENBURG
HARZ MTS.
Magdeburg
Goslar
Oder R.
POLAND
KINGDOM OF GERMANY
SILESIA
Cologne
Aachen
LOWER
LORRAINE
THURINGIA
Saale R.
Elbe R.
Rhine R.
Frankfurt
Main R.
Bamberg
Prague
BOHEMIA
Trier
Mainz
Würzburg
Worms
PALATINATE
FRANCONIA
MORAVIA
UPPER
LORRAINE
Strasbourg
Danube R.
Ratisbon
AUSTRIA
Augsburg
SWABIA
BAVARIA
Vienna
FRANCE
Constance
STYRIA
A L P S
CARINTHIA
Saône R.
KINGDOM OF BURGUNDY
(KINGDOM OF ARLES)
TYROL
CARNIOLA
Trieste
Rhône R.
Legnano
LOMBARDY
Brescia
Milan
Pavia
Po R.
Adige R.
Venice
HUNGARY
Drava R.
Danube R.
Danube R.
Avignon
Alessandria
Roncaglia
Ferrara
Arles
Genoa
Canossa
Bologna
Ravenna
ROMAGNA
Zara
KINGDOM OF ITALY
Pisa
Florence
Ancona
Assisi
SERBIA
Adriatic Sea
TUSCANY
Siena
Ragusa
CORSICA
(to Pisa)
PAPAL
STATES
Rome
Anagni
Tagliacozzo
Bari
Melfi
APULIA
Naples
Amalfi
Salerno
Taranto
SARDINIA
(to Pisa and Genoa)
KINGDOM OF THE
TWO SICILIES
(Hohenstaufen, 1194)
CALABRIA

Medieval Germany and Italy

At the Death of Frederick II, 1250

■ Battle sites

─── Boundary of the Holy Roman Empire

Kingdom of the Two Sicilies

Papal States

Claimed by papacy

Venetian possessions

Palermo
SICILY
Syracuse
Mediterranean Sea

another of his innovations: the training of members of the lower classes to serve as administrators, the so-called *ministeriales.* The Church had used such men to run its great estates. Now the kings used them to run the lands of the crown. Though they were rewarded with land, it was often not hereditary and so not a true fief, and they therefore remained dependent directly on the crown, becoming a social group peculiar to Germany. Soon the nobles were complaining that the king listened only to low-born fellows.

Henry III (reigned 1039–1056) chose Goslar in the Harz Mountains as the permanent royal residence. Henry IV (reigned 1056–1106) ordered a survey of crown lands (not *all* of the land of Germany, and so less comprehensive than the Domesday Book) to discover how much money he could count on. By the 1070's the German monarchy was comparable to that of Norman England and more effectively administered than the French monarchy would be for more than a century. Whereas in France the Carolingian counts had become feudal lords in their own counties, the German dukes had no such feudal position. In Germany no free man had to become a vassal of the duke; many small and large estates continued to be owned outright by free men. Allods, as these nonfeudal lands were termed, were more common in Germany than else-where in western Europe; and, though the social distinction between rich and poor was great, both were more often free of feudal ties than anywhere else. The German free landowners, without a counterpart in France or England, resisted the policies of the kings.

They were further strengthened by their role as guardians or "advocates" of new monastic foundations, of which perhaps six hundred were founded during the eleventh century. The advocate had jurisdiction over the monastic tenants, and also obtained substantial revenues in exchange for protecting the foundations. To keep these new monasteries, sources of wealth and power, out of royal hands, their founders often made them the legal property of the pope. A nobles' revolt in Saxony, put down by Henry IV in 1075, signalized the nobles' hatred of the royal church, the ministeriales, and royal centralizing practices in general.

THE INVESTITURE CONTROVERSY   The real ruin of the German monarchy came with the Investiture Controversy. This began in 1049, when Henry III installed Pope Leo IX, a close relative, on the papal throne. Leo IX not only was thoroughly committed to an intensive program of monastic reform sponsored by an order of monks active at Cluny in Burgundy, but also, together with his younger assistant, Hildebrand, favored the purging of secular influences from the entire church hierarchy. Ironically, the emperor was sponsoring reformers whose greatest target would be his own imperial system of government in Germany. When Hildebrand himself became pope in 1073 as Gregory VII, he determined to secure the canonical (legal) election of all bishops and abbots. This would have meant the end of the German system of royal selection and appointment, and of the subsequent ceremony in which the emperor, a lay-man, conferred on the prelate his insignia of office (for bishops, a ring and a staff), thus *investing* him. The pope opposed lay investiture. Yet the emperor's government in Germany depended on lay investiture, on the sale of church offices, and on many other corrupt practices.

Pope Gregory VII, a statesman of great vigor, shrewdness, and passion, believed that, as wielder of supreme spiritual authority, the pope had jurisdiction over temporal things as well. Any temporal prince who defied him he condemned as a follower of Antichrist. To many pious men this seemed a new and radical claim. The emperor's pamphleteers—conservatives—attacked it.

The papal pamphleteers—revolutionary innovators—attacked them in turn. In 1059, the papacy had established the College of Cardinals and given it the role of electing new popes. This deprived the emperors of their former role and gave Gregory a real advantage over his opponent. Gregory could also count on the support of the German nobles, always hostile to their ruler, and on an alliance with the new Norman rulers of southern Italy.

In 1075, Gregory forbade lay investiture. Emperor Henry IV and his bishops responded by declaring Gregory's election as pope null and void. Gregory then excommunicated Henry and declared him deposed, and deprived of office all bishops who supported him. To prevent Gregory from accepting the German nobles' invitation to visit Germany, Henry secretly went to Italy. At the castle of Canossa, Gregory kept him waiting outside for three days, barefoot and in sackcloth, before he let him enter to do penance and receive absolution (1077). Though the drama and symbolism of this famous episode seem to show the power of the pope, the fact is that Henry had forced Gregory's hand. The pope had had to absolve him, and once absolved Henry could no longer be deposed.

Illumination from a twelfth-century chronicle. Top: Henry IV and his antipope expelling Gregory VII from Rome. Bottom: Gregory's death.

Though Gregory later deposed Henry again, and supported his rival in a German civil war (1077–1080), Henry triumphed, marched to Rome, which he took in 1084, and installed an antipope who crowned him emperor. Gregory's Norman allies arrived too late, and the pope died in defeat in 1085. But Gregory's successor renewed the struggle, supporting civil war in Germany. Henry V (reigned 1106–1125) made peace with his own nobles, conceding them many of the gains they had won in the revolt against his father in the hope that he could then proceed to defeat the Church. But he changed the character of the German monarchy, for, once freed from the restraints imposed by the crown, the nobles indulged in private warfare and the ravaged crown lands could not be reassembled or put into order.

It was the great German nobles who dictated to the emperor the settlement of the Investiture Controversy reached with the pope at the Concordat of Worms (1122). Henry V renounced the practice of investing bishops with the clerical symbols of ring and staff, but, with the pope's permission, continued to bestow the *regalia* (worldly goods pertaining to the bishop's office). The emperor received an oath of fealty from each new bishop before he was consecrated. Moreover, in Germany the emperor or his representatives were to be present at episcopal elections, and so continued to exert a strong influence. In Italy and Burgundy, the emperor had less power: consecration would take place *before* the regalia were conferred, and the emperor could not attend episcopal elections. This compromise ended the overt struggle over investitures.

During the civil war, the German nobles had pretended that there was no king in Germany because the pope had deposed him. They extended their powers and ran their own affairs without reference to the monarchy. Feudal castles multiplied, free peasants fell into serfdom, lesser nobles had to seek the protection of greater. The feudalizing processes that had gone on in ninth- and tenth-century France were now operating in eleventh- and early twelfth-century Germany. Employing their own ministeriales, the great German nobles, or princes, increased the number of their vassals and pyramided their monastic "advocacies." The aftermath of the Investiture Controversy was the beginning of the German territorial principalities and what is known as German *particularism*.

In Italy, the struggle led to the rise in importance of the communes, sworn associations of lesser nobles banded together to resist the local bishops in the towns of the north, where they began to usurp the powers of city government. In Lombardy the pope supported them, in Tuscany the emperor. Everywhere they threatened imperial authority.

THE HOHENSTAUFENS   In 1138, by choosing a Swabian, Conrad III of Hohenstaufen, as emperor, the German nobles precipitated a long-lasting feud between Conrad's family, called Waibling (Ghibelline in Italy) because of their ancestral castle, and that of a rival claimant, Henry the Proud, duke of Saxony and Bavaria, of the family of Welf (Guelf in Italy). Feudal warfare in Germany resumed. Conrad III's nephew, Frederick I of Hohenstaufen (1152–1190), known as Barbarossa ("redbeard"), strove to rebuild the monarchy. Because the Investiture Controversy had ended the possibility of governing Germany through the bishops, and Frederick's own royal lands in Germany were not extensive enough to give him the base he needed, he focused his attention on Italy and Burgundy, marrying the heiress to the latter in 1156, and making Switzerland, with its control over the Alpine passes into Italy, his strategic center.

He tried to turn Swabia into a kind of German Île de France, at first conciliating his Welf rival, Henry the Lion, who became the leader of a great wave of eastward German expansion against the Slavs and ruled almost independently across the Elbe. Frederick eventually curbed Henry by the same feudal means that Philip Augustus would use against John of England. He received complaints from Henry's vassals, summoned Henry into the royal court to answer the claims, and when Henry did not appear deprived him of his holdings (1180). Frederick was able to break up the great Welf territorial possessions. But he could not add them to the royal domain, as Philip Augustus would hold onto Normandy, because he did not control his vassals so effectively. The Welf lands were parceled out among the German nobles. In 1180 also, all Frederick's immediate vassals were recognized as princes of the empire. The new feudal order had obtained recognition.

Frederick made six trips to Italy. He helped the pope put down Arnold of Brescia, a rebel against papal rule in Rome (1143) who favored the return of the Church to apostolic poverty and simplicity. In 1155, the pope crowned Frederick emperor after a famous argument over whether Frederick would hold the pope's bridle and stirrup as well as kiss his foot (Frederick lost). Soon afterward (1158) Frederick tried at the Diet of Roncaglia to define the imperial rights (regalia) in Italian towns: what role did he have in appointing dukes and counts, in coining money, in collecting taxes? Many of Frederick's claims, though several centuries old, had not been regularly exercised by recent emperors, and Frederick was more interested in asserting his rights in principle than in exercising them in practice. Opposed by the pope and the Lombard League of communes under Milan, Frederick was forced to fight a long war. Defeated at Legnano in 1176, he finally made the Peace of Constance with the towns in 1183. The towns retained the regalia within their own walls, but outside the walls they retained only such rights as they had already bought or might in the future buy from the emperor: they recognized Frederick as suzerain, and their municipal officials were to take an oath of loyalty to him.

In 1190, Frederick was drowned while on a crusade. He had been so powerful for so long that the legend soon arose that he was not dead but asleep in a cavern with his great red beard flowing over the table on which his arm rested: some day "the old emperor" would awake and return to bring glory and union to Germany.

Four years before his death, Frederick had married his son Henry VI to the heiress of the flourishing Norman kingdom in Sicily and southern Italy. Here the descendants of a small band of eleventh-century Norman adventurers had built a rich and powerful realm of mixed Catholic, Orthodox Greek, and Muslim population, tolerating all faiths, and issuing its public documents in Arabic, Greek, and Latin, but governed in the efficient Norman manner. Its kings appointed the members of the curia regis, who were not hereditary, and royal officials called justiciars gave justice to the provinces.

By taking over this Norman state together with his German and north Italian lands, Henry VI (reigned 1190–1197) surrounded the papal territories in central Italy. He frustrated an effort by the papacy, the Welfs, and the English to take Sicily away from him, holding Richard the Lionhearted for ransom and securing Sicily by 1194. He was building a fleet to invade the eastern Mediterranean and attack Byzantium when he died suddenly in 1197. To support his grandiose projects and to get the backing of the German princes for the succession of his son, Frederick II, he had to offer the German nobles in their fiefs the same sort of hereditary right he was asking them to recognize. In England or France the problem would not have arisen, because the royal succession was established.

The minority of Frederick II was marked by civil war (1197–1215), in which the great pope Innocent III (reigned 1198–1216) determined to destroy the German-Sicilian link and to revive the claim of Gregory VII that papal confirmation was needed to legitimize any emperor. Frederick II's uncle, Philip of Swabia, maintained by contrast that an emperor elected by the princes was legitimate by virtue of his election alone. Richard the Lionhearted and Innocent backed a Welf, Otto, against Philip. Philip Augustus of France backed

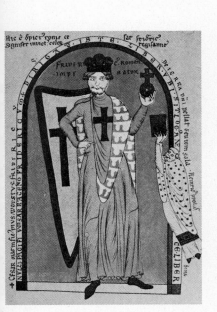

Frederick Barbarossa portrayed as a crusader, from a Bavarian manuscript of 1188.

Philip of Swabia, who was assassinated in 1208. Once on the imperial throne, however, Otto undertook to conquer Sicily, a conquest that the pope was most anxious to prevent. Innocent therefore turned to the young Frederick II, whose position was soon consolidated by the victory of his French ally, Philip Augustus, over the Welf and English forces at Bouvines (1214).

FREDERICK II   Intelligent and cultivated, speaking Arabic and Greek as well as half a dozen other languages, deeply interested in scientific experiment, the extraordinary Frederick II collected wild animals and women, wrote poetry in the Italian vernacular and a textbook on how to hunt with falcons. He was a brilliant and cynical statesman, perhaps the most interesting monarch of medieval history. He preferred his civilized southern kingdom of Sicily, and inherited his father's dream of creating a great Mediterranean empire. To these ambitions he sacrificed the hard-won rights of the crown in Germany. To obtain the consent of the German bishops and abbots to the coronation of his son, Henry, as king of Germany in 1220, Frederick II gave away the royal rights of levying customs dues, coining money, and exercising justice. He promised also to exclude from imperial towns runaway serfs from church lands, and to build no new towns on such lands. In 1231, the secular princes exacted from Frederick a similar privilege in their favor. Germany was then condemned to six centuries of particularism.

In Sicily, however, Frederick imposed his own tightly centralized monarchy on his subjects, carrying further the policies of his Norman predecessors and buttressing his actions by reference to Roman law, with its lofty conception of the imperial position. He founded a university at Naples to train future officials in Roman law. Like William the Conqueror in England, he assumed title to all property. He wiped out feudal custom, forbidding trial by battle as absurd. He organized his army and navy on a paid basis rather than a feudal one, anticipated modern methods of finance, collected tariffs on imports and exports, and—like the emperors at Byzantium—instituted imperial monopolies in certain industries, such as silk.

THE PAPAL TRIUMPH   Against this most unmedieval monarch the papacy, threatened by his holdings, waged steady and eventually successful war beginning in the 1220's. Pope and emperor quarreled over Frederick's slowness in going on a crusade and over his plans to extend imperial administration to all Italy, including Rome. Troops hired by the pope attacked Frederick's south Italian lands. Both sides circulated violent propaganda pamphlets, the pope calling Frederick a heretic, Frederick calling the pope a hypocrite and urging all kings of Europe to resist the Church. On one occasion (1241) Frederick's fleet captured a delegation of more than a hundred prelates on their way to a council called by the pope to depose him. Eventually he was deposed, but the struggle went on after Frederick's death in 1250. In 1266 the papacy imported into Italy Saint Louis's brother, the ruthless and able Charles of Anjou, who defeated and killed Frederick's illegitimate son, Manfred, and established himself as ruler of the south Italian lands. Then, in 1268 Charles defeated the last of Frederick's descendants, his legitimate grandson, Conradino, executing him soon afterwards. Angevin rule over Naples lasted down to 1435, even though the Aragonese took Sicily in 1282.

With the extinction of the Hohenstaufens the papacy had destroyed the Holy Roman Empire begun by Frederick I and given an Italian rather than a German base by Henry VI and Frederick II. But within forty years Philip the Fair, grandnephew of the papal instrument of vengeance, Charles of Anjou,

Emperor Frederick II, in the ship on the left, watching his soldiers assaulting churchmen on their way to the council summoned by Gregory IX.

would puncture the inflated temporal claims of the papacy and take it off to Avignon. In Germany, the imperial throne remained vacant from the death of Conrad IV, the son of Frederick II, in 1254, to 1273. The German princes enjoyed the absence of an emperor, and utilized the interregnum to consolidate their powers and extend their usurpation of former crown rights. The old links with Italy were greatly weakened, and the earlier form of the imperial idea disappeared. An allodial nobility, the Investiture Controversy, and the imperial preoccupation with Italy had ensured that princely particularism would emerge as the ruling force in Germany.

III

The Church and Civilization

Noble and peasant and townsman, in England or on the Continent, all belonged without question to the Christian church. Only the Jews were apart; they suffered occasional persecutions and such disabilities as having to live in a separate quarter or ghetto. When heresy arose, the temporal powers joined with the Church in attacking it. For the medieval man, religious and political governance were the "two swords" of God, equally indispensable for maintaining human society. Which was the greater? Gregory VII and Innocent III and Boniface VIII said that the spiritual power outshone the temporal as the sun the moon, but often had trouble making good so extreme a claim. Henry II and John in England, the Emperors Henry IV and Frederick II, Saint Louis and Philip the Fair all struggled against papal pretensions.

The Reformers

CLUNIACS AND CISTERCIANS   In the tenth century, as we have seen, the papacy had become a prize for local Roman politicians, while concubinage, simony (the sale of church offices), and other forms of corruption were growing among the clergy. From this decline the Church was rescued by a reforming movement that began at the monastery of Cluny in France (founded 910). At Cluny the monks reverted to the strict Benedictine rule; from Cluny reformers went out to reform the monasteries and to found more than three hundred "daughter" houses inspired by the same ideals and all under the attentive rule of the "mother" abbey. Eventually men trained in the Cluniac spirit reached the papal throne itself as nominees of Emperor Henry III. They established the principle of clerical celibacy, which has preserved Catholic priests from the natural tendency of fathers to provide property for their offspring. The reformers checked, though of course they did not completely root out, simony.

We have seen Gregory VII (Hildebrand) expand the ideas of reform into a generalized effort to root out secular influences from the entire church, which would then move forward under militant papal leadership. The Lateran Synod of 1059 issued the decree establishing the College of Cardinals, a group of certain key clerics (cardinal from *cardo,* "hinge"), who were to elect each new pope. The system remains in force today. When it was instituted it did away with imperial interference with papal elections: henceforth the emperor was notified and could approve of the cardinals' choice, but he could no longer impose his own candidate. The Investiture Controversy over German appointment of bishops was a natural sequel.

The Cluniac movement was only the first of several waves of reforming zeal that swept the medieval church. By the early twelfth century the first wave of zeal had spent itself. The Cluniac order had become rich and powerful, and its original concern for asceticism and morality had grown feeble. A similar pattern was repeated by the successors of the Cluniacs as the leaders of reform, the Cistercians. Founded in the late eleventh century, the mother house at Citeaux (Cistercium) in Burgundy lay in a desolate spot transformed into a garden by the labor of the monks. The great Cistercian leader was Saint Bernard (1091–1153), who in 1115 led a small band to Clairvaux, an equally unpromising site, and from there exercised an extraordinary influence over his age. The king of France took his advice; a whole crusade set out at his bidding. In contrast to the Cluniacs, the Cistercians gave daughter houses their self-rule, but within a century they too had become wealthy and lax.

FRANCISCANS AND DOMINICANS By then another wave of reform had already begun, with a new emphasis appropriate to a changing society. Unlike the Cluniacs and Cistercians, the friars of the new orders founded by Saint Francis (1182–1226) and Saint Dominic (1170–1221) did not intend to live apart from the world and reform monasticism from within. Instead, they went to the increasing populations of the new towns and cities, often neglected by the Church, and so often hostile to its rich and worldly clergy. Such anticlerical sentiment sometimes led to movement of protest, some of them heretical, like that of the Waldensians, who in the 1180's taught that laymen could administer the sacraments, and exalted the authority of the Bible alone.

Gentle, charming, and ascetic, Saint Francis, son of a merchant family, had undergone religious conversion in his youth. He loved everything that God had created—men, birds, flowers. Francis prescribed for his followers total poverty: they were to have no monastic house but were to go and preach, and were to rely on charity for their food and shelter. Francis called his order Friars Minor ("little brothers"), and their dependence on alms led to the term *mendicant* friars. In 1210, Innocent III approved Francis's foundation, but even before Francis died (1226) the papacy against his wishes permitted a revised rule, and land and buildings and worldly concerns preoccupied some of the friars to the dismay of the rest. Though Francis had repudiated book-learning and books, later Franciscans often studied in the universities and became distinguished scholars.

Saint Dominic, a Spaniard, founded his own mendicant order in 1216. From the beginning study was a cardinal duty of his followers, who were to educate the laity of the world by preaching to them. The Dominicans were given the name Order of Preachers. Their monastic houses or priories (for they, too, soon began to acquire property) were governed by monks elected by the members, and the officials of each priory in turn elected the superior officials of the order.

The reforming movements of the eleventh, twelfth, and thirteenth centuries within the Church helped to keep piety constantly renewed, dispelled the threat of mass disaffection, and played a major role in the intellectual as well as the social life of the age. Dominicans and Franciscans served as the staff of the permanent papal tribunal of the Inquisition formed in 1233 to find, interrogate, judge, and punish suspected heretics and to deliver those who persisted in their heresy to the secular authorities to be burned at the stake.

The Church and Education   It was the Church that alone directed and conducted education in medieval Europe. Unless destined for the priesthood, young men of the upper classes had little formal schooling, though the family chaplain often taught them to read and write. Their training was in war and hunting, and sometimes in the problems of managing their property. But even in the Dark Ages the monastic schools educated future monks and priests, and the Cluniac reform, with its increased demand for piety, stimulated study and the copying of manuscripts. Medieval men reckoned that there were seven "liberal arts," divided into the *trivium* (grammar, rhetoric, dialectic) and the *quadrivium* (arithmetic, geometry, astronomy, and music), the first three including much of what we might call humanities today, the last four corresponding to the sciences. Only a few monastic schools in the eleventh century were prepared to offer instruction in all seven, and in general monks thought of their work as the preservation rather than as the advancement of knowledge.

The cathedral schools, on the other hand, whose teachers were often less timid about studying pagan writings from the great classical past, fostered a more inquiring spirit. In France during the eleventh century at the cathedral schools of Paris, Chartres, Rheims, and other towns, distinguished teachers now were often succeeded by men whom they had trained themselves, and distinguished pupils went on to join or found other schools. Scholarship no longer depended on the occasional advent of a single first-class mind. In Italy, where the connection with cathedrals was not so close, the medical school at Salerno had a tradition stretching back into the Dark Ages; at Bologna law became the specialty, beginning as a branch of rhetoric and so within the trivium. Students were attracted to Bologna from other regions of Italy and even from northern Europe, and in the early twelfth century, as education became fashionable for young men ambitious for advancement in the Church or in the royal service, the numbers of students grew rapidly.

UNIVERSITIES   The student body at Bologna organized itself into two associations: students from the near side of the Alps and students from the far side, and the two incorporated as the whole body, the *universitas,* or university. As a corporate body, they could protect themselves against being overcharged for food and lodging by threatening to leave town; they had no property, and could readily have moved. If the students did not like a professor, they simply stayed away from his lectures, and he starved or moved on, for he was

Scenes of student life in the Middle Ages, from *Statenbuch des Collegium Sapentiae.*

dependent on tuition fees for his living. Soon the *universitas,* that is to say the students, fixed the price of room and board in town, and fined professors for absence or for lecturing too long. The professors organized too, and admitted to their number only those who had passed an examination, and so won a *license* to teach, remote ancestor of all our academic degrees.

In Paris and elsewhere in the north, the cathedral schools were the immediate forerunners of the universities, and it was the teachers, not the students, who organized first, as a guild of those who taught the seven liberal arts and who got their licenses from the cathedral authorities. By the thirteenth century pious citizens had founded in Paris the first residence halls for poor students, who might eat and sleep free in these "colleges." The practice crossed the Channel to Oxford and Cambridge. As in later times, the authorities of these medieval universities stoutly defended themselves against encroachment by the secular power; there was often friction between town and gown, as irrepressible high spirits among the students led to rioting and disorder.

THE QUESTION OF UNIVERSALS   Much of the learning taught and studied in the Middle Ages seems strange to us today, and it requires imagination to understand how exciting the exercise was to men discovering it for the first time. At the turn of the eleventh century, Gerbert of Aurillac, who spent the last four years of his life as Pope Sylvester II (999–1003), stood out as the most learned man of his day; the smattering of mathematics and science that he had been able to pick up caused his contemporaries to suspect him of witchcraft. His own main interest lay in logic, and he turned back to the work of Boethius (see Chapter 3). For the first time, across the gulf of five hundred years, a probing mind moved into the portions of Aristotle that Boethius had translated, and discovered in logic a means to approach the writings of the ancients and of the church fathers in a systematic way. By the end of the century churchmen could debate whether it was proper to use human reason in considering a particular theological question (for example, was Christ present in the sacramental wafer and wine?), and in all efforts to explain away inconsistencies in the Bible and the Fathers in general. Even those who attacked the use of reason used it themselves in making new definitions that enabled them to argue that bread and wine could indeed, in a certain way, become flesh and blood.

Once the new method became available, the men of the late eleventh and early twelfth centuries employed it largely in a celebrated controversy over the philosophical problem of universals. A universal is a whole category of things; when we say *dog* or *table* or *man,* we may mean not any specific individual dog or table or man, but the idea of all dogs, tables, or men: dogdom, tabledom, mankind. The question that exercised the medieval thinkers was whether universal categories have an existence: *is* there such a thing as dogdom, tabledom, or mankind?

If you said no, you were a nominalist; that is, you thought dogdom, tabledom, mankind were merely *nomina, names* that men give to a general category from their experience of individual members of it. We experience dogs, tables, men, and so we infer the existence of dogdom, tabledom, mankind because the individual members of the category have certain points of resemblance; but the category, the universal, has no existence in itself. If you said yes, you were a realist; that is, you thought that the general categories were real and so did exist. Many realists took this view a large step further, and said that the individual dog, table, or man was far less real than the generalizing category or universal or even that the individual was a mere reflection of one aspect of the category, and existed by virtue of belonging to the category; a

182

man exists only because he partakes of the nature of mankind, a dog because he partakes of the nature of dogdom.

If one transfers the problem to politics, and thinks of the state and the individual, one can see at once how great its practical importance may be. A nominalist would say that the state is just a name, and exists only by virtue of the fact that the individuals who make it up are real; he would argue that the state must then serve its subjects, since after all it is only the sum of their individualities. A realist would say that the state is the only real thing, that the individual subjects exist only so far as they partake of its general character, and that the state by virtue of its existence properly dominates the individual. In religion, an extreme nominalist, arguing that what one can perceive through one's senses is alone real, might even have trouble believing in the existence of God. An extreme realist would tend to ignore or even to deny the existence of the physical world and its problems. Moderate realists have to start with faith, to believe so that they may know, as the English Saint Anselm put it.

Peter Abelard (1079–1142), a popular lecturer in the University of Paris, tried to compromise the question. He argued that universals were not merely names, as the nominalists held, nor did they have a real existence, as the realists held. They were, he said, concepts in men's minds, and as such had a real existence of a special kind in the mind, which had created them out of its experience of particulars: mankind from men, dogdom from dogs, and so on. His compromise between nominalism and realism is called conceptualism. Abelard insisted on the importance of understanding for true faith; he put reason first, and thus understood in order that he might believe, instead of the other way around. His most famous work, *Sic et Non* (Yes and No), lists over 150 theological statements and cites authorities both defending and attacking the truth of each. When Scripture and the Fathers were inconsistent, he seems to argue, how could a man make up his mind what to believe unless he used his head? A rationalist and lover of argument, Abelard was none the less a deeply pious believer. The mystical Saint Bernard, however, suspicious of reason, believed him heretical, and had his views condemned and denounced repeatedly.

Thomas Aquinas

By the time of Abelard's death in the mid-twelfth century, the Greek scientific writings of antiquity—lost all these centuries to the West—were on their way to recovery, often through translations from Arabic into Latin. In civil law, the great Code of the emperor Justinian became the text commonly used in the law schools. In canon law, the scholar Gratian published at Bologna about 1140 what became the standard collection of decrees, and reconciled by commentary apparently contradictory judgments.

In the second half of the century came the recovery of Aristotle's lost treatises on logic, which dealt with such subjects as how to build a syllogism, how to prove a point, or how to refute false conclusions. Using these instruments, medieval thinkers were for the first time in a position to systematize and summarize their entire philosophical position. Yet the recovery of Aristotle posed certain new problems. For example, the Muslim Averroës, whose comments accompanied the text of Aristotle's *Metaphysics,* stressed Aristotle's own view that the physical world was eternal; since the soul of man—a nonphysical thing—was essentially common to all humanity, no individual human soul could be saved by itself. Obviously this ran counter to fundamental Christian teaching. Some scholars tried to say that both views could be true, Aristotle's in philosophy and the Christian in theology; but this led directly into heresy. Others tried to forbid the study and reading of Aristotle, but without success. It was the Dominican Albertus Magnus (1193–1280), a German, and his pupil Thomas Aquinas (1225–1274), an Italian, who—in massive multivolume works produced over a lifetime—succeeded in reconciling the apparent differences between Aristotle's teachings and those of the Christian tradition. They were the greatest of the Schoolmen, exponents of the philosophy historians call Scholasticism.

Aquinas's best-known writings were the *Summa Theologica* and the *Summa contra Gentiles*. He discussed God, man, and the universe, arranging his material in systematic, topical order in the form of an inquiry into and discussion of each open question. First he cited the evidence on each side, then he gave his own answer, and finally he demonstrated the falsity of the other position. Though Aquinas always cited authority, he also never failed to provide his own logical analysis. For him reason was a most valuable instrument, but only when it recognized its own limitations. When reason unaided could not comprehend an apparent contradiction with faith, it must yield to faith, since reason by itself could not understand the entire universe. Certain fundamentals must be accepted as unprovable axioms of faith, although, once they had been accepted, reason could show that they are probable.

If a man puts a series of arguments together and comes out with a conclusion contrary to what orthodox Christians believe, he is simply guilty of faulty logic, and the use of correct logic can readily show where he erred. Indeed, Aquinas delighted in the game of inventing arguments against accepted beliefs, matching them with a set of even more ingenious arguments, and then reconciling the two with an intellectual skill suggesting the trained athlete's ability in timing and coordination.

Here is a simple example of the mind and method of Aquinas. He is discussing the specific conditions of "man's first state," and comes to the question: what were babies like in the state of innocence before the Fall of Man? Were they born with such perfect strength of body that they had full use of their limbs at birth, or were they like human babies nowadays, helpless little wrigglers? In the Garden of Eden, one might think that any form of helplessness would detract from perfection and that God might well have made the human infant strong and perfect, or might even have had men and women born adult. Aquinas did not think so; even his Eden was as "natural" as he could make it:

By faith alone do we hold truths which are above nature, and what we believe rests on authority. Wherefore, in making any assertion, we must be guided by the nature of things, except in those things which are above nature, and are made known to us by Divine authority. Now it is clear that it is as natural as it is befitting to the principles of human nature that children should not have sufficient strength for the use of their limbs immediately after birth. Because in proportion to other animals man has naturally a larger brain. Wherefore it is natural, on account of the considerable humidity of the brain in children, that the sinews which are instruments of movement, should not be apt for moving the limbs. On the other hand, no Catholic doubts it possible for a child to have, by Divine power, the use of its limbs immediately after birth.

Now we have it on the authority of Scripture that *God made man right* (Eccles. 7:30), which rightness, as Augustine says, consists in the perfect subjection of the body to the soul. As, therefore, in the primitive state it was impossible to find in the human limbs anything repugnant to man's well-ordered will, so was it impossible for those limbs to fail in executing the will's commands. Now the human will is well ordered when it tends to acts which are befitting to man. But the same acts are not befitting to man at every season of life. We must, therefore, conclude that children would not have had sufficient strength for the use of their limbs for the purpose of performing every kind of act; but only for the acts befitting the state of infancy, such as suckling, and the like.*

This apparently trivial passage contains much that is typical of Thomism, as the Scholastic philosophy of Aquinas is termed. It is close to common sense, yet it grants a clear supremacy to "truths which are above nature," which we hold by faith and receive through divine authority. It expresses the belief that God usually prefers to let nature run its course according to its laws, and that there is a "fitness" in human action conforming to these laws of nature. Finally it makes an appeal to authority, in this case the Old Testament and Saint Augustine.

Mysticism

In all periods there are many human beings who distrust reason and prefer to rely upon the emotions or the instincts. Not only did Aquinas's rationalism arouse considerable hostility in his own day, but the voices of antirationalist mystics were raised on behalf of their own views. Saint Bernard of Clairvaux, the mystic in action, as we saw, fought Abelard's apparent exaltation of reason. Saint Francis the mystic distrusted books and told his brethren to throw them away, to rely on love, to discipline the mind as well as the body. Aquinas's Franciscan contemporary Bonaventura (John of Fidanza, 1221–1274) preached to his students in Paris that the human mind, as an organ of Adam's sinful and unredeemed descendants, could understand only things of the physical world. Only by divine illumination could men hope to gain cognition of the divine or supernatural. Prayer, not study, love and longing for God, not reason—this was the answer of Bonaventura, as it always is for mystics. Yet Bonaventura was an accomplished philosopher, quite able to deal on even terms with his rationalist opponents. In his *Voyage of the Mind to God* he echoes Augustine and the earlier Platonists: the grace of God helps the mind achieve the degree of love it needs to undergo the ultimate mystical experience of a kind of union with the divine.

Political Thought

The medieval thinker believed that the perfection of the kingdom of heaven could not possibly exist on earth, where compromise and imperfection are inescapable. Full equality could not exist on earth. The twelfth-century *Policraticus (Statesman's Book)* of the English philosopher John of Salisbury (ca. 1115–1180) gives us a view of the order of rank in human society. The prince (or king) is the head of the body of the commonwealth; the senate (legislature) is the heart; the judges and governors of provinces are the eyes, ears, and tongue; the officials and soldiers are the hands; the financial officers are the stomach and intestines; and the peasants "correspond to the feet, which always cleave to the soil." This figure of speech, or, in more ambitious terms, this organic theory of society, has remained a great favorite with those who oppose change. For obviously the foot does not try to become the brain, nor is the hand jealous of the eye; the whole body is at its best when each part does what nature meant it to do. The field worker, the blacksmith, the merchant, the lawyer, the priest, and the king himself all have been assigned a part of God's work on earth.

Medieval thought thus distinguished among vocations, but it also insisted on the dignity and worth of all vocations, even the humblest. It accepted the Christian doctrine of the equality of all souls before God and held that no man

* *The "Summa Theologica" of St. Thomas Aquinas,* 2nd ed. (London, 1922), Vol. IV, Pt. I, Quest. XCIX.

could be a mere instrument of another man. Even the humblest person on this earth could in the next world hope to enjoy a bliss as full and eternal as any king's. Furthermore, medieval political theory by no means opposed all change on earth. If existing conditions were bad, it was a sign that originally good conditions had been perverted; the thing to do was to restore the original good, God's own plan.

A relatively rigid and authoritarian society needs a sovereign authority whose decisions are final. But the medieval West never gave unquestioning acceptance to a single and final authority, although both popes and emperors competed for the position. Both sides enlisted medieval thinkers; in the strife of propaganda the imperialists insulted the papalists and the papalists insulted the imperialists. Each side had to find backing for its claims to authority, and some of the arguments ring familiarly even in modern ears.

Marsiglio of Padua (ca. 1275–1343), the author of *Defensor Pacis (Defender of the Peace),* an imperialist pamphlet, maintained that the only true source of authority in a commonwealth was the *universitas civium,* the whole body of the citizens. Marsiglio probably did not mean to be so modern as he may seem. He still used medieval terms, and the constitutionalism, the notions of popular sovereignty, that have been attributed to him are a long way from our notion of counting heads to determine political decisions. But Marsiglio did in all earnestness mean what a great many other medieval thinkers meant: no man's place in the order of rank, even if he is at the top of it, is such that those of lower rank must always and unquestioningly accept what he commands. The feudal relation itself was an admirable example of medieval insistence that the order of rank was not one of mere might. Lords and vassals were held together by a contract binding on *both* parties.

IV
Literature and the Arts

Latin Literature

In literature and the arts, as in the social and economic life of medieval men, the eleventh century provides a convenient turning point for the student. Latin, as we have abundantly seen, continued to be the language of the Church and of learned communication everywhere in western Europe. In fact, men wrote it far better and more fluently than they did in the earlier Middle Ages, when, with the exception of the Carolingian period, literacy was in some measure kept alive by the half-literate. All the churchmen we have been discussing in this chapter—John of Salisbury, Abelard, Bernard, Aquinas, and the rest—wrote Latin even when corresponding informally with their friends. Schoolboys, often destined for the Church or they might not have been schoolboys at all, began their academic lives by learning it. It was also the language of the law and of politics: all documents, such as a title deed to a piece of property, a royal enactment, a treaty of peace, or a letter from one monarch to another or between laymen and clerics, were still written in Latin as a matter of course. Sermons were written and delivered in Latin, hymns were composed and sung in Latin, and much verse was still written in Latin, even extremely colloquial or satirical verse, such as the famous student songs of the twelfth century, still preserved in a single manuscript found in a German monastery.

These songs, all anonymous, are called Goliardic because the authors—mostly, we imagine, wild young renegade clerics wandering about Europe from one lecturer to another—claimed to be in the service of a certain Golias, a kind of satanic figure perhaps deriving originally from the Old Testament giant, Goliath, whom David slew with a stone from his sling. Their verses mocked the form and the values of the serious religious poetry of the time, and goodhumoredly, though very roughly, satirized the clergy and the Church and even the Bible. No doubt the Goliardic verses in praise of wine, women, and song shocked the virtuous, as they were intended to do. Here is the way in which the Confession of Golias, so called, defined the highest good:

My intention is to die
　　In the tavern drinking;
Wine must be on hand, for I
　　Want it when I'm sinking.

Angels when they come shall cry
　　At my frailties winking:
"Spare this drunkard, God, he's high,
　　Absolutely stinking." *

Vernacular Poetry: Northern France

But if Latin persisted and was widely used for all literary purposes, the period after the eleventh century marks the gradual triumph of the vernacular languages all over Europe for the literature of entertainment, of belles lettres. Whereas *Beowulf,* coming from a Britain never thoroughly Latinized, was our only important literary vernacular poem during the early Middle Ages, now such poems began to appear in ever greater numbers on the Continent as well. A particularly celebrated one is *The Song of Roland,* of about four thousand lines, written in Old French, whose earliest surviving manuscript was probably written down a little after the year 1100. The poem tells of the exploits of Roland, a peer of Charlemagne, against the Muslims on the Spanish border and in the face of treachery.

In the *Song of Roland,* human beings have replaced the monsters of *Beowulf* as the enemy; the landscape has brightened; a more intense Christian piety softens some of the worst violence: Roland sees to it that his comrades slain by the infidel receive a Christian blessing. It is human treachery—by the villainous Ganelon—that brings down tragedy on the heroic forces of Charlemagne, leaving Roland and the king grief-stricken. The highest virtue in the poem is loyalty to one's lord: a quality that was the first necessity in a feudal society which only the knight's loyalty to his suzerain saved from anarchy. And, as the knight was always defined as a mounted man, a man on a horse, so the unwritten but generally accepted code that during these centuries came to govern his behavior in more and more elaborate detail as time went on was called *chivalry,* from the word that means a horse: chivalric actions are those knightly deeds to be expected from a mounted man. In Roland's deep loyalty to his lord, Charlemagne, we find something new: a love for "sweet France," a patriotic note of love for country struck at just about the earliest moment that we can speak of Europeans as having a country.

Many other songs were sung about Charlemagne's captains, and stories told about them; and other such "cycles" of stories also evolved at the same period around other great heroes. King Arthur of Britain, far more legendary than Charlemagne, was of course one of the most famous, and the exploits of his knights were celebrated not only among Arthur's fellow Celts in Wales, Ireland, and Britanny but in France as well, by such poets as Marie de France

---

* From *The Goliard Poets* by George F. Whicher. Copyright 1949 by George F. Whicher. Reprinted by permission of New Directions Publishing Corporation.

and Chrétien de Troyes. From France they passed in the thirteenth century into Germany, where Wolfram von Eschenbach wrote a splendid long poem about King Arthur's knight Sir Percival, and gave new impetus to an old tradition that would not culminate perhaps until Wagner's opera of the nineteenth century. If Wagner found inspiration in the Arthurian cycle, so did Tennyson, Edwin Arlington Robinson, and a host of other moderns, always ready to retell a well-known story in a way that would speak afresh to the psychological attitudes of new generations.

Similarly, the men of the thirteenth century rediscovered the story of the Trojan war, an event already almost three thousand years in the past. It was of course not yet Homer, himself still unknown in the Latin West, but two rather humdrum summary accounts in Latin supposedly by one Dares the Phrygian and Dictys the Cretan (imaginary figures, both of them) that supplied the impetus to the revival of interest in Troy. And current or recent events, like the Crusades, led to dozens of other poetic narratives of adventure. In all these poems, collectively called the *Chansons de Geste*—songs of action—and chiefly written in northern France, we encounter again the same chivalric virtues of loyalty and courage that were celebrated in the *Roland.*

Provence and Courtly Love

In southern France, things were gentler. No doubt the sunny climate, the greater leisure, and the proximity to the cultivated Muslims of Spain all played a part. Here lyric poetry flourished, with love as its favorite theme. But love in southern France soon had a curious code of its own: *courtoisie,* or courtly love. The singer's lady was never a properly attainable sweetheart, unmarried and perhaps ready to be won. She was always the wife of another; she was worshiped from afar; and the singer celebrated in ecstasy even the slightest kindness she might offer him. Her merest word was a command, and her devoted knight undertook without question even the most arduous mission she might propose to him, without hope of a reward. But a lady who failed to reward him, at least to some degree, was not playing by the rules of this elaborate and artificial game. The twelfth-century troubadours who sang in the southern French language (called Provençal after the large region of Provence, and quite a different dialect from that spoken in the north) were often half-humorous as they expressed their longings for the unattainable lady.

Aquitaine, in southwest France, was long a center for this form of lyric poetry. Duke William IX in the early twelfth century was himself a troubadour, and his granddaughter, Eleanor—the wife successively of Louis VII of France and then of Henry II of England—held "courts of love." Here, in sessions patterned mockingly on those of feudal courts of justice, the lovesick troubadours sang their songs and had their cases judged, and petitions from ladies and gentlemen crossed in love received mock-serious attention. So the southern French modified the general feudal attitude toward women as mere breeders of new generations of fighters, and made life more agreeable and far more sophisticated for all who heard the songs of courtly love.

The influence of the troubadours penetrated into Germany, where courtly love was soon called *Minne,* and its celebrants the minnesingers. Needless to say, few medieval nobles behaved according to the code, and yet portions of the conceptions fostered among the troubadours did become part of the developing notions of chivalry. In such a thirteenth-century figure as Saint Louis, we find as nearly as truly chivalrous figure as can have ever existed. His faithful biographer, Joinville, was himself the personification of a loyal vassal, as he accompanied his royal master on his ill-fated crusades. And Joinville's work is one of the two most important vernacular French prose documents of the thirteenth century, the other being the only slightly earlier account by Villehardouin of the Fourth Crusade and the capture of Constantinople. When historians began to write for their audiences in the language of every day rather than in Latin, the triumph of the vernacular was at hand.

In Italy, the original home of the Latin language, vernacular was somewhat slower to develop. But here too, at the sophisticated and cosmopolitan court of the emperor Frederick II (1215–1250) in Palermo, some of Frederick's chief advisers began to write love poetry in what they themselves called the "sweet new style" *(dolce stil nuovo),* and soon the fashion of writing at least that form of literature in the vernacular spread northward. But it was not until somewhat later, with Dante Alighieri (1265–1321) of Florence, that the vernacular Italian tongue scored its definitive triumph. It is significant to note that Dante himself felt impelled to write—in Latin—a stirring defense of vernacular Italian: *De Vulgari Eloquentia (Concerning the Speech of Every Day).* And for his own greatest work, *The Divine Comedy,* he himself chose Italian.

Among the writers in the Western tradition, Dante belongs with Homer, Vergil, and Shakespeare as a supreme master; so that it would be absurd to try to "appreciate" him here. Moreover, as a towering intellectual figure he heralds the new age of rebirth at least as loudly as he sounds the familiar medieval note; and we shall be discussing him again when we consider the Renaissance. It would distort our picture, however, not to examine here *The Divine Comedy* as a medieval book, a very long book, perhaps the most celebrated and in some ways the most typical of all medieval books.

Lost in a dark wood, in his thirty-fifth year ("halfway along the road of our human life"), Dante encounters the Roman poet Vergil, who consents to act as his guide through two of the three great regions of the afterlife of man: Hell and Purgatory. Descending through the nine successive circles of Hell, where the eternally damned must remain forever, the two meet and converse with individual souls in torment, some of them historic persons like Judas or Brutus, others recently deceased Florentines of Dante's own acquaintance, about whose sins he knew at first hand. In Purgatory, less sinful human beings are working out their punishment before they can be saved. The souls of the great pagan figures, born too early to have become Christians, are neither in Hell nor in Purgatory but in Limbo, a place on the edge of Hell, where Vergil himself must spend eternity. Here he introduces Dante to the shades not only of such ancients as Homer, Plato, and Socrates, but of characters in ancient myth and poetry such as Hector, Odysseus, and Aeneas.

When the poet comes to the gates of Paradise, Vergil cannot continue to escort him; so the guide to the final region of the afterlife is Beatrice, a Florentine girl with whom Dante himself had fallen desperately in love as a youth but whom he had worshiped only at a distance. Here Dante was consciously transforming one of the central experiences of his own life into literature in accordance with the traditions of the code of courtly love. In Paradise, of course, are the Christian worthies and the saints—Benedict, Bernard, Aquinas—and at the climax of the poem, a vision of God himself.

This voyage through the afterlife is designed to show in new pictorial vividness an ancient concept: that man's actions in this life determine his fate in the next. From the lost souls in Hell, who have brought themselves to their hopeless position ("Abandon Hope, All Ye Who Enter Here" reads the inscription over the gates of Hell), through those who despite their sufferings in Purgatory confidently expect to be saved and will indeed be saved, to those whose pure life on earth has won them eternal bliss, Dante shows the entire range of human behavior and its eternal consequences. It is a majestic summary of medieval Christian moral and ethical ideas, and has often been compared in its completeness and its masterful subordination of detail to general vision with the philosophical work of Aquinas. The *Divine Comedy* is a poetic and moving *summa*.

In the generation after Dante's death, the Italian authors Petrarch and Boccaccio became the chief intellectual and literary figures of Europe. We will consider them among the forerunners of the Italian Renaissance. Here, however, we must stop to pay tribute to a poet perhaps greater than they, one who knew Petrarch personally and had read many of Boccaccio's works, but who is nonetheless in many ways a medieval figure: Geoffrey Chaucer (1340-1400). In England, where the vernacular had always been strong, the Old English of the pre-Conquest period had by Chaucer's time evolved into a new form of the language usually called Middle English, quite recognizable to most of us today as an archaic version of the language we ourselves speak (although we may sometimes be perplexed by its forms). Chaucer is the supreme poet of Middle English, and surely the most brilliant English literary voice before Shakespeare. Not a scholar but an experienced man of affairs, who made several trips to the Continent on business for the king of England, and who eventually became Controller of Customs and Clerk of the King's Works, Chaucer left behind many literary works, including several allegorical poems, some of which satirize contemporary politics, and a long verse narrative love story full of passion and beauty, *Troilus and Criseyde*, deriving its characters from the Trojan War stories now so fashionable in western Europe.

But of course Chaucer's most celebrated work is the *Canterbury Tales*, and the student sometimes comes to feel that if nothing else had survived of medieval literature, we should still be able to learn most of what we know about it from the *Tales* alone. The *Tales* are told by a group of pilgrims on their way to the tomb of Thomas à Becket, the archbishop of Canterbury murdered under Henry II and now a saint. The pilgrims come from all walks of English life except the high nobility, and include a knight, a squire, a prioress, a clerk, a monk, a friar, a sailor, a miller, and others. In a brilliant prologue, Chaucer, who was himself one of the group, characterizes his fellow pilgrims, each of whom emerges as a living person. On the way from London, each tells at least one story consonant with his personality and experience.

The knight tells a romantic story of chivalric love: two cousins, Palamon and Arcite, both fall in love with a maiden whom they have barely glimpsed from the window of their prison cell. Deadly rivals thereafter, they continue to cherish their mutual strife, in prison and out, without the lady's ever being aware of them. When she learns, she does very little about it, and in the end one kills the other, and wins her as his own. It is indeed a strange story to us: the lady's passivity, the two knights' lovesickness unfed by any encouragement; but it is a true story of courtly love, and befits the experienced warrior who tells it. The miller tells a raw story of a young wife's deception of her elderly husband with a young lover, a barnyard anecdote, in effect, but full of liveliness and good humor. The prioress tells a saint's legend, the squire an (unfinished) story full of semiscientific marvels, and so on. Chaucer does not hesitate to satirize his churchmen: as we shall see, the fourteenth century was a period of much discontent with the English church, and the poet was striking a note that was sure to be popular. The sophistication, delicacy, power, passion, and humor that Chaucer commands put him in the same class with Dante, and with no other medieval writer in any country.

Architecture, Sculpture, Painting

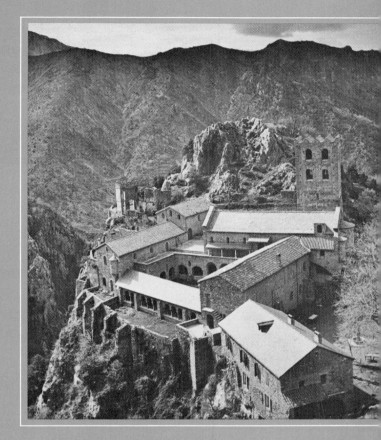

The monastery of St. Martin du Canigou high in the French Pyrenees, an early Romanesque building.

The Romanesque

ARCHITECTURE   In architecture,
the Romanesque style, evolving from
the Ottonian styles of the earlier period,
dominated the eleventh and most
of the twelfth centuries. The Gothic style,
following it and developing from it,
began in the twelfth century and continued
to prevail down to the fifteenth.
The transition between Romanesque
and Gothic is complex; and art historians
have recently begun to see the years
between about 1180 and about 1220,
especially in northern France,
as a fairly distinct period which they have
labeled transitional.*

But the whole matter of terminology
is difficult here: the term *Romanesque*
is sometimes rather loosely used
for buildings as early as the Carolingian
and Ottonian periods, but many prefer to use
pre-Romanesque and *proto-Romanesque*
for these, both terms suggesting,
quite properly, that we are on our way
to something that we have not yet
quite reached. Beginning in Lombardy, where
the first schools of craftsmen were formed, and from which the builders traveled wherever they
were needed and summoned, their skills and styles traveled across southern France to northern
Spain. One of the very earliest Romanesque churches, high up in the French Pyrenees, is St.
Martin du Canigou, built in the first quarter of the eleventh century. Like many of these new

* The concept was probably brought closer to general acceptance by an extraordinary exhibition of art called "The Year 1200,"
held in New York in 1970 to celebrate the hundredth anniversary of the Metropolitan Museum of Art, which concentrated upon the glories
and problems of these years.

buildings, it is a monastic church, far larger than most of the churches of the earlier period, and its interior provides examples of two important adaptations of earlier Roman architectural devices: the barrel or tunnel vault, or continuous round-arch roofing, now used for far larger spaces than before; and the groin vault, at first used in crypts only, and then later moved above ground to the main church. To the groin vault ribbing was sometimes added for strengthening. At St. Martin, the tower and cloister and body of the church are in harmonious balance, and all are adapted to the precipitous slope on which the church was built.

Most Romanesque churches had as their fundamental ground plan a Latin cross, with a long staff and shorter cross-arms; the shrine of the church, where stood the altar with the relics of the saint, was at the east end, and usually its walls formed a curved arc: this was the apse. Within this portion of the church also the choir sang. The arms of the cross extended north and south, usually from a point immediately west of the apse; these were the transepts. And the long portion of the cross, extending westward to the west front, was the nave, usually with an aisle at each side. Towers might be built over the crossing of nave and transepts, and at either side of the west front. Some churches had none or only one, some as many as six, if additional ones were built at the ends of the transepts. Around the interior of the apse—sometimes called simply "the choir"—there often opened a series of chapels, usually reflected in the exterior design by smaller arcs emerging from the apse wall, like bulges, little apses, or absidioles, as they are called. Of course, the ground plans varied greatly in detail from church to church, according to the wealth and taste of the community and the length of time that construction took, since as fashions changed, innovations could and would be incorporated in any church that remained a long time in the building.

Among the great Romanesque churches were those built at Mainz, Worms, and Speyer in western Germany by the Holy Roman emperors of the Salian line, of which we reproduce the ground plan of Speyer, mostly of the eleventh century, with later additions, and a view of the exterior of Worms as it is today.

One of the best ways to gain an impression of a great Romanesque monastery church, with its surrounding buildings is to examine the painstaking reconstructions made by a brilliant student of past architecture, Professor K. J. Conant. Here is Conant's drawing of his model of the entire complex of Cluny as it was in 1157. And to be compared with the church at Cluny is his reconstruction of the noble pilgrimage church of St. James (Santiago) at Compostela in far northwestern Spain.

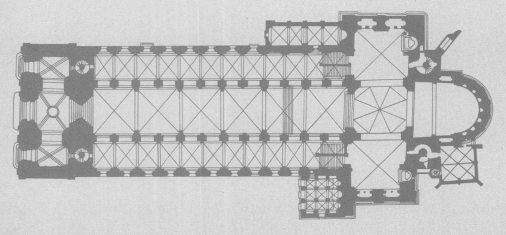

Ground plan of the Cathedral of Speyer in western Germany, begun ca. 1030.

The Cathedral of Worms, western Germany, begun in the eleventh century.

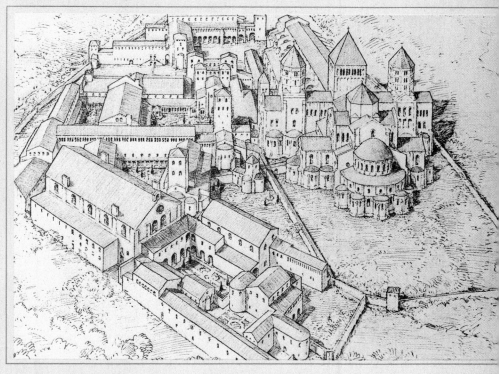

Above: Drawing of a model of the monastery of Cluny as constructed by Professor Conant.

Left: Santiago de Compostela, the goal of western European pilgrims: a drawing of a restoration to its medieval state.

To Compostela from all over
western Europe but especially
from France there flooded
in these years throngs of pilgrims
to worship at the shrine of the saint.
And along the routes, to accommodate
the pilgrims, hospices were built,
and monasteries and churches
flourished. It has long been realized
that Romanesque architecture spread
along these routes as well,
and "pilgrimage churches," great
Romanesque buildings at
which the pilgrims would stop
to worship along their way, were built
in many key centers. The interior
of Ste. Foi at Conques in
south-central France, with its groin
vaulting in the nave, is typical.

Variations on the typical Romanesque
church can be seen, for example,
in southwestern France, where
a group of churches, unlike those
anywhere else, have domed
roofs, sometimes with the domes
placed in a row above the nave, and,
sometimes, as at St. Front of Perigueux,
placed in a Greek (equal-armed)
cross pattern, with a central dome,
surrounded by four side domes, like
St. Mark's at Venice, itself
an imitation of the (lost) Church
of the Holy Apostles in Byzantium.
It has long been argued, and cogently,
that Greek influence was somehow
at work in this corner of France.
The effect upon the worshiper
standing under a roof made
up of a series of domes is entirely
different from that produced by the
ordinary Romanesque barrel or groin
vaulting, a point well illustrated

*Angoulême: The nave of a church whose
roof is a series of domes.*

by the interior of the Cathedral of Angoulême. That Romanesque was a truly international style despite its many variations may be seen in further examples, the interiors of two widely separated cathedrals: that of Pisa, in Italy, and that of Durham, in northern England.

SCULPTURE   A little before the year 1100, there began an extraordinary revival of European sculpture. While the tradition had never been lost, as we know from looking at monuments as late as the early medieval Irish and English crosses, and at the extraordinary figures at Cividale, the finest surviving examples of the art of sculpture before the Romanesque revival were the smaller examples in ivory and in metalwork that we have also noted. But now, quite suddenly, with joy and exuberance, the stones of the Romanesque churches we have been discussing came literally to life. The older classical columns usually had Corinthian capitals with their acanthus leaves. But now capitals began to blossom out with rosettes, palm-leaf ornament, and grapevines, and amidst the foliage there suddenly proliferated a whole race of marvelous beasts. Some were carved as if

Below: The nave of Pisa Cathedral, an Italian church of the Romanesque period.

Above: Durham: nave of the Cathedral. Romanesque (or Norman, as it is always called in England).

Man-eating dragon: capital of a column at the Church of St. Pierre, Chauvigny, France.

The Magi being waked from their dreams: from Autun.

they were illustrations to the popular bestiaries (collections of anecdotes about real and mythical animals, usually with a Christian allegorical explanation of the animals' incredible characteristics); some were taken from real life, and some from the teeming imagination of the sculptors. At such places as Chauvigny, in western France, lions and pelicans, horses and elephants, griffins and dragons, and mermaids and other weird monsters, savage harpies attacking each other, all now edified the beholder, or, as Saint Bernard stoutly maintained, distracted him from his real business in church: the capitals at his church of Clermont and at Cîteaux were severely plain.

Of course, scenes from the Bible also appeared on the capitals, and elsewhere in the churches, but now often interpreted with a freedom from the traditional ways of showing such subjects, and with a due consideration for the space available to the artist within the small compass of the top of a column. On some capitals, the three magi (wise men from the East) sleep happily under the same blanket with their crowns on. Judas hangs himself, while terrifying winged demons pull actually and symbolically at each end of the rope. And from the capitals, of course, the sculpture spread to the available large flat and vertical surfaces available to the artist in a Romanesque church: for example, to the arched space over the outside of the front portal, the tympanum, as it is called.

Here Christ himself could be shown enthroned, often with the Virgin and the saints at his side, and surrounding and beneath them a depiction of the Last Judgment, the souls of the damned

196

The west tympanum of the Cathedral of St. Lazare, Autun. (A detail of this relief is shown on page 156.)

being eternally rejected at the moment of the Second Coming of the Lord, while those of the blessed rise from the tomb to enjoy their eternal salvation. At Vézelay and Autun in Burgundy, at Conques and Beaulieu and many other Romanesque churches of the pilgrimage routes, such large-scale representations of this complicated composition gave the sculptor scope for his versatility at filling space and portraying what is after all the sublimest moment in the Christian's conception of his universe.

On the doorposts, and in the repeated hollow indented narrow arches around the portals (called *voussures*), sculptured ornament also took over. At Moissac and Souillac in southern France, a frantic series of grotesque beasts, each gripping and eating the next, climbs and struggles its way up an entire vertical column or doorpost. Human and animal heads look out side by side from the voussures surrounding the tympanum. In one region of southwest France, specially noted for its breeding of horses, it is horses' heads alone that ornament the church portals and façades. In the

197

cloister of San Domingo de Silos
in northern Spain, or in Chichester
Cathedral in southern England, one still can
see large plaques sculptured with splendid
representations of biblical scenes.
Romanesque sculpture is almost
always in relief rather than in the full round.

PAINTING   In the nature of things,
far less survives of Romanesque painting
than of Romanesque sculpture.
In the first place, when anti-Christian
vandals in later periods of revolution set
about the business of defacing
earlier Christian monuments, they naturally
found it somewhat easier to destroy
paintings by scraping them off the walls
or tearing out illuminations from books than
to shatter stone monuments completely.
In the second place, a painting
on a plaster wall, for example, deteriorates
faster with the passage of time than
does a piece of sculpture, especially one
that is indoors. However, enough survives,
often in out-of-the-way places,
to show that painting too experienced
a revival no less significant than sculpture.
In León in northern Spain, in many
churches of Catalonia, and in a few places
in England, France, and Italy,
wall paintings can still be seen from
this early period.

The stone panel in Chichester Cathedral showing
Mary and Martha kneeling before Christ at the
gates of Bethany.

Three bowing angels: fresco in the church of St.-
Savin-sur-Gartempe, France, illustrating a scene
from the Apocalypse.

Probably the most complete series still visible is in the abbey
church of St.-Savin-sur-Gartempe, not far from Poitiers
in western France, and only a few moments' drive
from the grotesque capitals at Chauvigny. At St.-Savin, the walls
and ceiling of the apse and the entire long barrel vaulting
of the ceiling of the nave were covered with an elaborate series
of paintings, the nave with scenes from the Old Testament:
Creation, the murder of Abel, Noah's Ark, the stories
of Abraham and Joseph, and the Tower of Babel; and the apse
with scenes from the New, including the deposition from
the Cross and the Resurrection. One may also consider
as a special kind of Romanesque

A scene from the Bayeux Tapestry, depicting the Norman fleet under William the Conqueror crossing the English Channel.

painting the unique and famous Bayeux tapestry (actually an embroidery) commemorating the Norman Conquest of England and made soon afterwards.

Such elaborate "programs" of painting as that at St.-Savin are more familiar to us from the monuments of Italy, where the painting often took the ancient form of mosaic, used by the Romans but perfected for Christian art and for wall decoration by the Byzantines. Just as in the earlier period Eastern influence produced the great mosaics in Ravenna, we find in the Romanesque period especially rich mosaic paintings in the churches of Norman Sicily, always open to Eastern influences, and still inhabited by and visited by many Greeks. In Palermo alone, the chapel of the royal palace of the Norman kings (Cappella Palatina), the church of the Martorana, and the magnificent nearby Cathedral of Monreale all display these Byzantine-influenced mosaic paintings against the usual gold ground, and present a rich variety of scenes. Not far away at

Mosaic scenes from Genesis: The west wall of the nave of the Cathedral of Monreale, Sicily, showing Byzantine and Muslim influence.

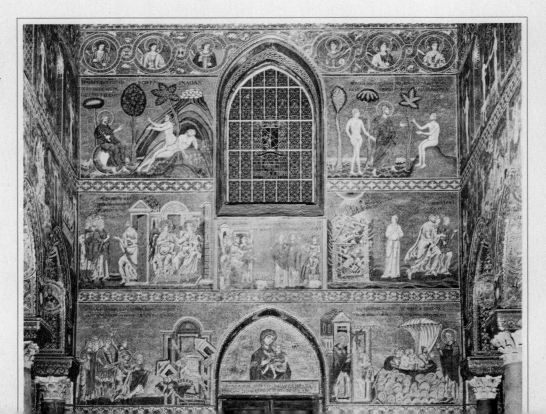

Cefalù is still another large church with mosaic decoration. The earliest surviving mosaics at St. Mark's in Venice—also intimately linked with Byzantium, as we know—date shortly after the beginning of the thirteenth century.

The Transition to Gothic

ARCHITECTURE   We turn now briefly to the changes that came over the Romanesque beginning in the late twelfth century. In architecture, the arches, from being round, now gradually rose to points at the peak, and similarly the roofs, once barrel-vaulted (or barrel-vaulted with groins and ribs), now also rose more and more sharply, as the smooth flow of the arc was sharply broken, and two loftier curves now met instead at a point. The continuous Romanesque barrel vault pressed down upon its supporting walls with even stress, and the walls had to be made very strong, with few openings, and often with buttresses—stone supports built at right angles to the main wall to take part of the outward push. But the chief feature of the newer medieval architecture always known as Gothic was precisely this pointed arch, a new device by which the builder could carry his buildings to soaring heights. The vaulted ceiling now rested upon a series of masonry ribs, in groups of four, two rising from each side of the wall, and each group supported by a massive pillar. Four pillars therefore could now be made to take the place of a whole section of solid Romanesque wall, and the spaces between the pillars could be freed for windows. From the beginning, therefore, Gothic churches were far lighter inside than Romanesque churches.

Outside too, a new effect of increased lightness and soaring height was achieved by moving the vertical buttress of the Romanesque period away from the walls of the church, and by bridging the gap between buttress and church wall with an arched support that looked as if it were actually flying between the now distant vertical and the lofty masonry wall, part of whose outward thrust it was designed to take. These "flying buttresses" also freed the builder to soar upward. Into the new window spaces made possible by the new architectural devices the craftsmen of the thirteenth century and later fitted a new form of painting: the window in multicolored (stained) glass, glittering with gemlike color in ruby, sapphire, and emerald, and showing biblical episodes or episodes from the life of the saint whose church they illuminated.

Gothic architecture flourished for at least two centuries everywhere in Europe. Its first and perhaps greatest moments came in northern France, with the building—all between the 1190's and about 1240—of the cathedrals of Chartres, Reims, Amiens, Notre Dame of Paris, and other celebrated churches. Sometimes the ambition of a designer extended beyond his control of engineering: the architect of Beauvais, who managed to build the loftiest apse and transepts of any Gothic church, found that he could not get his nave to stand up; so it fell, and what remains still looks like an exercise in defiance of the law of gravity.

Open and vast, but solidly built, soaring upward according to well-worked-out and usually well-understood mathematical architectural proportional formulas, the Gothic cathedral terminates in aerial towers. Though its great windows let in the light, the stained glass keeps the interior dim and awe-inspiring. In England, York and Canterbury, Salisbury and Wells, Ely and Winchester among a good many other cathedrals still stand as the best of island Gothic, fully comparable with

Amiens: The nave.

Chartres Cathedral, whose later tower (left) illustrates the overripe look of Gothic architecture in its decline.

the best on the Continent. With the passage of time in the fourteenth and fifteenth centuries ornamentation grew richer, decoration became more intricate, literally flamelike, or "flamboyant," and Gothic architecture on the Continent moved toward its decline. The later tower at Chartres illustrates this overripe look; in England, however, the later richer Gothic has given us such marvels as King's College Chapel in Cambridge and the Henry VII Chapel at Westminster Abbey in London.

King's College Chapel, Cambridge.

"Style 1200": Two of Nicholas of Verdun's enameled plaques made for the Klosterneuburg altarpiece—Christ enthroned, and the mouth of Hell. In the former, note the folds of the draperies and the genuine bodies beneath.

SCULPTURE   Of sculpture in the years between 1180 and 1220 it has been recently said that "for practically the first time since ancient Greek and Roman times, draperies curl and caress the bodies underneath; limbs themselves are proudly and successfully shown as organic entities; strength becomes a thing of muscles rather than size alone; physiques are neither camouflaged nor ignored, but studied and presented to our eyes in an almost overpowering beauty. Faces become truly alive, eyes shine with an inner light, gestures seem to develop an entirely new expressive poetry of their own. Drama is supreme." * Refusing to call this style either Romanesque or Gothic, and discarding even the name "transitional," but preferring simply the slightly awkward term "Style 1200," recent scholars point to the work in metals of Nicholas of Verdun and of sculptors working in the valley of the Meuse, where France, Belgium, Holland, and Germany are close together, as marking the beginning of the new school; but more generally northern France, western Germany, and England all saw its activity.

* Thomas P. F. Hoving, in his Foreword to *The Year 1200: A Centennial Exhibition at the Metropolitan Museum of Art* (New York: The Metropolitan Museum of Art, 1970), I, vii.

Gradually during this period, sculpture in the round became more and more common, beginning with figures that were carved fully in the round from the mid-sections of columns, engaged in the façade or the portal of a church only at the top and at the base. The lifelike representation of drapery, the firm balance of the figures on their feet, are principal characteristics of these new statues, chiefly occurring in northern France. Similar influences are shown elsewhere in metalwork and in manuscript illumination, rather than in monumental sculpture, and it is agreed that the influences from outside that help make the development possible must be sought in Byzantine art, then itself undergoing a kind of classical renaissance, and available to Western eyes through renewed and intensified contacts between East and West by pilgrims, travelers, and warriors during the period of the Crusades. What we have here is an artistic revival more splendid and more complicated even than had hitherto been suspected.

Right: The Last Judgment: a page from the psalter made for Ingeborg, Danish wife of King Philip Augustus of France (reigned 1180–1223), a further representation of "Style 1200."

Left: "Style 1200": Silver-gilt figure of Saint Simon sculpted by Nicholas of Verdun for the Shrine of the Three Kings, Cologne.

Medieval music was essentially church music, which began in the sixth century with Gregorian chant or plainsong. Plainsong was simply a series of musical tones, separated by no set rhythmic interval, sung in unison. It was used in church services as a setting for the psalms and other prose. But apparently there were also hymns in metrical or verse form that could be accommodated to a simple tune. As Europe emerged from the Dark Ages, music, like the other arts, grew more and more complex. Our present method of musical notation—the staff—was invented, or at any rate developed and taught, by an eleventh-century Italian monk, Guido of Arezzo. Church music developed both melody and harmony—the sounding of two or more notes simultaneously—until the peak of balanced form and matter was reached in the thirteenth century. Later medieval church music sometimes resembles an extremely complex musical puzzle.

Conscious secular musical composition begins in the Middle Ages with the minstrels, who often elaborated popular tunes. By the end of the fourteenth century we get something like the modern composer, for example the Italian Landini, who wrote songs, called madrigals, set for two voices. Music, like the other arts, was anonymous, but the cautious historian can say only that this anonymity may be simply a result of the gaps in our historical record.

Reading Suggestions on Western Medieval Europe

SOCIAL AND ECONOMIC FOUNDATIONS

R. S. Lopez, *The Birth of Europe* (Lippincott, 1967). Basic work by a ranking economic historian.

The Cambridge Economic History, Volumes I and II (Cambridge University, 1944, 1952). Detailed survey of the economy of medieval Europe by various experts.

P. Boissonade, *Life and Work in Medieval Europe* (*Torchbooks). A very good introduction, written by a French scholar in the 1920's.

L. White, Jr., *Medieval Technology and Social Change* (*Galaxy). Scholarly, readable, and suggestive study.

H. Pirenne, *Medieval Cities* (*Anchor). Excellent short essay by a Belgian scholar who wrote several other works on the social and economic life of the Middle Ages.

S. Painter, *Medieval Society* (*Cornell). Handy introduction by a very good scholar.

POLITICS: WORKS TOUCHING MORE THAN ONE COUNTRY

C. Brooke, *Europe in the Central Middle Ages, 962–1154* (Holt, 1964). Excellent up-to-date survey.

S. Painter, *Rise of the Feudal Monarchies* (*Cornell). Good introduction for the beginner.

C. Petit-Dutaillis, *Feudal Monarchy in France and England from the Tenth to the Thirteenth Century* (*Torchbooks). Standard study by a French expert of the early twentieth century.

W. Ullmann, *Principles of Government and Politics in the Middle Ages* (Barnes & Noble, 1961). Ambitious synthesis, not acceptable to all specialists; by the author of other controversial studies in the field.

C. H. Haskins, *The Normans in European History* (*Norton). By a celebrated historian and teacher of the early twentieth century; still very much worth reading.

Amy Kelly, *Eleanor of Aquitaine and the Four Kings* (*Vintage). Learned and lively book about the ranking feminine personality of twelfth-century France and England.

THE FRENCH MONARCHY

R. Fawtier, *The Capetian Kings of France* (*Papermac). Most up-to-date account.

J. Evans, *Life in Medieval France* (Oxford, 1925). Good picture of French society.

A. Luchaire, *Social France at the Time of Philip Augustus* (*Torchbooks). A famous old account, stressing the seamy side of life about 1200.

THE ENGLISH MONARCHY

G. O. Sayles, *The Medieval Foundations of England* (*Perpetua). Excellent basic study. With H. G. Richardson, Sayles is co-author of *The Governance of Medieval England from the Conquest to Magna Carta* (Edinburgh, 1963), a brilliant and provocative analysis.

A. L. Poole, *From Domesday Book to Magna Carta, 1087–1216,* and F. M. Powicke, *The Thirteenth Century, 1216–1307* (Clarendon, 1951, 1953). Very useful volumes in the indispensable Oxford History of England.

D. M. Stenton, *English Society in the Early Middle Ages* (*Pelican); A. R. Myers, *England in the Late Middle Ages* (*Pelican); H. M. Cam, *England before Elizabeth* (*Torchbooks). Good brief popular accounts by sound scholars.

D. C. Douglas, *William the Conqueror and the Norman Impact upon England* (*University of California). The last word on 1066 and all that. Frank Barlow, *William I and the Norman Conquest* (*Collier). A shorter and more popular account.

B. Wilkinson, *The Constitutional History of England, 1216–1399,* 3 vols. (Longmans, 1948–1952). Magisterial treatment of a much debated topic.

G. L. Haskins, *Growth of English Representative Government* (*Perpetua). A clear account of a most difficult and vital subject.

G. C. Homans, *English Villagers of the Thirteenth Century* (Russell & Russell, 1960). Interesting sociological study.

THE GERMAN MONARCHY

G. Barraclough, *The Origins of Modern Germany* (*Capricorn). Best general treatment of medieval Germany in English; Barraclough also translated and edited important revisionist essays by German scholars in *Medieval Germany*, 2 vols. (Blackwell, 1938).

J. Bryce, *The Holy Roman Empire* (*Schocken). First written as an undergraduate honors essay more than a century ago, and still worthwhile.

J. W. Thompson, *Feudal Germany* (University of Chicago, 1928). A standard work, now somewhat outdated.

E. Kantorowicz, *Frederick the Second, 1194-1250* (R. R. Smith, 1931). Scholarly and imaginative treatment. The scholarship has won wide respect; the imagination has not.

CIVILIZATION

H. O. Taylor, *The Medieval Mind,* new ed. (Harvard University, 1949). A great inclusive work, now somewhat outdated.

Henry Adams, *Mont-Saint-Michel and Chartres* (*several editions). A highly personal introduction to the values of medieval civilization by the famous American intellectual. Many of its conclusions have been challenged by experts; see, for example, E. Mâle, *The Gothic Image: Religious Art in France in the Thirteenth Century* (*Torchbooks).

M. DeWulf, *Philosophy and Civilization in the Middle Ages* (*Dover). Popular lectures by a ranking scholar of an older generation.

D. Knowles, *The Evolution of Medieval Thought* (*Vintage). Stresses the continuity between classical and Scholastic thought.

C. S. Lewis, *The Discarded Image: An Introduction to Medieval and Renaissance Literature* (Cambridge University, 1964). A subtle commentary, revising traditional interpretations.

K. S. Drew and F. S. Lear, *Perspectives in Medieval History* (Chicago, 1963). Five American medievalists sum up their generation's views.

H. Rashdall, *The Universities of Europe in the Middle Ages,* 3 vols. (Clarendon, 1936). The classic detailed study of its subject.

C. H. Haskins, *The Rise of Universities* (*Cornell). Delightful short essays.

———, *The Renaissance of the Twlefth Century* (*Meridian). An important revisionist work, stressing "modern" elements in medieval civilization.

A. C. Crombie, *Medieval and Early Modern Science,* 2 vols. (*Anchor). A standard succinct account.

A. E. Gilson, *Reason and Revelation in the Middle Ages* (*Scribner's). By a distinguished French Catholic scholar, author of many other important works sympathetic to the Middle Ages.

M. D. Chenu, *Toward Understanding St. Thomas* (Regnery, 1964). Standard French work on Aquinas.

H. Daniel-Rops, *Bernard of Clairvaux* (Hawthorne, 1964). Excellent account.

ART

Kenneth J. Conant, *Carolingian and Romanesque Architecture, 800-1200* (Pelican, 1959). The classic general work by a great authority.

The Year 1200: A Background Survey, ed. Florenz Deichler, 2 vols. (Metropolitan Museum of Art, 1970.) Well-illustrated volumes putting forth new and still controversial theories.

FICTION AND BIOGRAPHY

Chaucer, *Canterbury Tales* (many editions). Perhaps the best literary introduction to medieval civilization.

Bryher, *The Fourteenth of October* (Pantheon, 1952), and Hope Muntz, *The Golden Warrior* (*Scribner's). Good novels about the Norman conquest.

Eileen Power, *Medieval People* (*Anchor). Biographical sketches of a half-dozen individuals from various walks of medieval life.

Helen Waddell, *Peter Abelard* (*Compass). Novel about the famous affair with Héloïse.

C. Whitman, *Peter Abelard* (Harvard University, 1965). Interesting narrative poem.

Z. Oldenbourg, *The World Is Not Enough* and *The Cornerstone* (*Ballantine). Realistic novels about French feudal families.

five

The Medieval World: Eastern Europe

In this chapter we introduce two other civilizations, that of the Eastern Christian society centering on Byzantium, and that of the Muslims. Once again the eleventh century provides a turning point, for it was then that the West undertook a prolonged campaign against the Muslim and Orthodox East: a campaign that temporarily destroyed the Byzantine Empire, so weakening it that the Ottoman Turks could complete their conquest in 1453. Yet in the East, the medieval period really extended down to the end of the seventeenth century. We recognize this fundamental continuity here by carrying our discussion well past the end of the western European Middle Ages, dealing with both Ottoman history after the conquest of Byzantium and the Russian society that owed so much to Byzantine civilization.

I

Life in Byzantium

At the far southeastern corner of Europe, on a little tongue of land still defended by a long line of massive walls and towers, stands a splendid city. Istanbul it is called now, a Turkish corruption of three Greek words meaning "to the city." After 330, when the Roman emperor Constantine, abandoning Rome, decided to make it his capital, it was often called Constantinople, the city of Constantine, but it also retained its earlier name, Byzantium. For more than eleven hundred years thereafter it remained the capital of the Roman Empire, falling to the Turks in 1453.

The waters that surround it on three sides are those of the Sea of Marmora, the Bosporus, and the city's own sheltered harbor, the Golden Horn. A few miles north, up the narrow swift-flowing Bosporus, lies the entrance into the

Black Sea. To the southwest of the city, the Sea of Marmora narrows into the Dardanelles, the passage into the Aegean and thus the Mediterranean. Together, the Dardanelles, the Sea of Marmora, and the Bosporus not only connect the Mediterranean with the Black Sea but separate Europe from Asia. These are the Straits, perhaps the most important strategic waterway in European diplomatic and military history, dominated by "the city." To the Slavs, both of Russia and of the Balkans, who owe to it their religion and their culture, the city has always been "Czargrad," city of the emperor. This was the center of a civilization in many ways similar to that of medieval western Europe, yet in other ways startlingly different.

The State

THE EMPEROR Byzantium called itself New Rome. Its emperors ruled in direct succession from Augustus, and its population, while predominantly Greek in race, language, and origin, called itself Rhomaean, Roman. Despite pride in this Roman heritage, many non-Roman elements became increasingly important in Byzantine society. After Constantine himself had become a Christian, the emperor was of course no longer considered a god. But he was ordained of God, and his power remained divine. As there could be but one God in heaven, so there could be but one emperor on earth. The Roman pagan tradition of the god-emperor was modified but not abandoned.

In theory, the will of God manifested itself in the unanimous consent of the people, the senate (established at Constantinople in the Roman pattern by Constantine himself), and the army to the choice of each new emperor. In practice, the reigning emperor usually chose his heir, often his own son, by coopting him during his own lifetime, as he had done at Rome. Byzantine dynasties sometimes lasted several centuries. But politicians often intervened: they imprisoned and exiled emperors, murdered them, blinded them (which made them ineligible to rule again), and enthroned their own candidates.

Each new emperor was raised aloft on a shield as a sign of army approval, so becoming *imperator,* commander in chief. By the mid-fifth century, he was also formally crowned by the patriarch of Constantinople. He would swear to defend the Christian faith, and in addition to the crown received a purple robe and purple boots. In the seventh century, the emperor began to call himself *basileus,* king of kings, in token that he had defeated the Persians. Later still, he added the term *autokrator,* the autocrat. Empresses bore corresponding feminine titles and in general played an important role. Three times in Byzantine history women ruled without a male emperor.

A conspiracy by a rival might overthrow the emperor, but autocracy as such was not challenged. Divinely awarded powers entailed immense earthly responsibilities. An elaborate and rigid code of etiquette governed the emperor's every activity every day of the year; he spoke and commanded through brief established formulas. His subjects ceremoniously fell on their faces as they approached him with a courtier holding them by each arm, and the emperor would be acclaimed with song and silver trumpets whenever he appeared in public.

As agent of God, the emperor ordered the periodic recompiling of the Roman law. Justinian (527–565) had his lawyers codify all the laws since Hadrian (117–138) in the *Code;* even bulkier was the *Digest,* a collection of authoritative legal opinions. The *Institutes,* a handbook, served to introduce students to the larger works. While all these were in Latin, Justinian issued his own new laws (the *Novels*) in Greek. In the eighth century, the emperors issued the *Ekloga,* a new collection, more Christian in its provisions with regard to family matters, somewhat less severe and less Roman than its pre-

The emperor Justinian surrounded by attendants: a mosaic from the sixth-century Byzantine Church of San Vitale, Ravenna.

decessors. Under Leo VI (886–912) appeared the *Basilics,* last of the major compilations. The emperor was supreme judge, and all other judges had power only as derived from him. Many emperors enjoyed and prided themselves on their willingness to judge ordinary cases brought them by their subjects. The emperor's palace was the center of the state, and the officials of the palace were the state's most important functionaries. Every official had a title giving him a post in the palace hierarchy and a rank among the nobility. Many of the greatest and most influential officials were eunuchs, an oriental feature disturbing to most Western visitors.

THE ENEMIES   As defenders of the faith, the Byzantine emperors fought one enemy after another for eleven hundred years. Sometimes the invaders were moving north and west from Asia: Persians in the seventh century, Muslim Arabs from the seventh century on, and Turks beginning in the eleventh century. Persians and Arabs successively seized the East Roman provinces of Syria and Egypt, and the Arabs kept them. Though western Europe too experienced Muslim invasions in Sicily and Spain, Charles Martel's victory at Tours in 732 (see Chapter 3) was less decisive than that of the Byzantines in 717, when Emperor Leo III thwarted an Arab siege of Constantinople. Had it not been for the Byzantine resistance to the Muslims over the long centuries, we might all be Muslims today.

The Byzantines fought other Asians too: the Huns of the fifth century, the Avars of the sixth and seventh, the Bulgars of the seventh and later, the Magyars of the ninth and later, and the Pechenegs and Cumans of the eleventh, twelfth, and thirteenth centuries. All these were initially Turkic or Finnish or Mongolian nomads, fierce, swift-riding, savage horsemen who invaded imperial territory. Sometimes the enemies were native Europeans, like the Slavs who first appeared in the sixth century and filtered gradually southward into the Balkans and Greece.

In the northeastern Balkans, the Hunnic tribe of the Bulgars conquered the Slavs, who then absorbed their conquerors; by the tenth century the Bulgarians were thoroughly Slavic. The Bulgarians and the Slavic Serbs to the west of them fought long and exhausting wars against Byzantium. So did the Russians, another Slavic people, whose Scandinavian upper crust was gradually absorbed by a Slavic lower class. They floated in canoes down the river Dnieper, and sailed across the Black Sea to assault Byzantium from the water in 860. Beginning in the eleventh century the Byzantines had to fight western Europeans: Normans from south Italy, crusaders from all the Western countries, freebooting commercial adventurers from the new Italian towns. Against all these the Byzantines held their own until the late eleventh century, when Turks and Normans inflicted simultaneous severe defeats. Even then Constantinople held out, and was never taken by an enemy until 1204, when a mixed force of Venetian traders and western European crusaders seized it for the first time.

ARMY, NAVY, DIPLOMACY   Only a state with phenomenally good armies and navies could have compiled so successful a military record. The Byzantines were adaptable, learning and applying lessons from their successive enemies. Carefully recruited and trained, well armed and equipped, served by medical and ambulance corps, by a signal corps with flashing mirrors, and by intelli-

A thirteenth-century manuscript illumination illustrating the use of Greek fire.

gence agents behind the enemy lines, often commanded by the emperor himself, the Byzantine land forces were over the centuries the best in Europe. At its height the Byzantine fleet too played a major role, equipped as it was with a real secret weapon: Greek fire, a mysterious chemical compound squirted from siphons mounted on the prows of ships, which set enemy vessels aflame and terrified their sailors. Like other Byzantine institutions, the navy suffered a decline in the eleventh century from which it never recovered, and the Italian city fleets replaced it as the chief Mediterranean naval power.

The Byzantines fought only if they had to, preferring diplomacy, which they raised to a high level of subtlety. First Persia, and then to some extent the Muslim caliphate, were the only states that the Byzantines regarded as comparable to their own in prestige. All others were barbarians: so Byzantium either disputed or scornfully ignored the claim of Charlemagne and his German successors to the title of emperor. There could be but one emperor and he ruled at Byzantium.

Since negotiations with barbarian states were necessary, a kind of "office of barbarian affairs" kept imperial officials supplied with intelligence reports on the internal feudings among each barbarian people, so that a "pro-Byzantine" party might be created among them and every advantage taken of their internal stresses. When the emperor sent arms to the chieftain of a foreign tribe, the act was the equivalent of adoption. The emperor could make the paternal relationship still stronger by inviting the barbarian to Byzantium, standing sponsor for him at his baptism, and bestowing upon him splendid insignia of office in the palace hierarchy. The imperial court, solemn and dazzling, overawed the simple foreigner.

THE ECONOMY   Armies, navies, and diplomacy cost money, and Byzantium was enormously rich. It was a center of trade: from the Black Sea coastal lands came furs and hides and slaves; from the Far East, spices and precious stones; from western Europe, especially Italy, merchants eager to buy for gold the goods in Byzantine markets. Silk manufacture, for long a closely guarded secret of the Persians, came to Byzantium in the sixth century when—as the story goes—two monks brought from Persia silkworms' eggs hidden in a hollow cane. Thereafter, the emperors maintained a monopoly on the manufacture and sale of silk, and of the purple dye and gold embroidery that were needed by dignitaries of church and state in West and East alike.

The emperors forbade the export of gold, and maintained their reserves at a high level. The nomisma, the Byzantine gold coin, was standard currency in the whole Mediterranean world and was never debased until the crisis of the eleventh century; it remained stable for eight hundred years. Constantinople's glitter and sophistication made a great contrast to the prevailing rural way of life in the West. Silken garments, palaces and churches aglow with marbles and mosaics, precious stones lavishly used in decoration were the dazzling reflection of a thriving commerce and industry and a substantial revenue.

Money came in from state property in land: farms, gold and silver mines, cattle ranches, quarries. It came from booty seized in war or property confiscated from rich men in disgrace, and from taxation: on land and persons, sales and profits, imports and exports, and inheritances. From Diocletian the Byzantines inherited the concept that land and labor were taxable together: in order to be taxable each unit of land had to have its farmer to work it; in order to be taxable as a person, each farmer had to have his land to work. While this system promoted the binding of the peasant to the soil as a serf, large private landowners flourished because the state leased large tracts of land, leaving the landowner to supply the labor. The treasury assigned marginal land or abandoned farms to the nearest landowner, who became responsible for the taxes on them. Only the proprietor of rich and productive acreage could be expected to take on the responsibility for the less productive. Yet, though the large private estate predominated, the small private freeholder seems never to have disappeared entirely.

THE CAPITAL AND THE FACTIONS   As the capital, Constantinople had its own special administration, under a prefect of the city, or *eparch*. He was mayor, chief of police, and judge rolled into one, responsible for public order, inspecting the markets, fixing fair prices for food, and supervising the lawyers, notaries, moneychangers, and bankers as well as the merchants. Each trade or craft was organized into a guild or corporation with its own governor under the prefect.

From Rome Byzantium inherited rival parties of chariot racers, each with its own stables, equipment, and colors, the Blues and the Greens. They raced each other regularly in the Hippodrome, a vast stadium attached to the imperial palace. Blues and Greens represented not only rival sporting groups but opposing factions on all the political, religious, social, and economic issues of the day, so that every chariot race was the occasion for a public demonstration. In general the Blues were the party of the aristocracy, strict orthodoxy, and the better neighborhoods, while the Greens represented the lower classes, the less orthodox, and the poorer quarters. The cleavage existed in all the great provincial cities of the empire, but in Constantinople it took on special virulence. The political demonstrations sometimes became riots, when bands of one faction would invade the quarter of the other and burn down houses. The Nika revolt of 532 (so called from the rioters' shout of "victory") almost overturned the emperor Justinian. It was not until after the mid-seventh century that the emperors managed to control the Blues and Greens.

Religion and Civilization

In the Byzantine world, religion governed men's lives from birth to death. It pervaded intellectual life; the most serious questions that intellectuals tried to settle were theological, zestfully attacked by powerful and subtle minds. It dominated the arts and literature, and also economic life and politics: the position taken on a theological question often determined adherence to a political faction. What was the relationship of the Father to the Son? (The Arian controversy, see p. 119.) What was the relationship between the human and divine natures of Christ? (The monophysite controversy, see p. 120.) The right answer meant salvation and immortality, the wrong, damnation and eternal punishment. But men lined up on these issues in part according to the city they lived in and according to their social and economic position. In foreign affairs, too, the emperor went to war as champion of the faith, with a sacred picture borne before him, an icon (image) of the Virgin, perhaps one of those which legend said had been painted by Saint Luke or perhaps one not made by human hands at all but sent from heaven.

As we have seen, religion played a not dissimilar role in the medieval West. But the relationship between church and state was different in the East. The very abandonment of Rome by the emperor had permitted the local bishops to create the papal monarchy and in effect challenge Western kings and emperors. In Constantinople, however, the emperor remained in residence. Constantine summoned the Council of Nicaea (325), paid the salaries of the bishops, presided over their deliberations, and gave the force of law to their decrees. When he legislated as head of the Christian church in matters of Christian dogma, he was doing what no layman in the West would or could do; he still had some of the attributes of the Roman pontifex. In the East the emperor regularly deposed patriarchs and punished clerics. Constantine's successors were often theologians themselves; they enjoyed argument and speculation on theological questions and sometimes even legislated on matters of faith without consulting churchmen.

In short, the Church in the East was a kind of department of state, and the emperor was the effective head of it as he was of the other departments. The situation that prevails when a single authority plays the role of emperor and pope is called caesaropapism, a term often applied to Byzantium. From time to time, it is true, the patriarch of Constantinople challenged the emperor successfully. Moreover, absolute though they were, none of the emperors could impose new dogma without church support or risk offending the religious susceptibilities of his people. Some scholars therefore prefer not to apply the term *caesaropapism* to Byzantium; but the exceptions seem to us less important than the rule.

The Byzantines assumed, to a far greater extent than the western Europeans, that the individual had very little chance of salvation. In the East more than the West, monasticism became *the* Christian life, since to become a monk was to take a direct route to salvation. Worldly men, including many emperors, became monks on their deathbeds. Monks enjoyed enormous popular prestige, and often influenced political decisions; monks staffed the highest ranks of the church hierarchy; rich and powerful laymen, from the emperor down, founded new monasteries as an act of piety. Often immune from taxation, monasteries acquired vast lands and precious objects.

For the laity the sacraments of the Church provided the way to salvation. In the East every religious act took on a sacramental quality. Every image, every relic of a saint, was felt to preserve in itself the essence of the holy person. So God was felt to be actually present in the sanctuary; he could be reached through the proper performance of the ritual. In the East the emphasis fell on mystery, magic, rituals, a personal approach to the heavenly Saviour, more than on the ethical teachings of Christianity. Once a believer has accepted the proper performance of a magical action as the right way to reach God, he cannot contemplate any change in it; if the old way is wrong, one's parents and grandparents are all damned.

THE SCHISM   A slight difference in the wording of the liturgy, it is sometimes argued, caused the schism, or split, between the Eastern and Western churches that took place in 1054. The Greek creed states that the Holy Ghost "proceeds" from the Father, and the Latin adds the word *filioque,* meaning "and from the Son." But this and other differences might never have been noticed and might not have led to schism had it not been for the political issues at stake also.

After the monophysite provinces of Syria and Egypt had been lost to the Muslims in the seventh century, a new religious controversy raged in Byzantium over the use of sculptured and painted sacred images, and the nature and amount of reverence that a Christian might pay them. Something very like idolatry was widespread in the East, and twice for long periods in the eighth and ninth centuries the emperors adopted the rule that all images must be banned (iconoclasm, that is, image-breaking). The impulse came from the puritanism of the soldiers, country boys from Anatolia and Armenia who took seriously the Old Testament prohibition against worshiping graven images and who were able to install their officers on the imperial throne. The popes, who felt that images were educational and might be venerated (but of course not worshiped), condemned iconoclasm. In the end, the emperors restored the images, but not before an iconoclastic emperor had punished the pope by removing southern Italy with its rich church revenues from papal jurisdiction and placing it under that of the patriarch of Constantinople. Even more decisive than iconoclasm was the papacy's fear that the Byzantine emperor could not defend the pope or Italy against Lombards and Muslims. As we know, Pope Stephen II decided to turn instead to Pepin and Charlemagne (see p. 128).

Again, in the 860's, competition between papal and Byzantine missionaries to convert the Bulgarians led to a political quarrel. It was only then that the Greeks "discovered" the Roman "error" in adding *filioque* to the creed. When the papacy fell into corruption during the tenth century, the Byzantines became accustomed to going their own way without reference to the bishops of

The archangel Michael: sixth-century ivory figure probably made at Constantinople.

Rome. And when the reforms of Hildebrand reestablished a powerful papacy in the eleventh century, the Byzantines found that the Normans were turning over to papal jurisdiction churches and church revenues in the areas they had conquered in Byzantine southern Italy. The ambitious and vigorous popes welcomed the return of both souls and income. The Byzantine patriarch, unhappy at his losses, revived the *filioque* controversy as a pretext for pushing his more solid grievances. But the pope sent to Constantinople a most unbending emissary. In 1054 cardinal and patriarch mutually excommunicated each other. Despite many efforts, the churches have never been reunited for more than a very brief period since the schism. Only in the mid-1960's did hope revive for a genuine reconciliation.

In general, Greeks and Westerners (who were called Latins or Franks) detested each other. To the visiting western European, no doubt envious of the high Byzantine standard of living, the Greeks seemed soft, effeminate, and treacherous. To the Byzantine, the Latins seemed savage, fickle, and dangerous, barbarians like other barbarians. This antagonism made the schism even harder to heal.

BYZANTINE CIVILIZATION   Like the civilization of the West in the Middle Ages, that of Byzantium was derived from Greece and Rome. Yet in the West long centuries passed during which nobody knew Greek. During all this time the Byzantines preserved ancient Greek works of philosophy, science, and literature, copied and recopied them, and rendered them the homage of constant study. Had it not been for Byzantium, Plato, Aristotle, Homer, and Sophocles would have been lost, to the great impoverishment of our own cultural inheritance.

Byzantine learning, unlike that in the West before the twelfth-century growth of universities, was not confined to monasteries. Secular libraries and schools never disappeared in the East. The teacher occupied an important position in society; many of the emperors were themselves scholars and lovers of literature. Though the pious Justinian closed the university at Athens because of its strong pagan traditions, the imperial university at Constantinople supplied a steady stream of learned and cultivated men to the bureaucracy and the law courts. It emphasized secular subjects, while the patriarch presided over a theological school of his own.

The Byzantines were creative writers, although their literature has remained little known. From the tenth or eleventh century there survives an epic poem about a warrior who had fought the Muslims in Asia Minor two or three hundred years before, Basil Digenes Akritas. Half Greek, half Muslim (*Digenes* means "of two races"), he conquers wild beasts and brigands along the frontier (*Akritas* means "a frontiersman") and engages in single combat with a magnificent Amazon (female) warrior. The author, while no Homer, is fully comparable to the author of *The Song of Roland.* In prose, the most striking Byzantine achievement was that of the historians who set down the record of the empire over the centuries in a fashion sometimes violently partisan but extraordinarily valuable to the modern student. Nothing in the medieval West corresponds to their work.

Naturally, theological writing loomed large at Byzantium. The hotly debated controversies of the early period produced volumes much too difficult for most people to understand but immensely influential in determining the policies of Byzantine leaders. Theologians drew up the rule for monks, trying to moderate the ascetic zeal of the extremists. Saints' lives, written often for a popular audience, took the place the novel has in our society. The hero

The interior of the Church of Santa Sophia.

undergoes adventures, trials, agony of various sorts, and reaps the ultimate rewards of his own piety and virtue. These saints' lives often supply valuable bits of information about daily life and popular attitudes.

Unique among the saints' lives is a tenth-century tale of an Indian king who tries to prevent his son Ioasaph from learning about Christianity by shutting him away in a remote palace. But a wise monk, Barlaam, penetrates to his retreat and converts him by instructing him in the faith and telling him ten moral tales illustrating the Christian life. A christianized version of the life of Buddha, *Barlaam and Ioasaph* had traveled from India across Asia before it was turned into Christian legend and transmitted by the Byzantines to the West. The stories Barlaam tells are also Indian in origin, and have entered our literature too: one, for example, is the casket story of Shakespeare's *Merchant of Venice*. The very name "Ioasaph" is the same as the Indian word "Boddhisattva," which means a person destined to attain Buddhahood. Prince Ioasaph was canonized as a saint in both the Orthodox and Roman Catholic churches, so that through this legend Buddha himself became and has remained a Christian saint.

In the plastic arts the Byzantine achievement is still visible. The Church of Santa Sophia in Constantinople was designed to be "a church the like of which has never been seen since Adam nor ever will be." The dome, said an early observer, "seems rather to hang by a golden chain from heaven than to be supported by solid masonry," and Justinian (527–565), the emperor who built it, was able to exclaim "I have outdone thee, O Solomon!" The Turks, who seized the city in 1453, ever since have paid Santa Sophia the compliment of imitation; the mosques that throng present-day Istanbul are all more or less copies of it. In plan it is a fusion of the Hellenistic or Roman basilica with a dome taken from Persia, a striking example of the blending of Greek and oriental elements. In decoration, the use of colored marbles, enamel, gold, silver, and jewels, and the glowing mosaics on the walls and ceilings, reflect the sumptuousness of the Orient.

The tourist of today wishing to see a Byzantine church of Justinian's time need not go all the way to Istanbul. On the Adriatic coast of Italy, south of Venice, at Ravenna (capital of the Byzantine exarchate until 751; see Chapter 3), there are three smaller churches of the sixth century with superb mosaics still well preserved, including portraits of Justinian himself (see p. 208) and of his Empress Theodora. And at Venice, first the client, then the peer, and finally the conqueror of Byzantium, St. Mark's is a true Byzantine church of the later period, whose richness and magnificence epitomize perhaps better than any surviving church in Istanbul itself the splendor of later Byzantine architecture.

The creation of the world: mosaic scenes from Genesis in St. Mark's, Venice.

Along with the major arts of architecture and mosaics went the so-called minor arts, whose level the Byzantines raised so high that the term *minor arts* seems almost absurd. The silks, the ivories, the work of goldsmiths and silversmiths, the enamel and jeweled bookcovers, the elaborate containers made especially to hold the sacred relics of a saint, the great Hungarian sacred crown of Saint Stephen, the superb miniatures of the illuminated manuscripts in many European libraries—all testify to the endless variety and fertility of Byzantine inspiration.

II

The Fortunes of Empire, 330–1081

Against this general background, we turn now to examine the course of Byzantine history between 330 and the end of the eleventh century, the year 1081, when the decline of imperial strength could be plainly seen. This long stretch of 751 years may be divided into several shorter periods, beginning with that running from 330 to 717.

From 330 to 717

Constantine's immediate successors were Arian heretics. The first truly orthodox emperor after him, Theodosius the Great (reigned 379–395), proclaimed orthodox Nicene Christianity to be the sole permitted state religion. Although the empire East and West was united under Theodosius, his sons Arcadius (395–408) and Honorius divided it, with Arcadius ruling at Constantinople. It was never again fully united in fact, although in theory it had never been divided.

Until the accession of Justinian in 527, the eastern portion of the empire used Germans as troops in its own armies, and at the same time usually managed to deflect the new blows of invaders so that they fell chiefly upon the West. Though the Huns and the Persians presented a challenge, the cities of the East continued prosperous, and government operated undisturbed. The only warning of internal weakness came from the monophysite controversy, in which the real issue was whether Alexandria would successfully challenge Constantinople for leadership.

With Justinian (reigned 527–565) we encounter an emperor so controversial that his own historian Procopius, in addition to several works praising him to the skies, wrote a *Secret History,* never published in his own day, violently denouncing him. Justinian's armies reconquered North Africa from the Vandals, Italy from the Ostrogoths, and part of southern Spain from the Visigoths—a last desperate effort to reunite all of Rome's Mediterranean lands. Both the long-drawn-out campaigns and a vast new system of fortifications proved extremely costly. The focus of imperial attention on the West permitted the Persian danger on the eastern frontier to grow to the point where Justinian's immediate successors could not check it, while in Europe Slavs and Avars were able to dent the Danube line and filter into the Balkans.

Justinian began a process of administrative reorganization that his successors would finish. In the provinces of the Roman Empire he reversed the system of Diocletian and Constantine, and occasionally entrusted both civil and military power to a single officer. After Justinian's death the military emergency caused in Italy by the invasion of the Lombards and in North Africa by the savage native Berbers forced the authorities to create large military districts, the exarchates of Ravenna and Carthage, whose commanders, called exarchs, also served as civil governors.

In the early years of the seventh century, internal bankruptcy and external attacks from the Persians seemed to threaten total destruction, when Heraclius (610–641), son of the exarch of Africa, sailed from Carthage to Byzantium and seized the throne. He absorbed heavy losses, as the Persians took Antioch, Damascus, and Jerusalem, bearing off the True Cross in triumph. Soon afterwards they entered Alexandria, and Egypt too was gone. After 622 Heraclius began a great counteroffensive, defeating the Persians on their own territory, recapturing all the lost provinces, and returning the True Cross to Jerusalem in 629.

But only a few years later, the new movement of Islam exploded out of Arabia and took away once more the very provinces that Heraclius had recaptured from the Persians. In both the Persian and the Muslim victories over Byzantium the disaffection of monophysite Syrians and Egyptians played a major part. From Egypt the Muslims pushed on westward and took Carthage in 698, putting an end to the North African exarchate. Muslim ships began to operate from Cyprus and Rhodes. In northern Italy the Lombard kingdom had increased its power, while Lombard duchies threatened in the center and south. Heraclius' work and that of Justinian were seemingly undone.

The Reorganization of the Seventh and Eighth Centuries

The loss of Syria and Egypt required the transformation of Asia Minor into a reservoir of military manpower and a stronghold of defense. The perpetual raids of Slavs, Avars, and Bulgars into the Balkan provinces made the emergency the more acute. The emperors now extended to their remaining territories in Asia Minor and the Balkans the system of government previously introduced into the two exarchates, dividing them into what we would call army corps areas, with the local military commanders also exercising civil authority.

These new military districts were called *themes,* from a word meaning a permanent garrison. In each theme, many scholars believe, the troops were recruited from the native population; in return for their services, the yeoman farmers were granted land, but they might not dispose of it or evade their duties as soldiers. Their sons inherited the property along with the obligation to fight. Commanding generals of the themes, though in theory responsible to the emperor, often revolted, and in the seventh and eighth centuries many of them seized the throne. The imperial government strove to combat this danger by dividing up the large original themes into smaller ones. From seven big themes at the end of the seventh century, the number mounted to about thirty smaller ones by the year 900. From the start, one of the themes was naval. The emperor also asserted more and more direct supervision over the civil service departments.

The new system embodied a change in concepts of taxation. Since immigration and settlement had apparently put an end to the labor shortage of earlier centuries, it was possible to begin separating the land tax from the tax on persons. The latter was transformed into a hearth tax, which fell on every peasant household without exception. For purposes of the land tax, each peasant village was considered a single unit. Imperial tax assessors regularly visited each village, calculated its total tax, and assessed the individual inhabitants the portion of the tax that each would owe. The community as a whole was held responsible for the total tax, and often the neighbor of a poor peasant or of one who had abandoned his farm would have to pay the extra amount to make up the total.

Thus, in the period 330–717, the emperors, despite their efforts, failed to reconquer the West and to reconstitute the Roman Empire of Augustus.

Worse still, theological controversy, reflecting internal political strain, combined with Persian and Arab aggression, cost the empire both Syria and Egypt and forced a complete reorganization of the machinery of state, still incomplete in 717.

From 717 to 867

In 717, Leo III defeated the Arabs, who were besieging Constantinople itself. Thereafter the struggle against the Muslims gradually became stabilized along a fixed frontier in Asia Minor. But the Muslim capture of Crete and Sicily opened the way for pirate raids against the shores of imperial lands in Greece and southern Italy. In northern Italy, the Lombards extinguished the Exarchate of Ravenna in 751, and Byzantine rule was interrupted by the alliance between the Franks and the papacy. The Byzantine *dux* (originally, army commander) of Venetia moved his headquarters to the famous island of the Rialto and thus became the forerunner of the *doges* of Venice.

In the Balkans, the Bulgarians had long been engaged in intermittent warfare against Byzantium. In 811, their ruler, Krum, defeated the imperial armies and killed Emperor Nicephorus I (802–811), the first emperor to fall in battle since Valens at Adrianople in 378. Krum had Nicephorus' skull lined with silver, and used it as a drinking cup. Despite their primitive paganism, the Bulgarians nonetheless wanted to be converted to Christianity, an essential step for any ambitious ruler or state in the medieval world. Yet the Bulgarian rulers hesitated to accept Byzantine missionaries, for fear of Byzantine political influence.

Simultaneously another Slavic people, the Moravians, living in what is now Czechoslovakia, reached the same stage. But they feared the encroachments of their powerful neighbors, the Germans, and in 862, to avoid German influence, sent to Byzantium for missionaries. The emperor Michael III sent to Moravia two missionaries, Cyril (or Constantine) and his brother Methodius, who had invented the Slavic alphabet, still in use today and called Cyrillic. At the same time, Boris, ruler of the Bulgarians, asked for Christianity from the Germans. But the attempts of the two Slavic peoples to avoid being converted by their powerful neighbors failed. The Germans and Roman Catholicism triumphed in Moravia, and Boris had to yield to the Byzantines, though within the fold of the Eastern church he unified his people and consolidated his power.

For Byzantine internal development the years during which iconoclastic emperors held the throne (726–787 and 813–842) were the most critical. Beginning in Anatolia as a puritan reaction against excessive or superstitious adoration of religious pictures and images, iconoclasm later took on a violent anti-monastic aspect, since Byzantine monks were great defenders of the images. The images were twice restored by imperial decree (each time by an empress) as they had twice been banned by imperial decree. As a result of the struggle, the Byzantines drew more careful distinctions between superstitious adoration paid to images and proper reverence. When the controversy ended, it was tacitly understood that no more religious statues would be sculptured in the round, though the religious pictures that we call icons were permitted. Thus, containment of the Arabs, conversion of the Bulgarians, and the convulsions of iconoclasm characterized the period 717–867.

From 867 to 1081

In Byzantium the people developed a deep loyalty to the new ruling house that was established in 867 by the Armenian Basil I (867–886) and called the Macedonian dynasty. As political disintegration began to weaken the Muslim world, the Byzantines went over to the counteroffensive in the tenth century.

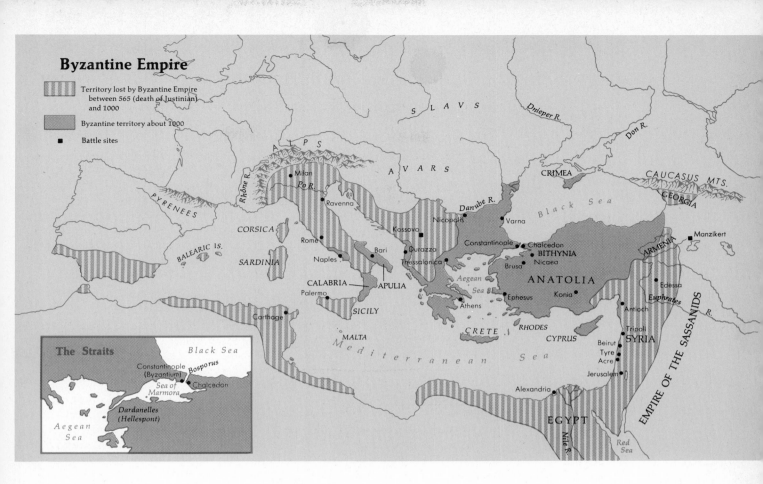

Their fleets and armies recaptured Crete (961), and soon afterward Antioch and much of northern Syria after three centuries of Arab domination. A new Muslim dynasty in Egypt, which took over in Palestine also, stopped the Byzantine advance short of Jerusalem. But, much like the later Crusaders from the West, the Byzantine emperors hoped to liberate Christ's city from the infidel. While pushing back the Muslims, the Byzantines allied themselves with the Armenians, penetrated the state of Armenia, and at the end of the period annexed it. This was an error in judgment: what had been a valuable buffer against the Turks of Central Asia who were beginning to raid into eastern Asia Minor now lay open to attack. In the face of the Muslim threat from Sicily, the Byzantines reestablished themselves in southern Italy, and dominated the neighboring Lombard duchies until the early eleventh century, when the Normans gained a foothold in the peninsula.

Meantime, ambitious Bulgarian rulers initiated a bitter hundred years' war against Byzantium, during which they tried to make themselves emperors by conquering Constantinople. Toward the end of the tenth century, the conflict became more intense under a Bulgarian ruler named Samuel. In 1014 the emperor Basil II (976–1025) captured fourteen or fifteen thousand Bulgarian prisoners and savagely blinded ninety-nine out of every hundred, allowing the hundredth man to keep the sight of one eye to lead his miserable fellows home. At the ghastly sight of his blinded warriors, Samuel fell dead. Basil II took the appropriate name of Bulgarslayer, and shortly afterward Byzantium made Bulgaria a conquered province.

The great expenditures of money and manpower of the Bulgarian war weakened Byzantium for the military disasters that were to come. But the Bulgarian decision to accept Christianity from Constantinople, and the subsequent Byzantine military conquest of the country, helped to determine where the line between East and West would be drawn for all future history. The Bulgarians are an Orthodox people to this day, and their architecture, their literature, and their art throughout the Middle Ages directly reflected the overpowering influence of Byzantium. Similarly, more than three hundred years later, the western neighbors of the Bulgarians, the Serbs, also took their faith from the Greek East after an initial flirtation with the Latin West.

Under the early emperors of the Macedonian dynasty the large landowners flourished. Nobles with great estates, "the powerful," constantly bought up the holdings of "the poor" and made the peasantry once more dependent upon them. The growing power of "the powerful" threatened the state in two important ways: it was losing its best taxpayers—the free peasants—and its best soldiers—the military settlers.

During the tenth and eleventh centuries, a great struggle developed between the emperors and "the powerful." Repeated imperial laws striving to end the acquisition of land by "the powerful" could not be enforced; in times of bad harvest especially, the small free proprietor was forced to sell out to his rich neighbor. Basil II forced "the powerful" to pay all the tax arrears of the delinquent peasants, thus relieving the village communities of the heavy burden that was so difficult for them to bear, and placing it on the shoulders of the rich. But a few years after Basil died, this law was repealed under the influence of "the powerful." As the landlords got more of the free military peasants as tenants on their estates, they became virtual commanders of private armies. To reduce the landlords' power, the imperial civil servants tried to cut down the expenses of the army, in which the landlords were now playing the leading role.

This strife weakened the imperial defenses. The Normans drove the Byzantines from the Italian peninsula by taking the great southern port of Bari in 1071. In the same year, after three decades of raids across the eastern frontier of Asia Minor, the Seljuk Turks defeated the imperial armies at Manzikert in Armenia and captured the emperor Romanos IV. Asia Minor, mainstay of the empire, now lay open to the Turks, who pushed their way almost to the Straits and established their capital in Nicaea. Meanwhile other Turkic tribes, Pechenegs and Magyars, raided southward into the Balkans almost at will. The situation was desperate in 1081, when there came to the throne one of the "powerful" magnates of Asia Minor, Alexius I Comnenus.

Thus between 867 and 1025, the Byzantine Empire reached its height. The emperors went over to the offensive against the Muslims and regained much territory and prestige. They fought the grim Bulgarian struggle to its bloody conclusion and strove to check the power of the great landlords. From 1025 to 1081 came a period of decline, accelerating as the period drew to a close, in which the triumph of the landowners was accompanied by—and related to—external military disaster.

III

Islam before the Crusades

Islam (the Arabic word means "submission") is the most recently founded of the world's great religions. Its adherents (Muslims, "those who submit") today inhabit the entire North African coast of the Mediterranean, sections of tropical Africa, part of Yugoslavia and Albania, the entire Middle East, Pakistan and parts of India, the Malay Peninsula, Indonesia, and the Philippine Islands, to say nothing of Russian Central Asia and portions of China. From the point of view of Western civilization, relationships with the Muslim world have been of crucial importance ever since Mohammed founded Islam in the early seventh century.

Mohammed

Sixteenth-century Persian miniature showing Mohammed, his face veiled, ascending to Paradise.

The Arabia into which Mohammed was born about the year 570 was inhabited largely by nomad tribes, each under its own chief. They raided each other's flocks and lived on the meat and milk of their animals, and on dates from the palm trees. They were pagans, who worshiped sacred stones and trees. Their chief center was Mecca, fifty miles inland from the coast of the Red Sea. In a sacred building called the Kaaba, or cube, they revered idols, especially a small black stone fallen from heaven, which perhaps was a meteorite.

Mohammed was born into one of the poorer clans of the Kuraish, a trading tribe that lived by caravan commerce with Syria. Early orphaned, he was brought up by relatives, and as a young man he entered the service of a wealthy widow much older than himself, whom he later married. Mohammed was then free to devote himself to his divine mission, though we do not know exactly how he came to believe that he was the bearer of a new revelation. On his caravan journeys he no doubt observed and talked with Christians and Jews. He spent much time in fasting and vigils, and suffered from nervousness and hysteria. He became convinced that God was revealing the truth to him, having singled him out to be his messenger. The revelations came to him gradually over the rest of his life; he cast them in a rhythmic, sometimes rhyming prose, and included entertaining stories from the Old Testament of the Hebrews and from Arabian folklore.

Some little time later Muslim revelation was put together as the Koran, or "book." The chapters were not arranged in order by subject matter, but put together mechanically by length, with the longest first. This makes the Koran difficult to follow, and a large body of Muslim writings explaining it has grown up over the centuries. Mohammed regarded his revelation as the confirmation of Hebrew and Christian scriptures, as a religion designed for all men, the perfection of both Judaism and Christianity, the final revelation and synthesis of God's truth.

Mohammed was a firm monotheist, yet he did not deny that his pagan fellow Arabs had previous knowledge of God. He declared only that it was idolatry to worship more than one God, and he believed the trinity of the Christians to be three Gods and therefore idolatry. A major innovation for the Arabs was Mohammed's idea of an afterlife, which was to be experienced in the flesh. The delights of paradise for Mohammed are fleshly indeed, and the punishments of hell are torture.

The requirements of Islam are not severe. Five times a day in prayer, facing toward Mecca, the Muslim must bear witness that there is no God but God and that Mohammed is his prophet. During the sacred month of Ramadan—perhaps suggested by Lent—he may not eat or drink between sunrise and sunset. He must give alms to the poor. And, if he can, he should be least once in his lifetime make a pilgrimage to the sacred city of Mecca. This was, and is, all, except for regulation of certain aspects of daily life—for example, the prohibition against strong drink, and other rules about food and its preparation, mostly taken from Jewish practice. The rest is social legislation: polygamy is sanctioned, but four wives are the most a man, save for the Prophet himself, may have; divorce is easy for the husband. The condition of women and of slaves, however, was markedly improved by the new laws.

At first, Mohammed preached this faith only to members of his family, then to the people of Mecca, who repudiated him scornfully. In 622, some pilgrims from a place called Yathrib, two hundred miles north of Mecca, invited Mohammed to come to their oasis. This move from Mecca is the famous *Hegira* from which the Islamic calendar has ever since been dated; 622 is the Muslim year 1. Yathrib, to which he went, had its name changed to al-Medina, *the* city, and became the center of the expanding new faith. God told Mohammed to fight against those who had not been converted. The holy war, or *jihad,* is a concept very like the Christian crusade: those who die in battle against the infidel die in a holy cause. In 630, Mohammed returned to Mecca as a conqueror, cleansed the Kaaba of all the idols except the black stone, and incorporated it into his religion. Two years later, in 632, he died; perhaps one-third of Arabia had by then become Muslim. Only one century later, Charles Martel was battling Mohammed's coreligionists in far-off France; the great Byzantine Empire was locked in a struggle with them for its very existence; and Islam had reached India.

Expansion

Scholars used to think that this startling expansion was due to the zeal of converts to the new faith; now they usually contend that overpopulation of the Arabian peninsula set off the explosion of the Arabs. In fact, Arabs had been quietly emigrating for some time before Mohammed, settling in Iraq, Palestine, and Syria. The new faith served to unify them, but, while Islam might now be the battle cry of the emigrants, their motives seem to have been the age-old ones of conquest for living space and booty. Toward Christians and Jews the Muslims generally were tolerant, regarding both as "peoples of the Book."

Syria and Persia were conquered almost simultaneously during the decade after Mohammed's death. The Syrian province, disaffected from Byzantium by monophysitism, fell easily. And the Persians, because of their weakness after recent defeats at the hands of Heraclius, failed to put up the resistance that might have been expected. In 639–640, the Arabs took Egypt, the major Byzantine naval base, which was monophysite in religion and, like Syria, ripe for conquest. Launching ships, they now seized the islands of Cyprus and Rhodes and began attacking southern Italy and Sicily. Moving west across North Africa, they took Carthage in 698. In 711, under the command of Tarik, they launched the invasion of Spain across the Straits of Gibraltar ("Rock of Tarik"). By 725, the first Muslims had crossed the Pyrenees, to meet Charles Martel at Tours seven years later. Meanwhile, they had been spreading east from Persia and in 724 reached the Indus and the western frontiers of China. Simultaneously, they moved south from Egypt and North Africa into the little-known desert regions of Central Africa. Of all this territory only the Mediterranean islands and Spain were ever permanently reconquered by Christians.

Disunity

The wide variety in the lands and peoples conquered and the internal dissensions among the conquerors made it impossible for the Arabs to establish a unified state. After Mohammed's death, they disagreed over the succession, finally choosing his eldest companion, Abu Bakr, as caliph (*khalifa,* the representative of Mohammed). The next two caliphs were also chosen from outside Mohammed's family, to the distress of many Muslims. By 656, when the third caliph was murdered, those who favored choosing only a member of Mohammed's own family had grouped themselves around Ali, son-in-law of

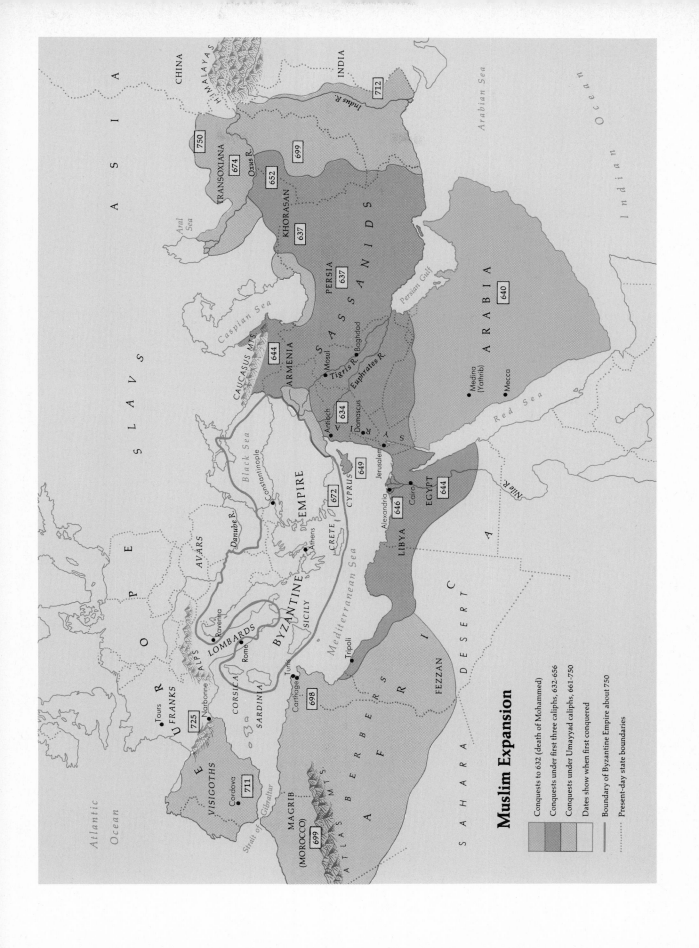

Muslim Expansion

Conquests to 632 (death of Mohammed)

Conquests under first three caliphs, 632–656

Conquests under Umayyad caliphs, 661–750

Dates show when first conquered

Boundary of Byzantine Empire about 750

Present-day state boundaries

Atlantic Ocean

E U R O P E

S L A V S

A S I A

CHINA

HIMALAYAS

INDIA

Indus R. 712

TRANSOXIANA 750

674

Oxus R.

Aral Sea

699

KHORASAN 652

637

Caspian Sea

PERSIA 637

SASSANIDS

ARABIA 640

Arabian Sea

Indian Ocean

CAUCASUS MTS.

ARMENIA 644

Mosul

Baghdad

Tigris R.

Euphrates R.

Persian Gulf

Medina (Yathrib)

Mecca

Red Sea

AVARS

Danube R.

Black Sea

Constantinople

BYZANTINE EMPIRE

Athens

CRETE 672

CYPRUS 649

Antioch

Damascus

Jerusalem

S Y R I A 634

Nile R.

Alexandria

Cairo

EGYPT 644

646

Mediterranean Sea

Tripoli

LIBYA

FEZZAN

Ravenna

LOMBARDS

ALPS

Rome

SICILY

SARDINIA

CORSICA

Tunis

Carthage 698

FRANKS

Tours

Narbonne 725

VISIGOTHS

Cordova 711

Strait of Gibraltar

ATLAS MTS.

MAGRIB (MOROCCO) 699

B E R B E R S

A F R I C A

S A H A R A   D E S E R T

the prophet; they were known as Shiites (Sectarians). Opposed to them were the Sunnites (traditionalists), who favored the election to the caliphate of any eligible person and who also advocated supplementing the Koran with commentaries called "traditions," which were disapproved by the Shiites.

In 656, Ali was chosen caliph; civil war broke out, and Ali was murdered in 661. His opponent Muawiya, of the Umayyad family, leader of the Sunnites, had already proclaimed himself caliph in Damascus. Thus began the Umayyad caliphate (660–750), which was on the whole a period of good government, brisk trade, and cultural advance under Byzantine influence. (It produced the famous "Dome of the Rock" mosque in Jerusalem.) The civil service was manned by Greeks, and Greek artists worked for the caliph; the Christian population, except for the payment of a poll tax, was better off than it had been under Byzantium.

Shiite opposition to the Umayyads, however, remained strong. The Shiites felt it their duty to curse the first three caliphs, who had ruled before their hero, Ali, and who were deeply revered by the Sunnites. The Shiites were far more intolerant of the unbeliever, conspired in secret against the government, and were given to self-pity and to wild outbursts of grief for Ali's son Husein, who was killed in 680. Southern Iraq was then the center of Shiite strength.

From these eastern regions came the leadership of the plot that in 750 was responsible for the murder of the last of the Umayyad caliphs, together with ninety members of his family. The leader of the conspirators was Abu'l-Abbas, not a Shiite himself, but the great-grandson of a cousin of Mohammed. The new Abbaid caliphate soon moved east to Baghdad, capital of present-day Iraq, and the days when Islam was primarily an Arab movement under Byzantine influence were over. At Baghdad, the caliphate took on more and more the color of the Persian Empire, in whose former territory it was situated. Its Christian subjects were on the whole, though, well treated.

The rest of the Muslim world slipped away from Abbasid control. One of the few Umayyads to escape death in 750 made his way to Spain and built himself a state centered around the city of Cordova. Rich and strong, his descendants declared themselves caliphs in 929. Separate Muslim states appeared in Morocco, in Tunis, and in Egypt, where still another dynasty, this time Shiite, built Cairo in the tenth century and began to call themselves caliphs. Rival dynasties also appeared in Persia itself, in Syria, and in the other eastern provinces. At Baghdad, though the state took much of its character and culture from Persia, power fell gradually into the hands of Turkish troops. The Seljuk Turks emerged supreme from the struggle for power when they took Baghdad in 1055. Although the caliphate at Baghdad lasted down to 1258, when the Mongols finally ended it, the caliphs were mere puppets in Turkish hands.

Islamic Civilization

Many of the regions conquered by the Arabs had been parts of the Byzantine or Persian empires, and had an ancient tradition of culture. The new religion and the Arabic language brought to them by the conquerors often stimulated new artistic and literary development. The requirement of pilgrimage to Mecca made Muslims a mobile people and encouraged the exchange of ideas from all quarters of the Islamic world. Everybody who wanted to read the Koran had to learn Arabic: translation of the book was forbidden. Since Arabic is an extraordinarily flexible and powerful instrument, it became the standard literary language of the whole Islamic world. The Muslims gave poetry the highest rank among the arts.

Like both Roman and Greek Christianity, Islam was convinced of its innate superiority to all other religions and ways of life. Like the Byzantines, the Muslims aspired to dominate the civilized world, which they thought of as divided between those lands already part of Islam and those lands still to be conquered. Like the Byzantine emperor, the caliph was an autocrat, a vicar of God, chosen by a mixture of election and the hereditary principle. The caliph, however, could not add to or change the religious law, although the Byzantine emperor sometimes pronounced on dogmas. Both courts stressed show and ceremony, largely derived from the Persian tradition. Christians and Muslims, however strong their mutual hatred, felt themselves to be worshipers in two religions that were on the same level of intellectual advancement and that held similar views on creation, human history, the last judgment, and the instability of everything mortal. When at peace with the Muslims, the Byzantines thought of them as the successors of the Persians, and as such the only other civilized people.

Learning, Literature, and the Arts

The reign of Mamun (813–833) is often said to mark the high point in the civilization of the caliphate. In Baghdad, he built observatories, founded a university, and ordered the great works of ancient Greek and Indian scientists and philosophers translated into Arabic. The Muslims developed medicine beyond the standard works of the Greek masters. They wrote textbooks on dieases of the eye, on smallpox, and on measles, which remained the best authorities until the eighteenth century. Avicenna (980–1037) was famous for his systematization of all known medical science and also for his philosophical and poetic writings.

Muslim scientists adopted Indian numerals, the ones that we use today and call Arabic. The new numerals included the zero, a concept unknown to the Romans, without which it is hard to see how higher mathematical research could be carried on. The Muslims began analytical geometry, and founded plane and spherical trigonometry. They made much progress in algebra, which is itself an Arabic word, as, for example, are alcohol, cipher, alchemy, zenith, and nadir.

In philosophy, the Muslims eagerly studied Plato, Aristotle, and the Neoplatonists. Like the Byzantines and the western Europeans, they used what they learned to solve theological problems about the nature and the power of God and his relationship to the universe. Efforts to reconcile philosophy and religion occupied the great Spanish Muslim Averroës (ca. 1126–1198), whose commentaries on Aristotle, translated from Arabic into Latin, were available to the Christian West well before the original Greek text of Aristotle himself.

Spanish Christians complained that their fellow Christians were irresistibly attracted by Muslim poetry and its portrayal of life in the desert, with its camels and horses, its warfare and hunting, its feasts and drinking bouts, and its emphasis on love. Arabic love poetry, as developed in Spain, influenced the troubadours across the Pyrenees in France and so indirectly the minnesingers in Germany (see p. 188). Some of the greatest masterpieces of Western love poetry thus find their ancestry in the songs of Spanish Muslims. Besides poetry there is a great deal of interesting autobiography and excellent history in Arabic. The fiction is limited to a few subjects—the adventures of a rogue, the sad misfortunes of a pair of lovers, or exciting incidents of life in the capital, with the caliph participating. These tales were collected in the celebrated *Arabian Nights* together with stories of Indian and Jewish origin, as well as some that derive from the Greek classics and from Hellenistic works.

In the arts, the Muslims adapted Byzantine churches in building mosques, which needed a front courtyard with a fountain where the faithful must wash

Mosque of the emperor Suleiman the Magnificent, Istanbul, sixteenth century.

before entering. All that was necessary inside was a quiet and dignified place to pray and rest, with a small niche in the wall showing the direction of Mecca, and a pulpit from which the Koran might be read aloud. Since the muezzin's call to prayer summoned the faithful, slender towers or minarets were built next to the mosque. Beautiful and elaborate geometric patterns, in wood, stone, mosaic, and porcelain tile, characterized the interior decoration, which also utilized the highly ornamental Arabic script, particularly the names of the first four caliphs and passages from the Koran. The great mosques of Damascus, Cairo, Jerusalem, and Cordova are perhaps the finest surviving specimens, but there are thousands of others all over the Muslim world.

The Gothic architecture of the West owes a still largely unexplored and unacknowledged debt to the pointed arches and ribbed vaults, the stone tracery (often called arabesque), and the other striking features of these buildings. In the architecture of the Norman period in Sicily we can see direct traces of Muslim influence, as of course we can in Spain, whose entire civilization has been permanently shaped by the Muslims. Through Sicily and Spain came Greco-Roman and Muslim science, philosophy, and art. In music, the Morris dance, for instance, is simply a "Moorish dance"; lute, tambourine, guitar, and fanfare are all words of Arabic origin. When we consider all the contributions of the Byzantines and the Muslims to medieval Western culture, we are altogether justified in saying that much light came from the East.

IV
The Crusades

Precedents for the Crusade

In the last quarter of the eleventh century, the relationships between Roman Christendom, Greek Christendom, and Islam entered upon a long period of crisis. One striking new development was that the pope in 1095 proclaimed a Holy War against the Muslims, a war for the Cross, or Crusade, with the recovery of the Holy Sepulcher as its ultimate aim. The idea itself was not new. The Byzantines regarded their wars against the Muslims as sacred campaigns for the faith, and had once almost reconquered Jerusalem. In Spain, Christian had been fighting Muslim ever since the invasion of 711; the small Christian states pushed southward whenever they could. When the Cordovan caliphate weakened just after the year 1000, the abbey of Cluny prodded French nobles to join the Spanish Christians and war on the Muslims. The pope offered an indulgence for all who would fight for the Cross in Spain. The fighting in Spain continued on into the twelfth century, the Christians recovering a large area of central Spain. Another precedent for the crusades was the warfare of the Normans against the Muslims in Sicily.

Moreover, Christians had been undertaking expeditions of another kind to the Holy Land ever since Constantine had become converted: these were the pilgrimages to the scenes of Christ's life and Passion. Indeed, Constantine's mother, Saint Helena, discovered the True Cross there. Even the Muslim conquest of the seventh century did not interrupt pilgrimages for long. Charlemagne, for example, had excellent relations with Caliph Harun al-Rashid (785–809), who allowed him to endow a hostel at Jerusalem for pilgrims. The belief grew that pilgrimage would bring God's pardon for sin. Cluny fostered pilgrimages, and large organized groups flocked eastward in the tenth and eleventh centuries; one of them was seven thousand strong.

Stable conditions in both Muslim and Byzantine dominions were needed for the safety of the pilgrims. Yet the late eleventh century brought civil strife at Byzantium and the catastrophes of Bari and Manzikert (see p. 220). Seljuk Turks flooded Asia Minor; Normans crossed the Adriatic to attack the Dalmatian coast; Pechenegs poured into the Balkans. Amidst intrigue and disorder Alexius I Comnenus (reigned 1081–1118), a general and a big landowner, came to the Byzantine throne. He made an expensive alliance with Venice—giving the Venetians special trade concessions and a quarter of Constantinople to live in—and held off the Normans. But he could do little about conditions in Asia Minor or Syria, where civil wars among the Turks and brigandage on the highways made pilgrimages very dangerous.

Besides their concern for the pilgrims, the vigorous reforming popes of the later eleventh century felt that the schism between Roman and Greek churches was intolerable. In 1073, Gregory VII himself sent an ambassador to Constantinople, who reported that the Byzantine Empire too was anxious for a reconciliation. Gregory planned to send Western armies to help the Byzantines against the Turks, and even intended to take personal command and bring about a reunion of the churches. It was only the quarrel with the German emperor Henry IV (see p. 175) that prevented Gregory's acting on the project. Here, more than twenty years before the First Crusade, we have all the essential elements: a holy war under papal sponsorship to be fought in alliance with the Greeks against the Muslims in Asia.

The First Crusade

In 1095 envoys from Emperor Alexius I Comnenus came to a papal council and asked for help against the Turks, stressing the sufferings of the Christians in the East and arguing that the time was ripe to defeat the weakening Turkish power. Eight months later at the Council of Clermont (1095) Pope Urban II proclaimed the First Crusade. In his sermon to the crowd he emphasized the anguish of the Greek Christians and the hardships faced by pilgrims. He also mentioned the riches that might be gained, and promised that any sinner who might be killed doing this work of God would receive automatic absolution and could count on salvation. His audience greeted his oration with cries of

"God wills it." Thousands of volunteers took a solemn oath, and sewed crosses of cloth onto their clothes.

As it turned out, the expedition that Urban launched was only the first of a series continuing for almost two centuries. Crusaders battled the Muslims, most often in Syria and Palestine, but also in Egypt, North Africa, and Portugal. Under the command, sometimes of kings or emperors, sometimes of lesser nobles, the armies won some successes, but more often they failed. Reinforcements flowed to the East in almost a constant stream. Therefore the practice of calling certain specific expeditions the Second, Third, or Fourth Crusade, and so on up to the Eighth, is really not very accurate, though it is convenient.

After Clermont, an undisciplined mob of ignorant and often starving peasants under a certain Peter the Hermit poured eastward to Constantinople. The Byzantines, who had hoped for the loan of a few hundred well-trained knights, were appalled at this mob. The crusaders burned houses and stole everything that was not chained down, including the lead from the roofs of the churches. Alexius Comnenus shipped them out of Constantinople and across the Straits as fast as he could. In Asia Minor they were eventually massacred.

Meanwhile, a considerable number of great lords had also enlisted, of whom the most famous were Godfrey of Bouillon (duke of Lower Lorraine) and his brother Baldwin, Count Raymond of Toulouse, and Bohemond, a

Fourteenth-century manuscript illumination showing Godfrey of Bouillon before Jerusalem in 1099. At the left is Peter the Hermit.

Norman prince from southern Italy. Far better equipped and disciplined than Peter the Hermit's forces, the armies led by these lords began to converge on Constantinople by different routes. Alexius was willing to have the Western lords carve out principalities for themselves from the Turkish-occupied territory they hoped to conquer, but he wanted to recover Byzantine territory and to dominate whatever new states the crusaders might create, so he extracted from each great Western lord an oath of liege homage to him.

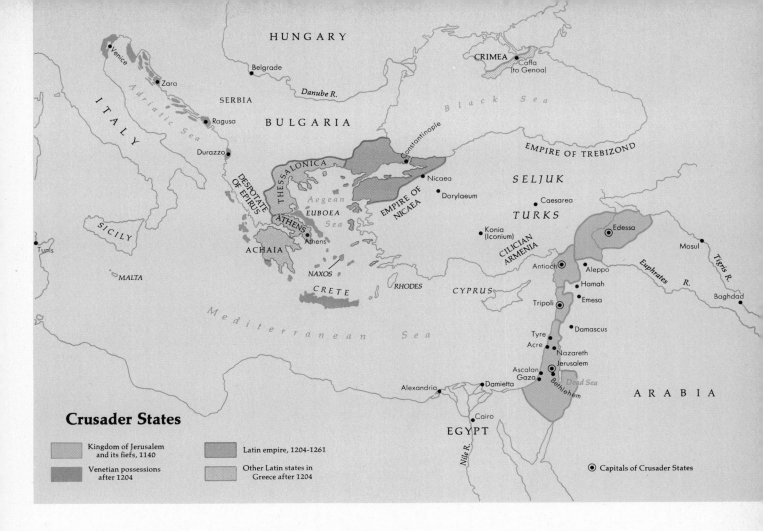

Crusader States

- Kingdom of Jerusalem and its fiefs, 1140
- Venetian possessions after 1204
- Latin empire, 1204-1261
- Other Latin states in Greece after 1204
- ⊙ Capitals of Crusader States

Once in Asia Minor, the crusaders took Nicaea, the Seljuk capital, in 1097, and at Dorylaeum captured the Seljuk Sultan's tent and treasure. Baldwin, brother of Godfrey, marched to Edessa, a splendid ancient imperial city near the Euphrates, and was accepted by its local Armenian rulers as its count (1098). This was the first Crusader State to be established. Meanwhile the main body of the armies took Antioch after a long siege, and Bohemond now became its prince and thus the ruler of a second Crusader State. Finally, in July 1099 the crusaders took Jerusalem itself by assault, and massacred its Muslim and Jewish inhabitants.

THE CRUSADER STATES   Godfrey of Bouillon would not consent to wear a royal crown in the city where Christ had worn the crown of thorns, and he accepted the title only of "defender of the Holy Sepulcher." But Jerusalem became the third of the Crusader States. Godfrey's brother, Baldwin of Edessa, became first King of Jerusalem in 1100. Venetian, Genoese, and Pisan fleets now assisted in the gradual conquest of the coastal cities, ensuring sea communications with the West. In 1109, the son of Raymond of Toulouse founded the fourth and last of the new states, centering around the seaport of Tripoli. The king of Jerusalem was the suzerain of the other three rulers, but was often unable to enforce his authority. The Byzantine emperors never relinquished their rights.

The holdings of the Westerners lay within a narrow Syrian coastal strip extending from the Euphrates River to the Egyptian borders, more than five hundred miles long and seldom as much as fifty miles wide. From the Muslim cities of Aleppo, Hamah, Emesa (Homs), and Damascus, all just inland from the strip, and from Egypt, danger constantly threatened. Yet the crusader lords often ignored the common defense, fighting with one another in alliance with neighboring Muslims. At strategic places they erected superb castles, among the finest ever built.

The crusaders established a purely feudal government, whose institutions may be studied in the *Assizes of Jerusalem,* written down in the thirteenth century, when the Crusader States were dying. The great officers of the realm were the officers of the king's household: seneschal, constable, marshal. The high court of the barons adjudicated disputes and acted as council of state for the king's business. The Italian commercial cities, as colonial powers, had quarters of their own in the coastal cities, with privileged status. Revenues were raised by carefully collected customs dues, by monopolies, by a poll tax on Muslims and Jews, and by a land tax on the native population. Ecclesiastical organization was complex—the two Latin patriarchs of Jerusalem and Antioch each had a hierarchy of subject Roman Catholic archbishoprics and bishoprics. Greek, Syrian, and Armenian churches continued to exist, each with its own clergy, in addition to the Muslim and Jewish faiths.

The crusaders created new "military orders" of religious knights: the Templars were founded about 1119 to afford protection to pilgrims on their way to the Holy Places. The knights took the vows of poverty, chastity, and obedience, and were given headquarters near the Temple of Solomon—hence their name. Saint Bernard himself (see p. 180) inspired their rule, based on that of his own Cistercians and confirmed by the pope in 1128. A second order, founded shortly after, was attached to the ancient Hospital of Saint John of Jerusalem, and was therefore called the Hospitalers. Made up of knights, chaplains, and serving brothers, under the command of a master, with subordinate provincial commanders both in the East and at home in the West, the two orders put into the field the most effective fighting forces in the Holy Land. A purely German group became the Teutonic Knights.

The orders quickly acquired fortresses and churches and villages of their own; Western monarchs endowed them with lands in Europe. Sometimes allied with Muslims, they quarreled with the nobility and clergy of the Holy Land, with new arrivals, with the Italian cities, and with one another. Eventually the rich orders forgot their original vows of poverty so far that they engaged in banking. In the early fourteenth century, Philip IV of France destroyed the Templars (see Chapter 4). The Teutonic Knights, most of whose fighting was done along the eastern Baltic shore, were disbanded only in 1525; some of their lands and many of their attitudes passed to the modern state of Prussia. The Hospitalers moved first to Cyprus, then to Rhodes, and were driven to Malta by the Turks in 1522, where they continued until Napoleon's seizure of the island in 1798.

THE MUSLIM RECONQUEST The disunion of the Muslims did more than the castles or military orders to keep the Crusader States alive. Beginning in the late 1120's, Zangi, governor of Mosul on the Tigris (the town that gives its name to muslin), succeeded in unifying the local Muslim rulers. In 1144, he took Edessa, first of the Crusader cities to fall; it was never to be recaptured. Two years later, Zangi was assassinated, but the Muslim reconquest had begun.

As an answer to the loss of Edessa, Saint Bernard himself preached the so-called Second Crusade in Europe. He aroused enormous enthusiasm, and for the first time Western monarchs—King Louis VII of France and King Conrad III of Germany—came to the East. But the armies of the Second Crusade were almost wiped out in Asia Minor. When the remnants reached the Holy Land, they found themselves in conflict with the local Christian lords, who sabotaged the siege of the key Muslim city, Damascus (1149). In 1154 Zangi's son, Nureddin, took Damascus, and Muslim Syria was united against the Latins.

In Egypt, one of Nureddin's generals became vizier (minister). When this general died in 1169, he left his office to his nephew Saladin, the greatest Muslim leader of the crusading era, renowned for his generalship and chivalry. Saladin brought the Muslim cities of Syria and Mesopotamia under his control and distributed them to members of his own family. Internal decay in the Kingdom of Jerusalem and a squabble over the throne gave Saladin his chance, and a violation of a truce by a crusader lord gave him his excuse. In 1187 Jerusalem fell, and soon there was nothing of the kingdom left to the Christians except the port of Tyre.

The Later Crusades

These events elicited the Third Crusade (1189–1192). The Holy Roman Emperor, Frederick Barbarossa, led a German force but was drowned in Asia Minor (1190) before reaching the Holy Land. Some of his troops, however, continued to Palestine. There they were joined by Philip Augustus of France and Richard the Lionhearted of England, deadly rivals in the West (see Chapter 4). Each was at least as interested in thwarting the other as he was in furthering what was supposed to be the common cause. The main operation of the Third Crusade was a long siege of the seaport of Acre, which was finally successful in 1191. Jerusalem itself could not be recaptured, but Saladin signed a treaty with Richard allowing Christians to visit it freely. A small strip of seacoast with Acre as its center remained in the hands of the Crusaders as a pitiful remnant of the Kingdom of Jerusalem. The cities of Tripoli and Antioch, their surrounding territories greatly shrunken, were also preserved.

When Saladin died in 1193, his dominions were divided among his relatives, and the Christians obtained a respite. But from the end of the twelfth century, the story of the Crusades and of the Crusader States in Syria is a mere epilogue. Innocent III's great effort at a Fourth Crusade was, as we shall see, diverted away from the Holy Land. The failures in the East were partly balanced by the successes in Spain, where, by the end of the thirteenth century, the Muslims were reduced to the Kingdom of Granada in the southeastern corner of the peninsula. Far to the northeast in the Baltic region, the

Krak des Chevaliers, a crusader fortress built by the Hospitalers and taken by Saladin in 1188.

pagan Lithuanians and Slavs received the attention of the Teutonic Knights.

The zeal that had driven men toward the Holy Land was diluted, perhaps most of all, by the struggle between the papacy and its European opponents—the Albigensian heretics of southern France and the Emperor Frederick II (see Chapter 4). Now the pope was offering to give those who would fight against a purely European and nominally Christian enemy the same indulgence as he offered to those who fought the infidel. This brought disillusionment, especially when combined with the spectacle of repeated military failure and internal Christian dissension in the Holy Land itself.

The high point of tragic futility was the famous Children's Crusade of 1212, when throngs of French and German children went down to the Mediterranean in the expectation that its waters would divide before them and open a path to the Holy Land, along which they could march to a bloodless victory. When this failed to happen, several thousand pushed on to Marseilles and other seaports where many were sold into slavery.

The Fifth Crusade (1219–1221) was a vain attempt at the conquest of Egypt, which had become the center of Muslim strength. The sophisticated Western emperor Frederick II led the Sixth Crusade. Speaking Arabic and long familiar with the Muslims, Frederick secured more for the Christians by negotiation than any military commander since the First Crusade. In 1229, his treaty with Saladin's nephew restored Jerusalem to the Latins again, except for the site of the Temple, where stood the great mosque of the Dome of the Rock. The Muslims restored Bethlehem and Nazareth and made a ten-year truce.

But because Frederick II was on bad terms with the papacy (see Chapter 4), the Christians put Jerusalem under an interdict when he visited it to crown himself king. The ruler of Egypt now took into his service several thousand Turks from Central Asia, displaced by the invasions of Genghis Khan and his Mongols, then raging through western Asia and eastern Europe. These Turks took Jerusalem in 1244; it remained in Muslim hands until 1917. The Mongols themselves appeared in the neighborhood of Antioch and forced the ruler of the principality to pay tribute.

Now Louis IX of France launched the Seventh Crusade. Saint Louis himself was taken prisoner in Egypt (1250) and had to pay a very heavy ransom. In 1250 also, the household troops of the Egyptian sultan, called Mamluks (slaves), took power in Egypt. Soon after, the Mongols, fresh from victories in Asia, where they had extinguished the Abbasid caliphate in Baghdad (1258), invaded Syria and were defeated in 1260 by the Mamluk general Baibars, who then gradually took the Christian fortresses. Antioch fell in 1268. Baibars delayed his advance in fear of a new crusade (the Eighth) of Saint Louis in 1270, but resumed it when Louis landed in Tunis and died there. The Mamluks took Tripoli in 1289 and Acre in 1291, massacring sixty thousand Christians. The Christian settlements were wiped out, but they were not deeply mourned even in western Europe, from which so much blood and treasure had flowed for their establishment and defense.

The Meeting of East and West

From the first, crusaders had had mixed motives: the wish to make a pilgrimage and to win indulgence, the desire for gain and the love of adventure. Some intended to return home, others to stay. A new world neither Eastern nor Western but compounded of both was growing up in the narrow strip of crusader territory. As one crusader put it:

God has poured the West into the East; we who were Westerns are now Easterns. He who was a Roman or a Frank is now a Galilean or Palestinian. He who was from

Rheims or Chartres is now a Tyrian or an Antiochene. We have all forgotten our native soil; it has grown strange unto us.*

A Muslim reports an old crusader knight who

presented an excellent table, with food extraordinarily clean and delicious. Seeing me abstaining from food, he said, "Eat, be of good cheer! I never eat Frankish dishes, but I have Egyptian women cooks and never eat except their cooking. Besides pork never enters my home."†

Once Christians and Muslims had begun to mix, the spirit of tolerance moved both. Each side respected the valor of the other. The Latins were never numerous enough to cultivate the soil of Syria, and needed the labor of the Christian and Muslim peasants. The natives were also most useful in commerce.

As time passed, some Westerners married Easterners, and a race of half-breeds came into existence. Even those who did not intermarry often had their houses, palaces, or churches built by native craftsmen. They wore oriental clothes, let their beards grow, and ate squatting on carpets, Eastern-style. They enjoyed watching the Muslim dancing girls, hired Muslim physicians, joined Muslims in tournaments and hunts, shared certain shrines, and debated the theology of one another's religions. To pilgrims freshly arrived from the West, these easternized Westerners were suspect, yet the visitors who went back to the West probably had a greater effect on European society than did those who stayed in the East. From Marseilles alone, the ships of the Hospitalers and the Templars carried six thousand pilgrims a year, so many that the shipowners of the port sued the knightly orders for unfair competition.

Arabic words in Western languages testify to the concepts and products borrowed by the Westerners—in commerce: bazaar, tariff, the French *douane*, the Italian *dogana* (a customs house, from the Arabic *diwan*, the sofa on which the officials sat); in foods: sugar, saffron, rice, lemons, apricots, melons, and pistachios; in manufactured goods: cotton, muslin, damask (from Damascus), and many others. All the new products proved a stimulus to the markets and fairs of the West. Venice and Genoa, the ports from which much of the produce of the East was funneled into Europe, prospered. So did the cities of Flanders, whose own manufacture of woolen goods was stimulated by the availability of Eastern luxuries for trade. Letters of credit and bills of exchange became more and more necessary as commercial arrangements grew complex. Italian banking houses sprang up with offices in the Holy Land, and the orders of knighthood—especially the Templars—joined in the money trade.

Some historians believe that the Crusades helped to weaken and impoverish the feudal nobility and that the monarchies thereby benefited. Certainly kings were able to tax directly for the first time, as a result of the need to raise money for the expeditions to the Holy Land. The papacy was no doubt strengthened in its climb to leadership over all Western Christendom by the initiative it took in sponsoring so vast an international movement and by the degree of control it exercised over its course; yet this short-run gain may have been outweighed by a long-run loss. The religious motive was increasingly diluted by worldly considerations. The misuse of the crusading indulgences for purely European papal purposes and the cumulative effect of failure and incompetence in the Holy Land surely contributed to a disillusionment with

* Fulcher of Chartres, quoted by Archer and Kingsford in *The Crusades* (New York, 1895), p. 170.
† *Memoirs of Usamah Ibn-Munqidh*, trans. P. K. Hitti (Princeton, 1930), p. 170.

the papal concept of the Crusades. Moreover, the discovery that all Muslims were not savage beasts, that profit lay in trade with them, and that living together was possible must have led Christians to question statements to the contrary even when issued by Rome.

The influence of the Crusades upon western European art and architecture was slight. It was greater in the writing of history and personal memoirs, especially in the vernacular languages. In the thirteenth century, French, not Latin, was used by Villehardouin in his account of the Fourth Crusade against Constantinople, and Joinville wrote his moving and vivid life of Saint Louis, including an account of the Seventh Crusade. Still more important was the great increase in geographical interest and knowledge; our first reliable maps and the beginnings of European journeys to the Far East date from the crusading period.

The fourteenth- and fifteenth-century Europeans who fought against the Ottoman Turks, who explored the West African coasts and rounded the Cape of Good Hope, emerging into the Indian Ocean and fighting Muslims there, who eventually crossed the broad Atlantic with the mistaken idea that they would find at the other side that old hypothetical ally against the Turks, the lord of the Mongols, were the direct descendants of the crusaders of the earlier period. It is perhaps as a colonizing movement, inspired, like all else in the Middle Ages, largely by the Church, that the Crusades are best considered. The Westerners called the Crusader States in Syria *Outremer,* the "land beyond the sea." The crusaders were as truly overseas colonists as the followers of Columbus.

V

The Fortunes of Empire, 1081–1453

During its last 372 years, the fate of the Byzantine Empire rested increasingly on the actions of western Europeans. Pisans and Genoese joined the Venetians as privileged residents of Constantinople; the empire came to depend on them for its merchant marine and navy. The floods of crusaders rendered the Byzantines first uneasy, then insecure. Popular hatred mounted until it broke out in a series of violent acts, culminating in the capture of Constantinople by the Fourth Crusade in 1204. The crusaders set up a "Latin Empire" and drove the Byzantine into exile. After the Byzantine leaders returned to power in 1261, they were unable to shake off the economic and military dominance of the Westerners. Twice—in 1274 and 1439—the Byzantine emperors had to conclude a formal "union" with the Church of Rome, only to have it repudiated by the forces of Greek public opinion. Mutual hatred between Christians played a major part in the final downfall of Byzantium.

Byzantine Feudalism

"The powerful," in the person of Alexius Comnenus, had captured the throne in 1081. Thereafter the accumulation of lands and tenants—who could serve as soldiers in the landlords' private armies—seems to have gone unchecked. As early as the middle of the eleventh century the emperor granted land to be administered by a magnate in exchange for military service. Such a grant was called *pronoia.* Although it was not hereditary, and although no pronoia was held except from the emperor directly, there was a fundamental similarity between the pronoia and the Western fief. Military service now depended on the holders of pronoias.

A form of feudalism thus became the characteristic way of life on Byzantine soil. In the cities, imperial police officials or local garrison commanders often formed petty dynasties of their own, acting as virtually independent potentates. Many individual Western knights entered imperial service. Western concepts of feudalism were apparent as early as the oath exacted by Alexius from the crusaders (see p. 228); and Alexius' successors acted as feudal suzerains of the Latin principality of Antioch.

Along with political feudalism went economic ruin and social misery, which mounted steadily during the twelfth century. Periodic reassessment of the taxes gave assessors unlimited opportunity for graft. They demanded food and lodging, presents and bribes; they would seize cattle on the pretext that they were needed for work on state projects, and then sell them back to the owners. The Aegean coasts and islands became nests of pirates, preying not only on merchant shipping but also upon the population on shore. Bands of wandering monks, at odds with the secular clergy, and without visible means of support, acted like brigands.

Toward the end of the twelfth century, these processes reached a climax. In 1171, the emperor Manuel I Comnenus (1143–1180) made a desperate effort to rid the capital of Venetian merchants by arresting more than ten thousand. But the emperor was soon forced to restore Venetian privileges. In 1182, a passionate wave of anti-Latin feeling led to a savage massacre by the Constantinople mob of thousands of Westerners who were resident in the capital. In 1185, the Normans of Sicily avenged this outrage by sacking Thessalonica, second city of the Byzantines. The last of the Comnenian dynasty, Andronicus I (1183–1185), was torn to pieces by the frantic citizens of Constantinople as the Norman forces approached the city walls. The weak dynasty of the Angeloi succeeded. Four years later, in 1189–90, the crusading forces of Frederick Barbarossa nearly opened hostilities against the Greeks; his son, Henry VI (see Chapter 4), prepared a fleet to attack Byzantium, but died in 1197 before it could sail.

The Fourth Crusade

In 1195, Alexius III deposed, blinded, and imprisoned his elder brother, Emperor Isaac Angelus (1185–1195). Three years later Pope Innocent III called for a new crusade. Count Baldwin of Flanders and numbers of other powerful lords took the Cross. The Venetians agreed to furnish transportation at a high price, more than the crusaders could pay, and also to contribute fifty armed warships, on condition that they would share equally in all future conquest. The shrewd old doge of Venice agreed to forgive the debt temporarily if the crusaders would help him reconquer Zara, a town on the Dalmatian side of the Adriatic which had revolted against Venice. So the Fourth Crusade began with the destruction of a Roman Catholic town, in 1202. Angrily, the pope excommunicated the crusaders, but worse was to follow.

The son of the blinded Isaac Angelus, known as the young Alexius, had escaped to the West and was trying to recruit assistance to overthrow his uncle, the usurper Alexius III, and to restore Isaac. The brother of the late Henry VI, Philip of Swabia, candidate for the Western imperial throne, had married a daughter of Isaac, and so welcomed his brother-in-law Alexius. Young Alexius offered to pay off the rest of the crusaders' debt to Venice and to assist their efforts in the Holy Land if they would go first to Constantinople and free his father; this proposal suited the ambitions of both the Venetians and the many sympathizers of Philip of Swabia among the crusaders.

In July 1203, the crusaders took Constantinople by assault. Isaac was set free and his son the young Alexius was crowned as Alexius IV. When he failed to pay off his obligations to the crusaders, they drew up a solemn treaty (March

Two of the gilded bronze horses taken by the Venetians from the Hippodrome at Byzantium and installed at St. Mark's Cathedral, Venice.

1204) with their Venetian allies; they agreed to seize the city a second time, to elect a Latin emperor, who was to have a quarter of the empire, and to divide the other three-quarters evenly between the Venetians and the non-Venetians. Then came a second siege, a second capture, and a dreadful sack of Byzantium. What was destroyed in the libraries we shall never know. Many relics and some notable works of art were sent to the West, among them the famous gilded bronze horses from the Hippodrome still to be seen over the door of St. Mark's in Venice.

The Latin Empire

After the sack, the Latins elected Baldwin of Flanders as their first emperor, and the title continued in his family during the fifty-seven years of Latin occupation. The Venetians chose the first Latin patriarch and kept a monopoly on that rich office. The territories of the empire were divided by treaty, with the Venetians claiming the coastal towns and strategic islands. A strange hybrid state was created, in which the emperor's council consisted half of his own barons and half of members of the Venetian merchant colony under the leadership of their governor. Though in theory the Latin emperors were the successors of Constantine and Justinian, and wore the sacred purple boots, in practice they never commanded the loyalty of the Greek population and could not make important decisions without the counsel of their barons.

As neighbors they had hostile Greeks and a new Bulgarian Empire, whose ruler promptly took Baldwin prisoner and had him murdered. Across the Straits, Greek refugees from Constantinople set up an empire at Nicaea. The Latins could not concentrate upon the enemies in Asia because of the threat from Europe. Outnumbered, incompetent as diplomats, slow to learn new military tactics, miserably poor after the treasures of Byzantium had been siphoned away, the Westerners could not maintain their Latin Empire, especially after the popes became involved in the quarrel with the Western emperor Frederick II. The Greeks of Nicaea recaptured Constantinople (1261) and reestablished the Byzantine Empire.

Meanwhile, however, the Latins had fanned out from Constantinople, establishing a series of principalities where the externals of Western feudal society were faithfully copied. Templars, Hospitalers, and Teutonic Knights had lands in Greece. The laws were codified in the *Assizes of Romania,* like the *Assizes of Jerusalem* a valuable source book of feudal custom. As in the Latin states of Syria, intermarriage took place between Latins and Greeks, but the native population never became reconciled to alien domination. Most of the feudal states in Greece were wiped out during the Turkish conquest in the fifteenth century, and none existed after the sixteenth.

Byzantium after 1261

The Greeks of Nicaea, under Michael VIII Palaeologus (reigned 1261–1282), found Byzantium depopulated and badly damaged, while the old territory of the empire was mostly in Latin hands. He and his successors could reconquer only occasional fragments on continental Greece or the islands. In Asia Minor the frontier remained near Konia, the Seljuk capital. Michael VIII staved off the threat posed to his empire by Charles of Anjou, a younger brother of Saint Louis, to whom the popes had given the south Italian kingdom of the Normans and Hohenstaufens. Just as Charles was about to invade from Sicily, Michael helped precipitate the revolt of 1282, known as the Sicilian Vespers. The Sicilians massacred Charles' French troops, and the Aragonese from Spain took over Sicily.

The incompetent and frivolous successors of Michael VIII added materially to the decline of the empire, now little more than a small Balkan state. Wars among rival claimants for the throne tore the empire apart internally. Social unrest appeared, and for a few years in the 1340's Thessalonica was run as a kind of independent proletarian republic. In the 1350's the leader of the Serbian state, the lawgiver king Stephen Dushan, proclaimed himself emperor of the Serbians and Greeks. In 1355, he was about to seize Constantinople and make it the capital of a new Greco-Slavic state when he suddenly died. The Genoese and the Venetians, usually at war with each other, interfered at every turn in the internal affairs of the empire.

The Ottoman Advance

The Ottoman Turks gave the empire its final blow. Ablest and luckiest of the groups to whom the Seljuk Empire in Asia Minor was now passing, the Ottomans in the last quarter of the thirteenth century settled on the borders of the province of Bithynia, across the Straits from Constantinople. The discontented population of this region turned to them in preference to the harsh and ineffectual officials of the Byzantine government. As time went on, many Greeks were converted to Islam in order to avoid the payment of tribute. They taught the nomadic Turkish conquerors some of the arts of a settled agricultural life; the Turks, in turn, adopted Byzantine practices in government.

The corporations of the Akhis, a combination of craft guild, monastic order, and social service agency, built hostels for travelers in the town of Anatolia. There they staged religious dances and read the Koran, presenting Islam at its most attractive and thus aiding the conversion of Christians. Within a generation or two it is highly likely that the original Ottoman Turks had become greatly mixed with the native Greeks of Anatolia.

Meantime, the Ottomans were engaged in warfare with the Byzantines; they built a fleet and began raiding in the Sea of Marmora and the Aegean. They were invited into Europe by one of the rival claimants to the Byzantine throne, who in 1354 allowed them to settle in the Gallipoli peninsula. Soon the

Ottomans occupied much of the neighboring province of Thrace and, in 1363, moved their capital to the European city of Adrianople. Constantinople was now surrounded by Ottoman territory, and could be reached from the West only by sea. In order to survive at all, the emperors had to reach humiliating arrangements with the Ottoman rulers, in some cases becoming their vassals.

The Byzantine Empire survived down to 1453 largely because the Ottomans chose to conquer much of the Balkan region first, putting an end to the independent Bulgarian and Serbian states in the 1370's and 1380's. The final defeat of the Serbs at the battle of Kossovo on June 28, 1389, has long been celebrated by the defeated Serbs themselves in poetry and song. June 28, St. Vitus' day, is their national holiday, and the day on which the archduke Francis Ferdinand was assassinated by the Serb nationalists in 1914.

Ottoman conquests were delayed for half a century when a new wave of Mongols under Timur or Tamerlane emerged from Central Asia in 1402 and defeated the Ottoman armies at Ankara, the present-day capital of Turkey. Like most Mongol efforts, this proved a temporary one, and the Ottoman armies and state soon recovered. In 1453 Sultan Mohammed II ordered a great siege of Constantinople. As final defeat seemed inevitable, the Greeks with their Latin auxiliaries took communion together inside Santa Sophia for the last time, and the last emperor, Constantine XI, died bravely defending the walls.

On May 29, 1453, the Ottomans poured into the city. Mohammed II, the Conqueror, gave thanks to Allah in Santa Sophia itself, and ground the altar of the sanctuary beneath his feet. Thenceforth it was to be a mosque. Shortly thereafter, he installed a new Greek patriarch, and proclaimed himself protector of the Christian church. During the centuries that followed, the Orthodox church for the most part accepted the sultans as successors to the Byzantine emperors. But the empire that traced its origins to Augustus had come to an end.

VI

The Ottoman Successor State, 1453–1699

The Ottoman sultans ruled over the same territory and the same subjects as the Byzantine emperors. In many ways their state was a successor state to Byzantium. The Ottoman fondness and capacity for war, their rigid adherence to custom, and their native Turkish language came from their far-distant past in Central Asia. From the Persians and the Byzantines, who themselves had been influenced by Persia, the Ottomans seem to have derived their exaltation of the ruler, their tolerance of religious minorities, and their practice of encouraging such minorities to form independent communities inside their state. From Persia the Turks took much of their literary language, and from Islam they took the sacred law and their approach to legal problems, the Arabic alphabet with which they wrote until the 1930's, and the Arabic volcabulary of religious, philosophical, and other abstract terms. All the wellsprings of their inheritance—Asian, Persian-Byzantine, and Muslim—tended to make them an exceptionally conservative people.

Civilization

THE SLAVE SYSTEM The most unusual feature of Ottoman society was the advancement of slaves to the highest position within the state. Except for the sultan himself, all the major officials of government and of the sultan's household, as well as all the officers of the army and large bodies of picked

Sultan Mohammed II (ruled 1451–1481): detail of a painting by Gentile Bellini.

troops, were slaves, almost always the children of Christians. They were picked in their early youth for their promising appearance and were especially educated for the sultan's service. As slaves, they owed advancement to the sultan, and could be instantly removed from office and punished by death at any moment in their careers. Every four years from the late fourteenth to the early seventeenth century specially trained officers, each with a quota of places to fill, visited the Balkan Christian villages and took away the ablest appearing youths, from ten to twenty years old. Two considerations made this less dreadful than it seems at first: since a married boy was ineligible, marriage was always an escape; moreover, unlimited opportunities were open to the chosen boys. In poverty-stricken villages, being chosen was sometimes regarded as a privilege. We know of cases where Muslim families paid Christian parents to take their sons and pass them off as Christian in the hope that they would be selected. Once taken, all these youths were converted to Islam, and most of them seem to have become good Muslims. No born Muslim could in theory ever be recruited into the system, since the law said that no born Muslim could be a slave.

This ruling class of slaves was carefully educated. Of the seven or eight thousand chosen annually, all got systematic physical and military training. About a tenth received higher education, and the very cream of the crop became pages in the sultan's own household and attended his palace school, where they were taught languages, Muslim and Ottoman law, ethics, and theology, as well as horsemanship and military science. All left school at the age of twenty-five, and the graduates of the picked schools were then given jobs in the administration; the rest became *spahis* or cavalrymen. There was always plenty of room for advancement, since many were killed in war and at the top levels many were demoted, dismissed, or executed for inefficiency or disloyalty. Splendid financial rewards awaited any man lucky enough to rise to one of the top posts.

At the lower level, the less intelligent slaves were often drafted into the janissaries (from the Turkish words *yeni cheri*, "new forces"). Their training emphasized physical endurance, and they served not only as infantrymen in the army but as shipyard workers, palace gardeners, and the like. They lived in special barracks and had special privileges. A source of strength, they also posed a constant potential danger to the state. At the height of Ottoman military successes, the sultans could put into the field formidable armies, sometimes amounting to more than a quarter of a million men.

The Sultan's harem was a part of the slave institution since all the women in it were slaves, together with their household staffs. The sultan's consorts, as slaves, gave birth to the heir to the empire, so that each new sultan was by birth half-slave. The sultan picked his favorite, not necessarily his eldest, son to succeed him, and the custom arose that the heir to the throne must kill all his brothers and half-brothers upon his succession. Every son of a sultan knew as he was growing up that he either must obtain the throne himself or be killed by whichever of his brothers did obtain it. In 1595, for instance, Mohammed III killed no fewer than nineteen brothers and half-brothers.

THE FOUR PILLARS OF ADMINISTRATION   Ottoman writers thought of the state as a tent resting on four pillars. The first was the viziers, varying in number, to whom the sultan actually delegated many powers. They presided over the council of state, kept the great seal, and could sometimes make decisions on policy. The second pillar was the financial officers, organized to collect revenues: the poll tax on the Christians, one-tenth of all produce, and many of the old Byzantine taxes on commerce, as well as special levies, including money realized by confiscating the great fortunes of disgraced officials. The third pillar was the chancery, a secretariat that affixed the sultan's signature to documents, and prepared, recorded, and transmitted them.

The fourth pillar, unlike the other three, was not a department of state manned by slaves born as Christians. It was composed of the judges, all of whom were born Muslim. Islam itself had responsibility for all legal matters and for education. One-third of state lands were set aside as religious property. Each tract had its own purpose: the support of mosques, of charitable or educational institutions, and even of inns or public baths. Income from such property supported the entire class of *ulema*, the learned men of Islam.

Among the ulema were the *muftis,* or jurists, who answered questions that arose in the course of lawsuits. The grand mufti in Istanbul, whom the sultan himself consulted, was known as the Sheikh-ul-Islam, the "ancient" of Islam, and outranked everybody but the grand vizier. Since he could speak the final word on the sacred law, it may be said that he exercised a kind of check on the absolute power of the sultan. He alone could proclaim the beginning of war, or denounce a sultan for transgression of the sacred law and summon his subjects to depose him. The opinions of the muftis were collected as a body of interpretative law. The general acceptance by all Muslims of the supremacy of the sacred law and the reluctance of the muftis to accept change helped to account for the failure of the Ottoman system to develop with the times. There are no full-scale "reformations" in Ottoman history until the twentieth century.

WEAKNESSES OF THE SYSTEM   The effectiveness of the entire structure depended upon the character of the sultan. Harem upbringing and ruthless family antagonisms did not produce wise and statesmanlike sultans. Rather, more and more sultans became weaklings, drunkards, debauchees, and men of little political experience or understanding. Harem intrigue played a great role in the state.

Efficient operation of the administration depended upon maintaining the slave system by excluding from participation the born Muslim sons of the slave ruling class. But in practice this rigid exclusion broke down early, and born Muslims, attracted by the possibilities of gain and power, were admitted. Since they could not be regarded as slaves, the chief restraints that kept the machine running thus faded. Insubordinate soldiers also sped the decay of the state, as turbulent janissaries frequently deposed sultans.

Finally, in a society where religion was the only test of nationality, all Orthodox Christians were automatically regarded as Greeks, and lived under the control of the patriarch. As time passed this alienated many Slavs and Romanians who might otherwise have been loyal subjects.

The Empire

EXPANSION, TO 1566   The core of the Ottoman state was the same as that around which the Byzantine Empire had been built—Asia Minor and the Balkans. From this core before the death of Mohammed II in 1481, the Turks expanded across the Danube into modern Romania, seized the Genoese outposts in the Crimea, and made this southern Russian region a vassal state under its Tatar rulers. But they failed to take either the great Hungarian fortress of Belgrade, key to a further advance into central Europe, or the island fortress of Rhodes in the Mediterranean, stronghold of the Hospitalers and key to a further naval advance westward.

Sultan Selim I (reigned 1512–1520) nearly doubled the territories of the

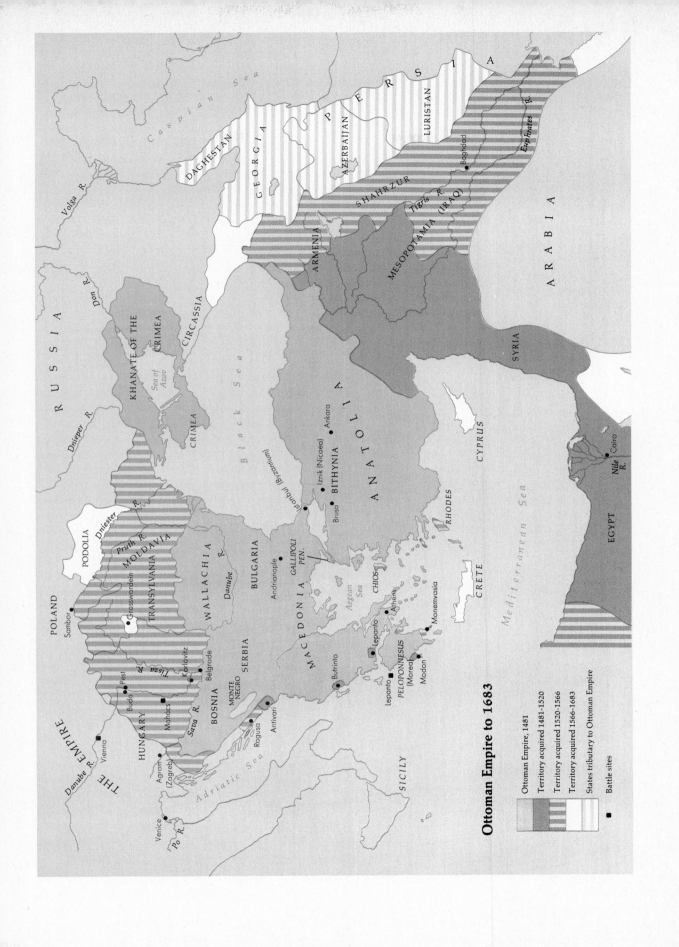

Ottoman Empire to 1683

Ottoman Empire, 1481
Territory acquired 1481–1520
Territory acquired 1520–1566
Territory acquired 1566–1683
States tributary to Ottoman Empire

■ Battle sites

empire—in Asia, at the expense of the Persians, and in Africa, where Egypt was annexed in 1517 and the rule of the Mamluks ended. From them the sultan inherited the duty of protecting Mecca and Medina, and he also assumed the title of caliph. The character of the Ottoman state was substantially altered by these acquisitions, for the overwhelming majority of the population was now Muslim, mostly Arabs, often more fanatical than the Turks.

The advance into Europe was resumed by Suleiman the Magnificent (reigned 1520–1566), who participated in the dynastic wars between the Hapsburgs and the French Valois, and even affected the course of the Protestant Reformation by the threat of a military invasion of Germany (see Chapter 7). In 1521, Suleiman took Belgrade, and in 1522, Rhodes, thus removing the two chief obstacles to westward advance. In 1526, at Mohács in Hungary, he defeated the Christian armies, and the Turks entered Buda, the Hungarian capital on the middle Danube. In September 1529, Suleiman besieged Vienna, posing a threat to Christendom greater than any since Leo III and Charles Martel had defeated the Arabs in the early eighth century. But the Ottoman lines of communication were greatly overextended, and Suleiman had to abandon the siege after two weeks. He retained control over the south-central portion of Hungary and added other lands north and east of the Danube. In North Africa he acquired Algeria, which remained an Ottoman vassal state in the western Mediterranean until the nineteenth century. In Asia he defeated the Persians, annexed modern Iraq, including Baghdad, and secured an outlet on the Persian Gulf.

In 1536, a formal treaty was concluded between France and the Ottoman Empire, the first of the famous "capitulations," so designated because it was divided into "articles" or "little heads" (Latin, *capitula*), not because it was a surrender. It permitted the French to buy and sell throughout the Ottoman dominions on the same basis as any Ottoman subject. They could have resident consuls with civil and criminal jurisdiction over Frenchmen in the Ottoman Empire. In Ottoman territory, Frenchmen were to enjoy complete religious liberty and were also granted a protectorate over the Holy Places, the old aim of the Crusades. The Orthodox church resented the Roman Catholic gains, and the dispute would survive to precipitate the Crimean War in the nineteenth century. These capitulations gave France a better position in the Ottoman Empire than that of any other European power; their terms paralleled those of earlier Byzantine trade treaties with Venice and Genoa.

DECLINE, 1566–1699   After Suleiman, the Ottoman system deteriorated, despite occasional periods of Turkish success. The Ottoman capture of Cyprus in 1571 led to the formation of a Western league against the Turk, headed by the pope. In the same year the league won the great naval battle of Lepanto, off the Greek coast, but failed to follow up the victory, thus permitting the Turks to recover.

Within the Ottoman state, the sale of government offices had become a regular practice by the end of the sixteenth century, and the repeated rebellions of janissaries were jeopardizing the sultan's position. Had it not been for the Thirty Years' War (1618–1648), which preoccupied the states of western Europe (see Chapter 8), the Ottoman Empire might have suffered even more severely in the first half of the seventeenth century than it did. Several sultans were deposed within a few years; the Persians recaptured Baghdad; rebellion raged in the provinces.

Yet a firm sultan, Murad IV (1623–1640), temporarily restored order through the most brutal means, and what looked like a real revival began with the accession to power of an able family of viziers, the Köprülüs. The first Köprülü ruthlessly executed 36,000 people in a five-year period (1656–1661), hanged the Greek patriarch for predicting that Christianity would defeat Islam, rebuilt the army and navy, and suppressed revolt. Between 1661 and 1676 the second Köprülü led the Ottoman navy to a triumph in Crete, taken from Venice. The Ottomans temporarily won large areas of the Ukraine from the Russians and Poles, only to lose them again in 1681. In 1683, the Ottomans again besieged Vienna, with all Europe anxiously awaiting the outcome. For the second time in two centuries, the Ottoman wave was broken, and Europe began a great counteroffensive. The Hapsburgs drove the Turks out of Hungary, and the Venetians seized the Peloponnesus, while the Russians made their first effective appearance as enemies of the Ottomans. Although the Köprülüs had galvanized the Ottoman armies into a last successful effort, they did not touch the real evils of the Ottoman system.

In 1699 an international congress at Karlovitz on the Danube confirmed Ottoman territorial losses. From then on the European powers could stop worrying about the Ottoman menace, which had preoccupied them ever since the fourteenth century. The importance of the Ottoman Empire was no longer its military potential, but its diplomatic position as a power in decline over whose possible disintegration and division the states of Europe might squabble and negotiate. With the meeting at Karlovitz, what we call "the Eastern question" began. Forced onto the defensive, the Ottoman Turks had to go outside their slave family for administrators. Against their will they came to rely for diplomacy upon Christian Greeks, born negotiators, with generations of experience in commerce, who retained the talents of their Byzantine ancestors.

VII
Medieval Russia

Of all the achievements of the Byzantines perhaps the most remarkable was their impact on the Slavic world. As old Rome civilized and eventually christianized large groups of "barbarians" in western Europe, so Constantinople, the new Rome, civilized and christianized the Slavs. Many of the problems that beset the West today in its dealings with the Soviet Union arise from the fact that the Soviet Union is still essentially Russia, a country in the Orthodox and not in the Western tradition, a country that still shows the effects of having experienced its conversion from Byzantium.

Rus and Byzantium

Into the great plains of European Russia, lying between the Baltic and the Black Sea—where movement is easiest along the north-south courses of the rivers—Scandinavians called Rus began to penetrate in the eighth century. We know few details of their conquests of the peoples then living on the steppe, mostly Slavs but also Lithuanians and Finns. The Old Russian Primary Chronicle, compiled during the eleventh century, reports that during the 850's the struggling tribes of the steppe actually invited the Scandinavians in to keep order, and that Rurik, a Danish warrior, accepted. Moving south along the Dnieper River from the Baltic area and the trading center of Novgorod, the Scandinavians seized the settlement called Kiev and made it the center of a state, at first loosely organized and especially devoted to trade. And in 860, for the first time, a fleet of two hundred of their warships appeared off Constantinople. In this and later clashes, the Byzantines were victorious.

The Primary Chronicle also preserves the texts of the trade treaties between Byzantium and the Russians. While the Byzantines took precautions to protect their lives and property from the wild barbarians, they wanted the furs and timber that the Russians brought them. In the trade treaty of 945, some of the Russians were already Christians, for they swore by the Holy Cross. But the conversion of the Russians as a whole occurred in the 980's in the reign of Vladimir. Like Boris the Bulgarian before him, Vladimir felt that the old worship of forest and water spirits and a thunder god was inadequate. The Primary Chronicle tells how Vladimir surveyed Islam, Judaism, and the Christianity of the Germans (Roman Catholicism) and finally chose the Christianity of Byzantium because of the awe-inspiring beauty of Santa Sophia and the services held there. No doubt Vladimir was also moved by the opportunity to marry a Byzantine princess, and so to acquire some of Byzantium's prestige. In one day he threw down all the idols in Kiev and had the entire population forcibly baptized in the waters of the Dnieper.

The Impact of Conversion

Conversion meant the introduction of priests, a new and important social class. The clergy had jurisdiction over all Christians in cases involving morals, family affairs, or religious questions. Christianity brought with it the advanced concept that crime should be punished by the state rather than avenged by the victim or his family. The Church introduced the first education, and churchmen, using the Cyrillic alphabet, wrote the first literature, chiefly ecclesiastical. Byzantine art-forms were imported and imitated; the great church of Santa Sophia at Kiev is in its way as magnificent as its prototype at Constantinople. Culture was confined to the few cities and to the monasteries, for paganism died slowly in the countryside. In the early period, the archbishops of Kiev were Greeks from Byzantium, but the Russian church soon asserted its practical independence. From the first it became a large landowner, and monasteries quickly multiplied.

In the West every educated priest, no matter what his native tongue, knew Latin and had access to Latin classics and the Latin church fathers. The Russian priests had no such advantage; since Slavic was used in the liturgy, few of them learned Greek. Sermons, saints' lives, some chronicles, and *Basil Digenes Akritas* (see p. 213) were translated from Greek and circulated in Slavic, but they were no substitutes for the classics or the Fathers. Indeed, in the nineteenth century an influential group of Russian thinkers argued that the Byzantine faith had fostered stagnation and intellectual sterility; their opponents, however, argued that it had given the Russians spirituality, a willingness to bend to God's will, and other great virtues. It would be hard to deny that conversion from Byzantium cut Russia off from access to the treasure house of Western culture and was in some measure responsible for Russian "cultural lag."

Kievan Society and Politics

Kievan Russia developed a society rather similar to that in medieval western Europe. The entourage of the prince, which began as a Scandinavian war band, gradually became a group of councilors appropriate to a settled state. The law codes reflected social conditions: arson and horse theft were more heavily punishable than murder. Because the Byzantines paid cash for the Russian forest products, Kiev had more of a money economy than manorial western Europe.

The Kievan ruling house contracted dynastic marriages with the royal families of Sweden and France, and made alliances with the Holy Roman emperors. Merchants from the West appeared in the area, especially at Novgorod ("new town") in the north and at Kiev itself. Had the Russians been able to maintain and develop these promising lines of communication, they might have overcome whatever handicap had been imposed by Byzantine Christianity. But they were denied the opportunity.

When a Kievan prince died, his sons divided up the land as if it were their private property—a custom that caused the fragmentation of territory and authority. The mutually hostile petty principalities thus established weakened Kievan society in the face of outside dangers. In the eleventh century, the Turkic tribe of Polovtsy or Cumans appeared on the southern steppes. The warring Russian princes made the tragic mistake of hiring bands of Polovtsy. The sole surviving heroic poem of the Kievan period, the *Song of the Expedition of Igor,* quite comparable with the French *Song of Roland* (see p. 187), reproves the princes for introducing the infidels and compounding chaos. Shortly after 1200, the Mongol Tatars made their appearance, and the Kievan state as such disappeared. It bequeathed to later Russians the ideal of unity, the common heritage of language, and the Christian faith.

Early Russian architecture: the Church of the Savior, Novgorod.

Politics from 1200 to 1450

THE WESTERN LANDS AND NOVGOROD   During the confused 250 years following the collapse of Kiev, Russian national life continued in several centers. The southwestern region, including Kiev itself, became a virtually independent principality, distinguished by an unruly nobility who hampered all efforts of the princes to consolidate their power in the face of pressure from their Polish and Lithuanian neighbors. A parallel development marked the northwest region, centering around the cities of Polotsk and Smolensk. By the early fourteenth century, the grand duke of Lithuania held nominal rule over most of these western lands. Still mostly pagan, the Lithuanians in some measure took over the language and attitudes of their more advanced Russian vassals. In 1386, a famous dynastic marriage united Lithuania with Poland, and the influence of the Polish Roman Catholic church and the Polish nobility now superseded that of the Orthodox Russians.

The western lands comprised feudal Russia, where the local nobles, Russian or Polish, ruled their lands without interference from the grand duke of Lithuania. The economic base was manorial like that in the West, and restrictions on the movement of peasants appeared here long before they did elsewhere in Russia. Feudal decentralization and the heavy Polish-Catholic influence meant that the western lands could never become the center around which Russia could reunite.

The northern regions of Russia, between the Baltic shore and Lake Ilmen, and stretching far north and northeast over empty wastes to the Arctic Ocean and Siberia, lay under the dominion of the town commonwealth of Novgorod. Long before Kiev collapsed, Novgorod cherished a tradition of municipal independence; its city council became its most powerful institution. Novgorod traded with the West, especially Germany, exchanging its forest products for cloth and metalwork. Since its soil was infertile, it depended on the area to the southeast, around Moscow, for grain. Novgorod's inability to solve its social and economic problems deprived it of a chance to unify Russia. A few rich merchant families came to control its council and struggled with each other for power; the poor, meantime, might be sold into slavery for debt or turn brigand. In the fifteenth century, when Poland-Lithuania and the principality of Moscow competed, the upper classes supported the Poles and Lithuanians, and the lower classes supported Moscow. In 1478 Moscow conquered Novgorod, wiped out the upper classes, and took away the bell, symbol of town independence.

A Russian prince and his body-guard.

MOSCOW AND THE TATARS   After the collapse of Kiev the principality of Moscow to the northeast was still a newly settled frontier area. Though agriculturally poorer than the fertile southwest, it was richer than the north and could provide food enough for its people; it also had flourishing forest industries. Since neither cities nor a nobility had developed to any marked extent, the pioneers turned to the prince for leadership.

This was also the region most exposed to the Tatars. By the early thirteenth century, Genghis Khan had consolidated a large number of the Mongolian nomads of Central Asia; he then led them into the steppes of southern Russia, defeating Russians and Polovtsy together in 1223. His nephew Baty returned in the 1230's, sacked Moscow in 1237 and Kiev in 1240, and moved on into the western Russian regions and Poland, Hungary, and Bohemia. The success of the Tatars seems to have been due to their excellent military organization and deceptive battle tactics. Though Baty defeated the Poles and the Germans in 1241, political affairs in Asia drew him eastward, and the Tatars never again appeared so far to the west. At Sarai, near the great bend of the Volga, he founded the capital of a new state—the "Golden Horde," which accepted the overlordship of the far-off central government of the Mongols, in Peking.

In Russia the Tatars laid waste to the land while they were conquering it, but after the conquest they shifted their emphasis to levying tribute. It was not to their interest to disturb economic life, so long as their authority was recognized. They drafted some Russian recruits for their armies, but generally made the Russian princes responsible for the delivery of men and money, and stayed out of Russian territory except to take censuses, survey property, and punish the recalcitrant. The tributary Russian princes, on assuming office, traveled to Sarai to do homage. The expensive burden of tribute and the humiliating sense of subservience fell most heavily upon the region of Moscow.

Toward the end of the fourteenth century, as the Mongol Empire grew feebler, the Russians became bolder. The first Russian victories over the Tatars, scored by a prince of Moscow in 1378 and 1380, were fiercely avenged; yet they served to show that the Tatars could be defeated. When the Golden Horde disintegrated in the early fifteenth century, three Tatar states were formed from its debris: one at Kazan on the middle Volga, which blocked the course of the river to Russian trade for another century and a half; a second at Astrakhan at the mouth of the Volga on the Caspian; and a third in the Crimea, which later became a vassal of the Ottoman sultan.

Though some argue that the Tatar impact was beneficial to Russia because it eventually enabled the prince of Moscow to centralize his power, it seems certain that the conquest also had a very serious negative effect. The Tatars, despite their military efficiency, were bearers of a lower culture than the Russians of the Kievan period had already achieved; when their power was finally shattered in the fifteenth century, Russian civilization was far behind that of the West. To the retarding effect of Byzantine Christianity had been added the tremendous handicap of two centuries of cultural stagnation.

The Muscovite State

During these two centuries, the princes of Moscow assumed leadership. They were shrewd administrators, who married into powerful families and acquired land by inheritance, by purchase, and by foreclosing mortgages. They established the principle of seniority, so that their domain was not divided among their sons and the tragedy of Kiev was not repeated. They developed useful relations with their Tatar overlords, who chose them to collect the tribute from neighboring princes and to deliver it to Sarai. The princes kept a close watch

MEDIEVAL EASTERN EUROPE

246

on the Tatars, so that when the moment of Tatar weakness came they could take advantage of it. They could truthfully claim to be the agents of liberation and champions of Russia.

Finally, and very possibly most important, the princes of Moscow secured the support of the Russian church. In the early fourteenth century the metropolitan archbishop deliberately transferred his see to Moscow, and made it the ecclesiastical capital of Russia. When the effective line of Muscovite princes faltered temporarily, the metropolitan administered the principality loyally and effectively until the princely house recovered. Ivan III of Moscow (reigned 1462–1505) put himself forward as the heir to the princes of Kiev and declared that he intended to regain the ancient Russian lands that had been lost to Catholic Poles and Muslim Tatars—a national and religious appeal. His wars took on the character of a purely Russian crusade. Many nobles living in the western lands came over to him with their estates and renounced their loyalties to the Lithuanian–Polish state. In 1492, the Prince of Lithuania was forced to recognize Ivan III as sovereign of "all the Russians."

In 1472, Ivan had married the niece of the last Byzantine emperor, Constantine XI. He adopted the Byzantine title of autocrat, used the Byzantine double-headed eagle as his seal, and began to behave like a Byzantine emperor. He sometimes used the title *czar* (Caesar) and no longer consulted his nobles on matters of state but reached decisions in solitude. Italian architects built him an enormous palace, the Kremlin, a building set apart, like the one at Byzantium.

In short, from the late fifteenth century on, we find the czars acting like autocrats. Perhaps constant war helped foster autocracy: a national emergency prolonged over centuries naturally led to a kind of national dictatorship. Unlike the nobles of western Europe, those of Muscovy did not unite to fight

Medieval and Early Modern Russia

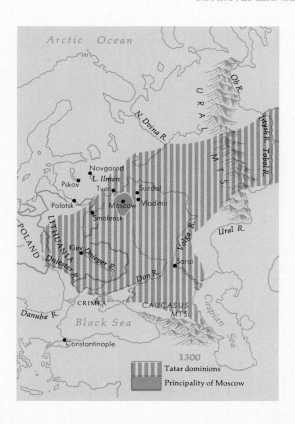

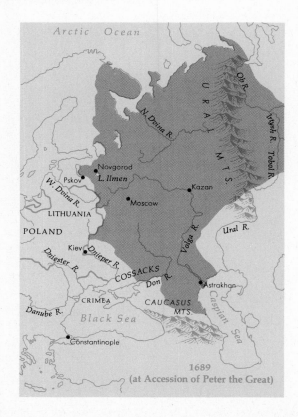

the rising monarchy for their privileges, but split into various factions, with which the monarch could deal individually. In the West, the Church itself was a part of feudal society, and jealous of its prerogatives; in Russia it became the ally of the monarchy and a department of state. Russian churchmen knew all about Rome's claim to world empire and Constantinople's centuries-long position as "new Rome." With the fall of Constantinople to the Turks, they elaborated a famous theory that Moscow was the successor to the two former world capitals:

> The Church of Old Rome fell because of its heresy; the gates of the Second Rome, Constantinople, have been hewn down by the infidel Turks; but the Church of Moscow, the Church of the New Rome, shines brighter than the Sun in the whole Universe. . . . Two Romes have fallen, but the Third stands fast; a fourth there cannot be.*

Between the accession of Ivan III in 1462 and the accession of Peter the Great in 1689, the autocracy succeeded in overcoming the opposition of the old nobility. This was done in part by fostering a class of military service gentry who owed everything to the czar. Their estates, at first granted only for life in exchange for service, eventually became hereditary. The estates of the old nobility, which had always been hereditary but for which they had owed no service, became service estates. Thus, by the end of the period, the two types of noble and the two types of estate had by a gradual process become almost identical. The hereditary nobles often owed service; the military-service nobles often had hereditary land.

This tremendously important social process was accompanied by another, which is really the other side of the coin—the growth of serfdom. Economic factors and political unrest had forced more and more peasants to become dependent on large landowners. The peasants would accept contracts that involved a money loan and that required rent in produce and service on the landlord's lands. By the early seventeenth century it had become customary that the peasant could not leave his plot until he had paid off the loan. Since the debt was often too big for him to repay, he could in practice never leave.

The process was enormously speeded up when the czars gave estates to the military service gentry, who received help from the government in keeping farmers on the land. Since the peasants paid most of the taxes, it was easier for the government to collect revenues if it kept the peasants where they were. Gradually it was made harder and harder for a tenant to leave his landlord, until by 1649 the avenues of escape were closed and the serf was fixed to the soil. The landlord administered justice, had police rights on the estate, and collected the serfs' taxes. He himself could sell, exchange, or give away his serfs, whose status became hereditary. Together with the absolute autocracy, the institution of serfdom was the most characteristic feature of Russian society, and its consequences are still with us today.

IVAN THE TERRIBLE AND THE TIME OF TROUBLES   Most of the disorders of sixteenth- and seventeenth-century Russia had their origin in the long reign of Ivan IV, the Terrible (1534–1584). Ivan succeeded to the throne as a small child, suffering helplessly the indignities inflicted on him by rival groups of intriguing nobles. When Ivan was strong enough to assume power, he regulated the rapacity of the provincial administrators who had oppressed the population.

* Quoted by A. J. Toynbee, in *Civilization on Trial* (New York, 1948), p. 171.

He also convoked the first *zemski sobor* (land assembly), a consultative body consisting of nobles, clerics, and town representatives, to assist particularly with important questions of war and peace. Comparable to the various assemblies of the medieval western European world, the zemski sobor under Ivan seems to have met only once.

In 1564 Ivan created a fantastic new institution: the *oprichnina,* or "separate realm," which was to belong to him personally, while the rest of Russia continued to be administered as before. His new officers (called *oprichniks*), grimly dressed in black, and riding black horses, bore on their saddlebows a dog's head (for vigilance) and a broom (symbolizing a clean sweep). These forerunners of the secret police waged a relentless war on the nobles, confiscating their estates, exiling them, killing them off. By the time of Ivan's death Russian administration had degenerated to a state approximating chaos. Pathologically cruel, Ivan had seven wives and murdered his own son in a fit of rage. Yet Ivan extended Russian authority to the east against the Tatars, thus opening the whole Volga waterway to Russian commerce and facilitating expansion further east, into Siberia.

The few foreign observers who knew the Russia of Ivan could foresee collapse. And the czar himself wrote in his last will: "The body is exhausted, the spirit is ailing, the spiritual and physical wounds multiply, and there is no doctor to cure me."* With the death of his imbecile son Fëdor (1598), the Moscow dynasty, descended from the Kievan princes, died out. Fëdor's able brother-in-law, Boris Godunov (reigned 1598–1605), could not deal with the legacy of disorder, especially after a famine and plague began in 1601. Brigands roamed the countryside, a pretender under Polish protection claimed to be a son of Ivan the Terrible, and Russia was launched on the "Time of Troubles" (1603–1613).

The pretender himself ruled briefly as czar, but was murdered within a year. New pretenders arose; civil war continued as Poles and Swedes intervened. Polish forces took Moscow, and the king of Poland planned to become czar. In answer to an appeal from the patriarch, a kind of Russian national militia assembled, drawn from the prosperous free farmers of the middle Volga region. Under the combined command of a butcher and a nobleman, the militia drove the Poles from Moscow in 1613. The prospect of foreign Catholic rule had produced an explosion of Russian national sentiment.

THE FIRST ROMANOVS A *zemski sobor* now elected Michael Romanov czar. From the election of Michael in 1613 to the Russian Revolution of 1917, the Romanovs held the throne. Michael succeeded with no limitations placed upon his power by the zemski sobor; he was an elected autocrat. For the first ten years of his reign the zemski sobor stayed in continuous session to give the new dynasty the semblance of popular support it needed. But the zemski sobor never transformed itself into a parliament, and after 1623 it was summoned only to help declare war or make peace, to approve new taxation, and to sanction important new legislation. It endorsed the accession of Michael's son Alexius (1645–1676), and in 1649 it confirmed a new law code. After 1653 Alexius did not summon it again, nor did his son, Fëdor (1676–1682). Its last meetings were in 1682.

The early Romanovs were neither distinguished nor talented. The ill-defined departments of the central government often had overlapping areas of

A contemporary portrait of Ivan the Terrible.

* Quoted by M. T. Florinsky, *Russia: A History and an Interpretation,* Vol. I (New York, 1953), p. 208.

competence. Provincial governors milked the long-suffering population, and local efforts at self-government were in practice limited to the choice of officials who collected taxes for the central authorities. Opposition came not from articulate citizens but from the oppressed and hungry peasantry, who burned manor houses and killed landlords or tax collectors. Such uprisings were almost never directed against the czar; often indeed the peasant leaders would arouse their followers *in the name* of the czar, or pretend to be czars.

During the sixteenth and seventeenth centuries Russian pioneers, in search of furs to sell and new land to settle, led the way in the tremendous physical expansion of the Russian domain. Russian frontiersmen known as Cossacks (a Tatar word meaning "free adventurer") organized themselves for self-defense against the Tatars. Two Cossack republics arose, one on the Dnieper, the other on the Don, living in a kind of primitive democracy relatively independent of Moscow. As time passed, more Cossack groups formed in the Volga, in the Urals, and elsewhere.

The most dramatic expansion rapidly took the Russians eastward into the Urals and across Siberia to the Pacific. Far more slowly, because of Tatar, Turkish, and Polish opposition, the Russians also moved southeast toward the Black Sea. Repeatedly Russians and Poles fought over the old west Russian territory of the Ukraine, but by 1682 the Poles were beginning to yield. The Swedes still blocked the Baltic exit into the North Sea. On the southern steppes the Russians struggled against the Crimean Tatars. The Turks, overlords of the Tatars, held the key fort of Azov, controlled the Black Sea, participated in the wars over the Ukraine, and now became perennial enemies of the czars.

THE CHURCH AND FOREIGN INFLUENCES   The Church remained the partner of the autocracy. The czar controlled the election of the metropolitan of Moscow, and after 1589 that of the newly proclaimed patriarch of Moscow. Czar Alexius appointed to the patriarchal throne a cleric named Nikon, whose arrogance aroused protests from both the clergy and the laity. He seriously advanced the theory that, since the spiritual realm was superior to the temporal, the patriarch was actually superior to the czar. In the West the more powerful popes had maintained this view, but in Byzantium or in Russia few churchmen ever dared. In 1666, a church council deposed Nikon, who died a mere monk, and Peter the Great was to abolish the patriarchate largely because he wished to silence Nikon's claims forever.

By 1500 the Russian monasteries owned more than a third of the land available for cultivation. Opposition to monastic worldliness arose within the Church itself. But those who favored monastic poverty also wished to enforce the noninterference of the state in monastic affairs. To preserve its rights to control the monasteries in other respects, the government of the czar therefore opposed the reforming movement that it would otherwise have acclaimed.

The Church, almost alone, inspired the art and literature of the Muscovite period. The icon, inherited from Byzantium, was the type of painting that flourished. Historical chronicles were written by the monks, and theological tracts attacked both Catholics and Protestants, whose doctrines were known in the western regions. This limited literature was written in Old Church Slavonic, the language of the liturgy but not of everyday speech. There was no Russian secular learning, no science, no flowering of vernacular literature, no lively philosophical debate.

Slowly and gradually, during the sixteenth and seventeenth centuries foreigners and foreign ideas penetrated into Russia. The small group of talented

Italians who built the Kremlin in the late fifteenth century had little lasting influence. Ivan IV welcomed the English and encouraged them to trade their woolen cloth for Russian timber, rope, pitch, and other naval supplies, which helped build the Elizabethan fleets that defeated the Spanish Armada. The English taught the Russians some industrial techniques and supplied a large number of officers, mostly Scots, for the czar's armies. In the mid-seventeenth century the Dutch displaced them as the leading foreign residents, managing their own glass, paper, and textile plants in Russia.

The foreign quarter of Moscow, always called "the German suburb," grew rapidly. German, Dutch, Danish technicians—bronze founders, textile weavers, clockmakers—received large salaries from the state. Foreign physicians and druggists became fashionable, though the common people thought they were wizards. Merchants continued to enjoy special privileges much to the disgust of their native competitors. A few nobles began to buy books, assemble libraries, and learn Latin, French, or German; some began to eat salad and take snuff and even to converse politely. Some Russians went abroad to travel, and most of these refused to go home. The lower classes, however, distrusted and hated the foreigners, and jeered at them on the street.

The most dramatic outburst of antiforeign feeling was precipitated by learned clerics from the Ukraine and Greece who recommended to Patriarch Nikon that the Holy Books be corrected in certain places where the texts were unsound. Many Russians were horrified. With their deep regard for the externals, the rite, the magic, they were now told that they were spelling the name of Jesus wrong, and using the wrong number of fingers in crossing themselves. Opponents of change split away from the Church, and some twenty thousand of them burned themselves alive, convinced that the end of the world was at hand, since Moscow, the Third Rome, had become heretical, and there would be no fourth. Survivors settled down and became sober, solid citizens, called Old Believers, many of them merchants and well-to-do farmers. Some later Russian governments persecuted them. The influx of foreigners thus not only introduced the Russians to Western technology well before the advent of Peter the Great, but also profoundly split Russian society and the Russian church.

Reading Suggestions on Eastern Medieval Europe

BYZANTIUM

G. Ostrogorsky, *History of the Byzantine State* (Rutgers, 1957). A brilliant historical synthesis, with rich bibliography.

A. A. Vasiliev, *History of the Byzantine Empire, 324-1453*, 2 vols. (*Wisconsin). A good comprehensive work.

J. M. Hussey, *The Byzantine World* (*Torchbooks). Useful shorter sketch.

The Cambridge Medieval History, IV, Parts I and II (Cambridge University Press, 1966 and 1967). Collaborative work by many excellent scholars treating Byzantium and its neighbors, and its government, church, and civilization.

D. Obolensky, *The Byzantine Commonwealth: Eastern Europe, 500-1453* (Praeger, 1971). Treats the peoples in the Byzantine orbit as well.

J. B. Bury, *A History of the Later Roman Empire, 395-802,* 2 vols. (Macmillan, 1889). A celebrated old study; a revision of the first volume (*Dover) is the best work on the period 395-565.

———, *A History of the Eastern Roman Empire, 802-867* (Macmillan, 1912). Distinguished scholarly treatment.

R. Jenkins, *Byzantium: The Imperial Centuries, A.D. 610 to 1071* (Random House, 1967). Sound account of the fortunes of Byzantium at their height.

C. Diehl, *Byzantine Portraits* (Knopf, 1927). Excellent essays on personalities.

———, *Byzantium: Greatness and Decline* (*Rutgers). Another thoughtful study.

J. M. Hussey, *Church and Learning in the Byzantine Empire, 867-1185* (Oxford, 1937). An excellent introduction to the subject.

S. Vryonis, Jr., *The Decline of Medi-*

eval Hellenism in Asia Minor and the Process of Islamization from the Eleventh through the Fifteenth Century (University of California, 1971). Recent learned study of a difficult, little studied, and important subject.

A. Grabar, *Byzantine Painting* (Skira, 1953). Superb reproductions of mosaics and frescoes.

D. Talbot Rice, *The Art of Byzantium* (Thames and Hudson, 1959). A splendid picture book.

ISLAM

F. Rahman, *Islam* (Weidenfeld & Nicholson, 1966). Sound comprehensive introduction by a Muslim scholar.

H. A. R. Gibb, *Mohammedanism: An Historical Survey* (*Galaxy). A meaty introduction by a great authority.

————, *Studies in the Civilization of Islam* (*Beacon). A collection of perceptive essays.

B. Lewis, *The Arabs in History* (*Torchbooks). Crisp and suggestive survey.

W. Montgomery Watt, *Muhammad: Prophet and Statesman* (*Oxford). Clear and informative study.

T. Andrae, *Mohammed: The Man and His Faith* (*Torchbooks). A scholarly appreciation and interpretation.

K. Cragg, *Call of the Minaret* (*Galaxy). Analysis by a Protestant missionary.

THE CRUSADES

A History of the Crusades: Vol. I, *The First Hundred Years,* ed. M. W. Baldwin; Vol. II, *The Later Crusades, 1189–1311,* ed. R. L. Wolff and H. W. Hazard (University of Pennsylvania, 1955, 1962). Collaborative and authoritative work.

S. Runciman, *A History of the Crusades,* 3 vols. (*Torchbooks). The most comprehensive treatment of the topic by a single scholar.

J. L. LaMonte, *Feudal Monarchy in the Latin Kingdom of Jerusalem* (Medieval Academy, 1932). Important study of crusader political institutions.

W. Miller, *The Latins in the Levant: A History of Frankish Greece, 1204–1566* (Dutton, 1908), and *Essay on the Latin Orient* (Cambridge, 1921). Two good studies of Westerners in Greece.

THE OTTOMAN EMPIRE

E. S. Creasy, *History of the Ottoman Turks* (Khayats, 1961). New edition of a good general account that was first published in the 1850's.

H. A. R. Gibb and H. Bowen, *Islamic Society and the West,* Vol. I, Parts 1 and 2 (Oxford University, 1950, 1956). Scholarly survey of Ottoman institutions.

E. Pears, *The Destruction of the Greek Empire and the Story of the Capture of Constantinople by the Turks* (Longmans, 1903). A solid work, not superseded by later studies.

H. A. Gibbons, *The Foundation of the Ottoman Empire* (Century, 1916), and P. Wittek, *The Rise of the Ottoman Empire* (Luzac, 1958). Two perceptive studies of the forces accounting for the rapid development of the Turkish state.

A. H. Lybyer, *The Government of the Ottoman Empire in the Time of Suleiman the Magnificent* (Harvard University, 1913). Lively pioneering study, now outdated.

MEDIEVAL RUSSIA

V. O. Kluchevsky, *A History of Russia,* 5 vols. (Dent, 1911–1931). The greatest single work on the subject, poorly translated.

M. Florinsky, *Russia: A History and an Interpretation,* Vol. I (Macmillan, 1953). A good textbook, solid and accurate.

G. Vernadsky, *Kievan Russia and The Mongols and Russia* (Yale, 1948, 1953).

Vols. II and III of the Yale History of Russia; authoritative and complete.

G. P. Fedotov, *The Russian Religious Mind,* 2 vols. (Harvard, 1946, 1966). A study of the Kievan period from a most unusual point of view.

SOURCES

Procopius, 7 vols. (Loeb Classical Library, 1914–1940). Writings of a major historian who lived through the events recounted.

Digenes Akritas trans. J. Mavrogodato (Clarendon, 1956). The Byzantine frontier epic.

A. J. Arberry, *The Koran Interpreted* (*Macmillan). The best modern translation.

William, Archbishop of Tyre, *A History of Deeds Done beyond the Sea,* 2 vols. (Columbia University, 1943). The best contemporary account of the Crusades.

Memoirs of the Crusades (*Everyman). Eyewitness accounts of the Fourth Crusade and of the crusade of Saint Louis.

Memoirs of Usamah ibn-Munqidh (Columbia, 1929). An Easterner observes the Western invaders.

The Life and Letters of Ogier Ghiselin de Busbecq (C. K. Paul, 1881). By the Hapsburg ambassador to Suleiman the Magnificent.

The Russian Primary Chronicle, Laurentian Text trans. S. H. Cross (Medieval Academy, 1953). Our oldest source for early Russian history.

The Correspondence between Prince A. M. Kurbsky and Tsar Ivan IV of Russia and *Kurbsky's History of Ivan IV,* both ed. J. L. I. Fennell (Cambridge, 1955, 1965). Formerly regarded as the fundamental sources for the political theories of the czar and his opponents. Recent scholarship has demonstrated that they are probably later forgeries.

six

Transition to a New World:

Late Middle Ages and Renaissance

The transition from the medieval to the modern world begins with the fourteenth and fifteenth centuries. Everywhere in the West we find the hastening growth of a materialistic spirit. In France and the Low Countries, in Germany, and in England, the prevailing mood was one of depression and uncertainty, as old institutions decayed and people became unsure and pessimistic about the future. By contrast, in Italy—where feudalism and manorialism had never gained so strong a hold—the exuberant life of the city-states produced a spirit very like that of the greatest days of ancient Greece. Here, in spite of the cynicism and brutality of politics, the mood was one of optimism. Italy gave civilization a new impetus that would inspire the regions north of the Alps.

We begin with the economy and with society: depression, plague, and agricultural decline accompanied commercial advances. As the hired mercenary replaced the feudal noble in the battlefield, the rich townsman gradually inherited his economic influence. We continue with politics: in France, England, and Spain the centralized new national monarchies triumphed. In Germany, particularism developed still further. In Italy the towns became the centers of the national life. We conclude with the Renaissance, the unparalleled flowering of literature and learning, of painting, sculpture, and the other arts, beginning in Italy but soon spreading northward.

I

The Economy and Society of the Fourteenth and Fifteenth Centuries

Depression in the West

Just as the population growth of the eleventh century helped to advance the European economy (see Chapter 4), so a population decline in the fourteenth and fifteenth centuries helped to shrink both the supply of labor and the market for products. Large-scale warfare caused most regimes to debase their coinage, leading to inflation and wild price fluctuation. One can sense everywhere except in Italy that the optimism of the thirteenth century shifted to a mood of deepening pessimism in the fourteenth and fifteenth. Nobody really understood what was going on, uneasiness prevailed, and many people strove to deny that any changes were taking place.

More and more, money underlay social relationships as it never had during the earlier period. For the peasant in good times, the gain was great: it was more agreeable to pay cash than to owe physical labor. But then in hard times, when there was no cash to pay, his loss was great. The security of serfdom, the inherited right to work and live on certain land and to eat its produce, had diminished, sometimes to the vanishing point. Often the peasants would simply move off the land and try to sell their labor in the towns. Since the price of farm products fell off while the prices of other commodities rose, the landowner was caught in a squeeze.

The Black Death (bubonic plague) of 1348-1349 and subsequent plagues speeded these tendencies. Disease wiped out between a fifth to a third of the population, especially in thickly settled regions. Having suddenly become scarce, manpower grew expensive. Peasants found they could force the landlords to commute for cash the services they still owed; the landlords, in turn, strove to hold on to whatever services they could and sought the help of governments in keeping wages down. In France, in England, in Florence, we shall encounter wild outbreaks of social unrest. In towns, it was the same: the guilds refused to admit new members; employers and city governments fought to keep wages down. It was not until the later fifteenth century that things gradually got better. In France and England and in much of western Germany, the services owed by the peasantry were now commuted into cash payments, and serfdom was nearing an end, though in eastern Germany the landlords frequently attempted to enforce their old rights. Still further east, as we have seen (Chapter 5), the bonds of serfdom were actually tightening.

Commercial and Industrial Innovation

THE HANSE, VENICE, GENOA   During the long depression and slow recovery, we find much new experimentation in commercial methods and organization. Among the most striking was the Hanseatic League, an association (Hanse) of north German seaport trading towns that began by occasionally consulting among themselves and ended by organizing a real federation in the fourteenth century. The cities of Lübeck, Bremen, Hamburg, and Wisby (on the island of Gotland in the Baltic) joined with the German traders abroad in Novgorod, London, Venice, and Bruges to protect and increase their business. They put down piracy and brigands; tried to secure monopolies in fish, timber, amber, furs, and metals; assessed themselves for common expenses; and fought and won a war (1367-1370) against Denmark, which tried to impose tolls on Hanseatic ships. The Hanse regularly called meetings of its representatives at Lübeck, sent its diplomatic agents abroad to negotiate, and did not hesitate to use force to drive English intruders, for example, out of Norwegian fishing grounds (1406). Of course rivalries between the Hanse's own members did not disappear, and the shift of trade routes to the Atlantic after 1500 helped dry up Hanseatic prosperity.

Venice, by dint of long and repeated warfare, especially against Genoa, and as a result of earlier colonial conquests, dominated the Mediterranean trade as the Hanse did the Baltic. Venice was the marketplace for the spices, silk, sugar, and cotton of the East, and the woolen cloth of the West. In the huge government-operated shipyard, the Arsenal, shipbuilders improved the traditional long, narrow, oar-propelled galley into a faster and more capacious merchant

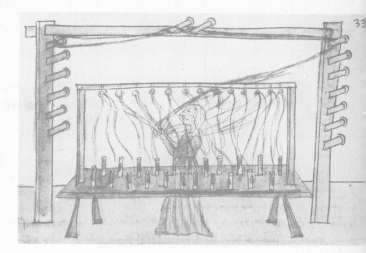

Silkworkers. Illustrations from an Italian manuscript of 1487.

ship. Four galleys a year in this period sailed to Flanders, four to Beirut in Syria, three to the Black Sea, traditional preserve of the Genoese, and about three dozen others to all the major ports of the Mediterranean. The Flanders service (begun in 1317), calling also in London and Southampton, was the first regular all-water service between Italy and northwestern Europe. The Venetians had their own ambassador resident in London, a step soon to be copied by other states.

Genoa, too, had many enterprising merchants. Benedetto Zaccaria, for example, in the 1340's obtained from the Byzantine emperor concessions of alum, a chemical essential in the manufacture of woolens. He built his own fleet to transport alum to the woolen factories in the Low Countries, established a company town with medical services and a population of three thousand at the alum mines in Asia Minor, and in Italy organized a woolen-manufacturing plant of his own. He then obtained a second monopoly, the mastic plant (a luxury useful in perfume and chewed like chewing gum) on the island of Chios; he kept mastic prices high by limiting the supply. He became so influential that he married his son into the imperial house at Constantinople, and finally flew his own flag.

The manufacture of woolen cloth in the towns of Flanders and North Italy was of course the largest industry of western Europe in the fourteenth century. In Florence 30,000 workmen produced 100,000 pieces of cloth a year for their bosses, about 200 "masters" of the guild. Since there were no machines, all their work was literally "manufactured," made by hand. At Venice the building of ships in the famous Arsenal was in itself an industry. At Florence there was already industrial strife, with the poorest workmen, the "Ciompi," actually staging a revolution in 1378. Western Europe, though still in a preindustrial phase, since there had been no large-scale development of machinery, had already embarked on capitalism.

Capitalism

BANKERS AND MERCHANT PRINCES Zaccaria's operations—like those of Hanseatic or Venetian merchants—were clearly capitalistic. These men built up their capital in cash and in goods; they used credit on a large scale; they went in for long-range planning; they took heavy risks; they went all out for profits; they counted their labor as part of their costs. One should not overestimate the "modern" features of their operations any more than one should imagine medieval factories as comparable in technology with those of later centuries. But equally, one should not fail to see that their economic attitudes and methods were often the same as ours.

Credit came then, as now, from bankers, but the risks were larger then, and the profits also. Florentine bankers charged 266 per cent annual interest on a loan they thought to be really risky; in 1420 an effort to cut interest rates to a maximum of 20 per cent proved a failure. All this of course came in a period when the Church regarded the loan of money at interest as the sin of usury. Contrary to widespread belief, the Jews did *not* dominate the field of banking; only in Spain did they play a role, and then not after 1492. The Templars were the leading bankers until they were destroyed by Philip the Fair (see Chapter 4). Then came the Italians, called Lombards (though many came from Tuscany); their memory is preserved in London's Lombard Street. Florentines handled the papal revenues, seeing to it that income from distant lands flowed safely into Rome. The Bardi and Peruzzi families financed both sides in the Hundred Years' War, and went bankrupt when Edward III of England defaulted on his debts in the 1340's. The Medici, who began in the wool business and then added silk and spices to their interests, had branches of their bank in sixteen cities in Italy and abroad. In Genoa, the Bank of St. George (founded 1407) took over much of the Mediterranean business of Spanish Jews. In Barcelona, in London, everywhere in cities, men in the profession of making money breed upon money won wealth, power, and influence.

Jacques Coeur (1395–1456) of Bourges obtained the favor of Charles VII of France when that monarch was only a refugee (see p. 261). He ran a fleet of trading vessels to and from the Levant, became the director of the mint and chief fiscal agent of the crown, and financed the last campaigns of the Hundred Years' War. He built up a business empire of textile workshops and mines, bought landed estates from impoverished nobles, loaned money to half the dignitaries of France, and arranged noble marriages for his middle-class relatives. But he had too much power; and too many highly placed people owed him too much money. He was disgraced on a trumped-up charge, and died in papal service on an expedition against the Turks.

Jacques Coeur's slightly later German counterparts were the Fugger family of Augsburg. Beginning as linen weavers, this mighty financial dynasty in the late 1400's became bankers for the popes and the Hapsburgs. Soon they had mining concessions scattered throughout central Europe and made a colossal fortune. It was not until 1607, after the Hapsburg ruler Philip II of Spain had defaulted on his debts, that the Fuggers were ruined. The Fuggers had the modern spirit of social service, and built for the deserving poor of Augsburg a garden village called the Fuggerei.

The New Materialism

THE IMPACT ON FEUDALISM   The business class, the bourgeoisie, began to assume an ever greater role, not only in the economy but in political life. Sometimes its members actually came to power, as in Venice or Florence or the Hanseatic towns; sometimes, like the Bardi or the Fuggers, they financed those who wielded power. Often their talents helped a monarch further his interests: Jacques Coeur helped Charles VII; Charles' successor, Louis XI (reigned 1461–1483), depended on the bourgeoisie; so did Henry VII, the first Tudor monarch of England. Similarly, the middle classes, with their wealth and their interest in letters and the arts, moved into the role of patron hitherto reserved for the Church and a few great princes. Bourgeois materialism also pervaded the Church, and many popes were indistinguishable from the economic and political magnates of the day in their attitudes toward money, power, and the arts.

In the upper levels of the feudal world, the new materialism played havoc with old established attitudes and relationships, though often those affected

An Italian bank at the end of the fourteenth century.

hardly realized what was happening. Some nobles lost all but the name of noble, as their manors could no longer support them. Their descendants, finding their pockets empty, their status vanishing, were often altogether declassed. Even those who retained or increased their wealth found that in the new monarchies they had to put their obligations to the monarch ahead of their duties to any other suzerain, and so did their vassals.

Moreover, cash transformed warfare. In the great struggles of the fourteenth and fifteenth centuries it was no longer practical to rely on the feudal levy, which was required to fight for a limited time only, and had only miscellaneous equipment. War now required professional troops, who would fight on indefinitely, and could be properly trained and equipped. Commutation of a vassal's military service for money to pay regular troops became a regular practice. Even if a vassal of the king actually did fight, he now did so on the basis of an indenture, stipulating that he would fight for pay. Not only monarchs offered such inducements to their troops; great lords recruited private forces in the same way.

This military system is sometimes called *bastard feudalism,* because, while superficially resembling feudalism, it had become something quite different. Both in France and in England, in the fifteenth century, great rival parties of nobles with private armies fought for the control of the central government. The standards of chivalrous conduct that had softened the harshness of earlier feudal periods became corrupt or disappeared. Lords no longer even had as their ideal the maintenance of the peace or the protection of the poor. New knightly orders were founded in the fourteenth and fifteenth centuries: the Gater in England, the Star in France, the Golden Fleece in Burgundy. But all the protestations that these were devout chivalrous bodies with pious work to do could not conceal the fact that they did little and were simply exclusive clubs that all ambitious nobles yearned to join.

THE IMPACT ON THE CHURCH Snatched off to Avignon in 1305, the papacy remained there under seven successive popes down to 1377. Though the charming city on the Rhone, deep inside French territory, thus became a papal enclave, their absence from Rome cut the popes off from the ancient source of their spiritual authority. In their magnificent palace and amidst the ostentation of their court, with its smoothly functioning diplomatic service and bureaucracy dedicated to collecting money from Christendom, they too were deeply affected by the materialism of the time. From 1378 to 1409 there were two lines of popes, one at Rome and one at Avignon, and in 1409 a third was added. In this Great Schism, the rulers of Europe decided which pope they preferred on the basis of their national interest. The French supported the Avignonese; the English, naturally enough, the Roman; the Scots, hostile to England, the Avignonese; and so on.

Against this scandal, the Church rallied in the Conciliar Movement, a series of councils beginning at Pisa in 1409 and continuing at Constance (1414-1417) and Basel (1431-1449). At Constance the unity of the papacy was restored with the election of Martin V (1417-1431), who returned to Rome. The long crisis had given rise to a school of thinkers who urged that the popes yield their autocratic power within the Church and act as constitutional monarchs, with the general councils serving as a kind of parliament. But the restored popes stoutly refused to yield any of their traditional power; and, though often cultivated and able, the popes of the late fifteenth century were also usually corrupt, cynical, and ruthless—for example, the notorious Alexander VI, the Borgia pope (reigned 1492-1503).

Protests against the wealth of the clergy, frequent throughout the Middle Ages, multiplied in this period of ecclesiastical decline. Echoing the Waldensians (see Chapter 4), John Wycliffe (d. 1384) in England and John Hus (1369–1415) in Bohemia strove for reform. Hus wanted to rid his fellow Czechs of German clerical domination; he was given a safe-conduct to attend the Council of Constance and answer for his opinions, but once there was tried and executed. His Czech followers went underground. Girolamo Savonarola (1452–1498), a Florentine Dominican, led a puritanical reform movement against the vices of the age, calling Alexander VI a devil and a monster. Though for a brief period (1497–1498) he virtually ruled Florence, in the end he failed and was executed.

II

The Making of the New Monarchies

The Hundred Years' War

ROUND I Ever since 987, the Capetian kings of France had regularly produced sons and heirs who survived to take the throne. In 1328 this streak of luck ran out. Three sons of Philip the Fair (see Chapter 4) ruled in succession for the years between 1314 and 1328; then the throne passed to a nephew of Philip the Fair, Philip VI of Valois (reigned 1328–1350). But Philip the Fair's daughter Isabelle had married Edward II (reigned 1307–1327) of England, and this made Edward III (reigned 1327–1377) Philip the Fair's grandson. Did not he have a better claim to the throne of France than a mere nephew? In order to dispose of Edward's claim, French lawyers cited a Frankish law of the sixth century (the Salic law) that a woman could not inherit land; therefore, they argued, Isabelle never had any rights in France to pass on to Edward.

Although Edward III took this decision as pretext for war, there were other good reasons for the French and English to fight. England still possessed the rich French province of Aquitaine, and the French kings constantly encroached there upon the rights of their vassal, the king of England, just as they encroached on other vassals' rights elsewhere. The English wanted to get back all that John had lost to Philip Augustus (see Chapter 4). Moreover, in Flanders, where the count was a vassal of France, the French had been backing the count and many of the wealthy merchants in a quarrel with other merchants and most of the workers in the woolen industry, backed by the English. Since England exported raw wool to Flanders and bought back manufactured goods, Edward could cut off supplies, thus causing unemployment in Flanders. But since the English crown taxed the wool going and coming, Edward III hurt his own pocketbook too. Jacob van Artevelde, leader of the pro-English party, rose against the French, organized his own government, and recognized Edward III as king of France in exchange for military help and the promise of a steady flow of wool.

In response to Flemish pressure, Edward launched what proved to be the Hundred Years' War (1338–1453). The English won the major battles, and at times controlled most of France. But the French developed a standing army supported by a system of direct taxation, and eventually expelled the English and unified France under a strong national monarchy supported by the middle classes.

After winning command of the Channel (1340), the English invaded France in 1345, and by superior tactics, including the effective use of the longbow, defeated the French at Crécy (1346) and took Calais. After an eight-year truce, marked by the ravages of the Black Death (1348–1349), the English repeated their success at Poitiers (1356), this time taking prisoner King John of France (reigned 1350–1364). John's son, the future Charles V, the Wise (reigned 1364–1380), became regent.

The defeats brought bitter criticism of the French monarchy: the Estates-General (see Chapter 4) insisted not only on specifying what sort of taxes might be levied (sales tax and salt tax), but also on having their own men collect them. For the first time they scheduled future meetings "to discuss the state of the realm," and they also demanded that the regent Charles dismiss and punish his advisers and substitute a twenty-eight-man committee from the Estates. When Charles hesitated, Etienne Marcel, a Parisian bourgeois who was leader of the Estates, led a revolution in the capital, the first of many in French history, and forced Charles to yield in 1357.

Marcel allied himself with a violent peasant uprising, the *Jacquerie* (from the popular name for a peasant, Jacques Bonhomme, "James Goodfellow"), which broke out in 1358. Charles's forces put down the Jacquerie, and Marcel was killed. Although the Estates had dominated France during 1356 and 1357, they had imposed no permanent principle of constitutional limitation upon the king. Nor did the members of the three estates—clergy, nobles, townsmen—trust each other or share the same interests. Even members of a single estate were divided by conflicting regional interests. Thus the Estates-General did not take the road toward becoming the French counterpart of the English parliament.

In 1360, by the Treaty of Brétigny, Edward III renounced his claim to the French throne, but only in exchange for all southwestern France plus Calais. The treaty, however, never really went into effect, since the French did not pay the huge ransom required for King John. John died in captivity (1364), and when the war resumed, the French made substantial gains. By the time Charles V died (1380), they had ejected the English from all except a string of seaports including Bordeaux and Calais. For the first time since 1340 French ships could sail the Channel and raid the English coast. In domestic affairs Charles V was also successful, getting the Estates to agree that the existing taxes would be permanent.

ROUND II But Charles VI (reigned 1380–1422) went insane. A stuggle broke out between his brother, the duke of Orléans, and his uncle, the duke of Burgundy, who had been given this duchy by King John. In 1407, the Burgundians murdered the duke of Orléans, and Count Bernard of Armagnac, father-in-law of the new duke, took command of the royal party. Known thereafter as Armagnacs, they commanded the loyalty of Frenchmen in the south and southwest, and of the great nobles; they were anti-English. The Burgundians, who were pro-English, controlled the north and east, and had the support of the upper bourgeoisie in the towns. Furthermore, the duke of Burgundy had inherited the County of Flanders in 1381, and thus had become very rich.

In alliance with the Burgundians, the English reopened the war. Henry V of England (reigned 1413–1422) won the battle of Agincourt (1415) and reconquered Normandy, thus undoing the work of Philip Augustus and Charles V. In Paris, the Burgundians massacred the Armagnacs, whose partisans fled in disorder to set up a rival regime south of the Loire, with the heir to the throne, the future Charles VII, as its nominal head. The English reached the peak of their success in the Treaty of Troyes (1420), whereby Charles VI cast off his son as illegitimate, and adopted Henry V as his heir and as his regent during his lifetime. Henry married Charles's daughter, and retained all his conquests north of the Loire until he should inherit the whole of France on the death of

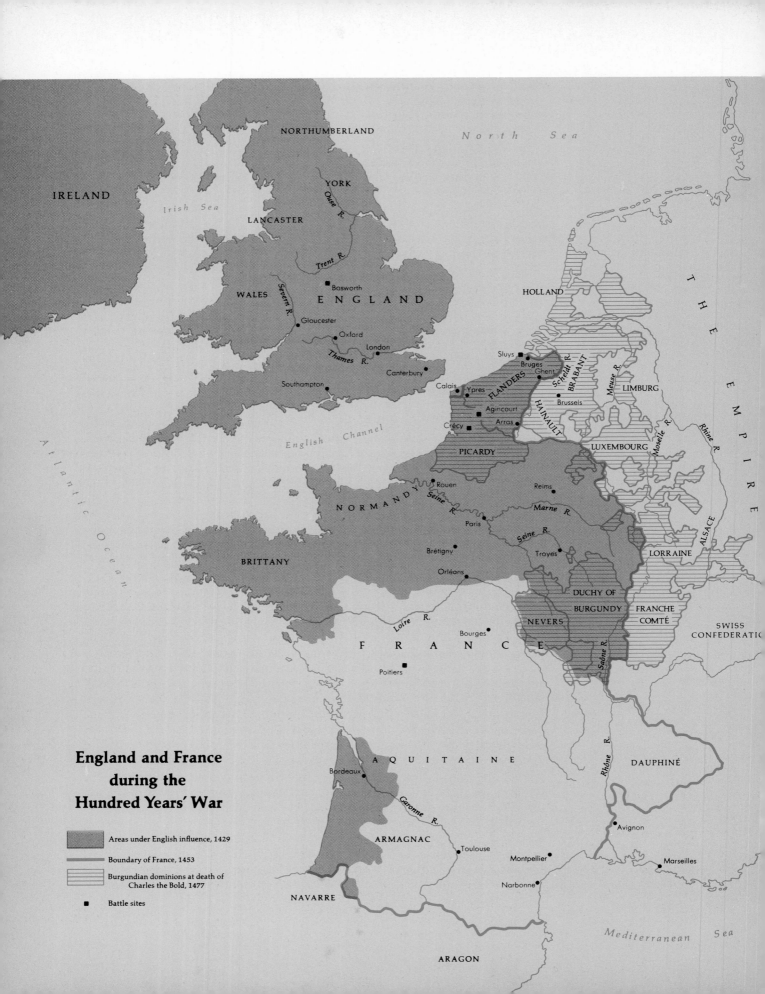

IRELAND

NORTHUMBERLAND

North Sea

Irish Sea

YORK

Ouse R.

LANCASTER

WALES

Severn R.

Trent R.

• Bosworth

E N G L A N D

• Gloucester

• Oxford

• London

Thames R.

• Canterbury

• Southampton

English Channel

HOLLAND

Sluys

Bruges

Ghent

Scheldt R.

BRABANT

Meuse R.

LIMBURG

Calais

Ypres

FLANDERS

• Brussels

LUXEMBOURG

Agincourt

HAINAULT

Arras

Moselle R.

Rhine R.

Crécy

T H E   E M P I R E

PICARDY

ALSACE

Atlantic Ocean

N O R M A N D Y

• Rouen

Seine R.

Reims

• Paris

Marne R.

Seine R.

LORRAINE

BRITTANY

• Brétigny

Troyes

• Orléans

DUCHY OF

FRANCHE

Loire R.

NEVERS

BURGUNDY

COMTÉ

SWISS
CONFEDERATIO

• Bourges

F R A N C E

Saône R.

• Poitiers

Rhône R.

DAUPHINÉ

England and France during the Hundred Years' War

A Q U I T A I N E

• Bordeaux

Garonne R.

• Avignon

Areas under English influence, 1429

ARMAGNAC

• Toulouse

Boundary of France, 1453

• Montpellier

• Marseilles

Burgundian dominions at death of
Charles the Bold, 1477

• Narbonne

■ Battle sites

NAVARRE

Mediterranean Sea

ARAGON

Charles VI. This fantastic settlement would have ended French national sovereignty.

When Henry V and Charles VI both died in 1422, the regent for Henry's heir, Henry VI, prepared to march against the pitiful Charles VII, the rightful king of France, who ruled at Bourges with Armagnac support. At this juncture, the miracle of Joan of Arc saved France. The visionary peasant girl who reflected the deep patriotism of the French put heart and strength into the demoralized forces of Charles VII. Saints and angels told her she must bring Charles to be crowned at Reims. Inspired by her presence, French troops drove the English out of Orléans and Charles was crowned. Joan was later captured by the Burgundians, sold to the English, turned over to the French Inquisition, and burned as a witch at Rouen (1431). The papacy itself reversed the verdict against her in 1456 and made her a saint in 1920.

Her cause triumphed despite her own martyrdom. In 1435 Charles VII and the Burgundians concluded a separate peace; without the Burgundian alliance, the English could not win, and Paris fell to the French (1436). France still suffered from the depredations of private companies of soldiers in the countryside and from the unruliness of factions among the nobles. Charles VII, however, was able to win from the Estates (1439) not only the right to have an army but also the *taille,* a tax to be levied directly on individuals and collected by royal agents. He got money also from Jacques Coeur and chose as his closest advisers members of the bourgeoisie. With his new army Charles retook Normandy and Aquitaine. When the Hundred Years' War finally ended in 1453, Calais alone of French territory remained in English hands.

France: Louis XI

Charles's son was Louis XI (reigned 1461–1483), plainly dressed, crafty, penny-pinching, hard-working, a constant traveler about his kingdom, inquisitive and cautious, accessible and ruthless. He put the seal on the work that his father's bureaucrats had accomplished. He had reason enough to be impatient with the quarrels of nobles, and so trusted only bourgeois advisers whom he could control. He kept the army in fighting trim, but hated the thought of risking it in war. His great achievement was settling the problems posed by the existence on his eastern and northern borders of the great collection of territories controlled by the duke of Burgundy—the Duchy of Burgundy itself and the adjacent Free County (Franche Comté), and most of the Low Countries. Though divided by Alsace and Lorraine, this sprawling realm could have been the basis for a "middle kingdom" between France and the Empire.

Philip the Good of Burgundy (reigned 1419–1467), who had inherited most of it, and his heir Charles the Bold (reigned 1467–1477) hoped to use its great wealth for just this purpose. Louis XI subsidized the Swiss, who also were threatened by Charles's expansive plans, and the Swiss forces defeated Charles the Bold and killed him (1477). France took Burgundy and the Franche Comté; Charles's daughter, Mary, inherited the Low Countries, and took them with her as dowry when she married Maximilian of Hapsburg, who later became Holy Roman emperor. Burgundian ambition and hostility to France were now united to the empire, and in subsequent generations would trouble Louis XI's successors. But Louis himself had consolidated French territory and given it a strong central administration.

England

EDWARD II AND EDWARD III   For England, too, the Hundred Years' War was the major preoccupation of the fourteenth and fifteenth centuries. English internal development moved along different lines from the French. Under the weak and inept Edward II (reigned 1307–1327), dominated by his favorites and his

LATE MIDDLE AGES AND RENAISSANCE

261

French queen, the barons revolted again (1311) as they had under his grandfather Henry III, and virtually reenacted the Provisions of Oxford of 1258 (see Chapter 4). They established as the real rulers of England twenty-one Lords Ordainers, who had to assent to all appointments and to any declarations of war. But the barons were as selfish and grasping as the king's bureaucrats had been. Edward's queen, Isabelle, led a revolt against him; he was imprisoned and murdered.

Edward III (reigned 1327–1377) needed a constant supply of money to fight the French; since Parliament voted it without opposition while objecting to all other royal forms of money-raising, he summoned Parliament often. By the middle of the fourteenth century, the knights of the shire and the burgesses regularly met together, apart from the great lords and clergy. Though little is known about the details of the process, this gradual coalescence of knights and burgesses is the origin of the House of Commons. A similar coalescence of higher clergy and earls and barons, lords spiritual and lords temporal, is the origin of the House of Lords. By the end of the fourteenth century, the knights and burgesses chose a chairman to conduct their meeting and report their deliberations to the king: the Speaker of the House of Commons.

Because the king had so often asked them for money, the Commons gradually began to make certain assumptions: that he must do so, that they might withhold the money unless certain conditions were fulfilled, and that they might sometimes say how it should be spent and later check to see if it had been. The British tradition that money bills originate in the Commons had its foundation here. Moreover, the first foreshadowing of the legislative rights of the Commons can be found in the knights' and burgesses' device of drawing up a single petition embodying all their individual petitions. They would send this omnibus document to the Lords, who, if they approved, would forward it to the king for his decision. Finally, the Commons began to impeach royal officials for misconduct, and the Lords would acquit or condemn the accused. Usually such an impeachment meant only that one faction of the powerful Lords had become influential enough to rally a majority of Commons in trying to ruin individual members of an opposing faction.

In Edward III's reign a great economic crisis arose, in part out of the ravages of the Black Death, which killed almost half the population. A terrible shortage of manpower resulted; crops rotted in the fields and good land dropped out of cultivation. The agricultural laborers of England, aware of their suddenly increased bargaining power (and of the wealth gained by their masters from the French war), began to break the bonds of serfdom, or left home and flocked to the towns. In 1351, Parliament passed the Statute of Laborers, an attempt to fix wages and prices as they had been before the plague, to prevent workmen from quitting, and to force the unemployed to accept work at the old rates. It failed, and the labor shortage hastened the end of serfdom and paved the way for the disorders that took place under Edward's successor.

To enforce the Statute of Laborers, Edward III appointed the first justices of the peace, chosen from the gentry in each shire. They received no pay, but served from a sense of duty or a wish for prestige. The old shire and hundred courts disappeared. In later centuries, and down almost to our own times, the justices of the peace dominated English rural life.

Because the Avignonese popes were thought to be instruments of the French, Parliament in 1351 passed a statute restricting the appointment of aliens to church offices in England, and in 1353 checked the appeal of legal cases to the papal courts. Dislike for the papacy, the widespread economic discontent, and a growing sense of national identity can all be seen in England's first real heresy, which appeared at the end of Edward III's reign. John Wycliffe, an Oxford scholar, advocated a church without property in the spirit of the early Christians. He wanted to abolish or weaken most of the functions of the priests, so that the individual could have direct access to God. He and his followers—called Lollards (babblers)—also translated the Bible into English, in defiance of the long-established supremacy of Latin. English became the language of the courts (1352), was taught in the schools (1375), and was used to open Parliament (1399). Love for a native language was always and everywhere a fundamental part of quickening national feeling.

RICHARD II Under Richard II (reigned 1377–1399), grandson of Edward III, peasant discontent reached an intensity comparable to that of the French Jacquerie. Many landlords were still trying to enforce serfdom. In 1378, 1379, and 1380 the crown imposed a poll tax (head tax) on every person over fifteen; the rich scarcely noticed it, but the poor bitterly resented it. In 1381, the peasants revolted, burned manor records to destroy evidence of their obligations, and marched on London. Their demand for the end of serfdom and the confiscation of clerical wealth reflected the widespread influence of Wycliffe's ideas among the lower classes. In the capital, Richard II, who was fifteen years old, showed heroism by interviewing the peasants' leaders and promising to fulfill their demands. In the end, however, the revolt was harshly suppressed; had it been economically possible to restore serfdom, the authorities would have done so.

Meantime, the great nobles took advantage of Richard's youth to conspire against each other to seize power. More and more each of them became a commander of his own private hired army. Gradually, the feudal practice of a lord's calling for military assistance on vassals of his own social class gave way to the new practice of simply hiring strong-arm men. These were social inferiors, had no feudal ties, held no fiefs, but were bound by written indenture and a retaining fee. The custom, known as *livery and maintenance,* was forbidden by statute in 1390, but continued to flourish. Every time there was an interlude in the Hundred Years' War, these plundering mercenaries came to England from France and continued their disorderly behavior.

One of the noble factions was called Lancastrian, after the duke of Lancaster, John of Gaunt, one of Edward III's sons and uncle of Richard II. Two other uncles, the dukes of Gloucester and York, also had their factions. In 1387, Gloucester defeated Richard's forces and in 1388 forced a packed Parliament to condemn the royal ministers for treason. Richard himself made an effort at absolutism in 1397, arresting Gloucester, packing Parliament with his own supporters, pushing through severe antitreason laws, many of them retroactive, and confiscating the estates of Henry, exiled son of John of Gaunt. This royal highhandedness precipitated a revolution. Henry returned to England with troops, gained wide support because of Richard's behavior, defeated and deposed Richard, and became Henry IV, first monarch of the House of Lancaster.

LANCASTER AND YORK Henry IV (reigned 1399–1413), preoccupied with rebellions against him, made no effort to tax or legislate without parliamentary approval. Moreover, he and his successors recognized that they needed parliamentary support; the nobles in turn used Parliament as an instrument to prevent a recurrence of Richard II's tyrannous behavior, and to further their own interests. Henry V (reigned 1413–1422), whose great victories in France were won at the expense of neglecting England, died young, and left as his heir the infant Henry VI (reigned 1422–1461), who proved mentally unstable as he grew up. Disaster followed.

The English defeats in the war with France were accompanied by quarrels at home between Queen Margaret of Anjou and her noble English allies on one hand (the Lancastrians), and Richard, duke of York, a great-grandson of Edward III who was heir to the throne until Henry VI had a son in 1453. These quarrels led directly to the dreary Wars of the Roses (1455–1485), named for the red rose, badge of the House of Lancaster, and the white rose, badge of the House of York. Without too severe an impact on the daily life of the ordinary man, the nobles and their private liveried armies slaughtered each other in droves for three decades.

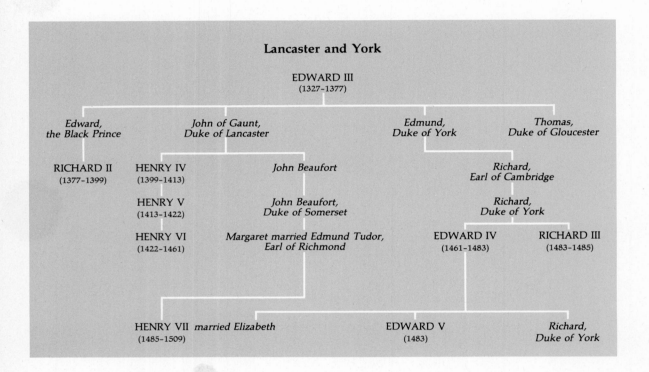

Parliament became the tool of one or the other faction. Even the throne repeatedly changed hands: in 1461, the earl of Warwick, leader of the Yorkist side, put on the thone the son of Richard of York, Edward IV (1461–1483); but quarreled with him and in 1470–1471 staged a revolution that briefly restored Henry VI. Edward IV soon regained control, and Henry VI and Warwick were killed. Edward IV might well have restored stability, but himself died in 1483 while still young. The throne passed momentarily to his son, Edward V, and then to Edward IV's brother, Richard III (1483–1485), last of the Yorkist kings, whose responsibility for the murder of the "little princes of the Tower"— Edward V and his younger brother—is still a matter of controversy. In 1485, on Bosworth Field, Richard III was defeated and killed by Henry Tudor, an illegitimate great-grandson of John of Gaunt, the Lancastrian leader. Henry became King Henry VII (1485–1509), and promptly made his tenuous claim to the crown stronger by marrying the Yorkist princess Elizabeth, daughter of Edward IV.

HENRY VII   With Bosworth Field the Wars of the Roses at last ended, and England had a tough, new-style monarch who could not only command but enforce his commands. Henry VII forbade livery and maintenance, and private armies disappeared; he kept the nobles from intimidating litigants in cases before the royal courts. He appointed a special administrative court within the King's Council, the Court of Star Chamber (so called from the stars painted on the ceiling of the room in which it met), which bypassed the customary procedures of the common law, including trial by jury. Although Henry was striking at local resistance, local abuses, and local privileges, the Star Chamber procedure could easily become tyrannical, trampling on the rights of defendants. Its worst period did not come until the seventeenth century (see Chapter 8), however, and under Henry VII most Englishmen probably found little fault with its activities.

Henry and his self-made middle-class officials, whom he kindly rewarded with lands confiscated from the Yorkists, managed to double the royal revenue. "Morton's Fork," a practice attributed to the archbishop of Canterbury, an able lawyer, penalized high churchmen when they were summoned to make payments to the king. The richly dressed were told they could obviously afford to pay heavily; the poorly dressed that, since they were economical, they too could make a large contribution. Threatening foreign governments with loss of the valuable trading privileges enjoyed by their merchants, Henry's bureaucrats secured comparable advantages for English traders abroad, especially in Italy. Henry VII had the support of the growing middle classes, and, like Louis XI in France, he restored the prestige of the monarchy and made it the rallying point of English national feeling.

During the last half of his reign of two dozen years, Henry VII had so well managed his finances that he had to summon Parliament only once, in 1504. When it did not give him all the money he wanted, he did not press the issue. Although the vigor of Tudor policies, as pursued by Henry and his successors, often takes the student's attention away from Parliament, the Tudors could not and did not wish to alter the unique English tradition that the monarch could not levy taxes or make law without consulting Lords and Commons.

Spain

Though both France and England had been raked by severe internal troubles, they had long been national states with established and accepted centralized monarchial institutions. By contrast, Spain, as a result of its history, had no national identity until the fifteenth century. The gradual and painful reconquest of the peninsula from the Muslims has often been compared to a Crusade that lasted more than five centuries. The little Christian kingdoms in the north, however, often put more energy into fighting each other. By the middle of the fifteenth century, when the Muslims were confined to the Kingdom of Granada in the south, there were three separate and often mutually hostile Christian kingdoms.

Castile, in the center of the peninsula, had scored some of the major victories over the Muslims. But its kings shared their authority with the *Mesta*, a powerful organization of sheep ranchers, and the nobles and the towns were also independent-minded. Castile had a counterpart of Parliament or the French Estates-General—the *Cortes*, with all three estates represented. Portugal, to the west, once a Castilian province but independent since 1179, looked out to the Atlantic and to commerce and exploration overseas. Aragon, in the northeast, comprised both backward mountain areas and the vigorous commercial towns of Catalonia, especially Barcelona. Aragon, with a long tradition of trade and conquest in the Mediterranean, had ruled Sicily since 1282 and

took Naples in 1435. At home, the Catalans championed autonomy and made trouble for the king of Aragon in his Cortes.

When Ferdinand, heir to Aragon, married Isabella, heiress to Castile (1469), the dynastic alliance made possible union of the two largest states of Spain. Castilians and Aragonese, however, did not even speak the same language (Catalan still today thrives in Catalonia), and royal power was weak in both states. While Ferdinand looked outward to the Mediterranean and was relatively tolerant in his religious attitudes, Isabella focused her attention on Castile and was fanatically pious. She summoned the Cortes only when she could not avoid it, and appointed her own council, to which she gave large powers. She allied herself with the towns, using their militias as troops rather than relying on feudal levies from the nobles. She met opposition from three large military brotherhoods similar to the crusading orders of knighthood (see Chapter 5), founded by nobles to fight the Muslims; Isabella controlled them by having Ferdinand made the commander of all three.

Ferdinand and Isabella made a firm alliance with the Church. Isabella's chief minister, Cardinal Ximenes, archbishop of Toledo, was instrumental in executing her policies, which included a thoroughgoing reform of the Church itself. From the papacy, the Spanish crown obtained the right to dispose of ecclesiastical appointments and of some church revenues. In 1478, the Inquisition was imported into Spain, where it served as an instrument of Isabella's aims: Spanish unity and universal Catholicism. Jews and Muslims, who had long enjoyed toleration and had become prosperous, were its first targets. In 1492, Jews were offered the choice between baptism and exile. In the same year Granada fell, and the last Muslim foothold in Spain was eliminated. Ten years later, the remaining Muslim residents of Spain were offered the same choice as the Jews.

To avoid exile, many Jews and Muslims became nominal Christians, conforming outwardly to escape the harsh punishments of the Inquisition, but inwardly loyal to their old faiths. Many others did go into exile, and cost Spain some of its ablest and most productive people. The year 1492, which marks the fall of Granada and the onset of persecution, also marks Columbus' first voyage. The Spanish monarchy and its future colonial empire already bore the stamp of the bigotry that would prove both a strength and a weakness in the generations to come.

III
Particularism

Germany

In Germany, no "new" monarch made his appearance. Rudolf of Hapsburg (reigned 1273–1291), the first emperor chosen after the Interregnum (1254–1273; see Chapter 4), came of a family of lesser nobles whose estates lay mostly in Switzerland. Rudolf cared nothing for imperial politics but wanted to enlarge the family holdings and to secure a hereditary monarchy for the Hapsburgs in Germany. He acquired Austria, and his descendants ruled at Vienna until 1918. Because his own interests lay in the southeastern portions of the empire, Rudolf made concessions to the French in its western lands, in order to win their support. Thus the French moved into the region east of the Rhone and obtained a foothold in Lorraine. Those who supported this eastern-based, pro-French policy of Rudolf may be called the Hapsburg party. Those who opposed it—chiefly the rich and powerful archbishops of the Rhine valley and other princes in western Germany—were anti-French and anti-Hapsburg.

This whole development helped perpetuate particularism: the gravitation of political power to the rulers of the many particular territorial units composing the empire, at the expense of the central authority. The imperial office sometimes went to a Hapsburg, and sometimes to members of other houses: Nassau, Luxembourg, Bohemia, the Wittelsbach family of Bavaria. During the fourteenth century, the central monarchy became simply another territorial princedom, since the German princes wanted to be emperor chiefly because the title would help them add to their possessions. They won a great victory in 1356, when the emperor Charles IV issued a "Golden Bull," proclaiming that the imperial dignity was of God, that the emperor was to be elected by the German electoral princes, and that their choices needed no confirmation by the pope. The seven electors thereafter were the archbishops of Mainz, Trier, and Cologne, the count palatine of the Rhine, the duke of Saxony, the margrave of Brandenburg, and the king of Bohemia. Each of the electors would have full rights of coinage in his own territory, and there would be no appeal from the decisions of his court: he would be all but sovereign.

Within each of the many German principalities, the prince faced the threat of the nobility, now strengthened by the addition to its numbers of the former ministeriales (see Chapter 4), who had acquired lands, feudal rights, and titles. Within the state of Brunswick, for example, the duke had to face in minature the same problem from the knights, towns, and clergy—the "estates"—that the kings of France and England faced. Power shared with the estates meant increasing disorder, as urban-rural antagonism increased, robber barons infested the roads, and local wars became common.

But in the decades after 1400 the princes combatted the estates by adopting the rule of primogeniture and the indivisibility of their princedoms. Increased use of Roman law helped them assert their claims to absolute control over public rights and offices. Gunpowder and artillery, now coming into use, made it impractical for an unruly vassal to defy his prince successfully inside medieval fortifications. By the end of the fifteenth century, the German princes had achieved, inside individual principalities, orderly finance, indivisible hereditary domains, and taxation granted by the estates; cooperation with the estates had replaced hostility. The empire as such had lost its meaning. Territorially it had lost control not only over the western lands gained by the French but also over Switzerland, where, beginning with a revolt in 1291, a confederation of cantons had taken form with a weak central authority and wide cantonal autonomy. In 1438, the title of emperor passed permanently to the House of Hapsburg. Though the emperors who followed immediately were weak, Maximilian (reigned 1493–1519) not only reestablished strong Hapsburg rule in Austria and its dependencies, but arranged for his children and grandchildren a stunning series of dynastic marriages that would make his grandson, Charles V, the ruler of half of Europe. Thus German national sentiment could not overcome the particularism of the princes and the dynastic interest of the emperors.

Italy

In Italy, the struggle between popes and emperors had promoted the growth of communes or city-states, much like those of ancient Greece. In the twelfth and thirteenth centuries, the communes had been mostly oligarchic republics, dominated by nobles and rich businessmen. Within the ruling group, in each town, the pro-papal Guelf faction struggled against the pro-imperial Ghibelline faction, while smaller businessmen and artisans fought their own fight against the ruling oligarchy as a whole. Just as the city-states of Greece went through a phase of government by tyrant, so those of late medieval Italy mostly passed from oligarchy to depotism. Sometimes a despot seized power; sometimes the struggling factions in the town invited him in. Often he was a *condottiere,* a captain of the mercenary troops hired to fight the city-state's enemies.

The city-state was characteristic of northern Italy. The south comprised the Kingdom of the Two Sicilies (the island plus Naples and its large territories on the mainland), which had experienced Byzantine, Muslim, Norman, Hohenstaufen, and Angevin domination during the course of the Middle Ages. Sicily passed to Aragon in 1282, Naples in 1435. Though some of the Aragonese rulers, notably Alfonso the Magnanimous (reigned 1416–1458), were generous patrons of learning, the Two Sicilies never recovered the prosperity or the cultural leadership they had enjoyed in earlier days.

Similarly, central Italy, consisting chiefly of the Papal States, went into eclipse during the "Babylonian Captivity" at Avignon. The government of Rome fell into the hands of the great nobles; twice, in the middle of the fourteenth century, they put down attempts by Cola di Rienzi to establish a kind of republic with himself as tribune of the people. It was another century before popes Nicholas V (1447–1455), Pius II (1458–1464), and Sixtus IV (1471–1484) were able to restore Rome to its old position as a center of learning and of power.

The Borgia pope Alexander VI (1492–1503), whose son Cesare gave him much political and military assistance, not stopping at the use of poison, broke the power of many Roman princely families and of the lords of central Italy, and reasserted papal political supremacy in the papal lands. Pope Julius II (1503–1513) actually took the field in command of the papal troops. But papal temporal power would soon suffer severe blows abroad as the result of the Reformation, and at home as the result of the long wars between the Hapsburgs and the Valois kings of France, in which Italy became a battleground.

MILAN, FLORENCE, VENICE   The northern city-states emerged in the later Middle Ages as the centers of Italian political life. Milan, strategically located in the fertile Lombard plain, meeting place of the routes over the Alps from the

Drawing of a condottiere by Leonardo da Vinci.

Cesare Borgia.

north, manufactured the best velvets and the best armor in Europe. It had led the opposition to Frederick Barbarossa in the twelfth century, and then pushed its holdings south into Tuscany. In 1277 Milan substituted for its previous republican government a despotism by the rich and high-handed Visconti family. Extending their rule to include Genoa, intermarrying with the royal houses of England and France, the Visconti dukes at the turn of the fifteenth century had most of northern Italy in their hands.

In 1447, the direct Visconti line died out, but Francesco Sforza, husband of the illegitimate daughter of the last Visconti, made himself duke in 1450. His son, Ludovico (reigned 1479–1500), called il Moro, "the Moor," was a clever diplomat and great patron of art and learning who made the mistake of becoming embroiled in the Italian projects of the French (see p. 325) and ended his days in a French prison.

On the banks of the Arno in Tuscany, midway between Milan and Rome, Florence shared with Milan and Venice the leadership of Italy. The rich merchants and bankers of the town were mainly Guelfs, the older nobility with estates in the environs and great palaces in town mostly Ghibelline. A bloody seesaw struggle raged through most of the thirteenth century, while prosperity grew, and the gold florin (minted first in 1252) replaced the Byzantine gold nomisma as standard coinage in Europe. By 1282, the Guelfs had placed political power in the hands of the seven major guilds, including banking and wool-making, and a law of 1293 closed off the last possibility of noble participation in government, as all those not actually practicing their professions were expelled from the guilds. The Guelfs themselves now split, the Black Guelf extremists favoring repeal of the law of 1293, and the White Guelf moderates taking a position approximating that of the Ghibellines. The continuing factional struggle claimed many victims, among them the poet Dante (1265–1321), permanently exiled with many fellow White Guelfs from his beloved Florence.

The politically unprivileged sought to make Florence more democratic. They failed because the lesser guilds, with their lower-middle-class membership, could never join with the poor workmen in a joint alliance against the entrenched oligarchy. Bank failures and the Black Death of the 1340's led to revolutions, including a serious uprising of the Ciompi in 1378, but the ruling oligarchy returned to power (1382–1434), buying the towns of Pisa and Leg-

View of Florence at the end of the fifteenth century.

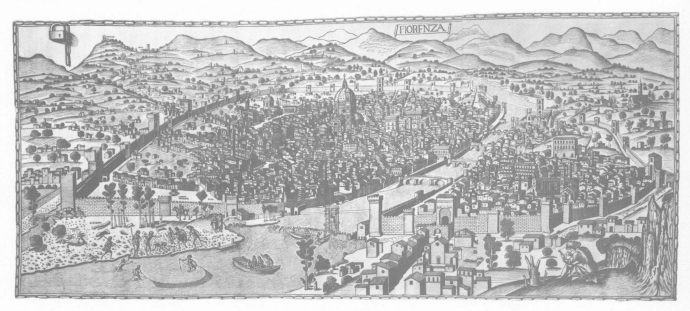

Terra-cotta bust of Lorenzo de' Medici by Verrocchio.

horn, which gave the Florentines access to the sea. Military reverses brought to power in 1434 Cosimo de' Medici, member of a family with large woolen and banking interests, who was none the less a champion of the poor.

Between 1434 and 1494, the Medici ran Florence, introducing a progressive income tax to lighten the burden of the poor. Though Cosimo was a despot, he ruled quietly by managing to pack the city council, traditionally chosen every two months through random drawing of the names of eligible citizens from leather bags. Cosimo's grandson, Lorenzo de' Medici (reigned 1469–1492), earned his name of "the Magnificent" by his lavish patronage of all the arts, his charm, tolerance, intelligence, and wisdom. In 1474 the Pazzi family, rivals to the Medici, obtained the valuable concession of receivers of papal revenues, as a result of a quarrel between Lorenzo and Pope Sixtus IV, which led to an attempt (1478) to assassinate Lorenzo. The fierce Medici vengeance against the Pazzi precipitated a papal interdict on Florence and the excommunication of Lorenzo. A general upheaval in Italian city-state relationships followed. After Lorenzo's death in 1492, economic decline, the French invasions, and two expulsions and two returns of the Medici family marked the history of Florence, now a petty state despite its transformation (1569) into the Grand Duchy of Tuscany.

Third of the great north Italian states, Venice had founded an overseas empire along the eastern Adriatic shore and in Greece and the Aegean (see Chapter 5). This expansion led to fighting with the Genoese during most of the later thirteenth and the fourteenth centuries. Venice was governed by a doge, in the early Middle Ages appointed by the Byzantine emperor, and later elected. After 1171, he was appointed by an elected assembly of 480 members, which became the Great Council. In 1297, the members of the Council restricted future membership to the descendants of those who had served during the preceding four years, plus certain other families. These names were listed in the Golden Book, and all others were permanently excluded from the government. A rebellion in 1310 led to the creation of an inner Council of Ten, especially charged with maintaining security.

The doge now became chiefly a ceremonial figure, who, for example, annually "married" the Adriatic in a famous ceremony, by throwing a ring into the sea. Despite the tight control of the great families and their ruthlessness, Venice was by no means insensitive to the welfare of its poorer subjects. It enjoyed great stability: no despots overthrew the oligarchy; no factionalism tormented its citizens. Its imposing fleets challenged Turks as well as Genoese. Money poured in, and Venice's wealth, power, and unique location made it a city unlike any other.

THE LESSONS OF DESPOTISM: MACHIAVELLI   In the cynical age of Louis XI of France and Henry VII of England, the Venetian oligarchs and Italian despots like the Sforza, Borgia, and Medici served as models for statesmanship. The Venetian diplomatic service, with its shrewd ambassadors sending detailed and informative reports from abroad, soon had its imitators. The Italian despots' reliance on mercenaries foreshadowed the general use of paid troops and the abandonment of the old feudal levies. The balance of power precariously maintained in the peninsula by the Italians served as a model for the new European monarchies. Italy was in a real sense the "school of Europe" in statesmanship. Yet the very balance among the Italian states made it impossible for them to unite in the face of a foreign threat, and the French invasion of 1494 ushered in a new period of French, Spanish, and Hapsburg competition in the disunited peninsula.

The young Machiavelli.

Summing up the lessons that long observation of Italian political behavior had taught him, Niccolò Machiavelli (1469–1527), a Florentine diplomat who had served the Florentine republic in the early 1500's and was exiled when the Medici came back in 1512, wrote his celebrated book, *The Prince*. Arguing that men in general were "ungrateful, voluble dissemblers, anxious to avoid danger and covetous of gain," he advised a prince "not to keep faith when by so doing it would be against his interest," but to be as deceitful and unscrupulous as Ludovico Sforza, Lorenzo the Magnificent, or especially Cesare Borgia, the son of Pope Alexander VI. Was Machiavelli perhaps being satirical and might he mean the opposite of what he said? Some scholars think so, but it seems improbable. His overriding aim was to expel the French, Spanish, and Hapsburg intruders and to unify Italy, and he was ready to sanction any means to gain that end. He was also hoping, though vainly, to regain political favor.

In a second work, *The Discourses* on the Roman historian Livy, Machiavelli dealt not with the immediate Italian crisis, but with the problem of building a lasting government. In this context, he prescribed not a single all-powerful prince but magistrates elected by the people, whom he regarded as more prudent and stable than a prince. The contradiction between *The Discourses* and *The Prince* is more apparent than real: in *The Discourses* Machiavelli was discussing the ancients with all their republican civic virtue, in *The Prince* the modern Italians who had, he was convinced, lost theirs. For this loss Machiavelli blamed the Church: not only the worldly papacy with all its temporal interest, but Christianity itself, which by exalting humility and a contempt for this world, and by focusing on the City of God, had left men less well prepared than the pagans to fight, work, and die for their country here on earth.

In defending secularism and power politics, Machiavelli was only preaching what others had already practiced. Louis XI, Henry VII, Ferdinand of Aragon, and the successful German princes and Italian despots were all Machiavellians in action before Machiavelli himself set down the theories. Machiavellianism seemed an essential part of the age, the era of the Renaissance.

IV

The Renaissance: Literature and Learning

The Meaning of "Renaissance"

Renaissance means "rebirth." When men have applied the term to the extraordinary flowering of letters and the arts begun in fourteenth-century Italy and spreading at varying speeds and with varying intensity to the other countries of Europe, they have wanted it to mean a rebirth of classical culture, a return to the standards of the Greeks and Romans of antiquity, and a repudiation of everything for which the Middle Ages had stood. Not so long ago most people believed that, when Constantinople fell to the Turks in 1453, refugee Greek scholars brought to the West the precious manuscripts of the classics and taught the West to appreciate them. Then suddenly a continent cloaked in darkness and inhabited by barbarians was illuminated by a blaze of light that enabled the ignorant brutes to behold the truth and to transform themselves into cultivated skeptical gentlemen.

We have learned enough now to see that this view is largely wrong. No very large migration of Greeks took place after 1453; many more had migrated earlier. In the twelfth century, the Western rediscovery of the classical heritage was already well under way, and in the thirteenth Aquinas and others had already incorporated Aristotelian philosophy into the Christian scheme. The so-called barbarian Middle Ages had seen a great Christian civilization come to maturity. Some scholars indeed have pointed to earlier "rebirths" and refer to the "Carolingian Renaissance," the "Renaissance of the Twelfth Century," and even to tenth- and eleventh-century renaissances. It is, however, just as misleading to regard the whole medieval period as a series of rebirths culminating in a great rebirth as it is to overestimate the suddenness and originality of the transition.

Transition there certainly was: a period in which the world was growing less medieval and increasingly modern. *Renaissance* is not a bad name for the civilization of the transition period if we understand our terminology: a movement away from devoutness, caste consciousness, otherworldliness, and credulousness, and toward secularism, individualism, skepticism, and materialism. This does not mean that all scholars or artists of the Renaissance suddenly appear totally devoid of medieval qualities or totally imbued with modern ones. It does mean that most could be found moving away from the older standards, somewhere on the path toward the newer ones. Some men moved fast and far along all these lines; other men far on some lines and not at all on others. The new secular drift has been well described as "art for art's sake, politics for politics' sake, science for science's sake." Men were writing, painting, studying, and participating in the active life nor primarily as a means of glorifying God or attaining salvation hereafter, but as ends in themselves.

The Vernacular Triumphs; Dante

Latin remained the language of the Church and the international language of scholars, and classical scholarship flourished indeed as never before, and extended rapidly to Greek as well as Latin writings. But at the same time, the vernacular tongues of Europe, whose progress we have been watching throughout the Middle Ages, now came into general literary use. When Italian, with Dante, won general acceptance in Italy at the end of the thirteenth century and the beginning of the fourteenth, the triumph of Italian in the home of Latin was in itself symbolic of the transition to a new age.

And Dante, whose *Divine Comedy* we studied (p. 189) as the greatest of all medieval works of literature, is of course simultaneously regarded traditionally as the first of the Renaissance men. Sometimes he wrote in Latin: his *De monarchia*, for example, is a long treatise yearning for the restoration in Italy of the medieval empire that had forever disappeared. In another treatise in Latin, *De vulgari eloquentia (On the Common Speech),* he stoutly defended the use of the vernacular language. And in the *Divine Comedy* he put his precepts into practice, writing in Italian.

Humanism and Dante's Successors in Italian Literature

In Italian universities the students called their law teachers by a slang word, *legista* or *jurista*—the "law guy," one might translate it. *Humanista* was their word for the teachers of grammar, rhetoric, and the other humane studies—the "humanities guy." And the learned men of the new period called themselves humanists, often exhibiting a passion for the classics quite different in its violence and devotion from anything in the previous centuries of scholarship. Humanists rediscovered texts hitherto lost—the Roman historians Tacitus and Lucretius, for example. At an extraordinary rate they multiplied copies of texts already known, so that knowledge of the texts was diffused far beyond the narrow circle of medieval scholars who previously had had access to them. Most striking was the quickening in Greek studies. Despite the long contacts between Europe and Byzantium, almost nobody in the West before the late fourteenth century knew Greek or cared about Greek literature; the earlier translations of Greek often came from an intermediary Arabic version and consisted of medical, scientific, and Aristotelian philosophical works.

The generation of humanists that immediately followed Dante was headed by Petrarch (Francesco Petrarca, 1304–1374), more steeped in the contemporary adoration of the classics and, like Horace, for example, who had boasted that his poems were a monument more lasting than bronze, much preoccupied with his own fame among the generations that would come after him. Petrarch collected and copied manuscripts, discovered some lost letters of Cicero, and even wrote letters of his own to Cicero and other ancient writers. Imitating Vergil, he composed a Latin epic to celebrate Scipio Africanus, conqueror of the Carthaginians. He tried hard to learn Greek and employed a teacher, but to his sorrow never mastered the language.

Portrait of Dante attributed to the school of Giotto.

Crowned with laurels by the "Senate" (city council) of Rome, Petrarch would have been painfully surprised to discover that posterity remembers best, not the Latin works that he himself valued most, but the Italian sonnets (little songs) he wrote in honor of his beloved Laura. These charming verses gave definitive form to the Italian sonnet: fourteen lines, divided into an octave and a sestet, each with its own rhyme scheme. Petrarch admired the beauties of this world, as most Renaissance men did, but he too remained in many ways a man of the Middle Ages, turning for inspiration as much to Saint Augustine's *Confessions* as to Cicero. Yet like many humanists he felt that the scholastic philosophers had missed the forest (the spirit of Christianity) in their concern for the trees (the detail of controversy).

Petrarch's famous pupil, Boccaccio (1313–1375), was also a hard-working humanist, who discovered a lost manuscript of Tacitus, succeeded in learning Greek, and taught at the University of Florence. When the Florentines wanted to find a man who had mastered Dante's *Divine Comedy* and could give public lectures on it, they selected Boccaccio. Having started life as apprentice in his

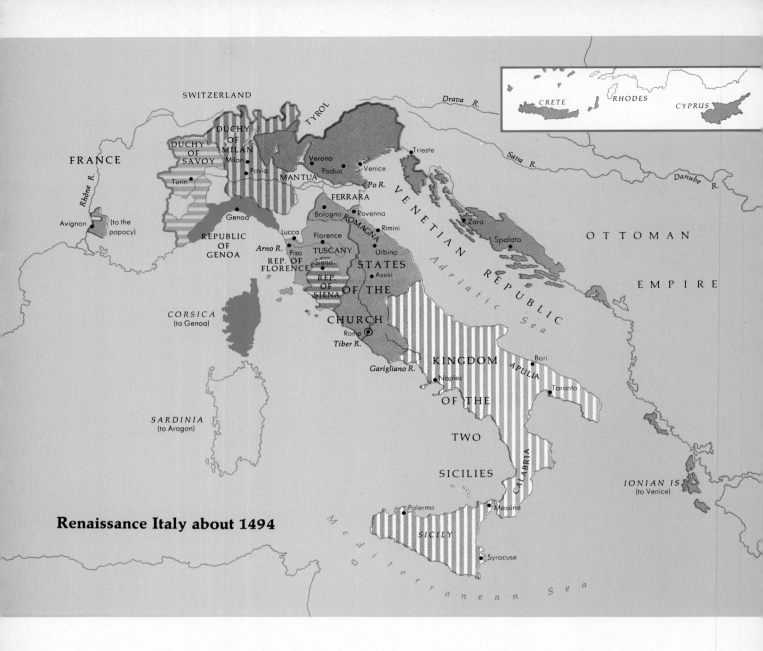

Renaissance Italy about 1494

father's banking business, he came to detest the sharp practices he saw, and to scorn the pious professions of the hypocritical rich. Boccaccio is most celebrated for his vernacular work, *The Decameron,* a series of stories told during ten days by a company of ten lively young people fleeing Florence to escape the Black Death of 1348. In these tales we find wronged husbands and clever adulterous wives, cheating merchants and frivolous youths, lustful priests and cynical apprentices, a convincingly sinful cast of characters given to all the human failings, treated with an earthy lightheartedness. Boccaccio of course did not invent all the *Decameron* stories: he took old fabliaux (traveling-salesman jokes that everybody knew) and gave them literary form.

The Scholars

It was in the years immediately after Boccaccio's death that the main Greek revival took place in Italy under the powerful impetus given by Greeks from Byzantium. Manuel Chrysoloras came to the West in the closing years of the fourteenth century to get help for the Byzantines against the Ottoman Turks, and between 1396 and 1400 lectured in Florence and Milan on Greek literature and the proper methods of translating it into Latin. George Gemistos Plethon, a scientist and Platonist, attended the Church Council of Florence in 1437, and encouraged the teaching of Greek in the universities. Homer and the other poets now were translated into Latin, as were philosophers other than Aristotle, notably Plato and the Platonists. In 1462, Cosimo de' Medici founded a "Platonic Academy" in Florence, a sort of center for advanced study in Platonism, where the researches of a small circle of scholars were subsidized. Here Marsiglio Ficino (1433–1499) translated Plato and taught Platonism. In the teachings of the Neoplatonists of the third century A.D. and later, Ficino and his school found something very like Christian mysticism, and they broadened their approach to philosophy and religion to include those whom the Neoplatonists had revered, Pythagoras and his followers, and the almost mythical "Wise Men" of the ancient Near East. Ficino's pupil, the brilliant and short-lived Pico della Mirandola (1463–1494), who knew Hebrew and Arabic in addition to Greek, and studied Jewish allegory, Arab philosophy and medieval Scholasticism (which, almost alone among humanists, he respected), hoped by examining the varied beliefs and ideas of the past to find a set of keys to man and the universe, the common denominator of faith. Pico's effort was typical of the best in humanist scholarship.

But the humanists were more than scholars: they themselves wrote voluminous letters, speeches, poems, and treatises on grammar and rhetoric, history, politics, education, and religion. They proclaimed an ideal of eloquence; as professional rhetoricians, they were convinced that classical models supplied the best guides. Many of them had contempt for the learning of their medieval predecessors, whose ideas on life and learning they did not share. But many others had a deep regard for medieval scholastic thought, and continued to study it. By the mid-fifteenth century many lawyers and doctors and other professional men were humanists as well. Only a few humanists were what we would term "free-lance" writers; most were either teachers or acted as secretaries to princes or city governments. In any role, however, they prided themselves on writing correct Latin letters and speeches, much as their medieval predecessors had done.

Lorenzo Valla (ca. 1405–1457) is probably the most celebrated Italian humanist, who tackled biblical scholarship among other subjects with the methods of the new scholarship. Translator of Herodotus and Thucydides, author of a handbook on Latin style, historian of the reign of Ferdinand of Aragon, and a practicing philosopher and professor, Valla was immensely learned and courageous, and also petty and vindictive. He enjoyed the favorite contemporary game of trading insults with his fellow humanists. His great achievement was to prove that the Donation of Constantine (see Chapter 3), the basis since the eighth century for sweeping papal claims to temporal power, was a forgery. Valla showed that the Latin of the document could not possibly be as early as the time of Constantine, and pointed to several glaring anachronisms: for instance, the Donation referred to Constantinople as a "patriarchate," when in fact, in 314, the purported date of the document, Valla argued, "it was not yet a patriarchate, nor a see, nor a Christian city, nor named Constantinople, nor founded, nor planned. . . ." Valla published his exposure in 1440, as secretary to Alfonso the Magnanimous of Naples, whose claim to Naples was being challenged by the pope on the basis of the Donation. Not only did the pope not condemn Valla as a heretic, which one might have expected at any time during the Middle Ages, but it was he who later commissioned Valla to translate Thucydides.

During the fourteenth and fifteenth centuries, Italian humanists took their new attitudes and skills northward out of Italy. They came as diplomats, as visiting lecturers, and even on business, and found themselves in great demand. Northerners came to Italy on private or public business. In the less urbanized, less Roman, more "Gothic" north the new humanistic enthusiasm spread rapidly especially among intellectuals, high churchmen, the nobility, and the kings and princes.

Conrad Celtis (1459–1508) wrote verses begging Apollo, master of the Muses and god of the sun, to leave Italy and come to Germany, where he was so badly needed, and urged young German students to vie with the Italians. Johannes Reuchlin (1455–1522), who launched a revival of Hebrew letters, was attacked for it by anti-Semites, and the episode gave rise to vigorous humanistic satirical defenses of Reuchlin, and a controversy that in many ways foreshadowed the Reformation that would soon begin in Germany.

Petrarch himself had lived for a time in Avignon, but the true flowering of French humanism was postponed until the early sixteenth century, when Francis I (1515–1547) as king was caught up in the enthusiasm for the classics. Guillaume Budé, a learned scholar, played a major role in the revival of Greek, and under his prodding, the king founded a college where Greek was taught as well as Latin and French, and a great library which became the nucleus of the present Bibliothèque Nationale. Lefèvre d'Étaples (1455–1536), who studied the Greek church fathers, was close to those who later turned to religious reform. In letters, François Rabelais (ca. 1494–1553; see Chapter 7) and the urbane essayist Michel de Montaigne (1533–1592) were fully men of the Renaissance.

Three Englishmen who had studied in Florence brought the new humanistic learning to England about 1500, by launching at Oxford programs of study like those of which they themselves had been the products. And one of these Englishmen, William Grocyn, became the teacher of the "Prince of Humanists," Desiderius Erasmus (1466–1536), a Dutchman, who studied, taught, and lived at Oxford, Cambridge, and Paris, in Italy, Germany, and Switzerland. Erasmus knew Greek so well that he published a scholarly edition of the Greek New Testament. He carried on a prodigious correspondence in Latin, and compiled a series of *Adages* and *Colloquies* to give students examples of how to write Latin. But he cared for content as well as style, and sneered not only at the "knowledge factories" of the grammarians but at the mutual admiration society of his fellow humanists, who were "scratching each other's itch." Erasmus played no favorites; he satirized any group or class inflated by a sense of its own importance—merchants, churchmen, scientists, philosophers, courtiers, and kings. In appraising human nature, however, Erasmus tempered criticism with geniality, and concluded that we must cherish particularly the few outstanding individuals who have led great and good lives. Christ heads his list of great men; Cicero and Socrates rank very high. Plato's account of the death of Socrates moved Erasmus so deeply that he almost cried out, "Pray for us, Saint Socrates."

Erasmus joined love of the classics with respect for Christian values. Both testy and vain, he had little use for the finespun arguments of Scholasticism and was a tireless advocate of what he called his "philosophy of Christ," the application, in the most humane spirit, of the doctrines of charity and love taught by Jesus. Yet though Erasmus always considered himself a loyal son of the Church, he nevertheless helped to destroy the universality of Catholicism. His edition of the Greek New Testament raised disquieting doubts about the correctness of the Vulgate and therefore of Catholic biblical interpretations.

Hans Holbein the Younger's portrait of Erasmus.

His attacks on the laxity of the clergy implied that the wide gap between the professed ideals and the corrupt practices of the Church could not long endure. A famous sixteenth-century epigram states: "Where Erasmus merely nodded, Luther rushed in; where Erasmus laid eggs, Luther hatched the chicks; where Erasmus merely doubted, Luther laid down the law." Erasmus was still in his prime when Luther "laid down the law" in 1517 and launched the Protestant revolt (see Chapter 7).

Science and Medicine

In the history of science the fourteenth, fifteenth, and sixteenth centuries were a time of preparation for a larger revolution, as scientists absorbed, enlarged, and modified the knowledge handed down to them from the Middle Ages and antiquity. In the fourteenth and fifteenth centuries Aristotelian studies continued to be pursued vigorously at Paris and Padua. The humanists for the first time translated Galen, Ptolemy, Archimedes, and other scientists from Greek into Latin.

But the humanists' worship of classical antiquity tended to put old authorities high on a pedestal, beyond the reach of criticism. How could one improve on the medicine taught by Galen during the second century A.D.? Galen, for example, said that the blood moved from one side of the heart to the other by passing through invisible pores in the thick wall of tissue that divides the organ. Galen was wrong, as Harvey was to discover in the seventeenth century: the blood gets from the one side to the other by circulating through the body and lungs. But Galen's theory of invisible pores was enough to keep Leonardo da Vinci (1452–1519) from anticipating Harvey. Leonardo's anatomical studies led him to the brink of discovery; then he backed away, for he was certain that Galen must have been right.

Leonardo, in fact, illustrates both the shortcomings and the achievements of Renaissance science. He took notes in a hit-or-miss fashion, without the modern scientist's concern for the systematic cataloging of observations and for the publication of findings and speculations. Yet he projected lathes, pumps, war machines, flying machines, and many other contraptions, not all of them workable, to be sure, but all highly imaginative. He did not always bow before established authority, as he did before Galen. His geological studies convinced him that the earth was far older than the men of his time thought it to be; the Po River, he estimated, must have been flowing for about 200,000 years to wash down the sediments forming its alluvial plain.

In medicine, the University of Padua maintained a lively tradition of scientific inquiry that presaged the seventeenth-century triumphs of the experimental method. A young Belgian named Vesalius (1514–1564), who taught at Padua, rejected Galen's notion of invisible pores in the wall of tissue within the heart because he could not find such pores. In 1543, Vesalius published the splendidly illustrated *De humani corporis fabrica (Concerning the Structure of the Human Body),* largely accepting older authorities, but also pointing out some of their shortcomings.

Astronomy

In 1543 Copernicus launched modern astronomical studies with *De revolutionibus orbium coelestium (Concerning the Revolutions of Heavenly Bodies).* Born in Poland of German extraction, Copernicus (1473–1543) studied law and medicine at Padua and other Italian universities and spent thirty years as canon of a cathedral near Danzig. His work in mathematics and astronomy led him to attack the generally accepted hypothesis of the geocentric (earth-centered) universe derived from Ptolemy and other astronomers of antiquity. He now advanced the revolutionary new hypothesis of the heliocentric (sun-centered) universe.

The concept of the geocentric universe included an elaborate system of spheres. Around the stationary earth there revolved some eighty separate circles (crystalline spheres) containing some of the heavenly bodies, each moving on an invisible circular path, each transparent so that we mortals could see the spheres beyond it. This imaginative and symmetrical picture of the universe had been questioned before the time of Copernicus, as scientists had trouble making it agree with the observable behavior of heavenly bodies. Copernicus used both these earlier criticisms and his own computations to arrive at the heliocentric concept.

Once Copernicus had reversed the roles of the sun and the earth, his universe retained many Ptolemaic characteristics. Its heavens were still filled with spheres revolving along their invisible orbits. Only they now moved about a stationary sun, instead of the stationary earth. Though Copernicus dedicated his book to the pope, Christendom viewed it with dismay and found it hard to accept the disappearance of the earth-centered and man-centered universe. Yet Copernicus only began the revolution in astronomy, which was to be carried much further in the next century by Galileo and Newton.

Technology

The most important Renaissance contribution to technology was printing. The revolution in book production began in the fourteenth century, when Europeans imported paper from China and found it to be cheaper than the lambskin or sheepskin previously used. Next, engravers made woodcuts or copper plates that could produce many copies of the same drawing. Then sentences were added to the cuts or plates. Finally, almost certainly in the German Rhineland during the 1440's, movable type was devised. Each piece of type was simply a minute bit of engraving; it could be combined with other pieces to form words, sentences, a whole page, and then salvaged to be used again. This crucial invention used to be credited to Gutenberg; some scholars disagree.

By 1500, Italy alone had seventy-three presses employing movable type. The most famous of them was the Aldine Press in Venice (founded by Aldus Manutius, 1450–1515), which sold at reasonable prices scholarly editions of the classics printed in a beautiful typeface reportedly based on the handwriting of Petrarch. Everywhere the printing press suddenly made both classical and vernacular literature available to large numbers of people who could never have afforded hand-copied manuscripts. Without the perfection of printing, Erasmus might not have become the arbiter of European letters, and Luther might not have secured the rapid distribution of his antipapal tracts and sped the Reformation on its way.

Another technical innovation was gunpowder, brought from China, and used in the fighting of the early 1400's, notably the later campaigns of the Hundred Years' War. Firearms and artillery doomed both the feudal knight and the feudal castle. At sea, important aids to navigation came into general use, particularly the magnetic compass and more accurate sailing charts. By the close of the fifteenth century, Europeans possessed the equipment needed for the oncoming age of world discovery.

V

The Renaissance: The Arts

Main Characteristics of Renaissance Art

Exploiting both the humanistic enthusiasm for classical antiquity and the growing secularism of the age, and aided by technical advances, artists of genius now produced an extraordinary number of masterpieces. They released painting and sculpture from their previous subservience to architecture in the West. The individual picture or statue emerged as an independent work of art rather than as a part of a larger whole; the individual painter or sculptor sometimes reveled in an artistic self-assertion that was quite unmedieval. Reflecting the classical revival, the fashion in building changed from the soaring Gothic to adaptations of the ancient Roman temple, emphasizing symmetry and the horizontal line. Reflecting the expanding wealth and materialism of the age, palaces and private residences began to rival cathedrals and churches in magnificence.

The arts as a whole, like society and culture in general, became less Christian and more secular than they had been during the Middle Ages. For patrons, artists turned increasingly to men of state and business; for subjects they chose not only the traditional Virgin, Christ, and saints but also pagan gods and their own patrons. Interest in the things of this world, however, did not exclude concern with the next world; the Renaissance was *both* worldly *and* otherworldly.

The artists of the Renaissance, even more than its writers and thinkers, displayed an extraordinary range of talents and interests. They produced both secular and sacred works; they copied classical models and launched bold experiments in artistic expression; some of the very greatest were also the most versatile. Giotto painted, designed, and ornamented buildings, wrote verses, and did handsomely in business. Leonardo was a jack of all trades and a master of many—painter and sculptor, musician and physicist, anatomist and geologist, inventor and city planner. Michelangelo executed heroic frescoes and heroic statues, and helped to plan St. Peter's. In sculpture the Renaissance rivaled the golden centuries of Greece. In painting, it was more than a rebirth; it transformed a rather limited medium of expression into a thrilling new aesthetic instrument.

Renaissance Painting, Sculpture, and Architecture

Painting

GIOTTO AND HIS SUCCESSORS   Before 1300, Italian painters had generally followed Byzantine models: their work, while often splendid in color and drawing, was also flat and two-dimensional. Giotto (ca. 1270–1337), though not entirely forsaking the Byzantine tradition, experimented to make painting more lifelike and less austere. He learned much from the realistic statues of Italian sculptors, who, in turn, had been influenced by the striking sculptures of French Gothic cathedrals. We may take as examples the frescoes Giotto executed for the Arena Chapel at Padua. In *Return of Joachim to the Sheepfold,* the dog greets his returned master with his right forepaw raised to scratch a welcome. In *The Lamentation,* the mood of grief is intensified by the angels who are

Giotto's "Return of Joachim to the Sheepfold."

Giotto's "The Lamentation."

flying above the dead Christ and seem to be beating their wings in a transport of sorrow. By varying the brightness of his colors and introducing new contrasts of light and shade, by studying perspective and foreshortening, Giotto gave his paintings a quite unmedieval three-dimensional quality, and caused his human subjects to appear lifelike.

Giotto was no anonymous craftsman, content to work in obscurity, but a many-sided man, hungry for fame, and famous in his own day for his verses and his witty remarks as well as for his artistic accomplishments. His artistic commissions netted him a fortune, which he augmented through lending money, running a debt-collection service, and renting looms (at stiff fees) to poor woolen-weavers. Giotto had many connections with the great and wealthy; he won the patronage of Roman cardinals, the king of Naples, and the guilds and millionaires of Florence.

In the two centuries after Giotto, more and more despots, kings, and merchant princes joined the ranks of patrons. In Florence, the government, the wealthy magnates, and the churches and monasteries all engaged in a campaign for civic beauty. Lorenzo the Magnificent subsidized the great painter Botticelli as well as the humanists of the Platonic Academy. Il Moro, the Sforza

Grotesque faces: a drawing from the notebooks of Leonardo.

Masaccio's "The Expulsion from Paradise."

Botticelli's "Primavera."

despot in Milan, made Leonardo da Vinci in effect his minister of fine arts, director of public works, and master of the revels. After the collapse of Il Moro's fortunes, Leonardo found new patrons in Cesare Borgia, the pope, and the French kings Louis XII and Francis I. The popes, who employed Leonardo, Botticelli, Michelangelo, and many others, intended to make Rome the artistic capital of the world.

In subject matter, the sacred and the secular could often be found in the same picture. In a Florentine chapel, for instance, Giotto placed round a religious fresco a border of medallions portraying the sponsors, the banking family of the Peruzzi. Giotto's successors often introduced into a sacred painting a portrait of the person who had commissioned it. Usually the patron assumed a duly reverent posture, but with a hint of the ambition that had won him worldly success and permitted him to afford the luxury of subsidizing a work of art.

Following many of Giotto's new techniques and perfecting others of his own, Masaccio (1401–ca. 1428) was influenced by the anatomical realism employed by sculptors, and, for example, showed Adam and Eve expelled from Eden with facial expressions and bodily attitudes showing the shame they were feeling at their punishment, while the light and shadow in contrast (*chiaroscuro*) on their bodies heightened the dramatic effect.

Botticelli (1445–1510), a superb draftsman and master of color, seemed to have brushed in separately every hair on the head of his human subjects. Like other Renaissance artists in the treatment of pagan and classical themes, Botticelli exhibited great delicacy. In his *Primavera*—a pagan allegory of spring, one finds nothing carnal despite much nudity.
Mercury, the Three Graces, a surprisingly wistful Venus, the goddess Flora, bedecked with flowers, and Spring herself, blown in by the west wind, are all youthful, slender, almost dainty, with the air of otherworldly sweetness for which Botticelli is famous. Botticelli seems to have moved in the circle of Pico della Mirandola, and his paintings often suggest an aspiration to some lofty Platonic realm. Yet he threw some of his own paintings of nudes onto the flames at the demand of the puritanical Savonarola.

LEONARDO, MICHELANGELO, TITIAN   The major trends that we have been following in patronage, subject matter, and technical proficiency reached a climax with the masters of the High Renaissance. We may take three of them as examples—Leonardo, Michelangelo, and Titian. Leonardo da Vinci completed relatively few pictures. His scientific activities and his innumerable services for his patrons took a large part of his time and energy. Some of his surviving paintings are badly damaged, notably *The Last Supper,* a fresco executed on the wall of the refectory of a monastery in Milan. Fortunately, one may discover Leonardo's superb talent and his extraordinary range of interests in the voluminous collections of his drawings and notebooks. The drawings include every sort of sketch, from preliminary work for paintings through realistic human embryos and fanciful war machines to mere doodles.

From an intensive study of human anatomy Leonardo drew up rules for indicating the actions of human muscles and for establishing the proportions between the parts of the human body. He combined a zeal for scientific precision with a fondness for the grotesque that recalls the gargoyles of a Gothic cathedral; he did many sketches of the deformed and of people suffering intense strain and anguish. He made *The Last Supper* in part an exercise in artistic geometry, arranging the apostles in four groups of three men each around the central figure of Christ, and keeping the background deliberately simple. Older painters had usually shown the solemn yet peaceful moment of the final communion, and had suggested the coming treachery of Judas by placing him in isolation from the others. Not Leonardo. He chose the tense moment when Jesus announced the coming betrayal, and he placed Judas among the apostles, relying on facial and bodily expression to convey the guilt of the one and the consternation of the others.

Leonardo got on fairly amicably with his patrons. By contrast, Michelangelo Buonarroti (1475–1564) quarreled repeatedly with the imperious pope Julius II (reigned 1503–1513); it took all the pope's cajolery to get Michelangelo to complete a fresco for the ceiling of the Sistine Chapel in the Vatican. The Sistine ceiling is in every respect a prodigious piece of work. The area is approximately fourteen by forty yards, and Michelangelo covered it with 343 separate figures. He executed the whole in the space of four years, working almost single-handed, assisted only by a plasterer and a color mixer, painting uncomfortably on his back atop a scaffolding, sometimes not bothering to descend for his night's rest.

For this massive undertaking Michelangelo boldly chose the grandest scenes from Genesis—the creation of the sun and moon, God hovering over the waters, the creation of Adam and of Eve, the eating of the forbidden fruit, and the expulsion from Paradise. In this vast gallery of nudes in all types of poses, Michelangelo summed up all that Renaissance art had learned about perspective, anatomy, and motion. The Sistine ceiling also comes close to summarizing man's concepts of God; no medieval artist would have thought of representing the deity so directly. God appears repeatedly, draped in a mantle, an ever changing patriarch. Hovering over the waters, he is benign; giving life to the motionless Adam or directing Eve to arise, he is gently commanding; creating the sun and moon, he is the all-powerful deity, formidable and urgent as a whirlwind.

Both Michelangelo and Leonardo had received their artistic training in Florence. Their contemporary, Titian (1477–1576), who was identified with Venice, for eighty years enjoyed almost unbroken professional success and produced an average of one picture a month. He painted frescoes for the headquarters of the German merchant colony in Venice, portraits of rich merchants, altarpieces and madonnas for churches and monasteries, and a great battle scene for the palace of the doge. By the middle decades of the sixteenth century, Titian was receiving offers from half the despots of Italy and the crowned heads of Europe. Titian transferred to paint much of the flamboyance and pageantry of Venice, using rich, intense colors, particularly reds and purples. A gallery of his portraits, at once elegant and revealing of character, would make a splendid introduction to the high politics—and politicians—of the sixteenth century.

NORTHERN EUROPEAN PAINTING   As with humanism, the fame and influence of the Italian painters helped to stimulate northern European artists. This northern Renaissance, however, also grew out of native traditions of Gothic art passed down from the Middle Ages. It centered in southern Germany and in the Low Countries. Its leading artists were Albrecht Dürer (1471–1528) and Hans Holbein (ca. 1497–1543), Germans both, and Pieter Brueghel the Elder (ca. 1520–1569), who was born near Brussels. Dürer received commissions from the emperor Maximilian. Armed with an introduction from Erasmus, Holbein moved to England, where he won the custom of humanists,

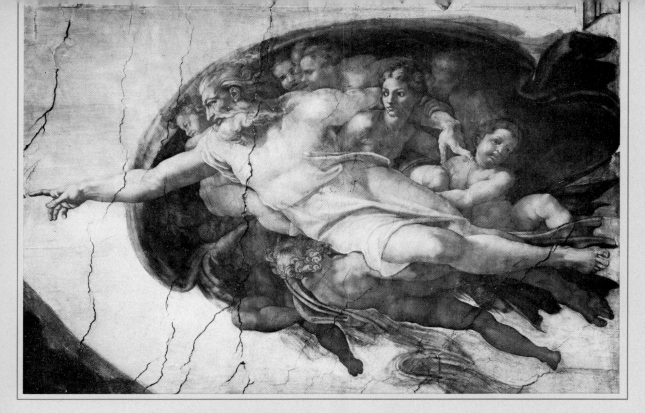

God: detail from The Creation of Adam, from Michelangelo's ceiling for the Sistine Chapel.

Titian's portrait of Emperor Charles V.

aristocrats, and the court of King Henry VIII. Brueghel had the support of businessmen in Antwerp and Brussels.

Dürer was in many ways the Leonardo of Germany. His realistic yet compassionate portrait of his aged and homely mother might almost have come from Leonardo's sketchbook. He collected monkeys and other tropical specimens, painted the Virgin in the unusual pose of a *Madonna with Many Animals,* and wrote treatises on perspective and human proportions. By sensitive use of line and shading Dürer revolutionized the hitherto primitive techniques of copper engraving and

285

woodcuts. These innovations permitted the reproduction of drawings in many copies, enabling an artist to illustrate a whole edition prepared by the new process of printing. They brought Dürer closer than any Italian painter to the rapidly expanding public of readers; they made him in effect the first artist in history to become a "bestseller."

Brueghel delighted in scenes of peasant life—weddings, dances, festivals, skating parties—and also enjoyed painting a series of landscapes showing the cycle of farming activities during the various seasons. Northern art also retained the old medieval fascination with the monstrous and supernatural. Dürer, in a series of sixteen woodcuts, depicted the Four Horsemen and the other grim marvels of the Apocalypse. Brueghel's *The Triumph of Death* is a nightmarish landscape; and his bizarre *Battle of the Angels and the Demons* is full of "things" whose nearest relatives populate the science fiction and the surrealist art of the twentieth century—coats of arms that actually fight, shellfish that fly, hybrids with insect wings, artichoke bodies, and flower heads. Most of these

fantasies were designed to teach
a moral lesson; they were
sermons in paint or ink.
The painting of northern
Europe demonstrates
once more the medieval
aspects of Renaissance men.

Dürer's engraving "Knight, Death, and Devil."

Pieter Brueghel the Elder's "The Triumph of Death."

Two Renaissance equestrian statues of condotti-eri—Donatello's of Gattamelata (above) and Ver-rocchio's of Colleoni (below)—shown with their Roman model, the statue of the emperor Marcus Aurelius in the Piazza del Campidoglio (right).

Sculpture

Renaissance painting owed its three-dimensional qualities to the painters' knowledge of sculpture; indeed Giotto, Leonardo, and Michelangelo were accomplished sculptors as well as painters. Sculptors, too, turned to classical models and secular themes, studied human anatomy, and experimented with new techniques. Donatello (ca. 1386–1466), a Florentine, produced an equestrian statue of the condottiere Gattamelata in Padua that illustrates these changes: the subject is secular; the treatment is classical (Gattamelata looks like the commander of a Roman legion); and the material is bronze, not the traditional stone. Another of Donatello's most celebrated works, the David in bronze, was the first statue of the male nude for more than a thousand years: David is a handsome young man, not at all a divinely inspired giantkiller. In

his statue of Mary Magdalen, called by one critic "an emaciated monster," Donatello did indeed make his subject all skin and bone, lank hair, and tattered clothing; but Mary Magdalen is a saint who looks the part.

In the next generation, Donatello's self-conscious rival, another Florentine, Verrocchio (1435–1488), deliberately chose the same or similar subjects: a David, a saint (Thomas, who had doubted Christ), and a condottiere: Colleoni, whose superbly arrogant figure on horseback dominates the square before the Church of Saint John and Saint Paul (Zanipolo) in Venice. Verrocchio was for fourteen years the teacher of Leonardo.

Donatello's statue of Mary Magdalen.

Three Renaissance statues of David. From left to right, by Verrocchio, Donatello, and Michelangelo.

It was Michelangelo, however, whose genius brought sculpture to the highest summit it had reached since the Age of Pericles, perhaps the highest in the whole record of the art. Early in his career, when the government of Florence invited him to create something beautiful from an enormous chunk of marble that another artist had seemingly spoiled, Michelangelo produced the renowned colossal statue of David. Late in his career, he met another exacting challenge in carving the figures of Dawn, Day, Dusk, and Night that adorn the tombs of the Medici family in Florence. The figures recline on sloping cornices yet do not seem about to slide off; they are relaxed but have enormous latent power. In portraying the Virgin grieving over the dead Christ—the *Pietà*—Michelangelo brilliantly solved the difficult technical problem of posing a seated woman with a corpse lying across her lap, and he triumphantly called attention to his feat by executing the work in highly polished marble. The face of Mary is sorrowful yet composed, and younger than that of the dead Christ. She is the eternal Virgin, Michelangelo explained, and so is always youthful and does not grieve in the manner of an earthly mother.

Born a quarter of a century later than Michelangelo, and not his equal, Benvenuto Cellini (1500–1571) was, however, a Renaissance artist of tremendous versatility. The popes, King Francis I

Cellini's statue of Perseus.

of France, and the Medici duke of Tuscany all acted as his patrons. His autobiography, revealing his energy, arrogance, and devotion to high living, is a famous document of the period, never yet fully exploited for what it tells us of the psychology of the men of his time. Engraver and goldsmith, who made lavish creations in precious metals and jewels, Cellini became a sculptor on a larger scale only in middle age, when he confounded the skeptics by producing a bronze statue of Perseus, holding the snaky head of Medusa, that is still one of the great sights of Florence, where it stands outdoors in the Loggia dei Lanzi on the main square.

Architecture

In 1546, at the age of seventy, Michelangelo shouldered one more artistic burden: he agreed to be the chief architect of St. Peter's. He died in 1564 long before the great Roman basilica was finally completed in 1626, and his successors altered many of his details. But the great dome, the key feature of the whole structure, and the basic Greek-cross ground plan with four equal arms followed his design. Instead of Gothic towers, St. Peter's has Michelangelo's dome, which rises 435 feet above the floor below yet is dwarfed in mass by the immense building underneath. The great windows, pointed arches, and high-flung vaults of medieval churches sometimes create an impression of strain and instability; not so St. Peter's with its round arches, heavier walls, stout columns, and its Renaissance symmetry.

Left: The dome of St. Peter's, Rome, by Michelangelo.

Below: Brunelleschi's dome for the cathedral of Florence.

A relatively late Renaissance building, St. Peter's illustrates long-standing Renaissance architectural practices. Architects had long been studying the profuse remains of buildings from antiquity that crowded Rome itself and other Italian cities, and had made it a practice to copy and adapt them. Brunelleschi (1377?–1446) had been the pioneer, and his monumental dome for the cathedral of Florence his major achievement, a real engineering tour de force, and one that Michelangelo had daily seen from his youth in his native city. Humanistic study of the writings of the ancients on geometry, especially Plato and Pythagoras, gave Renaissance architects knowledge of the Greek

Palladio's Palazzo Chiericati, Vicenza.

Palazzo Farnese, Rome.

concepts of perfect ideas and perfect geometric forms. Palladio (1518–1580), the foremost architectural theorist of the age, praised the Greek-cross plan for churches because of its symbolic values. If the apses (at the ends of the four arms) were rounded, and if the spaces between the arms were filled with rounded chapels, then the whole structure became an almost perfect circle. And the circle, according to Palladio, "demonstrates extremely well the unity, the infinite essence, the uniformity, and the justice of God."* Some scholars have detected a shift in religious emphasis in the change from the plan of the Latin cross, shaped like a crucifix, to the circled Greek cross; the medieval stress on the sacrifice of Christ yields to the Renaissance celebration of the perfection of God.

The lavish residences built during the Renaissance celebrated success in business or politics. Moreover, the growth of effective government meant that a man's home could be a showplace and no longer had to be, quite literally, his castle. Elaborately symmetrical villas now ornamented the countryside; in the cities rose the *palazzo* or palace, often not a royal or official structure but a private townhouse, combining business offices and residential apartments. Rome and Florence were dotted with them; in Venice they lined the Grand Canal from one end to the other. The usual palazzo was three-storied and rectangular, with its windows arranged in symmetrical rows. It became standard practice to ornament the first floor with Doric columns, the second with Ionic, and the third with Corinthian, thus using all three classical "orders" of capitals one above the other.

The fame of Italian builders soon spread throughout Europe, even to distant Moscow, where Italian experts supervised the remodeling of the Kremlin for Ivan III. Most countries did not copy the Italian style outright but grafted it onto older native architecture. The resulting compound produced some very striking buildings, particularly the great sixteenth-century chateaux of central France, which gracefully combine elements taken from the Gothic church, the feudal castle, and the Italian palace.

* Rudolf Wittkower, *The Architectural Principles of the Age of Humanism* (London, 1949), p. 21.

A musical composition, like a building, has its basic skeleton or form, its overall line, and its surface decorations and embellishments. Medieval sacred music had achieved very complex and elaborate combinations of form, line, and decoration. The center of Gothic music in the late Middle Ages was northern France and the Low Countries. By the fifteenth century French and Flemish musicians were journeying to Italy, where a process of mutual influence developed. The northerners took up the simple tunes of folk songs and dances; the Italians, in turn, added a strain of Gothic complexity to their austere plainsong. The end product was the beautiful sacred music of the Italian composer Palestrina (ca. 1525–1594), which was at once intricate in the northern manner and devout in the Italian.

Even in music the secularism and individualism of the Renaissance exerted an influence: the Flemings based their Masses on popular tunes. Moreover, Renaissance music was no longer anonymous; the day of the celebrated individual composer like Palestrina was at hand. And, like other artists, composers and performers of music experimented. They developed or imported a variety of new instruments—the violin, double bass, and harpsichord; the organ, with its complement of keyboards, pipes, and stops; the kettledrum, which was adopted from the Polish army; and the lute, which had originally been developed in medieval Persia and reached Italy by way of Muslim Spain.

Music played its role at almost every level of Renaissance society. The retinue of musicians became a fixture of court life, with the dukes of Burgundy, Philip the Good and Charles the Bold, leading the way. In German towns "mastersingers" organized choral groups; the most famous of them, Hans Sachs, a cobbler in Nuremberg in the 1500's, was later immortalized in Wagner's opera *Die Meistersinger*. But the mastersingers followed directly in the tradition of the thirteenth-century minnesinger, and princely patronage of music went back at least to the twelfth-century court of Eleanor of Aquitaine and its chivalric troubadours. In music the Renaissance did not make the sharp break with the recent past that distinguished the plastic arts, but built on the legacy it had received from the Middle Ages.

It is difficult to summarize an era as complex as the Renaissance. While no one man, nor single masterpiece of art or literature, was fully representative of it, its distinctive values and ideals were presented most sympathetically in a dialogue of manners published in 1528, *The Courtier* by Baldassare Castiglione (1478–1529). Although Castiglione, like a medieval man, believed the profession of arms to be the proper one for a gentleman, he recommended a quite unmedieval moderation and balance, and prescribed a humane and literary education in Latin and Greek. His courtier was to be a "universal man" like Leonardo. Castiglione was both reviving the old classical ideal of the well-rounded individual, "the sound mind in the sound body," and anticipating modern champions of the humanities and a liberal education.

Castiglione sang the praises of beauty: of God's physical world, of man, a little world in himself, and of the world of art. "The world," he says, is praised when one acclaims "the beautiful heaven, beautiful earth, beautiful sea, beautiful river, beautiful woods, trees, gardens, beautiful cities, beautiful churches, houses, armies. In conclusion, this comely and holy beauty is a wondrous setting out of everything. And it may be said that good and beautiful be after a sort one self thing. . . ." * A medieval man might also have coupled the good and the beautiful, but he would have stressed the good and the ways in which

* *The Courtier*, T. Hoby translation modernized (1907), p. 348.

God led man to righteousness. Medieval man had a vision of God's world. The Renaissance man, for whom Castiglione so eloquently speaks, had a vision not only of God's world but also of nature's world and man's world.

Reading Suggestions on the Late Middle Ages and the Renaissance

GENERAL ACCOUNTS

W. K. Ferguson, *Europe in Transition, 1300-1520* (Houghton, 1962). A comprehensive survey by a Canadian scholar.

D. Hay, *Europe in the Fourteenth and Fifteenth Centuries* (*Holt). Up-to-date.

E. P. Cheyney, *The Dawn of a New Era, 1250-1453* (*Torchbooks), and M. Gilmore, *The World of Humanism, 1453-1517* (*Torchbooks). Good introductory accounts, with very full bibliographies; the first two volumes in the series "The Rise of Modern Europe," edited by W. L. Langer.

J. Huizinga, *The Waning of the Middle Ages* (*Anchor). A remarkable re-creation of the atmosphere of an entire period of European history, with particular stress on France and the Low Countries.

G. Mattingly et al., *Renaissance Profiles* (*Torchbooks). Lively sketches of nine Italian figures including Petrarch, Machiavelli, Leonardo, Michelangelo.

ECONOMICS AND SOCIETY

W. K. Ferguson, *The Renaissance* (*Holt). Excellent short survey, stressing the social and economic background.

Miriam Beard, *A History of Business*, 2 vols. (*Ann Arbor). With good sketches of Renaissance millionaires.

A. W. O. von Martin, *Sociology of the Renaissance* (*Torchbooks). Instructive study of Italian society in the 1300's and 1400's.

F. C. Lane, *Venetian Ships and Shipping of the Renaissance* (Johns Hopkins, 1934). An exceptionally interesting monograph.

R. de Roover, *Rise and Decline of the Medici Bank, 1397-1494* (*Norton). A case history of the profits and pitfalls of Renaissance finance.

R. Ehrenberg, *Capital and Finance in the Age of the Renaissance: A Study of the Fuggers and Their Connections* (Harcourt, 1928). Another instructive case history.

THE NEW MONARCHIES

G. Mattingly, *Renaissance Diplomacy* (*Penguin). A stimulating study concerning the origins of modern diplomatic techniques.

E. Perroy, *The Hundred Years' War* (*Capricorn). The authoritative book on the war; an excellent introduction to French history during the fourteenth and fifteenth centuries.

A. J. Slavin, ed., *New Monarchies and Representative Assemblies* (*Heath). A wide sample of views on constitutional developments.

May McKisack, *The Fourteenth Century* (Clarendon, 1959), and E. F. Jacob, *The Fifteenth Century* (Clarendon, 1961). Scholarly and detailed volumes in the Oxford History of England.

A. R. Myers, *England in the Late Middle Ages, 1307-1536* (*Penguin). Brief survey.

E. F. Jacob, *Henry V and the Invasion of France* (*Collier). A good popular treatment.

C. W. S. Williams, *Henry VII* (Barker, 1937). A solid study of the first Tudor monarch.

B. Wilkinson, *The Constitutional History of Medieval England, 1216-1485*, 3 vols. (Longmans, 1948-1964). Detailed scholarly treatment.

S. B. Chrimes, *English Constitutional History* (*Oxford). Reliable short survey.

J. H. Elliott, *Imperial Spain, 1469-1716* (*Mentor). An excellent survey of Spain.

J. H. Mariéjol, *The Spain of Ferdinand and Isabella* (Rutgers, 1961). Readable study by a French scholar.

GERMANY AND ITALY

G. Barraclough, *The Origins of Modern Germany* (*Capricorn). The best general treatment of medieval Germany in English.

D. Hay, *The Italian Renaissance in Its Historical Background* (*Cambridge). An up-to-date introduction.

J. C. L. de Sismondi, *A History of the Italian Republics* (*Anchor). Famous old account from the early Middle Ages to the Renaissance.

J. A. Symonds, *The Age of the Despots* (*Capricorn). Another famous old account, the first volume of an extended study of Renaissance Italy.

H. Baron, *The Crisis of the Early Italian Renaissance* (*Princeton). Monograph affording many insights into Italian politics.

M. B. Becker, *Florence in Transition*, 2 vols. (Johns Hopkins, 1968). Study of the fourteenth century, superseding all previous scholarship.

F. Schevill, *Medieval and Renaissance Florence*, 2 vols. (*Torchbooks) and *The Medici* (*Torchbooks). Clear and useful.

C. M. Ady, *Lorenzo de' Medici and Renaissance Italy* (*Collier). A brief, popular account.

DeL. Jensen, ed., *Machiavelli—Cynic, Patriot, or Political Scientist?* (*Heath). Introduction to the many conflicting interpretations of the author of *The Prince*.

J. R. Hale, *Machiavelli and Renaissance Italy* (*Torchbooks). Good short biography.

INTERPRETATIONS OF THE RENAISSANCE

K. H. Dannenfeldt, ed., *Renaissance— Medieval or Modern?* (*Heath). A good sampler.

G. C. Sellery, *The Renaissance: Its Nature and Origins* (*Wisconsin). Clear and helpful survey.

W. K. Ferguson, *The Renaissance in Historical Thought: Five Centuries of Interpretation* (Houghton, 1948). Stimulating.

J. Burckhardt, *The Civilization of the Renaissance in Italy*, 2 vols. (*Torchbooks). The classic defense of the Renaissance as unique and revolutionary.

F. Chabod, *Machiavelli and the Renaissance* (*Torchbooks). With a fruitful chapter, "The Concept of the Renaissance."

L. Olschki, *The Genius of Italy* (Cornell, 1954). Solid essays on many aspects of the Renaissance.

LITERATURE AND LEARNING

P. O. Kristeller, *Renaissance Thought*, 2 vols. (*Torchbooks). Valuable study, emphasizing its diversity.

H. O. Taylor, *The Humanism of Italy*

(*Collier). Excerpted from the author's highly regarded *Thought and Expression in the Sixteenth Century.*

R. R. Bolgar, *The Classical Heritage and Its Beneficiaries from the Carolingian Age to the End of the Renaissance* (*Torchbooks). The last third of this scholarly study treats the Renaissance.

G. Highet, *The Classical Tradition: Greek and Roman Influences on Western Literature* (*Galaxy). A lively survey.

J. Huizinga, *Erasmus and the Age of the Reformation* (*Torchbooks). Excellent.

A. Hyma, *The Christian Renaissance* (Shoe String, 1965). Study of an aspect of the era often neglected.

Marie Boas, *The Scientific Renaissance, 1450–1630* (*Torchbooks). Helpful account.

H. Butterfield, *The Origins of Modern Science, 1300–1800* (*Free Press). Controversial study, minimizing the scientific contribution of the Renaissance.

G. Sarton, *Six Wings: Men of Science in the Renaissance* (*Meridian). Appreciations by a famous historian of science.

A. C. Crombie, *Medieval and Early Modern Science,* Vol. II (*Anchor). A good survey.

L. Thorndike, *Science and Thought in the Fifteenth Century* (Columbia, 1929). By a specialist on medieval science.

THE ARTS

G. Vasari, *Lives of the Artists* (*several editions). Famous biographies of Italian painters, sculptors, and architects.

H. Wölfflin, *The Art of the Italian Ren-*aissance: A Handbook for Students and Travellers* (*Schocken). By a ranking expert of an earlier day.

B. Berenson, *The Italian Painters of the Renaissance* (*Meridian). Essays by a famous collector and enthusiast.

F. Antal, *Florentine Painting and Its Social Background* (Kegan Paul, 1948). An attempt to relate art to economic and social currents.

K. M. Clark, *Leonardo da Vinci* (*Penguin).

J. S. Ackerman, *The Architecture of Michelangelo* (*Penguin). Brilliant scholarly study, beautifully illustrated and written to appeal to the layman.

O. Benesch, *The Art of the Renaissance in Northern Europe* (Harvard, 1945). Good work on the artists in their time.

E. Panofsky, *Studies in Iconology: Humanistic Themes in the Art of the Renaissance* (*Torchbooks), and *The Life and Art of Albrecht Dürer* (Princeton, 1955). By a distinguished and stimulating scholar.

R. Wittkower, *Architectural Principles in the Age of Humanism* 3rd ed. (A. Tiranti, 1962). A study of major importance.

E. J. Dent, *Music of the Renaissance in Italy* (British Academy, 1935). By a great authority.

SOURCES

J. Froissart, *Chronicles of England, France, and Spain* (*Dutton). A great narrative source of late medieval history.

The History of Comines, trans. T. Danett, (D. Nutt, 1897). Account of Louis XI and Charles the Bold by a contemporary of both.

Machiavelli, *The Prince* and *The Discourses* (*Modern Library).

J. B. Ross and M. M. McLaughlin, eds., *The Portable Renaissance Reader* (*Viking). A wide-ranging anthology.

W. L. Gundesheimer, ed., *The Italian Renaissance* (*Spectrum). Selections from eleven representative writers.

Erasmus, *The Praise of Folly* (*Ann Arbor).

P. Taylor, ed., *The Notebooks of Leonardo da Vinci: A New Selection* (*Mentor).

A. H. Popham, ed., *The Drawings of Leonardo da Vinci* (*Harvest).

FICTION

G. B. Shaw, *St. Joan* (*Penguin). Perhaps more successful as drama than as history.

Josephine Tey, *The Daughter of Time* (*Dell). Fascinating effort to rehabilitate Richard III of England; by a writer of detective stories.

D. Merezhkovsky, *The Romance of Leonardo da Vinci* (*Signet). The best novel on the Renaissance, romanticized but actually based on Leonardo's notebooks.

V. Hugo, *Notre Dame de Paris* (*several editions), and W. Scott, *Quentin Durward* (*Signet). Celebrated Romantic novels set in the France of Louis XI.

N. Balchin, *The Borgia Testament* (Houghton, 1949). Autobiography as Cesare might have written it.

seven

Transition to a New World: Religious Upheaval,

Imperial Expansion, Dynastic Conflict

I

The Protestant and Catholic Reformations

Luther

Though all aspects of the past may arouse our emotions to some extent, most of us can remain relatively detached until we come to the issues that engage us in this chapter. Here even the terms in common use betray involvement: the Protestant refers to the Protestant *Reformation,* the Catholic to the Protestant *Revolt.* Even the secularist or skeptic can hardly claim to be impartial, for he inevitably feels that Protestantism, if only because it did shatter the unity and conformity of medieval Catholicism, prepared the way for men like him to exist. Old exaggerations, old slanders from the partisan struggle of the times are still bandied about: that Luther led a revolt against the Church so that he, a monk, could marry; that the Catholic clergy sold salvation; that Henry VIII broke with the pope so that he might marry.

LUTHER'S REVOLT   On October 31, 1517, Martin Luther (1483–1546) nailed his Ninety-five Theses to the door of the court church at Wittenberg in Saxony. The action touched off what proved to be a major social, economic, and intellectual revolution. Neither Luther nor other later major leaders like Calvin intended such a revolution. They conceived of themselves not as starting *new* churches but as going back to the true *old* church as reformers. Again and again, as we know, the Catholic church had faced reform movements like the Cluniac, the Cistercian, the Franciscan, and had absorbed them. In the fourteenth and fifteenth centuries Wycliffe and Hus had almost created separate, or schismatic, churches. The Conciliar movement, in the early fifteenth century, had challenged papal authority, though it had failed to subordinate the pope to the views of a general council.

Luther's action, however, led to the organization of a separate church outside the Catholic communion. Within a generation after 1517, dozens of sects or denominations in addition to the Lutheran came into existence: Anglican, Calvinist, Anabaptist, and many others. We take this multiplicity so much for granted today that it is worth emphasizing how great a departure it was in the sixteenth century, what a real revolution from medieval religious unity.

Son of a German peasant who became a miner and eventually a prosperous investor in mining enterprises, Luther studied law in his youth; then in 1505, at the age of twenty-two, he had a shattering experience. Caught in a severe thunderstorm and greatly frightened, he prayed to Saint Anne for help, and pledged himself to become a monk. Once in the monastery, however, he underwent a major personal crisis: he was sure he was a lost soul without hope of salvation. Though he submitted to the monastic discipline of his order and made a pilgrimage to Rome in 1510, none of the good works (i.e., deeds) he did could free him from the gnawing fear that he could not attain God's grace, and that he must therefore be destined for hell.

Modern psychoanalytic scholars such as Erik Erikson have recognized in Luther's agony a clinical case of what they call "identity crisis." It was only when his confessor told him to study the Bible that Luther, from his readings in the Epistles of Saint Paul and in Saint Augustine, found an answer to his anxiety: he must have faith in God, faith in the possibility of his own salvation. The Roman church had of course always taught this. What was new about Luther was his emphasis on *faith alone, to the exclusion of works.* The promise that faith alone might mean salvation had a particular attraction in an age of doubt and gloom, rather like the era when men had first turned to Christianity.

Luther then began to question practices that in his view were abuses tending to corrupt or weaken faith. He cast his questions in the form of the Ninety-five Theses, written in Latin and in the manner of the medieval Scholastics as a challenge to debate. The specific abuse that he attacked he called the "sale" of indulgences, particularly the activities of Tetzel, a Dominican who, with papal authorization, was conducting a "drive" for contributions to rebuild St. Peter's in Rome.

The theory of indulgences did *not* concern forgiveness for sins: only God could forgive a sin; no indulgence could assure such forgiveness. But repentant sinners had to do penance on earth and suffer punishment after death in purgatory, in order to prepare for heaven. The theory of indulgences *did* concern remission of such punishment. The Church claimed that Christ, the Virgin, and the Saints had performed so many good works that the surplus constituted a Treasury of Merit. A priest could secure for a layman a draft, as it were, on this heavenly treasury. This was an indulgence and could remit penance on earth and part or all of the punishment in purgatory. Such an indulgence was "granted" by the priest; any monetary contribution thereupon made by the recipient was a freewill offering. But Luther said that Tetzel was selling indulgences.

To the man in the street it seemed as though a sinner could obtain *not only* remission of punishment *but also* forgiveness of sin, if only he secured enough indulgences, and that this depended on his money gifts to Tetzel. In the Ninety-five Theses, Luther objected vehemently both to Tetzel's perversion of indulgences and to the whole doctrine behind them. He thus minimized the importance of good works at a moment when many ordinary believers were

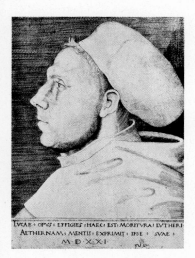

Martin Luther: engraving by Lucas Cranach the Elder.

trying to increase their stock of such works by drawing on the Treasury of Merit. Christian theory usually insists on the need for *both* faith and good works. Luther's emphasis on faith drove his papal opponents into a corresponding extreme emphasis on works, and this in turn drove him, in moments of excitement, to deny the uses of works and to insist on faith alone. Since "works" include all earthly ecclesiastical organization and the priestly way of doing things, Luther before long was denying that priests are necessary. He had enunciated the doctrine of the priesthood of all believers; in popular terms, "every man his own priest."

Pope Leo X (1513–1521), the son of Lorenzo de' Medici but lacking much of the family brains and decisiveness, was naturally alarmed by the financial implications of Luther's actions as well as by the critical importance of the issues that they raised. In 1518, Luther defied a papal emissary, and refused to recant some of his propositions on indulgences. In 1519, at Leipzig, in debate with the learned theologian John Eck, who accused him of disobeying the authority of the popes and church councils, Luther said that popes and councils were not necessarily authoritative. He said he accepted certain views of Hus that the Council of Constance had declared heretical. In 1520, in his *Appeal to the Christian Nobility of the German Nation,* Luther called the term "spiritual estate," as used to describe the clergy, a "lie," and declared that "all Christians are truly of the spiritual estate, and there is no difference among them save of office."

When Leo X issued a bull condemning Luther's teaching, Luther burnt it. In 1520 he was excommunicated, and the emperor Charles V and the imperial diet solemnly declared him an outlaw at Worms. Once again he was asked whether he would recant. His reply contained his most famous words:

Your Imperial Majesty and Your Lordships demand a simple answer. Here it is, plain and unvarnished. Unless I am convicted of error by the testimony of Scripture or (since I put not trust in the unsupported authority of Pope or of councils, since it is plain that they have often erred and often contradicted themselves) by manifest reasoning I stand convicted by the Scriptures to which I have appealed, and my conscience is taken captive by God's word, I cannot and will not recant anything, for to act against our conscience is neither safe for us, nor open to us.

Hier stehe ich. Ich kann nicht anders. Gott helff mir. Amen. [On this I take my stand. I can do no other. God help me. Amen.]*

The empire and the papacy took their drastic actions in vain, for Luther was already gathering a substantial following and becoming a national hero. He had the protection of the ruler of his own German state, the elector Frederick the Wise of Saxony, and was soon to secure the backing of other princes. In the next few years he translated the Bible into vigorous and effective German, and remodeled the church in Saxony according to his own views. His revolt was a success.

THE REASONS FOR LUTHER'S SUCCESS   More than theology was at issue in Luther's revolt. The Catholic church that Luther attacked was, as many Catholic historians grant, at the time in one of its more worldly periods. Especially in its center at Rome, it had come under the influence of the new wealth of the Renaissance and the new fashions of good living. The papacy, triumphant over the councils, had been drawn into Italian politics, and the Rome Luther visited in his younger days was a shocking spectacle of intrigue, display, and corrup-

* *Documents of the Christian Church,* ed. H. Bettenson (New York, 1947), p. 285.

Title page of Luther's "Appeal to the Christian Nobility of the German Nation."

tion. Some part of Luther's success lay in the fact that he was attacking practices abhorrent to decent men, and reasserting the primacy of the spirit over materialism.

There was a second great reason for his success: in the name of good Germans he was attacking the practices of Italians and Italianate Germans. In the eyes of Luther and his followers, Tetzel was not only performing theologically and morally outrageous acts; he was raising money to enrich Italy:

For Rome is the greatest thief and robber that had ever appeared on earth, or ever will. . . . Poor Germans that we are—we have been deceived! We were born to be masters, and we have been compelled to bow the head beneath the yoke of our tyrants. . . . It is time the glorious Teutonic people should cease to be the puppet of the Roman pontiff.*

What Luther started, a good many German princes soon took out of his hands. They stood to gain, not only by cutting off the flow of German money to Italy, but by confiscating Catholic property, especially monastic property, which was not needed for the Lutheran church. Moreover, Luther gave them a new weapon in their eternal struggle against their feudal overlord, the emperor. The princes were also moved by Luther's German patriotism. One of them at least, Philip of Hesse, who married a second wife without divorcing his first, found Luther elastic enough not to condemn his bigamy.

Luther's personal energy, courage, and intelligence were of major importance. He wrote the pamphlets that did for this revolution what Tom Paine and the Declaration of Independence did for the American. He wrote his *Appeal to the Christian Nobility of the German Nation* in the vernacular German, not the academic Latin, so that it became a bestseller. Luther's translation made the Bible a part of German life. Its language became one of the bases of modern literary German. The Lord's Prayer in his sonorous German, and his great hymns, notably *A Mighty Fortress is Our God,* enabled the individual German to feel that Christian observance belonged to him personally. Luther's marriage to a former nun and his raising of a large family dramatized the break with Rome. And behind all this was his passionate conviction that he was doing what he had to do: *"Ich kann nicht anders."*

The forces that opposed Luther were relatively weak. Clerical opposition centered in the top levels of the Catholic bureaucracy: Pope Leo X was only its willing instrument. Many moderate Catholics were anxious to compromise and avert a schism. Erasmus, for example, who remained a Catholic, fully recognized how much the papacy was hated in Germany, acknowledged the need for reform, and said of Luther "God has given us a radical physician." Had there been at the head of the Catholic church a pope willing to reform and to make concessions not harmful to the Church as God's chosen instrument on earth, even Luther might perhaps have been reconciled. Yet, as in all the great modern revolutions, the moderates—gifted, numerous, and active though they were—could not hold up against the extremists. Once Leo X had excommunicated Luther in 1520, the way to compromise was probably blocked, for Luther's associates could have been won away from him only by concessions too great for a Catholic hierarchy to make.

Politically, the Catholic opposition in these critical years found its leader in the young emperor Charles V (reigned 1519-1556). Grandson on his father's side of the emperor Maximilian and Mary, daughter of Charles the Bold of Burgundy, and on his mother's side of Ferdinand and Isabella, Charles of

* Ibid., pp. 278-279.

Hapsburg was the fruit of a series of marriages that gave rise to the Latin epigram "Let others wage wars; thou, happy Austria, marry." * Together with the Hapsburgs' lands in Austria and elsewhere and their claim to the title of emperor, Charles V inherited the Low Countries, Spain and the Spanish lands overseas, and parts of Italy. This was geographically the nearest thing to a European superstate since Charlemagne, and Charles V wanted to make it a political reality. The activities of Luther's princely German supporters threatened his hold over Germany; moreover, Charles, though by no means a mere papal instrument, was a devout Catholic. He decided to fight, and he had to spend the rest of his reign fighting.

WAR AND REBELLION IN THE 1520's   Charles V entrusted the government of the Germans to his younger brother Ferdinand, who formed alliances with Bavaria and other Catholic German states to oppose the Lutheran states. Thus began a long series of combinations, the fruits of which were the religious wars of the next few generations, and the enduring territorial division of Germany into, roughly, a Protestant north and east and a Catholic south and west. But the imperial Hapsburg power also had to fight against the Ottoman Turks and the French, and so could not steadily concentrate on defeating the Lutherans in Germany.

In Germany, below the level of the princes, the knights espoused Luther's cause. Some of them held castles and small estates direct from the emperor and were in theory just as "independent" as a greater prince. Others were vassals of some greater lord. Some were younger sons, who were feeling the decline of their status caused by changing economic and social conditions (see Chapter 6). Under the leadership of Ulrich von Hutten and Franz von Sickingen, they rose in 1522, in what is called the Knights' War. Troops of the western German archbishoprics put them down, but their struggle added to the disorder of the period.

Worse still was the Peasants' Rebellion of 1524–1525, not unlike the French Jacquerie of 1358 or the English Peasants' Revolt of 1381: like them directed against the remaining burdens of the manorial system, like them without competent military commanders, and like them ruthlessly suppressed. It centered, not in the eastern German regions where serfdom had been completely enforced, but in the southwest, where the peasants had begun to emancipate themselves and wanted to finish the process. Much as Wycliffe and the Lollards had influenced the English peasants, Luther's preaching stirred those in Germany. More than their English counterparts of the fourteenth century, the German peasants had educated leaders with a revolutionary program of their own which they embodied in the "Twelve Articles." Couched in biblical language, the articles seem moderate enough today: each parish should choose its own priest; tithes and taxes should be lowered; the peasants should have the right to take game and firewood from the forests; and so on.

Horrified at the peasants' interpretation of the Bible that he had translated into German for them, Luther denounced the peasant rebels in unbridled terms as "murderous thieving hordes." The princes, who of course agreed with him, joined with Lutheran-minded cities in the Schmalkaldic League, founded in 1531, and pursued the war against Charles V. Though the emperor in 1547 defeated the League using Spanish troops, he was unable to take

Woodcut from a Lutheran attack against the Peasants' Rebellion, 1525.

* *Bella gerant alii, tu, felix Austria, nube!*, which is a perfectly good hexameter, a line of verse in the meter of Vergil's *Aeneid*.

advantage of his victory because it would have made him too powerful to suit even his own fellow Catholics, the pope and the Catholic German princes, and would, as we shall see, have upset the European balance of power. So by 1555, as his reign drew to an end, Charles V was forced into the compromise Peace of Augsburg on the religious issue, which left the Lutherans in power in the German states where there was a Lutheran prince (see below, p. 326).

Luther's own respect for established political authority helps account for the political success of the Lutheran movement. He once said, "The princes of the world are gods, the common people are Satan." This conservatism is quite consistent with Luther's fundamental spiritual position. If the visible external world is subordinate to the invisible spiritual world, the best one can hope for here on earth is that good order be maintained. Kings, princes, authority, custom, law: all existing institutions are preferable to discussion and dissension.

The princes of northern Germany and the Scandinavian kingdoms reciprocated. They superintended and hastened the process of converting the willing to Lutheranism and evicting the unwilling. By the mid-sixteenth century Lutheranism had become the state religion of these regions, and, as such, it was often the docile instrument of political rulers.

In organizing his own church, Luther showed the same conservatism. After all, the logical extreme of the priesthood of all believers is no church at all, or as many churches as there are individual human beings; in Saxony, reformers influenced by Luther tried out these anarchical concepts before Luther himself and the moderates intervened. Luther's new church often simply took over the existing church buildings. It did have priests; but they were free to marry, a sign that they had no more sacramental powers than other men. The Lutherans retained two of the sacraments: baptism and the Eucharist, both specifically mentioned in the Bible, but deprived them of their miraculous quality. Veneration of saints and relics, fasts, pilgrimages, monastic orders all vanished. Yet the forms of worship retained much that had been traditional. To Luther this new church was not merely an alternative to the Church of Rome, it was the *one true Church,* a return to early Christianity before Rome had corrupted it.

Zwingli

Only a year after Luther nailed his theses to the door at Wittenberg, a Swiss priest named Ulrich Zwingli (1484–1531), a humanist trained in the tradition of Erasmus, launched a quieter reform in Zurich. It produced no single organized church, but extended and deepened some of the fundamental theological and moral concepts of Protestantism. Like Luther, Zwingli objected to the idea that priests had miraculous powers not possessed by laymen. But he felt that the social conscience of enlightened people led by good pastors would achieve a common discipline that would promote righteous living. Like Luther, Zwingli opposed priestly celibacy, fasts, monasticism, confession, and indulgences. He thought the appeal to saints and the use of incense, candles, and images were "superstition." He began the process of making the church building an almost undecorated hall, of making the service a sermon and responsive reading, and of abolishing the Catholic liturgy.

Zwingli's chief point of difference with Luther was sacramental. The Catholics believed in transubstantiation: that the bread and wine of the communion miraculously became in *substance* the body and blood of Christ, although their chemical makeup—their accidents—remained unchanged. Luther denied the miracle of the Mass, and believed in consubstantiation: that the body and blood were somehow *present* in the bread and wine. Zwingli believed

Zurich at the time of Zwingli: panel painting by Hans Leu the Elder.

what has become the usual Protestant doctrine: that the bread and wine merely *symbolized* the body and blood.

Zwingli won over the government of Zurich and most of its citizens; and many of the other German-speaking towns of Switzerland became Protestant. But the Catholic cantons went to war against the Protestants, and Zwingli was killed in 1531. Though the individual Swiss cantons were allowed to choose their form of worship thereafter, Protestant leadership had suffered a severe blow.

Calvin

It recovered a decade later, when John Calvin (1509–1564) took power in Geneva. French-born and Paris-educated, Calvin was a classicist and lawyer, converted from Catholicism by his reading of Erasmus and Luther. He took refuge in the Swiss town of Basel, and there published his *Institutes of the Christian Religion* (1536), a complete summary of his theological and moral views and a work of great influence in spreading Protestant thought. Both Calvin and Luther rejected good works as a way to salvation. But, where Luther emphasized the view that a man could save himself by faith, Calvin emphasized the awe-inspiring majesty of God and the littleness of man.

In fact, Calvin said, man cannot save himself by faith, or by anything else, since God alone can save. God from the beginning predetermined—predestined—who among men would be saved and who eternally damned. He had chosen very few, his "elect," for salvation; no man could attain it by his own merit. Nor was there any way for a man to know certainly whether he was among the elect. Of course, he *could* be sure, if he led a life contrary to Christian morality, that he was damned. But no matter how moral a life he led he could never be sure that he was saved; he just *might* possibly be among the elect. This was the only crumb of comfort Calvin's system held out.

CALVINIST PRACTICE   Stern logic, rigorous morality, an Old Testament conception of God, and emphasis on strict observance of commandments characterized Calvinist views and Calvinist behavior. The French-speaking city of Geneva asked Calvin in 1541 to help in a rebellion against its Catholic bishop and the count of Savoy. From 1541 until his death twenty-three years later, Calvin

Two views of John Calvin. Left: by an unknown painter, 1534. Right: caricature by Giuseppe Arcimboldo, 1566.

was the supreme ruler of the city. Geneva became a theocracy, literally a government by God, in practice a system in which the church governed all aspects of the citizen's life. Protestant refugees from other parts of Europe came to learn from Calvin. John Knox (1505–1572) took the system back to Scotland; others took Calvinism to Holland, to France, to England (whence it crossed the Atlantic to Massachusetts), and to Hungary and Poland.

In the Low Countries, Calvinism became in the second half of the sixteenth century the symbol of Dutch nationalism against the Spanish rule of Charles V's heir, Philip II (see p. 321). In France, Calvinist ideas led to the foundation of churches called Huguenot (perhaps from the German word *Eidgenosse,* "covenanted"), chiefly in the old southwestern strongholds of the Albigensian heresy (see Chapter 4). Here, as elsewhere in Europe, the Protestants would have to fight not for toleration but for supremacy. Few men of the time could conceive of subjects of the same ruler peacefully practicing different religions.

Where the Calvinists controlled an area, they censored, interfered, and punished; they were petty tyrants, denying the individual much of his privacy, pleasure, and individualism. They were sure they were God's agents, doing God's work. These firm believers in the inability of human efforts to change anything were the most ardent workers for change in human behavior. The world to them was a serious place, and they were sure that music, dancing, gambling, fine clothes, drinking, and the theater were to Satan's liking. Sexual intercourse, they said, had as its sole purpose the perpetuation of the race, not the pleasure of the participants. This philosophy of life is called Puritanism. Within each man the struggle raged between the temptations of the world and his "Puritan conscience"; in his dealings with others, the Puritan tried not only to coerce but also to convert. We shall encounter Puritanism again in sixteenth- and seventeenth-century England.

The English Reformation

HENRY VIII   In England, the signal for religious overturn was very different from Luther's Ninety-five Theses. Henry VIII (reigned 1509–1547), the second Tudor king, badly wanted a male heir, and his wife, Catherine of Aragon, aunt of the emperor Charles V, had not produced one. His legal case for separation was thin: Catherine had been married first to his deceased brother, Arthur, and Henry now "discovered" after twenty years of marriage that canon law

RELIGIOUS UPHEAVAL, IMPERIAL
EXPANSION, DYNASTIC CONFLICT

forbade marriage with a deceased brother's widow. Henry, who had published an attack on Lutheran ideas, for which the pope had declared him Defender of the Faith, tried hard to obtain an annulment from the pope. But the pope was unwilling to risk offending Charles V, whose troops were in control of Rome at the time (1527). In 1533, the obliging archbishop of Canterbury, Thomas Cranmer, pronounced the marriage annulled, and Henry married Anne Boleyn. The pope excommunicated Henry and declared the annulment invalid. Henry broke relations with the papacy and, by the Act of Supremacy (1534), became "supreme head" of the Church of England.

In these drastic actions, Henry had the support of Parliament, which voted the Act of Supremacy. This is the clearest proof that there was more than the king's private life involved. Had it not been for the substantial body of anti-papal opinion among Englishmen, Henry could not have acted as he did. In fact, antipapal and more generalized anticlerical sentiment was nothing new in England. The ideas of Luther and other Protestants had won the sympathies of a good many Englishmen, though many others, including Thomas More (1478–1535), author of *Utopia,* favored reform only within the Church. (More lost his head for opposing the Act of Supremacy.)

One target of the English anti-Catholics was the monasteries, many of which were wealthy and corrupt. By closing them and confiscating their property, Henry VIII won the favor of the nobles and gentry to whom—at a price— he passed on the loot. The confiscation and redistribution of monastic properties virtually amounted to a social and economic revolution, binding the recipients more closely to their benefactor, the king, and greatly increasing their wealth.

Yet all through, Henry considered himself a Catholic, not a Protestant. In his eyes and in those of some of its communicants today, the Church of England remained a Catholic body. Except for the abolition of monasteries and the break with Rome, Henry was determined to make no change. In this way he stimulated two kinds of opposition: from Catholics like More who felt that Henry had gone much too far, and from militant Protestants who felt that Henry had not gone nearly far enough, and who wanted to introduce clerical marriage and the use of English in the ritual, and to abolish auricular confession (i.e., confession spoken into the ear of a priest in private) and the invocation of saints. Partly because so many of its members were now complacent with their new riches, Parliament did what Henry wanted. In 1539 it passed the Six Articles, reaffirming clerical celibacy, confession, and four other important Catholic points of doctrine and ritual, and making their denial heresy. But by this definition there were far too many heretics to be rooted out, and England became the scene of wide religious experiment and variation.

RELIGION AND THE LATER TUDORS When the frail young Edward VI (reigned 1547–1553) succeeded his father Henry VIII, the government for a time turned more strongly Protestant. The Six Articles were repealed in 1547, and in 1549 Parliament passed an act requiring uniformity of church services, and introduced an official prayer book. Cranmer, still archbishop of Canterbury and a convinced Protestant (he had married), published the Forty-two Articles of Religion in 1551. But when Edward VI died, the crown passed to his half-sister, the Catholic Mary Tudor (reigned 1553–1558), daughter of Henry VIII by Catherine of Aragon. A plot to put her cousin, the Protestant Lady Jane Grey, on the throne failed, and Mary as queen tried to restore Catholicism.

When she announced her intention of marrying the very Catholic Prince Philip of Spain, who was, however, to be without power in England, a rebel-

Catherine of Aragon (above) and Anne Boleyn.

RELIGIOUS UPHEAVAL, IMPERIAL EXPANSION, DYNASTIC CONFLICT

lion broke out. Mary suppressed it. Lady Jane Grey was executed, and Mary married Philip. A Catholic became archbishop of Canterbury, and Cranmer was burned at the stake. Perhaps three hundred in all lost their lives in Mary's persecutions, which won her the celebrated sobriquet of "Bloody Mary."

When she died in 1558, her half-sister Elizabeth, daughter of Henry VIII by Anne Boleyn, succeeded her as queen (reigned 1558–1603). Elizabeth was a Protestant, and soon after her accession all of Mary's Catholic legislation was repealed and all of Henry VIII's laws regarding the Church were reenacted. In 1563 Parliament adopted the Thirty-nine Articles, modified from Cranmer's Forty-two of 1551. The Articles rejected clerical celibacy, auricular confession, papal supremacy, and the use of Latin. They required that the laity receive communion in both wine and bread, whereas the Catholic church gave only the bread. Though they rejected Catholic doctrine on the Eucharist, they also rejected Zwinglian symbolism: the members of the Anglican church would receive the Eucharist as the body and blood of Christ. The Articles avoided the Lutheran doctrines of justification by faith and the priesthood of all believers.

Ever since, the Thirty-nine Articles of 1563 and the Elizabethan prayer book have remained the essential documents of the Anglican faith. At the time, however, Elizabeth was faced by Catholic opposition, both within England and abroad, where Spaniards and Scots, in particular, were hostile. Even more serious was the opposition of Protestants who wanted to purify the Church of England of what they considered papist survivals. Some of these Puritans were moderates, who were willing to retain bishops if the ritual were simplified. Some were Presbyterians, who accepted the full Calvinist theology and wanted to abolish bishops and substitute synods of elders (presbyters) as the government of the church. Some were radicals—called Brownists after their leader Robert Browne—who wanted each congregation to be an independent body, and who anticipated the later Congregationalists and Independents. Elizabeth tolerated all but Catholics at one extreme and Brownists at the other.

Indeed, the Church of England has ever since reflected the wide range of religious sentiment in the country. It has always had "High Church" communicants who think of themselves as Catholics, and "Low Church" communicants who are far more Protestant in outlook, as well as those of intermediate opinion. It retains a modified form of the Catholic hierarchy, with archbishops and bishops, though of course it does not recognize papal authority, and its clergy may marry. Moderation—of ritual, hierarchy, discipline—has been its outstanding characteristic. But it has also had many people who emphasize earnest evangelical piety, social service, plain living, and high thinking: Puritans who have not left the church.

The Radical Left: Anabaptists and Unitarians

Among those touched by Luther's teachings in Germany were some who took quite literally his doctrine of justification by faith, and fell into the anarchy which he avoided. Since each man was to find in his own conscience God's universal law, all written law was to be rejected: these people were *Antinomian* (from the Greek "against law"). They did not believe in class distinctions or in the customary forms of private property. Some of them practiced polygamy: if they took several wives, it was clear that God wanted them to, since they wanted to. In 1534–1535 a group of these radicals under the leadership of a Dutch tailor, John of Leiden, took control of the city of Münster in western Germany, where John was crowned as "King David" and kept a kind of harem in attendance. They were put down by force, and John was killed.

These radicals believed that the Catholic sacrament of baptism for infants was invalid, since no infant could "understand" the significance of the act. By "understanding" they did not mean an intellectual process but emotional or instinctive comprehension and participation. Therefore they baptized again anybody who joined them: as an adult, he was now for the first time able to "understand" what he was doing, and this kind of baptism alone had validity. Thus arose the name *Anabaptists* (from the Greek for "baptizing again"); later generations were not baptized until they came of age, and so the prefix *ana-* was dropped. Most of the sixteenth-century Anabaptists were by no means so wild or fanatical as the followers of John of Leiden. They established communities and lived as they thought the early Christians had lived—working, sharing, and praying together.

The wide divergence of beliefs and practices among the sixteenth-century groups loosely called Anabaptist arose in part because many very earnest and ignorant people were for the first time reading the Bible for individual guidance, and—especially in the apocalyptic books of the Old Testament and in the Book of Revelation—were finding just about anything they were looking for. Many Anabaptist groups broke sharply with the old forms of worship; their congregations no longer remained quiet during the services, but shouted or danced. All sang hymns with great fervor. The sermon became very important, and was often highly charged emotionally with hopes of heaven and fears of hell. Some of the sects expected the Second Coming of Christ immediately. Some shared among themselves what little property they had, and so were communists of a sort.

Distrusting the state, refusing to take oaths on grounds of conscience, coming mostly from the poorest classes, occasionally going to such radical extremes as those at Münster, the Anabaptists frightened the conventional and the comfortable in society. They became the objects of vigorous persecution, which made no distinction between the socially dangerous and the brave, quiet, humble Christians among them. Their high sense of community, their asceticism, their sober, industrious behavior have outlived the excesses of the more eccentric, and can be seen today among Baptists, Quakers, Mennonites, Moravians, and a good many other sects.

Close to the Anabaptists, too, was one other strain of Protestantism: Unitarianism, the denial of the Trinity and of the full divinity of Christ. Its most famous advocate, the Spanish mystic Michael Servetus (1511–1553), stressed the humanity of Christ without depriving him of his divine attributes altogether. He hoped thereby to make it easier for individual human beings to feel a sense of mystic identification with Christ, and thus achieve salvation. Both Catholics and Protestants found these views alarming. Calvin had Servetus burnt at the stake in Geneva in 1553 for heresy. Another Unitarian, however, the Italian Socinus (Sozzini, 1539–1604), preached successfully among Poles and Hungarians. Present-day Unitarians in England and the United States are not the direct heirs of the mystic tradition of Servetus: imbued instead with the rationalism of the eighteenth-century Enlightenment, they believe that Christ was simply a particularly inspired human being, but not divine.

Protestant Attributes

From Henry VIII (who almost certainly never thought of himself as a Protestant) through Luther, Zwingli, and Calvin to John of Leiden and Servetus is a broad spectrum indeed. What did these Protestants have in common? All repudiated the claim of the Roman Catholic church to be supreme. Each was convinced that his own church was the true successor of Christ and the Apostles. Even the Antinomians, who believed that each man carried the truth in his own bosom, went on to say that if one could sweep away the obstacles to truth, each man would find the *same* truth in his own bosom. Some

Protestants were prepared to educate humanity in the correctness of their own beliefs, and so convert it; others could not wait: so Calvin, having been persecuted himself, persecuted Servetus. Religious tolerance and the peaceful coexistence of many churches—concepts that we today take for granted—were rare indeed in the sixteenth and seventeenth centuries.

All Protestants reduced the ritual and other external manifestations of belief. The seven sacraments of the Catholic church were diminished, often to only two, baptism and the Eucharist; the various sects differed widely in their views on the meaning of the sacraments. "Papist" practices like the veneration of saints, the saying of rosaries, and the making of pilgrimages disappeared among all Protestants. The more radical banished music and painting, and greatly simplified church architecture and decoration. All Protestants appealed from an established order to a "higher law," so echoing Luther's appeal from works to faith. All had at least a tinge of individualism, which they bequeathed to the modern world.

Protestantism and Progress

Friends of Protestantism often maintain that there was also something fundamentally "modern" and "progressive" about the Reformation that set it off from the "medieval" and "stagnant" centuries that preceded it. They contrast the predominantly Protestant world of the United States and Britain and the lands such as Canada largely settled by Englishmen, which enjoy economic prosperity, democratic constitutional government, progress in the sciences, with Catholic nations, which they regard as poorer, less stable, less advanced. And where they find a Catholic nation that has some Protestant qualities, such as France, they attribute this to the presence of a strong anticlerical tradition. Within the Protestant countries themselves men have often believed that they owe their prosperity and success to their Protestantism.

Yet the original sixteenth-century Protestants shared with Catholics most of the basic Christian concepts. Neither Catholic nor Protestant believed that life on earth was improving or should improve. They were not rationalists: Luther threw his ink bottle at the devil, Calvinists killed witches. They were just as intolerant as the Catholics and, like them, believed in rank and status. Lutheranism and Anglicanism were hierarchical and conservative; Calvinism was deeply undemocratic in its view of the small number of the elect, and authoritarian in its theocracy. Only the radicals in the sixteenth century, with their appeal to the Bible, voiced demands for political and social equality, and many of them were less concerned with this world than with the next.

What Protestantism did, however, was to challenge authority and start all sorts of men, many of them in humble circumstances, thinking about fundamental problems. And Protestant moral ideas fitted in with the strengthening of a commercial middle class. Max Weber, a twentieth-century German sociologist, has traced the connection between Protestant ethics and the "spirit of capital," the spirit that animated the middle classes who were to lay the foundations of modern Western democracy. Capital accumulation of course means that profits are not spent but "plowed back" into the business. If plowing back reduces the costs of production, still more capital accumulates. In its simplest terms this means hard work and no play all along the line, especially at the top.

Much evidence can be advanced to support Weber's thesis. The Calvinists in particular preached that the devil lies in wait for idle hands, and that work keeps a man from temptation to run after women, or play silly games, or drink, or do many other things unpleasing to God; moreover, work in itself is a kind of pleasing tribute to the Lord. Luther, too, glorified work, and affirmed the dignity of the vocation a man is called to, however humble. All this is quite contrary to the feudal, chivalric contempt for the work of the fields and the countinghouse. The Calvinists in particular also discouraged the kind of consumption that would interfere with capital accumulation. They frowned upon the fine arts, the theater, expensive clothing, and beautiful and "useless" objects in general.

The Calvinist countries had a maximum number of working days in the year; they kept the Sabbath most rigorously, but they eliminated the numerous religious holidays, sometimes even Christmas. The Scots, the Dutch, the Swiss, the New England Yankees—all of them with a strong Calvinist background—have long had a popular reputation for thrift, diligence, and driving a hard bargain. Many Protestant theologians rejected the Catholic view that all interest was usury, and the medieval idea of a "just price" (see p. 158), in favor of something much closer to our modern notions of free competition in the market, where God would certainly take care of his own.

Finally, the Calvinist focus on the other world as the supreme goal, but one that could never be *certain* for any individual, helped shield the newly rich Calvinist from the temptation to squander his money and imitate a free-spending, loose-living aristocrat: if he did this, he could be pretty sure he was not of the elect. So the faith itself tended to give cohesion to the middle class. Family fortunes founded on hard work and maintained by reinvestment tended to hold together for several generations.

Not all the evidence, however, supports Weber's thesis. Banking, for example, began before the time of Luther in Catholic countries such as Italy, southern Germany, and Belgium, which Protestants never won over. Nor is there any complete correspondence between Protestantism and capitalism on the one hand and Catholicism and slower industrial development on the other: compare the Catholic Rhineland with its great modern industries to Protestant East Prussia, a rural agricultural region. Resources remain important too: had Italy turned Calvinist this still would not have given Italy coal and iron; had England remained Catholic, it would still have had them. Yet, with all allowances made, it does seem that the "Protestant ethic" gave a little extra push to the economic development of the Protestant regions, and helped to start the West on its modern path.

The Catholic Reformation

At first, the Catholic authorities tried to deal with the Reformation by suppressing it. But the Protestant movement itself had begun within the Church, and many Catholics not dissatisfied enough to leave the Church still wanted reform within it. The sixteenth century saw a revival, notably in Spain but elsewhere as well, of mysticism and popular participation in religion. These diverse forces produced the Catholic Reformation. Protestant historians often call it the Counter-Reformation, but it was far more than a defensive or negative movement. Though it failed to restore the medieval unity of Christendom, it did preserve and reinvigorate Catholic beliefs and practice.

Politically speaking, the house of Hapsburg, in both its Spanish and German branches, supplied the secular support for the Catholic movement. The French monarchs also helped preserve France as a Catholic country, and in the seventeenth century (see Chapter 8) France would witness a great Catholic revival. Other ruling houses, too, in Germany, Italy, eastern Europe, gave the Catholic faith their powerful support. And once again, as so often during the Middle Ages, there arose a series of new orders of the regular clergy, a revival of the old monastic ideals of austere simplicity and social service. In the 1520's, while the struggle with Luther was still young, an earnest group at Rome

Ignatius Loyola: the only authentic portrait of the saint, by Claudio Coello.

founded the Oratory of Divine Love, dedicated to the deepening of spiritual experience through special services and religious exercises. The Oratory inspired the foundation of the Theatines, an order designed particularly to advance the education of the clergy. In the same decade a new branch of the Franciscans appeared, the Capuchins (hooded friars), to lead the order back to Francis' own ideals.

By far the greatest of the new orders was the Society of Jesus, founded in 1540 by the Spaniard Ignatius Loyola (1491-1556). Loyola, who had been wounded in battle as a soldier, intended the Jesuits to be an army for the Church. His *Spiritual Exercises* emphasized absolute obedience to higher authority (the hierarchy of the Church), and displayed a realistic middle-of-the-road estimate of what can be expected of ordinary human beings in this world, cautioning against undue emphasis even on the truth of a religious controversy lest a delicate balance be upset.

Always the center of controversy, the Jesuits have been accused by their enemies of devotion to worldly power, and of a willingness to use any tactics to win. This last is indeed a slander, for the Jesuits have never underestimated the hold that moral decency has on human beings. They not only struck shrewd blows for Catholicism in Hungary, Poland, England, and Holland, trying to win back souls lost to the Protestants, but moved with the expanding frontiers of the West to India, to China, to Japan, to North America to win new lands and new converts. They were preachers, teachers, social workers, martyrs, always disciplined, never lapsing into the kind of fleshly worldliness that had been the fate of other monastic orders.

The Church used also an old weapon, the Inquisition, in its struggle with Protestantism. In its papal form, this tribunal goes back to the Albigensian Crusade of the early thirteenth century (see Chapter 4), and in its Spanish form to Isabella's efforts in the fifteenth century to make Jews and Muslims conform (see Chapter 6). These medieval courts used medieval measures of torture, and perpetrated horrors against former Muslims in Spain and against Protestants in the Low Countries. As weapons against Protestantism, however, the Inquisition in particular and persecution in general were not effective. The Inquisition was most active in Italy, Spain, and Portugal, persecuting heretics in regions where Protestantism was never a threat; while in those areas that the Church eventually won back—Poland, parts of Hungary and Germany— it accomplished its victory chiefly in other ways.

Catholics did not yield to doctrinal pressure from Protestants. The Protestant tendency toward some form of the "priesthood of the believer" hardened Catholic insistence on the unique powers of the ordained priest. The Church did not even change its views on indulgences, but reaffirmed them—not, of course, as a money transaction but as a spiritual return for spiritual efforts. The Council of Trent, called by Pope Paul III in 1545 and meeting on and off for twenty years, gave formal voice to the total refusal to compromise with Protestant doctrine. It reaffirmed all seven sacraments, transubstantiation, the importance of both faith *and* works, and the authority of both the Bible and unwritten tradition; it also forbade individuals to interpret scripture contrary to the teaching of the Church. Though it was intended to provide a chance for reconciliation, certain conservative Protestants, while invited, never came. Liberals, even liberal Catholics, have always felt that the Council was a rubber stamp in the hands of the popes and the Jesuits.

The Council of Trent and the reforming popes of the later sixteenth century did effect in Catholic practice the kind of reform that the Cluniacs had put through five centuries earlier, enforcing priestly celibacy, combatting simony,

310

and improving the training of priests. The Council also founded the *Index*, a continuing list of books that Catholics must not read because of peril to their faith; it included the writings of anticlericals like Machiavelli and Boccaccio, as well as those of heretics and Protestants. Since the civil authorities were enlisted to prevent the publication and circulation of anything contrary to the faith, this amounted to censorship of the press. Under Pius V (reigned 1566–1572) a standard catechism, breviary, and missal were drawn up to embody the work of the Council of Trent for purposes of instruction. The whole Catholic system had been greatly tightened. The papacy had ceased to be the corrupt center against which Luther and others had inveighed, nor did it ever again become so.

Divided Christendom

Once the Catholic Reformation had been launched, the Protestants gained little more territory. By the end of the sixteenth century, the territorial division between areas dominantly Catholic and areas dominantly Protestant was much as it is now. England, Scotland, Holland, northern and eastern Germany (with a southern projection in Württemberg and Switzerland), and Scandinavia were predominantly Protestant. Ireland, Belgium, southern Germany and the Rhine valley, the Hapsburg lands, Poland, Italy, and the Iberian peninsula were predominantly Catholic. But there were Catholic minorities in England, Scotland, and Holland; there were Protestant minorities in Ireland, France, and some of the Hapsburg lands; and the two faiths interpenetrated most confusedly in greatly divided Germany.

To some extent the religious differences contributed to the growth of national patriotism. Where a specific form of religion became identified with a given political unit, religious feeling and patriotic feeling reinforced each other, especially in a struggle for independence. So Protestantism heightened Dutch resistance to the Spaniards; Catholicism, Irish resistance to the English. In states already independent, religion often strengthened patriotism. England since Elizabeth I—despite its Catholic minority—has taken pride in being a Protestant nation, Spain in being Catholic. In the campaign of the Spanish Armada and the other great wars to which we turn later in the chapter, religion and politics were both at issue, together with competition for overseas trade and empire.

II
The First Overseas Empires

In the mid-fifteenth century, Western society began an expansion which within 250 years or so revealed to Europe almost the whole world. It was the first time—except perhaps for a few half-legendary Viking voyages—that Westerners had crossed the oceans. For the first time western Europeans traveled far outside the orbits of the only two other societies—the Byzantine and the Muslim—that they had so far encountered, and into touch with a bewildering variety of races, creeds, and cultures, from naked savages to cultivated Chinese.

The Europeans were superior in military strength to the peoples they met, and so were able to extend their influence around the world in a quite unprecedented way. They had guns; but non-Europeans could quickly acquire these, and did. More important, European technological superiority was mixed with superior political and military organization in a combination very difficult to imitate. Half a dozen competing Western nations, eager to destroy one another, shared in the superiority. In the Far East, Portuguese, Spaniards, Dutchmen, Frenchmen, and Englishmen intrigued against each other, and other Western nations later joined. But not until the twentieth century did there arise an Asian nation, Japan, that could compete.

Why did this great movement begin just when it did? There were technological reasons: the magnetic compass that makes navigation possible even when the sun and stars are hidden was known by the early fifteenth century, and by the end of the century had become a regular piece of ship's equipment. Shipbuilders were building vessels longer and narrower than the older types of Mediterranean ship, better adapted to ocean swells. There were economic–political reasons: the Ottoman conquest had to some extent interfered with the trade routes through the Near East, although Venice and Genoa had agreements with the Turks. The very predominance of the Italians in the Levant attracted the rising Western states to try the Atlantic waters.

And there were surely also reasons of another sort. This rise of a scientific investigating spirit impelled men, if for instance they heard about the existence of unicorns, to go and look for some. Columbus deliberately set out across the unknown ocean to prove his theory that because the world is round one can travel from Europe westward and reach Asia. In sum, those who carried out the expansion had motives as mixed as those of the crusaders (see Chapter 5); like the crusaders, they were, in part, convinced that they were also doing God's work.

The Portuguese

EAST BY SEA TO THE INDIES   The first of the great pioneers in this modern expansion was Prince Henry of Portugal (1394–1460), known as "the Navigator." Deeply religious, he wanted to convert to Christianity the peoples of Asia, already known in the West through the reports of overland travelers such as Marco Polo the Venetian (ca. 1264–ca. 1324) and others. Since the thirteenth century many Europeans had believed that most Asians were already Christian, and needed only to be brought into touch with Rome. While there were indeed some Christians in Asia, descendants of refugees from the theological controversies in fifth-century Byzantium (see Chapter 3), the medieval legend of Prester (Priest) John, the great Christian ruler somewhere in the distant East, remained only a legend. Henry the Navigator also wanted to promote Portuguese commerce and national power. Carefully he and his fellow workers planned each successive expedition and equipped it with the best instruments available.

The Portuguese had already discovered the Atlantic islands—the Azores, Madeira, and the Canaries. Creeping southward along the west coast of Africa, they now doubled Cape Verde in 1445, and thought they could circumnavigate Africa by turning east. By 1472 they had reached the end of the west African bulge, and had seen that the coastline turned south once more. In 1488 Bartholomew Diaz was blown far south in a storm and rounded the Cape of Good Hope. In 1497, Vasco da Gama followed him, worked his way north along the east coast of Africa, and came to an area of Arab traders who knew how to sail across the Indian Ocean to India. Ten months and fourteen days out from Lisbon, da Gama reached the Indian coast. The Portuguese had an ocean route to the East.

On the next great voyage toward India in 1500, Pedro Cabral—no longer feeling the need to creep along the west African coast—stayed out in the Atlantic after rounding the western African bulge, and was blown so far west that he made a landing in Brazil. It may be that this was not so accidental as it seems. By 1500, the Spanish were well launched in exploration, and Columbus' voyages were well known. In 1493, after Columbus' first voyage, Pope Alexander VI had granted to Spain all lands south and west of a north-south line drawn in the Atlantic between the Azores and the Cape Verde Islands. In 1494, the Portuguese, by the Treaty of Tordesillas with Spain, had succeeded in having this line moved 370 leagues further west. Brazil thus fell into the sphere of the Portuguese, who may have known about it all along and who only announced their landing there after Cabral's voyage. In any case, it was now determined that Brazil alone in Latin America would be Portuguese; everything else lay on the Spanish side of the line.

The main Portuguese push, however, was toward India and the Far East. By the first years of the sixteenth century Portugal owned a string of fortified trading posts along the Indian coast and had won control of navigation of the Indian Ocean from the Muslims. Affonso de Albuquerque established Goa as the capital of the Portuguese holdings (it was lost by the Portuguese to Nehru's India only in 1962), and began to organize communications with southeastern Asia and China. By 1557, the Portuguese had a base at Macao near Canton, which they still possess. They first landed in Japan in 1542 or 1543, introduced firearms, and opened trade relations. Portugal, then, had assembled a colonial empire.

AFRICA, INDIA, AND CHINA   The Africa the Portuguese had opened up was hot, relatively poor, and thinly populated. The coastal stations they and later European voyagers established carried on a flourishing slave trade, as did the Arabs in northern and northwestern Africa. The Africans of the great west African continental bulge had been in touch with North African Muslim traders, who had introduced Islam, and who came to Timbuktu on the upper Niger to acquire gold and slaves. The states of Ghana and Mali of our own day when they became independent took the names of black empires which ruled over these west African regions in the European Middle Ages. In contrast, central and southern African tribes were largely still in a Stone Age culture, so primitive that few Europeans made any effort to understand them. By and large Africa offered little immediate commercial attraction to the Portuguese. India, China, and much of southeast Asia, by contrast, were thickly populated, with great wealth accumulated in a few hands, and with much to offer the Europeans in the way of luxuries like silks and spices. Moreover, here were the seats of very ancient and very advanced civilizations.

India, known only vaguely to the West during the Middle Ages through the intermediary of the Arabs, proved to be the home not of Christians but of people belonging to faiths unknown to the Europeans. This in part no doubt accounted for the contemptuous attitude of the Portuguese and later Europeans, a contempt reinforced by the Westerners' military superiority. India itself was politically disunited. In the north, Central Asian Turkish invaders, wrongly called Mogul (from *Mongol*), were consolidating their foreign rule. In the south, where the Europeans appeared, the local rulers fought each other in bitter rivalry. There was vast diversity among the populations: some tribesmen in the south were at the Stone Age level; some in the northern highlands were similar to the nomadic warriors of Central Asia. In the Indus and Ganges valleys there was a wealthy Hindu society, in part dominated by Muslim invaders.

Among the Hindus the institution of *caste* prevailed—the determination of status by birth. The Europeans found the Indians divided into more than a thousand separate castes, including at the bottom a group of "untouchables." The two ruling castes at the top were the Brahmins or priests, and the Kshatriya or warriors. Marriage between castes and all social mobility were in theory impossible.

The Brahmins presided over a faith that believed in the evils of fleshly life and the attainment of salvation by mystic transcendence in ascetic denial. A sinful life here on earth brings reincarnation in a lower animal form; a virtuous one, reincarnation in a higher form, until—some believed—final union with the perfect might be attained. These doctrines were overlaid and contaminated by a popular belief in a multiplicity of gods and goddesses and by a rigid and complex Brahmin ritual. In the sixth century B.C. a great religious leader, Gautama Buddha, had led a movement against these corruptions. Though Buddhism, one of the great religions of the world, accepts the Brahmin concept that the world of the flesh is bad, it finds salvation, the *nirvana* of peaceful release from the chain of earthly birth and rebirth, in a life ascetic but not withdrawn, a life of charity and good works. In India Buddhism died out, but it spread to China, Japan, and southeastern Asia. In China and Japan, Mahayana Buddhism ("Great Vehicle") prevailed, emphasizing that Buddha wished to make nirvana available to everyone. In southeast Asia and Ceylon, Hinayana Buddhism ("Lesser Vehicle") emphasized detachment from the world, expecially for its monks, and relied more heavily on ritual. An offshoot from this is Zen Buddhism, a stoic form of the faith that developed originally in Japan.

Chinese civilization first arose in the valleys of the Yellow and Yangtze rivers several thousand years before Christ. Like the Mesopotamian civilization (see Chapter 1), it was subject to incursions from the nomads of Asia, against whom the Chinese built the famous Great Wall in the third century B.C. Though the nomads at frequent intervals broke through and conquered the Chinese, eventually the Chinese absorbed each wave of invaders and transformed them into Chinese. Less than a century after the Portuguese

The Great Wall of China, built in the third century B.C.

arrived in Macao this happened for the last time, when the Manchus came down from the north and in 1644 established their own dynasty—the last, which held power until 1911—on the throne at Peking. Like their predecessors from outside, the Manchus were speedily made over into Chinese rulers.

Well before this, Chinese culture had gradually spread southward and eastward to the region of Canton, to Korea, and across the sea to Japan. Chinese society was tightly cemented by a communal village organization characterized by strong family ties that continued almost without change until the Communist takeover of 1949-1950.

China was always ruled by an emperor, the "Son of Heaven," and by a bureaucracy of intellectuals, the mandarins, who were selected by rigorous examinations in classic Chinese literature and philosophy. Though open in theory to anybody with talent, the mandarin class in fact required so expensive a preliminary education that very few poor men's sons managed to rise into it. Worldly and realistic, with little mysticism or interest in an afterlife, the Chinese, it has been said, never had a religion. Confucianism, a code of manners and morals, prescribing temperance, decorum, obedience to the wise and good, governed the behavior of the ruling classes. And if the Chinese proved more resistant to westernization than people of any other land intruded upon by Westerners, this may well be because of their confidence— not misplaced—that in the arts of life, including painting and the making of ceramics, they were already superior to anybody else in the human race.

THE PORTUGUESE EMPIRE   The Portuguese, bursting for the first time into these lands so strange to Europeans, created a trading empire, not an empire of settlement. Along the coasts of Africa, India, and China, they established a series of posts, or "factories," over which they raised the Portuguese flag as a sign that they had annexed these bits of territory for the Portuguese crown. To the inhabitants they offered relatively cheap mass-produced articles: guns, knives, and cloth. In return they got gold and silver when they could, spices, silks and other luxuries, and cotton and slaves. The principles first followed by the Portuguese later became general among the colonizing powers: the mother country produced the manufactured goods, the colonies the raw materials; foreigners were excluded from the trade between the two. These policies were applications of the economic philosophy called mercantilism, which we shall soon examine in more detail.

Relatively few land troops were needed to keep the natives under control and ward off rival European powers. But the Portuguese needed and built a large and powerful navy to protect their vessels from piracy at sea; in the early days of overseas expansion, a power would often unofficially turn pirates loose to prey on the shipping of its rivals. The Portuguese did not settle large numbers of their own people in their colonial outposts or rule the inhabitants directly, but left the old chiefs and ruling groups pretty much as they had found them. Except for a few natives who learned the language, the masses were little affected by the Western goods and ideas brought to their shores.

But, like the other colonial powers later, the Portuguese did try to convert the natives to Christianity. Christian missionaries worked hard and devotedly, often becoming very fond of their charges. Some of the Jesuits in China, the first European intellectuals to live in that very civilized land, seriously believed that a reconciliation between Christianity and Confucianism was just around the corner. Often the missionaries, anxious to protect the natives, conflicted with the traders, eager to exploit them. The missionaries, however, made comparatively few converts in the vast populations of India and China.

RELIGIOUS UPHEAVAL, IMPERIAL
EXPANSION, DYNASTIC CONFLICT

315

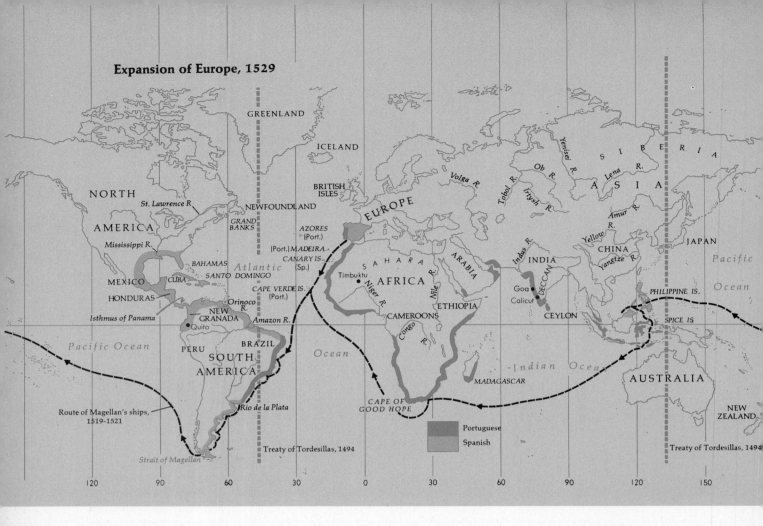

Expansion of Europe, 1529

GREENLAND

ICELAND

NORTH
AMERICA

St. Lawrence R.

NEWFOUNDLAND
GRAND
BANKS

BRITISH
ISLES

EUROPE

SIBERIA

ASIA

Volga R.

Tobol R.

Ob R.

Yenisei R.

Lena R.

Irtysh R.

Amur R.

Mississippi R.

AZORES
(Port.)

(Port.) MADEIRA
CANARY IS.
(Sp.)

SAHARA

ARABIA

CHINA

JAPAN

Atlantic

BAHAMAS
SANTO DOMINGO

Timbuktu

AFRICA

Indus R.

INDIA

Yellow R.

Pacific
Ocean

MEXICO
HONDURAS

CUBA

CAPE VERDE IS.
(Port.)

Niger R.

Nile

Goa
Calicut

DECCAN

Isthmus of Panama

Orinoco
R.

ETHIOPIA

CEYLON

PHILIPPINE IS.

Quito

NEW
GRANADA

Amazon R.

CAMEROONS

Congo
R.

SPICE IS.

Pacific Ocean

PERU

BRAZIL

SOUTH
AMERICA

Ocean

Indian Ocea

AUSTRALIA

MADAGASCAR

Route of Magellan's ships,
1519-1521

Rio de la Plata

CAPE OF
GOOD HOPE

Portuguese
Spanish

NEW
ZEALAND

Strait of Magellan

Treaty of Tordesillas, 1494

Treaty of Tordesillas, 1494

120   90   60   30   0   30   60   90   120   150

In the seventeenth century the Portuguese would lose ground to the French, Dutch, and English, more advanced than they in industrial and banking techniques. But they did leave as a lasting monument a famous epic poem, *The Lusiads* (1572), by Camoëns, commemorating their overseas expansion. And they kept their trading stations: Timor in the East Indies, Goa, Macao. In Africa their empire, almost 800,000 square miles—Angola and Portuguese Guinea in the west, Mozambique in the east—has despite rebellions continued to exist down to our own day, long past the moment when other empires have been dissolved.

The Spaniards

WEST BY SEA TO THE INDIES   Second to Portugal in exploring and colonizing came Spain. Ferdinand and Isabella commissioned Columbus (1451–1506) largely as a way of catching up with Portugal. Genoese-born, and competently self-educated in navigation and geography, Columbus was not the only man to think that one could reach the Far East by sailing west. Ancient Greek geographers had believed the earth was round, and the belief revived during the Renaissance. Toscanelli had published a map at Florence in 1474, and Behaim one at Nuremberg in 1492 showing the earth as a globe—without the Americas, of course, and with the combined Atlantic and Pacific much narrower than they are in fact. But the ingenuity and persistence with which Columbus promoted the idea of sailing west in order to go east were strikingly novel. He was commissioned not only to reach the Indies but to discover and secure for Spain new islands and territories, a mission that probably reflects old legends about Atlantis or other lost continents and islands beyond the Azores.

RELIGIOUS UPHEAVAL, IMPERIAL
EXPANSION, DYNASTIC CONFLICT

Of course Columbus did not reach the Indies, but a New World. On October 12, 1492, after a voyage of a little more than two months with three small ships, he made a landfall on one of the Bahama Islands, and continued on to discover the islands of Cuba and Santo Domingo (Hispaniola). On his second voyage, in 1493, with seventeen ships and fifteen hundred colonists, he explored further in the Caribbean, and laid the foundations of the Spanish Empire in America. On his third voyage, in 1498–1500, he reached the mouth of the Orinoco on the north coast of South America, and was sent home in irons after difficulties with the royal governor. He was released on his return to Spain, and in 1502–1504 made a fourth and final voyage, reaching the mainland of what is now Honduras. He died in Spain in 1506, unaware that he had reached not Asia but two new continents, which received the name of another Italian in Spanish service, Amerigo Vespucci, a far more prolific writer of letters about his own explorations.

During the next few years many other explorers discovered that the new continents were a barrier to the westward voyage. In 1513 Balboa saw the limitless Pacific from the Isthmus of Panama. The new problem was how to get *through* the Americas by sea and into the Pacific, and the promising openings—Chesapeake, Delaware, Hudson, St. Lawrence—all proved to be nothing but river mouths after all. There was a Northwest Passage waiting to be discovered, but it was usually ice-choked, and it was not actually found until the 1850's by the Englishman Sir John Franklin, who died in the Arctic wastes. The Southwest Passage, around the southernmost tip of South America, however, was found by Ferdinand Magellan, a Portuguese in the service of Spain, on an extraordinary voyage that began in 1519 and lasted until 1522. It took him through the strait that still bears his name, into and across the Pacific amid dreadful hardship, and to the Philippines, where he was killed. But one of his captains sailed on across the Indian Ocean and home around the Cape of Good Hope to complete the first circumnavigation of the globe. The Philippine landing brought Spain into the Far East.

In the New World, the Spaniards soon explored by land, and annexed great territories. Led by the conquistadores, who were explorers, soldiers, and administrators, they conquered the only two civilized regions of the New World. Hernando Cortés took the Aztec empire of Mexico (1519) and Francisco Pizarro the Inca empire of Peru (1531–1533). In dramatic, toilsome, and often bloody adventures, many conquistadores opened up other regions of the vast and strange New World for Spain: Quesada in what is now Colombia; Ponce de León looking for the fountain of youth in Florida; Coronado, de Soto, and Cabeza de Vaca in the southwestern portions of the United States; Mendoza in the La Plata region of Argentina and Uruguay; Valdivia in Chile; Alvarado in Guatemala. Although throughout Central and South America millions of people of Indian stock survive today, and are often proudly conscious of their heritage, the structure of the Aztec and Incan civilizations—unlike that of China or India—disintegrated or disappeared before the often brutal conquest of the Spaniards.

THE LATIN EMPIRES OF THE NEW WORLD   Before the end of the sixteenth century the Spaniards and, in Brazil, the Portuguese had completed the foundation of the first colonial empires of settlement. But only in the La Plata region and in central Chile did a European population replace the natives. Elsewhere a crust of Spanish or Portuguese settlers formed at the top of society and made their European language the language of culture. From the union, formal or informal, of Europeans and natives arose a class called *mestizos,* mixed bloods. In

Machu Picchu, ancient Incan city in the Andes of Peru. Corn and potatoes were grown on the terraces.

many areas the Indians maintained their stock and their old ways of life almost untouched. But in the Caribbean the Indians were exterminated, and in Brazil they proved inadequate as a labor force. In both cases large-scale importation of black slaves from Africa added another element to the racial mixture.

The physical features of South America broke it into separate regions. Between Argentina and Chile the great chain of the Andes, crossed only with great difficulty through high mountain passes, prevented a political union. The Andes and the great tropical rain forests of the Amazon Basin divided the colonies of La Plata from those of Peru and Colombia (New Granada). Similar mountain formations determined the creation of small states in Central America. Even had Brazil been settled by Spaniards, it would almost surely have remained separate because of the difficulty of communications with the rest of the continent.

The Spaniards put their colonial administration under two viceroys, one of Peru, with his capital at Lima, and the other of "New Spain," with his capital at Mexico City. The viceroy at Lima ruled over all of Spanish South America except Venezuela. The viceroy at Mexico City ruled all the mainland north of Panama, the West Indies, Venezuela—and—far across the Pacific the Philippines! In each capital, and also in Guatemala, New Granada, Quito, the Philippines, and elsewhere, there were *audiencias,* advisory councils that also operated as courts.

This regime seems highly centralized, but in view of the vast areas and the varied peoples under its control, it could not be absolute in practice. The citizens were consulted in assemblies and before long the colonial bureaucracy was largely managed by colonials—men who had been born overseas and had never seen Spain. It was impossible for the mother country to enforce mercantilist practices completely; not only did domestic industry grow in the colonies, but in time the local officials connived at trade with other Europeans: English, Dutch, and French.

In the sixteenth century, the Spaniards were interested chiefly in mining and exporting to Spain the rich and easily accessible deposits of gold and silver in Mexico and Peru. The crown got a fifth of all metals mined. Except for jewelry and other crafts, the precious metals were doing the natives no good; but they did the Spaniards little good either, as it turned out, since Spain spent the vast resources to finance a vain bid for European supremacy. By the seventeenth century sugar, tobacco, chocolate, cotton, and hides were flowing to Europe in exchange for manufactured goods. The chief beneficiaries of this trade were the Creoles (Americans born of pure European stock) and the mestizos, but not the Indians.

All over Latin America the Indians fell to the bottom of the social system. Especially in the Caribbean, but to a degree everywhere, the initial European policy of using native labor proved disastrous for the natives, who died in droves from diseases to which they had no immunity. Tragedy also marked the installation of the *encomienda,* a semimanorial system of forced labor, and the efforts to regiment native labor on plantations. Most Spanish colonists were hard-boiled and tough with the natives.

The record of contact between whites and nonwhites everywhere in the world, however, was marked by harshness and brutality. The Spaniards were perhaps no worse than other nationalities, and they did occasionally make an effort to mitigate the cruelties. In 1542 the enslavement of the natives was forbidden. Other laws, though often flouted, at least were designed to protect the natives, who found a warm champion in the distinguished humanitarian bishop of Chiapas in Mexico, Bartholomew de las Casas (1474–1566), "Father of the Indians." Everywhere in New Spain missionaries were active; the Indians, unlike the Asian or African masses, were converted to Catholicism. In Paraguay the Jesuits set up among the Guarani Indians a benevolent despotism, a utopia of good order, good habits, and eternal childhood for the Guarani. On the northern fringes of the Spanish world, where it was to meet the Anglo-Saxons, a long line of missions in California and the American southwest held the frontier.

In contrast to the Spanish settlements, the Portuguese in Brazil were far less urbanized. When the black slaves were imported, no color line was drawn, and the races became more thoroughly mixed in Brazil than in any Spanish colony except Cuba. The Dutch, French, and British all tried to get chunks of Brazil away from the Portuguese, and the three northern South American states of Surinam (Dutch Guiana), French Guiana, and Guyana (formerly British Guiana) survive today as evidence of this effort.

Competition Begins

Portugal and Spain were the only two European countries to found colonial empires during the sixteenth century. France and England were just beginning their explorations, and did not enter the competition in earnest until the seventeenth century. Verrazzano, an Italian in French service, in 1524 explored the North American coast in what is now Canada, and between 1534 and 1541 Jacques Cartier several times sailed into the St. Lawrence River, proceeding as far as the site of Montreal. But the French did not for the moment follow up these efforts by settlement.

Nor were the English any quicker to pursue the opportunities in North America, although their agents, the Italians John and Sebastian Cabot, had in 1497 and 1498 touched on Nova Scotia, Newfoundland, and the American coast as far south as Delaware. Instead, the English began some six decades later to challenge the Spaniards to the south. In the 1560's, John Hawkins, despite opposition, made three voyages into Spanish territory to sell slaves. His nephew Francis Drake attacked Spanish shipping on his celebrated trip around the world (1577–1580)—the first by an Englishman—when he touched on California and claimed it for England under the name of New Albion.

The pace now quickened, as Martin Frobisher explored Labrador and the regions to the north and west, Sir Humphrey Gilbert (1583) claimed Newfoundland for England, and other English explorers began to search for the Northwest Passage, continuing to plunder Spanish commerce. In 1584, Sir Walter Raleigh tried to found a settlement on Roanoke Island (North Carolina), but neither his colonists nor a second group sent out in 1587 survived. All these efforts only faintly foreshadowed the great English seventeenth-century settlements in North America.

III

The New Monarchies and the Wars of the Sixteenth Century

By the end of the fifteenth century, the Spanish, French, and English monarchies dominated western Europe. The Holy Roman Empire of the Germanies, occupying much of central Europe, had no comparable internal unity. Yet under the Hapsburgs the Germanies, too, entered into competition for supremacy. Italy, with its city-states, attracted outsiders by its riches and its civilization. Between the Hapsburg lands and the French lay the zone of fragmentation which the Burgundian dukes of the fifteenth century had almost cemented into a major state (see p. 261). Out of this zone have come the modern nations of Holland, Belgium, Luxembourg, and Switzerland. To the east, Muscovite Russia was just coalescing as a state, and the feudalized, Catholic kingdom of Poland occupied vast areas. To the southeast, the Ottoman Turks were already ensconced in the Balkans, threatening Italy and central Europe. In short, the picture has become a recognizable one, though the unification of Germany and Italy into nations, the entrance of Russia onto the European stage, and the gradual expulsion of the Turks from Europe all still lay far in the future.

In succession, individual states tried to dominate the entire western portion of the continent, and break down what was already becoming a "system" of states. In the sixteenth century, Spain, in the seventeenth and eighteenth and down to 1815, France, in the twentieth, Germany, tried either to absorb or to control the other states, to limit their sovereignty. Each time, the threatened states sooner or later joined in a coalition, overthrew the threat to stability, and restored the system. Each time, England—not itself a continental power after the Hundred Years' War—intervened to support or lead the coalition against the aggressor. What we have been describing is called the preservation of the "balance of power." Whenever one power has sought to overthrow the balance on the continent of Europe, it has in the end been thwarted.

During the sixteenth century, the "New Monarchies" of Spain, France, and England evolved, each in its own way, toward a more and more centralized regime. All had central foreign offices, paid professional armies, and paid professional diplomats and spies. All had paid professional civilian bureaucrats, a central financial system with some control over taxation, and a central legal system that tried to render uniform justice. In each, the monarch had inherited the throne, and passed it on without question to his nearest heir. Everywhere he claimed the right to make final decisions, and overshadowed the traditional assembly—Spanish Cortes, French Estates-General, English Parliament. The efficiency of absolutism, however, was limited by poor communications and by the continued survival of many medieval local privileges and local ways of life.

RELIGIOUS UPHEAVAL, IMPERIAL
EXPANSION, DYNASTIC CONFLICT

CHARLES V AND PHILIP II   The sixteenth century was the Spanish century, when Spain tried and failed to upset the balance of power—first of all the European nations to do so. For most of the century she was ruled by Charles V (1516–1556—technically, Charles V as emperor and Charles I as Spanish monarch) and by his son, Philip II (1556–1598). Brought up in the Low Countries, Charles came to Spain a stranger who hardly spoke the language. He brought with him a Flemish entourage who did not conceal their contempt for this old-fashioned, divided, slow-moving land.

Three years after inheriting Spain from his maternal grandfather, Ferdinand of Aragon, Charles inherited the empire on the death of his paternal grandfather, Maximilian (1519). Soon there was an outburst of indignation at his leaving Spain and spending Spanish money and the lives of Spanish troops for purposes that were not Spanish. In 1520, a group of Spanish cities, led by Toledo, revolted. The rebels, called the *Comuneros,* included many nobles hostile to the king and many members of the lower classes with strong radical aims. They were put down in 1521 (the upper-class rebels had been frightened by the radicalism of the lower), and Charles thereafter simply tried not to antagonize the Spaniards.

Philip II, on the other hand, was profoundly Spanish in character and attitudes. Personally self-denying and extremely hard-working, he was a religious fanatic. He changed the internal administration of Spain, devising a system of consultative councils with a council of state at the top, all manned by nobles. But the decisions were his alone and were put into effect by his personal secretariat and the local authorities, who were not noble. Especially in Castile, Philip diluted the power of the Cortes almost to nothing: nobles and priests no longer could attend, since they paid no taxes, and the delegates from the towns could do little by themselves.

Philip thought he did not need to ask the Cortes for money because of the wealth that came from the tax of one-fifth on the cargoes from the New World, from his own royal estates, from the sale of offices and titles, and even from a royal percentage of the profits of the sale of papal dispensations, not unlike indulgences. He spent it all on foreign wars, and left Spain almost bankrupt in 1598. His vast domains—divided Spain, the Low Countries, lands in Italy, and the overseas empire in America and the Philippines (named after Philip himself)—had no common organs of consultation; the richest of his subjects were tax exempt; there was no accumulated Spanish administrative experience that prevented graft or promoted efficiency.

SPANISH REGIONALISM AND MERCANTILISM   Spanish regionalism (see Chapter 6) was so extreme that the separate provinces often levied customs dues on each other's goods, and had no arrangements for extraditing criminals to each other. In the extreme north, the provinces that the Muslims had never conquered retained many jealously guarded privileges, the *fueros.* Aragon had its own chief justice, the *justicia major,* nominated by the crown, but possessing within the province authority like that of the United States Supreme Court, and holding office for life.

Had Charles V and Philip II devoted themselves and their wealth to uniting and developing Spain, they might have accomplished wonders. Spain had great agricultural potentialities and mineral resources, notably iron. With its head start on overseas imperial development and its flourishing navy and merchant marine, it had a tremendous opportunity. But the monarchs spent their efforts and their gold in trying to dominate Europe and to extirpate Protestantism. The Spanish infantry, the best in Europe, had to be paid every-

Marble bust of Philip II, from the workshop of Leone Leoni.

RELIGIOUS UPHEAVAL, IMPERIAL EXPANSION, DYNASTIC CONFLICT

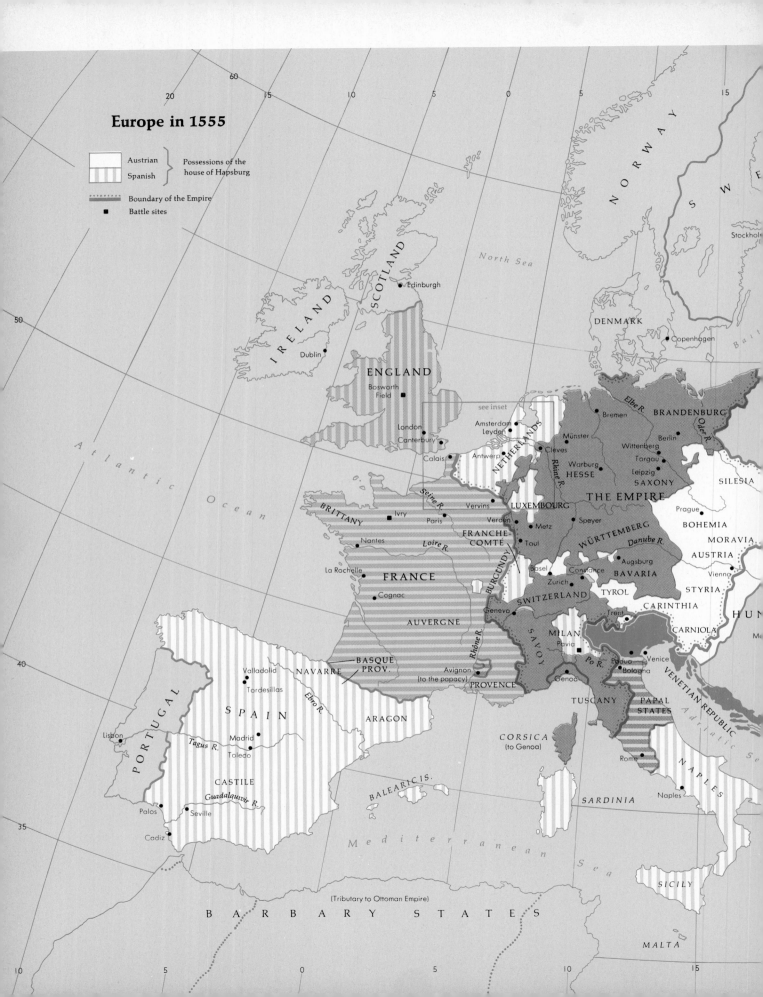

Europe in 1555

Austrian	Possessions of the
Spanish	house of Hapsburg

······ Boundary of the Empire

■ Battle sites

North Sea

NORWAY

SWE...

Stockhol...

DENMARK

Copenhagen

Batt...

Edinburgh

SCOTLAND

IRELAND

Dublin

ENGLAND

Bosworth
Field ■

London

Canterbury

Calais

*Atlantic

Ocean*

BRITTANY

Nantes

La Rochelle

Cognac

Ivry ■

Paris

Seine R.

Amsterdam

Leyden

Antwerp

NETHERLANDS

Cleves

Rhine R.

Bremen

Münster

Wittenberg

Berlin

Torgau

Leipzig

Elbe R.

Oder R.

BRANDENBURG

Warburg

HESSE

SAXONY

SILESIA

LUXEMBOURG

Verdun

Metz

Vervins

Toul

FRANCHE-
COMTÉ

THE EMPIRE

Speyer

Prague

BOHEMIA

MORAVIA

Danube R.

WÜRTTEMBERG

Augsburg

Basel

Constance

BAVARIA

AUSTRIA

Vienna

FRANCE

Loire R.

AUVERGNE

BURGUNDY

Zurich

SWITZERLAND

Geneva

Rhône R.

SAVOY

TYROL

Trent

STYRIA

CARINTHIA

CARNIOLA

HU...

Milan

Pavia ■

Po R.

Padua

Bologna

Venice

VENETIAN REPUBLIC

Adriatic Se...

Valladolid

Tordesillas

NAVARRE

BASQUE
PROV.

Avignon
(to the papacy)

PROVENCE

Genoa

TUSCANY

PAPAL
STATES

NAPLES

Lisbon

PORTUGAL

Tagus R.

Madrid

Toledo

SPAIN

Ebro R.

ARAGON

CORSICA
(to Genoa)

Rome

CASTILE

Guadalquivir R.

Palos

Seville

Cadiz

BALEARIC IS.

SARDINIA

Naples

M e d i t e r r a n e a n   S e a

(Tributary to Ottoman Empire)

B A R B A R Y   S T A T E S

SICILY

MALTA

Inset map labels:

ENGLAND

North Sea

London

Canterbury

Amsterdam
Leyden
Utrecht

Armada sea fight

Bruges
Calais
Boulogne

FLANDERS

Antwerp

Guinegate

ARTOIS

NETHERLANDS

Scheldt R.

Cambray

Cateau-
Cambrésis

FRANCE

60

55

50

Main map labels:

25 30 35 40 45

E N

TEUTONIC
ORDER

Volga R.

Moscow

Oka R.

W. Dvina R.

R U S S I A

PRUSSIA

L I T H U A N I A

Ural R.

Warsaw

POLAND

Vistula R.

Kiev

U K R A I N E

Dnieper R.

Don R.

KHANATE

Volga R.

55

45

Dniester R.

MOLDAVIA

OF THE

TRANSYLVANIA

CRIMEA

Caspian Sea

40

RY

Belgrade

WALLACHIA

Danube R.

Black Sea

50

MONTE-
NEGRO

O T T O M A N

Constantinople

E M P I R E

Salonika

Tigris R.

35

Lepanto

Athens

Aegean Sea

Euphrates R.

PELOPONNESUS

ONIAN IS.

(to Venice)

RHODES

CRETE

CYPRUS
(to Venice)

20 25 30 35 40 45

where it went, and the drain was never made up. Although expenditure on armed forces can stimulate economic productivity, it did not do so in Spain. The vast sums from the New World, while enabling her to fight her wars, passed out of her hands and into those of foreign bankers and merchants to pay for manufactured goods needed by Spanish colonies.

In accordance with the mercantilist ideas of the time, Spain forbade the colonies to engage in manufacturing. But she did not develop her own industrial production to supply the colonies; instead she bought goods abroad, thus helping the industries of other states and sometimes tempting their citizens to attempt a little smuggling into the Spanish dominions. In Spain, there was little room for individual economic initiative; the government controlled all enterprise, especially the colonial trade, with detailed regulations. The Castilian Casa de Contratación (House of Trade) licensed every export and import to and from the colonies. Equally important was the whole attitude of the Spaniards. They retained a medieval contempt for business and preferred war, politics, religion, art, or living like an *hidalgo,* a nobleman (*hijo de algo,* "son of somebody"). Numerous holidays, the siesta, the thronging soldiers, priests, monks, and other economically unproductive persons, combining with monopoly, bureaucracy, and the lack of encouragement to new enterprise stimulated the exact opposite of Weber's "capitalist spirit" (see p. 308), and in the long run disqualified Spain for competition with those nations that had it.

SPANISH LITERATURE AND PAINTING   Yet the sixteenth-century man could not see all this. What he saw was the richest of states, with the best of armies and a magnificent literature and art. Spanish culture reflects a spirit strange to those who know the books and paintings of other countries: a serious, darkly passionate, unsmiling spirit, fascinated with death and all the details of death, preoccupied with honor and "face," agonized and pious, intensely proud. Loyola the Jesuit represents this Spanish spirit. So do Saint Theresa of Avila (1515–1582), the ascetic and mystical girl who reorganized the Carmelite nunneries and wrote her autobiography, and Saint John of the Cross (1542–1581), her disciple. They do not withdraw from the world of the senses like the ascetics of the early Church, but combat and try to transcend the necessity of living in the flesh.

In a very different way, Miguel de Cervantes (1547–1616), whose *Don Quixote* (1605) is one of the few universal books, carries the mark of this Spanish spirit. Cervantes gently satirizes the concepts of chivalric behavior that have addled the pate of his poor old hero: anyone that does a disinterested deed, in these degenerate times, Cervantes seems to say, is a crazy man tilting with windmills. And yet there was something magnificent about self-denial and chivalry and protecting the innocent that we in our superior wisdom have lost. Speaking for earthy common sense is Don Quixote's devoted squire, Sancho Panza, sharing the mad adventures of the Don but protecting him from their worst consequences, never forgetting that man after all must eat.

The Spanish spirit was caught by a painter, El Greco (1541–1614), not a Spaniard at all but a Greek, born Domenico Theotokopouli on the island of Crete and trained both in the Byzantine tradition of the Aegean world and at the school of Titian in Venice. He settled at Toledo in 1575, and lived there the rest of his life. His long, thin figures, with their eyes often turned upward in piety or simulated piety, the greyish flesh tones, often contrasting with the brilliant colors of landscape and dress, suggest the Spanish combination of energy and otherworldliness that created the Inquisition and built and misused the first overseas empire.

El Greco's "Fray Felix Hortensio Paravicino."

THE ITALIAN ADVENTURE OF CHARLES VIII AND LOUIS XII Far more centralized both by geography and history than Spain, France also spent most of the sixteenth century in war: foreign wars against the Hapsburgs down to 1559, and religious civil wars from 1562 to 1598. From his father, the canny Louis XI (see Chapter 6), Charles VIII (reigned 1483–1498) inherited a well-filled treasury, a good army, and a docile nobility. By marriage in 1491 he added to the crown the province of Brittany. Secure at home, he decided on foreign adventures. He had inherited the claim of the Angevins to the throne of Naples. Italy, with its great material riches and its political instability, was very tempting. In 1494–1495, Charles led his armies triumphantly all the way to Naples, but then a coalition formed against him: the Holy League of the papacy, the empire, Spain, Venice, Milan, and England. Charles was forced to withdraw. His cousin Louis XII (reigned 1498–1515), who succeeded him, had a Visconti grandmother, and so a claim to Milan against the Sforzas. In 1499 Louis took Milan, avoided the isolation that had ruined Charles's campaign, and allied himself with Ferdinand of Aragon to share the conquest of Naples. But the allies fell out, and Ferdinand's forces drove Louis out of Naples (1503).

With the greedy French in Milan and the greedy Spaniards in Naples, fresh interventions and new illustrations of the workings of the balance of power were only a matter of time. In 1508 Louis joined with Ferdinand, the emperor Maximilian, and the pope in the League of Cambrai to seize the rich possessions of Venice in the Po valley. But the League broke up when the pope and Ferdinand had what they wanted, and the pope now formed a Holy League (Ferdinand, Venice, Maximilian, England) *against* France. In 1513, Henry VIII's invading forces defeated the French at home and the Swiss defeated them in Italy. So Louis XII, like Charles VIII before him, had to withdraw, and the Sforzas returned to Milan. The Italian campaigns were the prelude to the great series of Hapsburg-Valois wars that began under Charles V of Hapsburg and Francis I (reigned 1515–1547), successor of Louis XII as king of France.

FRANCIS I AND THE HAPSBURG-VALOIS WARS Dashing, self-indulgent, energetic, extravagant, Francis was a Renaissance despot thoroughly at home in the age of Machiavelli. He began his reign with a brilliant victory over the Swiss that brought Milan back to France. In 1520 he held the celebrated ostentatious meeting with Henry VIII near Calais, the "Field of the Cloth of Gold," so called because of the splendor that surrounded the monarchs. But Francis was soon preoccupied with Charles V, whose enormous territories surrounded France. The struggle that broke out in 1521 was inconclusive until 1525, when the imperial forces defeated Francis at Pavia and took him prisoner. He was held in Madrid until he renounced all claims to Milan, Genoa, and Naples, and ceded Burgundy to Charles (1526). Francis soon repudiated the settlement after allying himself with the pope, Venice, and the Sforzas in the League of Cognac, and the war resumed. In 1527, Charles' Spanish and German mercenaries, restless at being unpaid, and commanded by a great French noble, the constable of Bourbon, who had quarreled with Francis I, sacked Rome. The horrors of the sack shocked contemporaries, who said it was worse than anything since the one by Alaric the Visigoth in 410 (see Chapter 3). By the Treaty of Cambrai (1529) Francis renounced his claims to Italy and other territories and paid a large indemnity; Charles promised to postpone any demand for Burgundy, and set free Francis' sons, whom he was holding as hostages. In 1530, Charles was crowned emperor by the pope. Despite the Lutheran disturbances in Germany, and the French threat, Charles was now at the height of his power.

Twice more (1536–1538 and 1542–1544) in the lifetime of Francis I and Charles V, Hapsburg and Valois renewed their struggles. After the death of the Sforza ruler of Milan (1535), Francis revived his claim there, and Charles invaded southern France. Francis, "eldest son of the Church," first allied himself with Suleiman the Magnificent, the Ottoman sultan, who menaced the imperial forces both in the Mediterranean and on land in Hungary. This was a perfectly Machiavellian action: Francis not only won valuable commercial concessions from the Turks (see Chapter 5) but also seriously embarrassed his enemy, Charles.

War broke out again in 1542 over Charles's investment of his son Philip as duke of Milan, and the capture and execution by Charles of two French secret agents on their way to Istanbul. The Ottoman fleet used French naval bases, and this time the Catholic Francis I also allied himself with the Protestant duke of Cleves, one of the German princes in rebellion against the Catholic emperor. The turmoil inside Germany made it impossible for Charles V ever to count on much German assistance against the French. In this war, Henry VIII joined Charles against Francis, partly in revulsion against the Franco-Turkish alliance, and for a time Paris was threatened. But, obeying the principles of the balance of power, the English did not want Charles too strong, and did not give him all the help they might have; Paris escaped capture.

THE SECOND ROUND: AUGSBURG AND CATEAU-CAMBRÉSIS   Once this particular war was over, Charles was temporarily free to concentrate his strength against the German Protestants. Victories over them led in 1552 to another Hapsburg–Valois war, as Henry II of France (1547–1559), son of Francis I, continued the Protestant alliance. Henry seized the imperial fortresses of Metz, Toul, and Verdun on the northeastern border of France, and held them against Charles. Unable to knock out the Protestants, Charles allowed in 1555 the religious Peace of Augsburg, which recognized them as established in those regions they had already won. The principle was that called *cuius regio, eius religio,* which may be freely rendered as "Whoever is the ruler of an area may require that it follow his religion." If the elector of Saxony is Lutheran (as he was), Saxony is Lutheran; if the duke of Bavaria is Catholic (as he was), Bavaria is Catholic. The peace failed to solve the problem of what should happen to the property of Catholic bishops or abbots who were converted to Protestantism. Also, it made provision for no religion but Catholicism and Lutheranism.

Charles V abdicated in 1556, and spent the last two years of his life in a monastery. The Austrian territories and the title of emperor passed to his brother, Ferdinand; Spain and the rest of the Hapsburg lands went to his son, Philip II. The last of the Hapsburg–Valois wars was fought between Philip and Henry II of France between 1556 and 1559. The English, fighting on the side of Spain, lost Calais, their last foothold in France (1558). By the Treaty of Cateau-Cambrésis (1559) the French retained Calais and also Metz, Toul, and Verdun. In the same year Henry II died of a wound received in a tournament; he was followed on the throne by his three sons—Francis II (1559–1560), Charles IX (1560–1574), and Henry III (1574–1589)—who were greatly influenced by their strongly Catholic mother, the Florentine Catherine de' Medici. Under the sons of Henry II the French monarchy underwent its worst crisis since the Hundred Years' War: the Wars of Religion, precipitated by the existence of a powerful French Protestant minority, the Huguenots.

THE FRENCH WARS OF RELIGION   Protestantism in France made a great appeal to the nobles, almost half of whom were Huguenots at the peak of the move-

Henry IV (Henry of Navarre).

ment, and to the middle classes in the towns. It affected the great masses of the peasantry much less. Regionally, it was strong in the south (where it did win many peasants), while it scarcely penetrated Brittany, Normandy, or the region of Paris. Conversion to Protestantism for the nobility was not exclusively a matter of conscience and conviction: the new faith also offered a chance to challenge the centralizing Catholic monarchy and its agents. For the French monarchy, Protestantism offered no temptations, as it had to the German princes. In France, beginning in 1438, the kings had asserted their rights over the French church, and by the Concordat of Bologna (1516) Francis I had won from the papacy the right to choose bishops and abbots. Conversion to Protestantism could have brought the kings no more.

Between 1562 and 1589 there were no fewer than eight religious wars. The most savage episode was the Saint Bartholomew's Day massacre (1572) when the Protestant leader Coligny and thousands of other Protestants in Paris and the provinces were dragged from their beds and murdered. As the struggle continued, the great noble house of Guise assumed the command of a Catholic League, while a Huguenot prince, Henry of Navarre, the nearest male heir of the childless King Henry III, took command of the Protestants. The prospect of a Protestant succession caused the Catholic League to redouble its efforts. The Catholics negotiated with Spain, the Protestants with England. The monarchy, though Catholic, found itself threatened not only by the Protestants but by the intransigence of the Catholic League and the ambitions of the Guises, who sought to put on the throne the uncle of Henry of Navarre, not only a Catholic but a cardinal. This prospect horrified public opinion generally.

In the War of the Three Henrys (King Henry III, Henry, duke of Guise, and Henry of Navarre), an insurrection in Paris (1588) drove Henry III out of the city, which then acclaimed Guise. Henry III arranged the murder of Guise, was forced by the Catholic League to take refuge with Henry of Navarre, and was in turn murdered. Henry of Navarre—still a Protestant—became King Henry IV (reigned 1589–1610), first of the House of Bourbon. He defeated the Catholics, besieged Paris, and was persuaded that if he himself should accept Catholicism he could at least obtain toleration for the Huguenots. In 1593 he did so, although he probably did not make the celebrated remark attributed to him: "Paris is well worth a mass"; in 1594 the city surrendered.

In 1598 Henry IV issued the Edict of Nantes, giving the Huguenots not full freedom of worship by any means but a measure of toleration unequaled in any other Catholic country. Citizens of certain cities and towns, and nobles having the old feudal judicial rights, might exercise their religion freely. Public worship by Huguenots was forbidden in and around Paris and in all archiepiscopal and episcopal cities. Religious concessions alone would probably not have been enough to persuade the Huguenots to lay down their arms. They obtained also certain fortified towns in the southwest, where they were strongest, notably the port and fortress of La Rochelle, and thus won recognition as a political party in arms, entitled to defend itself. The Edict of Nantes brought religious peace to France.

This compromise peace would probably have been impossible had it not been for the long and exhausting wars that had disrupted France for almost forty years. The men who worked hardest to bring it about were moderates, usually practicing Catholics themselves. Michel de l'Hospital (1507–1573) believed that it was un-Christian to try by force to impose religious conformity, although he could not believe that men of different faiths could live peacefully together. He appealed to Protestant and Catholic to submerge their differences in their common Christianity. Jean Bodin (d. 1596) similarly longed for a strong centralized monarchy tempered by the limitations imposed by history and tradition, and thought that the quarreling factions should submerge their differences in loyalty to the French crown. These men and many who shared their views were known as *politiques,* political moralists.

THE FRENCH RENAISSANCE   Despite almost constant warfare, sixteenth-century France experienced a cultural renaissance, which began in large measure under the influence of Italian models. The French humanist François Rabelais (1494–1553), who began life as a monk, studied the classics, practiced and taught medicine, and created two of the greatest comic figures in literary history, the giant Gargantua and his son Pantagruel. Gargantua helped to found a wonderful unmonastic monastery, the Abbey of Thélème, whose motto was "Do What Thou Wilt," and whose happy inmates got up and went to bed when they wished, ate and drank and worked and slept whenever they felt like it, and did anything else they pleased. Exuberant, fleshly, optimistic, Rabelais is often obscene. His language comes pouring out in a torrent of synonyms, full of energy, almost tiring to read. But he recommends more than self-indulgence: Gargantua wants Pantagruel to learn everything—Arabic, Latin, Hebrew, Greek, all the arts and all the sciences, with the true humanist zeal for discovery. Typical of another strain in humanism was the reasonable, self-analytical, and somewhat skeptical Michel de Montaigne (1533–1592), an essayist who was one of the first great stylists of French letters.

Perhaps the single most characteristic monument of the Renaissance in France was the great chateau, in which the grim fortress of medieval days was transformed into a residential palace, often charmingly domesticated, retaining its thick walls and its towers, which now served a decorative rather than a defensive purpose. The Loire valley is the site of many. Two of the most celebrated are Chambord, built by Francis I, and Chenonceaux, built on a bridge over a small river, which Henry II gave to his aging but still beautiful mistress, Diane de Poitiers, and which Catherine de' Medici took from Diane after Henry's death. In sculpture, Jean Goujon returned to the classical nude as the inspiration for his statues—of Diane de Poitiers as well as of anonymous nymphs. In painting, the French, though producing no artists of the stature of the great Italians and Spaniards of the sixteenth century, did enjoy a school of portraitists, including Clouet and Fouquet, that left sensitive and realistic likenesses of the men and women of the Valois court.

The Château of Chambord, built by Francis I in the Loire Valley.

For the court Francis remodeled the Louvre, the royal residence in Paris. As a patron of the arts, he employed both Leonardo da Vinci and the famous Florentine sculptor, goldsmith, rake, and autobiographer, Benvenuto Cellini. Catherine de' Medici continued the Italian influence: in behavior as well as in decoration the court echoed Italian originals.

England

THE TUDOR MONARCHY OF HENRY VIII AND ELIZABETH   Henry VIII (reigned 1509–1547), the instigator of the Anglican Reformation, is perhaps the most familiar figure in sixteenth-century history: fat, lavishly bejeweled, with shrewd little eyes staring out of his broad face fringed with beard, his velvet hat jauntily cocked. Six times married, self-willed and intelligent, personally extravagant, he was yet economical where it counted. While the Spanish royal house squandered its wealth in war, Henry contented himself with much cheaper pleasures. He never risked big English armies on the Continent, but intervened inexpensively to maintain the balance of power when necessary. Rewarding his followers with the proceeds of confiscated monastic properties (see p. 305), he created a whole new class of loyal nobles, replacing those exterminated during the Wars of the Roses. He continued the policies of his father, Henry VII, strengthening the central administration and maintaining adequate supervision of the justices of the peace, who continued to be the keystone of English local government (see Chapter 6).

Henry's parliaments granted him what he wanted. The Tudor House of Lords had a safe majority of his newly ennobled men, who, together with the bishops of the new church (after 1534), owed their place in the House to him. As for the House of Commons, a small minority of the people chose these knights of the shire and burgesses of the towns. In the countryside, only freeholders voted, not the majority of the residents, who were tenant farmers or agricultural workers; the country gentlemen and squires chose their representatives from among their own number. In the towns, too, the franchise was usually a narrow one.

Queen Elizabeth I: "The Rainbow Portrait."

Yet the very combination of knights of the shire and burgesses meeting together made the Tudor House of Commons unique among contemporary European assemblies, since the third estate on the Continent usually represented townsmen only. In England, too, unlike the Continent, only the eldest sons of noblemen, who actually inherited the title, could sit in the House of Lords, while the younger ones, as gentry, had to seek representation in the Commons. Finally, the English Parliament, unlike continental assemblies, had during the Middle Ages acquired the right to legislate, especially on money. Why did the Tudor parliaments not quarrel with the monarch, as the Stuart parliaments would do in the seventeenth century? In part because they owed the king so much gratitude, but partly also because the Tudor monarchs, Henry VIII and Elizabeth I particularly, were skillful, dignified, persuasive, and popular, symbolizing in their own glittering persons the national sense of patriotism and of hostility to Spain and the Roman church.

We have already seen how Elizabeth I (reigned 1558–1603) completed the establishment of the Church of England upon acceding to the throne at the death of her half-sister Mary. But Elizabeth did more: her name has become a synonym for the flowering of English achievement and self-confidence in every field of endeavor. Proud, cool, and remarkably intelligent, she loved flattery but never let it lead her astray when important matters were at stake. She more than held her own among her contemporaries as a Machiavellian statesman. Her people loved her more than did those who knew her best. She never married, and in her early years she played off foreign and domestic

RELIGIOUS UPHEAVAL, IMPERIAL EXPANSION, DYNASTIC CONFLICT

329

suitors against each other with excellent political results. Like her father, she enjoyed getting her successes as cheaply as possible. Under her able ministers Burleigh and Walsingham she maintained and heightened the administrative efficiency of her government.

THE SPANISH THREAT AND MARY QUEEN OF SCOTS   Elizabeth's chief problem was the hostility of Philip II, who had been married to her Catholic half-sister Mary, and who resented both the very existence of a Protestant England and the beginnings of English penetration into the Spanish New World. Had Philip been able to concentrate on England, especially early in Elizabeth's reign, her position would have been precarious indeed. But at first he hoped to marry Elizabeth; then he hoped to capitalize on her fears that the French would succeed in backing Mary Queen of Scots against her; then he was delayed by a great Dutch revolt.

Mary Stuart, Queen of Scots, was the great-granddaughter of Henry VII. Her grandmother was Henry VIII's sister Margaret, who had married King James IV of Scotland. Her father was James V, who had married a Guise, and who left Mary as his heiress. She was not only a Catholic and half a Guise (and so of the extreme Catholic faction in France), but she lived in France, while her mother acted as regent for her in Scotland. She married the short-lived King Francis II of France (reigned 1559–1560) and took the title of queen of England as well as queen of Scots. Since Catholics regarded Elizabeth, daughter of Henry VIII by Anne Boleyn, as illegitimate, Mary might have given Elizabeth a very anxious time if she had been able to combine Scottish with French support.

But in 1555 John Knox returned to Scotland from Geneva, and found the ground ready for Calvinist preaching. The Scots had come to associate Catholicism with the hated French influence; in 1557 Scottish nobles signed the first covenant to defend Protestantism; in 1559 they revolted against Mary's mother, Mary of Guise; and in 1560 Elizabeth helped them oust the French troops. So when Mary Stuart returned to Scotland in 1561, after the death of Francis II, she found a Presbyterian church, the authority of which resided in the elders of each congregation, who could not be easily dominated by a monarch. Mary's reckless love affairs, punctuated with murder and scandal, made her extremely unpopular. In 1568, she was forced by revolution to take refuge in England, where Elizabeth put her into confinement. Her very existence was a threat to Elizabeth, who had her executed in 1587 for involvement in an alleged plot. Mary left behind her infant son, later James I of England (and VI of Scotland).

THE DUTCH REVOLT AND THE ARMADA   Meantime, the Dutch had staged a great revolt against Philip II. Charles V had resided in the Low Countries by preference, and had confirmed their traditional privileges. Philip, who was thoroughly Spanish, tried to curb the feudal and municipal liberties of the Netherlands. The more pressure he applied, the more Calvinist his subjects became; the more Protestants there were, the more he sent Spanish garrisons and tried to enforce edicts against heretics. The Dutch were also a seafaring commercial people determined to conduct their trade free from the jealous restrictions of Spanish mercantilism.

So economic considerations joined religious and political ones to precipitate a revolt by a league including nobles, rich townsmen, and members of the lower classes. They proudly called themselves Beggars, a name that had first been applied to them with scorn. In 1567 Philip sent an army under the stupid

The battle between the English fleet and the Spanish armada, 1588.

and ruthless duke of Alva, who tried but failed to hold down the thoroughly disaffected population by force alone. Alva's punitive Council of Troubles only forced the southern provinces (modern Belgium) to join the northern (Holland) in revolt. The Beggars had the support of virtually the whole population, from William the Silent, prince of Orange, down.

In 1578 Philip sent the duke of Parma to effect a compromise, and he did win back the southern provinces by political concessions; they remained basically Catholic. But the northern Protestant provinces could have been won over only by religious concessions more radical than Philip II was by temperament able to make. In 1581 the Dutch declared themselves independent of Spain. The assassination of William the Silent (1584) gave them a national Protestant martyr and strengthened their determination.

It was at this point that Queen Elizabeth came to the aid of the Dutch. She had always sympathized with them, but had so far hesitated to take on the powerful Spaniards, especially for fear that the French Catholic party and the Spaniards might unite against her. But a series of crude Spanish plots against Elizabeth's life and throne had aroused public opinion. In 1585 Elizabeth sent troops to Holland. After she executed Mary Queen of Scots (1587), Philip declared open war. The great armed fleet (armada) that he sent out in 1588 met its defeat in the English Channel at the hands of a lighter, skillfully maneuvered English fleet; a great storm north of Scotland scattered and destroyed what was left of the Spaniards. The battle marked the fading of Spanish preponderance in Europe, the beginning of English maritime greatness, and the decisive step in achieving Dutch independence. Protestants everywhere took heart and called the great storm that had sent Philip's galleons to the bottom "the Protestant wind." Desultory fighting continued in Holland after Philip's death in 1598 and down to 1609, when a truce established the virtual independence of the Dutch.

IRELAND   Elizabeth's last years were marked by a great crisis in Ireland. Henry VIII had put the Irish Parliament completely under English control, and Henry VIII's Act of Supremacy, combined with the decision (1542) that the king of England was also king of Ireland, required the Catholic Irish to acknowledge the English monarch as head of the Church. Ireland was an ancient

Celtic feudal land, where most of the Norman and English settlers had been assimilated to Irish ways, spoke the native Irish Gaelic, and remained Catholic. Chieftains regarded themselves as local kings, commanded the loyalty of their followers in war, and were still incited to battle by a professional class of bards. Ireland had only a few Protestant English inhabitants settled near Dublin. Thus the insurrection of 1597 led by "the O'Neill," whom Elizabeth had made earl of Tyrone, was a serious affair. It was not suppressed until 1601, and the Irish Question in its various phases has remained to trouble the English crown into our own day.

THE ENGLISH RENAISSANCE   The solid administration, economic prosperity, and steadily growing national feeling of the Elizabethan age was accompanied by a renaissance that had actually begun under Henry VIII, and was the latest of the European renaissances. It took its start, as all of them did, with the classics; more than the others, it was chiefly literary. Saint Thomas More, Shakespeare, Francis Bacon, Edmund Spenser, Ben Jonson, and others are part of the birthright of English-speaking peoples. They vary greatly among themselves, but Shakespeare by common consent towers not only above all the rest but above everybody else of any age, save perhaps Homer or Dante.

To admirers of order and precision the Elizabethans appear excessive, undisciplined, even uncouth. The plots of Elizabethan tragedies are often bloody, and the dramatists sometimes seem to love words for their own sake. Yet the Elizabethans in their exuberance were bursting with life and with a passionate love of country. Shakespeare sums up the Englishman's patriotic pride, in the famous lines given to John of Gaunt in *Richard II:*

This royal throne of kings, this scepter'd isle,
This earth of majesty, this seat of Mars,
This other Eden, demi-paradise,
This fortress built by Nature for herself
Against infection and the hand of war,
This happy breed of men, this little world,
This precious stone set in the silver sea,
Which serves it in the office of a wall
Or as a moat defensive to a house,
Against the envy of less happier lands,
This blessed plot, this earth, this realm, this England.

Reading Suggestions on Religious Upheaval, Imperial Expansion, Dynastic Conflict

THE REFORMATION

H. G. Koenigsberger and G. L. Mosse, *Europe in the Sixteenth Century* (Holt, 1968). Recent survey; good bibliographies.

G. R. Elton, ed., *Reformation Europe, 1517–1559* (*Torchbooks). A recent general history, with a selective bibliography.

E. H. Harbison, *The Age of Reformation* (*Cornell). Admirable.

H. J. Grimm, *The Reformation Era, 1500–1650* (Macmillan, 1954). A good American textbook, with a thorough critical bibliography.

H. Holborn, *A History of Modern Germany*, Vol. I: *The Reformation* (Knopf, 1959). Scholarly, readable, and up-to-date.

O. Chadwick, *The Reformation* (*Penguin). A very good popular account.

A. G. Dickens, *Reformation and Society in Sixteenth-Century Europe* (*Holt). Useful emphasis on social history; good illustrations.

R. H. Bainton, *The Reformation of the Sixteenth Century* (*Beacon). By a sound Protestant historian, fully abreast of modern research.

————, *Here I Stand: A Life of Martin Luther* (*Apex). Sympathetic, scholarly, and readable.

E. Erikson, *Young Man Luther* (*Norton). An important book by a distinguished psychoanalyst who is also a historian.

J. Courvoisier; *Zwingli: A Reformed Theologian* (*John Knox). Good study of an important and neglected figure.

G. Harkness, *John Calvin: The Man and His Ethics* (*Apex). A good introduction.

J. Mackinnon, *Calvin and the Reformation* (Longmans, 1936). Solid longer study.

E. H. Harbison, *The Christian Scholar in the Age of Reformation* (*Scribner's). Helpful exploration of the connection between intellectual and religious history.

A. G. Dickens, *The English Reformation* (*Schocken), and T. M. Parker, *The English Reformation to 1558* (*Oxford). Good introductions.

F. M. Powicke, *The Reformation in England* (*Oxford). A scholarly study.

G. H. Williams, *The Radical Reformation* (Westminster, 1962). An indispensable big book concerning the Anabaptists and other radicals.

H. Daniel-Rops, *The Catholic Reformation*, 2 vols. (*Image). Admirable work by a French Catholic historian.

A. G. Dickens, *The Counter-Reformation* (*Holt). Sound survey by a Protestant.

L. W. Spitz, ed., *The Protestant Reformation* (*Spectrum). Excellent selections, with good commentary.

Max Weber, *The Protestant Ethic and the Spirit of Capitalism* (*Scribner's). Celebrated controversial work on the interrelation of religion and economics.

R. H. Tawney, *Religion and the Rise of Capitalism* (*Mentor). Revision of the Weber thesis by an English intellectual associated with the Labour party.

E. Troeltsch, *Protestantism and Progress* (*Beacon). By one of the most important religious philosophers of modern times.

OVERSEAS EMPIRES

J. N. L. Baker, *A History of Geographical Discovery and Exploration*, rev. ed. (Barnes & Noble, 1963). Standard work of reference.

J. H. Parry, *Age of Reconnaissance* (*Mentor) and *Establishment of the European Hegemony, 1415-1715* (*Torchbooks), and *The Spanish Empire* (Knopf, 1966). First-rate works by an expert.

B. Penrose, *Travel and Discovery in the Renaissance* (*Atheneum). Good survey.

C. R. Boxer, *The Portuguese Seaborne Empire, 1415-1825* (Knopf, 1969) and *Four Centuries of Portuguese Expansion* (*California). By the leading authority on the subject.

S. E. Morison, *Admiral of the Ocean Sea*, 2 vols. (Little, Brown, 1942). The best book on Columbus.

H. H. Hart, *Sea Road to the Indies* (Macmillan, 1950). Treating da Gama and other Portuguese explorers.

C. McK. Parr, *So Noble a Captain* (Crowell, 1953). A scholarly treatment of Magellan and his circumnavigation.

J. H. Brebner, *The Explorers of North America, 1492-1806* (*Meridian). A good brief account.

H. R. Trevor-Roper, ed., *The Age of Expansion: Europe and the World, 1559-1660* (Thames & Hudson, 1968). Sumptuously illustrated collaborative volume.

B. Davidson, *Africa in History* (Macmillan, 1969), and R. Oliver and J. D. Fage, *A Short History of Africa* (*Penguin). Helpful introductions to the subject.

D. F. Lach, *China in the Eyes of Europe: The Sixteenth Century* (*Phoenix). Lach has published companion volumes on India, Japan, and Southeast Asia (*Phoenix).

K. S. Latourette, *China* (*Spectrum). Excellent introduction.

G. B. Sansom, *Japan: A Short Cultural History*, rev. ed. (Appleton, 1962). Stimulating introduction by a distinguished British expert.

A. L. Basham, *The Wonder That Was India* (*Evergreen). A sober and careful analysis of medieval India.

I. R. Bladen, ed., *The Portable Prescott* (*Viking). Excerpts from the accounts of the conquest of Mexico and Peru by a famous American historian.

C. H. Haring, *The Spanish Empire in America* (*Harbinger). The best general study of the subject.

R. E. Poppino, *Brazil: The Land and People* (*Oxford). Recent social and economic study.

MONARCHY AND WARFARE IN THE SIXTEENTH CENTURY

G. H. Sabine, *A History of Political Theory*, rev. ed. (Holt, 1950). An admirably lucid survey.

J. W. Allen, *History of Political Thought in the Sixteenth Century*, 3rd ed. (*Barnes & Noble). More detailed treatment.

C. W. C. Oman, *A History of the Art of War in the Sixteenth Century* (Dutton, 1937). Highly interesting study.

S. T. Bindoff, *Tudor England* (*Penguin). Short scholarly introduction.

J. D. Mackie, *The Earlier Tudors, 1485-1558* (Clarendon, 1952), and J. B. Black, *The Reign of Elizabeth* (Clarendon, 1936). Somewhat longer historical accounts.

J. J. Scarisbrick, *Henry VIII* (California, 1968), and Lacey Baldwin Smith, *Henry VIII: The Mask of Royalty* (Houghton, 1971). Two excellent new works, the latter requiring a certain preliminary knowledge.

J. E. Neale, *Queen Elizabeth* (*Anchor). The best volume on the famous queen; by a scholar who has written several specialized works on political life during her reign.

E. Jenkins, *Elizabeth the Great* (*Capricorn). Focusing on the queen as a person.

G. Mattingly, *The Armada* (*Sentry). Topnotch account.

J. Ridley, *Thomas Cranmer* (*Oxford). Biography of Henry VIII's collaborator.

J. Lynch, *Spain under the Hapsburgs*, Vol. 1 (Oxford, 1964). An up-to-date and scholarly treatment of sixteenth-century Spain.

R. Trevor Davies, *The Golden Century of Spain* (*Torchbooks). Sound popular introduction to the sixteenth century.

K. Brandi, *The Emperor Charles V* (*Humanities). A comprehensive account.

C. Petrie, *Philip II of Spain* (Norton, 1963). Good biography.

L. Goldscheider, *El Greco* (Phaidon, 1954). Well-illustrated study of the artist who expressed so well the Spanish style.

P. Geyl, *The Revolt of the Netherlands, 1555-1609* (*Barnes & Noble). By a celebrated Dutch historian who regretted the separation of the Dutch and the Flemings.

C. V. Wedgwood, *William the Silent* (*Norton). Sympathetic biography.

J. E. Neale, *The Age of Catherine de' Medici* (*Torchbooks). Short and lucid introduction to a complex era.

Q. Hurst, *Henry of Navarre* (Appleton, 1938). The standard biography of Henry IV.

SOURCES AND FICTION

H. S. Bettenson, ed. *Documents of the Christian Church* (*Oxford). An admirable compilation, useful for the Reformation.

R. H. Bainton, *The Age of the Reformation* (*Anvil). Selections from the great men and great books of the era.

Lew Wallace, *The Fair God* (*Popular). Thriller on Aztec Mexico.

C. S. Forester, *To the Indies* (Little, Brown, 1940). Excellent novel on Columbus.

R. Sabatini, *The Sea Hawk* (Houghton, 1923). Good melodramatic novel of life on the main in the late sixteenth century.

S. Putnam, ed., *The Portable Cervantes* (*Viking). Excerpts from a widely acclaimed translation of *Don Quixote*.

eight

The Seventeenth Century: War, Politics, and Empire

Ancient Greek mythology tells of Proteus, a sea divinity on whom it was difficult to keep one's grasp. To avoid capture he would turn into a flapping fish, a wriggling serpent, a bird, a trickle of water, or a ribbon of sand. The problems of the sixteenth and seventeenth centuries seem truly Protean. The internal history of each state is at once the story of the local dynasty and of other dynasties intervening in its affairs, so that domestic issues suddenly become foreign issues. Problems of conscience arise, so that what looks like a political issue proves to be largely religious, or what looks religious proves to be mainly political. Economic and social values are involved with both politics and religion, so that a wealthy bourgeois, excluded from political power by the aristocracy, may be tempted to refuse his nominal ruler financial support, to desert the ruler's religion, to listen to the siren voice of foreign agents, or even to take arms in open rebellion.

In the last chapter we saw that the French nobles who turned to Calvinism did so in part to maintain their traditional privileges against the encroachments of the king. Elizabeth helped the Dutch against the Spaniards partly because the Dutch were fellow Protestants, but more because of Philip II's threat to herself. The Catholic Reformation failed to win back some areas of Europe because the Hapsburg monarchy headed the Catholic cause, and many powerful persons who otherwise would have helped Rome could not bear at the same time to help the Hapsburgs. The papacy itself was determined to avoid Hapsburg domination. The Peace of Augsburg of 1555, the triumph of Henry IV in France, and the execution of Mary Queen of Scots all contributed to the containment of Hapsburg power. Yet none of these interlocking problems was finally resolved when the Hapsburg leader of the late sixteenth century, Philip II, died in his colossal monastic palace of the Escorial in the bleak hills near Madrid, in 1598, with an open coffin standing at his order beside his bed, and a skull grinning at him beneath a golden crown.

I

The Thirty Years' War

The Dutch played a part of outstanding importance in the international affairs of the seventeenth century. In 1609 they concluded their successful revolt against Spain by negotiating a truce for twelve years that made their state virtually independent. The United Provinces, which made up the Dutch republic, were, however, united only in opposition to Spain. Each of the seven provinces preserved its local traditions of government and sent delegates (the *Hooge Moogende,* High Mightinesses) to the Estates-General, which behaved like a diplomatic congress rather than a central legislature. Each province had its own *Stadholder* as executive, though several of them often elected the same man to the office. After the truce of 1609, Maurice, prince of Orange, son of William the Silent, was chosen Stadholder by five of the seven. Religious differences also divided the Dutch nation. There was a large Catholic minority, and the Protestant majority was badly split between orthodox Calvinists and moderates called Arminians (after Arminius, a Dutch theologian), who believed that what a man did on earth might change God's original intentions about his individual fate: predestination, therefore, was conditional.

The Dutch were the world's best businessmen; by the early seventeenth century they controlled most of the coastwise shipping of Europe. They went into the wine business in France and into the fishing grounds of the Arctic. In 1602 they organized the Dutch East India Company, and soon launched other ventures overseas. The Bank of Amsterdam (1609) minted its own florins, which became standard in Europe; its services to its depositors were so much in demand that Amsterdam became the financial capital of Europe. The Dutch invented life insurance, and made it a big business. Diamond-cutting, ship-building, gin-distilling, and tulip-growing all made the Dutch provinces rich and famous. Their opulent middle-class way of life is mirrored in the great paintings of Hals, Vermeer, and Rembrandt.

It was no wonder that Philip II's successors in Spain dreamed of reconquering the United Provinces. Spanish strength was visibly declining in the seventeenth century, as a result of the country's bad administration, its underdeveloped economy, and all the other chronic difficulties discussed in Chapter 7. Nevertheless, Spain could still draw on important resources—the wealth of the Americas, the reserves of military manpower in her north Italian possessions, and the loyalty of her Catholic Belgian provinces. After the Dutch revolt, the Spaniards wanted to stabilize a line of communications between their Italian and Belgian lands, so that men and money could move over the Alps and down the Rhine, which flowed through the lands of some rulers who were friendly and others who were hostile to the Hapsburgs. To deny this communication line to the Spaniards was a great goal both for the Dutch and for the French: the Bourbons did not relish the idea of being surrounded by Hapsburg territory any more than the Valois had done.

Thus the key to the situation was Germany—by the early seventeenth century a truly fantastic conglomeration of states. Some of the German principalities had been divided and subdivided until an ostensibly independent princeling might rule over only a village or a few hundred acres of forest. Free cities acknowledged no authority but the emperor; some held huge lands outside their walls, others not. The Church governed certain cities and regions, and

The emperor Rudolf II, king of Bohemia 1575–1611, shown with the electors on a Bohemian enameled glass beaker.

The Bohemian Period, 1618–1625

these too varied greatly in extent. There were more than two thousand governing authorities; but since many of the smaller ones combined or reached understandings locally, this number can be reduced to perhaps three hundred.

Particularly influential in Germany were the seven electors, who chose each new emperor and enjoyed other prerogatives. One elector, the king of Bohemia, was in practice always a Hapsburg, so that the imperial family always had at least one vote at election time. The three Rhineland electors—the archbishops of Mainz, Trier, and Cologne—were Catholic, and the electors of Saxony and Brandenburg were Lutheran. The elector of the Palatinate, with his capital at Heidelberg, was a Calvinist; his lands, in a rich vineyard area along the Rhine, constituted a major block to the Hapsburg plan of securing communications to the Low Countries. In addition, some princes who were not electors exercised much influence, especially the great Catholic duke of Bavaria, Maximilian.

Triumphant German particularism paralyzed the central institutions of the empire. The imperial diet, consisting in theory of all the independent German rulers, always quarreled when it met; some princes refused to accept its decisions. The emperor was virtually forced to bypass the diet, and attempted to rule by decree and pressure. Altogether, Germany did not possess the machinery to resolve the religious difficulties stemming from the Augsburg settlement of 1555 (see p. 326).

The Peace of Augsburg had not recognized Calvinism; yet Calvinism spread rapidly after 1555, horrifying both Lutherans and Catholics. Calvinist princes ignored the provision in the peace against proselytizing, and proved equally vigorous in Lutheran and in Catholic regions. Sudden conversion of a prince meant sudden conversion of his subjects, or else persecution. The consequences were riots and disorder, followed by the formation of the Calvinist Protestant Union (1608) and the Catholic League (1609) under Maximilian of Bavaria. It was not surprising that war broke out in Germany in 1618, three years before the truce between Spain and the Dutch was due to elapse.

In 1618 the head of the Protestant Union was the Calvinist elector of the Palatinate, Frederick, who was married to the daughter of James I of England. Frederick hoped to break the Catholic hold on the empire upon the death of the emperor Matthias (reigned 1612–1619), who was old and childless. If there could be four Protestant electors instead of three when Matthias died, the majority could then install a Protestant emperor. Because three electors were Catholic archbishops, the only way to get an additional Protestant was to oust the one lay Catholic elector, the king of Bohemia. The king-elect of Bohemia, Ferdinand, was a strongly Catholic Hapsburg prince, already chosen by Matthias to be his heir.

Bohemia presented its own special problems. The native Czechs expressed their national defiance of the Germans in part by following the faith that John Hus had taught them (see p. 258), the chief feature of which was utraquism, the practice of giving the laity communion in wine as well as in bread. While Lutherans, Calvinists, and utraquists were tolerated, Catholicism remained the state religion. Though Ferdinand guaranteed freedom of Protestant worship, the prospect of his becoming king of Bohemia and then emperor alarmed the Protestants. The arrest of some Protestants who had lost two legal cases touched off a revolt, which began with the famous Defenestration of Prague (May 23, 1618), when the angry rebels actually threw two Catholic imperial governors out of a window into a courtyard seventy feet below. They landed on a pile of dung, and escaped with their lives.

The hanging of thieves during the Thirty Years' War: a contemporary engraving.

The Czech rebels set up their own government and offered the crown of Bohemia to the elector Frederick of the Palatinate. The inept Frederick went off to Prague, leaving badly defended the Rhineland territories that the Spaniards most wanted and that they occupied in 1620. Meantime, Catholics in Bohemia, Spain, and Flanders rallied against the rebels with money and men. After the emperor Matthias died in 1619, the electors chose the Hapsburg Ferdinand to be emperor (Ferdinand II, reigned 1619–1637). Maximilian of Bavaria, head of the Catholic League, joined Ferdinand, in return for a promise of Frederick's electoral post; even the Lutheran elector of Saxony joined the Catholic Ferdinand, who also secured the neutrality of the Protestant Union. In Bohemia, Maximilian and the Catholic forces won the battle of the White Mountain (November 8, 1620). Frederick, derisively nicknamed "the Winter King," fled, and Ferdinand made the Bohemian throne hereditary in his own family. With the aid of the Jesuits, he enforced Catholicism and abolished toleration for utraquists and Calvinists, but granted it temporarily to Lutherans because of his obligations to the elector of Saxony. He executed the Czech leaders of the rebellion and permitted terrible destruction in Bohemia.

The continued presence of Spanish forces in the Palatinate posed a threat to others. The Protestant king Christian IV of Denmark (1588–1648) feared the Hapsburgs would move northward to the Baltic; the French faced a new Hapsburg encirclement; and the Dutch, menaced by an immediate Spanish attack, were worst off of all. They made an alliance with Christian IV, and another with the fugitive Frederick of the Palatinate, agreeing to subsidize his reconquest of his Rhenish lands. Had Frederick accepted a proposal of the Spanish to return to the Palatinate under their auspices, there might have been no Thirty Years' War; but he turned it down. When fighting resumed, Frederick was routed again, whereupon Ferdinand transferred the Palatine electorate to Maximilian (1625).

In France, meantime, Cardinal Richelieu, who was emerging as chief minister of Louis XIII (reigned 1610–1643), fully recognized the Hapsburg danger. Richelieu was ready to arrange a dynastic marriage between the future Charles I of England and Louis XIII's sister, Henrietta Maria, and to make an alliance with other Protestants—Frederick, the Dutch, Christian IV of Denmark, and also Gustavus Adolphus, the Lutheran king of Sweden. Richelieu could count on the understanding of Pope Urban VIII, who felt that the fulfillment of Hapsburg ambitions would be bad for the interests of the Church. By the summer of 1624 the new coalition was in being. But Spanish victories in

Holland (1625) and the unwillingness of Gustavus Adolphus to serve under the Danes spoiled the plan. Christian IV now had to fight for the Protestants alone, thus inaugurating the Danish phase of the war.

Count Wallenstein: a portrait by Van Dyck.

In the new phase Catholic military operations fell into the hands of Count Wallenstein, who had recruited a private army, which lived off the land by requisitions and open plunder. Born a Protestant and converted to Catholicism, Wallenstein had bought up a quarter of the lands in Bohemia after Ferdinand's suppression of the Czech rebellion and now dreamed of creating a new-model monarchy in Germany. Together with the forces of Maximilian and the Catholic League under the command of Count Tilly, Wallenstein's armies defeated the Danes and moved northward into Danish territory.

In 1629 the emperor Ferdinand dramatized his successes by the Edict of Restitution and the Treaty of Lübeck. The Edict reaffirmed the religious Peace of Augsburg, still making no provision for Calvinists, and declared that the Catholics were entitled to recover all ecclesiastical property that had passed to the Lutherans since 1551—a vast amount of land and wealth. It meant changing boundaries throughout northern and western Germany, and dispossessing many whose wealth rested on former Church property. In the Treaty of Lübeck Christian IV acknowledged defeat, and undertook not to interfere again in German affairs; he received his lands back. Wallenstein further enriched himself by increasing his own land holdings. But the Hapsburgs had moved into regions hitherto Protestant and only on the periphery of imperial interest, and they had shown that in victory they would revert to religious extremism.

More and more Ferdinand became indebted to his ambitious general Wallenstein, and less and less could he control him. Wallenstein planned to found a new Baltic trading company with the remnants of the Hanseatic League (see Chapter 6), and by opening the Baltic to the Spaniards make possible a complete Spanish victory over the Dutch. When Ferdinand asked Wallenstein for troops to use in Italy against the French, Wallenstein, intent on his northern plans, at first refused to send them because Gustavus Adolphus of Sweden had decided to attack the imperial forces in Germany.

Soon Ferdinand dismissed Wallenstein, and so placated Maximilian of Bavaria. The imperial troops defeated the French in Italy, and the emperor was able to make the French agree not to help the Dutch or the Swedes. If Ferdinand had next revoked the Edict of Restitution and placated the Protestants, peace still might have been possible. But he refused. Maximilian and Tilly were now in command of the imperial armies, and Gustavus Adolphus was invading. The Swedish phase of the war was beginning.

Highly intelligent, physically powerful, competent in every way, Gustavus Adolphus (reigned 1611–1632) had tamed the unruly Swedish nobility, given his country an efficient government and a sound economy, taken lessons from the Dutch in military tactics, and proved himself and his armies against Russians and Poles by establishing a Swedish foothold on the south shores of the Baltic. A Lutheran, tolerant of Calvinists, he brought a large, well-disciplined army of Swedes, Finns, and Lapps, and added to them all the recruits, even prisoners, that he could induce to join his forces. Sharing their hardships, he usually restrained them from plunder. Richelieu agreed to subsidize his forces, and Gustavus agreed not to fight Maximilian and to guarantee freedom of worship for Catholics. The Protestant electors of Saxony and Brandenburg denounced the Edict of Restitution, and mobilized, in part to revive the Protestant cause, but also in part to protect the Germans against the Swedes.

Protestant hesitation ended after the terrible sack of Magdeburg by the Catholic forces of Tilly in May 1631, accompanied by a fire that left the city in ashes. Tilly himself may not have been responsible for the massacre of twenty thousand or more Protestants: no doubt, the imperial troops simply got out of hand. But even in an atrocious war, this episode was recognized as a fearful atrocity, and the Catholic cause, far from gaining, lost as a result.

The elector of Brandenburg had to ally himself with Gustavus, and so did the elector of Saxony, threatened by Tilly's starving troops. At Breitenfeld, in September 1631, Gustavus defeated Tilly. This, together with a defeat of the Spaniards off the Dutch coast, turned the tide against the Hapsburgs. Now the Saxons invaded Bohemia and recaptured Prague in the name of Frederick of the Palatinate, while Gustavus invaded the Catholic lands of south central Germany, taking Frankfurt and Mainz, and obtaining the alliance of many princes and free cities. In the crisis, Ferdinand turned back to Wallenstein, who consented to return to his command.

Gustavus had been more successful than Richelieu, his sponsor, had expected; indeed, too successful, since not only the Hapsburgs but Maximilian and the Catholic League, still friends of France, were suffering from the Swedes. Gustavus was planning to reorganize all Germany, to unite Lutheran and Calvinist churches, and even to become emperor—aims opposed by all the German princes. But the strength of Gustavus' position declined: his allies were untrustworthy and his enemies, Maximilian and Wallenstein, drew together. In November 1632 the Swedes won the battle of Lützen, defeating Wallenstein; Gustavus Adolphus, however, was killed.

Once more a moment had arrived when peace might have been possible, yet the fighting, and the plague, famine, and death accompanying it, continued. The pope, suspect among the cardinals as hostile to the Catholic cause, wanted peace. Richelieu preferred war, in order to further French aims in the Rhineland; the Swedes needed to protect their heavy investment and come out of the fighting with some territory; the Spaniards hoped that Gustavus' death meant that the Hapsburg cause could be saved and the Dutch defeated. Gustavus' chancellor, Oxenstierna, an able diplomat, was recognized by the German Protestants in 1633 as chief of the Protestant cause.

Wallenstein negotiated with the enemies of the empire (he wanted the French to recognize him as king of Bohemia); his army began to dribble way, and he was again dismissed by the emperor Ferdinand, who suspected him of treachery. On February 24, 1634, an English mercenary in the imperial service murdered Wallenstein and won an imperial reward. At Nordlingen, in September 1634, the forces of Ferdinand defeated the Protestants, thereby lessening the influence of Sweden and making Cardinal Richelieu the chief strategist for the Protestant cause, which now became the Bourbon cause.

The Swedish and French Period, 1635–1648

The remaining years of the Thirty Years' War were years of Hapsburg-Bourbon conflict, a sequel to the Hapsburg-Valois wars. The Protestant commander had to promise future toleration for Catholicism in Germany, and undertake to keep on fighting indefinitely in exchange for French men and money. More and more the original religious character of the war became transformed into a purely dynastic and political struggle. The armies themselves on both sides were made up of a mixture of men from just about every nationality in Europe; they fought as professional soldiers, changing sides frequently, and taking their women and children with them everywhere.

In 1635 the emperor Ferdinand at last relinquished the Edict of Restitution

Europe in 1648

Legend:
- Brandenburg-Prussia
- Austrian Hapsburg lands
- Spanish Hapsburg lands
- Swedish possessions
- Venetian possessions
- Ottoman Empire
- ··········· Boundary of the Holy Roman Empire
- ■ Battle sites

60
10
5
0
5
15

55

20

50

NORWAY

Oslo

S
W

Stockholm

SCOTLAND

Edinburgh
Dunbar Berwick

North Sea

DENMARK

Copenhagen

Baltic

ULSTER

Drogheda

IRELAND

Dublin

Wexford

Preston Marston Moor

Lübeck

POMERANIA

Danzig

Hamburg

ENGLAND

Nottingham

see inset

Texel

Bremen

Elbe R.

BRANDENBURG

Cavaliers

Worcester

Naseby

UNITED
NETHERLANDS

Osnabrück

Münster

WEST-
PHALIA

Magdeburg

Berlin Frankfort

Lützen Breitenfeld

Oder R.

Approximate division line
between Puritans and Cavaliers
in England, May 1643

London

Puritans

Rhine R.

SAXONY

THE

SILESIA

SPANISH
NETHERLANDS

Mainz

PALATINATE

Heidelberg

Prague

BOHEMIA

MORAVIA

Atlantic Ocean

45

Rocroy

Seine R.

Paris

Verdun

Metz

EMPIRE

AUSTRIA

15

Nantes

Orléans

Toul

Strasbourg

Nördlingen

Danube R.

Vienna

STYRIA

Loire R.

F R A N C E

ALSACE

BAVARIA

FRANCHE-
COMTÉ

SWITZERLAND
VALTELLINE

TYROL

CARINTHIA

HUN

Bordeaux

Geneva

SAVOY

PIEDMONT

MILAN

Po R.

Venice

CARNIOLA

VENETIAN REPUBLIC

40

PORTUGAL

Burgos

Avignon
(to the papacy)

Genoa

Florence

PAPAL
STATES

Ragusa

Lisbon

Tagus R.

S P A I N

Madrid

Ebro R.

Marseilles

CORSICA
(to Genoa)

Rome

NAPLES

Barcelona

BALEARIC IS.

Naples

Guadalquivir R.

Valencia

M e d i t e r r a n e a n   S e a

SARDINIA

Seville

35

Granada

Palermo

10

SICILY

ALGIERS
(Tributary to Ottoman Empire)

TUNIS

MALTA

5

0

5

10

15

FINLAND

25   30   35   40   45   50

E
N

L. Onega

Gulf of Finland

INGRIA

• Novgorod

ESTONIA

LIVONIA

• Pskov

COURLAND

W. Dvina R.

LITHUANIA

Königsberg

• Vilna

• Smolensk

Moscow •

Oka R.

R U S S I A

Ural R.

55
45

PRUSSIA

• Warsaw

P O L A N D

Vistula R.

Kiev •

Dnieper R.

Volga R.

Don R.

Dniester R.

MOLDAVIA

CRIMEA

Caspian Sea

40

TRANSYLVANIA

GARY

Belgrade •

WALLACHIA

Danube R.

Morava R.

50

MONTE-
NEGRO

Black Sea

Vardar R.

O T T O M A N

Salonika •

Constantinople •

E M P I R E

35

Aegean Sea

Tigris R.

IONIAN IS.
(to Venice)

Athens •

RHODES

Euphrates R.

(to Venice)

CYPRUS

CRETE

20   25   30   35   40   45

North Sea

Zaandam
Haarlem
Leiden   Amsterdam
Schiedam   Rotterdam

UNITED NETHERLANDS

Bruges •

Calais •

Antwerp •

Scheldt R.

Meuse R.

SPANISH
NETHERLANDS

Cambray •

Rhine R.

F R A N C E

and made a compromise peace with the elector of Saxony. Most of the other Lutheran princes signed also. Alarmed by the imperial gains and by the renewed activity of the Spaniards in the Low Countries, Richelieu made new arrangements with Oxenstierna in Germany and a new alliance with the Dutch. No longer confining himself to the role of subsidizer, he declared war on Spain. The war would go on, though the only German allies the French and Swedes still had were a few Calvinist princes.

A great Dutch naval victory over Spain (1639) put an end to the power of the Spanish navy, which had been declining for some years. The power of Spain was further sapped by unrest in Catalonia and by the revolt (1640) of Portugal, which Philip II had annexed in 1580 and which now proceeded to reestablish its independence. The death of Richelieu (1642) and of Louis XIII (1643) did not alter French policy. Within a few days after the death of Louis, the French defeated the Spaniards at Rocroy so thoroughly that Spain was knocked out of the war, and in fact out of the competition for European hegemony. The dreams of Charles V and Philip II ended here.

Two peace conferences now opened: between Hapsburgs and Swedes at Osnabrück, and between Hapsburgs and French not far away at Münster. At Osnabrück proceedings were delayed by the sudden Swedish invasion of Denmark, where Christian IV had shown his jealousy of rising Swedish power. At Münster, the French refused to treat with a Spanish delegate: they wished to make peace with the Austrian Hapsburgs only. The Baltic quarrel petered out when Christina, Gustavus Adolphus' daughter, who greatly wanted peace, became queen of Sweden in 1644.

The problems for settlement were many and delicate, the negotiations complex; differences between the allies that had been unimportant during open warfare proved critical when it came to a religious settlement. The meetings dragged on for several years while the fighting and destruction continued. The Dutch made a separate peace with the Spaniards, and pulled out of the French alliance after they learned of secret French negotiations with Spain hostile to their interests. French victories forced the wavering emperor Ferdinand III (reigned 1637–1657) to agree to the terms that had been so painstakingly hammered out, and on October 24, 1648, the Peace of Westphalia put an end to the Thirty Years' War.

The Peace of Westphalia: Impact of the War

The religious terms of the peace extended the *cuius regio eius religio* principles of the Peace of Augsburg to Calvinists as well as Lutherans and Catholics. The year 1624 was designated by compromise as the normal year for establishing the status of Church property; for the Protestants this was a great improvement over the Edict of Restitution. States forcibly converted to Catholicism during the war won the right to revert to Protestantism; the Protestants of the Hapsburg lands, however, won no toleration at all.

Territorially, France secured Alsace and sovereignty over Metz, Toul, and Verdun. Sweden received most of Pomerania, along the Baltic shore of Germany, a large cash indemnity with which to pay the huge armies still mobilized, and three votes in the German Diet. As recompense for the loss of Pomerania, Brandenburg received the archbishopric of Magdeburg and several other bishoprics. The family of Maximilian of Bavaria kept the electorate of the Palatinate and a part of its territory; the rest was returned to the son of Frederick, who was restored as an elector, thus raising the total number of electors to eight. German particularism gained, as the individual German states secured the right to conduct their own foreign affairs, making treaties among themselves and with foreign powers if these were not directed against the emperor. The Dutch and Swiss republics were recognized as independent.

Despite the peace, the danger was great that fighting would resume. Sweden had 100,000 soldiers in arms in Germany, of whom only a few were Swedes; the rest were professional fighting men, whose whole life was war. A similar problem of demobilization and resettlement faced the imperial authorities. Many soldiers engaged themselves as mercenaries to any ruler who would hire them, and some simply became brigands. Moreover, since the treaty did not provide a means for enforcing the religious property settlement, any attempt to recover lost property might provoke a new fight. The huge amount of money to be paid the Swedes gave rise to such bitterness that this too endangered the peace.

For more than two centuries after 1648, the Thirty Years' War was blamed for everything that later went wrong in Germany. We now know that the figures given in contemporary sources are inflated and unreliable; sometimes the number of villages allegedly destroyed in a given district was larger than the whole number of villages that had ever existed there. Also scholars traditionally failed to note that the economic decline in Germany had begun well before the war opened in 1618. Yet, even when we make allowances for these early exaggerations, we must note that contemporaries everywhere in Germany felt the catastrophe to have been overwhelming. The over-all diminution in population was from about 21 million in 1618 to less than 13½ million in 1648; the suffering of individuals was indeed extreme. Some historians have attributed to the disasters of the war the long delay in achieving German national unity, a consequent lack of experience in orderly self-government, a yearning for authority, an eagerness to obey, and even a kind of national inferiority complex. Though suggestive indeed, and certainly to be pondered as the student encounters the problems of more recent German history, these generalizations by their very nature remain unprovable.

Once the war was over, the nobility sometimes succeeded in forcing the peasants back onto the soil by denying them the right to leave the village or to engage in home industry. In general the war made little change in the social hierarchy of Germany. Politically the main change was probably the shrinking of the power of the empire: the recognition that individual German states could, in effect, conduct their own foreign policies limited direct Hapsburg power to Hapsburg lands. Bavaria, Saxony, and especially Brandenburg-Prussia would now be able to emerge as powers in Germany. Non-Austrian Germans harbored bitter resentment against the Hapsburgs for having fought a terrible war simply to protect family interests. Particularism, which had flourished at least since the Golden Bull of 1356, now received yet another long lease on life.

All these issues remained to trouble Europe again, to make more fighting. Neither the pope, who denounced the Peace of Westphalia, nor many Protestants, who felt betrayed by its provisions, were satisfied with it. Its only merit was that it ended the fighting in a war that had become intolerable.

II
Revolution and Settlement in England

Background: The First Stuarts

SEVENTEENTH-CENTURY WAR, POLITICS, AND EMPIRE

England's small part in the Thirty Years' War is explained by the domestic crisis that grew under James I (son of Mary Stuart, whom Elizabeth had executed in 1587) and culminated under his son Charles I in a prolonged civil war and the execution of the king. Thereafter, for eleven years, England was a kind of republic, until Charles's son, Charles II, was restored, and the Stuart family got a second chance. How was it that less than half a century after the death of the enormously popular Elizabeth, Englishmen would be executing their king?

Like the Thirty Years' War, the English Civil War is Protean. James I was a Scot and so a foreigner, and far less popular than Elizabeth. He believed that he ruled by divine right. Kings, he said, were God's "vice-gerents* on earth, and so adorned and furnished with some sparkles of the Divinitie." James was an articulate pedant constantly repeating his views in speaking and writing. While his son, Charles I, was personally far more attractive, he understood no more than his father the kind of compromises the Tudor monarchs had made in order to keep their Parliaments contented. The character of the first two Stuarts had a great deal to do with the breakdown of the monarchy.

Politically speaking, the English king, like other contemporary European monarchs, strove to make the royal administration strong. Unlike the continental rulers, however, James and Charles found themselves infringing on what the gentry in Parliament and in the countryside felt to be their established rights. At the same time the royal effort to force submission to the Church of England alienated those Protestants who could not accept the Church. So political and religious questions were knit together.

Since the English king was obliged to ask Parliament for funds, quarrels over money proved very important. But it was perhaps more important that Charles I lacked a bureaucracy of the kind that ruled France for Richelieu and Louis XIII. The unpaid English justices of the peace rendered justice in the parishes, administered poor relief, and indeed managed the administration in the countryside. From the same class of gentry came the knights of the shires and burgesses who made up the House of Commons, and included so many "Puritans," or English Calvinists. The same important people and their relatives were alienated from the monarch on many issues. Finally, the actual outbreak of civil war was closely connected with foreign policy: Parliament had become suspicious that the king was pro-Spanish and pro-Catholic, and had ceased to trust him on diplomatic issues.

Actually both parties to the quarrel were trying to make revolutionary changes in the traditional system. The crown was trying to make England more like a continental divine-right monarchy, in which the king was the earthly representative of God. The idea, as old as the Roman Empire, was strongly revived in the sixteenth and seventeenth centuries; it was quite different from the Tudor compromise of a strong monarch working with and through his Parliament and satisfying the goals of the gentry and commercial classes. The parliamentarians who revolted against the Stuarts were trying to secure for a legislative body final authority in the execution of policy as well as in the making of law. This was something equally new, not only for England but for the Western world as a whole.

The Reign of James I

All the issues that led to the final explosion may be seen in an earlier phase during the reign of James I (1603–1625). About the House of Commons he once remarked "I am surprised that my ancestors should ever have permitted such an institution to come into existence. I am a stranger, and found it here when I arrived, so that I am obliged to put up with what I cannot get rid of."† When the Commons expressed national grievances against certain legal but

* The word is "gerents," not "regents"; it comes from Latin *gerere*, "to manage" or "to bear."
† G. Davies, *The Early Stuarts, 1603–1660* (New York, 1937), p. 17.

outworn rights of the crown, James acted as though they were personally insulting him. He tried to develop sources of income outside parliamentary control, and Parliament insisted on the principle that it had to approve any new methods of raising revenue. When Parliament did not enact legislation he wanted, he would try to get the courts to declare the measure legal.

One case, seemingly on a small point, involved a question of principle: John Bate, a merchant, refused to pay duty on imported currants. The judges ruled that there was no parliamentary authority for James to levy these customs duties, but that nonetheless he had the right to levy them. In a matter concerning the common good, they ruled, the king had absolute power, and all foreign affairs, including foreign trade, fell within this category. So James's officials joyfully began to levy sales taxes without parliamentary authority, and when Parliament showed alarm at the prospect that James might make himself financially independent, he tried to forbid discussion of the question. Finally, James dissolved his first Parliament, which had sat from 1604 to 1611. Another met briefly and quarrelsomely in 1614, but thereafter none was elected until 1621. In the interim, to raise money, the king relied to some extent on "benevolences," supposedly free gifts granted by the subject to the monarch when he asked for them, but often in fact extracted under pressure.

Portrait of James I by Daniel Mytens, 1621.

James behaved as if Parliament had no legitimate concern in foreign affairs, and for years, in the face of the popular hatred for Spain, tried to arrange a Spanish royal marriage for his son Charles. In 1621 when Parliament petitioned James instead to go to war with Spain and marry Charles to a Protestant, he replied angrily that this was none of their business and threatened to punish the "insolent behavior" of anybody who continued to discuss the question in Parliament. The members admitted that the king alone had the right to make war and peace and to arrange for the marriage of his son, but declared that they wished to call his attention to the European situation as they saw it. James answered that this was merely a way of concealing their real intention to usurp royal prerogative.

The House of Commons then presented the Great Protestation (1621), which denied the king's right to imprison its members at will, and asserted their right to discuss and resolve any question touching the state. James dismissed Parliament and imprisoned three of its leaders. In fact James was right in alleging that the Commons were making a new claim, but the unpopularity of his Spanish policy made their protest a popular one. And James himself threw his case away in 1624, when—the Spanish match having fallen through—he summoned Parliament, gave it a complete report on foreign affairs, and asked its advice on just those questions he had been ready to punish them for discussing.

In religion James was determined to enforce conformity to the Church of England. He rejected a moderate appeal presented by Puritans inside the Church: to relax or make optional certain requirements of the ritual. This probably reflected the majority sentiment in the House of Commons, but James told the Puritan leaders (1604) that he would make them conform or harry them out of the land. He summed up his view as "no bishop, no king," stressing his belief that each depended on the other. And if the bishops did depend on the king for their continued support against the Puritans, he no less depended on them, for they preached his views of divine right and from the pulpit kept urging obedience to the royal will. One great service was rendered the English-speaking world by James's love of uniformity: between 1604 and 1611 a commission of forty-seven scholars prepared the King James version of the Bible, a major influence in the shaping of literary English.

Charles I (reigned 1625–1649) shared his father's theories of monarchy, though he proved it more in action and less in words. His first Parliament voted him only a fraction of what he asked for and needed for the war against Spain (1625), which it had itself urged on James. Soon Charles found himself fighting the French as well, and the English forces suffered a severe defeat (1627). Charles raised money by forced loans, always unpopular, and arrested some who refused to contribute; the courts upheld the legality of both loans and arrests. In 1628 both houses of Parliament produced the Petition of Right, which listed alleged royal infringements of ancient statutes and asked for a redress of grievances: no royal taxes without the consent of Parliament, no billeting of troops in private houses, no imprisonment without a charge or legal protection. The king assented.

But by his assent, he later said, he had meant only to affirm previously existing rights, not to hand over any new ones. Nor was his assent to the petition a law. Indeed, after Parliament had voted the subsidies he asked for, he went right on collecting customs duties that Parliament had not voted. Parliament protested. Sir John Eliot, leader of the House of Commons, attacked Charles's religious policies, denouncing the bishops as unfit to interpret the Thirty-nine Articles (see p. 306), thus in effect claiming the right for Parliament to determine the religion of England. Amid protests Charles dissolved Parliament in 1629, and had Eliot and others arrested; Eliot died in prison, the first martyr in the parliamentary cause.

For the next eleven years (1629–1640) Charles governed without a Parliament. He totally failed to sense the rising popular support for the views of Eliot and the Puritans. To him any subject who did not adhere to the Church of England was disloyal; the whole duty of a loyal subject consisted in obeying king and bishop. Like James, he referred questions of legality to the courts, but if the judges did not say what he wanted to hear, they were dismissed and replaced by judges who would.

To save money and postpone indefinitely the recall of Parliament, Charles made peace with France and Spain. He revived obsolete medieval (but perfectly legal) ways to collect money: he forced all those who owned land worth forty pounds a year and who had not been knighted to pay large fines; he said that large areas now in private hands were in fact royal forest, and collected fines from their owners; he enforced feudal wardships. All this aroused the wealthy against him. He also regularly collected from all of England an imposition called ship money, which had been traditionally levied only on coastal towns to pay for defensive ships. John Hampden, a rich gentleman from Buckinghamshire, an inland county, refused to pay it, and lost his case (1637). But the case dramatized the issue, since the judges who found for the king echoed the divine-right theory, saying the the king is *lex loquens,* a speaking law.

Charles's unpopularity grew, as his archbishop of Canterbury, William Laud, vigorously enforced conformity: Laud drove the Puritans from their pulpits, censored all but approved books on religious subjects, and aroused a storm of disapproval. The Puritans denounced the established ritual as popish and contrary to the Bible, and gave their resistance the color of martyrdom.

In Scotland, by reannexing in 1625 all the church and crown land that had fallen into private hands since 1542, Charles with one stroke aroused the Scotch nobility that had acquired the land in the interim. English and Scots often disliked each other, the English thinking of the Scots as barbarous and greedy, the Scots of the English as too rich for their own good and inclined to popery. A plan of James I to create a constitutional union between the kingdoms had failed early in his reign. Unable as usual to gauge public opinion, Charles decided in 1637 to impose a Book of Common Prayer on the Scots, who rose in their wrath, as if "the Mass in Latin had been presented."

In March 1638 the Presbyterians of Scotland banded together in a Solemn League and Covenant (its members were called Covenanters) to defend their faith; in November, a general assembly—despite royal objections—abolished episcopacy and prescribed a definitive ritual for the Scottish Kirk (church). The Covenant united almost all Scots, who insisted all along that they were undertaking nothing against Charles as their king. In fact, however, it was impossible simultaneously to uphold Charles as king and to abolish bishops; Charles went to war in Scotland (the first "Bishops' War," 1639), and at once the question of paying for the campaign arose. In 1640 Charles summoned Parliament once more.

Reforms of the Long Parliament

The Short Parliament of 1640 would vote no money until the piled-up grievances of almost forty years were settled; Charles refused all compromise, and dissolved it. But a defeat in Scotland forced him to promise to buy off the Scots, and, since he could not find the money, he had to summon another Parliament. This was the Long Parliament, which sat for twenty years, 1640–1660. It began by arresting the most powerful royal favorite, Thomas Wentworth, earl of Strafford, who was tried for high treason without a verdict being reached and who was eventually sacrificed by Charles to the passions of the public and executed. Archbishop Laud was imprisoned and later executed.

Parliament now passed the Triennial Act, providing machinery for summoning Parliament if the king did not summon it within three years after a dissolution. It also passed a revolutionary act making it illegal for Charles to dissolve the present Parliament without its own consent. It abolished the Court of Star Chamber (see p. 265), reversed the judgment against Hampden in the ship money case, abolished ship money, reverted to the forest boundaries of 1623, and declared it illegal to require anybody to become a knight. All of this Charles assented to, but hated; many suspected that he would bide his time and do away with these laws.

The Long Parliament, however, could not agree on church affairs; the Lords would not accept a bill excluding bishops from their house, largely because they resented the Commons' interference. A "root and branch" bill abolishing bishops altogether had passionate defenders and a good many lukewarm opponents. The Commons favored, but the Lords did not, various regulations of ritual and Sabbath observance. The extreme radicalism of some of the Puritans began to produce a reaction among the milder ones.

The king's position was improving when it was damaged by an Irish Catholic revolt that began in October 1641 with a massacre of some thirty thousand Protestants who had been settled in Ulster by James I and, ironically enough, had been oppressed by Strafford, acting as governor for Charles I. Parliament, suspecting that Charles had encouraged the Irish rebels, was unwilling to entrust to royal command the army that would put down the revolt, and threatened to take the appointment of officers into its own hands. Finally, Parliament produced a monster list of grievances, the Grand Remonstrance in 204 clauses (December 1641).

The House of Commons voted to print the Grand Remonstrance and so advertise its anger to the public; it began to discuss the appointment of a "lord general" who would have power to raise and pay troops; it talked of impeaching the queen (the French princess Henrietta Maria) on suspicion of instigating the Irish rebellion. Charles unwisely tried to arrest five leading members of

Commons for treason and for complicity with the Scots. He took the unprecedented step of entering Parliament with a group of armed men, but found that the five had taken refuge in the privileged City of London. They returned to Parliament in triumph (January 1642). Charles did consent to a bill removing bishops from any temporal position and depriving them of any private law court. But he refused other parliamentary demands, including the "Nineteen Propositions" of June 1642, which would have enabled Parliament to veto appointments to the great offices of state, to approve the education and marriages of the royal children, to consent to all appointments of new peers, and to dictate further reform of the Church.

England was now dividing into two camps that would fight a civil war. Leadership of the Commons passed to the Independents, who were Brownists or extreme Calvinists (see p. 306); around Charles there gathered a party loyal to the Church and to him, including members of both houses. When Parliament announced that the cost of its own military operations would be borne by its opponents, many who had been neutral joined the king. Yet for Charles money continued to be the problem, as he depended on gifts from rich individuals. The north and west of England were largely royalist, the richer and more populous south and east, including London, largely parliamentarian.

In recent years, English historians have engaged in a sharp controversy with respect to the economic motives of the parliamentary side. Though stimulating and entertaining, much of the writing has tended to reflect the individual author's political position on twentieth-century questions in England. So present-day Labour party proponents have argued that the Puritans of the Civil War included the most enterprising, advanced, and successful members of the gentry, to which present-day Tories have tended to answer that the gentry who backed the Puritans were actually those on the way down in the economic competition, and unable to face inflation, the enclosure of lands for sheep-raising, and other economic threats. Neutral scholars tend to enjoy the argument, but to accuse both sides of oversimplification: economic motives alone did not determine a man's allegiance in the English civil war any more than they have in any other complex political and social and religious struggle.

Civil War, 1642–1649

In the civil war the early advantage lay with the king, but his inability to win quickly a decisive victory cost him the war in the end. His peace with the Irish rebels in 1643 and his intention of using Irish forces in England increased the fear of "popery" that all along had driven neutrals toward Parliament, and helped it reach a "Solemn League and Covenant" with the anti-Catholic Scots. This brought Scottish forces into England against Charles, in exchange for a promise to make English and Irish religion as nearly like Scottish Presbyterianism as possible. Parliament won the battle of Marston Moor (1644) largely owing to the specially trained cavalry led by Oliver Cromwell, one of the radical Puritan gentry. Soon after, Cromwell reorganized the parliamentary forces into the "New Model" army. At Naseby (1645) his Roundheads (so termed from their close-cropped hair) decisively defeated the Cavaliers (royalists).

In 1646 Charles surrendered to the Scots, and stalled for time by launching prolonged negotiations with them and with Parliament. Dissension now developed among his opponents, as the army, representing the radical, Independent (Congregationalist) wing of Puritanism, quarreled with the moderate Presbyterian leadership of Parliament that had begun the civil war. The Independent members (about sixty) and the speakers of both houses fled London and joined the army, which marched on London and forcibly restored them to their places. Even more radical than Cromwell and the Independents was one faction in the army called Levellers, who advocated a universal franchise and relief from social and economic grievances.

In December 1647 the king secretly agreed with the Scots to establish Presbyterianism in England for three years and to suppress the Independents. Parliament thereupon renounced its allegiance to the king, and a second civil war began. The Presbyterians, who had formerly supported Parliament, now joined the royalists and the Scots against the army; most Englishmen, however, seem to have remained neutral. In August 1648 Cromwell thoroughly defeated the Scots at Preston Pans, and ended the second civil war. The army took possession of Charles; Colonel Pride, acting on its behalf, excluded 140 Presbyterian members from Parliament in "Pride's Purge," leaving only about 60 Independents as members. The "Rump," as this much abbreviated body was called, created a special court to try the king. In January 1649 Charles was tried, condemned, and executed. While the killers of the king believed that they were acting as agents of God, the execution created a new wave of sympathy for the king both in Europe and at home.

The Rump now abolished the monarchy and the House of Lords. England was a republic, styled the Commonwealth (1649–1653), ruled by a Commons comprising only about a tenth the original membership of the Long Parliament. This minority regime depended for support on the radical army of Cromwell, who was the dominant personality of the republican experiment. Cromwell himself with the utmost ruthlessness began the reconquest of rebellious Ireland (1649–1650). Next he turned to the Scots, who supported Charles I's son, Charles II; Cromwell defeated them at Dunbar (1650), and Charles II himself at Worcester (1651). The effort at restoration ended; Charles fled to France in disguise. Finally there was a war with the Dutch, precipitated by the Navigation Act of 1651, a mercantilist measure that struck a heavy blow at the Dutch carrying trade by forbidding the importation of goods into England or the colonies, except in English ships or in ships of the country producing the goods. The Dutch War, fought at sea, ended in a victory for England.

But England itself remained Cromwell's greatest problem. Government by Rump and army aroused much bitter opposition. To grant an amnesty to the royalists and to enact conciliatory reforms seemed to be impossible in the face of parliamentary opposition. Though the Rump under pressure did fix a date for new elections, its members voted to keep their own seats in the new Parliament and to pass on all other representatives who might be chosen. Discarding the last pretensions to be acting legally, Cromwell and his musketeers dissolved the Rump (1653), thus earning the eternal hatred of the extreme republicans. Then the army itself elected a Parliament of members nominated by Congregational ministers in each county, which was called the Nominated or Barebone's Parliament.

The House of Commons as shown on the Great Seal of England used by the Commonwealth, 1651.

After a few months, the members of the new Parliament resigned their powers to Cromwell, who became lord protector of England, thus inaugurating the second phase of the republican experiment—the Protectorate (1653–1660). At first he governed under a written constitution, the Instrument of Government, drawn up by some of the army officers. Since the Instrument limited voting to those with an estate worth £200, the new Parliament proved to be an upper-class body. It wanted to amend the Instrument and proved so uncooperative that Cromwell—who believed that only a military dictatorship could govern England properly—dissolved it in 1654. After a royalist uprising in 1655, Cromwell ordered Catholic priests exiled, forbade Anglicans to preach, and divided England into eleven military districts. The major-general in command of each not only collected the taxes and policed his district but served as censor of public morals. Horse-racing, cock-fighting, and bear-baiting, were prohibited (the last, as Macaulay later said, not because it gave pain to the bear but because it gave pleasure to the spectators); alehouses, gambling-dens, brothels were closed or regulated severely; the theater was forbidden.

Englishmen hated this Puritan regime and its attempts to impose Calvinist morality by force. The revulsion of opinion was evident in the parliamentary election of 1656. Even when the army had purged parliamentarians of whom it did not approve, those who were left still produced the "Humble Petition and Advice," revising the Instrument of Government in the direction of traditional English monarchy. It asked Cromwell to become king (he refused), gave the House of Commons the right to exclude any elected member, and created a second house to be nominated by Cromwell. Though Cromwell accepted some of the amendments, he dissolved this Parliament, too (1657).

Cromwell died September 3, 1658, and was succeeded as lord protector by his son, Richard, who proved unable to reorganize the army and weed out the most fanatical extremists. The army forced Richard to recall the Rump, and resign (May 1659). As tension grew between the army officers and the Rump, royalist activity increased. In October, General Lambert expelled the Rump, and set up a Committee of Safety to govern England. But a popular reaction soon set in against the assumption of such a major political role by the military. General George Monck (or Monk), a leading Cromwellian officer who had always upheld the principles of military obedience to properly constituted civil authority, emerged as the decisive figure in ending the political turbulence. In December 1659, the army gave in, and restored the Rump for the third time; Monck allowed the members excluded by Pride's Purge to take their old places.

The partially reconstituted Long Parliament prepared to restore the monarchy as the only barrier to chaos. At Monck's suggestion, the exiled Charles II issued the Declaration of Breda, promising a free pardon, confirmation of all land sales during the civil wars, payment of the soldiers' back pay, and liberty of conscience; Charles added, however, that on each point he would be bound by what Parliament wanted. A new Parliament, chosen in free election, summoned the king home in a burst of enthusiasm; Charles II (1660–1685) arrived in London on May 29, 1660.

The English Revolution in Review

Revolutionary changes had occurred in England since 1642. Divine-right monarchy had been challenged, and a constitutional and representative government set up, based on a legislature backed by politically active private citizens. Though the Stuarts were restored, no English king ever again could hope to rule without a Parliament or reinstate the Court of Star Chamber or take ship money, benevolences, and other controversial taxes. Parliament thenceforward retained that critical weapon: ultimate control of the public purse by periodic grants of taxes.

Moreover, minority groups had gone much further toward political and social democracy. The Levellers put forward a program that was later carried by emigrants to the American colonies, and that favored universal suffrage, progressive taxation, separation of church and state, and protection of the individual against arbitary arrest. A more extreme group called the Diggers actually dug up public lands near London and began planting vegetables in a kind of communistic enterprise. They were driven off, but not before they had got their ideas into circulation. The Fifth Monarchy men, the Millenarians, and a dozen other radical sects preached the Second Coming and the achievement of some kind of utopia on earth.

During the English struggles the Puritans urged freedom of speech and of the press, although when they came to power they often failed to practice what they had preached. Another basic liberal idea to emerge from the civil war was religious toleration. Some of the Puritans believed that compulsion should not be exercised to secure conformity, and at least one sect held that religious toleration was a positive good. The Quakers—more properly, the Religious Society of Friends—led by George Fox (1624–1691), were Puritans of the Puritans. They eschewed all worldly show: for example, they regarded the polite form "you" as hypocritical, and so addressed all men as "thou" or "thee." They took so seriously the basic Protestant doctrine of the priesthood of the believer that they did entirely without an ordained ministry, and encouraged any worshiper to testify in a kind of sermon if he felt the spirit move him. The Friends were—and still are today—pacifists, who abstained from the use of force and would have no part in war.

The Restoration

Although many of the ideas advanced during the civil wars were much too revolutionary to win easy acceptance, the Restoration settlement showed a high degree of political tolerance. Except for a few revolutionaries, including surviving judges who had condemned Charles I to death, Parliament pardoned all those who had been involved in the civil war or the republican regimes. It made every effort to injure as few people as possible in settling the claims of royalists and churchmen to their former lands. Parliament appeared to be maintaining its political supremacy, and in the central administration there were the first foreshadowings of what eventually would become the cabinet.

Religion, however, was quite another matter. Though personally rather disposed to toleration, Charles II governed a country where very few people were yet ready to accept it. Not only were bishops restored but Parliament proceeded to enact a long series of repressive acts. The Corporation Act (1661) required all magistrates to take the sacraments according to the Church of England. The Act of Uniformity (1662) required clergymen and teachers to subscribe to the Book of Common Prayer; those who refused were known as Nonconformists or Dissenters. The Conventicle Act (1664) limited to five the number of persons attending a Nonconformist meeting outside a private household, and the Five Mile Act (1665) forbade those who had not accepted the Act of Uniformity to come within five miles of any town unless they swore a special oath.

Much of this was impossible to enforce; it placed the Dissenters under disabilities but did not cause them great suffering. The Test Act of 1673 required that all officeholders take communion in the Church of England and renounce transubstantiation (the Catholic doctrine of the Eucharist). But the practical English found ways around this. One was "occasional conformity," whereby a Dissenter whose conscience was not too strict might take Anglican communion occasionally, while worshiping as a Presbyterian or Congregationalist most of the time. Another way, common after 1689, was to allow Dissenters to hold office, and each year pass a special bill legalizing their acts.

The revulsion against Puritanism carried over into all aspects of the Restoration period. Where the Commonwealth and Protectorate had forbidden all theatrical performances, the Restoration thoroughly enjoyed them, the more indecent the better. Charles II himself and his court led cheerfully immoral lives. Everywhere in Europe there was a trend back toward Catholicism: in Sweden, for instance, Gustavus Adolphus' own daughter, Christina, had abdicated and become a Catholic (1654). Charles II sympathized with Catholicism, and in 1672 tried but failed to remove disabilities from both Catholics and Dissenters. He greatly admired the flourishing monarchy of Louis XIV across the Channel. Without the knowledge of Parliament, he made a secret treaty with Louis (1670) and promised, in exchange for an annual subsidy, to support the French in their wars and to become a Catholic as soon as he could. His brother James, duke of York and heir to the throne, openly practiced Catholicism.

English popular suspicion of the Roman church, however, was still strong. In the late 1670's a series of disclosures about alleged "Popish" plots to murder the king and restore Catholicism aroused great popular excitement. One faction in Parliament wanted to exclude the Catholic and pro-French James from the succession; these "exclusionists" were called *Whigs* (a Scotch variant of "wigs"). They included many well-to-do urban merchants and certain very powerful peers, who hoped to enhance their own political influence if the monarchy itself should be weakened. Supporting Charles and the succession of James were the landed gentry, lesser lords and country gentlemen who had been pro-Stuart all along and who suspected the newly rich townsmen. They were called *Tories* (a Gaelic term for "robber").

*James II
and the Glorious Revolution*

James II (reigned 1685–1688) alienated even the Tories who had sucessfully opposed his exclusion. He put down an ineffectual effort of a bastard son of Charles II, the duke of Monmouth, to invade England (1685), but then sent a savage judge, Jeffreys, to try and punish those suspected of sympathizing with Monmouth. These trials were the "Bloody Assizes." Disregarding the laws, James appointed Catholics to high office, and judges appointed by him declared that he was acting legally. His Declaration of Liberty of Conscience (1687), extending religious toleration, was issued without parliamentary approval or support; James claimed to be acting on the basis of his right of "dispensation."

When a son was born to James (June 1688) and the prospect of a Catholic dynasty loomed, seven Whig and Tory leaders decided to act. They offered the throne jointly to James' daughter Mary, who was a Protestant, and to her husband William of Orange, Stadholder since 1673 of six of the seven Dutch provinces and the most vigorous enemy of Louis XIV. When William landed in November 1688, James soon had to flee to France. Elections were held, and the elected body (technically a "convention," not a Parliament, since a royal summons must be issued to elect a Parliament) formally offered the throne to William and Mary. They ruled as William III (1689–1702) and Mary II (1689–1694).

When issuing the invitation, the "Convention Parliament" accompanied it with the Declaration of Rights, summing up what was won in the long struggle with the Stuarts: Parliament alone makes or suspends laws; the king has no power of "dispensation"; he cannot tax without Parliament. Freedom of election, freedom of debate, freedom of petition, frequent elections, no trial without jury, no excessive bail—all these Parliament declared to be the rights of Englishmen, and all William and Mary accepted. Parliament made them into laws as the Bill of Rights (1689), adding that no Catholic could become king of England in the future.

The sum total of the events of 1688–1689, almost bloodless, is called the Glorious Revolution. It was made secure by William's victory in Ireland over James II and an army of Irish Catholic insurgents with French supporters in the battle of the Boyne (1690). It was enhanced by a Toleration Act, allowing

Dissenters to practice their religion freely, but still excluding them from office (1689). After the Glorious Revolution three major steps still lay ahead before England could become a full parliamentary democracy. These were: first, the cabinet system, whereby a committee of the majority party would manage affairs of state—the work of the eighteenth and early nineteenth centuries; second, universal suffrage and payment of salaries to members of the Commons—the work of the nineteenth and early twentieth; third, curbs on the power of the Lords to veto legislation—the work of the twentieth.

William and Mary were childless, and Mary's sister Anne, who succeeded as queen from 1702 to 1714, had no living children. Parliament, fearing that James II's son, the Catholic "James III," would try to seize the throne, settled the succession upon the descendants of Sophia, granddaughter of James I, twelfth child of Frederick of the Palatinate (see p. 336), wife of the elector of Hanover. When Anne died in 1714, Sophia's son George, elector of Hanover, became king of England as George I, and his descendants have sat on the throne ever since. By excluding the elder Catholic line of succession, Parliament had shown who really made the kings of England.

There remained the danger that the Scots might prefer a Stuart monarch to a Hanoverian. Under Anne, in 1707, the old problem of Anglo-Scottish union which James I had failed to solve was worked out. Scotland accepted the Protestant succession, would send its own members to both houses of Parliament, and would join its cross of Saint Andrew with the English cross of Saint George on one flag, the Union Jack—symbol of Great Britain. Protestant fear of Catholic sovereigns made the settlement easy, and, despite occasional outbreaks of Scottish nationalism, the union worked well from the beginning. Wider economic and political horizons beckoned the able Scots, who have taken at least their share in governing and increasing the prosperity of the United Kingdom.

Tragedy, by contrast, was the continued lot of the Irish, whose support of the refugee James II led William III to revive the severe Cromwellian policy. Their Catholic worship was hampered by galling "penal laws" and their trade stifled by mercantilist regulation. Their misery was so acute that the Anglican Jonathan Swift made with bitter irony his famous "modest proposal" that they solve their economic problems by selling their babies to be eaten.

III

Divine-Right Monarchy in France

Henry IV, Richelieu, and Mazarin

During the first half of the seventeenth century, as we have seen, Europe still feared that a Hapsburg combination—Spanish and Austrian—would upset the balance of power. In taking the lead in every attempt to block this danger, the French in later years prepared to make their own bid for European supremacy. At home, France recovered quickly from the wounds of the sixteenth-century religious wars (see Chapter 7). Henry IV (reigned 1589–1610), witty, dashing, and popular, took a real interest in the popular welfare. His economic experts reclaimed marshes for farmland, encouraged the luxury crafts of Paris, and planted thousands of mulberry trees to foster the culture and manufacture of silk. They built the canals, roads, and bridges that made the French communications system the best in Europe. Faced with a great deficit on coming to office, Henry IV found an efficient finance minister in Sully (1560–1641), who gradually brought income up and expenditure down until they balanced. Monarch and minister even toyed with an advanced idea for a general European international Christian republic, including everybody but the Hapsburgs. This "grand design" thus had a practical bearing on the ambitions of the French, but it also was an ancestor of future leagues of nations.

Assassinated in 1610 by a madman, Henry IV was succeeded by his nine-year-old son, Louis XIII (reigned 1610–1643). During his minority, things went slack, as his mother, Marie de' Medici, acted as regent, and her favorites almost undid what Henry IV had accomplished. Finally in 1624 Richelieu became the king's chief minister. We have already seen him subordinating religion to the interests of France during the Thirty Years' War by his alliance with the Protestants. Richelieu made the interests of the state (*raison d'état*) govern his policy everywhere.

Though Richelieu subsidized and helped Lutherans and Calvinists in Germany, he felt that the Edict of Nantes (see p. 327) had given too many privileges to the Huguenots of France. The hundred-odd fortified towns in Huguenot hands seemed potential centers of disorder and a threat to his program of increased royal centralization. Foreseeing punitive measures against them, the Huguenots rebelled. It took Richelieu's forces fourteen months to reduce their key port of La Rochelle (1628), largely because there was no French navy to cut its communications. Over the next decade, Richelieu built both an Atlantic and a Mediterranean fleet for France. He also strove to curb the French nobility by ordering some of their chateaux destroyed and by forbidding their favorite pastime of dueling, but he by no means succeeded in taming them completely. He did successfully transfer responsibility for local administration from the nobles to royal officials, the *intendants,* who obtained greatly increased power to assess and collect taxes.

Though historians have disagreed in assessing Richelieu's services in France, all agree that subsequent French greatness under Louis XIV would have been unthinkable without him. His critics feel that he left too little place for government by discussion and for the participation of the middle classes in government, except for a few highly trained professional bureaucrats. His supporters praise the centralization and efficiency on which his successors would build. He himself hand-picked and trained his immediate successor, the Italian-born Cardinal Mazarin.

Succeeding to power after Richelieu's death in 1642, Mazarin soon faced the crisis caused by the death of Louis XIII (1643), whose heir, Louis XIV (1643–1715), was only five years old. Mazarin's foreign birth, his failure to pay obligations on government debts, and his piling up of a huge personal fortune antagonized the French nobility. This class by now consisted not only of the descendants of the feudal aristocracy—the nobility of the sword (*noblesse d'épée*)—but also of those who had been given titles because of their services as judges or administrators—the nobility of the robe (*noblesse de robe*)—who were not originally of aristocratic origin. The old nobility of the sword hated Mazarin partly for snobbish reasons, partly for keeping them out of power; the newer nobility of the robe worried about his fast-and-loose ways with money.

This discontent and the ambitions of rival cliques of nobles led to the complex disturbances known as the Fronde, 1648–1653 (the name refers to a slingshot used by Parisian children to throw mud at passersby). In the end, Mazarin and his bureaucrats were able to defeat both the old nobles and the newer official nobles of the law courts, among whom were many disgruntled investors. He maintained himself in power until his death in 1661. By then Louis XIV was twenty-three and ready for personal rule in the fullest sense of divine-right absolutism.

Triple portrait of Richelieu by Philippe de Champaigne.

It is not James I—despite all his theorizing on the subject—nor even Philip II of Spain whom we think of as *the* divine-right monarch, but Louis XIV, and not merely because he is supposed to have coined the famous summation of the theory: "L'État, c'est moi" (I am the State). God had from the beginning destined this descendant of Hugh Capet for the throne of France; to challenge his right to it was to challenge the structure of God's universe. Louis was able to act on these beliefs and be a divine-right monarch in part because of the revival of the concept from Roman law that God directs the affairs of states through his chosen agents. Moreover, the French monarchy had long taken the lead in striving to minimize the deep local loyalties that went so far back in time—to Normandy, Brittany, Burgundy, and so on—and to maximize a new transcendent loyalty to France as such. The subjects of the French crown spoke several different languages or at least dialects; they had no common educational system, or press, or political life. What they had in common was the king, a symbol of common "Frenchness," who collected taxes and raised armies. Frenchmen had to feel that he had a right to do these things, and was doing it *for* them, not just *to* them.

Though Louis is called absolute, he lacked the physical means for controlling in complete detail all the actions of all of his subjects. Indeed no ruler before the days of twentieth-century dictatorships, with all the totalitarian techniques of propaganda, surveillance, and terror, was ever absolute in this sense. Further limitations were placed on Louis's absolutism by medieval local survivals in language, law, customs, weights and measures—all of which stood in the way of real uniformity. Louis could not ride roughshod over city corporations that appealed to their ancient charters granting them immunities, or over guilds that could show a privileged status which they had "always" possessed. He could not force nobles and clergy to conform completely.

The French crown, however, shoved the nobles aside, deprived them of their political function, and left them only their social and economic privileges and their military careers. Louis XI had begun to tame them in the fifteenth century. Since they had helped to foment the religious wars, Henry IV's victory was a defeat for their program, and so was Richelieu's increased use of nonnobles as intendants, judges, and local officials. The crown usually granted such commoners titles of nobility which they could pass on to their sons. But they were still noblesse de robe, and lacked the prestige of the older noblesse d'épée.

The French church, too, had come under the control of the crown by gradual processes, and under Louis XIV was "Gallican," that is to say national, though of course Catholic. His bishops (like the bishops of Charles I) supported the divine-right monarchy. But the French clergy were not subject to royal taxation; of their own free will in their own assembly they voted gifts of money to the king. Louis abolished the religious toleration that Richelieu had left the Huguenots after taking away their fortresses and political privileges. In 1685 he revoked the Edict of Nantes. As a result, about fifty thousand Protestant families fled abroad. In Prussia, some of the exiles found a place in the military services, and their descendants fought against the French in the wars of the nineteenth and twentieth centuries. In Holland, England, North America, and South Africa the talents and skills of these refugees greatly strengthened the lands that received them. Some Huguenots remained in France, where they had to worship secretly.

Within the Catholic church itself, Louis had to contend both with enthusiastic mystics (Madame Guyon and the Quietists) and with the puritanical Jansenists, named after Cornelius Jansen, bishop of Ypres in the early seven-

Louis XIV.

The noblesse de robe: Municipal councillors of Toulouse.

teenth century. The Jansenists, who came close to Calvin's views on predestination, questioned the authority of both pope and king, since both were mere men. Their most distinguished spokesman was the scientist and philosopher Pascal. Though Louis contained the threat that they posed to uniformity, he did not succeed completely in suppressing the Jansenists.

Intent on his own glory, Louis worked hard and in his youth played hard. In middle age, after his Spanish queen's death, he contracted a morganatic marriage with Mme de Maintenon, former governess of his illegitimate children. She was a devout Catholic, and it seems certain that she influenced Louis's decision to revoke the Edict of Nantes. Louis installed the French court at Versailles, where he built a splendid palace on the site of a former hunting lodge. Almost half a mile long, the main buildings at Versailles housed a court of ten thousand nobles and their families, followers, and servants. It was a superb setting for *le Grand Monarque*.

So completely did Louis make Versailles the center of French social life that everything else in Europe seemed provincial, from the private country houses of the French nobles to the courts of all the other monarchs. The proper standard of sophisticated behavior for all Europe was set here: how to dress, how to speak French, what to read, what sort of story to tell, how far to go in gossip, what games to play, what food to eat at what times of day, what music to listen to, and what dances to dance. At every European court and in every private household with a pretense to gentility the master and mistress would ask what Versailles did before deciding.

Here Louis met with his ministers, the heads of departments like those in any modern state: war, finance, foreign policy, interior. They were directly

SEVENTEENTH-CENTURY WAR, POLITICS, AND EMPIRE

356

responsible to him and not to any legislative body; indeed, the Estates-General never met at all during Louis's entire reign of seventy-two years. From the top, the chain of command went down through the intendants, in charge of the *généralités,* or large province-sized administrative units, to smaller regional units and then to the towns and villages. Even the indefatigable Louis could hope to do no more than exercise a general supervision over details; but he was helped by the multiplicity of official forms that his subjects filled out; many thousands of them remain today duly filed in the French local archives. As members of the noblesse de robe, the intendants transmitted their titles and rank to their heirs, and so formed a new kind of privileged corporation, arrogating to themselves more power than the theory of royal absolutism ideally would have allowed, and so asserting provincial initiative against the monarchy.

The judges of the high courts of appeal, too, could not be removed by the king, and so exercised considerable independence. These courts were the *parlements,* of which the Parlement of Paris enjoyed the widest jurisdiction and the most prestige. By their function of registering each royal edict, the parlements claimed something like the power of judicial review; that is, they claimed the right to refuse to register an edict if they thought it violated the law of the land. Louis intimidated the Parlement of Paris by summoning the judges before him in a formal session (*lit de justice,* "bed of justice") and commanding them to register a royal edict. The claim that the parlements might throw out a royal edict, however, remained to plague his successors.

Mercantilism and Colbert: Economic Policy under Louis XIV

Just as France under Louis XIV exemplified widely held ideas of divine-right monarchy, so too the economic policies of his regime exemplified the widespread mercantilist theories and practices. Mercantilists held that hard money, gold and silver, was the basic wealth. Therefore the state should try to get as much of it as possible, and to arrange that more should come in than go out. It should maintain this "favorable balance of trade" by encouraging exports (which bring it cash from abroad) perhaps by bounties, and discouraging imports (which cause cash to flow out) perhaps by tariffs. Carried to its extreme, this would be absurd, since gold and silver cannot be much used by the state except as media of exchange.

But the mercantilists were not absurd; they were trying to make their own state as self-sustaining as they could. National production, they held, should provide the necessities of life for the population and the sinews of war for the armed forces. They favored rigorous planning and control, sweeping away the traditional ways of manor and guild and the medieval notion of the "just price" (see p. 158), and directing the economy instead by subsidies, grants of monopolies, government participation in industry, encouragement of research, and imposition of tariffs. They viewed the overseas colonies of the mother country as a source of necessary raw materials, possession of which made it unnecessary to import from rival states and encouraged manufacturing at home. For this reason the colonies must be strongly governed and their economies directed as the mother country saw fit.

Louis XIV's great exponent of mercantilism, his finance minister, Jean Baptiste Colbert (1619–1683), exercised more influence over his master than any other royal servant, though he met competition from other royal advisers, for example, Louvois, the war minister. Colbert supported new inventions, improvements in shipbuilding, technological education, the settlement of foreign experts in France, and the founding of new industries. This was the first major experiment in a modern controlled economy, and the result was prosperity.

Might France have done still better had her businessmen been left alone? Those who believe in the antimercantilist theory of free trade (*laissez faire*) argue that the mere removal of regulations would have enabled the individual entrepreneur and therefore the whole economy to enrich itself still further. But this rival theory was not practiced anywhere during Colbert's day.

His system gave France the economic leadership of Europe; during the eighteenth century she would lose this lead, partly because England adopted the new methods of power machinery and large-scale production of inexpensive goods. After Colbert, the French clung to the small-scale production of a large variety of products, chiefly luxuries and consumer goods. England also had the more easily exploitable resources, like coal, iron, and waterpower, and so got a head start in modern industrialization. Moreover, the expensive wars of Louis XIV built up a burden of debt that depressed the economy in the latter part of his reign and carried on into the eighteenth century.

The Wars of Louis XIV

As the real victor in the Thirty Years' War, France had achieved the defeat of the Hapsburgs and territorial enrichment at comparatively little cost. Prosperous and ambitious, Louis XIV set out to expand; thus France succeeded the Spanish and the Austrian Hapsburgs as the threat to the European balance of power. Louis did not envisage an organized world state in which everyone was his subject. But he did want to push French boundaries east to the Rhine, annexing the Spanish Netherlands and the Franche Comté (Free County of Burgundy); and as time went on, he hoped to secure Spain and the Spanish Empire. He also wanted to assert the predominance of France in every part of the globe and in every area of human life. He had agents in India, in Canada, in Holland, and on the Rhine. He regarded it as natural and proper that French culture, French taste in the arts, French social ways should influence all of Europe; to an astonishing extent they did so. But other European peoples came to feel that France was too threatening, and their rulers united against Louis XIV.

A legal quibble gave Louis the excuse for his first war, the War of Devolution (1667–1668). When he had married the daughter of Philip IV of Spain, his wife had renounced her rights of inheritance; but her dowry had not been paid, and Louis claimed that this voided her renunciation. After the death of Philip IV (1665), the queen of France, Louis claimed, ought to inherit her father's possessions in the Low Countries by virtue of an old Flemish law of "devolution." The threat to Belgium aroused the Dutch, who made an alliance with England and Sweden against France and thus joined their old enemies, the Spaniards, in supporting the balance of power. Louis made peace at Aix-la-Chapelle in 1668, collecting twelve fortified Flemish towns.

Furious at the Dutch, Louis bought off Charles II by a secret treaty in 1670 (see p. 352), and also made a treaty with the Swedes. Then he began his second war, the Dutch War (1672–1678), quickly occupying large areas of southern Holland. Six of the seven Dutch provinces elected William of Orange Stadholder, and decided that the office should be hereditary in his family. William allied himself with Brandenburg and with both Spanish and Austrian Hapsburgs, rallying enough forces against Louis to prevent a final and decisive French victory. At the Peace of Nijmegen (Nimwegen), 1678–1679, the Dutch lost no territory but had to promise future neutrality. Spain gave Louis the Franche Comté and some towns in the Spanish Netherlands.

Though the war was technically over, the superb French armed forces really dominated Europe. On the eastern frontiers, special French courts ("chambers of reunion") decreed further annexations of areas that could be shown to have belonged at any time to any of the territories newly acquired by France, and Louis's armies would then proceed to occupy these additional prizes. In this way France "reunited" Strasbourg (1681) and Luxembourg, all of Lorraine (1683), and the Rhineland bishopric of Trier (1684). These French aggressions in time of peace met with no resistance, partly because of the Ottoman siege of Vienna (1683) and its aftermath (see Chapter 5).

French pressure eastward continued as Louis now put in a farfetched claim to the lands of the Palatinate and insisted on pushing his own candidate for the archbishopric of Cologne (1688). The revocation of the Edict of Nantes (1685) had distressed the Protestants of Europe. Sweden, the Palatinate, Saxony, Bavaria, the Austrian and Spanish Hapsburgs, together with William of Orange, who was soon to be king of England, formed the League of Augsburg against Louis XIV. Thus his third war began: the War of the League of Augsburg, 1688–1697. After French occupation of the Palatinate, most of the land operations took place in the Netherlands; in Ireland (at the Boyne) and at sea, the English and Dutch defeated the French. The Treaty of Ryswick (1697) that ended the war deprived the French of much of the land "reunited" since Nijmegen, including Lorraine.

*The War
of the Spanish Succession*

But within four years Louis embarked on his last and most adventurous war. It had been clear for some time that the death of Louis's brother-in-law, the Hapsburg king of Spain, Charles II (1665–1700), who was without an heir, would create a crisis. The powers of Europe had agreed that a Bavarian prince would succeed, but he died first; they then arranged an elaborate partition that would have given Naples, Sicily, and Lorraine to France. But Charles II made a new will, leaving all the vast Spanish possessions in Europe and overseas to his great-nephew, the grandson of Louis XIV, Philip of Anjou. When Charles died in 1700, Louis could not resist the temptation: he proclaimed his grandson Philip V of Spain. At once, England, Holland, the Empire, and the German states formed a grand alliance against the French; they were joined before long by just about all the other states of western Europe.

The War of the Spanish Succession (1701–1713) was fought in Italy and overseas, and especially in the Low Countries. The allies gradually wore down the French. Queen Anne's great general, John Churchill, first duke of Marlborough and ancestor of Winston Churchill, together with Prince Eugene of Savoy, defeated France four times: at Blenheim (1704), Ramillies (1706), Oudenarde (1708), and Malplaquet (1709). But the defeats were not overwhelming, and Malplaquet alone cost the allies twenty thousand casualties, which in those days seemed "butchery" to the people of England. The death of the emperor Joseph (1711) meant that his brother Charles VI would be the legitimate heir to all the Spanish and Austrian possessions, that the old empire of Charles V would be recreated, and that the balance of power would be once more upset by the Hapsburgs. The English feared this as much as a total French victory. The Tories, who favored peace, came to power in England; Marlborough was removed from command, and negotiations for peace began. They culminated in the Treaty of Utrecht (1713)—like the Treaty of Westphalia (1648) before it and the settlements of Vienna (1815) and Versailles (1919) after it, a landmark in the diplomatic and territorial history of Europe.

By the terms of Utrecht, Philip V was accepted as king of Spain, but Louis promised that the crowns of France and Spain would never be united. He recognized the Protestant succession in England. In America, France gave up Newfoundland, Acadia (Nova Scotia), and the Hudson's Bay territory to England, but retained Quebec and Louisiana. From Spain the English obtained

Gibraltar, which they still hold, and the island of Minorca, which they returned later in the century, as well as a contract (the Asiento) to supply African Negro slaves to the Spanish colonies. Because the Austrian Hapsburgs lost their claim to the Spanish throne, they received the former Spanish Netherlands (Belgium), but the Dutch were allowed to maintain certain garrisons there to help defend themselves against a possible new French attack. The duke of Savoy was rewarded at first with Sicily, for which Sardinia was substituted in 1720; as kings of Sardinia, the dukes of Savoy would later unite the rest of Italy. The elector of Brandenburg was recognized as "king in Prussia."

Utrecht was on the whole a moderate and sensible peace. Yet it did not end overseas rivalry between the French and English; it did not really protect the Dutch; and it did not really satisfy the Hapsburgs, or settle the tangled affairs of Italy. French aggression was halted, but only temporarily, for it would be resumed at the end of the century under the impulse of the great Revolution (see Chapter 11). The wars of Louis XIV, however, despite their great cost in human life and in treasure, and despite the popular hatred aroused by the French in their drive into Dutch and German territories, were less savage than the Thirty Years' War or the wars of nationalism and revolution that would follow after 1789. Religion played a minor role, though Louis regarded himself as a Catholic champion, and William of Orange was hailed as a Protestant one. Hundreds of thousands of Catholics were lined up against Louis on the "Protestant" side. Louis's aggressions did not have the passionate quality of religious or political crusades: he was no Napoleon, no Hitler. His wars were in effect measured and "classical," as befitted le Grand Monarque.

IV
Europe Overseas

At Utrecht, Nova Scotia and Newfoundland changed hands as well as Gibraltar. Indeed, the last war of Louis XIV was almost a world war, fought not only to maintain the balance of power in Europe but to gain advantages and resources overseas. The increased concern with the world beyond Europe resulted from the faster pace of colonialism in the seventeenth century, when the English, French, and Dutch all joined the ranks of empire builders.

The Thirteen Colonies

The English got their first two permanent footholds in North America at Jamestown in Virginia (1607), and at Plymouth in Massachusetts (1620). At first similar to Spanish or Portuguese trading posts, these were established by English trading companies which vainly hoped to find gold and silver as the Spaniards had. Both settlements barely managed to survive the early years of hardship. Then the sparse native population was gradually replaced by immigrants of English stock. Tobacco and the resourcefulness of Captain John Smith saved Virginia; furs, codfish, and Calvinist toughness saved Massachusetts. Both gradually built up an agricultural economy and traded with the mother country. While neither received more than a few tens of thousands of immigrants from abroad, natural increase in a country of abundant land added to their numbers.

In 1664 the English defeated the Dutch in another round of the warfare for economic advantage that had broken out under Cromwell a decade earlier. They took over New Amsterdam, founded in 1626, which became New York; its important Dutch families—Stuyvesant, Schuyler, Roosevelt—would sup-

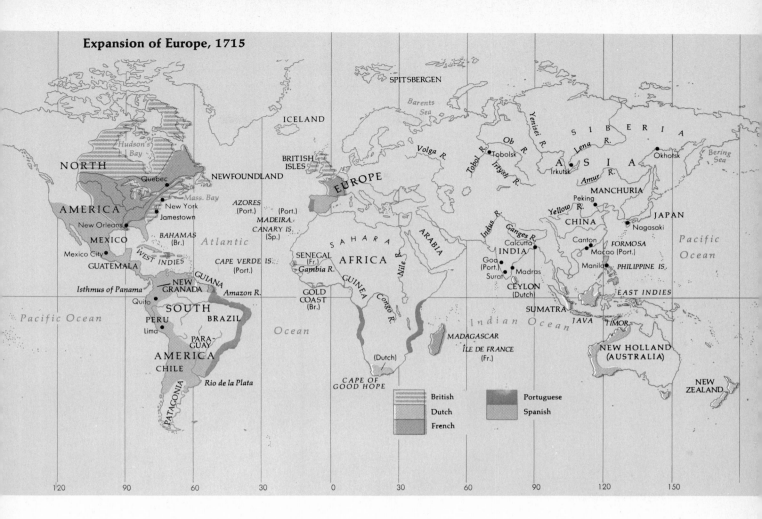

Expansion of Europe, 1715

British

Dutch

French

Portuguese

Spanish

ply some leading participants in American development. In 1655 the Dutch had already eliminated the Swedish settlement at Fort Christina on the Delaware, and here, too, the English ousted the Dutch. Pennsylvania, chartered in 1681 to the wealthy English Quaker William Penn, filled the vacuum left by the expulsion of the Swedes and the Dutch from the Delaware.

By the early eighteenth century, the English settlements formed a continuous string of thirteen colonies from Maine to Georgia. The new settlers came from all strata of English life except the very top. New England was for the most part settled by Calvinist Independents (Congregationalists), who believed in wide local self-government, and who set up their own Puritan state church, like Calvin's in Geneva or Cromwell's in England. Yet "heresy" appeared from the start, as Baptists, Quakers, and even Anglicans came to New England. The southern colonies, especially tidewater Virginia, were settled for the most part by Anglicans, used to the existence of frank social distinctions and to large landholdings. The Church of England became the established church in Virginia. Yet in the Piedmont section of Virginia and the Carolinas there were small farmers—"Scotch-Irish" Presbyterians, and Germans from Pennsylvania. Geography and climate played their part, making the South the land of one-crop plantations producing tobacco, rice, or indigo, while New England and the Middle Colonies went in for small farming, fishing, and small-scale industry and commerce.

In Maryland, founded partly to give refuge to Catholics; in Rhode Island,

SEVENTEENTH-CENTURY WAR,
POLITICS, AND EMPIRE

founded by Roger Williams and others unwilling to conform to the orthodoxy of Massachusetts; in Pennsylvania, founded by Quakers who believed in the separation of church and state, we find something like the religious freedom that was later to be embodied in the Constitution of the United States. During the eighteenth century, it came to be recognized that people might even be free not to belong to any formal religious organization.

The colonists, as men of the seventeenth century, accepted class distinctions as a matter of course. Yet the seeds of democracy were present. There was no titled colonial nobility, and the egalitarianism of the frontier and the career open to talent in the town balanced the privileged gentry in the coastal cities and in the Hudson Valley. Each colony had some sort of legislative body; government by discussion was firmly planted from the beginning. Though the crown was represented in most colonies by a royal governor, the English government, torn by revolutionary upheavals, exerted no continuing bureaucratic or absolute rule over the colonies, as the Spaniards and French did over theirs. The English royal governors bickered with the colonial assemblies, and often lost. Local government—in village and town and county—fostered wide popular participation. The English common law which provided for trial by jury and lacked bureaucratic administrative regulation reflected a very different tradition from that of the Spanish or French.

New France

To the north of the thirteen colonies, in the region around the Bay of Fundy and in the St. Lawrence Basin, New France was for a century and a half a serious threat to the English North American colonies. The St. Lawrence and the Great Lakes gave the French easy access to the heart of the continent, whereas the Appalachians stood between the English and the Mississippi. The French were also impelled westward by the fur trade; furs are goods of very great value and comparatively little bulk, easily carried in canoes and small boats. Moreover, led by the Jesuits, the Catholic French gave proof of a far greater missionary zeal than did the Protestant English. The priest, as well as the *coureur des bois* (trapper), led the push westward. Finally, the French in North America were guided in their expansion by a conscious imperial policy directed from the France of the Bourbon monarchs.

The result was that the French, not the English, explored the interior of the continent. The names and accomplishments of the French explorers, missionaries, and traders—Marquette, Joliet, La Salle, Frontenac, Cadillac, Iberville— are a part of our American heritage. By the early eighteenth century, the French had built up a line of isolated trading posts—with miles of empty space between, thinly populated by Indians—which encircled the English colonies on the Atlantic coast. From Quebec, one line of outposts led westward. From Mobile and New Orleans, in a colony founded at the beginning of the eighteenth century and named Louisiana after Louis XIV, lines led northward up the Mississippi to join with those from Canada and Illinois.

Yet, impressive though this French imperial thrust looks on the map, their territory was far too lightly held for them to be equal to the task of containing the English. French loss of Newfoundland, Acadia, and Hudson's Bay to England in the Utrecht settlement was a portent of this weakness. Theirs was a trading empire with military ambitions, and save in Quebec it never became a true colony of settlement. Frenchmen simply did not come over in sufficient numbers, and those who did come spread themselves out over vast distances as traders and adventurers. Frenchmen who might have come, the Huguenots who might have settled as did the Puritans, were excluded by a royal policy bent on maintaining the Catholic faith in New France.

The French, Dutch, and English intruded upon the pioneer Spanish and Portuguese both in the New World and in the Old. They broke the Spanish hold over the Caribbean and ultimately made that sea of many islands a kaleidoscope of colonial jurisdictions and a center of continuing naval wars and piracy. The West Indies, though today for the most part a seriously depressed area, were in early modern times one of the great prizes of imperialism. Here the cheap Negro slave labor that had replaced the exterminated Indian raised the great staple tropical crops—tobacco, fruits, coffee, and, most basic of all, cane sugar.

In India, the Mogul Empire proved strong enough to confine the Europeans on the whole to the costal fringes. Gradually in the course of the seventeenth century both the French and the English established themselves in India on the heels of decaying Portuguese power and wealth. The English defeated a Portuguese fleet in 1612, and immediately thereafter got trading rights at Surat on the western coast. Although the Mogul emperor, Aurangzeb, tried to revoke their rights in 1685, he soon found their naval and mercantile power too much to withstand. In 1690 the English founded in Bengal in eastern India the city they were to make famous, Calcutta. Meanwhile, the French had got footholds on the south coast near Madras, at a place called Pondichéry, and soon had established other stations. Early in the eighteenth century, the stage was set in India as in North America for the decisive struggle for overseas empire between France and Britain.

Both countries operated in India, as they had initially in North America, by means of chartered trading companies, the English East India Company and the French Compagnie des Indes Orientales. The companies were backed up by their governments when it was clear that bits of land around the trading posts had to be held and that the relation with India could not be a purely commercial one. Gradually, in support of their companies, both England and France became involved in Indian politics and wars. But neither country made an effort to found a New England or a New France in the East.

The Dutch, who operated the most profitable of all the East India companies, bypassed India but drove the Portuguese from the nearby island of Ceylon. In the East Indies proper, they built Batavia (from the Latin name for Holland) on the island of Java and founded an empire in Indonesia that lasted almost to our own day. Only after World War II did Batavia become Jakarta. When the Dutch reached Japan in 1609, the Japanese rulers were already suspicious of Christian penetration and irritated at the bickerings between Portuguese Jesuits and Spanish Franciscans. The Japanese gradually expelled

The island in Nagasaki harbor to which the Dutch were confined, 1699.

all Christians until in 1641 the Dutch alone were left, confined to an island in Nagasaki harbor. Japan had sealed herself off from the West until the mid-nineteenth century.

In Africa, the Dutch took over the Cape of Good Hope from the Portuguese in 1652 and settled there—the ancestors of today's Afrikaners in South Africa. The French, too, were moving into Africa, first into Senegal on the west coast (1626). In the Indian Ocean, Louis XIV annexed the large island of Madagascar in 1686, and in 1715 the French took the island of Mauritius from the Dutch, rechristening it the Île de France. The British broke into the competition by securing a foothold at the mouth of the Gambia River in West Africa (1662), and later added other acquisitions at French and Dutch expense. Thus a map of Africa and adjacent waters in the eighteenth century shows a series of coastal stations controlled by European states, but until the nineteenth century the interior remained untouched, save by slavers and native traders.

The Balance Sheet of Imperialism

Seen in terms of economics, the expansion of Europe in early modern times was by no means the pure "exploitation" and "plundering" of antiimperialist rhetoric. There *was* robbery, just as there was murder or enslavement. In dealing with the natives, the Europeans often gave much too little in exchange for land and goods of great value: the Indians sold the island of Manhattan to the Dutch for $24.00 worth of trinkets. And the almost universally applied mercantilist policy kept money and manufacturing in the hands of the home country. It relegated the colonies to the production of raw materials, a role that tended to keep even colonies of settlement in a relatively primitive and economically dependent condition.

Still, even with all these limitations, the expansion of Europe added to the goods available to non-Europeans. Although few Europeans settled in India or Africa, their wares, and especially their weapons, began gradually the process of Europeanizing the rest of the world. By the eighteenth century this process was only beginning, and, in particular, few of the improvements in public health that Europeans were to bring to the East had yet to come about; nor had any greater public order come to India and Africa. But, in the New World especially, there were signs of the westernization to come.

The West in its turn was greatly affected by the world overseas. The long list of imported items included foodstuffs above all, utensils and gadgets like pipes for smoking, hammocks and pyjamas, and styles of architecture and painting like bungalows and Japanese prints. Some of the novelties caught on more quickly than others. Tobacco, brought into Spain in the mid-sixteenth century as a soothing drug, had established itself by the seventeenth century as essential to the peace of mind of many European males. Potatoes, on the other hand, though highly nourishing and cheaper to grow than the staple breadstuffs, did not immediately catch on in Europe.

Among Westerners, knowledge of non-European beliefs and institutions eventually penetrated to the level of popular culture, where it is marked by a host of words—*powwow, kowtow, tabu, totem.* At the highest level of cultural interchange, that of religion and ethical ideas, however, the West imported little. The first impression of Westerners, not only when they met the relatively primitive cultures of the New World, but even when they met the old cultures of the East, was that they had nothing to learn from them. In time, some people began to respect the otherworldliness of Hinduism and the high but quite this-worldly ethics of Chinese Confucianism; others came to admire the dignity and simplicity of primitive peoples. But for the most part what struck the Europeans—when they bothered at all to think about anything more than money-making and empire-building—was the poverty, dirt, and superstition they found among the masses in India and China, the low material standards of primitive peoples everywhere, the heathenness of the heathens.

Yet, certainly, exposure to these very different cultures acted as a stimulus in the West. One of its first effects was to increase the fund of the marvelous, the incredible. The early accounts of the New World are full of giants and pygmies, El Dorados with gold-paved streets, fountains of eternal youth, wonderful plants and animals. All this was a great stimulus to the literary and artistic imagination, from the island of Shakespeare's *Tempest* to the Xanadu of Coleridge's *Kubla Khan,* two hundred years later. Science, too, was stimulated. A dip into any of the early collections of voyages gives an impression more of the realistic sense and careful observation of travelers than of their credulity and exaggerations. Here is the modern science of geography already well on the way to maturity, and here too are contributions to the modern social sciences of anthropology, comparative government, and economics.

The effects of expansion were harsh and unsettling as well as stimulating. The great new supplies of gold and silver from the Americas set in motion a secular trend toward price rises. This inflation accompanied, perhaps indeed "caused" or at least helped, general economic expansion. In this process, the merchants and financiers, "businessmen" in the broadest sense, gained; those on fixed incomes suffered; and the income of wage earners, peasants, and the like, while increasing, generally did not rise as fast as prices.

The Beginnings of One World

By the early part of the eighteenth century, there were still blank spots on the map of the world, especially in the interior of Africa and in our Pacific Northwest. Yet, in spite of this and in spite of the insignificance of the impression made by Europe on China and Japan, it was already clear that only one system of international politics existed in the world. From now on, all general wars tended to be world wars, fought, if only by privateers, on all the seven seas, and, if only by savages and frontiersmen, on all the continents. By the eighteenth century there was One World.

This was certainly not One World of the spirit. No common authority of any kind could reach all men; there were pockets of isolated peoples. And the masses of the world, even at its center in Europe, remained ignorant of, and uninterested in, what really went on in the hearts and heads of men elsewhere. But already Western goods penetrated almost everywhere, led by firearms, then followed by a great many other commodities; not all of them "cheap and nasty," as anticolonialists would claim. Already an educated minority was growing up everywhere, from professional geographers to journalists, diplomatists, and men of business, specialists who had to deal with the problems of the whole world.

Reading Suggestions on Seventeenth-Century War, Politics, and Empire

EUROPE IN GENERAL
    C. J. Friedrich, *The Age of the Baroque, 1610-1660;* F. L. Nussbaum, *The Triumph of Science and Reason, 1660-1685;* J. B.

Wolf, *The Emergence of the Great Powers, 1685-1715* (*Torchbooks). In the series "The Rise of Modern Europe," with full, up-to-date bibliographies.

    G. N. Clark, *The Seventeenth Century* (*Galaxy), and D. Ogg, *Europe in the Seventeenth Century* (*Collier). Older, briefer, and still useful surveys.

G. Renard and G. Weulersse, *Life and Work in Modern Europe* (Knopf, 1926). For the general economic background.

E. F. Heckscher, *Mercantilism*, 2 vols., rev. ed. (Macmillan, 1955). A famous and controversial work.

A. Vagts, *A History of Militarism* (*Free Press), and E. M. Earle, ed., *Makers of Modern Strategy* (*Atheneum). Both are helpful on seventeenth-century warfare.

F. L. Nussbaum, *A History of Economic Institutions in Modern Europe* (Crofts, 1933). Abridgement of Sombart's *Moderne Kapitalismus,* claiming that war is economically creative.

J. U. Nef, *War and Human Progress* (Harvard, 1950). Rebutting Sombart and arguing that war is economically destructive.

THE THIRTY YEARS' WAR

C. V. Wedgwood, *The Thirty Years' War* (*Anchor) Comprehensive account.

S. H. Steinberg, *The "Thirty Years' War" and the Conflict for European Hegemony* (*Norton). A somewhat briefer general treatment.

T. K. Rabb, ed., *Thirty Years' War: Problems of Motive, Extent, and Effect* (*Heath). Good introduction to the main controversies over the war.

H. Holborn, *A History of Modern Germany,* 2 vols. (Knopf, 1959, 1963). Volume I of this authoritative study goes to 1648; Volume II from 1648 to 1820.

M. Roberts, *Gustavus Adolphus,* 2 vols. (Longmans, 1953, 1958). Sympathetic study of the man and his reign.

ENGLAND

M. Ashley, *England in the Seventeenth Century* (*Penguin), and C. Hill, *The Century of Revolution, 1603–1714* (*Norton). Two sound surveys by experts.

G. Davies, *The Early Stuarts, 1603–1660,* and G. N. Clark, *The Later Stuarts, 1660–1714,* rev. eds. (Clarendon, 1949). More detailed scholarly treatments, in the Oxford History of England.

W. Notestein, *The English People on the Eve of Colonization, 1603–1660* (*Torchbooks). Admirable social history.

D. H. Wilson, *King James Sixth and First* (*Galaxy). Sound fresh study.

C. V. Wedgwood, *The King's Peace, 1637–1641; The King's War, 1641–1647; A Coffin for King Charles* (Macmillan, 1955, 1959, 1964). Detailed study of the Great Rebellion by a leading scholar.

M. Ashley, *Oliver Cromwell and the Puritan Revolution* (*Collier). Recent evaluation of a still controversial figure.

J. H. Hexter, *Reappraisals in History* (*Torchbooks), and L. Stone, *Social Change and Revolution in England, 1540–1640* (*Barnes & Noble). Good introductions to the recent controversy on the gentry and the Puritans.

A. Bryant, *King Charles II* (Longmans, 1931). Unusually sympathetic in tone.

F. C. Turner, *James II* (Macmillan, 1948). Balanced treatment of a ruler generally subject to partisan interpretation.

S. B. Baxter, *William III and the Defense of European Liberty* (Harcourt, 1966). Fine balanced study.

J. R. Tanner, *English Constitutional Conflicts of the Seventeenth Century* (*Cambridge). Full and scholarly.

G. P. Gooch, *English Democratic Ideas in the Seventeenth Century* (*Torchbooks). An older work, still worth reading.

FRANCE

J. D. Lough, *An Introduction to Seventeenth Century France* (McKay, 1961). Designed for the student of literature, but useful for anyone interested in the subject.

W. J. Stankiewicz, *Politics and Religion in Seventeenth Century France* (University of California, 1960). Good special study.

J. B. Wolf, *Louis XIV* (*Norton). Recent scholarly political biography.

A. Guérard, *France in the Classical Age: The Life and Death of an Ideal* (*Torchbooks). Stimulating interpretation of early modern France.

W. H. Lewis, *The Splendid Century* (*Anchor). Emphasizing society under Louis XIV.

C. V. Wedgwood, *Richelieu and the French Monarchy* (*Collier), and M. Ashley, *Louis XIV and the Greatness of France* (*Free Press). Good short introductions.

O. Ranum, *Richelieu and the Councillors of Louis XIII* (Oxford, 1963). An important monograph on administration.

C. W. Cole, *Colbert and a Century of French Mercantilism,* 2 vols. (Columbia, 1939). A solid, detailed study.

J. E. King, *Science and Rationalism in the Administration of Louis XIV* (Hopkins, 1949). Monograph showing the relations between intellectual and political history.

W. F. Church, ed., *The Greatness of Louis XIV: Myth or Reality?* (Heath). Samples the wide variety of judgments on *le Grand Monarque.*

EUROPE OVERSEAS

Cambridge History of the British Empire, Vol. 1 (Cambridge, 1929). Convenient account of developments up to the year 1783.

O. T. Black and H. T. Lefler, *Colonial America* (Macmillan, 1958). Good survey.

G. M. Wrong, *The Rise and Fall of New France,* 2 vols. (Macmillan, 1928). French Canada interpreted by a Canadian.

A. P. Newton, *The European Nations in the West Indies, 1493–1688* (Black, 1933). Reviews the days when the islands were prizes of empire.

B. H. M. Vlekke, *Nusantara: A History of Indonesia,* rev. ed. (Lorenz, 1959). Good account of Dutch imperialism.

A. Hyma, *The Dutch in the Far East* (Wahr, 1942). With emphasis on social and economic developments.

Note: See also titles cited in Chapter 7.

SOURCES AND FICTION

H. J. C. von Grimmelshausen, *Simplicius Simplicissimus* (*several editions). Picaresque novel of Germany during the Thirty Years' War by a seventeenth-century writer.

Pepys' Diary (*Macmillan). Abridgment of the famous diary by a Londoner.

R. Graves, *Wife to Mr. Milton* (*Noonday). Good novel about Milton, who was Cromwell's secretary.

W. H. Lewis, ed., *Memoirs of the Duc de Saint-Simon* (*Macmillan). Gossipy recollections of a touchy aristocrat.

Willa Cather, *Shadows on the Rock* (Knopf, 1931). Sensitive re-creation of life in New France by a fine American novelist.

A. Dumas, *The Three Musketeers* (*several editions). By the author of other rousing novels on seventeenth-century France.

W. M. Thackeray, *Henry Esmond* (*several editions). Famous novel set in England about 1700.

N. Hawthorne, *The Scarlet Letter* (*several editions). The best introduction to the Puritan spirit through fiction.

nine

The Arts and Sciences in the Classical

and Baroque Age

I

Introduction: "The Great Century"

When the French called Louis XIV *le Grand Monarque,* they also christened his epoch *le Grand Siècle,* the Great Century. As the last chapter showed, the glory of French feats in war and diplomacy had become decidedly tarnished by the death of Louis in 1715. But Paris and Versailles remained the supreme arbiters of taste throughout Europe in such matters as how to behave at court, what clothes to wear, what to eat and drink, what diversions to pursue, what dances to favor, what books to read, what plays to see, what music to hear. In the realm of culture the grandeur of France was undiminished, and le Grand Siècle truly continued for almost two hundred years, including most of the eighteenth century as well as the seventeenth.

The enduring success of this French cultural imperialism rested securely on the almost universal recognition of French as the language of cultivated men. Nearly everywhere on the Continent, even in remote Russia, sovereigns, aristocrats, and many intellectuals employed it in preference to their native tongue. While they did so in part out of envy or snobbery, they genuinely admired the elegance, clarity, and logic bestowed upon it by such formidable seventeenth-century writers as Descartes, La Rochefoucauld, Racine, and Molière, whom we shall encounter later in this chapter. German, for example, came close to disappearing as the language of educated Germans until it was restored to respectability by the writers of the Romantic generation at the close of the 1700's. King Frederick the Great of Prussia, the eighteenth-century hero of German nationalism, habitually spoke and wrote French. Though

An illustration from Abraham Bosse's "Le Palais Royal" (1640) gives a picture of French fashions and taste.

English suffered no such eclipse in the British Isles, it did not begin to compete with French for international status until the Victorian heyday of British imperialism. Even Shakespeare, whom we accept as one of the fixed stars in the firmament of world culture heroes, was very little appreciated outside Britain until the Romantic era, in part because the exuberant language of his dramas made them exceedingly difficult to translate into French.

In the grandest days of le Grand Siècle, however, neither the French language nor French culture exercised an absolute monopoly. Latin continued to be the vehicle of international science, as it had been since the Middle Ages. Newton chose it for his revolutionary *Principia Mathematica* (1687), and the eighteenth-century Swedish botanist Karl von Linné used it both for his system of classifying plants and animals by genus and species and for the name by which we know him, Carolus Linnaeus. Not only England and Sweden contributed to the roster of scientific "greats" but also Italy (Galileo), Holland (Leeuwenhoek), and Germany (Leibniz). Moreover, England, the Netherlands, Spain, and Italy, though outdazzled by France and especially by Versailles, maintained a lively artistic life of their own: witness, respectively, Wren and Hogarth, Rubens and Rembrandt, Velázquez, and Bernini. While the greatest monument of the neoclassical architecture of le Grand Siècle is Versailles itself—palace, gardens, and town—the finest specimens of the more innovative baroque and rococo styles will be found in Rome, in Germany and Portugal, and even overseas in Mexico and Peru. Still more examples could be cited, from literature, philosophy, and music, to demonstrate that France in the Great Century was no oasis surrounded by cultural deserts but the acknowledged capital of a vigorous and cosmopolitan intellectual and artistic life that had flourishing outposts elsewhere in Europe and the New World.

II
Literature

Classicism in France

Just as Henry IV, Richelieu, and Louis XIV brought greater order to French politics after the civil and religious upheavals of the sixteenth century, so did the writers of the seventeenth century discipline the French language and French literature after the extravagances of a genius like Rabelais. The Renaissance gave way to the Age of Classicism, which insisted on the observance of more rules, the authority of models from classical antiquity, and the employment of a more select vocabulary. Early in the seventeenth century the example of greater refinement in manners and speech was set by the *salon* (reception room) of the Paris mansion of an aristocratic lady, the marquise de Rambouillet. Later, proper behavior was standardized by the court ceremonial at Versailles and proper vocabulary by the famous dictionary of the French language which the experts of the Academy founded by Richelieu finished compiling in the 1690's after more than half a century of labor. Exaggerated notions of propriety outlawed from polite usage such terms as *spit* and *vomit* and obliged writers to seek for euphemisms to describe dozens of commonplace functions and matters. One could almost anticipate the genteel Victorian preference for calling the legs of furniture limbs, and, with some hindsight, one can also foresee the social cleavage that produced the revolution of 1789 in the enormous gap between the classical French of the court and the plainer, coarser language of the multitude.

On the other hand, the linguistic purification of the seventeenth century brought enormous benefits. Without its discipline French could never have won its unique reputation for clarity and elegance. The leading tragic dramatists of le Grand Siècle made obedience to all the classical do's and don't's not an end in itself but a means to probe deeply into the universal humanity of diverse personalities. Corneille (1606–1684) and Racine (1639–1699) usually chose plots from Greek mythology, wrote in the rhymed couplets called alexandrine (the iambic hexameter used for a poem about Alexander the Great), and observed the "unities" decreed by Aristotle's *Poetics.* They kept the action within the limits of one place, one twenty-four-hour span of time, and one topic. Within this rigid form the genius of Corneille and Racine created moving portraits of individuals upholding exalted ideals of honor or crushed by overwhelming emotion. The French tragedies of the seventeenth century rank second only to the Greek tragedies of the fifth century B.C. not merely because of their classical form but still more because of their psychological insights and emotional power.

Because Molière (1622–1673), the other great dramatist of the age, wrote

Painting of a Molière farce, with Molière himself shown at the far left.

comedies, he was less constrained to employ a dignified vocabulary and heed the other canons of classicism. He made the main characters of his satirical comedies not only sharply etched individuals but social types as well—the overrefined pedantic ladies of the salons in *Les Précieuses Ridicules,* the hypocrite in *Tartuffe,* the miser in *L'Avare,* the ignorant and self-important newly rich man in *Le Bourgeois Gentilhomme.* In Molière, as in all good satire, there is more than a touch of moralizing. Didactic overtones are also present in two other characteristic works of the Great Century. The *Fables* of La Fontaine (1621–1695) reworked in lively fashion tales borrowed from ancient times, thus vindicating the author's contention that while he imitated the classics he was by no means enslaved to them. The *Maxims* of La Rochefoucauld (1613–1680), cast in epigrammatic prose of classic purity, were less down to earth in language but even more disenchanted in their estimates of human nature: "We all have enough strength to bear the misfortunes of others," he wrote. "We generally give praise only in order to gain it for ourselves." "We always find something not altogether displeasing in the misfortunes of our friends."*

England

Seventeenth-century English literature also had its cynics, notably Wycherley, Congreve, and the other playwrights who wrote the witty, bawdy, and disillusioned plays we know as Restoration comedies. Under Charles II and his successors the pendulum of public taste and morality made a particularly violent swing in reaction to the midcentury Puritans who had closed down the theaters as dens of sinfulness. One of those Puritans, however, John Milton (1608–1674), the secretary of Oliver Cromwell, produced a truly major work of literature—*Paradise Lost,* the only English epic in the grand style that still attracts many readers. Though Milton was a classical scholar of staggering erudition, his often complex style and his profound belief in Christian humanism really made him a belated representative of an earlier literary age; he was the last great man of the English Renaissance rather than a pioneer of English classicism.

What was needed to prepare for the classical age of English letters was the modernization of the English language by pruning the elaborate flourishes, standardizing the chaotic spelling, and eliminating the long flights of rhetoric characteristic of Elizabethan and early seventeenth-century prose. Under the influence of John Dryden (1631–1700), English began to model itself on French, on its straightforward word order, on its comparatively brief sentences, free from long periodic clauses, and on its polish, neatness, and clarity. English letters were ready for the Augustan Age which lasted through the first half of the eighteenth century, when they could claim, with some exaggeration, a group of talents comparable to those of Vergil, Horace, and Ovid, all of whom had flourished under the Roman emperor Augustus. In the early 1700's Addison and Steele made the *Tatler* and *Spectator* vehicles for popularizing serious intellectual discussion; Alexander Pope (1688–1744) chose rhymed couplets, not for tragedies as Racine had, but for philosophical and satirical essays. The greatest of the Augustans was Jonathan Swift (1667–1745), author of the corrosive satire *Gulliver's Travels,* and a pessimistic and at times despondent genius whose convictions about human depravity went far beyond the moderation of the classical spirit. Recall, in *Gulliver,* the contrast between the noble and reasonable horses, the Houyhnhnms, and the brutish and revolting human Yahoos.

* *The Maxims of La Rochefoucauld,* trans. F. G. Stevens (London, 1939), pp. 9, 49, 173.

As the eighteenth century advanced, literature in the classical manner lost ground to more popular, less inhibited, and more emotional works. In England, particularly, the simplification of the language encouraged the development of fiction. Two of the earliest examples of the new genre were by Daniel Defoe—*Robinson Crusoe* (1719) and *Moll Flanders* (1722), both novels, though presented as autobiography, and both far removed from the refinements and elevated feelings of classicism. In 1749 Henry Fielding published the first great social novel, *Tom Jones,* with its realistic depiction of hard-riding, hard-drinking country squires and the toughs of London slums. Fielding, who was a magistrate in London, knew very well the characters he drew so faithfully. He also turned his biting realism to account in parodies of the sentimental novels of his countryman and contemporary Samuel Richardson (1689–1761).

A parodist could scarcely have found a more inviting target than the three gigantic novels which Richardson, a printer by trade, wrote late in life and cast in the form of letters by the chief characters. In *Clarissa Harlowe* (1748), for example, 2,400 pages of small print are devoted to the misfortunes of Clarissa, whose lover was a scoundrel, and whose greedy relatives were scheming to obtain her considerable property. Whatever disasters befell her, she never lost the ability to pour out her distresses on paper and move her readers to tears. With all Richardson's excessive emotionalism and preachiness, his descriptions of the struggles of passion and conscience carried such conviction that he greatly advanced the novel of "sensibility," so appealing to the large middle-class reading public.

In France the novel of sensibility had already begun to come into its own with Abbé Prévost's very popular *Manon Lescaut.* This tale of the vicissitudes of a young woman sent to the colony of Louisiana was brief and still deferred to the balance and moderation of the classical spirit. Much closer to Richardson in style and moral tone, and by a much more talented writer, was Jean Jacques Rousseau's lengthy novel about the conflict of love and duty, *La Nouvelle Héloïse* (1761). Because of the strict sexual morality Rousseau preached (though did not always practice), the new Héloïse, unlike her medieval namesake in the affair with Abelard, died in time to avoid adultery. On the French stage the retreat from classicism was marked by the *comédies larmoyantes* ("tearful comedies"), a popular blend of laughter, pathos, and melodrama. The way was being cleared for the Romantic writers who would largely dominate French literature in the early nineteenth century.

In Germany the dramas of Lessing (1729–1781) combined the middle-class appeal of Richardson with a devotion to moderation and toleration more in tune with the classical spirit. In his romantic comedy *Minna von Barnhelm,* the lively heroine pits her feminine values and charm against a Prussian officer in a fashion quite contrary to the stereotype of a masculine militaristic Germany. In the 1770's young German writers were associated in a movement called *Sturm und Drang* ("Storm and Stress") after an obscure play about a disturbed young man who fled Europe and fought in the American Revolution in hopes of finding himself. Yearning, melancholy, and despair were the dominant notes in the great landmark of the *Sturm und Drang* period, the immensely successful *Sorrows of Young Werther,* the youthful work of the celebrated Goethe (1749–1832). Napoleon later claimed to have read this lugubrious short novel seven times, always weeping copiously when the hero shoots himself because the woman he loves is already married. At the close of the century the Romantic movement continued to develop the themes of self-pity and self-destruction enunciated by Werther.

III   The Arts

Versailles.

Architecture: Neoclassical, Baroque, and Rococo

The great palace that Louis XIV built at Versailles is an admirable introduction to the medley of artistic styles prevailing in the seventeenth and eighteenth centuries. The exterior of the palace, with its symmetry and its columns, followed the classical models so long canonized by Renaissance builders. The geometrical layout of the gardens at Versailles, with their straight avenues and their carefully barbered shrubs and trees, heightened the sense of neoclassical order and proportion; only the fountains gave a welcome suggestion of exuberance and emancipation from restraint. Inside the palace, however, exuberance was everywhere—in the dramatic Hall of Mirrors, the majestic Staircase of Ambassadors (admirably designed to show the emissaries of lesser rulers that there could be only one Grand Monarque), and the acres of ceiling painted with smiling cherubs. This taste for theatricality and for lavish embellishments in interior decoration was a mark of the style called baroque.

St. Paul's Cathedral, London.

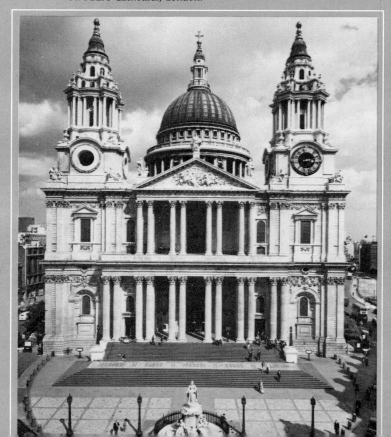

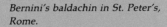

Bernini's baldachin in St. Peter's, Rome.

Derived from the Portuguese *barroco*, referring to a deformed or irregular pearl, *baroque* described the exaggerated and distorted elaborations of Renaissance neoclassicism. In architecture there was less reliance on the horizontal straight line and on balance and understatement, and more emphasis on the vertical and the curved line, on striking effects, and on the assertion of physical dominance. The palace of Versailles for all its enormous length seems a neoclassical understatement compared to the aggressiveness of higher and more baroque structures. A very moderate example of baroque, still under classical restraints, is St. Paul's Cathedral in London, designed and completed by Sir Christopher Wren to replace an earlier structure destroyed in the Great Fire of 1666. Even in present-day London, despite new skyscrapers, St. Paul's still dominates the City proper, the mile-square financial district.

More emphatic examples of baroque may be found in churches as far apart as Mexico and Austria. The city of Rome is studded with baroque monuments, many of them the work of the architect and sculptor Bernini (1598–1680). They include the great open spaces and curving colonnades of St. Peter's Square, which set off strikingly the imposing basilica designed in the neoclassical manner by Michelangelo and modified toward the baroque by the architects who succeeded him. More grandiose and aggressive than anything on the exterior of St. Peter's is the baldachin designed by

Right: Rococo architecture: the Amalienburg hunting pavilion at Nymphenburg, near Munich.

Far right: The Place de la Concorde, Paris.

Bernini for the interior. This canopy over the main altar is as high as an eight-story building, and is supported by enormous twisted columns of bronze, at once massive and restless.

In the eighteenth century the baroque evolved into the rococo, a term derived form the French word for seashells and often employing a shell motif in its intricate and florid ornamentation. Lighter and more elegant than baroque, rococo depended less on mass to create an effect and more on graceful line and elaborate decoration. Charming examples of rococo may be found in some of the smaller European palaces, those in the outskirts of Munich and Lisbon, for example; and a much-admired expression of the style is the delicate furniture called Louis Quinze (XV) after the king in whose reign rococo flourished. Rococo taste for the dainty and the exotic created a great vogue for things Chinese—Chinese scenic wallpaper, the "Chinese" furniture of Thomas Chippendale, and the painted scrolls, delicate porcelains, and other decorative items known collectively as chinoiserie. Eighteenth-century gardens often boasted pagodas, while the gardens themselves were moving away from the formal landscaping of Louis XIV to the more natural and wilder look of the English garden.

In the second half of the eighteenth century rococo lost ground to a revival of the neoclassical style stemming from the discovery in 1748 of the ruins of Roman Pompeii, well preserved under the lava of Vesuvius which had covered it since A.D. 79. In Paris classical models were used for the strikingly handsome and well-proportioned buildings flanking the Place de la Concorde (and the Parisian models were in turn copied 150 years later for the Free Library and Courts buildings facing Logan Circle in Philadelphia). In Britain the Adam brothers adapted Roman models most skillfully to design some of the most delightful townhouses and country mansions ever built, and in Virginia George Washington's residence at Mount Vernon was a relatively modest adaptation of the neoclassical. The popularity of "colonial" or "Georgian" buildings in our own century testifies to the lasting influence of the style.

Painting

In painting, a baroque amalgam of theatricality and otherworldliness had characterized the work of El Greco in late sixteenth-century Spain. The outstanding painter of seventeenth-century Spain, Velázquez (1599–1660), returned to the secular and realistic traditions of Renaissance art. He

executed forty portraits of the Hapsburg king Philip IV, not all of them flattering by any means, and some marvelous pictures of the royal children and the court dwarfs. By painting what the eye sees at a glance Velázquez created what one critic has called an effect of "optical" realism as opposed to the more detailed and cluttered photographic realism.

Above: Rubens' "Maria de' Medici, Queen of France, Landing in Marseilles."

Below: Velázquez' "The Maids of Honor."

Left: Rembrandt's "The Descent from the Cross."

In the Low Countries, the center of northern European painting in the 1660's, some artists also attained optical realism in their treatment of such everyday themes as the artist at work in his studio and the well-to-do businessman and his household. The Fleming Rubens (1577–1640) made

Above: Reynolds' "Mrs. Siddons as the Tragic Muse."

Left: Fragonard's "The New Model."

Hogarth's "The Orgy": a scene from "The Rake's Progress."

painting itself a big business, obtaining handsome commissions from French and English royalty, running a studio with two hundred students, and actually doing himself the brushwork on at least part of two thousand pictures. The grand scale on which Rubens worked, combined with his preference for painting rosy, fleshy nudes, made him a ranking painter of the baroque; these traits—and, according to his critics, his capacity for vulgar overstatement—are very evident in his celebrated series on King Henry IV and Queen Marie de' Medici installed in the Louvre. Rembrandt (1606–1669), the Dutch genius, exhibited a subtler baroque quality in his effort to involve the viewer directly in the action depicted. In successive sketches for *Ecce Homo,* when Pilate has the crowd choose between Christ and Barabbas, Rembrandt progressively eliminated the crowd, and the beholder of the final version comes to realize that he is one of the multitude choosing to release Barabbas. A devout member of the Mennonite sect of Anabaptists, Rembrandt is the only great Protestant religious painter, a rare exception to the rule that Protestant tradition has not welcomed the visual arts.

In the eighteenth century painting, like design, evolved from the baroque to the rococo. Two French artists, Watteau (1684–1721) and Fragonard (1732–1806), used Rubens-like flesh tones and applied them with a quick light touch that suggested improvisation; their subjects, too, were light, like the pampered flirtatious courtiers of Fragonard. In England neoclassical painting had a tireless and articulate advocate in Sir Joshua Reynolds (1723–1792), president of the Royal Academy, who laid down the rules for proper painting. In practice, fortunately, Sir Joshua and his contemporaries—Lawrence, Gainsborough, Romney—had sufficient talent to transcend the rules, and endowed their portraits of English aristocrats with real warmth. While these academic painters made the century the golden age of English portraiture, another English artist, William Hogarth (1697–1764), brushed aside neoclassical discipline and did in art what Fielding and Richardson did in the novel. Instead of catering to a few wealthy patrons, Hogarth won a mass market for the engravings he turned out in thousands of copies—*Gin Lane, Marriage à la Mode, The Rake's Progress,* and other graphic sermons on the vices to be found at every level of London society.

In art, the seventeenth and eighteenth centuries were perhaps something of an anticlimax after the great flowering of the Renaissance. In music, by contrast, the baroque was indeed a great century—two great centuries, in fact—the formative period of what we know as classical music, when the opera and oratorio, the sonata, concerto, and symphony, and the piano all made their appearance. Though the chief innovators were at first Italian, later on Germans, Austrians, and Englishmen made important contributions. In Venice, Monteverdi (1567–1643) composed the first important operas, a baroque fusion of music and theater, which gained such popularity that the city soon had sixteen opera houses. At Naples, the operatic capital of the later 1600's, conservatories (originally establishments for "conserving" orphans) stressed voice training; composers provided operatic vehicles to allow the "stars" to show off their vocal prowess; and the stars themselves constituted the final touch of unreality, since it was customary to have female roles sung by *castrati,* male sopranos, and male roles by women. From Italy Louis XIV imported to France Lully (1632–1687), musician, dancer, speculator, and politician extraordinary, who vied with Molière for the upper hand in directing the cultural life of the court. The operas that Lully composed to enhance the resplendence of the Sun King are now forgotten except for some delightful overtures and dances.

The baroque techniques of seventeenth-century composers were brought to perfection early in the next century by the German choirmaster Johann Sebastian Bach (1685–1750). Bach provided a wealth of material for the organ, part of it in the form of the fugue, an intricate version of the round in which each voice begins the theme in turn while the other voices are repeating and elaborating it. For small orchestras he composed the Brandenburg Concertos, in which successive instruments are given a chance to show their potentialities. And for choirs and solo voices he composed the Mass in B minor and two lengthy settings of the Passion of Christ according to Saint John and Saint Matthew.

In contrast to Bach's quiet provincial life was the stormy international career of his countryman, Handel (1685–1759). After studying in Italy, Handel passed most of his adult years in England trying to run an opera company. While he wrote more than forty operas, including *Xerxes,* with the celebrated "Largo," he is remembered best for the *Messiah* and other sacred works arranged for large choruses and directed toward a mass audience. These elaborate oratorios differed greatly from the earlier Italian oratorios, which had been done for the tiny prayer chapels called oratories.

While Bach and Handel composed many instrumental suites and concertos, it was not until the second half of the eighteenth century that orchestral music really came to the fore. New instruments appeared, notably the piano, which greatly extended the limited range of its ancestor, the harpsichord. New forms of instrumental music were also developed, largely by the Austrian Haydn (1732–1809), who wrote more than fifty piano pieces in the form of the sonata, in which two contrasting themes are stated, developed, interwoven, repeated, and finally resolved in a coda (Italian for "tail"). Haydn adapted the sonata for orchestra, grafting it onto the Italian operatic overture to create the first movement of the symphony. Opera itself was undergoing a revolutionary advance, thanks to another German composer, Gluck (1714–1787), who devised well-constructed musical dramas rather than vehicles to exhibit vocal pyrotechnics. Gluck kept to the old custom of drawing on classical mythology for heroes and heroines, but he invested shadowy figures like Orpheus, Eurydice, and Iphigenia with vitality and conviction.

The concerto, the symphony, and especially opera all reached a climax in the works of the Austrian Mozart (1756–1791), a child prodigy whose facility and versatility multiplied until his premature death as a debt-ridden pauper at the age of thirty-five. An evening sufficed for him to toss off the sprightly overture to *The Marriage of Figaro,* and two months during the summer of 1788 to write his final three symphonies. His orchestral works included a long roster of concertos, with the solo parts not only for the usual piano or violin but also for French horn or even bassoon.

In one opera, *The Magic Flute,* Mozart consciously strove to create a serious allegorical German work, but in his three most successful operas he kept to the tradition of Italian comic opera. These were the rococo *Così Fan Tutte* ("Thus Do All Women"); *The Marriage of Figaro,* based on Beaumarchais's famous satire on social caste, in which Figaro, the valet, outwits and outsings his noble employers; and, finally, *Don Giovanni,* a kind of "black comedy" depicting the havoc wrought by Don Juan on earth before his punishment in hell. Mozart composed with equal skill mournful and romantic arias for the Don's victims, a catalog of the Don's conquests for his valet ("A thousand and three in Spain alone"), and an elegantly seductive tune for the Don himself ("Give me your hand, my dear: I have a little chalet not far from here."). In the ballroom scene he has the orchestra play simultaneously three different tunes for three different dances—a minuet for the aristocracy, a country dance for the middle class, and a waltz (then considered quite plebeian) for the lowest order.

Music, like the novel or the engravings of Hogarth, was acquiring a broader social base and appealing to a wider audience. Where Bach had depended on a few aristocratic patrons, other composers moved further afield. Handel tried the very precarious venture of running his own opera company, as has been said, and the fortunate Haydn, when he left the princely estate of the Hungarian Esterhazy family, was able to score an equal success with the paying public of the London concert halls. The signs were multiplying that what R. R. Palmer has called the "age of the democratic revolution" was impending.

IV
The Scientific Revolution

The democratic revolution began in the thirteen colonies in 1776 and in France in 1789, but its roots reached farther back in European history. The assertions of "self-evident truths" and the jaunty appeals to "Nature and Nature's God" in the Declaration of Independence and the confident listing of the "rights of man and citizen" in the French Declaration thirteen years later required faith in the existence of truths and rights and a belief that men could understand the behavior of nature and of its god. This faith and this belief were part of the intellectual climate of the eighteenth-century Enlightenment which the next chapter will explore more fully. The Enlightenment, in turn, with its credo of reason, nature, and progress, would never have been possible without the revolutionary scientific advances of the seventeenth century.

New Attitudes and New Instruments

What made possible the accomplishments of Galileo, Pascal, Newton and other scientific luminaries of the 1600's was the development of new scientific instruments, new techniques, and, most fundamental of all, new attitudes toward science. The English intellectual and politician Francis Bacon (1561–1626), who was not a successful practitioner of science, was the tireless proponent of the need for the observation of phenomena and the patient accumulation of data. In *The Great Instauration* he wrote:

There are and can be only two ways of searching into and discovering truth. The one flies from the senses and particulars to the most general axioms, and from these principles, the truth of which it takes for settled and immovable, proceeds to judgment and to the discovery of middle axioms. And this way is now in fashion. The other derives axioms from the senses and particulars, rising by a gradual and unbroken ascent, so that it arrives at the most general axioms last of all. This is the true way, but as yet untried.

Bacon's untried way is what we call *induction,* in contrast to the *deduction* widely practiced in the Middle Ages. Deduction, of course, is not necessarily antiscientific, for it helps to account for the hunches propelling theoretical science forward. What Bacon attacked particularly was the inclination of deductive reason to accept general axioms as "settled" and "immovable." Ranking high among such established axioms were the views of the universe associated with two authorities of antiquity, Aristotle and Ptolemy. Bacon's Italian contemporary, Galileo (1564–1642), ridiculed blind acceptance of ancient authorities and thereby got himself embroiled with the Church.

Galileo was also one of the scores of individuals—some famous, some unknown or now forgotten—who contributed to the new instruments that permitted the more exact measurements and more detailed observations of inductive science. It is probable, for example, that Dutch glassmakers first put two lenses together and discovered that they could obtain a greater magnification. By 1610 Galileo was using the new device in the form of a telescope to observe the heavens, and by about 1680 the Dutchman Leeuwenhoek was using it in the form of a microscope to discover tiny creatures—protozoa— hitherto unknown. Working from the experiments of Galileo, other technicians developed such indispensable instruments of measurement as the thermometer and the barometer. Using the barometer, the Frenchman Pascal (1623–1662) proved that what we term air pressure diminished with altitude. From this he went on to counter the old adage "Nature abhors a vacuum" by showing that a vacuum is possible.

King Charles II of England roared with laughter on being told that members of his Royal Society were weighing the air. Yet the Royal Society for Improving Natural Knowledge, founded in 1662, and its French counterpart, the Académie des Sciences (1666), were important promoters of scientific investigation. The one, in characteristic English fashion, was a private undertaking, though with a royal charter; the other, sponsored by Colbert for the greater glory of le Grand Monarque and la Grande Nation, was a government institution, whose fellows received salaries and also instructions to avoid discussion of religion and politics. Both financed experiments and both published scientific articles in their "house organs," the *Philosophical Transactions* and *Journal des Sçavans* (savants). Elsewhere, too, learned societies flourished: in Rome the Accademia dei Lincei, and in Philadelphia the American Philosophical Society, started in 1743 with Benjamin Franklin one of its founders.

An international scientific community arose through the formal exchanges of the corresponding secretaries of such academies and also through the private correspondence among members and their acquaintances. Both professional men and aristocrats joined learned societies, and many a gentleman and an occasional lady dabbled in a private laboratory or observatory. Some did more than dabble, like the chemist Robert Boyle (1627–1691), son of an Irish earl, and Voltaire and his mistress, the marquise du Châtelet, who made a serious hobby of chemistry. The new advances in science were popularized in books and articles in the vernaculars and aimed at the educated lay public.

An example was the *Discourses on the Plurality of Worlds* by Fontenelle (1657–1757), the secretary of the Académie des Sciences, who also wrote valuable eulogies of deceased members, detailing their learned contributions.

The basic language of science—mathematics—was taking a great leap forward, meantime. In 1585, the Fleming Stevin published *The Decimal, Teaching with Unheard-of Ease How to Perform All Calculations Necessary among Men by Whole Numbers without Fractions*. A generation later, the Scot Napier formulated the *Marvelous Rule of Logarithms,* which shortened the laborious processes of multiplying, dividing, and taking square root. The Frenchman Descartes (1596–1650) worked out analytical geometry, which brought geometry and algebra together through the "Cartesian coordinates," as in the plotting of an equation on a graph. The mathematical achievements of the century culminated in a method of dealing with variables and probabilities. To this Pascal contributed his studies of games of chance, and in Holland insurance actuaries drew up tables to show the life expectancy of their clients. Then Isaac Newton (1642–1727) and the German philosopher Leibniz (1646–1716), apparently quite independently of each other, invented the calculus. Its practical value is underlined by the fact that without the calculus, and without Cartesian geometry, Newton could never have made the calculations supporting his revolutionary hypotheses in astronomy and physics.

Astronomy and Physics

In astronomy the heliocentric theory advanced by Copernicus in the sixteenth century proved to be only a beginning. It raised many difficulties, notably when observation of planetary orbits did not confirm Copernicus' theory that the planets revolved about the sun in circular paths. The German Kepler (1571–1630) opened the way to a resolution by proving mathematically that the orbits were in fact elliptical. Then Galileo's telescope revealed the existence of spots on the sun, rings around Saturn, and moonlike satellites around Jupiter. All this evidence of corruption in high places led Galileo to publish a book in 1632 defending the heliocentric concept and ridiculing supporters of the traditional geocentric theory. But the Church, headed by traditionalists, brought Galileo before the Inquisition, which placed his book on the *Index* of prohibited works and sentenced him to what amounted to perpetual house arrest. Despite the public recantation Galileo was obliged to make, he is reported to have had the last word, "and yet it does move"—the Earth is not stationary, as the Church insists, but a planet behaving like other planets.

An even more celebrated story recounts Galileo's experiment dropping balls of different weights from the Leaning Tower of Pisa to test Aristotle's theory that objects fall with velocities proportional to their weight. While the story itself may be apocryphal, Galileo did in fact disprove Aristotle. Galileo's studies of projectiles, pendulums, and falling and rolling bodies helped establish modern ideas of acceleration and inertia. These ideas were then formulated by Newton, a more accomplished mathematician than Galileo.

In 1687 Newton published the laws of motion, together with other great discoveries, in the *Principia Mathematica.* Since he had made many of these findings two decades earlier, when he was still an undergraduate at Cambridge or at home on a Lincolnshire farm after plague closed the university, Newton seems to fit the popular concept of physics as the young man's science par excellence. Newton went on to secure ample recognition, gaining a professorship at Cambridge, a knighthood, the presidency of the Royal Society, and a well-paid post as master of the mint. Even he was not quite a perfect culture hero, however, for he often devoted himself to experiments in alchemy and unsuccessful attempts to figure out the accurate dates of biblical events.

Newton.

Newton's greatest contribution was the law of gravitation. It followed from his laws of motion, which picture bodies moving not in straightforward fashion of themselves but only in response to forces impressed upon them. These forces are at work in the mutual attraction of the sun, the planets, and their satellites, which are thereby held in their orbits. Newton stated the formula that the force of gravitation is proportional to the product of the masses of two bodies attracted one to the other, and inversely proportional to the square of the distance between them. Newton also promoted the development of optics by using a prism to separate sunlight into the colors of the spectrum. He demonstrated that objects only appear to be colored: their color is not intrinsic but the result of reflection and absorption of light.

In the eighteenth century astronomy and physics consolidated the great advances they had made in the seventeenth. The versatile Benjamin Franklin (1706–1790) showed that electricity and lightning were really the same thing by obtaining an electrical charge in a key attached to the string of a kite flown during a Philadelphia thunderstorm. The experiment, which aroused a lively interest in Europe, was repeated at Versailles for the French royal family. The "Newton of France" was Laplace (1749–1827), one of the experts who prepared the metric system during the Revolution. He rounded Sir Isaac's investigation of celestial mechanics and explained the movements of the solar system in a series of mathematical formulas and theorems.

The Other Sciences

The mechanistic views affecting physics also invaded geology and physiology. In 1600 the Englishman Gilbert, in a study of magnetism, suggested that the earth itself was a giant magnet. In 1628, Harvey, the physician of Charles I, published his demonstration that the human heart is in fact a pump, and that it drives the blood around a single circulatory system. Harvey's theory, confirmed a generation later by the discovery through microscopic observation of the capillary connections between arteries and veins, discredited the hypothesis, handed down from Galen in classical Antiquity, that the blood in the arteries moved quite separately from that in the veins.

Work in biology was marked by the careful collection of specimens, the observation of microscopic organisms, and the Linnaean classification according to genus and species. All this was preparation for the great leap forward in biology to come during the nineteenth century. Modern chemical analysis started in the later eighteenth century with the Scottish professor Joseph Black (1728–1799), who exploded the old theory that air was composed of a single element by proving the existence of several discrete gases. Black's French contemporary, Lavoisier, (1743–1794), continued the study of gases, demonstrated that water was made up of hydrogen and oxygen, and went on to assert that all substances were composed of certain basic chemical elements, of which he identified twenty-three. Lavoisier served on the metric commission during the Revolution until he was executed for his role as one of the hated tax farmers under the Old Regime.

World Machine and Rationalism

One great reason why the developments discussed in the last few pages are called the scientific revolution concerns their revolutionary effects outside the realm of science. They dethroned religion and old established authority and exalted reason and innovation. The new mechanistic interpretation of the universe regarded God not as the incomprehensible Creator and Judge but simply as the chief architect of a world machine whose operations man could grasp if only he would apply his reason properly, as Newton had demonstrated. The new interpretation of man stressed the ways in which parts of the

Descartes: portrait by Frans Hals.

body performed the functions of a pump, a lever, or some other mechanical device; in 1748 La Mettrie, a French physician, actually produced a book entitled *L'Homme Machine* ("man a machine").

A century earlier, the rationalism and materialism engendered by the scientific revolution had already found a most articulate spokesman in René Descartes. When he was a young man, as his *Discourse on Method* (1637) relates, he resolved to mistrust all authorities, theological or intellectual. His skepticism swept everything aside until he concluded that there was one thing only he could not doubt: his own existence. There must be reality in the self engaged in the processes of thinking and doubting—in the famous formulation, *Cogito ergo sum* (I think, therefore I am). From this one indubitable fact Descartes reconstructed the world until he arrived at God, a deity poles apart from older patriarchal concepts, a supreme geometer whose mathematical orderliness foreshadowed the great engineer of the Newtonian world machine. But where Newton would proceed inductively, at least in part, by relying on the data compiled by earlier scientists in their observations and experiments, Descartes proceeded deductively, deriving the universe and God ultimately from *Cogito ergo sum*.

The world that Descartes reconstructed proved to be two separate worlds—that of mind and soul, on the one hand, and that of body and matter, on the other. We confront the famous Cartesian dualism, which the twentieth-century philosopher-mathematician Whitehead claimed so hypnotized succeeding generations of philosophers that modern philosophy was ruined by their futile endeavors to put matter into mind or mind into matter and thus resolve the dualism. Descartes himself claimed competence to deal in detail only with the material world, yet the way in which he dealt with it intimated that it was the only world that counted. Witness his boast that if given matter and space, he could construct the universe himself.

V

Conclusion

Scientist and rationalist helped greatly to establish in the minds of educated men throughout the West two complementary concepts that were to give the Enlightenment of the eighteenth century a pattern of action toward social change, a pattern still of driving force in our world. These were, first, the concept of a regular "natural" order underlying the irregularity and confusion of the universe as it appears to unreflecting man in his daily experience; and, second, the concept of a human faculty, best called "reason," obscured in most men by their faulty traditional upbringing, but capable of being brought into effective play by good—that is, rational—upbringing. Both these concepts can be found in some form in our Western tradition at least as far back as the Greeks. What gives them novelty and force at the end of the seventeenth century is their being welded into the doctrine of progress—the belief that all human beings can attain here on earth a state of happiness, of perfection, hitherto in the West thought to be possible only for Christians in a state of grace, and for them only in a heaven after death.

Yet protagonists of the older Christian ways continued to flourish and to be numbered among the movers and shakers of the Grand Siècle. One example is the energetic Frenchman Saint Vincent de Paul (1581–1660), who experienced seven years as a slave in a Turkish galley. While insisting on the observance of strict orthodoxy, Vincent also instituted the systematic care of foundlings, promoted missions to rural areas of France neglected by the Church, and launched the Daughters of Charity, an organization that would enable well-to-do women to undertake the good works Vincent believed their wealth and status obliged them to perform.

Another example was Blaise Pascal, the mathematician and experimenter, who also believed in charity, but in the sense of God's incomprehensible love rather than of philanthropic deeds. He became an eloquent spokesman for the high-minded puritanical Jansenist group of French Catholics. Pascal dismissed as unworthy concepts of God as a mere master geometer or super-engineer; he sought instead for the Lord of Abraham and the Old Testament prophets, and one night in November 1654 he found Him when he underwent a profound mystical experience in which he felt with absolute certainty the presence of God and Jesus.

A final example is Baruch Spinoza (1632–1677), who tried to reconcile the God of Science and the God of Scripture. Spinoza constructed a system of ethical axioms as rigorously Cartesian and logical as a series of mathematical propositions. He also tried to reunite the Cartesian opposites, matter with mind, body with soul, by asserting that God was present everywhere and in everything. His pantheism caused his ostracism in Holland by his fellow Jews and also by the Christians, who considered him an atheist; his rejection of rationalism and materialism offended intellectuals. Spinoza found few admirers until the Romantic revolt against the abstractions and oversimplifications of the Enlightenment.

Reading Suggestions on Culture and Science in the Seventeenth and Eighteenth Centuries

GENERAL WORKS

R. S. Dunn, The Age of Religious Wars, 1559–1689 (*Norton); L. Krieger, Kings and Philosophers, 1689–1789 (*Norton). Comprehensive surveys.

M. Ashley, The Golden Century (Praeger, 1969). Valuable introduction.

C. J. Friedrich, The Age of the Baroque, 1610–1660; F. L. Nussbaum, The Triumph of Science and Reason, 1660–1685; J. B. Wolf, The Emergence of the Great Powers, 1685–1715 (*Torchbooks). In the series "The Rise of Modern Europe," with full, up-to-date bibliographies.

J. D. Lough, An Introduction to Seventeenth-Century France (*McKay) and . . . to Eighteenth-Century France (*McKay). Enlightening surveys.

D. Maland, Culture and Society in Seventeenth-Century France (Scribner's, 1970). Another useful analysis.

A. Guérard, France in the Classical Age: The Life and Death of an Ideal (*Torchbooks). Lively interpretation.

W. H. Lewis, The Splendid Century (*Morrow). Especially valuable on social developments under Louis XIV.

LITERATURE AND THE ARTS

S. E. Bethell, The Cultural Revolution of the Seventeenth Century (Roy, 1951). A suggestive literary study.

V.-L. Tapié, The Age of Grandeur (Weidenfeld & Nicolson, 1960). Evaluation of neoclassicism and baroque.

G. Bazin, Baroque and Rococo Art (*Praeger). Concise manual by the author of the lavishly illustrated survey The Baroque (N.Y. Graphic Society, 1968).

M. R. Bukofzer, Music in the Baroque Era (Norton, 1947); E. M. and S. Grew, Bach (*Collier); A. Einstein, Mozart (*Galaxy); E. J. Dent, Mozart's Operas (*Oxford). Informative works on music.

THE SCIENTIFIC REVOLUTION

J. D. Bernals, Science in History (*MIT Press). See Vol. 2 for seventeenth- and eighteenth-century developments.

P. Smith, A History of Modern Culture, 2 vols. (Holt, 1930). A mine of information on often neglected topics.

H. F. Kearney, Origins of the Scientific Revolution (*Barnes & Noble). A many-sided introduction to this controversial topic.

H. Butterfield, The Origins of Modern Science, 1300–1800 (*Free Press). Provocative and controversial survey.

A. N. Whitehead, Science and the Modern World (*Free Press). An incisive and influential critique of what modern science really means and implies.

A. R. Hall, The Scientific Revolution, 1500–1800 (*Beacon). A solid account.

L. S. Feuer, The Scientific Intellectual: The Psychological and Sociological Origins of Modern Science (Basic Books, 1963). A stimulating interpretation from a more controversial point of view.

A. Wolf, A History of Science, Technology, and Philosophy in the Sixteenth and Seventeenth Centuries (Allen & Unwin, 1950). A standard account.

P. Hazard, The European Mind, 1680–1715 (Hollis & Carter, 1953). Especially dramatic study.

Index